Journal Entries

Throughout the text, you will be asked to ***stop and reflect on a particular question or issue.*** Pictorial representations of a journal and pencil signal that it's an important time to stop reading and think about the ideas and information being presented. This is especially important when observing children and educators. In these entries, you will be asked to recall a personal example of a principle just described, support a stance on an issue, consider an alternative idea, or create a professional response to a situation or an issue. The journal reflections can be used as individual writing exercises, for group discussions, and for peer dialogue.

The nature of this introductory text requires an overview of a broad scope of information. These highlighted boxes ***provide in-depth discussions of current research or issues in the profession.*** They expand upon the information in the chapters and encourage further exploration of critically important topics.

Your Professional Portfolio

At the end of each chapter is a ***set of ideas for materials and projects to include in a professional portfolio.*** They are ideal assignments for practicing and using the chapter information and skills, and will provide evidence of your understanding of the chapter's content. They are appropriate for self-assessment or course assessment.

Your Professional Library

At the end of each chapter is a ***brief list of suggested books and articles*** for you to extend understandings of the chapter content. The suggested readings focus on the primary ideas of each chapter and will be ideal for your ongoing professional development.

ANNOTATED WEB RESOURCES

Appendix A is a list of annotated web resources to enrich your learning of the field of early childhood education. Websites were selected to provide additional information and insights into topics of high interest and importance.

EARLY CHILDHOOD PRAXIS TEST

The six content categories of the Early Childhood Education Praxis Test are correlated with the chapters of this text. This matrix, which is included inside the back cover, provides an overview of where each of these content areas is presented.

Early Childhood Education, Birth–8

THIRD EDITION

Early Childhood Education, Birth–8

The World of Children, Families, and Educators

Amy Driscoll

CALIFORNIA STATE UNIVERSITY, MONTEREY BAY

Nancy G. Nagel

LEWIS AND CLARK COLLEGE

Boston • New York • San Francisco
Mexico City • Montreal • Toronto • London • Madrid • Munich • Paris
Hong Kong • Singapore • Tokyo • Cape Town • Sydney

Series Editor: Traci Mueller
Editorial Assistant: Janice Hackenberg
Developmental Editor: Sonny Regelman
Editorial-Production Administrator: Annette Joseph
Editorial-Production Coordinator: Holly Crawford
Editorial-Production Service: Lynda Griffiths
Photo Researcher: Katharine S. Cook
Text Designer: Carol Somberg
Composition Buyer: Linda Cox
Electronic Composition and Art: Omegatype Typography, Inc.
Manufacturing Buyer: Andrew Turso
Cover Designer: Kristina Mose-Libon

For related titles and support materials, visit our online catalog at www.ablongman.com

Library of Congress Cataloging-in-Publication Data

Driscoll, Amy.
Early childhood education, birth–8 : the world of children, families, and educators / Amy Driscoll, Nancy G. Nagel.—3rd ed.
Includes bibliographical references and indexes.
ISBN 0-205-41262-9
1. Early childhood education—Case studies. 2. Child development—Case studies. I. Title.

LB1139.23.D77 2005
372.21—dc22

2004045247

Printed in the United States of America

10 9 8 7 6 5 4 3 2 1 WC 09 08 07 06 05 04

Photo credits: pp. xxiv, 9, 22, 32, 74, 94, 374, 390: Tom Lindfors Photography; pp. 6, 54, 128, 144, 192, 195, 236, 239, 310, 340, 351: Courtesy of Amy Driscoll; pp. 13, 170: Will Faller; pp. 36, 114, 132, 180, 403: Getty Images, Inc.—PhotoDisc; p. 45: Dorling Kindersley Media Library; p. 49: Comstock Royalty Free Division; pp. 58, 162: Will Hart; pp. 64, 69, 77, 79, 82, 88, 90, 200, 204, 208, 210, 215, 217, 223, 229, 232, 276, 278, 279, 283, 285, 295, 306, 307, 315, 319, 323, 325, 331: Courtesy of Nancy G. Nagel; p. 97: Lawrence Migdale/Pix; p. 105: Elizabeth Crews/The Image Works; p. 124: Laura Dwight Photography; p. 141: AP/Wide World Photos; p. 147: Eddie Lawrence/Dorling Kindersley Media Library; p. 164: Robert Harbison; p. 211: Mentor Graphics Child Development Center; p. 241: Dana White/PhotoEdit; p. 246: Pearson Education/PH College; pp. 249, 336: Nancy Sheehan Photography; pp. 360, 363: Courtesy of Joy Lee; p. 381: James Shaffer/PhotoEdit; p. 409: Michael Newman/PhotoEdit; p. 417: Laima Druskis/Pearson Education/PH School.

Contents

Preface

This third edition has been written to provide you with a comprehensive introduction to the profession of early childhood education. Children and their families, as well as the educators who play important roles in their lives, will greet you as you explore the world of early childhood education. The stories in this book are about real individuals because they are the best way for you to learn about the broad scope of our profession. You will meet and observe them in their homes, their neighborhoods, and the various programs where the children spend their days. The children and families represent diverse ethnic and cultural heritages, family configurations, and beliefs and assumptions about child raising and education. The early childhood educators represent a range of professional roles, early childhood programs and settings, and philosophies about child development and education.

Throughout the chapters, we encourage you to observe children, families, and early childhood educators and to learn from them. Observations take the form of brief vignettes in the beginning chapters and extended cases in later chapters. The cases and vignettes provide a shared and common observation for you to process together with your peers, through class discussions and reflective writing. In the constructivist tradition, we nudge and encourage you to create your own knowledge and understanding of early childhood education as you reflect on your observations. A very important message we hope to communicate is that children and families are the most important source of information for the thinking, planning, decision making, and teaching in which you will engage in the future.

Be sure to review the inside front cover of this book. It will help you navigate the book using the symbols for **curriculum, guidance, assessment,** and **family communication and involvement.** There is also a symbol for **journal** reflections, signifying questions or prompts to encourage you to write or discuss your impressions about each chapter's contents. Notice our other features—**A Closer Look** and **A Conversation about Inclusion.** Finally, at the end of each chapter, there are suggestions for **Your Professional Portfolio** and **Your Professional Library.**

In this third edition, we have added several new features. One is an annotated list of important web resources. We have also correlated the Early Childhood Education Praxis Test with the content of each chapter in this book. In the inside rear cover of this book you will find those correlations in a chart that will be helpful as you prepare for taking the Praxis test. An additional highlight appears on the inside rear cover page—the core values of the Professional Code of Ethics from the National Association for the Education of Young Children. The entire code is found in Appendix B.

You may be wondering, *What is unique about this book?* or *What makes this text different from all the other choices out there?* or *Why did my instructor choose this book for my class?* One answer has to do with our choices of early childhood settings for you to visit as you read our book. We carefully selected centers and classrooms that exemplify the best practices in the profession. Some readers might contend that the programs in our chapters are ideal, and that is exactly our intention. We believe that beginning professionals, like you, need to observe and study the very best programs available so that you build your knowledge and understandings from excellent examples. Soon enough in your professional development you will realize that there are plenty of examples that contradict what you are learning about children and families. You will witness practices that do not feel right for children and that are not sensitive to families. In our combined (about 50) years of working with preservice teachers, we have never heard our students ask for an example of what *not to do.* Instead, our students have typically asked where they can observe the kind of programs they read and hear about—programs that exemplify the child development theories and research that they have been studying. We had those requests in mind when we wrote this book. We visited the kinds of places our students have longed to observe, and we described what we saw and heard as authentically as possible. The programs and professionals that we selected model what we are trying to teach through this text. We listened for the kind of thinking and decision making that we encourage you, a beginning professional, to prepare to do. Our hope is that you will delight in getting to know the real children, families, and educators in our book and will find them a rich source of insights and understandings, and that the programs you visit with us will help you envision what is possible for children and families and bring you inspiration for your future work.

You may be asking, *What new information will I find in this book?* and *What kind of changes have been made from the last edition?* First, we want you to know that a number of early childhood professionals reviewed both the first and second editions to check on how well the text works for your introductory courses in early childhood education. They examined the contents for clarity, for missing information, and for ways to make the information relevant for your experiences. In response to their reviews, we have developed several new areas of emphasis in this edition. They include the following:

- More descriptions of how technology is used in early childhood education to appropriately support children's development and learning
- Increased attention to children's physical/motor development with more examples of activities for children
- Findings from the latest research on children's developments in the arts and more classroom ideas to support that development
- Attention to the national curriculum standards in appropriate disciplinary areas
- Latest Head Start changes in policies and practices
- Guidelines from NAEYC for curriculum development
- New Standards for Professional Preparation from NAEYC

We hope that these additions will make this third edition even more useful for your professional preparation for your future role as an early childhood educator.

Throughout the chapters, we urge you to take an active role in your own professional development and to begin the observations, reflections, and decision making that characterize a professional. We sincerely hope that after reading this book, your continuing study and preparation will build on and expand the experiences we have shared together in this text. *Early Childhood Education, Birth–8* is designed to provide a comprehensive overview of the professional content to be studied by an early childhood professional. It is important to note that many of the content areas need further and intensive development. The best example is the study of child development. This book contains a chapter that describes typical development from infancy to age 8, a chapter that explains major theories of development, and various cases of children of different ages to highlight the development typically observed at each age. We do not consider those chapters and cases sufficient content for the extensive study of child development that is critical for the early childhood professional. We strongly urge you to use the content of this text as foundational information and to build on the ideas and concepts in future courses and experiences.

Acknowledgments

We wish to acknowledge those early childhood professionals who assisted our writing by welcoming us to their centers and schools, by interpreting their programs, by discussing their beliefs and practices, and by introducing us to the children and their families. We are grateful to the following families and early childhood professionals: Robin Lindsley, Francis and Akosa Wambalaba and family, Luke and George Kolln, Margaret Browning, Sue Patterson, Kristine Digman, Faridah Haron and Ibrahim, Ellie Noland and staff of Helen Gordon Child Development Center, Carolyne Westlake, Susana Grandjean, Lynn

Reer, Vicki Lawry, Tim Lauer, Candace Beck, Joy Lee, Vineeta Pahalad, Ann Gray, Nancy Johnson-Dorn, Jana Patterson, Nancy Anderson, Terri Wheeler, and Herb Martin.

We also acknowledge the careful and productive support of our students and assistants, Elizabeth Keniston, Stacey Malone, and Jennifer Cosio. In addition, we appreciate our excellent reviewers who contributed to the clarity, organization, and comprehensive quality of this text. For the first edition, the reviewers were Nancy File, Sante Fe Community College; Shelia Hendershot, Garden City Community College; Joan P. Isenberg, George Mason University; Penny Luken, Broward Community College; Frank Miller, Pittsburg State University; Colleen Olson, Cuyahoga Community College—Metro Campus; and Mary Rivkin, University of Maryland, Baltimore County. For the second edition, the reviewers were Elaine Camerin, Daytona Beach Community College; Diane E. Strangis, University of Florida; and Terry Swim, University of Akron. The reviewers for this third edition were Carla Ahmamm, Waubonsee Community College; Susan H. Christian, Patrick Henry Community College; and Tracy Keyes, Kutztown University.

We extend thanks to our editor, Traci Mueller, for her valuable feedback and encouragement during the planning and writing of this third edition. Nancy Forsyth, now the president of Allyn and Bacon, was instrumental in the early stages of this book. She nurtured its initiation with Allyn and Bacon, and we thank her.

Nancy dedicates this third edition to her husband, Ralph, and sons Marc and Scott Nagel with appreciation for their interest and support, and to her wonderful colleagues at Lewis and Clark College. Amy dedicates this writing to her mom, Virginia Smith, and her increasing number of grandchildren—Keeley, Riku, Keesha, Augustus, and Anna—they consistently delight and inspire her work.

Early Childhood Education, Birth–8

CHAPTER 1

What Is Early Childhood Education?

CHAPTER focus:

When you finish reading and reflecting on this chapter, you will be able to:

1. Describe a range of diverse early childhood education settings for young children and varied professional roles for working with those children and their families.
2. Describe some of the qualities possessed by an early childhood professional and conduct a self-assessment related to the professional role.
3. List the basic competencies needed by an early childhood professional.
4. Understand some of the major events and philosophies of the history and development of the early childhood education movement and profession.
5. Develop an initial plan for your own professional development of knowledge and skills.

"Individuality is a concentration of the whole world at the site of a individual" (Sewell, 1995, personal communication). The concept of individuality guides us as we begin this writing. Our hope is that it guides you as you prepare to care for children and their families. As we listen to the voices of society, we hear a yearning for community, a hope for relationships, and a sigh of isolation. In our work with young children and their families, we have the opportunity to respond to the yearning—to provide loving support, to model cooperation, and to build partnerships. As we participate in your professional development with this writing, we have similar opportunities and we will work to build a relationship with you as you read.

Building a Community of Early Childhood Professionals

We hope to interact with you to develop an early childhood education community. We welcome you to a profession of committed, caring, and competent individuals. This text is possibly different from other books you are using or have studied in the past, so we will describe how we intend to teach and mentor you as you begin your professional development.

A Text of Stories

We have chosen stories as a way of communicating with you in this book. As educators, we have learned that "when storytelling occurs, interpersonal collaborations, learning relationships, and connections are created" (Mello, 2001, p. 12). We think that stories build community and we want to begin to connect you to the early childhood educators' community. You will discover, or maybe you already have, that stories are "learning tools" that can link you and children to content, experience, and different worlds (p. 12). Story narratives are one of our human ways of making meaning, and as teachers, our stories are meant to "guide, focus, and reassure" (Mello, 2004, p. 8) you, our students. Stories are also easier to remember than other forms of information and we hope that you will remember the ideas of this book by recalling the stories.

We urge you to listen to our stories and picture yourself meeting the children and families, listening to their conversations, and feeling the spirit of their activities. Leave your surroundings and put your issues aside when you read. Put yourself into the homes and neighborhoods and schools so that your senses can experience the sights and sounds and scents. You will meet an infant named Luke and his dad, and will learn about Luke's family's concerns regarding his time in child care. A toddler named Ibrahim, whose parents are from Malaysia and Egypt, will stun you with his trilingual abilities. At a rural Head Start center, you will enjoy Felipe and his preschool activities. You will also visit his home and get acquainted with his mom and grandmother, who take such good care of him. You will fall in love with Keeley, who attends kindergarten in a public school for the arts. You will find yourself empathizing with her single mom and beginning to understand the challenges of raising a child alone. Erin Cheyenne is a surprisingly articulate 7-year-old whose parents have chosen to "home school" her until second grade. She and her parents will teach you much about what education can be. Finally, you will delight in Jodie, a 6-year-old who was diagnosed with Down syndrome at birth and who has tremendous ability to care for others. She also attends a public school and spends her day in an inclusive classroom that blends first and second grades. Her family will welcome you to their home and you will have the opportunity to hear their stories. You will also become acquainted with three brothers, Chimieti (7 years old), Otioli (5 years old), and Wamalwa (2 years old), and their parents from Kenya, as well as Angela Russo and her mom in Brooklyn, New York, who will introduce you to the community of professionals who help raise Angela. In addition to these children, you will meet the many children that we have encountered and observed during our combined 50 years of experience in classrooms and programs of all types.

Erin Cheyenne, Jodie, Keeley, Felipe, Ibrahim, and Luke are all real children, and their families were kind enough to let us share their stories with you. In a way, their conversations provide an opportunity for you to get to know them and us and our experiences with children. As you read the chapters, think about the children and families that you know and apply the ideas to their situations. That's just one suggestion for how to read our text.

Your Role in Reading This Book

As we tell the stories of this book, we promise to let you in on our thinking—what is going on in our heads. Since we won't be able to talk face to face, our intent is for our communication to be as clear as possible. We also want to interact with you. Get yourself a journal to use with this book—keep it nearby whenever you read these chapters. We will be posing questions, asking you to list ideas, and urging you to write what comes to mind when you hear or see the situations described in these chapters. Whenever you see the symbol, we expect you to think about and write your ideas before going on with your reading. If learning is active, understanding and memory are enhanced. Your participation (writing your thoughts) when you see the journal symbol will help you take an active learner role.

We do not intend to provide information for you to memorize or to answer every question we ask. When we tell stories or describe classroom situations, we often focus on curriculum and guidance. When you see this symbol c, it means that the story is about curriculum. When you see this symbol g, it means that the story is about guidance strategies. When you see this symbol a, it means that the educator is using assessment strategies. When you see this symbol f, it means that the educator is communicating with or involving families. We will tell stories, describe situations, and observe children and adults with you. We might ask you questions about topics that will require you to draw from your lifetime of experiences. Rather than tell you the "right" way to do things, we will provide as many options as possible. Then we will ask you to **respond**—to predict, to analyze, or to make recommendations. Sometimes we will ask you to **reflect**—to feel, to integrate ideas with your own experiences and beliefs, or to consider multiple perspectives or varied issues. We want you to make choices and to construct your own understanding. That is exactly the way we believe in teaching children, and we feel strongly that you should have the same kind of learning experience.

Teaching is a decision-making role, and we hope you will begin forming opinions and making decisions now, as you read this book and start your own professional development. In order to make all the decisions that teaching demands, you must first become a **reflective observer**—someone who watches and listens well and then questions what was seen and heard. In a classroom where teachers truly guide children's development and learning, there is constant action and interaction, and in the midst of it all, attention is paid to what is happening for each individual (Jones, 1993). In such a classroom, the teacher is not someone who tells and corrects, but someone who watches and asks, "What happened? What did you notice?" and reflects, "I noticed . . . " (Wasserman, 1990). An effective teacher never stops observing and asking.

Meet an Early Childhood Professional

We will begin by introducing you to a friend who is an outstanding early childhood education professional. It might be helpful for you to meet a real person who has the professional qualities we encourage you to develop. Robin is definitely a decision maker and a reflective observer—the ultimate early childhood professional. When you meet her later in this chapter, you will see her in a blended first/second-grade classroom in a public school.

Robin can be seen at every workshop or professional meeting that is scheduled—mostly in a very involved role. She questions her practices frequently and publicly. We still remember when she began questioning her morning calendar routine and the developmentally appropriateness of it for her first-graders. Morning calendar routines have been done by early childhood teachers for years and years, and most everyone just unhesitatingly accepted the practice. Not Robin! She questioned others about the value of the routine and asked herself about how well it matched the development of her children, then she made her decision. She decided to abandon the morning calendar routine, with its rote chorus of month, day, and year, because it had little meaning for her children. Robin is a risk taker in her work with children. She had 14 literacy centers in her classroom and was practicing *whole language* approaches long before we heard of the term. She blended her first-graders with the previous class of first-graders (now second-graders) after much studying and thinking, but before it became popular to mix different-aged children in groups.

The dining room table in Robin's home is never free of the most current children's books, latest curriculum materials, or stacks of recycled materials (for her construction center) she collects with a passion. If you talk with her, you find that she has read the latest book or journal about early childhood education. Most of us would like to slow her down a little—we worry about her burning out. Her human side is strong and her energy is boundless. Robin connects with others in a variety of other contexts—music, theater, antiquing, cooking, walks, and dancing. She also is a Big Sister and a member of her local church women's group.

The important quality we see in Robin is that she never finishes learning. She questions and probes all of the time. She does not accept every new approach that comes along, but she is curious. She consistently seeks improvement in what she does with children. Robin also serves as an advocate for children and families as well as for teachers. She has spoken to the legislature on behalf of children and teachers, and she has held offices in all of the major professional associations.

Recently, Robin received a prestigious national award for being an outstanding teacher. The award came with a generous amount of money, and with those funds, Robin opened *A Teacher's Space* in collaboration with her many early childhood educator friends. It is a storefront space with commercial materials for sale, a library, a workroom for laminating and producing materials, bins and bins of free recyclable materials, a meeting room for workshops and classes, and a place to relax and talk with other teachers.

Robin is exceptional but she is not the exception. You will meet many exciting early childhood professionals as you prepare to be one yourself. Some of them will be introduced to you in this book.

JOURNAL 1.1: Before joining our community, stop and think about your decision to take this course or begin your study in education. What are you thinking? How do you feel about making this decision? Why have you decided to study early childhood education?

Make a commitment right now to read this text with a questioning approach. Read the stories and practice being a reflective observer. Be actively involved in your learning. As we describe your options in early childhood education, try to visualize yourself working in the different programs—in other words, do some personal roleplaying!

Exploring the Options in Early Childhood Education: Programs and Roles

We are about to take you on a tour of early childhood education (ECE) programs, where you will be introduced to the many career choices available to you as an early childhood professional. There is a wide range of roles and responsibilities undertaken by early childhood professionals and there are many variations in ECE programs. Our first story, similar to a travelogue, takes you on a trip through the community in which we live. We will introduce you to early childhood professionals and give you the opportunity to observe some of the varied programs for children here in our part of the country. We will also share our stories of programs around the country that we have visited, so that you will have a broad picture of the range of programs waiting for you.

A Downtown Child Care Center

The community of Portland, Oregon, is a medium-sized city with all the advantages and disadvantages of an urban area. With respect to the early childhood education profession, Portland represents a typical metropolitan setting for viewing professional roles and programs. We begin downtown, amidst the city's office buildings and busiest traffic, where we find a very large child care center named Little Peoples. It is an example of a **proprietary care center,** meaning that it provides care and education for children and is designed to make a profit. Little Peoples fills an entire block at the street level. The floor-to-ceiling windows across the front and sides of the center allow the children to observe the downtown activity. On the outside, we see pedestrians observing the children. The center is bright with massive amounts of natural light (when it isn't one of Portland's famous rainy days) and the space is arranged with large play areas. Little Peoples opens at 7:00 A.M. to accommodate working parents and it closes at 6:00 P.M., when most workers are getting on the freeways to go home.

As we pass the center, two caregivers, Natasha and Jill, push the double doors open and emerge with six toddlers in strollers. The specially made strollers accommodate three children at once. A cool wind is blowing, so the children are wearing light sweaters and jackets. We hear the caregivers talking to the children: "Look at the big bus! There's lots of people in the bus. Listen to the bus."

Soon, half the toddlers are pointing to the bus and communicating in their own way about the scene. Angela is shouting quite clearly, "Bus—beep beep, beep." Jill responds, "Yes, the horn on the bus goes beep, beep, beep." She urges the children to wave back to the occupants on the bus who are now waving at the children.

At the intersection, the caregivers stop to discuss what direction to take for today's walk. Natasha reminds Jill that they planned to walk past the produce market because pumpkins and apples are in season. She steps in front of the strollers and tells the children, "We're going to see pumpkins and apples today. Can you make a pumpkin with your arms?" Angela and Dexter both lift their arms into a circle immediately, and others follow. Natasha also makes the pumpkin shape with her arms and begins singing a pumpkin song. She and Jill push the strollers for four blocks to the produce market.

We return to the center and watch the indoor activities. Preschool-aged children are involved in many different activities in one large room: Two children are painting at an easel, two others are sitting at a table with puzzles and Legos, several children are dressed up and playing in a dramatic play area, and a small group is cutting and pasting at a table with an adult who assists with the cutting and distribution of small mounds of paste. One child is wandering around and watching everyone else, and two boys are quietly wrestling on the rug. We look around the room and notice another adult who is comforting a child who appears to have a problem. In general, there's a calm about this place—only a slight hum of activity.

Everything in this place feels so new and shiny, so orderly. It is obvious that the facility was carefully designed and built for the child care activities we observe here. Wondering how old it is, we stop in at the office and are told that the facility is six years old, and that it is part of a commercial chain of centers. We also learn that the caregivers have a wide range of qualifications. Natasha has a bachelor's degree in child development, and several of the other caregivers have associate degrees in early childhood education from community colleges. Some have had experience at other centers. Others have some college credits, and many of the caregivers are attending the nearby university.

Professional Requirements

Little Peoples is not unique in its staff qualifications. The National Child Care Staffing Study (Whitebrook, Phillips, & Howes, 1993) surveyed 227 child care centers in four major cities and found that only 12 percent of the respondents held bachelor's degrees or graduate degrees in a field related to early childhood education, only 19 percent had some college education related to ECE, and 38 percent had no education at all related to the field. Most requirements governing child care programs are inconsistent when it comes to staff qualifications, so there is huge variation in the training backgrounds of child care personnel (National Center for Early Development and Learning, 2002). You could probably stop reading now and find yourself a job as a child care provider. You would definitely start learning on the job, but you would have few options regarding your future in ECE and you might not always be able to serve children well. We sincerely hope that you will not stop reading and that you will make a commitment to learn as much as you can about children and their families. We urge you to become an early childhood *professional.* Come with us and look at some other programs for children so that you will be able to make choices and decisions.

A Downtown Child Care Center for Children with Disabilities

This time, we are in the middle of Montreal, Quebec, Canada, and the downtown center is called Papillon (French for *butterfly*). It is an unusual child care center because Papillon is intentionally structured to serve an equal number of children with and without disabilities. It is also quite different from Little Peoples because Papillon is operated as a nonprofit center and sponsored by the Quebec Society for Handicapped Children. Papillon's location in a large metropolitan city and its reputation for excellent child care attracts a diverse population of families, thus children of many ethnic backgrounds attend the center. There are two official languages spoken by the children and adults of Montreal: French and English. However, there are many other languages spoken informally at Papillon. It will be interesting to listen and observe for just a few minutes.

We enter Papillon through a wide hallway bordered on each side by larger-than-usual cubbies for children's belongings. The floor is full of children struggling with boots and snowsuits. Several parents are helping their children and providing the usual encouragement ("Don't forget to bring your mittens home"). We hear French, English, Spanish, and Japanese spoken.

We notice a smiling 5-year-old, Teresa, arriving in a wheelchair. She is greeted by several teachers and she looks at us with an inquiring expression. *"Bonjour, comment ça va?"* she asks. We respond with our best French, telling her that we are fine, and she smiles. Her friend Natalie begins to remove Teresa's jacket, talking softly to her in French. When Natalie finishes, she places Teresa's belongings in Teresa's cubby and puts soft slipper-like shoes on her friend. Natalie wheels Teresa into the classroom and pushes her chair up to one of the amoeba-shaped tables. She then gathers paper and markers and seats herself at the table next to her friend. She places several colored markers and a paper on a raised stand in front of Teresa at the table. As we watch the two friends, we are touched by the opportunity that both of these children have for learning about differences. Later, we realize that this is the first of many advantages of **inclusion,** the integration of children with varying needs and abilities.

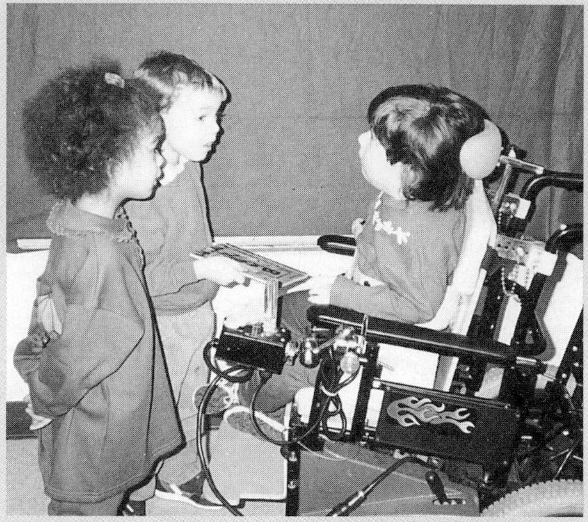

In an inclusive setting, children learn to appreciate differences.

Back in the hall, we hear "Ooh la la" from adults in response to the children's efforts and successes in removing their difficult, bulky, winter clothing. We also hear Gaby, one of the teachers, greet Robert, who is sitting on the floor fully clothed in his winter wear, and ask him, "Is anyone undressing you?" He shakes his head to indicate that no one is assisting. Gaby follows with, "OK, which leg is your prosthesis?" He points to his right leg and she carefully removes a boot from his right foot. She insists that he help by indicating where his clothes go. "Show me where your hook and your cubby are." Once Robert is ready for the day, Gaby encourages him to use the side rail, and he scoots down the hall to his classroom. As we reflect on this brief episode, we are aware of Papillon's goal of building self-confidence. Gaby provided Robert a chance to "be in charge," even while helping him (Driscoll, 1995).

Programs like Papillon are not unusual in early childhood education because there is agreement between our philosophy about children and the concept of inclusion. **Inclusion** is the idea that all children should be served in the same setting with an environment and a curriculum that is adapted to meet each child's varied needs. We will be talking about inclusion in almost every chapter because many professionals believe that early childhood educators are best able to achieve inclusion and support all children with the benefits it brings (Bergen, 2003, p. 65).

Papillon is the kind of place where you could learn a great deal about how to be an early childhood educator. That is also true of our next stop in Portland, because we are going to visit a university laboratory preschool.

A University Laboratory School

Our next stop, the university campus, is just five blocks away. There, we will visit the Helen Gordon Child Development Center, a university **laboratory school.** The center is in a lovely old home, now a historic site. Upon entering, there is the feeling of comfort and warmth that one gets when entering an old home. Two floors of large classrooms accommodate children ages 2 to 5. At least four adults are in each of the rooms—practicum students from the university and two preschool teachers per group. The center's status as a *laboratory school* means that there are always students engaged in fulfilling practicum or student-teaching requirements and faculty engaged in supervision or research projects. Also, there is a happy mix of children's conversations, singing, story reading, and laughter, and it carries through the halls of this center.

The activities are not very different from what we saw at the Little Peoples and Papillon, but there appears to be extensive adult/child interaction. The rooms feel different, too. The equipment looks old and very well used. There is an abundance of materials and well-defined **centers** (areas in which one kind of play is focused, such as a dramatic play center or a block center). The most noticeable difference is the presence of lots of blocks—and most of them on the floor, not on the shelves.

Several 4-year-old children are at a table, working with recyclable materials (paper-towel rolls, yarn, empty boxes, and so on). We hear Adam shout, "Look, Maya, I made a cage for my spider." Maya, the teacher, responds, "I can see that you worked hard on that. Tell me how you made it." Adam responds with descriptions of much cutting and gluing and "I used lots of tape" as Maya and some of the children listen. Bryna and Matt decide that they are going to make cages, too. Maya poses the question, "What other creatures could be in a cage like that?" The children erupt into a lively discussion of different insects and animals.

We take a peek outside the child development center and see that the entire yard is converted to a playground. There is a huge sand region, an area of tire swings and a slide, tricycles and a smoothly paved area for riding, and some space devoted to gardens. Beyond the tall fence surrounding the playground is the traffic of the city and the talk of students going to university classes. This outside area has that same well-used look that we saw inside the center.

Professional Requirements

The university context and the use of the Helen Gordon Child Development Center for demonstration purposes has an influence on the qualifications of the staff. All the head teachers have degrees in early childhood education and many of them are pursuing master's degrees. Their assistants have two-year associate's degrees in early childhood education. The center pays well and attracts such qualified personnel. The program quality observed at the center is in direct relationship to the preparation of its staff (National Center for Early Development and Learning, 2002) and its reputation attracts long waiting lists of children. Most of the parents feel that their children are challenged and are developing well, both cognitively and socially. There is ample evidence that high-quality early childhood programs benefit children in terms of school success, social and emotional competence, and improved opportunities for health (NAEYC, 1990c).

The Tradition of Laboratory Schools

Laboratory schools began as nursery schools in the 1920s, with the same purpose as they currently have. The Helen Gordon Child Development Center is very much a part of university life, as are many laboratory schools on campuses of universities, colleges, and community colleges. Some are associated with schools of education, some with departments of child and family studies, and others with departments of psychology, child development, and related disciplines.

All our local laboratory schools have a reputation for providing very high quality early childhood education programs. You probably have access to a laboratory school on the campus where you are studying. If you have not already visited the program, make it a priority for your beginning professional development as you study with us. Laboratory schools are ideal places to observe and begin learning about the profession. In our city, they are one of many good examples of early childhood education programs. Now it is time to see another example. Let's get ready to travel.

A Public School Early Childhood Education Center

Portland is a city divided by a river. We now cross one of the city's many bridges to see more examples of what is available for young children and their families. Close to the edge of a commercial area, in a section of the city marked by poverty, is an exceptional public school: Boise Eliot Elementary. It is one of Portland Public Schools' Early Childhood Education Centers, with classes for preschool children through third grade. The school is in a very large—almost imposing—old brick building. When we enter, the hallways feel familiar, much like they were when we went to school. However, once we enter the classroom area, there is a dynamic difference.

The hallway widens and is filled with equipment for woodworking, cooking, large motor activities, and so on. We learn that these areas are called the *commons* and that children in all of the adjoining classes use them. There is a distinctive smell of applesauce in this area. Children of different ages are in this common area engaged in varied activities. One teacher seems to be supervising them. She moves about, watching, commenting, or interacting with children, scanning their activities frequently. Adjoining this common area is a preschool classroom. Let's go and observe.

A Preschool Class

Inside the preschool room, children are gathered around a teacher as she writes their ideas about making applesauce. They have just come back to the room from the commons, where they washed and peeled apples, cut them into tiny pieces (very tiny), then mashed and cooked them into sauce. No wonder it smelled so good! We hear, "We squashed the apples" and "I'm a good peeler." Mac asks, "Is it cool yet, Miss Sabrina?" Two children go back to the commons area and get bowls of applesauce from the refrigerator. Soon, children are excitedly tasting their success.

Looking around the room, we notice that it is very similar to the one at the Helen Gordon Center. There are lots of centers: a block area, a dramatic play area, tables and shelves of art materials, a science corner, and a reading center. The room is cozy, with a little lamp and colorful pillows in the reading center. The dramatic play area offers many inviting accessories: a telephone, a typewriter, dishes and pots, dress-up clothes, child-sized furniture, and dolls. When the children finish eating, they scatter around the room and become quickly involved in play. Several children call out, "Grandpa's here," when they see a grey-haired man come into the classroom. He is immediately coaxed and pulled into the reading center and children bring books for him to read.

While keeping one eye on the children with Grandpa in the reading center, we browse the walls of this preschool classroom. We believe that a person can learn a lot about a program by studying the walls. Lots of examples of children's art, many of which look like they were hung by the children, decorate the walls. Sheets of photographs of the children engaged in activities are mounted with captions that sound like they were dictated by the children. We recall now that Miss Sabrina took some pictures of the children eating their applesauce. Now we know why. This is a room where we could spend a lot of time, but we must move on.

A Kindergarten Class

The next classroom is a kindergarten with one teacher and a teacher's aide. We also see a parent reading a book to a small group of children on an old sofa. Several children are drawing and writing in journals, some are "writing" with computers, and others are listening to story tapes. The teacher's aide, Jeremy, is sitting on the floor with five children looking closely at a basket of squash. They take turns touching the squash and describing its textures as Jeremy records their vocabulary on a large sheet of paper: *bumpy, ridges, rough, like little hills.*

The children's writing is hung in places all around the room. We see that some of it has been dictated to the adults and some of it is **invented spelling.** The kindergartners are encouraged to spell words as they sound, so the children invent their own spellings. It is evident that much of their work has been produced using computers. Many displays are around the room: on window sills, small tables, shelves, and hanging from the ceiling in mobile form. Those displays tell us that the children engage in projects, or in the **project approach,** in this classroom. Projects are focused studies of topics in which all of children's learning is integrated into the study. For example, there is evidence of a project about windows, with children's paintings of stained glass windows, photos of windows around the neighborhood and around the world, measurements of windows, and window-washing equipment in the display area.

Once again, the environment in this kindergarten tells us much about the activities of this class. As we prepare to leave, we see the children go into small groups (of three or four) and begin to have **Show and Tell time.** Some of the children have bags or boxes of items they have brought from home to show, while others tell about an event at home or an adventure in the neighborhood. Adults are in some of the groups but not in all. The children appear quite capable of conducting their own group activity, and we notice that they listen intently to each other. We would love to stop and listen to those conversations, but there is one more classroom to visit before leaving Boise Elliot School.

When topics are relevant to their lives, children are engaged and enthusiastic.

A Blended Class

The next classroom is a blended class of first-grade and second-grade children. Their teacher is Robin, whom you met at the beginning of this chapter. About half of the 23 children are sitting with Robin, talking about today's edition of the *Oregonian,* the local newspaper. They are especially interested in a story about children at another school. The children clamor to see the photos of the other children planting tiny trees. "Read what it says, please," asks Micah. Robin shows them the headline and asks if anyone can read it. Several children shout out the words *trees* and *children* and *school.* Robin assists them with the words *learn* and *neighborhood,* then asks the group to predict what the story is about. She guides them to see that the headline and the photos help them begin reading the story. Then she reads the news story to the group. During this time, the other children are at centers for painting, construction, card making, block building, and technology.

Thuy, one of the children in Robin's class, is sitting with her mother. Thuy and her family are recent refugees from Vietnam. After the newspaper discussion, Robin comes to Thuy and her mother and guides them around the room. She shows them examples of children's work or activity in each of her many centers, and Thuy's mom nods her head, acknowledging her understanding of what Robin is showing her. When they stop at the easels, Thuy shows interest, so her mother puts a painting apron on Thuy and encourages her to paint, speaking to her in Vietnamese. Thuy seems a little hesitant but proceeds to paint. Soon, one of the other children is chatting with her and encouraging her painting.

It looks like Thuy's mother is preparing to leave, and we see Robin packing a canvas bag of books for her to take home. She has selected simple children's books with little text, and adds some drawing paper and colored pens. They shake hands good-bye, and Robin goes immediately to Thuy's side, puts her arm around her, and talks about her painting. Just listening to her is comforting, and we predict that Thuy and her family will make a smooth transition to her new school.

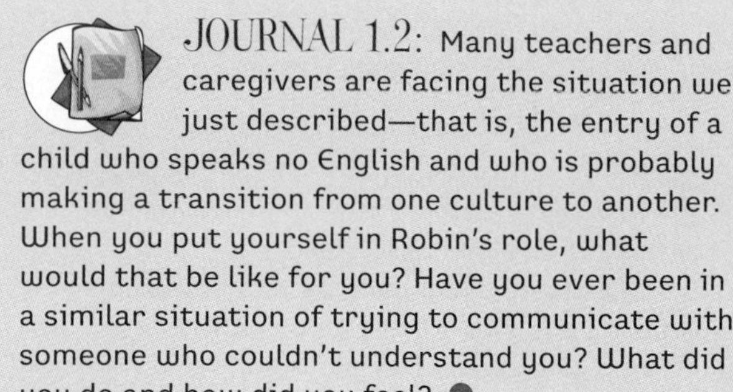

JOURNAL 1.2: Many teachers and caregivers are facing the situation we just described—that is, the entry of a child who speaks no English and who is probably making a transition from one culture to another. When you put yourself in Robin's role, what would that be like for you? Have you ever been in a similar situation of trying to communicate with someone who couldn't understand you? What did you do and how did you feel? ●

Professional Requirements

All the teachers at Boise-Eliot school have elementary teaching certificates, some with early childhood endorsements. Many of the teachers, like Robin, have master's degrees and years of experience. The teacher's aides have degrees in related programs—psychology, child and family studies, social work, and so on. Public school requirements for full-time teachers of young children are different depending on where you live. States vary tremendously in terms of certification requirements and the kind of preparation required for teaching young children. Some states require special certification and others require only an elementary teaching certificate.

Another kind of early childhood education program with varied requirements for its personnel is Head Start. Head Start programs are federally funded comprehensive programs that began in the 1960s during the War on Poverty. They were designed to counter the negative effects of poverty on young children and their families, and to offer high-quality early childhood education experiences for the children. Early in Head Start's history, it was realized that if parents weren't involved, the program would not be very successful. Head Start, then, is well known for its serious commitment to parent and family involvement. Our next stop is a Head Start center.

A Head Start Program

About 10 blocks from Boise-Eliot school is a rambling, dark brown house with multiple extensions—the site of a Head Start program. As we enter, we are once again greeted by the sounds of children. One group of 4- and 5-year-old children is approaching us and singing "This Old Man" as they climb the stairs. They gather just outside the building, sit on the grass, and listen as their teacher reminds them, "We're going to walk around our neighborhood today. What are we looking for?" Several children say, "Houses." Their teacher, Jonah, probes, "What do we want to notice about the houses?" Kim raises her hand and contributes, "We are looking for brick houses, wood houses, stone houses, and . . . " Joseph shouts, "And plastic houses." Jonah agrees and asks for volunteers to be recorders. Many children volunteer, so four recorders are easily available. Jonah gives each recorder a sheet with a picture of a different kind of house. He reminds the children that the recorders will make a mark every time the group sees a certain kind of house. "Then we will count the marks to see what is the favorite kind of house in our neighborhood. Which kind do you think will be the favorite?" he asks. After the predictions, Jonah nods to his teaching assistant, Melissa, indicating he is ready to leave. She gathers half of the group to walk with her, and the rest of the children leave with Jonah.

Back inside the Head Start center, we see a group of parents in a lounge area talking about their children and about the center. As members of the parents' advisory group, these individuals are responsible for policy decisions and recommendations to the center. Today, they are planning a transition program for children and families who will be moving on to kindergarten programs. We hear, "My older son had a terrible time when he left Head Start. I don't want that to happen to Tyrone." Another parent responds, "I think that we should spend some time visiting those kindergartens before we can decide what the children will need." Lots of head nodding and verbal agreement follow the suggestion.

Professional Requirements

Most Head Start programs are not associated with public schools and have different requirements for teaching positions. In fact, many of the program's paid staff begin their Head Start employment without baccalaureate degrees in early childhood education. Many Head Start teachers have or are working toward the Child Development Associate (CDA) credential (described in Chapter 13). Orientation, in-service, and other forms of on-the-job training and learning are a critical part of the structure of Head Start programs. Chapter 9 describes current qualifications for staff.

This is a good time to look at the different staff positions for professional roles in early childhood education and the educational qualifications desired for quality programs for children. Figure 1.1 displays a sample of some of the major roles in early childhood education. It would be ideal if we could tell you that you need specific qualifications for specific roles, but there is great flexibility in the profession at this time. Head Start has

FIGURE 1.1

Sample Differentiated Staffing Structure for Educational Personnel with Suggested Educational Qualifications

Staff Role	Relevant Master's	Relevant Bachelor's	Relevant Associate's	CDA Credential	Some Training	No Training
Director		Degree and 3 years' experience				
Master Teacher		Degree and 3 years' experience				
Teacher						
Assistant Teacher						
Teaching Assistant						

Note: This figure does not include specialty roles such as educational coordinator, social services director, or other providers of special services. Individuals fulfilling these roles should possess the knowledge and qualifications required to fulfill their responsibilities effectively.

Source: Reaching the Full Cost of Quality in Early Childhood Programs by B. Willer, 1990, Washington, DC: NAEYC. Copyright 1990 by NAEYC. Reprinted with permission from the National Association for the Education of Young Children.

a number of the specialty roles described at the bottom of Figure 1.1 and the qualifications for those roles may depend on the community of children and families, the availability of qualified professionals, and the program emphasis.

One of the major characteristics of Head Start programs is their **integration of services** for families. Many kinds of services (medical, dental, counseling, and housing assistance) are blended into the educational program and located all in one center to support families better. Let's visit another Head Start program. This one, in Alachua County, Florida, epitomizes service integration.

A Comprehensive Program for Families

The Family Services Center of Alachua County, Florida, is conceptualized as a "one-stop-shop" of family services. Through its on-site services and connections with other nearby facilities, over 750 preschool children and their families are served. It began in a complex of portable buildings with stairs and walkways connecting the units. In each of the buildings is a different kind of service for families.

The center has a Head Start program and its resources and services are shared with subsidized child care centers in the surrounding neighborhood housing projects. The nearby elementary school also has Head Start classrooms. Head Start is part of a huge collaboration between state-funded prekindergarten programs, early intervention classes, private child care and preschools, and public kindergartens and primary grades. Children benefit from the arrangement because there are more resources, easier transitions between programs, and high-quality programs due to combined expertise and consultation.

Back at the center there is also a health clinic with a nurse practitioner and a doctor. Their services include physicals, immunizations, well child care, family planning, and general medical care. In another building are adult education classes for family members. Many of the adults are working toward their general equivalency diplomas (GEDs) by fulfilling requirements and preparing to take exams. There are also technology classes and seminars in various topics such as nutrition, family finances, and music appreciation.

We listen to the conversations between Dr. Shelton Davis and a group of parents sitting in a semi-circle around him. We hear a parent share, "Eddie is 6 years old now and he's very complicated. He was two weeks overdue and when he was born, he looked old. He was so wrinkled, he just looked old. He was a baby that was always moving, like he does now. Sometimes it was like he was shaky, and he got frustrated easily. If I woke him up to feed him, he acted frustrated. If I stopped what he was doing to change him, he acted frustrated. Mostly, I just remember him as so active."

At this point, Eddie's mom and Dr. Davis talk about hyperactivity and its connection to nutrition and the need for fresh fruits and vegetables. Dr. Davis reminds the group, "You remember when you roleplayed hyperactivity and we had our bodies wiggling and moving?" Lots of heads nod, and another parent says, "I remember that it was impossible to notice or hear anything else but my own movement." The discussion continues and gets quite lively. It's obvious that there is mutual trust and caring among this group (Driscoll, 1995, p. 199).

JOURNAL 1.3: Think for a minute what it might be like to be very poor, to be a single parent with two young children, without transportation, and feeling isolated. What would be your major concerns? If representatives of a program like Head Start approached you, what would you want them to provide?

Just as the Portland Head Start program and the programs in Alachua County are quite different in the way they go about serving children and families, so are Head Start programs all over the country. Much depends on the community. Whether it is a tiny rural town or a crowded major city, you will consistently find that Head Start programs reflect the community of families in which they are located. When you meet Felipe and his family, you will visit his Head Start preschool and meet many of the professionals who make the program a success. For now, it's time to meet another professional and visit another setting.

A Family Child Care Facility

It's time to experience family child care, often called **day home,** so we leave the city and drive to one of the many suburban communities encircling the downtown area of Portland. In these sprawling neighborhoods, there are many family day homes for children. This alternative child care arrangement is another option for families. We park in the driveway of a family day home and it looks just like the other homes in this neighborhood. Once inside the front door, it is obvious that this home is different from most others in the neighborhood. Rather than the usual home furnishings, there is an abundance of toys and materials for children. There is even an easel set up in the kitchen. Two children are sitting at the kitchen table, coloring on large sheets of paper, and a child of 10 months is sitting in a highchair next to the table. One of the children, Xavier, tells us, "These are our placemats for lunch" as he colors his sheet. The family child care provider, Harriet, is also at the table, cutting apples on a wooden board. The wonderful smell of fresh bread baking fills the house. Harriet converses with the children and places small slices of apple on the highchair tray. She tells us that two children will be arriving for lunch from the kindergarten at the end of the block.

We wander through her home and see a number of accommodations she has made for the children. The bathroom has a little step stool at the sink, a stack of paper cups, and a rack of towels with children's names on them. Her living room has only a couch, a chair, and a TV wall unit. A large rug covers the floor and we see an assortment of colorful boxes of plastic blocks, Tinker Toys, puzzles, and Legos. In the adjoining dining room, there are no usual furnishings, only children's materials, a rocking chair, a bookshelf, and large pillows. On the wall are colorful creations by Xavier and Jesse, who are sitting in the kitchen. As we leave, we hear them singing a finger-play about apples and passing the apple slices around the table.

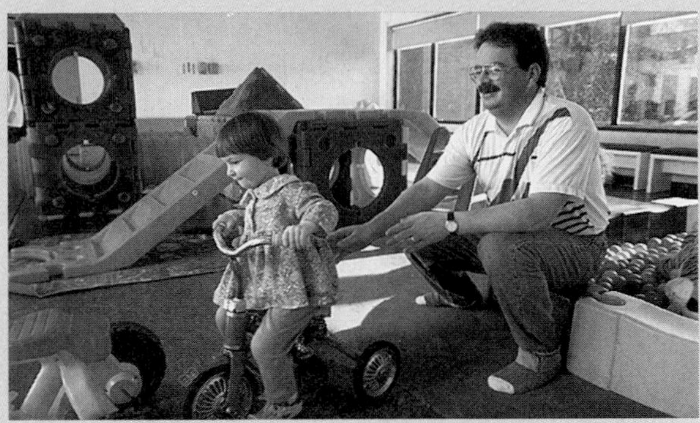

A very important part of early childhood education is parent involvement. What are the advantages of this dad spending time in his daughter's class?

Professional Requirements

As family child care gains recognition and regulation, the qualifications required for this child care arrangement are demanding attention. With more than 11 percent of children in child care being cared for in family child care settings, the staff is becoming increasingly important. Staff qualifications will vary greatly, depending on whether the home is regulated, licensed, or associated with a state or local agency. Licensing standards often specify staff qualifications, and training for family child care staff is offered by a variety of agencies and professional associations. It is difficult for family child care providers to take time off to attend workshops and other training sessions because they cannot leave parents without the needed care. Some providers seek weekend and evening training opportunities.

Professionalization of Family Child Care

Not so long ago, family child care was unregulated and invisible (Whitehead, 1994). Those who provided care in their homes were usually referred to as babysitters and viewed simply as custodial caregivers. Today, family care has become increasingly visible due to regulations, support from child care resources and referrals, and the connections of parents to family child care. Families have come to appreciate the benefits of family child care: proximity of care in one's neighborhood, small groups of children, a home environment, and a familylike structure. A study (1999) by the National Institute of Child Health and Human Development of early child care found that some of the "highest level of positive caregiving was provided by in-home caregivers, which included family members caring for one child, followed by home-based arrangements with relatively few children per adult" (p. 2). The results describing family child care look better for younger children, under 3 years of age, than for the preschool child who needs the socialization of group care. Experienced family child care providers are more likely to respond positively to toddlers' social bids and less likely to restrict toddlers than center caregivers (Kontos & Wilcox-Herzog, 2001, p. 90).

In addition, family home care providers have a very committed professional organization, the National Association for Family Child Care, with extensive offerings of workshops and classes in child development, developmentally appropriate practice, guidance and discipline, health and safety issues, and so on. For many of the experienced professionals in this type of arrangement, family child care represents an important alternative for children and families. Another alternative for families is parent cooperative programs, which we will look at next.

A Parent Cooperative Preschool

Our destination is a large church with an adjoining building that houses a **parent cooperative preschool, or nursery school,** a program in which the parents fulfill many of the planning and teaching responsibilities and the administration of the program. The two classrooms are filled with colorful and attractive play materials, many of which appear to be homemade rather than commercially produced. The place has a comfortable feeling and there is a quiet hum of children at work. Two fathers and three mothers are working with the children at this time. On one large table there are several large tubs of home-made play-dough and lots of kitchen and cooking utensils for molding and shaping the dough. The two adults and seven children sitting around the large table are very occupied with their play-dough creations, and the conversation is completely focused on their work. "Try rolling it," someone advises. "Look what I made," a child announces. Many play-dough snakes and cookies adorn the table.

Across the room, one of the mothers is reading to a small group of children. Another mom is guiding four children hard at work in the exploration center, filled with a variety of scales, rulers and measuring tapes, and very compelling objects to weigh and measure. One of the dads, Mr. Margolin, is sitting at the snack table, encouraging Alex as he spreads cream cheese on his bagel. He asks Alex if he knows what cream cheese is made of, and Alex shakes his head no. Mr. Margolin asks Alex if he likes other kinds of cheeses, and soon they are discussing swiss and cheddar, referring to "that white cheese with all the holes," and "the bright orange one we have on our tacos." It becomes obvious to us that the two are very comfortable together, and that Mr. Margolin spends a lot of time at the preschool.

Professional Requirements

There are no professional requirements for the parents working at this center, but cooperative programs generally schedule workshops and classes for the parents. The teacher requirements vary from one program to another and are often determined by the parents. Parent cooperatives reflect the neighborhood in which they are situated. The socioeconomic status of families influences the budgetary aspects of the program and, consequently, the salary and staff requirements. It's time now to drive to the outer limits of Portland to visit yet another type of child care center.

An Employer-Sponsored Child Care Center

We arrive at an area of business and industrial complexes—mostly newly constructed office buildings, manicured lawns and shrubbery, and huge parking lots. One complex is that of Mentor Graphics Corporation. The corporation has invested in quality child care for the children of those who work there. Such investments may be the way of the future.

We approach the Child Development Center building and are immediately impressed by the dynamic architecture, the festive quality of the building's design, and the convenient location for parents. We note the walking paths from the center leading to various office buildings. They are well used. The entrance of the Child Development Center is not like most of the places we have visited so far. It is definitely part of a business—streamlined in furnishings and space. Just inside the door where we sign in is a large window. We hear the usual sounds of children's play but the sounds are muffled. The volume increases as we approach the classrooms and peek in the large circular windows that allow those in the hallway to watch the classroom events.

An Infant Program

The Mentor Graphics center offers excellent care for infants, a rarity in available child care in most places. We decide to visit the infant room so that we can see what it takes to offer quality care to such young children.

Sue, the head teacher, greets us and introduces us to her assistant, Caryl, and to the babies.

Noah is on his stomach in front of a mirror, and Ivy is nearby, also on her stomach, reaching for a soft colorful ball. Two of the babies are in Caryl's lap listening to a story. Sue leaves me and takes Seth to a table for a diaper change. On the way, she stops and speaks to Luke, saying, "Look at Luke. See that happy face." Luke responds with a grin for Sue and for himself in the mirror.

As Sue changes Seth's diaper, she talks softly to him. She hands him the fresh diaper to hold and continues to talk.

Sue is an outstanding professional and is really the norm at Mentor Graphics. She has a master's degree in ECE, and Caryl has an associate's degree in ECE from a nearby community college. The staff is very committed and professional. They participate in many state and national workshops and are often the presenters for such sessions. The Mentor Graphics center is able to maintain such qualified staff because the pay is better than most centers and the benefits are quite attractive. Other corporate-sponsored child care centers will vary in terms of staff qualifications and corresponding quality.

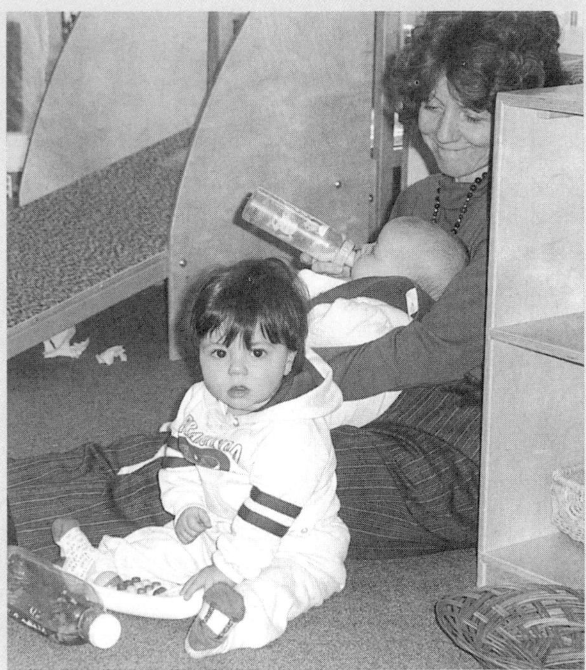

Why do you think it is so important for infant caregivers to be well prepared for their role?

Many educators in our community consider the Mentor Graphics center a kind of laboratory school. The environment, the curriculum, and the practices of the professionals are often called *state of the art,* meaning that they represent educators' best knowledge about early childhood education. You will get to spend much more time at this center in Chapter 7, but for now, let's focus on some obvious qualities of the program. For example, now that you have been in a variety of centers for children, have you noticed the number of adults in the classrooms, especially in the rooms with very young children (infants and toddlers)? When you count the adults and children, you come up with 1 adult for every 3 infants and 1 adult for every 4 toddlers. The Mentor Graphics center follows the recommendations of the National Association for the Education of Young Children (NAEYC), a group that you will come to know well. Table 1.1 shows those recommended child/staff ratios and group sizes. Notice how the ratio changes when the group is larger.

Other Forms of Employer-Sponsored Support

Although employer-sponsored child care is a hot topic in the corporate world and the early childhood education profession, it continues to be the least frequently provided employee

TABLE 1.1 **Recommended Staff/Child Ratios within Group Size***

Age of Children	Group Size										
	6	8	10	12	14	16	18	20	22	24	30
Infants (birth to 12 mos.)	1:3	1:4									
Toddlers (12 to 24 mos.)	1:3	1:4	1:5	1:4							
2-year-olds (24 to 30 mos.)		1:4	1:5	1:6							
2½-year-olds (30 to 36 mos.)			1:5	1:6	1:7						
3-year-olds					1:7	1:8	1:9	1:10			
4-year-olds						1:8	1:9	1:10			
5-year-olds						1:8	1:9	1:10			
Kindergartners								1:10	1:11	1:12	
6- to 8-year-olds								1:10	1:11	1:12	1:15
9- to 12-year-olds										1:12	1:15

*Smaller group sizes and lower staff/child ratios have been found to be strong predictors of compliance with indicators of quality such as positive interactions among staff and children and developmentally appropriate curriculum. Variations in group sizes and ratios are acceptable in cases where the program demonstrates a very high level of compliance with criteria for interactions (A), curriculum (B), staff qualifications (D), health and safety (H), and physical environment (G).

Source: NAEYC (1998). Accreditation criteria and procedures of the National Association for the Education of Young Children (p 47). Washington, DC: Author. Reprinted with permission of the National Association for the Education of Young Children.

benefit. Besides setting up an on-site center, employers can provide support for families and their child care needs in varied forms:

- Financial supplements or subsidies may be granted to help employees pay the cost of child care.
- Employers may issue vouchers to employees, who use them to purchase child care services.
- Contributions may be made to local child care centers that provide care for large numbers of employees' children. The contributions reduce the rates for families, so they are a kind of subsidy.
- Employers purchase child care services at nearby centers and make such services available to employees free or at reduced rates.
- Services that include information and counseling for families in need of child care may be provided.

All these forms of support ultimately make child care arrangements easier and more accessible for families. Other ways that employers can help is to provide flexible schedules, maternity and paternity leaves, and parent education programs. Many businesses and corporations have learned that their employees will be more satisfied and productive in their work if their children are well cared for.

Other Early Childhood Education Programs and Options for Families

We will return to the Mentor Graphics center when we study infants later in this book, so you will get to know Luke and the center very well. In the meantime, we need to move on before we run out of time for our travels. For efficiency reasons, we will simply describe some of the child care and preschool alternatives that you will find in the middle-class suburban neighborhoods in which we are traveling. In a number of the homes nearby, **nannies** live with families to take care of children. Nannies, which represent about 5 percent of the child care options, are usually trained in short-term programs for their work.

Some nannies, referred to as *au pairs,* come from Europe and usually stay for a year. This particular child care alternative is especially appropriate for parents who work flexible schedules or extensive hours. Often, nannies help with transportation to school and to activities such as scouts and lessons, and with a few household chores.

CHURCH-BASED PROGRAMS. The other options you will find in these neighborhoods are preschool programs: a school with a Montessori curriculum and a church-related school. We will describe Montessori ideas in detail in Chapter 4, so our discussion here will focus only on **church-based or church-related preschools.** Some claim that churches are the largest single provider of child care in the United States (Neugebauer, 1991a). They generally offer toddler groups, full- and part-time preschool classes, and full-day child care programs. In many of these programs, religious or spiritual development is subtly integrated into a traditional ECE curriculum. Staffing structures vary in church-related schools and the criteria for hiring is often influenced by program goals. A tremendous variation exists in this category of programs, but there is a common quality of providing a warm and loving environment for children.

INTERGENERATIONAL PROGRAMS. A unique approach to child care is through **intergenerational programs** in which seniors interact with young children. Intergenerational approaches use the strengths of one generation added to the energy and enthusiasm of another generation. These approaches often are used in community centers, shared-site programs, and other locations. The intergenerational activities may be ongoing or occasional and can involve children of all ages and seniors with varying degrees of independence. "Intergenerational child care is a wonderful blend—the richness of the past and the promise of the future" (Nazario, 1999, p. 1).

AFTER-SCHOOL PROGRAMS. Finally, in the broad category of child care are *after-school programs* or *school-age child care* for children whose parents' work schedules and school hours do not match. Such programs are also called *extended day* or *expanded learning programs.* Unfortunately, the need for such care arrangements is barely being addressed by actual programs despite widespread interest and involvement of public schools, communities, states, and federal funding (Seligson, 2001). It is clear that school-age child care needs consistent, professionally trained staff and carefully designed curricula. The National School-Age Care Alliance (NSACA) is currently focused on a national improvement and accreditation project to address quality issues for the care and education of school-age children.

A Community-Based Program for Homeless Children and Families

We return now to the downtown area because we want to show you one more program for children and families. This fairly new kind of program reflects some of the societal issues we posed at the beginning of this chapter. In downtown Portland, the YWCA offers a school for homeless children. These children often move from shelter to shelter, changing schools with every move. Having a school right in the shelter encourages a family to stay in one place and provides some stability for children. This school has been supported by extensive volunteer efforts and resources shared by other agencies. University students also assist here to help stretch the minimal budget available for this program. The shelter location supports an integration of services for the whole family—that is, some health services, parent education, assistance with housing, and school for the children. In Portland and in other cities, these schools have been successful in providing full and equal educational opportunities for homeless children.

As we look into the large living room, we see children snuggled on the couch with a young woman who is reading a story and asking questions about the characters. Three children are sitting on the floor around a coffee table with a dad. They have plastic poker chips and are using them to figure out math problems. A mom and her son are working with another adult on a project to weigh and measure the children in the group. Billy is recording the weight and height of each child. In a little side room, children are sorting clothes into piles for summer and winter. There is conversation about the color of the garments, the buttons, whether certain items will keep someone warm or not, and the children's likes and dislikes.

It is currently estimated that approximately 930,000 homeless students will need services such as those provided by the YWCA, with special liaisons for preschool children in programs like Head Start (Jacobson, 2002). We will discuss more issues of homelessness when we describe families and communities in Chapter 6.

PROGRAMS FOR TEEN PARENTS. Another kind of program in which we would observe early childhood educators is a program for teen parents, often in conjunction with a child care program. Such programs typically show positive gains for both the children and their parents, usually mothers. You will be prepared to work with infants and preschool children, but you will not have preparation for work with teenagers. If this interests you, you will need to explore the training needed to understand adolescent development and the psychological needs of teen parents (DeJong, 2003).

Summary of Professional Roles and Programs

PROFESSIONAL ROLES. As we visited Portland's early childhood education programs, you encountered a variety of professional roles. We advocate calling all who work with young children and their families *early childhood professionals.* The term reflects a concerted effort to recognize the status of those who work with young children. Although there are still some who regard these individuals as mere babysitters, there is an increasing recognition that these individuals deserve the respect, the rewards, and the responsibilities that accompany professional status. As you prepare for the profession and as you begin your career, you will encounter both kinds of thinking. It is important for you to be able to represent the profession by being able to describe why it is a profession. Keep that in mind as you read the stories to come and as you respond to the journal questions.

From the broad term *early childhood professional,* we move to the varied roles associated with the kind of programs in which individuals work and with the kind of preparation individuals have. You may see yourself becoming an early childhood teacher, a preschool or nursery school teacher, or a kindergarten or a primary grade teacher. If you intend to pursue one of those roles, you will need specialized preparation for your work and possibly a certification of your competencies. You will have responsibility for planning and implementing a developmentally appropriate program for children. Perhaps you will begin by working with a teacher as an assistant or associate teacher. Again, you will need some specialized training, but you will be in a supportive role of helping teachers. Maybe you will begin as a teacher's aide in classrooms, helping teachers and assistant teachers. You will not be required to have as much preparation, but you will be able to use your position to learn more about early childhood education. Another category of early childhood professionals are caregivers and their aides. These individuals have a variety of preparation, depending on the kind of program in which they work and the criteria for hiring. They have responsibility for basic care, protection, education, and guidance of young children; support for their families; and, in most cases, planning and implementing a developmentally appropriate program for children. In administrative roles in early childhood education, we find directors of child care and preschool programs, as well as principals of schools in which there are kindergartens and primary grades.

Although the work of early childhood professionals varies significantly, many feel that there are some common roles shared by all (Kostelnik, Soderman, & Whiren, 1993). "They all provide instruction to children, nurture and comfort children, offer medical assistance, keep records, work with parents, and cooperate with support staff" (p. 27) in the settings in which they work. Most of us would also agree that all early childhood professionals contribute to the general growth and development of children, and especially to their socialization and moral development.

JOURNAL 1.4: Think of all the professional roles you observed. What kind of early childhood educators do you know in your community? At this time, what role(s) appeals to you? ●

RANGE OF PROGRAMS. As you observed in our travels through the city, our profession, that of early childhood education, encompasses an enormous range of program options. It has been estimated that every day, 13 million preschoolers—including 6 million infants and toddlers—are in child care (Children's Defense Fund, 2003). It is not surprising that there is so much diversity in child care and preschool programs. That diversity has implications for you as you prepare to work with young children. You have many choices in your chosen career. Will you select a public or private facility? What size program interests you? Private home? Small group center? Large school? What about the length of your workday? Your choices range from full day to half day, every day to some days, and combinations thereof. For a more expansive overview, Table 1.2 gives you a look at every possible early childhood program with a description of the purpose and the age of the target population.

TABLE 1.2 Types of Early Childhood Programs

Program	Purpose	Age
Early childhood program	Multipurpose	Birth to grade 3
Child care	Play/socialization; baby-sitting; physical care; provides parents opportunities to work; cognitive development; full-quality care	Birth to 6 years
High school child care programs	Provide child care for children of high school students, especially unwed parents; serve as an incentive for student/parents to finish high school and as a training program in child care and parenting skills	6 weeks to 5 years
Drop-off child care centers	Provide care for short periods of time while parents shop, exercise, or have appointments	Infancy through the primary grades
After-school care	Provides care for children after school hours	Children of school age; generally K to 6
Family day care	Provides care for a group of children in a home setting; generally custodial in nature	Variable
Employer child care	Different settings for meeting child care	Variable; usually as early as 6 weeks to the beginning of school
Corporate child care	Same as employer child care	Same as employer child care
Proprietary care	Provides care and/or education to children; designed to make a profit	6 weeks to entrance into first grade
Nursery school (public or private)	Play/socialization; cognitive development	2 to 4 years
Preschool (public or private)	Play/socialization; cognitive development	2½ to 5 years
Parent cooperative preschool	Play/socialization; preparation for kindergarten and first grade; baby-sitting; cognitive development	2 to 5 years
Baby-sitting cooperatives (co-op)	Provide parents with reliable baby-sitting; parents sit for others' children in return for reciprocal services	All ages

(continued)

TABLE 1.2 *(continued)*

Program	Purpose	Age
Prekindergarten	Play/socialization; cognitive development; preparation for kindergarten	3½ to 5 years
Junior kindergarten	Prekindergarten program	Primarily 4-year-olds
Senior kindergarten	Basically the same as regular kindergarten	Same as kindergarten
Kindergarten	Preparation for first grade; developmentally appropriate activities for 4½ to 6-year-olds; increasingly viewed as the grade before first grade and as a regular part of the public school program	4 to 6 years
Pre-first grade	Preparation for first grade; often for students who "failed" or did not do well in kindergarten	5 to 6 years
Interim first grade	Provides children with an additional year of kindergarten and readiness activities prior to and as preparation for first grade	5 to 6 years
Transitional or transition classes	Classes specifically designed to provide for children of the same developmental age	Variable
Developmental kindergarten	Same as regular kindergarten; often enrolls children who have completed one or more years in an early childhood special education program	5 to 6 years
Transitional kindergarten	Extended learning of kindergarten preparation for first grade	Variable
Preprimary	Preparation for first grade	5 to 6 years
Primary	Teaches skills associated with grades 1, 2, and 3	6 to 8 years
Toy lending libraries	Provide parents and children with games, toys, and other materials that can be used for learning purposes; housed in libraries, vans, or early childhood centers	Birth through primary years
Lekotek	Resource center for families who have children with special needs; sometimes referred to as a *toy* or *play library* (*lekotek* is a Scandinavian word that means play library)	Birth through primary years
Infant stimulation programs (also called parent/infant stimulation and mommy and me programs)	Programs for enhancing sensory and cognitive development of infants and young toddlers through exercise and play; activities include general sensory stimulation for children and educational information and advice for parents	3 months to 2 years
Multiage grades or groups	Groups or classes of children of various ages; generally spanning 2 to 3 years per group	Variable
Dual-age classroom	An organizational plan in which children from two grade levels are grouped together; another term for multiage grouping and for maintaining reasonable student-teacher ratios	Variable
Learning families	Another name for multiage grouping. However, the emphasis is on practices that create a family atmosphere and encourage living and learning as a family. The term was commonly used in open education programs. Its revival signifies the reemergence of progressive and child-centered approaches	Variable
Junior first grade	Preparation for first grade	5 to 6 years
Split class	Teaches basic academic and social skills of grades involved	Variable, but usually primary
Head Start	Play/socialization; academic learning; comprehensive social and health services; prepares children for kindergarten and first grade	2 to 6 years
Follow Through	Extended Head Start services to grades 1, 2, and 3	6 to 8 years

TABLE 1.2 ***(continued)***

Program	Purpose	Age
Private schools	Provide care and/or education	Usually preschool through high school
Department of Children, Youth, and Families	A multipurpose agency of many state and county governments; usually provides such services as administration of state and federal monies, child care licensing, and protective services	All
Health and Human Services	Same as Dept. of Children, Youth, and Families	All
Health and Social Services	Same as Dept. of Children, Youth, and Families	All
Home Start	Provides Head Start service in the home setting	Birth to 6 or 7 years
Laboratory school	Provides demonstration programs for preservice teachers; conducts research	Variable; birth through senior high
Child and Family Resource Program	Delivers Head Start services to families	Birth to 8 years
Montessori school (preschool and grade school)	Provides programs that use the philosophy, procedures, and materials developed by Maria Montessori	1 to 8 years
Open education	Child-centered learning in an environment characterized by freedom and learning through activities based on children's interests	2 to 8 years
British primary school	Implements the practices and procedures of open education	2 to 8 years
Magnet school	Specializes in subjects and curriculum designed to attract students; usually has a theme (e.g., performing arts); designed to give parents choices and to integrate schools	5 to 18 years

Source: Early Childhood Education Today, Seventh Edition by G. Morrison, © 2003. Reprinted by permission of Prentice-Hall, Inc., Upper Saddle River, NJ.

The core of your preparation will be consistent, no matter what kind of program you choose to pursue for employment. Some additional skills or knowledge may be required, depending on your choice. That is our next and possibly our most important question. What do early childhood professionals need to know and be able to do? It is important to answer that question in this first chapter to give you some direction and to frame the remaining chapters. It is also important that we make certain to guide and support your development toward that knowledge and those skills. You must direct your efforts so that you are ready to fulfill the early childhood educator role.

What Do Early Childhood Educators Need to Know and Be Able to Do?

To answer the question of what you need to know and be able to do, we looked at two categories of information: competencies and characteristics. The competencies are simpler to address. They are straightforward lists of what you must know and be able to do. The characteristics are more complex because they begin to describe who you must be. They are not direct—we will have to interpret them together. That is where your individuality will come in. We can only guide—it is you who will be making the decisions.

Qualities and Characteristics of an Early Childhood Educator

A wealth of qualities and characteristics exist among early childhood educators. The diversity reflects the wide range of opinions represented within the profession. We begin with a set of recommendations about what makes a good preschool teacher, because we think that the statements apply to all early childhood professionals. Those qualities include:

> Good teachers are able to view themselves as learners.
> Good teachers are willing and able to grow.
> Good teachers are keen observers.
> Good teachers know the community in which they teach.
> Good teachers have something they care to teach.
> Good teachers have lots of energy.
> Good teachers are able to take risks.
> Good teachers possess a willingness to "mess around" and explore.
> Good teachers are flexible.
> Good teachers are filled with a sense of wonder. (Kramer, 1994, pp. 31–33)

Our book cannot influence your personality, but we do plan to address the first two qualities on Kramer's list. We care about how you see yourself as a learner and we will put our energy into nurturing you in your learner role. We hope to motivate your willingness to learn and grow by the kind of conversations we have in this book.

At all levels of education, it is very important to be a decision maker. We expect that the knowledge you gain from this book and from your coursework will be a foundation for the decisions you will make about children, their families, and your program. Recently, a set of primary-grade teachers were studied about their beliefs and practices (White, Buchanan, Hinson, & Burts, 2001). The researchers found that the majority of teachers expressed a strong sense of self. "They believed themselves to be competent, capable, and professional, and their autonomous characteristics enabled them to focus on the needs of children above all else" (p. 32). You may not be feeling competent or capable at this moment, but as you gather experiences and insights, you will begin to think of yourself with those characteristics.

Qualities of good teachers include inner security, intuition, and detachment (Cartwright, 1999). Perhaps you are surprised by the last descriptor—detachment—because it sounds like it's in contrast to the love and caring you want to have for children. Cartwright explains that when an educator or caregiver has "inner security and a mature self-awareness [and]

Can you see yourself as one of these early childhood professionals? They're happy, dedicated, patient, confident, and full of insight.

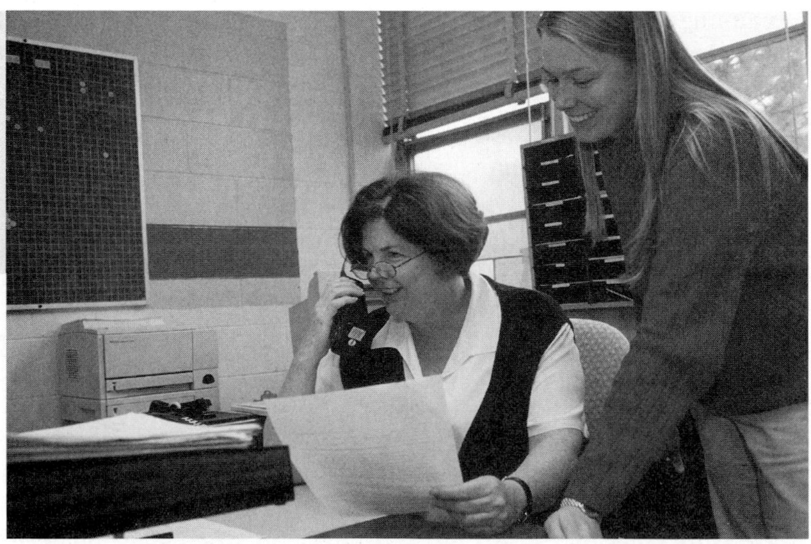

is at ease and fulfilled by her own adult development, she does not impose her personal needs onto her relationships with children" (p. 6). Your detachment can give children psychological space and help you make wise decisions based on knowledge of child development rather than on feelings prompted by the individual child. Ultimately, that means that you must have a knowledge base from which to draw. That takes us back to our question of what an early childhood educator needs to know.

JOURNAL 1.5: We hope that you have already begun to consider who you are in relation to the professional role of early childhood educator. We urge you to consider yourself, your personality, your previous experiences, and your strengths and limitations, especially in your interactions with others. Stop now and write about those qualities. Don't worry about format or sentences—just write everything that comes to mind about who you are. Describe how you feel about yourself. Later, take some time to assess your thoughts with friends. Ask someone you trust to describe your personal qualities. ●

A Common Core of Knowledge and Skills

Back to answering the questions! To begin with competencies, we turn to the common core of knowledge and skills needed by all early childhood professionals (Bredekamp, 1995) identified by the National Association for the Education of Young Children. To be prepared as an early childhood professional, you must have the knowledge and abilities to:

1. Demonstrate and apply a basic understanding of child development, including observation and assessment of individual children.
2. Establish and maintain an environment that ensures children's safety and their healthy development.
3. Plan and implement developmentally appropriate curricula.
4. Establish supportive relationships with children and implement appropriate guidance and group management.
5. Establish positive and productive relationships with families.
6. Support the uniqueness of each child, recognizing that children are best understood in the context of their family, culture, and society.
7. Demonstrate basic understanding of the early childhood profession and make a commitment to professionalism. (Bredekamp, 1995, p. 68)

NEW PREPARATION STANDARDS. In Chapter 11 we discuss the new Standards for Early Childhood Professional Preparation approved in 2001 by the National Association for the Education of Young Children and the National Council for the Accreditation of Teacher Education. Those standards also begin with child development understandings and the skills of observing and assessing young children and families. They affirm the importance of relationships with family, of developmentally appropriate curricula and teaching practices, and of professionalism. The standard that is unique in the new set is about content knowledge and processes in the disciplines of mathematics, science, and the arts. It will be important for you to be prepared for developing curricula in those areas, especially at a time when national and state subject matter standards define the outcomes for your future learners (Wheatley, 2003, p. 96). This represents a shift in the focus of our profession, and your future responsibility will be to balance your attention to academic content standards with your responsiveness to individual learners and appropriate teaching approaches (p. 100).

The competencies represented in the new standards require years of study and preparation, even though they may not appear that complex. Do you remember back in the beginning of this chapter when we were visiting the downtown child care center called Little Peoples? We described the frequent lack of qualifications for caregiver positions; that lack often accompanies other early childhood roles, as well. For a long time, we had no evidence that training and preparation—taking a course such as this one—could make any

FIGURE 1.2
Relationships between Caregiver/Teacher Characteristics, Program Quality, and Child Outcomes

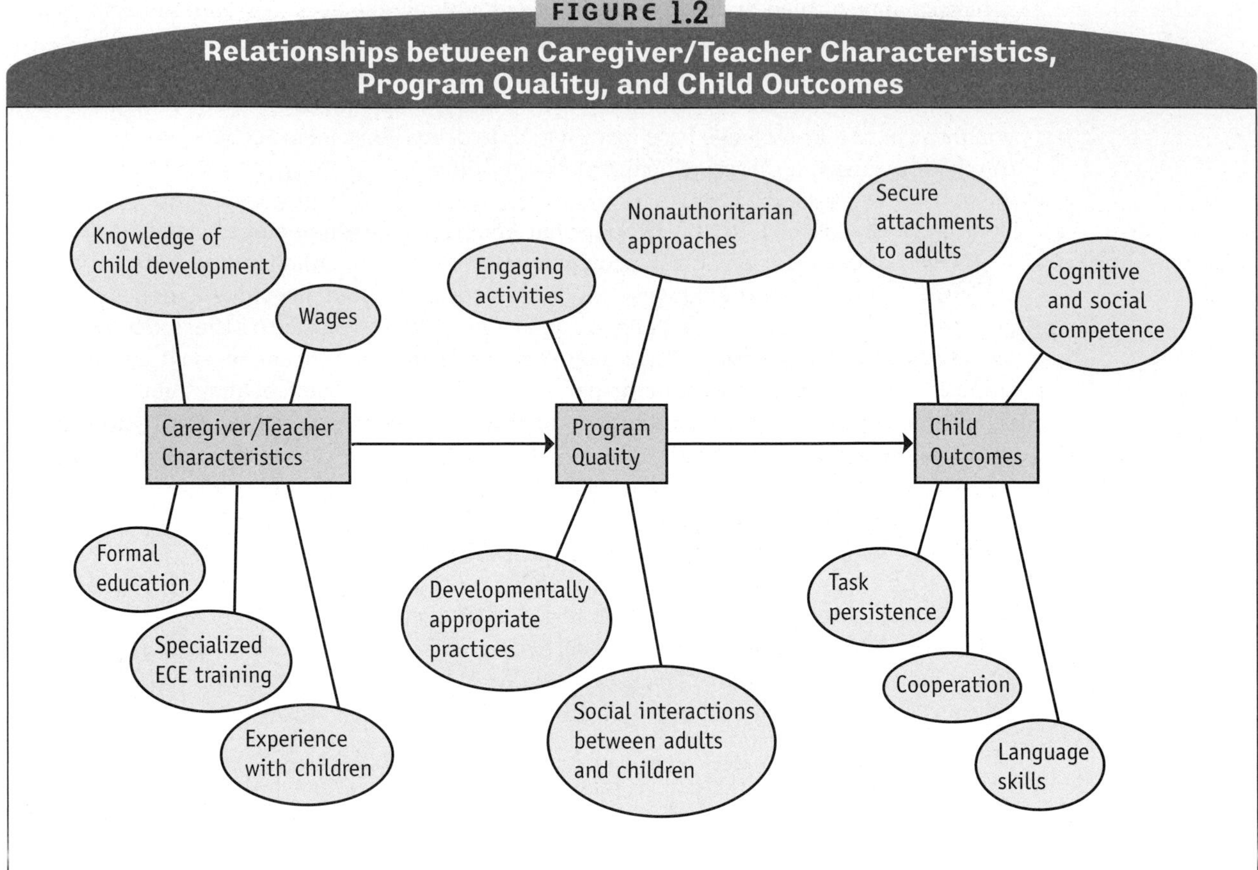

difference in the care and education of children. Fortunately, at this time, we have many studies and solid evidence that your preparation *will* make a difference. Take a look at the relationships in Figure 1.2 to understand what difference it will make if you take classes, go to workshops, read professional material, and participate in professional organizations.

By the year 2010, all states will require any early childhood educator who is responsible for children in centers and family child care to hold licenses. To attain a license, you will need to complete high levels of training and education and demonstrate competencies like those we've just discussed. You will also need to maintain your license by engaging in lifelong learning through workshops, conferences, readings, and so on.

History of Early Childhood Education and the Profession

One final collection of knowledge must be added to the list of what you must know as an early childhood professional, and that is the history of early childhood education and the profession itself. When you think about learning the history, you may question how relevant it is to your future work with children. Gordon and Browne (1993) make a convincing case for studying the history of our profession of early childhood education by pointing out that knowing its history provides a kind of support for our work. Knowing where current practices and philosophy originated will help you appreciate and understand the changes to and the challenges of our profession.

Because we think that you can learn better when you experience new information in context, much of the history of our profession is found in chapters that describe related current practices. For example, the history of kindergarten is found in Chapter 10, which focuses on Keeley, a kindergarten learner, and the history of Head Start programs is found in Chapter 9, which looks at Felipe, who attends a Head Start preschool program. As you begin your professional preparation, it will be good to look with us at the past with a broad lens so that when you encounter famous theorists, such as Piaget or Montessori, or visit programs like Head Start, you will have some understanding of how the thinking and events of the past shaped what we know today.

Ancient Civilizations of Greece and Rome

In our studies of the educational systems of the ancient civilizations for formative ideas and theories, we see that childhood at the time was brief (up to age 7) and that children were treated as adults at an early age. Both Plato and Aristotle appeared to appreciate the importance of early education, valued the development of mind and body, and saw the importance of play. Plato encouraged adults to observe children's play as a way of learning about children. In Rome, teachers were encouraged to use play to support children's intellectual development.

European Influences

Much of the philosophy of the educational system in general and early childhood education specifically can be traced to Europe from the Middle Ages to today's influence of Reggio Emilia.

MEDIEVAL TIMES AND THE RENAISSANCE. During the Middle Ages, societal views of children were such that the period of childhood was even more abbreviated. Much past infancy, children were seen as "miniature adults" (Vinovskis, 1993, p. 126). Childhood was not seen as a separate phase of development; in fact, young children received very little attention at all. They were expected to grow up as quickly as possible. Children learned from their parents or later as apprentices. There were few educational systems and the church controlled much of what was learned and believed about children. With the Renaissance came a revival of interest in learning, a lessening of the influence of the church, and an increase in the attention given to the individual and arts. It was at this time that the first humanist educators advocated a basic education for all children, including girls and the poor (Gordon & Browne, 1993, p. 6).

THE REFORMATION AND AGE OF ENLIGHTENMENT. The work of Martin Luther led to religious reform and strengthened the movement for universal education. Luther believed that schools must educate the "whole child"—that is, develop the child intellectually, physically, emotionally, socially, and religiously. Luther's reform influenced the development of the German school system, which would influence education throughout Europe and later in the United States.

A prominent and influential thinker of this time was John Amos Comenius, a bishop and educator. He gave us two critically important notions about children's learning: (1) children's development follows a natural order and education should follow that order and (2) children learn by doing, thereby affirming the value of play.

Comenius also produced some of the earliest educational materials for teachers and the first picture books for children. Through his books, he urged teachers to use sensory approaches in the learning process and to encourage children's study of nature. After the Reformation, many schools were developed and most children, rich and poor, learned to read and write. The influence of the church continued to lessen and people thought in more humane ways. Education and knowledge were prized and new theorists appeared to influence the education of children. The first of these was John Locke, primarily a philosopher, who described children's minds as "blank slates." His well-known *tabula rasa* theory, which contradicted the former notion that children were born evil, supported the importance of experiences and of parents, society, and education. Locke introduced the idea of individual differences, the importance of learning through the senses, and the value of modeling by loving, respectful adults. Although his ideas were not supported or popular, one can certainly see his influence in today's thinking about childhood.

A second important figure was Jean-Jacques Rousseau, a French philosopher and theorist. He, too, contradicted the notion that children were born with sin. In his famous book *Emile,* Rousseau described the education of a hypothetical child to adulthood. He urged educators and parents to respond to the needs and interests of the child. He believed that young children learned differently from older children or adults and that they needed direct experience and exploration. Rousseau advocated, as educators do today, natural, unstructured play, with minimal adult interference, so that children could learn and develop naturally. Current theories about children's active involvement in their own learning can be traced to Rousseau.

A third figure was the Swiss educator and theorist Johann Pestalozzi, who agreed with his colleagues about the right of all children to education. He believed that education should be adapted to each child's abilities, interests, and stage of development. Many of Pestalozzi's ideas provided underpinnings of early childhood education. Today we encourage children to explore and discover with their senses, and support their individually paced learning. We value integrated curriculum and the development of relationships. Pestalozzi's influence continues vividly in our profession (Feeney, Christensen, & Moravcik, 2000).

The fourth figure of the time was Friedrich Froebel, who is often referred to as the father of kindergarten. He envisioned schools as "children's gardens," hence the name kindergarten—places with play and toys for learning. Froebel, the originator of the idea that teachers needed preparation to guide children's play, began the first training school. His novel toys were called "gifts" and they included yarn balls, blocks, natural objects, and various shapes. He also designed materials called "occupations" that were used for handiwork activities, such as bead stringing, cutting, and sewing. Froebel introduced songs, finger-plays, stories, and games as part of the learning experience. He clearly saw the education of young children as a very different process from the education of older children. Fortunately, some of the graduates of his training school brought Froebel's ideas and his philosophy to the United States. You will learn more about the history of kindergarten in Chapter 10 when you meet Keeley and her kindergarten teacher.

Educational Developments in the United States

From Europe we move to the United States to look at the development of varied forms of early childhood education and the prominent ideas that shaped today's programs for young children.

OUR EARLIEST APPROACHES. In colonial New England, much of early education was the responsibility of parents. Some families, however, did send their youngest children to private dame schools run by women in their homes. There, children learned the rudiments of reading. Sunday schools were also created to provide moral training and literacy.

In the early 1800s, infant schools, patterned after Great Britain's infant schools, were established in the growing cities of New York, Philadelphia, and Boston. The intent of these schools was to emphasize a close, affectionate relationship between children and teachers and to downplay intellectual pursuits. Initially, the schools were developed to prepare children from disadvantaged homes using Pestalozzian methods. There were frequent attempts to integrate the infant schools into the public system but those attempts met with great resistance. Eventually, there developed a split in thinking about what and how children should be taught in the infant schools. Some teachers and parents stressed play, whereas others tried to teach the alphabet and reading with rote memorization and strict classroom discipline. This same debate continues to plague early childhood education even today. The controversy resulted in the demise of infant schools in the United States.

THE PROGRESSIVE EDUCATION MOVEMENT. The ideas of Rousseau and Pestalozzi were most influential in the movement to improve society through reform of education. John Dewey is the best-known spokesperson for progressive education and actually the first to influence the U.S. educational system. Like Froebel, Rousseau, and Pestalozzi, Dewey saw the need to focus on the child. He wrote about education at a time when childhood was not valued and was rushed so that children could work. Dewey's ideas are seen today in integrated curriculum, active learning, child-directed learning, the project approach, and group learning. He and other "modern theorists"—such as Piaget, Vygotsky, Bruner, and Montessori—influenced early childhood education as it is known today. You will read about those thinkers in Chapter 3, Theories of Development, and in Chapter 5 as we describe varied curricular models. Two other movements have been influential in the history of early childhood education in the United States: the nursery school movement and the beginning of child care services.

THE NURSERY SCHOOL MOVEMENT. Nursery schools in the United States were influenced by the work of the McMillan sisters in England. They, too, responded to the needs of poor children, focusing not only on care and education but also health care to address children's mental and physical development. The McMillans advocated active outdoor work and play and made great use of sandboxes, gardens, nature study, and other sensory experiences. Their nursery school ideas, together with Dewey's progressive education ideals, directly influenced the way nursery schools developed in the United States. Caroline Pratt's impressive City Country School in New York City opened in 1913 and is still a fine example of progressive early childhood education. You will visit City Country School in Chapter 5. Other prominent nursery schools include a laboratory nursery school directed by Harriet Johnson for the Bureau of Educational Experiments, the laboratory nursery school at Columbia University Teachers College directed by Patty Smith Hill, and the Ruggles Nursery School and Training Center in Roxbury, Massachusetts, directed by Abigail Eliot.

CHILD CARE BEGINNINGS. The earliest child care situations emerged as day nurseries in the nineteenth century primarily to serve immigrant children whose parents worked in urban factories. These day nurseries were not known for high-quality care with their untrained staff, high adult/child ratios, and very long hours. The care of children focused most often on minimal health requirements and safe environments. Much of the U.S. population did not support child care at that time because the prominent thinking was that children should be at home with their mothers. Later, during the Depression, another type of child care emerged, called emergency nursery schools. These schools were intended to provide child care relief to teachers, nurses, cooks, custodians, and others who needed employment (Feeney, Christensen, & Moravcik, 1996, p. 49). In the 1940s, the Lanham Act provided federally funded child care to support women working in defense plants. You will read about the Kaiser war nurseries in Box 1.1. At this same time, employer-sponsored child care also emerged in response to the needs of female workers. After World War II ended, most of the child care facilities either closed or were scaled down. Again, the belief was that children belonged at home with their mothers. Between that time and 1965, child care received little attention or support; however, by the 1970s, child care began to be a significant early childhood program responding to the growing needs of families. Throughout this book you will read about child care practices, visit an employer-sponsored child care center in Chapter 7, and learn about current public policies affecting child care in Chapter 13.

One final bit of history is the story of the National Association for the Education of Young Children. Its history can become part of your professional identity and we urge you to consider becoming a student member as part of your beginning professional development.

BOX 1.1 A Closer Look

The Kaiser War Nurseries—A Look at the Past for Lessons

In 1941, when women worked long days in factories to meet a huge demand for military supplies and to replace men who were serving in the armed forces, Congress passed the Lanham Act to provide federal funds to the states for many projects, including child care centers and nursery schools. The resulting creation of more than 2,000 nurseries serving approximately 600,000 children had a significant impact on public recognition of early childhood education.

The best known of the war nurseries were the Kaiser Child Service Centers at the Kaiser Shipbuilding Company in Portland, Oregon (Hurwitz, 1998). To meet the changing needs of a growing number of women working in the shipyards, the company decided to build on-site child care centers. Kaiser's two centers were built as state-of-the-art facilities and the cost of children's care was shared by the company and the parents. In a remarkably short time, the centers were ready for children and staffed with very qualified directors and personnel who were college graduates from universities and colleges across the country. Those staff members were paid at a rate equivalent to any college graduate's salary in the Kaiser Company. The centers also hired nurses, nutritionists, and family consultants to support 100 teachers and six group supervisors (p. 38). By 1944, approximately 1,000 children were cared for in each center.

Not only was the quality of care extremely high but also the cost of care was reasonable because of the Kaiser funding. The hours of care accommodated those parents who worked day shifts as well as those who worked night shifts. Every possible parent need was addressed, with infirmaries for sick children, immunizations, libraries, biweekly newsletters, a commissary for necessary care items, mending services, and a well-appreciated home food service (p. 39). Parents, mostly mothers, could order food from the centers when they brought children to the center and pick up the "precooked, prepackaged dinner when they picked up their children at the end of the day" (p. 39).

When you read about the Kaiser nurseries, you can't help but be impressed by the standards of care they provided and by the sensitivity shown to working families. You also can't help but wonder why such care and sensitivity is so rare today.

HISTORY OF THE NATIONAL ASSOCIATION FOR THE EDUCATION OF YOUNG CHILDREN (NAEYC). The NAEYC celebrated its 75th anniversary in 2001 and "affirmed that the original purpose—to create a movement to secure better educational environments and experiences for all young children"—had not been altered by the years (2001). The organization began in 1926 in New York City with a preliminary meeting chaired by Patty Smith Hill (who directed Columbia's nursery school and who wrote the song "Happy Birthday"). The meeting was attended by 25 members of the Committee on Nursery Schools. Two years later, 295 representatives from 24 states, the District of Columbia, Hawaii, and England attended, this time representing a wide range of professional roles associated with services to young children. By 1929, the loosely formed committee was inadequate. "People wanted to belong to a formal organization. As members of a variety of professions—nursery school people, pediatricians, home economists, social workers, nurses—they wanted an integrated association" (Hewes, 1996, p. 4). Their choices were to connect with the International Kindergarten Union (IKU), then being reorganized into the Association for Childhood Education (ACEI), or to form a new affiliation. The National Association for Nursery Education (NANE) was formed. It is said that the decision was influenced by the fact that the IKU was viewed as a group of female teachers, whereas the new nursery association included prominent men in its membership and was multidisciplinary (p. 5).

The NANE organization thrived until the 1940s, when its energy was affected by the demise of the Works Project Administration (WPA) nurseries and the demands of the war. Conferences were held every other year and membership went below 100. A mimeographed bulletin was sent to members to try to maintain connections but financial handicaps plagued the organization. Twenty years later, with a growing membership and the reality that financial resources were essential to the life of the organization, members and officers aggressively sought membership dues as well as funds from foundations. By 1964, the organization made its debut as the National Association for the Education of Young Children with the first copies of its journal, *Young Children,* and a membership of over 1,300 members. The NAEYC today is a dynamic professional organization with over 100,000 members, a bustling set of office buildings in Washington, DC, and a staff to address public policy issues, educational and professional development work, accreditation of centers and programs, the publication of *Young Children* and at least six books per year, and many other extensive professional services. The annual conference attracts a lively crowd of over 10,000 participants, with a workshop on every topic related to early childhood education and miles of displays of products and publications related to the profession. Attending the conference will be the professional experience of your lifetime.

During NAEYC's 75th anniversary year, members reflected on lessons learned over the years. Participants agreed that the "same truths emerge again and again and again" (NAEYC, 2001, p. 51). Those truths and lessons serve as good reminders to all of us as we think about our profession:

1. Individuals make a difference.
2. United and organized, individuals make a greater difference.
3. Setting and promoting standards makes a major difference.
4. Providing opportunities for experts to exchange information about child development and education makes an important difference .
5. Disseminating knowledge about children and what early childhood education should provide—to caregivers, teachers, parents, professionals in related fields, public policymakers, media, and the general public—is crucial. (pp. 51–52)

Perhaps that wisdom will encourage you to join NAEYC as a student member so that you can begin making a difference.

Professional Reflection

Our final answer to the question of what early childhood educators need to know and be able to do concerns professional reflection. It is important that professionals be reflective about their work with children and about their professional development. This is the time to start professional reflection, so that by the time you embark on your career, it is a habit.

Some of the staff development that has been done in Head Start programs has shown that teachers can make changes in their professional practices and their personal lives when they get in touch with their own childhood experiences and relate those experiences to their present lives (Jones, 1984, 1986). In Head Start programs, teachers often reflect on their own childhood experiences with respect to the goals and activities that they promote for children. We ask you to do some of that same reflection—to think about how you were treated, taught, and talked to with respect to health and safety issues. Those issues are a priority for Head Start and early childhood education in general.

Before you go on to the next chapter, we have a final activity for you. It is an opportunity to reflect on your future as an early childhood professional by thinking about your past.

JOURNAL 1.6: This reflection will consist of several tasks to engage you in reminiscing about your childhood and other life experiences that may have an impact on the kind of educator you will be. First, make a list of the messages you received as a child from your family or community—messages that communicated what to do and what not to do. Next, make a list of the messages you received when you started going to school—messages about what was important and what was not. Finally, make a list of all the people and experiences of your life that will influence the teacher you see yourself becoming. ●

Our reason for the preceding tasks comes from a belief that your past experiences, the influences of others, and your current ideas about teaching are a foundation for the preparation you are beginning. Bullough and Gitlin (1995; Bullough, 1994) have studied teachers and found that their personal biographies, or stories of their lives, reveal insights about their teaching. They say, "Who you are is important because it is through your prior experience that you will make sense of teaching and of children's backgrounds and abilities, formulate curriculum, frame problems for study, and ultimately negotiate a teacher role" (1995, p. 14). The events of your life will probably influence the decisions you make in your future work with children. This is an important time to bring those ideas and influences to the surface and reflect on them. When you finish this chapter, spend some time reflecting on your life thus far, or, better yet, write about your life history. See if you can pull out some themes that may have an effect on your future professional role. We encourage you to share those themes with your peers and with your instructor, because they are integral to how your preparation is planned. Remember that your stories are also important contributions to building that professional community that we are striving for in this journey together.

PRINCIPLES AND INSIGHTS: A Summary and Review

We wrote this chapter to show you the diversity of professional roles ahead of you and the range of professional settings in which you could choose to work with young children. It would be repetitive to summarize each type of program or to review the level of professional roles. Instead, we will emphasize the insights we want you to take into the next chapter and into your professional thinking. First, *you have choices* in early childhood education. That is part of the richness of the profession, as well as part of the complexity. Think of this feature as one of the main attractions to the profession and stay open to its diversity. Second, *preparation and education* are critical to the early childhood education profession and to your own professional development. You saw the differences that preparation and training can make. Be committed in your own thinking to lifelong learning and advocate for others to do the same. You can make a difference in the lives of children and in the profession. Finally, *know yourself.* As you observe children and adults, notice your reactions, your thinking, and your feelings. Maintain that reflective stance that you began in this chapter as you responded to the journal entries. Reflect on your life story, tell your stories to others, and begin building community.

In sum, you have many options ahead of you: varied professional roles, varied settings in which to work, varied models and mentors from which to learn, and varied ways to prepare for the profession. We look forward to this path we are taking together and we wish you well. Welcome to the community of early childhood professionals!

BECOMING AN EARLY CHILDHOOD PROFESSIONAL

At the end of each chapter we will suggest opportunities for your professional development that are related to the content of the chapter. The reflection in which you engage in each chapter needs to be extended beyond our stories. We encourage you to get out and observe in your community.

As you reflect, observe, and practice, we recommend documenting your experiences in a professional portfolio. That portfolio will be useful for self-reflection and assessment as well as for representing yourself when you begin your career. It is a very good professional practice to begin now. Our final recommendation is to develop a professional library. No matter how well you learn to be an early childhood educator, you will continue to encounter situations or problems for which you need new ideas or solutions. You will want to have books and other resources to browse for information or to be refreshed. Remember Robin? We hope that you will follow her example and read and study constantly to keep improving your practice. One of the most important qualities of an early childhood professional is that of being a lifelong learner. Developing your own professional library is a good step in that direction.

Your Professional Portfolio

1. An assessment of your personal qualities and capacity to fulfill the role of an early childhood educator would be an excellent first entry for your professional portfolio.
2. We encourage you to set some goals for your professional development. At regular intervals, return to those goals to assess your progress or to set new direction.

Your Professional Library

Some suggestions for books and other resources for this beginning stage of your professional development include the following books and articles:

Driscoll, A. (1995). *Cases in early childhood education: Stories of programs and practices.* Boston: Allyn and Bacon.

National Association for the Education of Young Children (NAEYC). (1990). *What are the benefits of high quality early childhood programs?* Washington, DC: Author.

Rand, M. K. (2000). *Giving it some thought: Cases for early childhood practice.* Washington, DC: National Association for the Education of Young Children.

Washington, V., & Andrews, J. D. (1999). *Children of 2010.* Washington, DC: National Association for the Education of Young Children.

CHAPTER 2

The Wonder of Children

Development and Dispositions

CHAPTER focus:

When you finish reading and reflecting on this chapter, you will be able to:

1. Describe major aspects of the development of an infant, a toddler, a preschooler, a child in kindergarten, and a child in the primary grades.
2. Draw implications from the development of each of the above children and plan a play activity or select a play material (toy) for each.
3. Define *disposition* and give a rationale for studying children's dispositions.
4. Recommend developmentally appropriate practices for each age group of young children based on those children's physical, cognitive, emotional, and social development.
5. Make an initial choice of an age group with which you would like to work and give a developmental rationale for your decision.

This chapter is about development and dispositions—two critical concepts for our study of children and the planning we do for their care and education. When we focus on the development of children, we learn what they are able to understand, do, feel, and be. With that understanding, we can set appropriate goals of knowledge, skills, and feelings and involve children in suitable activities. In addition to the learning goals that are typical for most early childhood education programs, we encourage you to include children's dispositions when planning for their education. You have probably heard the word *disposition* used in a context of describing someone you know. "She's got a sunny disposition" or "What a miserable disposition!" is commonly used. Based on those expressions, take a minute to think about what *disposition* might mean. In our conversations about children in this chapter, we will focus on both development and dispositions.

Introduction to Development and Dispositions

To begin to understand the concepts of *development* and *dispositions,* we are going to spend time observing a group of children. Unlike the groups we have observed thus far, this group is a mixed-aged group—that is, the children are not all the same chronological age. It is a class at the laboratory preschool we visited in Chapter 1, where we will see children from 3 to 6 years old. For a variety of reasons that include personality, social skills, play patterns, development, disposition, and age, these children work and play individually and together each day.

As you watch these children, keep in mind that you will see differences in their development and dispositions. Even if you have only a vague idea of what those concepts mean, we expect that you will begin to understand them by observing the differences in children. Remember: Children have a lot to teach us, if only we will pay attention.

Studying Children to Learn about Development and Dispositions

It is 8:12 A.M. and a sleepy-looking Adam, age 4, arrives at preschool, with his dad encouraging him to "have a good day" at the door. Adam hesitates at the door and waits for his teacher, Elena, to welcome him. Even with her cheerful, "Adam, we're so glad to see you," he remains at the door until she goes to him and takes his hand. Keeley, who is 5 years old, spots Adam and immediately begins organizing his play: "Adam, you're going to be the kid and I'm the bus driver. Pretend that you're waiting here for me to pick you up." Just moments before, Keeley brought 4-year-old Amanda into the bus play and resisted Amanda's attempt to be the bus driver. Not only has Keeley lined up six chairs in a row to create her bus but she also has a steering wheel and a hat for her accessories.

As the children are riding along, we hear Keeley ask, "Where do you want to get off?" Adam says, "Home," rather softly, but Amanda says, "Broadway Drive, please." Adam looks a bit unhappy and says that he does not want to play. He continues to sit in his bus seat, however, as Keeley engages other children in the bus play. After another two minutes, Amanda steps out of the bus and says emphatically, "I don't want to play any more." When the bus play ends, Keeley arranges the chairs in front of the puppet theater, then looks about the room. She approaches 5-year-old Olivia and 4-year-old Andrew, who are completing puzzles. "Those are easy puzzles," says Keeley. Andrew returns the boast: "I can do puzzles with a hundred pieces." "So can I," echo Keeley and Olivia. "Would you like to help me make a puppet show?" asks Keeley. "You can be the prince and princess and live in a castle with a gatekeeper," she continues. "Who will be our audience?" asks Olivia. "I'll get Miss Elena to watch us," Keeley responds as she looks for her teacher. Later, we learn that Keeley's puppet character is Merlin the royal magician. The other two children don't seem to know about Merlin, so she explains his role in the royal palace.

During this time, Adam has been sitting near the block area, playing with a few small blocks but mostly watching Leandra, age 4, and Ronald, age 3½, build a large structure. When their building looks like it is spreading in his direction, Adam scoots back away from it. When Miss Elena sits down on the floor next to him and asks him what he would like to do, he mumbles that he doesn't know. Together, they watch Leandra and Ronald drive little cars all over the block area and into their recently constructed parking garage. "Now we're parking and going to work" and "It's time to go home from work" are the dominant themes for about 10 minutes. Soon the two children begin playing independently of each other, building other structures and driving their cars.

JOURNAL 2.1: After watching these preschool children for just a few minutes, you can begin to predict and make assumptions about development and dispositions. Consider Keeley. How would you describe her disposition? What about Adam? Does Keeley's development seem to be what you would expect for a 5-year-old? Write your thoughts in your journal. ●

If you could watch Keeley and Adam for several days—which would be appropriate before coming to any conclusions about them—you would see that Keeley consistently is a "take charge" kind of child. She is an organizer, she is self-assured, and she is very social. These are some *dispositions* we would attribute to Keeley. However, if you watched Adam for several days, you would see a child quite different from the one you saw in the brief episode. On the morning we watched, Adam was just recovering from being ill and had returned to his class with some uncertainty. Generally, he is independent and energetic. You would likely describe Adam's dispositions as curious and sensitive if you could watch him on a day when he feels well. Now you are probably coming up with some understanding of the term *disposition.*

Defining Disposition

A *disposition* is a tendency to exhibit frequently, consciously, and voluntarily a pattern of behavior that is directed to a broad goal (Katz, 1993a). Another way of referring to a person's disposition is her *temperament.* In addition to promoting children's development in our work, dispositions are important goals for our efforts. Adam's parents have nurtured his disposition to be curious by providing a stimulating home environment and interesting experiences. From the time he was an infant, they gave him a lot of freedom to explore and ask questions. If you were to observe Keeley in her home, you would see that her disposition to take command and be self-assured has also been nurtured by her mother, who supports Keeley's control over her environment, her decision making, and her activities. Keeley helps plan the week's menus and determines how the furniture is arranged in her room. These individual dispositions of Adam's and Keeley's are further nurtured in their preschool program.

Defining Development

What did you notice about Keeley's development? Consider her language. Think about what she was able to do—that is, her physical and social skills. How does she handle situations emotionally? Over a period of time, you would see Keeley's consistent creation of dramatic play situations, her flexibility with changing conditions in the class, her ease in initiating conversations and activity with adults and children, her understanding of concepts and information, her frequent attempts to read, and her application of skills in puzzle making, painting, writing, climbing, and skipping. When you watched Keeley, did you notice her physical development, her cognitive development, her social development, and her emotional development?

Observing children's development guides our decisions about how to create their environments, select their instructional and play materials, plan their activities, and provide guidance when needed. What is **development**? A simple definition is the series of changes that occur in humans from birth to death. The most exciting aspect of being an early childhood professional is that you have the opportunity to observe and support those changes in young children.

Basic Principles of Development

With a reminder to attend to children's individuality, we move now to the basic principles of development. Many of the principles refer to *development* as *learning,* so we will use those words interchangeably. Each of the principles will be discussed before we describe the developmental characteristics of children at specific ages. The descriptions have been developed from years of observations by early childhood educators who have extensive experiences and expertise. As we continue observing children throughout this book, developmental characteristics will provide a beginning framework for what you will someday plan and provide for children. As you meet Luke, Felipe, and Jodie in later chapters, you will add detail to the framework and better understand their development.

Even with the constantly changing body of knowledge about child development, there is wide agreement about a few principles that help explain how children develop and learn. Later, in Chapter 3, we will talk about more sophisticated ideas and theories from important thinkers in our profession, but for now, let's look at six basic principles of development:

1. *Development and learning are characterized by individual variation.* This principle is the foundation of any theory of development. Children have different genetic makeups, they come from different home environments, they have different experiences, and they will grow and learn at different rates and in different ways. In Chapter 4, you will meet three brothers, Chimieti, Otioli, and Wamalwa. Even though they have

been raised by the same parents in the same home, they are vastly dissimilar. Their dispositions are different and their development has been different. "Each of them has been so individual—it certainly makes parenting interesting," said Francis, their father.

2. *Development occurs in a fairly predictable sequence.* Some say that development moves from awareness to exploration to inquiry to utilization (NAEYC, 1997a). Others describe the progression as moving from simple to complex, whether it be physical development or cognitive development. The progression has also been described as moving from general to specific. The word *predictable* does not mean that children do not move through the sequence in individual ways. For example, Chimieti and Otioli both liked to climb at a young age, but Wamalwa is far more adventurous and creative in his climbing pursuits than either of his brothers ever were.

3. *Children learn and develop well when their needs are met.* Those needs include physical and emotional needs as well as social needs. Maslow's hierarchy of needs reminds us that basic needs of food and shelter, as well as emotional safety and a sense of belonging, must be met before humans can begin to attain other needs. You will read about other ideas from Maslow in the next chapter. Ideally, children's needs would be met consistently at home and in schools or other programs, but we live in a society that does not assure that those basic needs are being met for all children. Consequently, those of us in the early childhood profession must often take care of hunger, fears, and loneliness in children before we can begin to teach or facilitate development. Remember when Adam came to his preschool after being ill? His insecurity kept him from joining in the play. He needed a lot of reassurance before he could truly participate.

4. *Children learn from interacting with the environment and with other children and adults.* The physical interactions children have as they touch, explore, manipulate, and experiment with the physical world around them promotes their physical and cognitive development. The social interactions children have as they watch, play, and work with others, and as they gradually cooperate with others promotes their cognitive, social, and emotional development. All the toys and materials you see in a preschool or child care center contribute to each child's development. The adults and the child's peers are major contributors to development.

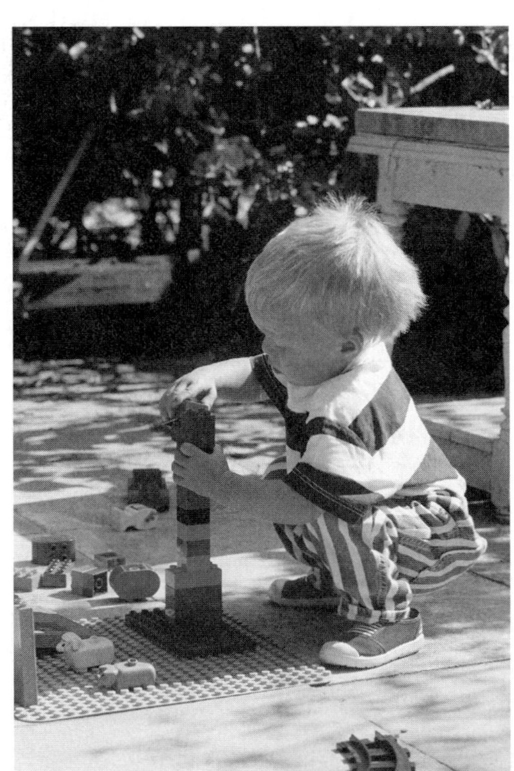
Observing children even briefly can reveal much about their development. What might you learn from watching this boy?

5. *Children learn from play.* Children's play, sometimes called "work" by them, promotes development in all aspects of growth. Play is the best context for children's learning and development in that it is open ended and free, children have control over it, it can be done alone or with others, it can even occur without any materials or equipment, and it can take place in many settings. Play comes naturally to children, so it makes sense that they learn from it.

6. *Children construct their own knowledge.* This idea is a fairly recent one. In the past, educators talked about children making discoveries as they played and interacted with others, but only recently have educators described what happens as children construct their own knowledge. It is what we are asking you to do in this book—that is, construct your own knowledge. In the beginning of this chapter, we did not define *disposition* for you. We hinted at its meaning, then we had you observe Keeley and see if you could describe her disposition. In other words, we left it to you to create your own definition, your own understanding. This principle is exemplified in our request to you to reflect on and respond to the journal entries every so often in each chapter. We're encouraging you to construct your own knowledge.

JOURNAL 2.2: Return for a minute to the scene in the mixed-aged class and watch Keeley and Adam again. See if you can find evidence of the basic principles of development in their play and interactions. Did you see them construct their own knowledge? What did they do? If Keeley and Adam did not have their basic needs met, what might you have seen them doing? ●

The basic principles we've listed are very broad; we will elaborate on them later. For now, we ask you to keep them in mind as we describe characteristics of each of the ages of children included in this book. We will be looking at children from birth to age 8, because those are the typical parameters of early childhood education. That is not to say that there are not some 10- and 11-year-olds out there who can be described with similar developmental descriptions. For our purposes of creating some generalizations about development, we will look at infants (birth to 24 months), toddlers (12 months to 36 months), preschoolers (3 to 5 years), kindergarten learners (5 to 6 years), and primary grade learners (6 to 8 years). You may have noticed an overlap between infants and toddlers, and that was intentional. Because children develop so differently, some children are considered infants at 18 months and others are considered toddlers at 18 months. The variety of early childhood programs classifies those two groups differently, so we tried to encompass all the possibilities.

Why Study Development?

The information we have today about child development comes from a wide variety of sources. It has been said that the body of knowledge about children's development doubles every three years. Today's knowledge comes from studies in psychology, sociology, linguistics, health, anthropology, history, and education. This may sound overwhelming, but it serves as a reminder of how important it is to be constantly watching children to learn about their development. Many research studies and significant theories about development will guide us as we observe children and make decisions about their learning. Why study development? The answer is decision making. Using what we know and observe about children's development guides our decisions about their environment, their activities, and how we interact with them.

USING DEVELOPMENTAL GUIDES. To assist us in understanding what we see when we watch children, there are normal **developmental guides**—indicators of what a typical 4-year-old or toddler looks like. Descriptions of **normative development**—what we know about so-called typical 4-year-old or 18-month-old children—are sort of an average developmental level. Talking about normative development comes with a caution to remember that each child is different. We must observe children with constant attention to the individuality of humans. There really is no such thing as a *typical* toddler or a *typical* 4-year-old. With young children especially, we know that development is happening so fast that their understandings and their skills change from day to day. For example, Keeley's language is expanding rapidly and her coordination is smoothing out right in front of her teacher's eyes. Her development may slow down for a few months and then suddenly accelerate. Children's rates of growth and development vary tremendously, so any developmental guidelines must take individuality into account.

PREVIEW OF DEVELOPMENTAL PROFILES. To begin, we will provide a developmental snapshot of each of the age groups we listed for early childhood education. The profiles will not be detailed. Perhaps you have been around children of all the ages described by early childhood. If so, you have a beginning understanding of what each age is like. If not, begin to take notice of children in your community—in the grocery store or library, on the bus, or in the center where you work.

In the chapters that follow, you will meet children of each age and observe them intensely at home and in a program or class where they spend their days. Those chapters will develop a more in-depth understanding of normative development of each age, while introducing the individual differences of the children in our stories. You will notice and describe their developmental characteristics, draw conclusions about them, and mentally plan environments and activities for them (constructing your own learning). We will also have in-depth conversations about the development of Ibrahim (Chapter 8), and Keeley (Chapter 10), and Jodie (Chapter 12) to get you ready for your role as an early childhood professional.

Studying Infants

Before describing infant development, it is appropriate to think about what happens before an infant is born. In today's society, with multiple stresses on families, with many teens giving birth, and with children born to adults who do not receive good prenatal care, your understanding of infant development would be incomplete without a look at the situation before birth.

Before Birth

The following factors help us focus on the situation before, during, and after birth that directly influence how a child will develop. They include:

- Family economics (resources, needs, and limits)
- Family support system
- Family health (physical, emotional, and social)
- Community and dominant themes within
- Educational levels of family members
- Cultural background of family
- Family size
- Family attitudes toward pregnancy, children, education

The behaviors and attitudes of parents directly influence the growth and development of a child before birth (Black & Puckett, 2000). Today's infants may be born to a homeless couple, to a drug-addicted family, or to a violent home. Birth may follow a pregnancy characterized and influenced by undernutrition, alcohol abuse, or depression about having an unwanted child. All of these factors will have an effect on how babies develop. In contrast, babies are also born to healthy parents, as you will see in many of our chapters. In most cases, babies are wanted and cherished. Their environments are often nurturing, stimulating, and secure. So what are infants like? How can we describe them in terms of development?

Infant Development

In the past, infants were not given credit for being able to do much, but today, people are aware of infants' incredible capacities. From the moment they are born, they must make a number of physiological adjustments that begin with breathing, eating, and eliminating. They adjust from a very secure, warm, and sheltered environment within their mothers to one of varied stimuli, less security, and different temperatures. For these reasons, the first four weeks, the **neonatal period,** is a critical period in infant development.

By the end of the neonatal period, the infant displays a number of inborn movements called **reflexes.** If you watch a newborn, you may see survival reflexes—such as breathing, rooting, sucking, and eye blinks—or primitive reflexes—such as grasping and the startle reflex (which occurs when a loud noise or sudden movement causes the arms to thrust out from the body).

PHYSICAL AND MOTOR DEVELOPMENT. An infant's physical development is marked by observable changes in weight and length as well as internal changes of the central nervous system, bones, and muscles. As the nervous system matures, the bones and muscles grow and become coordinated. Consequently, the first year of life is one of exciting motor development—that is, physical development focused on movement. Table 2.1 shows the changes, or developmental milestones, of motor development during the infant's first year. These changes in the infant's ability to move and manipulate his environment have many implications for the kind of environment he needs, the appropriate play materials, and the types of activities from which he can learn and enjoy.

TABLE 2.1 Developmental Milestones in Motor Control during the First Year

Age	Motor Development
Birth to 3 months	Supports head when in prone position Lifts head Supports weight on elbows Hands relax from the grasping reflex Visually follows a moving person Pushes with feet against lap when held upright Makes reflexive stepping movements when held in a standing position Sits with support Turns from side to back
3 to 6 months	Slaps at bath water Kicks feet when prone Plays with toes Reaches but misses dangling object Shakes and stares at toy placed in hand Head self-supported when held at shoulder Turns from back to side Sits with props Makes effort to sit alone Exhibits crawling behaviors Rocks on all fours Draws knees up and falls forward
6 to 9 months	Rolls from back to stomach Crawls using both hands and feet Sits alone steadily Pulls to standing position in crib Raises self to sitting posture Successfully reaches and grasps toy Transfers object from one hand to the other Stands up by furniture Cruises along crib rail Makes stepping movements around furniture
9 to 12 months	Exhibits "mature" crawling Cruises holding on to furniture Walks with two hands held Sits without falling Stands alone May walk alone Attempts to crawl up stairs Grasps object with thumb and forefinger

Source: The Young Child: Development from Prebirth through Age Eight by J. Black and M. Puckett, © 2000. Reprinted by permission of Prentice-Hall, Inc., Upper Saddle River, NJ.

If we asked you to list what kind of environment and materials you would provide for an infant, you might write *a safe place, soft surfaces,* and *carefully selected objects that can be held and tasted by the infant.* Each characteristic of infant development will give you an indication of what kind of setting and what sorts of activities and interactions are appropriate.

SOCIAL AND EMOTIONAL DEVELOPMENT. Normal social and emotional development of infants is characterized by the beginnings of trust and attachment, an array of emotions, crying and other forms of communication, and the start of social cognition. Each of these developments has important implications for the adults who interact with infants. Trust is learned by infants when their care is nurturing and predictable. The youngest infant soon realizes if she can depend on being comforted when upset, or changed when wet, or fed when hungry. This is the beginning of trust. In addition to trusting adults, infants learn to trust themselves. They learn that they have the capacity to get what they need by communicating with others. For example, an infant soon realizes that when she cries, one of the parents will comfort her; thus begins the baby's awareness of her ability to get what she needs.

Attachment is a complex kind of bonding and an emotional relationship between an infant and a significant adult (mother, father, or caregiver). The observable characteristics are mutual affection and the desire or need for proximity of each other. Emotionally healthy infants form attachments gradually during their first year. Bowlby (1962/1982) describes a sequence of four phases that characterize the development of attachment (Figure 2.1).

During phase 3, two related developments occur. Infants develop separation anxiety and stranger anxiety. For your work with young children, it will be important to understand these fears. **Separation anxiety** occurs when the attachment between infant and adult becomes quite intense. It is understandable, then, that the infant becomes very upset when separated from the adult. For a caregiver or other early childhood professional, the onset of separation anxiety means that the infant will need extra reassurance and support, gradual separations from the important adult, and well-established routines and rituals. **Stranger anxiety** is actually a healthy indication that the infant recognizes familiar adults and is insecure around those who are unfamiliar. Again, there are ways to ease the anxiety. Infants need long periods of unhurried time to get used to someone new. The security of a familiar object (blanket, stuffed animal, or toy) and familiar people (sibling, parent, or caregiver) help the infant become comfortable with someone new.

DEVELOPMENT IN AN UNHEALTHY BEGINNING. We have been describing what happens as healthy infants develop, but what occurs for those who do not have healthy beginnings? One characteristic that is in contrast to attachment is disorganization or conflicted feelings and behaviors expressing stress or anxiety. Not surprisingly, there is a connection between infant disorganization and parental neglect and abuse, maternal depression, low socioeconomic status, and no family support. In addition to the stress and anxiety observed in some infants, a **failure to thrive** characterizes some babies. Infants who are neglected or deprived of parental nurturance and stimulation fail to grow and develop normally. When you look back at those factors that influence how a child will develop, you can understand how those factors could result in deprivation or neglect. For instance, if family economics are drastic, and there is little food or heat in a home, it will be difficult to provide for a baby's needs. Likewise, if the family does not have a support system, new parents may become stressed by an infant's cry and not respond in healthy ways. Caring for an infant often requires 24-hour care and good physical and emotional health on the part of the adults. When the situation is supportive of infant development, babies are capable of rapid growth and development. They are able to accomplish so much in a short time. One area of rapid development that you cannot help but notice is infant communication. It is a developmental area that continues to be studied and is providing new insights about babies.

FIGURE 2.1

Bowlby's Sequence for the Development of Attachment

Phase 1 (Birth to 8–12 weeks)
Indiscriminate Responsiveness to Humans

During this phase, infants orient to persons in their environment, visually tracking them, grasping and reaching for them, and smiling and babbling. The infant often ceases to cry upon seeing a face or hearing a voice. These behaviors sustain the attentions of others and thus their proximity to the infant, which is the infant's goal.

Phase 2 (3 to 6 months)
Focusing on Familiar People

The infant's behaviors toward others remain virtually the same except that they are more marked in relation to the mother or perhaps the father. Social responses begin to become more selective, however, with the social smile reserved for familiar people. Strangers receive a long, intent stare. Cooing, babbling, and gurgling occur with familiar people. A principal attachment figure begins to emerge, usually the mother.

Phase 3 (6 months to 3 years)
Active Proximity Seeking

Infants show greater discrimination in their interactions with people. They become deeply concerned for the attachment figure's presence and cry when that person starts to leave. Infants will monitor the attachment figure's movements, calling out to them or using whatever means of locomotion they have to maintain proximity to them. The attachment figure serves as a base from which to explore and is followed when departing and greeted warmly upon return. Certain other people may become subsidiary attachment figures; however, strangers are now treated with caution and will soon evoke alarm and withdrawal.

During phase 3, two very predictable fears emerge. *Separation anxiety* occurs as the relationship between the infant and the attachment figure becomes more intense and exclusive. The infant cries, sometimes quite vociferously, upon the departure of the attachment figure and exhibits intense joy upon their reunion.

Stranger anxiety is another characteristic fear of phase 3. Occurring around 7 to 8 months, the infant's stranger anxiety is characterized by lengthy stares and subsequent crying at the sight of an unfamiliar person. Alarmed, the infant will cling tightly to the attachment figure and resist letting go.

Phase 4 (3 years to the end of childhood)
Partnership Behavior

Prior to this phase, the child is unable to consider the attachment figure's intentions. For instance, the suggestion that "I'll be right back" is meaningless to the child, who will insist on going along anyway. By age 3, the child has developed a greater understanding of parental intent and plans and can envision the parent's behavior while separated. The child is now more willing and able to let go and can be more flexible.

Source: The Young Child: Development from Prebirth through Age Eight by J. Black and M. Puckett, © 2000. Reprinted by permission of Prentice-Hall, Inc., Upper Saddle River, NJ.

INFANT COMMUNICATION. Research indicates that fetuses can hear their mothers from inside the womb and may even be able to distinguish differing patterns in the language that they hear (Golinkoff & Hirsh-Pasek, 1999, p. 47). It has been shown that infants can notice the difference in rhythms of different languages. Babies respond with excitement, vocalization, and eye contact to "baby talk" because it exaggerates sounds and facial expressions. By age 3 to 4 months, babies are "cooing" and making all sorts of sounds, especially in interactions with others. By 9 to 12 months old, babies carry on lengthy exchanges of language and are quite creative and persevering in making their wants and needs understood.

Infancy and Dispositions

Although infants go through rapid changes in some aspects of their development, their dispositions begin to emerge slowly. Individual temperaments might seem evident at birth, but a number of factors (feeding, mood of parents, comfort, order of birth) will probably influence a baby's true disposition. If you were to watch an infant for a period of time, you could probably predict her disposition. Recently, one of us observed a young adult with a very relaxed and accepting disposition. When we commented on her disposition, her mother recalled, "Even as a baby, she was like that."

Babies grow and develop so rapidly that those around them are usually amazed that the babies have become toddlers in such a short time. This fact is a great reminder to stop and watch babies now, for they will make tremendous changes rapidly.

Studying Toddlers

It is difficult to say when infancy stops and toddlerhood begins; in fact, it is different for every child, which is why we gave it a range of 12 to 24 months. For our purposes, let's say that a **toddler** is one who begins walking and talking. Some call **toddlerhood** a transition between infancy and childhood. It is a very exciting time to observe and care for a child, because so many major changes occur and growth is so noticeable. Certainly, you will never get bored around a toddler. When you meet Ibrahim and his toddler friends in Chapter 8, you will be amazed at the energy of their parents and teachers.

Toddler Development

During toddlerhood, children move from almost complete dependence on adults and others to the beginnings of self-reliance. They can move fairly well, do things for themselves, and express what they want. In addition to becoming self-reliant, toddlers begin to learn and comply with the rules and values of society; that is, they become socialized.

SOCIALIZATION. As children show that they can understand, social rules and values are actively imposed on them by parents and others. Learning theorists suggest that young children comply because they want to maintain closeness with parents and have their needs met. Some educators think that very young children comply with adult expectations and requests because they are born with the desire to please. This is especially reasonable if a child is in a pleasant and supportive environment and has loving caregivers. That same compliance of a toddler may be misinterpreted as a readiness for some new skill, so we urge caution when observing the child who goes along with a rule or routine.

JOURNAL 2.3: Make a list of situations in which adults try to get children to do things for which they are not ready. Now make another list, showing the reasons why adults expect and request such behaviors. ●

Toddlers begin to learn social rules and values (Honig, 2002) and become more competent in their interactions with adults and with other children (Howes, 1988). They can observe and interpret the actions of others, imitate them, and maintain a sequence of interaction with others. Most of the interactions of toddlers are **object centered,** meaning that they focus more on an object (such as a toy) rather than on an activity. One of the most obvious developmental changes in a toddler is his ability to separate from his parent or caregiver and go off to play or explore elsewhere. The toddler will often check to see if mom or dad is still in the room or will call out to her caregiver from across the room, but the distance appears to be comfortable. During toddlerhood, children also develop an ability called **social referencing.** This is the ability to "read" facial expressions and tones of voice as cues for what to do. Many a young child has looked up at a parent's face and expressed dismay at the parent's sad or angry facial expression.

During this stage, most toddlers begin talking; therefore, language development will demand much of our attention as we study this age group. In addition to learning words, toddlers begin to learn the rules, or conventions, for combining sounds into words and words into sentences. This is a fairly sophisticated process by itself, but it must be developed in the complexity of social situations that can change the rules, so it is an amazing accomplishment. Starting with the youngest toddler, we will look at the major tasks of language learning in a progression of typical development.

LANGUAGE DEVELOPMENT. The first task in language development is learning sound patterns. In infancy, we hear babies cry and coo and babble, and toward the end of the first year, we hear **patterned speech.** It sounds like babbling, but it has a pattern to it that resembles the intonation and form of the language that the child is hearing from those around him. Once the toddler recognizes and can produce a small number of **phonemes** (groups of sounds, the smallest speech units), he begins to say his first words and to recognize words.

Toddlers quickly develop **expressive language**—that is, the ability to produce language forms. That development follows a sequence. The child begins with a big language learning task—learning words and their meanings. The first words are, of course, the names of familiar people and items. Can you think of a list of predictable first words? Early vocabulary also includes social commands, such as "Me"; movement, such as "Go byebye"; and expressions of "No." During this learning period, parents and others who interact with the toddler influence the range of vocabulary and how it is used. Adult language patterns will often determine the toddler's language patterns. For example, if a parent asks a great number of "What?" questions of the toddler, the toddler will develop extensive vocabulary to label things.

The average toddler develops vocabulary slowly until about age 18 months, then the acquisition of new words increases dramatically. Between 1 and 2 years of age, the range of new words learned is between 100 and 1,000 words. That wide range is another reminder of individual differences. During this phase of toddlerhood, we hear young children attempting to make plurals of their words, or changing the tenses. They make a lot of mistakes in the process, often causing adults to chuckle at the attempts.

For most of toddlerhood, children are in a one-word stage, meaning that their speech is limited to using one word at a time. With their use of single words, however, toddlers may be communicating more than a simple label. For example, when a toddler points to her mother and says "Momma," she may simply be acknowledging her mother. But when she holds up her mother's scarf, and says "Momma," she may be saying "Momma's scarf," or when she tugs at her mother's hand and says "Momma," she may be saying "Momma, come." This is an example of a **holophrase,** and toddlers soon have a number of holophrases that communicate their needs and wants as well as enable them to hold a conversation with others. What you will learn about toddlers' speech is that you must not only listen well but you must also notice the situation, observe the toddlers' gestures, and be ready to guess. They want to talk with you, and their language development will be enhanced if you are able to respond appropriately to their early attempts at conversation.

At around 18 to 24 months of age, toddlers begin to put two words together into **two-word sentences.** They are usually very simple ideas and are generally expressed with a noun and a verb, and occasionally an adjective. Such sentences capture the gist of what the toddler wants to say, and adults again must maintain an awareness of the entire situation in order to interpret them appropriately. When you meet Ibrahim in Chapter 8, you will notice how his mother pays close attention to his talk in order to more accurately understand Ibrahim's ideas and needs. As an early childhood professional, you will need to follow her example and be a very good listener.

The stages of language development in Figure 2.2 go beyond two-word sentences, because some toddlers continue to develop their language and use **telegraphic sentences, joined sentences,** and even occasionally **overgeneralizations.** The figure shows the sequence of language development that you will observe when you spend time around toddlers and preschoolers.

Along with the development of language that has such dramatic growth during toddlerhood, there is also the beginning of a capacity for representation. The children begin to use symbols to represent things. Language use is one example of this capacity, but

FIGURE 2.2

Stages of Language Development

Sounds

From birth infants make and respond to many sounds. Crying, gurgling, and cooing are important first steps in the language-learning process.

Babbling

All of the sounds found in all languages are encompassed in children's first babbling. Gradually, babbling becomes more specific with native language syllables being consistently practiced. Before the end of their first year, children engage in pseudo-language, babbling that mimics the native language in its intonation and form.

Holophrases

The first word evolves to many single words or syllables that stand for a variety of meaningful sentences or phrases in different situations. *Car* said while looking out the window may mean, "Look at the car outside"; *car* said while standing next to the toy shelf may mean, "I want my toy car." A vocabulary of holophrases enables children to communicate with familiar caregivers. Children use successive holophrases to increase their communicative power: *Car* (pause) *go* to indicate "I want to go for a ride."

Two-Word Sentences

Two-word sentences appear between eighteen and twenty months of age and express ideas concerning relationships: "Mommy sock" (possessor-possession), "Cat sleeping" (actor-action), "Drink milk" (action-object), and so on. A vocabulary of about 300 words is typical.

Telegraphic Sentences

The next stage of language are sentences that are short and simple. Similar to a telegram, they omit function words and endings that contribute little to meaning: "Where Daddy go?" "Me push truck."

Joined Sentences

As language development proceeds, children join related sentences logically and express ideas concerning time and spatial relationships. They come to understand social expectations for language use and begin to use adult forms of language. Vocabularies expand rapidly, the ability to use words increases, and children intuitively acquire many of the rules of language. By age three children have vocabularies of nearly 1,000 words.

Overgeneralizations

As children become more sophisticated in their language, they overgeneralize rules in ways that are inconsistent with common usage; for example, "I comed home" for "I came home" (sometimes called *creative grammar*). Correct forms are temporarily replaced as rules are internalized.

Source: *Who Am I in the Lives of Children?* Sixth Edition by S. Feeney, D. Christensen, and E. Moravcik, © 2000. Reprinted by permission of Prentice-Hall, Inc., Upper Saddle River, NJ.

another is seen in pretend play. For example, toddlers will pretend to ride a large rectangular block or to drink out of a cylinder block. Young toddlers will play with actual objects, such as dolls, cars and trucks, and animals. Older toddlers (near 2 years) represent other things in their play—blankets and kitchen objects, for instance. When Keeley was 20 months old, she rolled up a cloth and carried it as a baby, and she expected everyone else to treat it like a baby.

PHYSICAL AND MOTOR DEVELOPMENT. Physically, toddlers do not grow as rapidly as they did during infancy, but their motor development is impressive. A young toddler walks unsteadily, partly because he still has some baby fat and because his legs make up only about 30 percent of his height. An early childhood classroom for toddlers often has furnishings that can be used for purposes of steadying and gaining balance. As a toddler develops and gains experience, his walking becomes well coordinated. From there, the toddler jumps, runs, and climbs. His large motor skills increase dramatically because his large muscles (in the arms, trunk, and legs) are maturing. He becomes more coordinated and can use wheel toys, explore climbing structures, and throw and kick balls.

During toddlerhood, small muscles also develop and mature. A toddler learns to manipulate objects well and begins building with blocks and other toys. His abilities to reach, grasp, manipulate, and release toys and other items become more precise during this de-

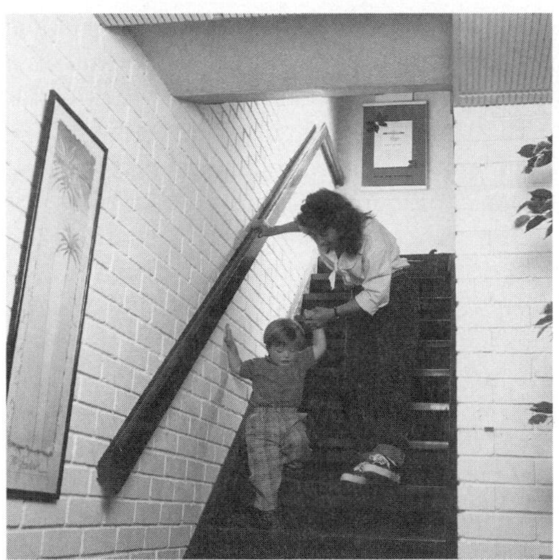
Toddlerhood is a time for rapidly developing motor skills and enormous amounts of determination.

velopmental period. It takes a great amount of experience or practice, so it is important to provide appropriate materials and activities for children at this age. At this time, the coordination of eyes and hands improves greatly, and the toddler begins to master tasks such as assembling simple puzzles, matching faces, and so on. Figure 2.3 summarizes some of the typical large and small motor skills that you will see when you watch the toddlers in Chapter 8.

Toddlers do not have well-developed **perceptual motor skills**—that is, the combination of what they see and the body movements to match what they perceive. They often bump into furniture or each other, or they try to stuff large toys into bags that are smaller than the toy. When they move to music, most toddlers do not really move to the rhythm or beat; they just move their bodies. At this age, children simply are not ready to process the information that they are taking in with their ears or eyes or touch. There is, however, one aspect of their experience that toddlers begin to organize and acknowledge: awareness of body and gender.

GENDER AWARENESS. It is not surprising that toddlers develop **body awareness** as they acquire and repeat new motor skills. From the time they are in the crib and discover that they can bang their bed against the wall by rocking back and forth, they become aware of their power and their ability to make things happen. As their motor activities increase, toddlers begin to form mental images of themselves. They also begin to touch body parts and later name those parts. This is the time when toilet training may begin, so there is much opportunity for the interest in body parts to heighten.

Toddler body awareness usually extends to curiosity about the body parts of others, such as their parents, siblings, and others in their lives. This is also a time when a toddler

FIGURE 2.3

Typical Large and Small Motor Skills of Toddlers

Young Toddlers (12–24 months)

Exercises physical skills
Likes to lug, dump, push, pull, pile, knock down, empty, fill
Enjoys pushing or pulling while walking
Likes to climb and can manage small indoor stairs
Manipulates in a more exploratory than skillful fashion
Shows interest in multiple small objects
Carries play materials from place to place
(by 2 years) Kicks and catches a large ball
(by 2 years) Strings large beads, turns knobs, uses twist motion

Older Toddlers (2 years+)

Shows skill in most simple large muscle activities
Engages in lots of physical testing: jumping from heights, climbing, hanging by the arms, rolling, galloping, doing somersaults, rough-and-tumble play
Throws and retrieves all kinds of objects
Pushes self on wheeled objects with good steering
Demonstrates good hand and finger coordination by 2½ to 3 years
Engages in lots of active play with small objects and explores different qualities of play materials

Source: The Right Stuff for Children Birth to 8—Selecting Play Materials to Support Development (pp. 47, 67) by M. B. Bronson, 1995, Washington, DC: NAEYC. Copyright 1995 by NAEYC. Reprinted with permission from the National Association for the Education of Young Children.

is able to tell you whether she is a boy or a girl; however, the toddler also thinks that she can change her gender identity. According to a female toddler, for example, putting on a man's hat changes her into a male. One of us still remembers a 3-year-old's drawing of himself as a girl, accompanied by his description of "I'm going to be a girl when I grow up."

The people around a toddler, both males and females, communicate messages about the child's **gender identity.** A great deal of the environment of a young child sends out information about what is expected of boys and girls, and those expectations are often different. By the second year of life, the play behaviors of children begin to display those different expectations. During this time, children's attention to body parts and comfortable responses from adults who use correct terms to name body parts and functions eventually lead to curiosity about why girls and boys are different. Toddlers are not ready for very elaborate or technical explanations—just simple answers given in a matter-of-fact manner.

JOURNAL 2.4: This is a time to check your sensitivities and comfort with children's bodies and gender awareness. Compose a response to a 2-year-old girl who asks you why her male toddler peer has a penis and she doesn't. What would you say to a 2½-year-old who asks, "How did the baby get in my mommy's tummy?" ●

Even if you are completely comfortable in giving answers to these questions, be sure to check with your class peers and instructor. You will probably hear an array of diverse responses and you may find that some feel much better and more appropriate for toddlers to hear than others.

Entire books are devoted to the developmental achievements of toddlerhood, but this brief section gives you a beginning glimpse of what a toddler is like. When you read about Ibrahim and his friends in Chapter 8, you will develop many more insights about this fascinating period as well as direction for how to promote toddler development in your early childhood professional role.

Implications of Toddler Development for Early Childhood Programs

All the developmental changes that occur during toddlerhood have implications for the adults who support these young children.

ENVIRONMENTS FOR TODDLERS. Toddler curiosity and the beginnings of independence require specific environments and behaviors on the part of adults. First, there are issues of safety. The physical safety of toddlers demands constant watchfulness and an environment that protects yet stimulates exploration. The National Association for the Education of Young Children (NAEYC, 1997a) demonstrates some of the important characteristics of that environment:

- Floor coverings are appropriate for the activities that occur there—shock-absorbent tiles for open areas where toddlers push and pull toys around and for art, eating, and water and sand play areas. Low-pile, easy-to-clean carpeting or nonslip area rugs cover areas for quiet play. (p. 86)
- The environment contains private spaces with room for no more than two children and that are easily supervised by adults. (p. 87)
- Care givers directly supervise toddlers by sight and sound, even when they are sleeping. (p. 89)
- Adults do safety checks of all areas both indoors and outside several times a day to assure that they are safe (e.g., electric outlets are covered, no objects are on the floor that a toddler could choke on, no splinters or nails are exposed on furnishings and equipment). (p. 89)

GUIDANCE FOR TODDLERS. Another kind of safety for toddlers is the issue of emotional security. These children are forming relationships, and their relationships with caregivers and educators is a critical one. The adults in the lives of toddlers need to be constant and committed to these youngsters. Toddlers are not yet good communicators, so adults need to know them well and be able to determine and respond to their needs and cues.

UNDERSTANDINGS FOR EDUCATORS. Another implication of toddler development is one of balancing opportunities for them to develop initiative, autonomy, and self-reliance with the routines, schedules, and rules that they seem to need. Toddlers want to try everything themselves, to do everything themselves, and to be in charge. At the same time, they have a limited capacity to communicate to others, to share or cooperate with others, and to take care of themselves. Bredekamp and Copple (1997) remind us, "A healthy toddler's inner world is filled with conflicting feelings—independence and dependence, pride and shame, confidence and doubt, self-awareness and confusion, fear and omnipotence, hostility and intense love, anger and tenderness, initiative and passivity" (p. 68). Those contrasts are a real challenge to the adults who intend to support the toddler. When toddlers feel that support, and know that they can count on those adults, they are able to face their own frustrations, struggles, and disappointments. Those adults need to make wise decisions about routines, schedules, and rules, so that they are a source of support to the toddler rather than a source of defeat. Listen to an early childhood professional who provides such support to toddlers:

Ethan: Testing Limits

Two-year-old Ethan has brought a wheelbarrow in from the playground and is pushing it around the room, banging into furniture and other children. He seems to have a lot of energy and is quite thrilled with his new skill with the wheelbarrow. After watching him for a brief time, Mimi, his caregiver, approaches him with, "Ethan, you are pushing the wheelbarrow so well, but we don't have enough room inside for the wheelbarrow." She quickly explains that the wheelbarrow may hurt his friends, and gives him a choice of taking it back outside or pushing a truck in the block area. She adds, "I would like to watch so you can show me how strong you are." Ethan pauses, holding tightly to the wheelbarrow, and tries to push it again. Mimi repeats his choices and says, "It's your choice, Ethan." He decides to go back outside, and he takes Mimi's hand, indicating that he wants her to accompany him.

That is the delicate balance of limitations and freedom that toddlers need from the adults in their lives in order to develop autonomy and initiative. For those who care for toddlers, that balance is one of the many challenges facing early childhood educators. Those challenges make toddler and infant care costly and not very accessible, or often mediocre and inadequate when affordable. Fortunately, children in the preschool years have many excellent care and educational programs to meet their needs.

Studying Preschool-Aged Children (Ages Three to Five Years)

We are now talking about a much wider age span, so we will see a great deal of development and growth. Children of ages 3 to 5 are grouped together because their growth and development are so fluid. Often, you can see a group of 3- to 5-year-olds and be unable to tell who is what age. The individual differences are so prominent by then that it is impossible to describe a typical 3-, 4-, or 5-year-old. We will provide a brief profile because you will be meeting a group of preschool-aged children in Chapter 9. By then, you will have developed a better understanding from watching and listening to them. We begin with their physical and motor development because it's so prominent.

Physical and Motor Development

LARGE MOTOR DEVELOPMENT. Some 3-year-olds are still developing the skills we described for toddlerhood, but others are well developed and have the capacity to run and jump. Age 3 is a time when fine motor skills such as cutting with scissors and drawing with crayons or markers are developing rapidly. Many 3-year-olds can copy simple shapes, draw faces, construct simple puzzles, and build with blocks. This is also a time for becoming independent or self-sufficient. These children need less help from the adults in their lives because they are developing the coordination and fine motor skills to do many tasks and because they have the motivation to try. By the end of age 3, children are ready for complex tasks that require extensive movement and coordination. In terms of motor development, preschoolers are ready for limitless physical activities. Their energy is overwhelming and their motor development is related to their abilities in other aspects of development.

By 4 and 5 years of age, the physical development of children is quite advanced, both in terms of skills and growth. These children are skilled at skipping, riding tricycles or bicycles, jumping, climbing, turning cartwheels, and throwing and catching balls. The body proportions of preschool children change significantly and that change contributes to these new skills. Their legs have lengthened and their bones have become harder and stronger. Consequently, they have increased body strength and coordination that enables them to perform various large motor skills. Gallahue (1982) describes the advances of motor development during preschool years with the following characteristics:

1. *Coordination.* The rhythmical integration of motor and sensory systems into a harmonious working together of body parts
2. *Speed.* The ability to move from one point to another in the shortest time possible over a short distance
3. *Agility.* The ability to move from point to point as rapidly as possible while making successive movements in different directions
4. *Power.* The ability to perform one maximum explosive force
5. *Balance.* The ability to maintain one's equilibrium in relationship to the force of gravity in both static and dynamic movement situations (p. 96)

SMALL MOTOR DEVELOPMENT. Just as the large muscles become stronger and more coordinated, the small muscles also develop so that fine motor skills become more controlled and precise. The fine motor development of preschoolers improves rapidly, enabling them to write letters and draw shapes with pencils. Some of the precision and coordination evident during this time is called **dexterity.** It can be seen as the children handle small puzzle pieces, master buttons and zippers, and use many adult tools, such as tweezers, tongs, and screwdrivers.

PERCEPTUAL-MOTOR DEVELOPMENT. Another aspect of motor development that becomes obvious during this time is **perceptual-motor development.** We are born with sensory abilities (sight, touch, hearing, smell, and taste) but our ability to interpret the information provided by our senses takes some time to develop. **Perceptual-motor movements** are a combination of what the child sees or perceives though her senses and the body movements that respond to those perceptions. The beginning of perceptual-motor development is the use of senses. Beginning at infancy, the capacity to take in sensory input is developing. It becomes well refined by the time children are preschoolers.

Two other aspects of perceptual-motor development are beginning during this time: body/spatial awareness and temporal awareness. Preschoolers are getting better about avoiding objects and furniture when they are on the move (referred to as **body/spatial awareness**). By age 4 or 5, they can run through an area and miss all of the obstacles, evidencing that they are better aware of their bodies and of the space surrounding them. In terms of **temporal awareness,** preschoolers begin to get a sense of time and sequence through the routines of their day. Most preschoolers will let you know if you skip an activity that is part of their usual sequence of events.

Young children take pride in their growing independence and motor skills. How might you respond to this child's accomplishments with his painting?

INDEPENDENCE. Motor development enhances the growing independence we see in a preschool classroom. The move toward independence or self-sufficiency continues rapidly with increased ability as preschoolers dress themselves, serve and eat meals, wash their hands and brush their teeth, and organize their own spaces (bedrooms, cubbies, toy shelves, etc.). This same independence means that preschoolers can begin taking more responsibility for themselves. In terms of health and safety, they are able to begin to understand concepts of nutrition and danger, and they can follow simple rules for their own well-being. Later, when we visit Felipe in his preschool, you will see that children of this age can get very involved in rules and quite demanding about their observance.

Nutrition and Physical Development

In addition to describing preschoolers' very prominent physical and motor development, we want to discuss a newly emerging body of research. Studies have gone beyond the relationship between nutrition and physical development to probe for impact on cognitive and social competencies. We know that many children in our country are malnourished, but recently we have become aware that many are misnourished (Marcon, 2003, p. 82)—that is, not consuming important nutrients. America's Children 2002 found that most children's (ages 2 through 5) diets are poor or in need of improvement, and as they get older, their diet becomes even more insufficient. With the condition of malnutrition or misnourishment are often other conditions, such as less supervision, less stimulation, and less education; thus, the effects of "even mild nutrition can have a negative impact on developmental outcomes" (p. 83). It is important to consider these concerns because you will need to be a very good observer of children's development, looking for signs of inadequate nutrition, especially when you watch the physical changes during the preschool span.

Social Development

Although preschoolers are still quite egocentric (involved in themselves), they are also quite social. A wonderful scene on a soccer field with a team of 4- and 5-year-old children illustrates these contrasts in development. The soccer game is underway and the children are running down the field toward one of the goals. Five-year-old Tony stops in the middle of the field and calls out to his parents on the side, "Can Eric come over to play today?"

The game continues as Tony's parents urge him to "watch the ball" and he remembers that he is part of a group effort, at least temporarily.

BEGINNINGS OF FRIENDSHIP. The preschool years are characterized by the beginning of friendships. Generally, by age 4, children can maintain friendships. Teachers and caregivers have noticed that children behave differently toward those children that they consider a friend and those that they do not consider a friend. With friends, young children often are more patient, more cooperative, more positive, and less disagreeable (Stroufe, Cooper, & DeHart, 1992). Preschoolers' abilities to begin and maintain friendships tell us that they have *social preferences.* By preschool, however, "approximately 10–24% of children are classified as unpopular, while 10–22% are classified as rejected, and 12–20% as neglected" (Kim, 2003, p. 234). These are children who typically do not have the following behaviors:

- Successful entry into the play of a group of children
- Effective verbal assertiveness
- Engagements in complex pretend plan
- Demonstration of positive affection toward peers

You may also note that these children display aggressive-hostile behavior, tease their peers, withdraw and play alone, and hover around other children's play. The first step in assisting these children is to observe their behavior consistently in order to determine what is keeping them from being accepted. From there you can teach children alternative behaviors, modeling the skills they need and creating environments that support all children's interactions with rules and constructive feedback. When you plan activities for preschoolers, provide many opportunities for practicing social skills so that all children can develop social competence.

SOCIAL COMPETENCE. Another significant development that we see in preschool-aged children is *social competence.* Social competence is related to the abilities we just described for children's friendships. Simply defined, it is the ability to engage with peers, to be liked and desired as a playmate, and to be able to interact with peers in mutually satisfying ways. Remember Keeley, who you met earlier in this chapter? She is a good example of a socially competent preschooler. She is liked and even admired by her young friends. Her mom constantly hears from other parents that their children "talk about Keeley all the time" and "want Keeley to come over." Keeley is friendly and emotionally positive. She gets a lot of attention from other children in her class and she wins struggles with her peers without ever being hostile. Closely observing a child like Keeley will give you ideas for how to support social competence in all children. Within that social development area, you will see many connections to children's cognitive development.

Cognitive Development

The intellectual development of 4- and 5-year-old children is marked by huge gains in understanding their world. Their use and understanding of symbols that began in toddlerhood is quite advanced. They write and draw symbols, as well as create and use symbols in their play. This is important development for understanding math and science literacy, which children of this age are beginning to pursue. This is a time of extensive "Why?" questions, as children explore their world and try to make meaning of their experiences. Many of the ideas expressed by preschoolers will strike us as humorous or strange, but these children are operating from a lack of information or misinformation. However, from ages 3 to 5 years, it seems that they are determined to gather as much information as possible. Preschoolers are active learners in ways that are different from the active learning of infants and toddlers. Although they maintain the physical and sensory aspects of their learning, they add concepts, vocabulary, and representation to the process. Thus, they actively construct meaning as they explore the world around them.

Instead of just observing and describing events around them, preschoolers try to explain the events.

CHARACTERISTICS OF PRESCHOOL THINKING. Although preschool cognition is becoming quite advanced, it is limited developmentally by three characteristics of preschool thinking. The first characteristic is **centration,** the tendency to consider only one piece of information when multiple pieces are relevant. Second is the preschoolers' lack of differentiation between reality and appearance, sometimes between pretend and real. Preschool teachers and caregivers are often asked, "Is it real or pretend?" when a story is read. The third characteristic is the lack of memory strategies. Some 4- and 5-year-olds begin to show some simple approaches to remembering. Keeley, for example, can be heard repeating to herself as she descends the stairs in her house, "Don't forget the backpack."

COGNITIVE CHANGES: DEVELOPMENT OF REASONING. One aspect of children's thinking that develops during preschool age is **causal reasoning.** This reasoning begins with children making explanations based on their observations—that is, by appearance. If it gets dark when the child goes to bed, then the reason it gets dark is so that people can go to bed. Later, this reasoning is influenced by an acknowledgment of powerful others (e.g., parents, sun, etc.). You may hear a child explain that the "sun made it get dark by going away." As children develop more concepts and vocabulary, their causal reasoning becomes more advanced and they are able to offer reasonable cause-and-effect explanations. When you observe preschoolers, you will notice that when they don't know the reason for something, they will invent one.

Other cognitive changes have been described by Piaget as he observed and discussed children's cognitive development. In the next chapter, you will read about preschoolers' abilities in the areas of conservation, serration, and classification. These are major developments in cognition and are especially relevant to the development of preschool-aged children.

Language Development

The language development of 4- and 5-year-olds is amazing. They can comprehend extensive vocabulary and concepts: spatial concepts, such as *beside* and *behind;* plural and singular forms of nouns, such as *mice* and *mouse;* and passive-voice sentences, such as *The plant was watered by Mary.* Their ability to follow directions continues to improve. Children of this age are curious about reading and are developing many of the skills necessary for reading. For instance, they can repeat stories after hearing them and they know that groups of letters represent words. The vocabulary of the preschooler is extensive—from 1,500 to over 2,000 words.

CHILDREN'S SCRIPTS. One of the most fascinating developments you will observe in a preschool class is the playing out of scripts. Children of preschool age have become familiar with scenes and accompanying dialogue of everyday activities, such as grocery shopping, going to the doctor's office, doing laundry at the laundromat, and so forth. You will hear them playing the roles with adult dialogue. Their language development comes through in these scenes; in fact, you can learn a great deal about their language by listening to their scripts. Listen to a pair of preschoolers playing out the family's morning:

Angela: "Honey, don't forget your briefcase for work. What time will you be home?"
George: "I have to go to work. Don't forget to make supper."
Angela: "Let's go out to dinner. I don't want to cook."
George: "I'm going to catch the bus. Bye."

Does any of this sound familiar? Most preschoolers' scripts are quite realistic and their use of language is accurate. Notice, however, that George wasn't working from the same script that Angela was using. Preschoolers may not listen to each other well but they definitely are paying attention to the adults and world around them.

Another aspect of language development that you will notice is the development of humor. Preschoolers enjoy jokes and riddles. They create jokes of their own and laugh hilariously at them. We adults go along with their jokes and usually laugh at the fact that the jokes are not funny. This ability is one of the enjoyable aspects of working with preschool-aged children.

Gender Development

Do you remember in our discussion about toddlers that they can tell you if they are a boy or a girl? You may also remember that gender isn't a constant for them. By age 3, most children identify themselves as a girl or a boy, but their concept of gender is not well developed. Most will not understand until the age of 5 or 6 that their gender is constant and determined by anatomy, not clothing, hairstyle, or toy preferences (Roberts & Hill, 2003, p. 39). These early years are critical for learning about gender and they are quite influenced by society's traditional gender role norms. The adults who are in the life of a preschool child will be communicating information about gender by the way they live their lives. Here again, the way adults respond to questions about gender will send important messages to children who are forming their own gender identities and taking on the beginnings of their own gender roles. Another important source of influence and information on children's understanding of gender is children's literature. Unfortunately, much of children's literature continues to present traditional stereotypes, so we must critically examine the books we provide for children. Figure 2.4 provides a kind of checklist for analyzing children's books for sexism in both illustrations and story content. Still another aspect of development that begins during preschool years is related to awareness of racial differences. Box 2.1 describes what research tells us about how young children respond to racial differences.

An entire book could be written about the development of 3-, 4- and 5-year-olds because so much growth and development is happening during this time. For now, however, you have a beginning sketch of some characteristics of this age. When you meet Felipe and his friends in Chapter 9, you will learn more about this age group. You will also observe how a preschool program accommodates the rapid development of children of this age. Considering the multiple facets of development that characterize the growth and learning of a preschool-aged child, you can understand why there are so many preschools with so many different kinds of programs.

FIGURE 2.4

Checklist for Analyzing Children's Books or Sexism

Checking the Illustrations

- Look at who is doing what in the pictures or photos. Are all the males leading, playing sports, or getting in trouble?
- Are the males rescuing the females?
- Are stereotypes communicated by the illustrations? Is the girl portrayed as meek or weak while the boy looks strong and in charge?
- Is there a token woman in a male-dominated setting or a token male in a female-dominated setting?

Checking the Content

- Could the story be told if the gender roles were reversed?
- Are female achievements based on their own initiative and intelligence?
- Is there cooperation between the sexes or competition?
- Are both sexes treated with respect?
- Are both males and females engaged in similar activities?

Source: Adapted from Roberts and Hill (2003, pp. 41–42).

BOX 2.1

Identity Development in Multiracial Children

For all children, identity development is a complex process—one that is influenced by numerous factors in childhood. For children of mixed racial, ethnic, and cultural heritage, it is even more complicated than for monoracial children (Schwartz, 2003, p. 12). The child's own qualities play a role in her or his ability to develop a cohesive and personally fulfilling identity. It helps to be resilient and to have self-esteem, it helps to have family stability and support from school and community, and it helps for a child to grow up around other multiracial families.

There are particular advantages and disadvantages for children of a multiracial background. One advantage is that of a broad cultural heritage and a broader sense of the world. They have the potential to have greater intergroup tolerance, language facility, and appreciation of minority group cultures. They also grow up able to identify multiple perspectives of a situation or both sides of a conflict (Schwartz, 2003, p. 12).

The disadvantages or challenges come primarily from society. Societal racism and a discomfort with interracial marriages can cause intense pressure on multiracial families and their children. Communities and even schools communicate negative messages to multiracial children—messages that compromise their sense of self and contradict identity development.

A key factor in the lives of multiracial children is how they are labeled—by themselves, by their parents, and by society in general (Schwartz, 2003, p. 10). Labels exert significant influence in the process of identity development. Within multiracial communities, parents choose different ways of identifying their children. Some families oppose racial labeling completely and classify their members as human. Other families help their children develop a biracial or multiracial identity based on the components of their particular background. They want their children to take equal pride in all of their heritages. And other families foster their children's identification with only one race, typically that of a minority group.

As of 1996, it was reported that more than 100,000 multiracial babies are born annually (Root, 1996)—a trend that is predicted to grow. In the next generations, the number of components of an individual's heritage will increase significantly, making racial distinctions less and less possible. Nonetheless, early childhood educators will need to continue learning about and respecting the beliefs, attitudes, and concerns of multiracial families. They will contribute significantly to the healthy identity development of multiracial children.

Studying Children in Kindergarten and Primary Grades (Ages Five to Eight Years)

Children of 5 to 8 years of age are beginning to make the transition to what is called *middle childhood.* These years are sometimes referred to as the *school years* because children of this age spend so much of their time in school. The physical growth during this period is not as dramatic as in the earlier years, but children in kindergarten and primary grades make exciting gains in terms of motor abilities. It is also a time of spectacular cognitive growth in the ability to handle complex mental tasks. Socially and emotionally, children of this age are developing the capacity for long-term relationships and secure adulthood. Most educational programs for this age begin to focus primarily on the cognitive aspects of learning, so let's begin with cognitive development. No less important will be our discussions of that social, emotional, and physical development.

Cognitive Development

If you remember our description of preschoolers' lack of memory strategies, it won't be surprising to you that from ages 5 to 8 years, memory abilities exhibit significant change. Children nearing middle childhood develop a variety of memory strategies that are increasingly effective. They also become aware of memory and its use. We saw that awareness beginning when Keeley was trying to remember her backpack.

CHANGES IN MEMORY SKILLS. The first change we see in middle childhood is the development of **basic memory processes**—that is, the routine acts of storing and retrieving information. These processes begin in infancy and continue through toddlerhood, but the capacity to remember is limited. By this age, the capacity increases enormously and children are accumulating knowledge—that is, processing information and storing it in memory, both recalled and constructed. When you ask a 6-year-old a complex question, his answer may be partly what he remembers and partly what he is inferring based on what he knows. This kind of recall, referred to as **constructive memory,** is a good indicator of how well children will remember information.

Earlier in this chapter, you heard Keeley using a memory strategy—repeating her mother's reminder to herself. At ages 5 to 8, children are able to use sophisticated memory strategies called **mnemonics.** The most common mnemonic is rehearsal, deliberately repeating over and over. We hear kindergarten children repeating their phone numbers and their addresses—an example of rehearsal. By ages 7 and 8, children use a great deal of rehearsal in their school learning and are ready for more advanced mnemonics. One of us still remembers the rhyme "Thirty days has September, April, June, and November . . . " and uses it for remembering how many days are in each month.

SIGNIFICANT ACHIEVEMENTS IN THINKING. One of the most impressive achievements of children of this age is their increasing ability to understand the views or perspectives of others. One welcomed effect of this new ability in their social interactions is they get along better. With this ability to see a situation from two perspectives comes the ability to focus on several aspects of a problem at the same time. These children are also able to reverse their thinking—that is, go through a series of steps and reverse them or realize that one step can undo another. In the next chapter, you will learn about Piaget's theories related to these achievements in thinking. Piaget explained for us how children's thinking changes as they mature during this time. Their achievements in thinking are very

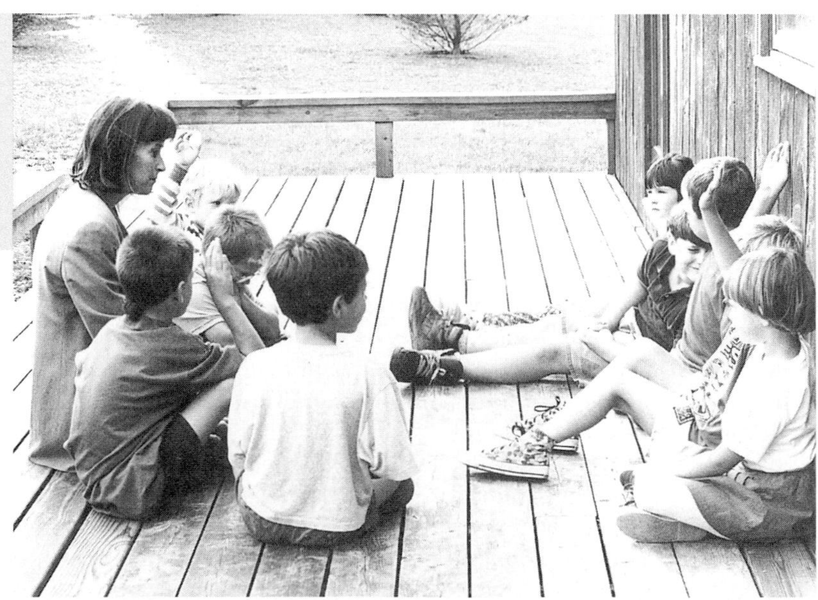

Children in kindergarten begin to understand the views of their friends and are able to get along well with one another.

influential in their abilities to learn math and science in kindergarten and primary grades, so it is important to be aware of their thinking capacities.

Another significant achievement of this age group is **concept acquisition.** Woolfolk (1995) defines **concepts** as categories used to group similar events, ideas, objects, or people, and states that "most of what we know about the world involved concepts and relationships among concepts" (p. 286). What is significant about the achievement of concept acquisition is that children of this age are able to work with abstractions (concepts). Concepts are vague and unlike the concrete learning that preschool children do so well. So, children in kindergarten and primary grades begin to move from physical examples to an understanding of complex concepts, such as numbers and time. Preschoolers often recite numbers and can count from 1 to 10 or more, but it doesn't mean that they understand what 1 is or what 10 is. By age 6 or 7, children's understanding of one-to-one correspondence and number is complete, but not until after age 8 are children reasonably accurate in placing events in a time sequence (Bredekamp & Copple, 1997). Concept acquisition means that children are moving beyond memorization to understanding. Gardner (1993a) says that they then have the capacity to "take knowledge, skills, and concepts and apply them appropriately in new situations" (p. 2). You can now see why we called this section Significant Achievements in Thinking.

Classification—the ability to group objects by common attributes—is another exciting capacity of this age. Children begin this ability by using one attribute, such as color or size, to classify objects and then extend the ability to classify using more than one attribute. For instance, in kindergarten, Matt sorts the blocks by shape, but in first grade, he may sort the large rectangles or the small red triangles, thus combining attributes. While in the primary grades, he may also master seriation, which is the ability to place objects in order of length, weight, or size. One of us observed a kindergarten/first-grade class in Victoria, British Columbia, in which the teacher asked the children to line up by height. Listen to what happened as the children struggled with a challenging task of seriation:

> The teacher, Mary, began, "I've been observing many of you measuring lately. You've been measuring your castles and measuring yourselves on our growth chart. We have an activity today to get you started using measurement. I want to see if you can form a line all together with the smallest child on this end and the tallest child on that end. You can do this any way you want."
>
> The children immediately began with ideas:
>
> "If you're not sure, you can stand back to back to measure."
>
> "Start with the smallest ones."
>
> "Start with three people and then get two more."
>
> For the next 10 minutes, three different children tried organizing the children into a line. They succeeded in arranging only four children. Then, one of the kindergarten children, a very petite girl named Sandy, loudly said, "I know what to do." The group allowed her to take over and she began adding children to the line of four children already arranged. Children followed her directions and stood still in their places. Sandy got lots of coaching from the other children as she estimated the "right spot" for each child, measuring with her hand on heads, and stepping back to verify her placements for each child. She succeeded in completing the line of children, then placed herself at the end as the shortest child, which she was. Mary clapped her hands with delight, "You did it all by yourselves." She grabbed a camera and took several pictures, encouraging children to talk about their experiences. Children stepped forward to look at the line of their classmates, and Sandy smiled to herself. (Driscoll, 1995, pp. 198–199)

As you will learn in the next chapter, a great deal of the cognitive development in middle childhood is influenced by children's social interaction. Both Piaget and Vygotsky (whom you will meet) have theorized about the effects of children learning from other children and from adults. Another great thinker, Jerome Bruner, adds discussion to the notion that others contribute to our individual learning processes, indirectly and directly. After reading more about cognitive development, you will be ready to be reacquainted with Keeley, who is now in kindergarten (Chapter 10), and to meet Jodie, a first-grade student, in Chapter 12. Jodie and her friends will help you understand the wide range of children's cognitive development in the primary grades. You will also observe their social and emotional development and see some distinctive differences and changes from the preschool children in Felipe's Head Start class (Chapter 9).

Social Development

This is a time for advances in self-understanding for children of ages 6 through 8 years. These children are able to assess their own personal abilities by making comparisons with peers. They are also able to see themselves in a social context—that is, as a member of a group. You will hear Keeley describing herself as, "I am friendly and nice to my friends." She refers to herself as a kindergartner. She might also say, "I'm Dani's friend" or "I'm the best writer in my class."

GENDER ROLE DEVELOPMENT. In addition to social comparisons and self-evaluation, children in kindergarten and primary grades are continuing their development of gender roles. Parents and other significant adults in children's lives continue to have a great influence on children's understanding of gender roles. Keeley insists that "girls can't play basketball or baseball" because she is surrounded by a group of adult males who play sports. None of the females in her life do so, so she is certain that girls can't play those sports. For children like Keeley, gender has become a *social construct*—that is, she is assigning or associating specific behaviors, attitudes, roles, and activities with one sex. Early childhood educators work to eliminate gender role constraints such as Keeley's assertion about girls and sports, and help each child reach his or her individual potential (Roberts & Hill, 2003, p. 39). Again, children's literature can provide models that challenge the gender role stereotypes that children are learning from society.

INFLUENCE OF TELEVISION ON CHILDREN'S GENDER ROLE SOCIALIZATION. Children learn about gender roles from multiple sources in addition to the adult models around them—books, songs, movies, and television, for example. Keeping in mind the number of hours that children watch television (30 hours a week for preschoolers), it has a significant influence. We know that television watching influences children's prosocial and antisocial behaviors as well as their attitudes about race and gender. Studies of television offerings found that two-thirds of characters are male, and women are frequently defined by their relationships with men. Even children's shows and cartoons depict females less often than males, less active than males, and in fewer lead roles than men. Gender stereotypes have been found in almost every kind of TV programming and in commercials. In sum, much of children's sense of what it means to be male or female in our society is influenced by television portrayals of males and females and those portrayals are characterized by gender biases and stereotypes (Witt, 2000, p. 324).

IMPORTANCE OF PEERS. Children of this age group begin to play, interact with, and prefer same-sex friends, but demonstrate the beginnings of attraction to the opposite sex. A great deal of kidding takes place about such topics as kissing and boyfriends and girlfriends. During this time, peer relationships begin to move into importance in competition with the family. Once children are in school all day, it makes sense that peers become so important. Many children spend as many hours with friends as they do with family members. Children learn from other children cooperation, relationships and friendships, and how to work and play in groups. By first and second grade, youngsters develop a sense of "groupness"—a beginning feeling of *we* and a collective identity. One often hears a preschooler or a kindergartner say, "I'm not inviting you to my birthday party." Social groups are already forming in kindergarten, but by first grade, they are more stable. It is easy to distinguish between those inside and outside the groups. When you watch Jodie in her class (Chapter 12), you will meet some of the children in her group.

Emotional Development

We can learn much about a child's emotional development by watching his or her social interactions. Personality characteristics and dispositions are quite visible when children are working or playing with others. What you also see is how those qualities affect peers and how peers respond to those qualities. Another aspect of a child's emotional development is reflected by a metaphor about children who are 6 to 8 years of age. They are described as a "commuter traveling back and forth between the outside world and the smaller more personal one of the family" (Chilman, 1966, p. 5). With such a context for their emotional development, it is not surprising to note that middle childhood is a time of emotional extremes. Children can be deliriously happy and excited one minute and miserably sad and morose the next.

ATTACHMENTS. This is a confusing time! The 6-, 7-, and 8-year-old wants constant attention and affection from parents and other adults and will regularly display exaggerated dependence. Simultaneously, that same child wants independence from those adults. To make things even more confusing, this child will use fairly negative behaviors to get attention and affection; thus, the interpretation of her development may be opposite of what she is actually communicating. To be specific, a 7-year-old may argue or use shocking language to get her mother to pay attention to her. Elkind (1994) thinks that some of this behavior may also be a kind of rebellion against the inequality of the parent/child relationship.

FEARS. The development of new fears and the disappearance of old fears go hand in hand with changes in cognitive development. As children begin to understand things, some fears are released. With new understanding and new information, however, come new fears. Children of this age won't express fears loudly or with intense emotion like toddlers or preschoolers, but they will exhibit **fear responses.** Those responses are characterized by anxiety, discomfort, and repression of the fear. You will see these children bite their nails, stop eating or sleeping, become very dependent, and even show signs of illness. Children in middle childhood boast of not being afraid and they become inattentive or distracted when they are afraid. There's that confusion again between what they really want and what they communicate.

Self-reflection on your own childhood fears will help you understand the many sources and influences on children's fears. Reflecting on your own experiences is often a way to understand others.

SELF-CONCEPT. This is a time of stability of self-concept, and self-concept is greatly influenced by what children believe others think about them. Remember the importance of peers! Children approaching middle childhood are self-critical and they compare themselves with others frequently. They need help in accepting their own feelings and in seeing how those feelings affect their relationships. Adults can provide support for emotional development by engaging in a healthy relationship with the children. If that relationship is characterized by mutual support, acceptance, empathy, and genuine understanding, the children will also develop those qualities.

During this time, children often engage in organized games and sports, and those activities can have a significant influence on the children's emotional development, especially self-worth. If those activities are not characterized by acceptance and sensitivity, a child's sense of self may be damaged. Most of us have observed too many Little League games and ballet recitals that satisfied adults but didn't respect children. Those experiences bring us to the final aspect of development: physical and motor development.

Physical and Motor Development

Children who are ages 5 to 8 advance in motor skills partly because of development and partly because they have many opportunities to use those abilities in games and sports. Think of the complexity of playing soccer, skiing, gymnastics, and so on. Many children of this age are physically ready and very enthusiastic and they develop coordination and complex motor skills. Gallahue (1982) recommends, however, that children should not be pushed into advanced sports activities or formalized participation before they are ready or interested.

Consider all of the benefits of these children's physical play and time out of the classroom.

In terms of small motor development, dexterity has increased and eye-hand coordination is enhanced. Small motor skills greatly influence school success. Making a variety of writing and drawing tools available to children will enhance their interest in these tasks. Children also need a balance of guided and unguided writing and drawing activities. This is an aspect of development in which you will observe enormous variation among a group of children who are exactly the same age.

The final aspect of physical and motor development to be considered is the perceptual-motor development we discussed during our focus on preschool children. Perceptual-motor abilities are well developed for kindergarten and primary grade children, and the level of refinement is dependent on the experiential opportunities the children have. Children of this age develop spatial and directional awareness as they participate in games and sports.

NEED FOR ATTENTION TO PHYSICAL DEVELOPMENT IN SCHOOLS. Physical development and motor abilities are not a priority in many elementary school programs, especially when the children move beyond kindergarten. This is partly due to dwindling resources in education. As an early childhood educator, you may have to become an advocate for children of this age to have opportunities for vigorous physical play. Research has suggested that there is a relationship between the many physical skills of middle childhood and children's cognitive and social development (Marcon, 2003, p. 86). In addition to planning and providing time and space for physical activities, remember to be a good model. Participate in some of those vigorous activities for your own health as well as to motivate children.

Often, children of this age are expected to sit for long periods of time because they have greater control of their bodies and longer attention spans, but long periods of sitting fatigue these children more than running, jumping, or bicycling does (Bredekamp & Copple, 1997). Programs and time set aside for physical action are essential in kindergarten and primary grades because children are refining their physical skills and expressing their physical power and control. Remember, too, that those physical activities can enhance self-confidence.

Individual Differences in Kindergarten and Primary Grades

All domains of development—physical, social, cognitive, and emotional—are connected or interrelated. So, when a 6-year-old develops new motor skills, it may result in changes in his social development. Especially during these early school years, development in one domain influences and is influenced by development in other domains (Bredekamp & Copple, 1997). Too many of the programs for kindergarten and primary grades focus on cognitive development and ultimately defeat the children's efforts to succeed.

RESPONDING TO VARIATIONS IN CHILDREN'S EXPERIENCES AND DEVELOPMENT. Because children of this age have accumulated five to six years of varying experiences and have been progressing in their development at very different paces, there is huge diversity among children in kindergarten and primary grades. One response to this is the mixed-aged class that you encountered earlier in this chapter. Whether you work in a mixed-aged class, a class of kindergarten-age children, a first-grade class, or a second-grade class, it's important to remember that those differences are a primary consideration for all of your decisions. The language of "developmentally appropriate practice" (Bredekamp & Copple, 1997) for 6- through 8-year-olds from the National Association for the Education of Young Children states our reminder well:

> Teachers have high (challenging but achievable) expectations and standards for every child's learning and development. To foster children's self-confidence, persistence, and other positive dispositions as learners, teachers adjust the rate and pace of the curriculum as well as the content so that all children engage in learning experiences in which they can succeed most of the time and yet are challenged to work on the edge of their developing capabilities.
>
> Teachers know each child well. As they plan learning experiences and work with children, they take into account individual differing abilities, developmental levels, and approaches to learning. Responsiveness to individual children is evident in the classroom environment, curriculum and teaching practices. Teachers make sure that every child has opportunities to actively participate and make contributions. (p. 162)

The implications of the wide range of development that occurs when children are in kindergarten and primary grades and of the individual differences in development offer a challenge to the way we prepare to teach or care for these children. Box 2.2 takes a closer look at an aspect of development that has become a focus of attention recently. It provides the kind of information you will need in order to make the multitude of decisions ahead

The Development of Self-Regulation in Young Children

Self-regulation has attracted the interest of both the general public and educators in recent years—most of the interest has been generated by stories of children who are "out of control." Self-regulation, often called *self-control* or *self-direction,* involves children's capacity for controlling emotions, interacting in positive ways with others, avoiding inappropriate or aggressive actions, and becoming an autonomous learner (Bronson, 2000, p. 32).

Existing research suggests that the beginning of self-regulation is evident at birth and is immediately influenced by both individual temperament and environment. Kopp (1982) describes a developmental progression from control of arousal and sensory motor functions to a beginning ability to comply with the suggestions of others by the end of the first year. During ages 3 and 4, self-regulation becomes more sophisticated, and by 6 to 8 years, children are capable of deliberate action, planning ahead, and conscious control (Bronson, 2000, p. 33). Self-regulation can be studied or explained from those same perspectives we describe for children's development in the next chapter.

Because we know that self-regulation influences children's social competence and success in school, it is important to look for ways to support and encourage its development. Much of what you will hear as "developmentally appropriate practice" is what young children need for their development of self-regulation. The kinds of support vary with children's age, but all domains of their development will influence self-regulation. For infants, there needs to be recognizable patterns in their interactions, signals for the essential routines in their day (such as food, comfort, and sleep), and the opportunity to test their ability to control or affect the environment. For toddlers, opportunities for exploration and autonomy are necessary along with role models of appropriate behavior sequences. The support that language can provide to toddlers as they carry out simple requests and label their own actions is also critical. For preschoolers and kindergarten children, the essential opportunities are for more complex directions, clear sets of rules, skill-appropriate responsibilities, understandable consequences of their actions, and again, positive role models. Finally, for primary grade children, opportunities for complex problem-solving strategies, individual choices, support for individual effort, and experiences with positive, trusting, and respectful adults are the supports needed for developing self-regulation.

of you. The decisions that we have been urging you to get ready for will be complex. Again, the more you know about and understand young children, the better you will be prepared to make those decisions. Our final topic, dispositions, is another individual aspect of development that will help you appreciate the uniqueness of each child.

Dispositions

As we described very early in this chapter, *dispositions* are inclinations and preferences. Only recently have teachers talked about dispositions as a consideration for their work with children and families. Dispositions will offer you greater insight to help you broaden that lens with which you view children. Often, a child's disposition may be his most obvious characteristic—the quality we first encounter. If someone like Adam has the disposition to be curious, his curiosity may be what we notice about him. It may even keep us from noticing other aspects of his development. So, our awareness of the presence of dispositions will help us see a more complete picture of a child.

Defining Dispositions

Before talking about how to use insights about dispositions, it is important to extend your understanding of what dispositions are. Some of the definitions of *disposition* from psychological literature suggest that it is an internal characteristic and that it is somewhat permanent. Katz and Raths (1985) think that disposition is connected to acts that may be so habitual and automatic that they seem intuitive and spontaneous. For instance, Keeley doesn't have to think about "taking charge" of her preschool peers—it seems to be intuitive and it definitely looks spontaneous. Others (Perkins, Jay, & Tishman, 1993) define dispositions as "people's tendencies to put their capabilities into action." Therefore, Keeley's "taking charge" in her preschool is a matter of using her ability to lead (her management skills, her social skills, and her creativity).

Finally, Katz and Raths (1985) suggest that dispositions are "patterns of action that require some attention to what is occurring in the context of the action, that is in a particular context and at particular times" (p. 10). Again, if we had observed Keeley over a period of time, we would see that her pattern had developed over time. We would currently see that pattern of "taking charge" occurring at particular time (during free play and center times) and in particular contexts (on the playground and at home with another child). We would see that she scans the room to find children who are not engaged or who will be open to her planning. We would also see that she often "takes charge" when others are having difficulty, so she is paying attention to what is happening and behaving accordingly. Dispositions are clearly an important aspect of who Keeley is and of each child's individuality.

Why Study Dispositions?

A number of psychologists and, more recently, early childhood educators think that dispositions are a critical goal of education, along with knowledge, skills, and attitudes. Their rationale is that without the disposition to do so, a child will not use all the knowledge and skills that we teach. This argument implores us to promote certain dispositions in the way we work with children. If we truly want children to be learners, to be listeners, to be readers, and to be caring individuals, they will need the dispositions to be all these things. Teaching them how to read or how to listen will not be enough. If you agree with the notion that dispositions are essential for learning, then you will need to begin thinking about how to encourage and support dispositions.

Nurturing the Disposition to Be Curious

"At no time in life is curiosity more powerful than in early childhood" (Perry, 2003, p. 26). Most of the children that you will encounter will arrive with curiosity and the desire to explore their world. Your challenge will be to nurture that disposition and not discourage it for the sake of safety, convenience, or conformity. You may be wondering about that statement, so we will provide examples.

- Setting up an environment for infants and toddlers to explore through touch and taste will require you to have daily routines for sterilizing toys and to arrange items on low shelves.
- Toddlers will explore with their bodies as they climb, poke, move, drag, or take apart, and the environment will need to be set up to support those behaviors.
- For all ages, you will need to provide the security of routines and setting while introducing frequent elements of novelty (Perry, 2003, p. 27). A new vase of flowers on the table, a new photo on the board, a mystery item on display, or an unusual piece of music will add novelty that stimulates curiosity.
- Finally, you will need to aware and sensitive to the differences in children's curiosity. Children's preferences, interests, and experiences will influence their curiosity and what stimulates it.

Nurturing the Disposition of Caring

Many of us in the early childhood profession are interested in the disposition of caring or being generous or helpful. That interest and commitment comes from concern about our society in general and about children's development. We know from research that humans are born with the capacity to be caring, and that even very young children demonstrate concern and comforting behaviors when other children are distressed. Research has documented that infants as young as age 10 months respond to another child's distress with sad looks and crying themselves (Zahn-Waxler & Radke-Yarrow, 1984). By children's second year, they tend to help and comfort other people frequently, but some children are much more inclined to do so than others. By preschool years, children become even more helpful, caring, and generous. If you observe a preschool class, you will likely see some children who are always caring for others and some children who do not seem to notice that others have any needs. For example, it appears to be automatic for Joely to respond whenever anyone else gets hurt or is upset, but we never see Adrian do so.

When caring behaviors are studied, it is clear that there are individual differences in young children's capacities to care and to demonstrate caring. Research also suggests that a number of factors explain or cause that variation among individuals: biological factors, cultural factors, and socializing effects of family, teachers, peers, and media (Eisenberg, 1992). As with curiosity, you will play an important role in children's development of the disposition of caring. There are specific ways to encourage children to be caring. Help children to recognize the feelings of others by drawing attention to someone's feelings, by letting them know that you care about their feelings, and by reminding them of experiences in their lives that are similar to someone else's experience (Schulman & Mekler, 1985). Provide lots of explanations about feelings. Acknowledge when children demonstrate caring and point out examples of kindness. And finally, remember that you are a powerful model with your caring behaviors whether you are with the children or interacting with another educator.

Teacher's Role in Children's Developing Dispositions

As a teacher, you will play a role in children's developing dispositions. This is not surprising, considering that many children will spend a significant amount of their day in your class or program. You, as a significant adult in their lives, will be a model for various dispositions. You will also be capable of promoting certain dispositions.

JOURNAL 2.5: Pause for a moment and think about the dispositions that you value. You may find them in your closest friends and family members. List them and then ask yourself if these are the dispositions you will want to nurture in young children. After some reflection, you may add a few to the list or take some off the list. ●

Professional Awareness

The important message we are sending to you is that you will play a key role in developing children's dispositions. Your example will contribute to their dispositions and the way you guide children's behavior will promote or discourage certain dispositions. Your first step is awareness. Respond to the reflection we prompted in Journal 2.5 often to maintain that awareness. Notice your behavior with children so that you are aware of your capacity to promote or discourage dispositions. That takes us back to your decision-making role, because you can make the decision to promote certain dispositions and to discourage others, but it will take watchfulness on your part. Begin now by noticing your responses to children, even as you observe them with us. Notice how you feel about the adults in our stories and what you value in their interactions with children.

PRINCIPLES AND INSIGHTS: A Summary and Review

We hope that the glimpses of children throughout this chapter have prompted enthusiasm for your future professional role. Our intent was to begin the process of understanding young children and their development. As you meet the children in the chapters that follow, they will teach you much more about development and individual differences, and you will learn about how to teach and guide children.

In addition to contributing to your knowledge of children and some beginning skills to use when working with them, we hope we have inspired you. Childhood is a time of wonder. We ask you to celebrate with us—celebrate childhood, child development, and the rich differences each of us brings to this world and to each other.

As promised, we provided only profiles of development for each of the age groups. To show you the whole and complete picture, it would have taken entire books about infant development and preschool development, but we wanted simply to begin your "picture" of each age group. What you can take from our descriptions is the certainty that there is a great deal of change occurring at each age, and those changes influence each domain of development—physical, social, emotional, and cognitive. We have already cautioned you about the individuality of children, so keep in mind that those characteristics we just described may not fit every child. We have another caution to describe for you. It's at the heart of a current and significant controversy that is drawing attention within the profession you are about to enter.

One of the dominant beliefs in the ECE profession is that knowledge of child development is the source of decisions for teaching and guiding young children. By *knowledge of child development,* we are referring to an individual child's development as well as child development in general. Stott and Bowman (1996) call this a "slippery base" for practice. Their concern is twofold. First, knowledge of child development is changing rapidly. Second, there are other rich sources of information that offer guidance to our professional practices. Consider the disciplines of sociology, anthropology, history, and public health as just a few possibilities for concepts and skills with which to work with children and families. If you are studying any of those disciplines in other courses, study them for insights about early childhood education. The complexity of our society, and consequently children and families, demands multiple perspectives for understanding them. In the chapters to come, we will integrate ideas from these disciplines to encourage you to broaden your thinking beyond child development.

The second discussion that is occurring in our profession centers on the concept of child development being both universal and cross-cultural in nature. This notion of cross-cultural development suggests that children's social, cognitive, physical, emotional, and language development are culturally influenced and constructed in important ways. We just described in this chapter characteristics of children at different ages that were culture free. Many of those characteristics would have looked or have been interpreted differently in some cultures. Cross-cultural child development takes into account not only the lives of children and the course of their development but also the lives of adults and the cultural and societal contexts in which those children and adults interact (New, 1994). An example of that wide lens for looking at children comes with our description of Keeley, the only child of a single working mom, who is being raised with an extended family of adults (Chapter 10). In Chapter 9, you will meet Felipe, one of three children in a Hispanic family that lives in a community in which the majority of residents speak Spanish. Our intent is to encourage you to see children in those cultural and societal contexts in which they are developing. If you truly become an observer (watching and listening) of children, you will begin to comprehend each child's ethnic and family characteristics and background.

You will need to accompany your sharp eyes and ears with basic knowledge of ethnic characteristics and individual family culture as a framework for your observations and questions. With broad perspectives of multiple disciplines and cross-cultural child development insights, you will be ready to make the decisions of an early childhood educator. You will truly be able to notice individual differences and accommodate those differences in the environment you provide, the activities you plan, and the interactions you have with children and families.

BECOMING AN EARLY CHILDHOOD PROFESSIONAL

This chapter is about child development and dispositions, which is a broad topic. There are volumes and volumes of research, theory, and information on child development. For your professional development, we have selected just a few resources and experiences so that you won't feel overwhelmed.

Your Professional Portfolio

1. Visit a toy store and make a list of toys suitable for an infant, a toddler, a preschooler, and a child in kindergarten or primary grades. For each of your choices, give a developmental rationale (a reason based on developmental characteristics).
2. Another item for your portfolio is a set of goals directed to building a solid foundation to your understanding of child development.

Your Professional Library

Bredekamp, S., & Copple, C. (1997). *Developmentally appropriate practice in early childhood programs.* Washington, DC: NAEYC.

Bronson, M. B. (1995). *The right stuff for children birth to 8: Selecting play materials to support development.* Washington, DC: NAEYC.

CHAPTER 3

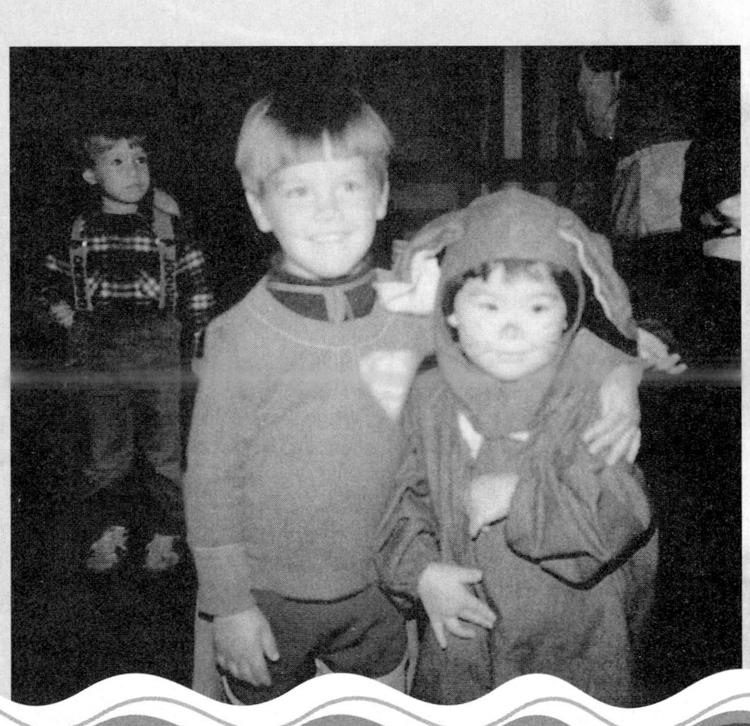

Theories of Development

Foundations for Practice

CHAPTER focus:

When you finish reading and reflecting on this chapter, you will be able to:

1. Define four areas of early childhood development: cognitive, language, social, and emotional.
2. Describe the major contributions associated with each developmental theorist.
3. Create an activity that supports growth in each developmental area.
4. Identify *theories in action* while you observe a preschool in the chapter.

When you spend much time in an early childhood setting, you soon notice that the teachers or caregivers interact with children in ways that create a recognizable pattern of responses, questions, and behaviors. These interactions grow out of specific developmental and learning theories. The environment, including activities and interactions, is based on understanding and interpreting theories of development.

Theories of Development at a Preschool

Jasmine, Scott, and Samantha are enrolled in the 4-year-olds class in the Creative Learning Cooperative Preschool. As in most cooperative preschools, parents work as teaching assistants or assist with other functions several times a month. They also hire the teacher and elect a school board.

As you enter the preschool early in the morning, you see Jasmine, Scott, and Samantha near the sink, mixing apple juice with water for the morning snack. Keith, the preschool teacher, is talking about changes in the taste of juice when water is added. Each child tastes a spoonful of juice from the juice can. "Yuk," says Scott. "I like it this way," shares Jasmine. "What if we used one tall container instead of two short ones?" asks Keith. He was thinking about Piaget's theory of conservation, or understanding that the same amount can be represented in different containers (in this instance, two short 32-ounce pitchers or one tall 64-ounce pitcher). Keith was also thinking about the use of language when children described the taste of the concentrated juice and their social interactions as they worked together on this task. Knowing that Scott was hungry, he paid attention to the children's emotional needs.

Why Study Theories of Development?

Keith, the teacher in the preschool you just visited, bases his curriculum planning, activities, and interactions with the children on his interpretations of theories of development. Early childhood professionals look to these theories as a foundation for their own belief systems and personal philosophies of early childhood education. These beliefs and philosophies are then translated into practice, resulting in the environment and interactions created for young children.

Theories come from many different disciplines of knowledge. As mentioned earlier, psychology, anthropology, sociology, physical development, health, linguistics, history, and education provide a knowledge base for planning programs for young children. Theorists and scientists in each of these fields contributed their work and findings. Their theories are analyzed and compiled into the growing body of knowledge about young children and their development.

From this knowledge base, early childhood professionals make numerous decisions about children and the type of environment that will nurture young children. For example, you might plan an activity in which young children have frequent opportunities to explore through music, art, books, tapes, manipulative activities, and talking and listening experiences. You would be including learning situations drawn from the theory of multiple intelligences, as discussed by Howard Gardner. Planning an experience where toddlers engage in guided verbal interactions around their activity facilitates their language development and supports the work of Lev Vygotsky, with his emphasis on spoken language.

This chapter describes major theorists from each developmental area. We selected these theorists based on their influence in their respective fields and in early childhood education. As you continue your study of child development, you will note that some theories may conflict with each other, as if saying the opposite about children. You may also notice that even the most respected theorists are criticized or ignored at times. Time spent learning from major theorists will assist you in clarifying the rationale for expectations for early childhood programs. An understanding of these theories will help you develop your own personal philosophy of what works best (and why) for the children in your care.

Integration of Developmental Theories

Observing young children at play, you will see that cognitive, language, social, and emotional development are integrated throughout their activities. Seldom do children use only one developmental area in isolation. For instance, 4-year-old Marc is busy at the dress-up center, talking to himself about putting his arms into a large coat. He is wearing a firefighter's jacket and hat and tells Samantha, "Let's hurry and put out the fire at the grocery store. We need to find a hose fast!" Samantha finds her raincoat and hops on a wooden truck with Marc. Off they go to put out the fire, which is actually the climbing structure outside. Their conversation continues about the fire and looking for a hose (a jump rope).

During this interaction, Marc was sharing his thoughts about the fire, looking around to see who might help put out the fire, and focusing on the task at hand. Although this might be described primarily as a social activity, there were many areas of development interwoven in the activity. Marc used language to describe the fire and the equipment needed to put out the fire, including self-talk. He was thinking about the organization and tools needed for fire fighting. At the same time, Marc worked cooperatively with Samantha, and certainly appeared to be enjoying this activity. Each of these behaviors might be classified separately as language development, cognitive development, social development, and emotional development. They were all integrated throughout Marc's activity of fire fighting. When we present the theories that follow, they may appear isolated as you examine one set of ideas, but the major intent is learning how these theories can be applied coherently in your work with young children.

Before you take your next trip to observe in a preschool, you will examine the developmental areas within cognitive, language, social, and emotional domains. Highlights of major contributors to the different developmental fields will first be discussed and then presented in a preschool setting.

Cognitive and Language Development

Cognitive development refers to the process of developing thinking and reasoning skills as children acquire language skills. This process results in changes in thinking that become increasingly complex (Woolfolk, 2004). **Language development** requires an understanding of words (meaning) and the structure of word groups (creating sentences), and is a tool for thinking. Cognitive development and language development are closely connected. Early childhood is a time of exploding use of language, both **receptive language** (what children hear) and **expressive language** (what children say). When a toddler begins to talk and express herself through words and phrases, new words seem to be added to her vocabulary each day.

Language shapes our thoughts and thinking. Jerome Bruner finds language and cognition to be intertwined, as did Lev Vygotsky, who saw language as "a logical and analytical tool in thinking" (Vygotsky, 1962). As an early childhood professional, you will want to know how children develop in these two areas and how you can support their development. Many early childhood educators agree that the work of Jean Piaget has greatly influenced the current thinking in child development and early childhood education, perhaps more so than any other theorist. Let's start with his work as you explore theories of development.

Piaget's Theory of Cognitive Development

Jean Piaget's (1896–1980) background was in biology and intelligence testing. He worked at Alfred Binet's experimental laboratory, where the first intelligence test was developed. While conducting intelligence tests with young children, Piaget became interested in the children's responses, particularly the wrong answers (Crain, 1980). The pattern of incorrect responses seemed to correlate with the age of a child, which led to Piaget's hypothesis that young children think in an entirely different way than older children and adults (Ginsburg & Opper, 1988). Piaget became interested in the child's view of environment and began to test his own three children to confirm his hypotheses about levels or stages of development. For example, Piaget believed that children younger than age 7 would not believe that a vertical stack of five books were the same as five books spread out over the rug area. Changing the layout of the books seemed also to change the number of books (physical property), according to children who have not yet reached an advanced stage of thinking. This concept, called **conservation,** is considered by Piaget as evidence of higher-level thinking.

Through his research, Piaget found that people's needs for creating order in their lives is a central drive (Piaget, 1952). He called this the drive for **equilibrium,** or a state of balance. To reach equilibrium, people have biological tendencies to organize and adapt.

TENDENCY TOWARD ORGANIZATION. Piaget proposed that each person is born with the ability to organize her thinking processes into structures and that the tendency to adapt to the environment is inherited. For example, **organization** allows you to represent your thinking into categories in order to make sense of your world. It would be impossible to deal with every encounter or object as an entirely new experience without drawing on your prior knowledge, which you previously categorized according to certain characteristics.

Let's say you are observing a 5-year-old at the zoo. Earlier, this child had been watching the bears; he has now moved on to the lion area. He keeps talking about the four-legged animals at the zoo. His experience has helped him organize these animals as four-legged creatures. Next, he encounters the parrots. Seeing only two legs, he asks you where the other two legs are. His organization of animals was built on the structure that the animals have four legs, so this new experience (the parrots) does not fit his organization, until he learns that parrots are classified as birds and have two legs. Thus, the child expands his thinking, but still uses his organization system based on the number of legs.

The structure or organizational system discussed here is called a **schema** (or *scheme*) and represents the way a person thinks about the world. An example of a simple schema would be when all flowers that are red are grouped into one category. A more complex schema would be built around the classification of flowers according to plant families. A schema assists you in organizing your thinking and provides a foundation or framework for future experiences.

TENDENCY TOWARD ADAPTATION. **Adaptation** refers to the way people adjust to their environment. As a biologist, Piaget brought ideas from the science world to educators. His thinking about adaptation prompted a look at the relationship humans have with their environment. Ongoing interactions with the environment constantly change people, as they change the environment. For example, when an infant tries to touch an object that is out of reach, she must adapt by moving toward the object or fussing until someone helps her. When she moves toward the object, she is adapting to the environment by changing her location. New experiences are added to the infant's repertoire and her organization schema. Adaptation becomes more refined and complex as she gains knowledge and skills.

Piaget's research on children's thinking led to his theory based on four stages of cognitive development, as shown in Table 3.1. He proposed that all children proceed se-

TABLE 3.1 Piaget's Stages of Cognitive Development

Stage	Approximate Age	Characteristics
Sensorimotor	0–2 years	Begins to make use of imitation, memory, and thought. Begins to recognize that objects do not cease to exist when they are hidden. Moves from reflex actions to goal-directed activity.
Preoperational	2–7 years	Gradually develops use of language and ability to think in symbolic form. Able to think operations through logically in one direction. Has difficulties seeing another person's point of view.
Concrete operational	7–11 years	Able to solve concrete (hands-on) problems in logical fashion. Understands laws of conservation and is able to classify and seriate. Understands reversibility.
Formal operational	11–15 years	Able to solve abstract problems in logical fashion. Becomes more scientific in thinking. Develops concerns about social issues, identity.

Source: Adapted from Barry J. Wadsworth, *Piaget's Theory of Cognitive and Affective Development/Foundations of Constructivism.* Published by Allyn and Bacon, Boston, MA. Copyright © 1989 by Pearson Education. Reprinted by permission of the publisher.

quentially through each of the stages of development, although at individual rates. Cognitive development is an active construction process, created by each child according to her experiences (Crain, 1980).

SENSORIMOTOR STAGE. The first stage, **sensorimotor,** includes children from birth to 2 years of age. Infants interact primarily with their immediate environment and learn through sensory actions, such as hearing, grasping, tasting, or seeing. Objects are real only when they are in sight or touched by the infant. During the first months of life, an infant has not yet developed the ability to mentally represent an object by thinking about it; the object must be present and be seen, touched, smelled, heard, or tasted in order to be "thought of" by the infant.

By the end of the sensorimotor stage, the child gradually begins to think of objects and processes as she moves into using prior knowledge and experiences to solve new situations. An example can be found in the following situation: An 18-month-old infant sitting in her high chair is picking up different crackers from the tray and placing them in her mouth, one by one. Whenever she picks up a goldfish-shaped cheese cracker, she chews it and then swallows. The round crackers, however, are spit back out onto the tray. After a few minutes of trial and error with the crackers, the toddler begins to throw the round crackers onto the floor and eat the goldfish-shaped crackers, without needing to taste them first. She learned to discriminate between the two types of crackers and eventually used her prior knowledge to discard the crackers she did not like.

PREOPERATIONAL STAGE. During the second stage of cognitive development, Piaget proposed that children from 2 to 6 or 7 years of age are at the **preoperational** level, where children have gained the ability and skills to represent images and objects without the object actually present. In other words, children at this stage will use objects during their play as symbols to represent objects not available. A 3-year-old might find a Frisbee outside on the playground and offer friends a piece of pizza, while another playmate might be sitting on a log and yelling, "Giddy-up horsee!" These children are involved in symbolic representation—using language to name their symbolic representations and inventing their own symbolic meaning for the object at hand.

Scott and Marc are utilizing several objects in their play as symbolic representations. What is one symbolic object you notice in the photo?

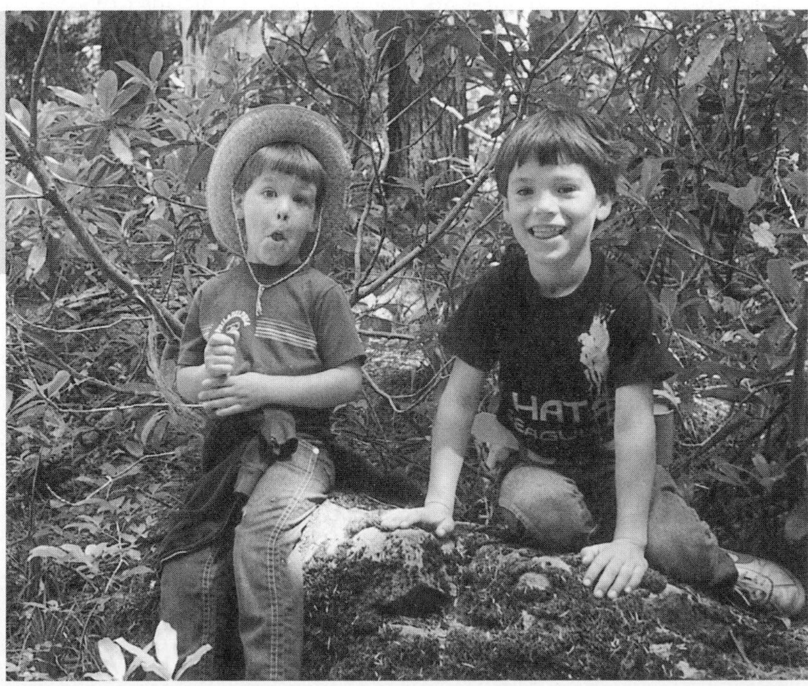

Other aspects of the preoperational stage include the development of beginning reasoning and **egocentricism** (the world revolves around one's self). Reasoning at this stage tends to be based on actual experiences and may not reflect logical rationale. For instance, Jason, a 4-year-old child, encounters a puddle of water near the sink in the playroom. Since it is raining outside, with puddles forming on the sidewalk, he decides that it must also have rained on this floor. Jason's reasoning is derived from his experience of walking in the puddle outside and watching the rain form puddles on the sidewalk. He transferred this outdoor experience to inside, when he determined the cause for the puddle on the floor.

Egocentricism could also be reflected in this related example. If another child told Jason that the water in the room came from spilling a glass of water, and Jason did not see anyone spill water, he might decide to hold on to his prior reasoning and explain the puddle from his own point of view. Children at the preoperational stage are not yet able to understand other people's viewpoints. This does not mean that the young child is selfish or self-centered, but rather that the child is firmly grounded in his own perspective, as this is what makes sense. Understanding that the child is relating to his personal perspective and experiences helps teachers and caregivers realize that explaining in length about sharing toys may not be as fruitful as short discussions and demonstrations of guidelines for sharing.

As the child progresses through the preoperational stage, he also becomes more **decentered** (and less egocentered), meaning he is able to look farther and farther beyond his own perspective. You might observe some 6-year-olds playing with younger children and talking to these children in shorter sentences, emphasizing certain words to help younger children understand. This is an example of decentering—that is, understanding the other person's perspective and acting on it.

CONCRETE OPERATIONS STAGE. From ages 6 to 12, the child enters the period of **concrete operations.** This stage is characterized by the child gaining the skills and concepts to understand conservation, reversibility, classification, seriation, and the ability to understand someone else's viewpoint. **Conservation** occurs when the physical elements of an object change, yet the object conserves most of its original property. A common example of conservation is found in holding up two identical balls of clay in front of a child. When you ask the child if these balls have the same amount of clay, he responds, "Yes." You then flatten one ball of clay and repeat the question. Typically, the child will decide that the flattened ball of clay is larger because it spreads out over a larger area. Thus, the shape of one of the identical balls of clay changed, but, until he grasps the concept of conservation, the child thinks of them as different amounts.

Reversibility is found in the logic that what is done with objects can also be undone or reversed. Reversibility can be represented with beginning addition. A 7-year-old child who understands reversibility would be able to show the relationship between 2 + 4 and 4 + 2 with blocks and discuss how they add up to the same amount. This same concept would also be introduced in subtraction, where children find that the 6 – 4 uses the same amount of blocks as 4 + 2 and that one equation "undoes" the other.

Classification begins with grouping objects according to one specific characteristic and then expands into a more complicated rationale for classifying. Young children often enjoy sorting like items into separate containers, which provides a structure for their beginning concepts of classification. Objects can be sorted according to shape, color, size, or use. This first step of organization helps children make sense of their world and promotes the understanding of connections and relationships. As children progress through this stage, they are able to increase the difficulty of their classification systems and use their own rationale for the classifications.

When objects are arranged in a sequential order based on one characteristic—such as age, length, or dates—we call this **seriation.** Our number system is a serial system, as it occurs in a specific order representing increasingly larger amounts. A group of 6- and 7-year-olds might make a chart that lists the months of the year according to their birth months, starting with the month with the most birthdays and moving in sequence to the month with the least number of birthdays. The chart represents seriation, with the months arranged according to the organizational schema of the number of birthdays per month.

Another change that occurs during the concrete operational stage is the child's beginning **understanding of other people's perspectives**. Children can now participate in a discussion about their favorite ice cream flavors and recognize that other people might have an opinion (or favorite flavor) that differs from their perspective. This is a wonderful age at which to discuss cultures and express appreciation for diversity in our world.

FORMAL OPERATIONS STAGE. The fourth and final stage of development, according to Piaget, occurs from age 12 through adulthood and is called **formal operations**, where people are dealing with abstract ideas, concepts, and issues. Much of the foundation for this stage was built throughout the prior three stages and is now expanded through the use of formal operations. Hypothetical situations and questions help older children sort their world and solve new problems that move beyond concrete thinking. The examination and exploration of important issues and concepts are teaching strategies that assist adolescents as they construct their attitudes and beliefs.

APPLYING PIAGET'S THEORY. If you incorporate Piaget's ideas when you set up your early childhood setting, you would include numerous opportunities for children to explore objects and their environment. When presenting the concept of *big* and *little* with a class of 3-year-olds, for example, you would make sure there were many concrete experiences available, such as objects, roleplaying, and pictures. Children learn from exploring their environment and from engaging in activities that allow them to make sense of their world. Simply telling a child what is *big* and what is *little* would produce very different learning. A learning environment where children are actively involved with materials helps them feel, see, draw, and categorize objects that are big or little. The involvement with materials is congruent with Piaget's belief that children learn through interacting with their environment.

Activities would also be designed to enhance the current cognitive development stage of the child. When a child is at the preoperational level, you would encourage her use of objects as symbols for objects that might not be available. For example, two children making a "pretend" breakfast on the play stove talk about the hot stove and remind each other not to touch the pan. They are using the play stove and pans as symbols of a real stove and cooking, and are engaging in language and activities built on symbolism.

Symbolic play is critical to learning, and activities should reflect the children's interests and developmental levels. When you listen to children at play and observe their approaches to problem solving, you are observing important information that helps you determine their current stage of development. This knowledge helps you plan a variety of activities that correspond to this level. While you watch students, you also realize that within a group of children of the same age, there will be differences among their levels of development. Planning developmentally appropriate activities for small groups and individuals shows your awareness of meeting the individual learning needs of each young child. You will visit a preschool later in this chapter and see how one early childhood educator applies Piaget's theories in his classroom.

PIAGET'S CONTRIBUTIONS AND LIMITATIONS. Piaget's theories about children and their thinking and development shifted educators' emphases on what children already know to examining how children come to know or learn. This shift greatly affected early childhood settings and interactions with children. The belief that acquisition of knowledge and true understanding in learning could be enhanced through activities and experiences had an impact on the curriculum of early childhood programs.

Piaget's ideas produced a schema or organizational structure of developmental levels useful for thinking about cognitive development of children. His work also challenged educators and psychologists to examine the origins of children's knowledge. Prior to Piaget's theories of cognitive development, much of the emphasis in early childhood learning had been based on what children already knew and building programs around their current knowledge. Piaget opened the way to explore how children come to learn new knowledge, which translates into providing activities and an environment that supports growth corresponding to the developmental levels.

Several limitations to Piaget's work have arisen recently. New research finds that infants exhibit behaviors earlier than Piaget established in his work. After all, Piaget did not have access to sophisticated experimental techniques that researchers now use to determine ages when cognitive stages are reached (Flavell, Miller, & Miller, 1993). Other researchers have suggested that Piaget underestimated young children's cognitive abilities. Work by Miller and Gelman (1983) found that preschool children are able to demonstrate they understand much more about numbers than was previously thought by Piaget. By reducing the amount of objects the children worked with and simplifying the directions, children were able to display that the number (amount) of objects stayed the same, whether the objects were spaced close together or moved apart from each other.

Important applications of Piaget's theory led to the acceptance of discovery learning, which is the role of play in early childhood, and to an increased awareness of the individual nature of learning and development. Piaget's work also laid the foundation for other cognitive developmental theories, such as the work of Jerome Bruner.

Bruner's Theory of Cognitive Development

In his early work, psychologist Jerome Bruner (born in 1915) studied perception (1951) and thinking (Bruner, Goodnow, & Austin, 1956). His research in these areas led him to propose that children learn as they seek meaning and make discoveries. As Bruner continued his study of cognitive development, he identified three stages of cognitive growth: the enactive, iconic, and symbolic stages (1966, 1971). These stages are outlined in Table 3.2.

ENACTIVE STAGE. During the **enactive stage,** the infant comprehends his world through actions, similar to the sensorimotor stage in Piaget's developmental levels. The infant responds to actions and objects through touch, taste, feel, smell, and sound.

ICONIC STAGE. When the child moves into the **iconic stage** (approximately 18 months to 6 years of age), he now views the world in concrete images. Whatever he sees must be true and real. A scary puppet looks real to a child in this stage.

SYMBOLIC STAGE. The final stage is the **symbolic stage,** where the child is able to draw from abstractions, language, and thinking to construct his world. He uses his knowledge gained through actions and images, but is able to move to higher levels of thinking and understand abstract ideas and concepts. You might notice this in a primary-level classroom, where children begin to read, write, and tell stories and remind each other what is real and what is "make believe." In their own imaginations, they are able to relate abstract ideas and share them with others.

DISCOVERY LEARNING AND INDUCTIVE REASONING. Bruner emphasized discovery learning and inductive reasoning as important instructional approaches for young children throughout all three stages of cognitive development. In Bruner's model of **dis-**

TABLE 3.2 Bruner's Three Stages of Cognitive Development

Stage	Approximate Age	Characteristic
Enactive	0–1½ years	Knows his or her world through senses
Iconic	1½–6 years	Knows his or her world through concrete images
Symbolic	6+ years	Knows his or her world through abstractions

covery learning, the child is an active player in discovering key principles of knowledge through her interaction with examples, materials, and/or problems. For example, a teacher or caregiver presents examples of pennies and other coins to a 5-year-old child. The child works with the coins, making connections and drawing her own meaning from the materials. She sorts the coins into different piles, discovering from another child the name of the brownish coins. She makes the generalization that all brownish coins are called pennies and the other coins are not pennies. When involved in discovery learning, the child builds her own structures and organizes her knowledge instead of passively accepting the teacher's reasoning or answers (Bruner, 1966, 1971).

If 5-year-old Antonio wants to find out what will float on water, the role of the teacher is to assist Antonio in gathering materials needed to test his hypothesis. He might also want assistance in designing an experiment that will help him discover if rocks, pencils, sticks, or a cookie will float. Antonio is actively exploring and experimenting to find answers to his question.

The teacher wants Antonio to discover the principle of gravity, weight, and buoyancy on his own, so she stops by to ask him about his findings. Through **inductive reasoning,** or drawing from specific examples to develop his own more general principles, Antonio talks about the heavy objects dropping to the bottom right away and the wood things staying on top of the water. Before he places a penny into the water, his teacher asks him to guess, or hypothesize, what will happen: "Will the penny float or sink?" She is encouraging Antonio to use his intuition based on his research, to think intuitively about the next step of his experiment, and to predict outcomes.

APPLYING BRUNER'S THEORY. An environment that reflects Bruner's ideas finds children actively pursuing their interests and testing ideas to find answers and solutions. The teacher or caregiver asks questions that require investigations and hands-on learning by the children. You see lots of equipment and materials available for children to use in a variety of ways. For example, Antonio used a small tub to test his floating theory. Later in the morning, Samantha was curious about the blocks in the play area and started drawing their shapes. She used the same tub to sort a box of blocks into two piles, one that contains shapes with four sides and one for shapes with more or less than four sides.

In an environment that supports Bruner's theory of learning, children expect to come up with their own answers and to share answers with others. They also expect to make mistakes, as they predict outcomes of their experiments based on their initial investigations and incomplete evidence. As an adult in this setting, you would ask many questions. Many of these questions will be **open ended,** with several possible answers. You would also expect the children to come up with ways to test their ideas and then connect their new learning with previous experiences.

Now we'll look at Vygotsky's work, which strongly supports the theory that children construct language and meaning from experiences with language through social interactions. Vygotsky stressed the importance of children's interactions with their environment to promote learning, as did Piaget and Bruner.

Vygotsky's Theory of Language Development

Lev Vygotsky (1896–1934) was a Russian psychologist whose contributions to early childhood study were in the field of the sociocultural aspects of learning. His work was based on the idea that society and culture influence what and how children learn (Bodrova & Leong, 1996). According to Vygotsky, human behavior must be studied within the social and historical context of the child (Dixon-Krauss, 1995). Teachers and caregivers need to include the social and cultural backgrounds of children when making educational decisions.

As a caregiver or teacher, it is important to move beyond your own culture and background and become knowledgeable of other cultures of the children with whom you work. For example, some Native American children may have been taught at home to support

These children are reading different books. They will then interpret the books and share their stories with their classmates.

others, even if there are personal costs for doing so. A Native American child in your care might not volunteer to give a correct answer if this made others in the group look as if they do not know as much. Awareness of cultural influences will help you in your interactions with children and their families and in your planning for learning activities (Bodrova & Leong, 1996). Box 3.1 presents a brief summary of a study that examined the influence of cultural context on a child's development.

Vygotsky presented the theory that children learn through their interactions with others, thus the people in their world hold great influence on their learning. Language is a

BOX 3.1

Does Cultural Context Influence Child Development?

If you were to observe a toddler in her home in San Pedro, Guatemala, and another toddler of the same age in Salt Lake City, Utah, you would note similarities and differences in their activities, behaviors, and development. "Each culture has its own system of norms and values in which the development and interactions of the children evolve" (Rogoff et al., 1993, p. 162). Rogoff and colleagues studied toddlers and their interactions with caregivers in four different cultural communities. Two of these communities included Salt Lake City and San Pedro. In this study, the researchers were attempting "to understand development in the context of children's everyday activities and culturally valued goals of development" (p. 9).

Expectations of the children led to variations in their development from culture to culture. For example, in San Pedro, where it is expected that young children will assist with household chores, 3 of the 14 toddlers helped their family by running errands, such as purchasing bread at a nearby store. None of the toddlers in Salt Lake City assumed such responsibility. In Salt Lake City, 10 of the 14 mothers of toddlers reported that they had instructed their child in walking or talking, whereas only 2 of the San Pedro mothers reported that they taught these skills. The mothers of the 14 toddlers in San Pedro indicated that their children learned to walk and talk by observing others or with parental encouragement.

The differences in reaching developmental milestones seem to be related to values and expectations expressed by the child's social and cultural community. According to Rogoff and colleagues (1993), "Goals of development vary according to local practices and values" (p. 151).

cultural tool, reflecting the child's physical and social environments (Bodrova & Leong, 1996). The use of language is critical for cognitive development. Children begin to develop higher levels of thinking when expressing their thoughts and ideas.

Older children and adults play a key role in the cognitive development of a child, often guiding the child to move to more complex ideas, concepts, or skills. When a child is working with others near the limits of her ability, support and guidance from others can help the child solve a new problem. This is called learning in the *zone of proximal development.*

THE ZONE OF PROXIMAL DEVELOPMENT. In his theory of the **zone of proximal development (ZPD),** Vygotsky believed that an educator could assist young children in moving to higher levels in their development by encouraging involvement in activities that are slightly more difficult than those the child can master alone (Bodrova & Leong, 1996). By working with capable peers or with adults who support them, children successfully complete more complicated activities and thus work at the level of potential development (Vygotsky, 1978). The ZPD theory is most often applicable to cognitive development, although it is certainly connected to language development. For example, when 2-year-old Kara wanted more apple, she said, "More." Her older brother replied, "You want more apple?" and Kara answered, "More apple." Through this shared interaction, Kara put two words together to make a phrase that communicated her request. Her brother's assistance to help her move beyond her current level of language use to a more complex level expanded her development, showing that Kara was in a zone of proximal development. Vygotsky finds language to be the foundation for higher cognitive processes (Berk, 2003).

JOURNAL 3.1: What is the difference between Kara's language experience with her older brother, compared to an adult correcting Kara's language by telling her, "No, you mean 'More apple' "? ●

Wood, Bruner, and Ross (1976) studied Vygotsky's zone of proximal development and used the term **scaffolding** to describe the assistance provided by the expert that helps the child move to a higher level of learning. The task itself is not changed, but the level or amount of assistance is gradually decreased until the child is able to perform the task independently. Bruner (1985b) finds the scaffolding provided by the expert (e.g., teacher, caregiver, or older child) to be important to the learning process. The scaffold provides a stable structure that enables a child to try out new knowledge with assistance, with the supports gradually decreased as the child becomes more capable. Scaffolding takes the form of directions, cues, modeling, or demonstrating, as well as many other learning guides. A young child learning to repeat a favorite nursery rhyme starts saying a few words along with his caregiver. After repeating the rhyme, he begins to say more and more words independently, while his caregiver leaves pauses in the rhyme to allow the child to "fill in the blanks." This is an example of scaffolding, where the support is gradually withdrawn as the child becomes more independent with his task.

EXPRESSIVE LANGUAGE. A second major contribution attributed to Vygotsky is the emphasis on expressive language as a child interacts with her environment. Children use the tool of language to master themselves and gain independence of behavior and thought (Vygotsky, 1986). If you listen to young children at play, you often hear them talking to themselves, whether explaining what will happen in their play or directing their own actions. According to Vygotsky, young children use their **self-talk** (private speech) for self-guidance and self-direction. We all use self-talk; in fact, as I am sitting at the computer, I often read sentences out loud to check for comprehension.

Language development and cognitive ability are affected by interactions children have with others. Infants begin responding to language at birth, and by 3 or 4 months of age, they will smile or turn toward the sound of a familiar voice. The interaction with the environment has a profound impact on language development, as children connect words

TABLE 3.3 Development of Language

Age in Months	Characteristics of Vocalization and Language
4	Coos and chuckles
6–9	Babbles; duplicates common sounds; produces sounds such as "ma" or "da"
12–18	A small number of words; follows simple commands and responds to no; uses expressive jargon
18–21	Vocabulary grows from about 20 words at 18 months to about 200 words at 21; points to many more objects; comprehends simple questions; forms 2-word phrases
24–27	Vocabulary of 200 to 400 words; has 2- or 3-word phrases; uses prepositions and pronouns
30–33	Fastest increase in vocabulary; 3- to 4-word sentences are common; word order, phrase structure, and grammatical agreement approximate the language of surroundings, but many utterances are unlike anything an adult would say
36–39	Vocabulary of 1,000 words or more; well-formed sentences using complex grammatical rules, although certain rules have not yet been fully mastered; grammatical mistakes are much less frequent; about 90 percent comprehensible

Source: F. F. Schachter and A. A. Strage, 1982, "Adults' Talk and Children's Language Development," in *The Young Child: Reviews of Research* (vol. 3, p. 83) by S. G. Moore and C. R. Cooper (Eds.). Washington, DC: NAEYC.

to concrete objects and activities and form a framework for their thinking and communicating. Table 3.3 highlights the language development of young children.

APPLYING VYGOTSKY'S THEORY. A classroom or environment set up around Vygotskian thinking would find the adult planning activities around guided or assisted discovery. Both Piaget and Vygotsky support discovery learning. The major difference is Vygotsky's incorporation of **guided learning;** that is, an adult or older child assists the child in the learning process. Piaget would have suggested that children learn through their individual interactions with the environment, choosing not to emphasize the roles of others as having an impact on learning, as Vygotsky proposed.

Language plays an active role in guided discovery, with the adult talking about the activity, asking questions, and encouraging the child to describe what he is doing throughout the activity. A rich context for language development includes time for reading, storytelling, sharing and discussions, and, when developmentally appropriate, introducing written symbols of language. There would also be many opportunities to interact and become involved in cooperative learning experiences. The voices of many children would be heard as they talked about their interactions and explained their activities to themselves, each other, and adults.

The teacher or caregiver would also be aware of each child's zone of proximal development and provide activities to engage the child in an activity that required assistance (scaffolding) from a peer or adult. To meet the children's learning needs, small group activities would be arranged according to the children's current level of development and their zone of proximal development.

Both cognitive development and language development have an impact on children's social and emotional development. Children need emotionally healthy lives in order to fully develop their cognitive and language skills. They also need frequent opportunities to interact with others as they grow socially. Let's turn our attention to social and emotional development and how you can support a young child's development in these areas.

Social and Emotional Development

Social and emotional development are at the heart of effective early childhood programs. Early childhood professionals acknowledge the importance of creating an environment that truly supports and encourages healthy social and emotional growth. **Social development** of a child reflects the standards and values of her family and of her society, where the child begins to learn acceptable or appropriate behaviors at birth and continues to learn behavior patterns through her relationships with others, adapting these behaviors to her unique personality (Gordon & Browne, 1993). These behaviors are established by the society within which the child lives and become the social expectations that guide social development and the child's interactions with others. **Emotions** are feelings, some of which are complex. At some time in your life, you have felt anger, fear, pride, satisfaction, sorrow, frustration, joy, confidence, hate, or love. Even as an adult, perhaps you have found it difficult to communicate some of these feelings. Young children's feelings grow out of their interaction with their environment and their responses to these interactions. Early childhood is the time when children learn to notice, accept, and express their feelings as they develop emotionally. The child is forming a sense of self.

The foundation for healthy social and emotional growth is established in a child's early years. As an early childhood professional, you have a great responsibility to understand theories of social and emotional development and to be able to translate these theories into sound practice. Many social and emotional behaviors are learned through responses to an individual's behavior, observations of adult or peer behaviors, trying out different roles through play, and opportunities for social interaction. The term **socialization** describes the process of learning which behaviors are appropriate for specific situations. Let's learn more about social development through Erik Erikson's theory of psychosocial development.

Erikson's Theory of Psychosocial Development

Erik Erikson (1902–1994) is considered to be a **psychosocialist,** one who believes that how individuals respond to the demands of society at different stages of life affects development and acquisition of skills and abilities to become contributing members of

What are some emotions this child might be experiencing?

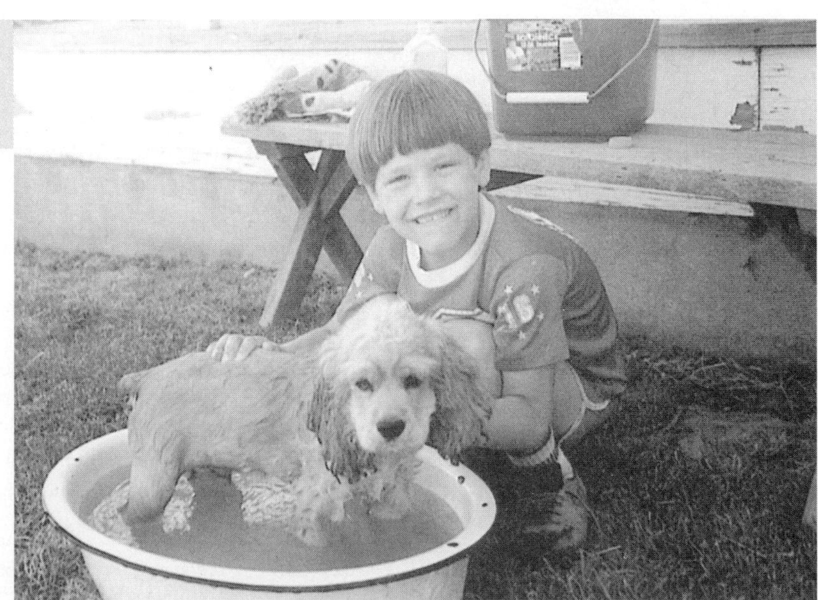

society (Berk, 2003). Erikson focused his attention on children's behavior. According to him, interpersonal relationships reveal the core of a person's makeup or personality (Maier, 1978). Based on specific behaviors, Erikson placed a child at a certain stage or level of development according to the description of that level and the match between the child's behavior and the level of development. Erikson's theory of human development is based on the concept that individuals move through development stages as they face problems or crises throughout their lives. When a person successfully solves conflict at earlier stages, then the person moves to the next life stage, as seen in Table 3.4. Achievement at each stage is dependent on learning and development at prior levels.

TRUST VERSUS MISTRUST. In the first stage of psychosocial development, **trust versus mistrust,** an infant is dependent on adults to meet all of her needs. When an adult responds to the cries or discomfort of the infant in a consistent manner, the infant develops trust for the world around her. Infants need consistent care provided by warm, responsive adults who attend to the infant when she is uncomfortable or in need, as well as times when she may want company or interaction with others. When the infant learns that she can depend on others for predictable care, she will then be able to develop trust. At this point, she has resolved the conflict of discomfort by trusting that an adult will help her. At approximately 12 to 18 months of age, she will then move into the second stage.

AUTONOMY VERSUS DOUBT AND SHAME. During the **autonomy versus doubt and shame stage,** children are generally from 18 months to 3 years of age, and are now testing their independence by assuming more self-responsibilities. This is a busy time, when toddlers explore a rapidly expanding world as they begin to walk and talk. They are also learning to dress and feed themselves, and begin toileting skills. Children at this age are also finding out what they like and do not like, and will clearly let others know their opinions, even as those opinions change frequently throughout the day.

Erikson believes that adults must provide guidance through support for the child's efforts at independence. If not, the child begins to doubt her own ability to master important tasks and skills, which would lead to lower self-confidence and self-esteem and result in shame and doubt. The role of the adult is critical in supporting and supervising this new independence, and in helping the child feel responsible and capable.

INITIATIVE VERSUS GUILT. From 3 to 6 years of age, the young child is in the **initiative versus guilt stage** and is ready to take initiative in planning some actions. He is

TABLE 3.4 Erikson's First Four Stages of Psychosocial Development

Stage	Approximate Age	Description
1. Basic trust vs. basic mistrust	Birth to 12–18 months	The infant must form a loving, trusting relationship with the caregiver, or develop a sense of mistrust.
2. Autonomy vs. shame/doubt	18 months to 3 years	The child's energies are directed toward the development of physical skills, including walking, grasping, and sphincter control. The child learns control but may develop shame and doubt if not handled well.
3. Initiative vs. guilt	3 to 6 years	The child continues to become more assertive and to take more initiative, but may be too forceful, leading to guilt feelings.
4. Industry vs. inferiority	6 to 12 years	The child must deal with demands to learn new skills or risk a sense of inferiority, failure, and incompetence.

Source: Adapted from Lester A. Lefton & Linda Brannon, *Psychology,* 8th ed., p. 106. Published by Allyn and Bacon, Boston, MA. Copyright © 2003 by Pearson Education. Reprinted by permission of the publisher.

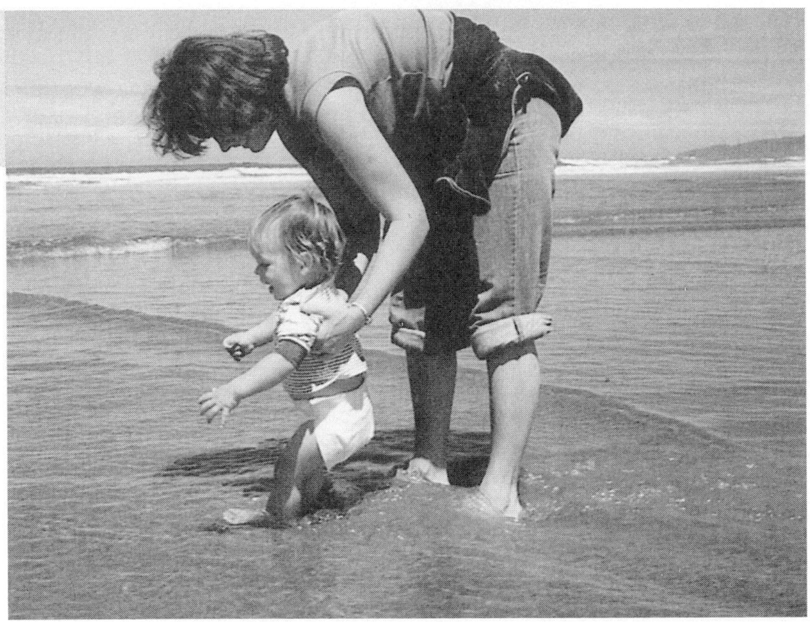

This infant is able to enjoy a new experience with someone he trusts.

interested in developing an idea and seeing it take place. Adults can encourage this curiosity and desire to take charge and help channel these activities into positive experiences. Erikson points out that if the child continually finds his actions result in "unhappy" events, he will develop guilt feelings.

Nurturing the child's independence and listening to his plans help the adult head off major problems and guide the child to successful ventures. For instance, a 5-year-old brings his favorite book to day care and wants to take it to the sandbox outside. Because of rain earlier in the day, the sand is wet. Wet sand is great for trucks and road building, but not so great for favorite books. You talk to the child about leaving the book in a special place and finding a construction truck or shovel to take to the sandbox. He agrees and makes sure his book is in a safe place before going outside to play. This exchange helped the child "save" his book and still take the initiative in bringing something out to the sandbox. It also helped avoid the guilt that could develop from ruining a favorite book.

INDUSTRY VERSUS INFERIORITY. During the elementary school years, from age 6 to 12, children enter the crisis of **industry versus inferiority** stage. This period is characterized by many new challenges and the introduction to learning the laws and expectations of society. Children are learning to read, to engage with a larger group of peers, and to master more and more complex skills. Productivity is necessary to complete assignments at school.

Children who are successful in their schoolwork and in other activities learn that industry and productivity are pleasant. When children find themselves repeatedly failing at school or in other settings, they begin feeling inferior and decide that they are inadequate. Helping children establish reasonable goals is an important learning tool. You want children to set realistic goals and maintain the motivation needed to reach those goals. Success must also be seen through the child's eyes in order for it to be believed. Helping children deemphasize mistakes and focus on the steps needed to progress helps them learn to solve problems and gain satisfaction from their accomplishments.

The final four stages of psychosocial development include identity versus role confusion, intimacy versus isolation, generativity versus stagnation, and ego integrity versus despair. These stages begin at puberty and continue through late adult life.

FACING CONFLICTS AND CRISES. Throughout each of Erikson's eight stages of psychosocial development, people face conflicts and crises. In Erikson's theory, **crises** occur when one needs to respond to a psychological challenge, which may mean adjusting behavior to meet society's expectations. The reaction to and resolution of these conflicts construct an individual's social development. According to Erikson, each person learns how to interact with others based on personal experiences with conflict, crises, and resolution of these problems. You form who you are and how you relate to others and to society by your experiences and responses to crises throughout these eight stages of development.

GENDER AND SOCIAL DEVELOPMENT. Moving through crises and stages of social development lead to the establishment of an individual identity. According to Erikson (1968), "Identity . . . is experienced merely as a sense of psychological well-being. Its most obvious concomitants are a feeling of being at home in one's body, a sense of 'knowing where one is going' and an inner assuredness of anticipated recognition of those who count" (p. 165). A major aspect of identity formation comes from the recognition of gender roles in one's life. Gender roles vary from society to society, which again points to the importance of studying child development within the context of social and cultural contexts.

In the United States, many adults are surprised to find that young children are still treated with different expectations according to their gender, even at a very young age. The perception of gender-typed behavior traits of women and men (e.g., women are more extroverted and emotionally sensitive, whereas men are assertive and aggressive) was studied in this country (Berk, 2002) and in Europe, Africa, Asia, and Australia (Williams & Best, 1990). These studies showed that stereotypes are still prevalent. Caregivers and teachers have a great impact in this area; for example, girls who have gone on to careers in science-related fields report that encouragement received from a teacher influenced their career choice (American Association of University Women, 1992). In his later work, Erikson (1974) noted that changes in society regarding gender roles have occurred since his earlier writing and he predicted that "modern life may come to permit a much freer inter-identification of the sexes in everyday life" (p. 333).

APPLYING ERIKSON'S THEORY. Erikson's theories bring important messages to your work with young children. Your understanding of the four stages or levels of development associated with early childhood and of the major crises associated with each stage will assist you in nurturing the social growth of young children in your care. Realizing that a toddler is attempting to establish her independence and take initiative in her activities helps you support her in reaching her goal. Recognizing that an infant is learning to trust others when you provide consistent and warm care lets you think about the far-reaching consequences of your interactions with this young child.

Erikson also emphasizes the significance of play and opportunities for children to take the initiative and to make choices in their play. Often, the primary role of the adult is to observe children at play and allow them to experience the consequences of their actions (of course, within safety limits). For example, establishing a time for "free play" helps young children learn to make choices of activities. They might also learn that other children choose this same activity and consequently toys or play space may need to be shared. Learning the social skills necessary for sharing through their own initiative is much more valuable than *being told* to share by an adult. You provide the support by establishing clear boundaries within which the children learn social expectations of different situations.

Play is also considered to be an environment where gender roles are acted out. We want to pay close attention to avoiding stereotyping of gender roles. All children should have access to dolls, trucks, science kits, balls, dress-up clothes, and quiet-time activities. The language of the adult can affect a child's interest in an activity. For instance, telling a girl that she should be a nurse instead of the doctor would be a flagrant example of gender typing that must be avoided. Many responses to children are made without recognizing the bias of gender typing. Gender-fair practices and encouragement to try out different roles in play activities must be a conscious effort made by caregivers and teachers, with tremendous implications in social development and the formation of identity. The environment and activities that caregivers and teachers create play a major role in social development: learning how to relate to others.

Social and emotional development are closely related. In order to interact positively with others, a child needs a healthy self-image. Maslow developed a hierarchy of emotional development that will be helpful as you create an environment that supports and promotes the social and emotional development of young children.

Maslow's Theory of Humanism

The work of Abraham Maslow (1908–1970) has presented important implications for the emotional development of children. Maslow's theory is considered **humanistic** because it is based on the belief that all people are motivated by fulfilling certain needs. Maslow studied the needs, goals, and accomplishments of successful people and used this information to construct a hierarchy, or ladder, of needs. In order for people to reach the highest level of self-actualization, all physiological needs and social-emotional needs must first be met. **Physiological** needs refer to what you need in order to be physically comfortable (e.g., food when hungry or a warm place to be when it is snowing outside). **Social-emotional** needs include feeling as if you belong to a group and are loved. When these needs are met, you may then move to higher levels toward **self-actualization,** where you realize your individual potential.

MASLOW'S SELF-ACTUALIZATION PYRAMID. According to Maslow (1987), people move through these six levels in a pyramid sequence as needs are met, as shown in Figure 3.1. Each person begins at the bottom level, with the most basic needs of food, shelter, and clothing, and then progresses to the sixth level. The sixth level represents self-actualization, where one focuses on attaining meaningfulness or goodness. Maslow claimed that a person moving through the levels will stop trying to meet a high-level need if the person becomes deprived of a lower-level need. The focus is then on satisfying the lower-level need first (Maslow, 1987).

Motivation to move to higher levels occurs after the basic needs are met at prior levels. For example, you may recall a time when you were extremely hungry—perhaps your busy schedule forced you to miss a meal. At that time, it would be difficult to think about

FIGURE 3.1
Maslow's Hierarchy of Needs

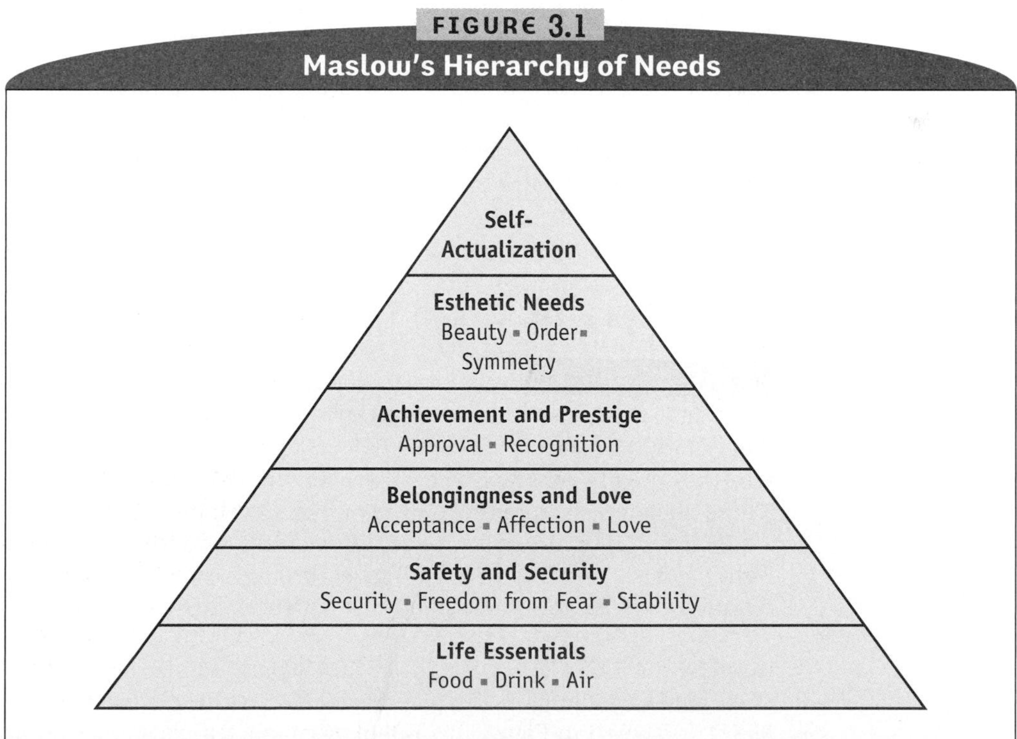

Source: Motivation and Personality by Abraham H. Maslow, © 1971. Reprinted by permission of Prentice-Hall, Inc., Upper Saddle River, NJ.

the beauty in the scenery outside your window as your stomach was growling. You were most concerned with taking care of your hunger. The same situation occurs with young children, who often do not have the ability to figure out how or where they will obtain food. When a young child is hungry and frustrated, you can imagine how difficult it would be for that child to be fully engaged in a learning activity.

APPLYING MASLOW'S THEORY. Maslow's theory brings helpful insights to those working with young children. For instance, when an infant is uncomfortable with a wet diaper, she lets you know by crying and squirming. This child would have difficulty focusing on the different objects in her mobile hanging above her play area. What she really wants is to get rid of the feeling of a wet diaper. Once the diaper has been changed and the baby is comforted, she might then be interested in looking around and reaching out for nearby objects.

The same is true with a child in a kindergarten setting. Think of a child entering a new school and not knowing any of the children or the teacher. He probably doesn't feel too safe or secure; in fact, he may want his parent, sibling, or caregiver to stay at school for a while to provide the needed security and safety. His teacher might spend some time showing him around the room and introducing him to a few children, watching to see if he begins to feel more comfortable. Again, the child needs to have his basic needs met (in this case, security and safety) before moving into a new and unfamiliar situation where he feels ready to explore and learn in his new classroom.

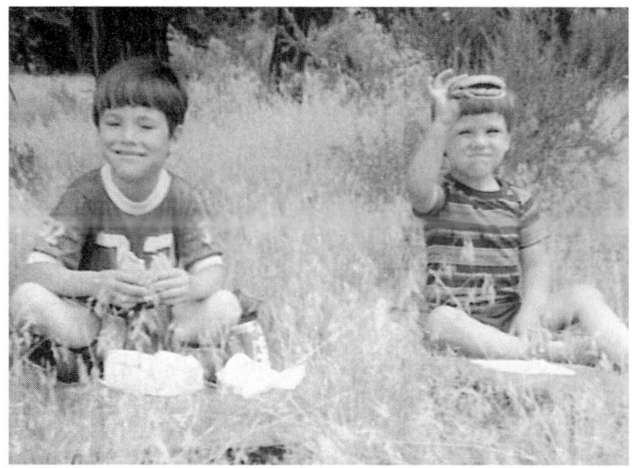

These children are content with a picnic on a summer day. Which of their needs, according to Maslow's hierarchy, appear to be met in this scene?

Caregivers and teachers working with young children find it critical to be attuned to these needs and to provide the support needed. This might mean finding a snack for a hungry child, keeping several sweatshirts available for cooler days, or spending extra time with a child who seems to need attention. Maslow's theory proposes that children who have their basic needs met are more likely to achieve positive self-images. Children who feel good about themselves are also more apt to be interested in socializing with others.

Within social and emotional development is the critical area of moral growth and development. Moral development is included within the broader category of social and emotional development, as moral development and reasoning strongly influence social and emotional interactions.

Kohlberg's Theory of Moral Development

Moral development influences understanding the impact of an individual's actions and decisions on others within society. Have you ever wondered how young children perceive what is right or wrong? Or how they make a decision about what is right or wrong? Or why they might choose to go ahead and do something that they know is considered wrong? These questions lead to thinking about the development of morals.

Piaget and Kohlberg have contributed to knowledge of children's moral development. Both theorists propose that children go through a sequence of levels as they develop more reasoning power and understand consequences for specific behaviors.

KOHLBERG'S STAGES OF MORAL REASONING. Perhaps the most widely accepted hierarchy of stages of moral development is the one developed by Lawrence Kohlberg (1927–1987), as shown in Figure 3.2. Kohlberg conducted his studies on moral reasoning by presenting a child with **moral dilemmas,** or situations where a child has to decide the best outcome for a problem situation where the situation has no seemingly right or wrong answer. The children participating in the study were asked to decide what a person involved in the

FIGURE 3.2

Kohlberg's Stage Theory of Moral Reasoning

Level 1: Preconventional Moral Reasoning

Judgment is based on personal needs and others' rules.

Stage 1 *Punishment-Obedience Orientation*
Rules are obeyed to avoid punishment. A good or a bad action is determined by its physical consequences.

Stage 2 *Personal Reward Orientation*
Personal needs determine right and wrong. Favors are returned along the lines of "You scratch my back, I'll scratch yours."

Level 2: Conventional Moral Reasoning

Judgment is based on others' approval, family expectations, traditional values, the laws of society, and loyalty to country.

Stage 3 *Good Boy–Nice Girl Orientation*
Good means "nice." It is determined by what pleases, aids, and is approved by others.

Stage 4 *Law and Order Orientation*
Laws are absolute. Authority must be respected and the social order maintained.

Level 3: Postconventional Moral Reasoning

Stage 5 *Social Contract Orientation*
Good is determined by socially agreed-upon standards of individual rights. This is a morality similar to that of the U.S. Constitution.

*Stage 6** *Universal Ethical Principle Orientation*
Good and right are matters of individual conscience and involve abstract concepts of justice, human dignity, and equality.

*In later work, Kohlberg questioned whether Stage 6 exists separately from Stage 5.

Source: "The Claim to Moral Adequacy of a Highest Stage of Moral Judgment" by L. Kohlberg, 1973, *Journal of Philosophy, 70,* pp. 631–632. Adapted by permission.

dilemma should do and why. The child's response would then indicate at which level the child was functioning: Level 1—Preconventional Moral Reasoning, Level 2—Conventional Moral Reasoning, or Level 3—Postconventional Moral Reasoning.

Similar to the descriptions of development in other domains, children and adults do not always reach the highest levels of development. Although the stages are loosely connected to age ranges, individuals move through stages at different times in their lives (Kohlberg, 1976). In early childhood settings, you will find most of the children operating at preconventional reasoning in Level 1, according to Kohlberg's model.

Moral development is closely related to cognitive and emotional development (Woolfolk, 2004). It would be difficult for a child who has not developed her ability to think at abstract levels to make moral decisions based on higher-level thought. Kohlberg recognized that thinking is required to make moral decisions. His work expressed the need to increase awareness of moral reasoning, both in one's own thinking and in that of others. At the same time, Kohlberg was cognizant of the role of moral reasoning within a democracy and the important role teachers play in facilitating the development of moral reasoning.

How do children learn moral reasoning? Witherell (1991) suggests that promoting genuine dialogue in the classroom or child care setting is a format to help children make sense of their world. Witherell finds that sharing stories serves as a springboard for discussing moral or ethical action. Other educators also see communication and dialogue about events occurring in the classroom, both within the curriculum and within the daily life of school (e.g., situations that arise during play), as important opportunities for discussions about moral reasoning. According to Kohlberg's stage model, young children make moral decisions based on avoiding punishment and an expectation of a reward for good behavior.

However, children need more than a "Yes, that's right" or a "No, that's wrong." To develop their moral reasoning, children need opportunities to stretch beyond their current abilities to reason and be encouraged to comprehend another's viewpoint (Berk, 2003). This suggests to early childhood professionals that very young children are attending to issues of right and wrong, which supports the rationale to respond to young children with their level of moral reasoning in mind.

APPLYING KOHLBERG'S THEORY. Some people feel that schools or other public settings should not include moral education in their curricula. In reality, caregivers and teachers continually communicate moral messages to children. The interpretation of rules and children's behaviors reflect moral judgments (DeVries & Zan, 1994). Young children grapple with moral issues based on observable behaviors and immediate consequences. A close look at the interactions and realities of a day-to-day life in a school or child care situation reveals the inherent inclusion of moral development and the need to attend to learning how to support healthy moral development.

Perhaps the most important consideration for adults working with young children is to respect each child and her individual values. Children at a young age are aware of justice and fairness in their environment and recognize when they are treated with respect or disrespect. Each child brings her own value system and stage of moral development with her to the child care setting or classroom and needs to know that her beliefs are honored.

When an adult understands that children might have a different perspective of right and wrong, they are better able to help a child learn to distinguish from acceptable and unacceptable actions. Learning from Kohlberg's theory of moral development will assist you in recognizing the stage in which a child might be currently operating. For example, when a 2-year-old takes another child's toy that was brought from home and runs to the other side of the room to examine the toy, you would not consider this "stealing." If a similar action occurred with an 8-year-old child in a store, then this likely would be considered taking an item that did not belong to him. In the case of the 2-year-old, you might briefly explain, "This is Trina's toy. Let's check with Trina to see if you can look at it with her." Children develop their personal value system through their experiences and observing the modeling of others—rarely from being told what to do or what not to do.

Within the early childhood setting, there must also be room for children to make decisions and learn from the results of their own decision making. When situations a 5-year-old child worked through did not seem to turn out quite right, brief discussions or sharing a story about a similar incident might be helpful. The focus of the discussion might be to look at possible alternative behaviors that the child might select if in a similar situation again.

The caregiver or teacher's role is also one of noting when actions, incidents, or behaviors occur that reflect conflicts in moral reasoning. Name-calling, pushing, taking toys, and not sharing are behaviors that occur in all early childhood settings. The response to these behaviors is how children reason about right and wrong. These conflicts become rich learning tools when used as discussion and reflection opportunities.

Another theory of social learning is behaviorism. Behaviorists consider interactions in the social environment an essential aspect of learning. According to behaviorists, a child's behavior is shaped by responses encountered in the child's environment.

Skinner's Theory of Behaviorism

The theory of **behaviorism** is based on the belief that learning is a change in observable behavior occurring as a result of experience (Woolfolk, 2004). Theorists in this field were interested in changes in behavior as a result of consequences from a child's interactions with his environment. B. F. Skinner (1904–1990) was a behavioral psychologist who developed the theory of operant conditioning (learning through responses and consequences).

OPERANT CONDITIONING. Have you ever found a piece of chocolate in the kitchen cupboard, bitten into it, and been unpleasantly surprised to find it was unsweetened chocolate meant for baking? You experienced an immediate consequence for your behavior. It is likely that you changed this behavior by reading labels or asking others about the chocolate before taking a large bite next time. This is an example of **operant conditioning,** where a consequence for behavior leads to changes in subsequent actions.

Skinner began his research with rats, which he placed in a Skinner Box and rewarded with food pellets when the rats touched a bar in the box. After a rat learned to press the bar for food, changes were implemented in the procedure. For instance, the rat may need to press the bar three times in succession to receive the food pellet, or the rat may have to listen for a tone before pressing the bar to receive food. To **extinguish** (or terminate) the behavior, food was not given when the bar was pressed and the rat no longer bothered to press the bar. By controlling the environment, Skinner was able to prove that **reinforcing** (providing a desirable consequence following a behavior) the rat's behavior led to changes in behavior. These experiments were the basis of his theory of operant conditioning, where behavior is influenced by the consequences following the behavior.

Consequences, the events that follow an action, lead to changed behavior. The use of **reinforcement** (use of consequences to alter behavior) or **punishment** (action that decreases the likelihood of the behavior occurring again) is purposely implemented to create change in behavior. Returning to the scientific experiments with the Skinner Boxes and rats, you will recall that the behavior of pressing the bar in the box resulted in food. The behavior (pressing the bar) resulted in a consequence that was reinforcing (food).

Operant conditioning is one form of behaviorism, with a focus on consequences that influence future behaviors (Woolfolk, 2004). Each day, you knowingly and unknowingly experience principles of behaviorism. A mother working with her toddler son on toilet training hugs him and gives him a cookie when he uses his potty chair. They both are delighted. This is an example of reinforcing behavior with a reward. The scientific application model of behaviorism (e.g., the rat experiment) might be construed as manipulative on the far end of the continuum of the use of behaviorism. It helps to remember that there is a continuum, or range, of behaviorism, with applications that may be appropriate in certain situations.

APPLYING SKINNER'S THEORY. In a preschool setting, you notice Stewart showing his painting to the teaching assistant, Marion. Marion responds, "What a beautiful sun you made." This response might be considered reinforcement by Stewart, who returns to the painting easel and continues painting suns. The child continues a behavior that is praised.

JOURNAL 3.2: What might be another reinforcement typically used in a preschool setting? How do you feel about the use of reinforcement in promoting learning? ●

In a different scenario at this preschool, Tracy keeps poking Brad. Marion walks over to Tracy and asks her to take a time-out. The time-out would be a punishment for the behavior of poking, with the plan that this consequence will decrease the behavior. Marion wants Tracy to eliminate, or extinguish, this behavior, so she creates a punishment (e.g., time-out).

A limitation in using operant conditioning with children is identifying reinforcements and punishments that matter to the child. Some children might be dissatisfied with the response Stewart received about his painting—perhaps they wanted Marion to notice the boats they had painted—so the comment on the suns would not be a reinforcement that would increase the likelihood of the behavior occurring again. With the poking incident, Tracy might like some quiet time, so time-out for her is not a punishment. She might also like to attract Marion's attention, so she might have seen that consequence as a reinforcement.

An even greater limitation is found in looking only at observable behavior and consequences. This approach to working with children minimizes the child's thinking and understanding of the situation. Making decisions based only on observable behavior and not on a child's interpretation of events or your interpretation of the child's reasoning raises some concerns about control and imposing one's judgments on the children in your care. Understanding the effects of praise, reinforcement, and punishment helps bring into focus a larger picture of working with young children. Recognizing the impact of one's statements—as simple as "Great work"—on a child's behavior helps the early childhood professional make decisions about the use of reinforcement and punishment in her setting. Children might come to expect reinforcement for their learning, which could affect learning if an adult were not present (Kohn, 1999).

By understanding the principles of behaviorism and operant conditioning, an early childhood professional can make decisions about when it is appropriate to use consequences, reinforcement, or punishment. Let's explore another important theory that influences early childhood education programs and the curriculum design within programs. Components from prior theories discussed in this chapter are incorporated into the model of multiple intelligences.

Multiple Intelligences Theory

The theory of **multiple intelligences (MI theory)** draws from each developmental domain and proposes there are at least eight separate human capacities that compose the plurality of intellect (Checkley, 1997). Instead of thinking of intelligence as a narrow measure, Gardner presents eight different intelligences, within which each person is capable of further development and growth.

Gardner's Theory of Multiple Intelligences

Howard Gardner (born in 1943) refers to **intelligence** as having more to do with solving problems and fashioning products within a naturalistic setting (Armstrong, 2000) than the artificial setting posed by most intelligence tests. The definition of intelligence as defined by an intelligence test is far more artificial than that posed by Gardner. Intelligence, as scored on tests, basically refers to what a person is born with; it is measurable and can be tested. Gardner's definition examines what a person does with an ability. In addition to the ability to solve problems and create products, a specific intelligence must also meet the following three criteria:

1. Is there a particular representation for this ability in the brain?
2. Do we know of populations that are particularly talented or particularly deficient in this ability?
3. Is there an evolutionary history of this intelligence that can be found in animals other than human beings? (Checkley, 1997)

Gardner's concept of intelligence is derived from an accumulation of knowledge about the human brain (Gardner, 1999). Every human being has the capacity for developing within each of the eight intelligences, but varying degrees of expertise are displayed with the different intelligences. In order to develop a program for young children based on MI theory, you would want to know more about the children's abilities, interests, and accomplishments within each of the eight intelligences, as outlined in Table 3.5.

THE EIGHT INTELLIGENCES. Let's look at each of the eight intelligences, according to descriptions by Gardner (1999), Checkley (1997), and Armstrong (2000). At the same time, teaching strategies that promote learning in each intelligence will be discussed.

Linguistic intelligence, the use of language, is seen in the ability to read, write, or talk to others. This intelligence is highly valued in schools. A primary focus in the early years of elementary school is literacy development, which demonstrates linguistic intelligence. Storytelling is a teaching strategy that allows the caregiver or teacher to weave in concepts, details, or goals that are appropriate to the children. Storytelling has been used for centuries and in many cultures as a medium to share knowledge.

TABLE 3.5 **Multiple Intelligence Theory Summary Chart**

Intelligence	Core Components	End-State Possibilities
Linguistic	Sensitivity to sounds, structure, meanings, and functions of words and language	Writer, orator
Logical-mathematics	Sensitivity to, and capacity to discern, logical or numerical patterns; ability to handle long chain of reasoning	Scientist, mathematician
Spatial	Capacity to perceive the visual-spatial world accurately and to perform transformations on one's initial perceptions	Artist, architect
Bodily-kinesthetic	Ability to control one's body movements and to handle objects skillfully	Athlete-dancer, sculptor
Musical	Ability to produce and appreciate rhythm and pitch; appreciation of forms of musical expressiveness	Composer, performer
Interpersonal	Capacity to discern and respond appropriately to moods, temperaments, motivations, and desires of others	Counselor, political leader
Intrapersonal	Access to one's own feelings, ability to discriminate among one's emotions	Psychotherapist, religious leader
Naturalist	Expertise in distinguishing among members of a species; recognizing existence of other species; and charting out relations among several species	Naturalist, biologist

Source: From *Multiple Intelligences in the Classroom,* 2nd ed., by Thomas Armstrong. Alexandria, VA: Association for Supervision and Curriculum Development.

Logical-mathematical intelligence refers to logic and mathematical ability. The ability to use numbers, understand patterns, and exhibit reason are the key characteristics of logical-mathematical intelligence. Certainly, mathematical learning is valued, as evidenced in school curriculum. *Categorization,* for instance, is a teaching strategy that is developmentally appropriate for young children and supports logical learning. Children as young as 3 and 4 years old enjoy sorting materials according to categories, some that they create and others created by those around them. A 4-year-old might sort items by color, then by size, and then according to use. Older children could also record their findings, creating charts and displays of their categorization findings.

Spatial intelligence is the ability to create a visual image of a potential project or idea and then act on this visualization. Think of bridge engineers or interior decorators who must be able to "see" their ideas before creating them. *Visualization* is a powerful teaching strategy in spatial intelligence. A kindergarten teacher might ask a young child to close her eyes and see a gingerbread man running from the fox before she begins to draw a picture to represent the scene. Visualization can also be used to rehearse the steps or sequence of a task before starting the activity.

Bodily-kinesthetic intelligence refers to the ability to use one's own body or parts of the body as a medium of expression or to solve a problem. A ballet dancer and an Olympic athlete are examples of people who have refined their bodily-kinesthetic skills or intelligence. The use of *manipulatives* in teaching math is an excellent example of the combination of bodily-kinesthetic intelligence with other intelligences. Many young children touch their fingers as they count, using their own teaching strategy for learning the sequence of numbers.

Musical intelligence is the ability to perform musically or to produce written music. People who are highly skilled in musical intelligence think in music patterns or see and hear patterns and are able to manipulate these patterns. Do you remember singing your ABCs? This is an example of a teaching strategy that helped you learn the alphabet. Songs for counting, colors, names, and other familiar objects promote learning through musical intelligence.

Interpersonal intelligence is the sensitivity one has toward others, along with the ability to work well with other people, understand others, and assume leadership roles.

Sharing is a way for young children to learn from each other and use their interpersonal intelligence. All ages benefit from sharing and interacting—children can share with peers as well as with children older or younger than them. Depending on the age of the child, caregivers or teachers should adjust their amount of involvement in the directions and guidance of the sharing situation.

Intrapersonal intelligence is the accurate understanding of one's self (who one is, what one wants, and a realistic sense of what one can do) and the ability to act according to this knowledge. *Modeling* true-felt emotions with young children provides an avenue for children to observe the range of emotions of others. Once a child reaches school age, curriculum is often presented in a neutral format, with little emotion shown by the teacher. Expressing joy, passion, disappointment, or other emotions sends a message that emotions are part of learning and are welcome in this setting.

Naturalist intelligence is used to discriminate among living things, such as plants or animals, as well as an understanding of other features of the natural world, such as weather or geology. Farmers, botanists, and hunters are examples of roles where this intelligence is used. Spending time outside on a regular basis facilitates naturalistic intelligence. Touching, seeing, and smelling plants outdoors is far different from looking at pictures of the same plants. Asking questions about the differences and similarities between the plants is appropriate for children as young as age 3 or 4. Young children are very observant and can use their categorization or classification abilities with the abundance of natural materials outside their setting.

Armstrong (2000) outlines four key points in MI theory: (1) People possess all of these intelligences, (2) most people have the potential to develop further in each of the intelligences, (3) the intelligences work together, and (4) there are numerous ways intelligence can be interpreted within each category. Gardner's work with multiple intelligences led educators to a new way of looking at intelligence and learning.

JOURNAL 3.3: In which of these eight intelligences do you feel the strongest? What might have led to your development in this intelligence? In which area are you most challenged? What might you do to improve in this area?

APPLYING GARDNER'S THEORY. When you nurture children's individual abilities and build rich learning activities, you provide experiences in multiple disciplines. You also provide different ways to learn the same material or knowledge. Some children might learn the names of colors best by sorting colors, others by classifying their crayons, others by painting and drawing, others by memorizing colors according to familiar objects (e.g.,

This preschool-aged child is using several senses to note the characteristics of a plant he found in his yard.

school bus yellow or stop sign red), and others by singing a song about colors. Your role is to ensure that you use different teaching strategies to reach all your learners.

Gardner (1993b) proposes that an individual-centered school should assess an individual child's abilities, goals, and interests to match to particular curricula and to the ways of learning that prove comfortable for that child. Children should also be involved in experiences that continually stimulate them as they develop within each of the intelligences. There are multiple ways to learn and a variety of ways to show what each child has learned.

With this approach to curriculum, you would plan different activities that involve several of the multiple intelligences in a setting that includes hands-on learning and opportunities for children to explore their environment. An example of stimulating multiple intelligences would be when young children listen to a story about making musical instruments (linguistic intelligence), play musical instruments (musical intelligence), dance to the music (bodily-kinesthetic intelligence), make one of several instruments (spatial intelligence and logical-mathematical intelligence), work together to create a band to play the grand finale (interpersonal and intrapersonal intelligence), and create instruments selected from the natural environment, such as reeds (naturalistic intelligence), differentiating which types and sizes of plant make the best sound and why. Of course, not all activities would include all eight intelligences, but planning around the eight intelligences prior to an activity will help you incorporate multiple intelligences throughout a project.

In the next section of this chapter, you will have an opportunity to watch these theories in an early childhood classroom setting. Get ready to observe a group of preschoolers involved in learning!

Theory into Practice: A Visit to Preschool

Now that you have some beginning ideas about theories of development that influence early childhood education today, you are going to resume your visit to the Creative Learning Cooperative Preschool and observe this group of 4-year-old children. This is your time to examine the major developmental theories "in action."

Starting the Day

As the children enter the preschool, their teacher, Keith, begins the morning by greeting each child with a personal comment. He tells Samantha, "I am so glad you shared your painting with 'new colors' with us. Today, we will all get a chance to try this out." The children also have news to share with Keith. Maria says to Keith, "My baby brother has a new tooth this morning." Keith replies, "Oh, a new tooth! A top tooth or a bottom tooth?"

Making New Colors

Today, this class of 4-year-olds is exploring the principle of creating new colors by combining two primary colors. Their interest came about when Samantha was finger painting and mixed several colors together and excitedly told the children that she made "new colors." The other children started talking about making "new colors" and were eager to try out some of their ideas.

Several learning centers are set up around the room, with a parent at each center. There are also some materials available on the counter, where children work independently and create their own activities. Some of these materials include transparent, colored pieces of plastic squares; food coloring and small jars of water; as well as crayons, chalk, paper, and some movable color wheels with primary colors.

JOURNAL 3.4: Which theorists would be pleased to see the materials set out on the counter and available for children to use without adult direction? Why?

You see that right inside the door, Marc and Matty are working together with felt marking pens. They are sharing a large piece of paper clipped to an easel. Both boys have a set of markers and are making little circles, then coloring the circles in with the same marker. Two days ago, Keith read a story about painters who mixed paint together and made a new color from two old colors. The boys were following this theme with their marking pens and were trying out different color combinations by making a new colored circle on top of the first colored circle. Keith walks over, noticing their colors, and talks about the old colors and the new colors with the boys. They all named the new colors together.

JOURNAL 3.5: What might Vygotsky say about the use of language in this color activity?

As Keith moved toward another group of children, Marc and Matty were heard talking about mixing three or more colors on top of their circles to see what would happen. After trying a few more combinations and getting muddier "new" colors, the boys began scribbling with the pens and chasing each other's marker pen lines around the paper. They then put the pens down and began looking for something else to do.

Samantha and Jamil are at the painting area right outside the door. They help each other put on paint aprons and ask a parent for paints and new paper on the easels. The parent brought over cups of finger paint and asked the children if they wanted to start by putting just one color on the paper. Samantha and Jamil both choose yellow paint, making large swoops on their paper. Jamil starts to paint on Samantha's paper and she tells him, "No." Samantha walks away to find Keith. Jamil then takes Samantha's cup of yellow paint away from her easel. Keith walks over and begins to talk quietly with Jamil.

Jamil gives the yellow paint back to Samantha and they continue painting. The incident seems to be forgotten. Samantha says, "This looks like a big banana." They then put their fingers into the container of red paint and add red on top of the yellow. Jamil exclaimed, "Wow! We made pumpkin orange!"

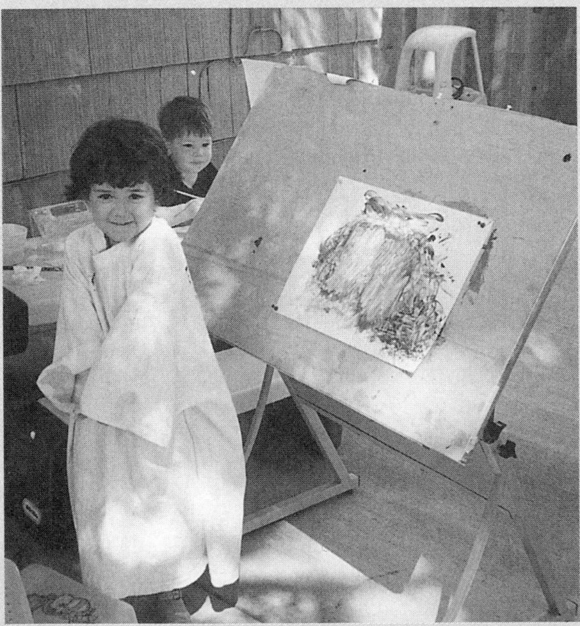

An outdoor art activity creates an enjoyable learning experience for Samantha and Nick.

Outside in the Play Area

You hear many children's voices, happily calling out to each other somewhere around the corner of the building. As you wander over to the side of the building, you see a large play yard with a climbing structure and an area where children are playing with balls. You notice two parents outside with the children. Sandy is watching the children at play while visiting with several children in a sandbox, and Rudy is playing a game with a soccer ball and four children. The game involves saying the name of another child and kicking the ball to that child across the circle. Giggles erupt when the ball heads to someone else other than the intended receiver.

In the sandbox, Scott, Tanisha, and Nick are making tunnels, roads, and parking lots with scoops and small shovels. There are yellow construction trucks moving through their building area, as they try out their highway system. They seem to be especially fond of the curves, as they go over and over the curves with small cars and trucks. Scott and Tanisha are talking about the roads and planning to add hills so they can try racing their cars around the curves and hills. You notice that Sandy is watching them, ready to help out if there are conflicts or "sandstorms."

Colors and Music

Near the windows, a parent, Ralph, is playing a guitar while Roberto, Danny, and Jessie are composing a song about colors in the rainbow. The beginning of their song starts off with, "Blue is blue, yellow is yellow, but yellow with blue makes green!" The children are singing and dancing to their song, while Ralph follows their lead in creating a tune on the guitar. Marc and Matty are drawn to the music and walk over to listen. They begin swaying to the music and join in the singing.

JOURNAL 3.6: Briefly describe several different intelligences you observed in the color and music activity, noting which activities connected to a specific area of intelligence.

Nalani, Scott, and Jeremy are busy mixing colored water in different clear containers. A parent is working next to them, making his own colored creations and listening to their talk. He occasionally identifies his discovery by saying, "Oh, I mixed red and blue water and now I have purple." The children watch him and then try out their own combinations. Nalani also talks about her experiment. She says, "My blue and red makes pretty purple water. Be careful, Nalani, keep your water from spilling."

The children continue to paint and watch each other's new colors appear. Nalani is intent on making lots of new colors. She seems to be expending a lot of energy and, as a result of her efforts, is getting tired. After mixing the colors into her container, Nalani quickly pours her colored water onto the floor. She looks around to see if any adult has noticed the puddle she just made. Now she begins talking to herself, "Nalani, no, no, bad to put water on the floor. Uh oh!" She then hurries away from the puddle.

JOURNAL 3.7: What type of moral reasoning might Nalani be applying in this situation and which of Kohlberg's stages seem to match her behavior? What would you do if you were the adult nearest to her? ●

It is the end of the morning now. The children and adults work together to clean up the different play areas. They had quite a busy morning, filled with many activities. The varied experiences involved colors and mixing colors. Gardner's theory of multiple intelligences was clearly attended to through the variety of activities around the theme of new colors, which supports the growth of intelligence in multiple ways.

Revisiting the Morning

Let's take a moment to reflect on some of our observations. In the first scenario, Marc and Matty used felt pens to make colors on the paper, and continued to draw circles and add new colors on top of the old colors. Because they were adding more and more colors, each combination created a brownish hue and they soon became bored with the activity. When Keith walked by and interacted with them about their two color combinations and named the colors with them, you observed their language use in color identification and an increased interest in the activity. You also observed that without new direction or guidance, they soon became bored with the activity and were ready to move to something different.

Both Piaget and Vygotsky would note that the children were interacting with their environment by experimenting with colors in various media, which supports each of their theories of discovery learning. Erikson would appreciate the choices of activities for the children, as well as opportunities for interesting interactions among the children and adults in the setting. Bruner would agree with Erikson—that children learn best when they choose their materials and discover principles independently. The materials available on the counter would enable children to choose what they needed to "prove" their ideas. Also, open-ended questions from adults would help children move toward proving their hypotheses or predicted outcomes of their experiments, again in alignment with Bruner's theory of discovery learning.

During the second scenario, the finger-painting activity, you saw guided direction provided by a parent. The results were interesting, and Samantha and Jamil expressed pleasure at creating a "new" color. Vygotsky would view this social interaction with a more knowledgeable adult as helping the child in the child's zone of proximal development, where guidance supported new learning. He would also appreciate the use of language throughout the activity, along with the many opportunities for children to name colors and shapes. Skinner might suggest a consequence or punishment, such as a time-out, when Jamil took Samantha's cup of paint. In this case, Keith chose to discuss with Jamil the feelings of others and to assist Jamil in moving toward an understanding of empathy or caring about the feelings of others.

As you continued to observe, you noticed that the children appeared engaged in their activities and felt free to leave one center and move to other sections of the room. They asked questions of the adults and of each other. You heard many conversations going on around the classroom. There was a sense of safety and security, with boundaries shared by the adults in relation to treating each other with respect. Maslow would find this atmosphere supportive of emotional growth, as indicated through the awareness of the teacher to the children's needs by welcoming them in the morning, offering snacks, and continually scanning the classroom to assure that children are safely engaged in interesting activities.

Many of the theorists' major ideas and each of the different developmental areas discussed throughout the chapter were represented in this brief snapshot of a preschool morning. Keith, the teacher, had planned the curriculum to reflect the children's interests as well as their developmental levels. The curriculum also reflected Keith's personal philosophy of theories of development.

PRINCIPLES AND INSIGHTS: A Summary and Review

Whether looking at cognitive, language, social, or emotional development, theorists tend to agree that humans develop in a gradual and sequential process. Theorists also agree that individuals vary in the rate of their developmental growth. Culture and society play a role in the context of development, with some cultures emphasizing certain skills or accomplishments that guide a child's learning.

Each of these areas of development overlap, with growth in one area affecting the learning occurring in other developmental areas. As the caregiver or teacher working with young children, you have a responsibility to create a rich learning environment based on the principles presented by theorists from each of the developmental domains. Gaining an understanding of these theories and approaches to learning will help you develop your own philosophy of working with young children, which translates into the daily activities and experiences you create with and for them.

Piaget's work altered the way adults view the learning of young children. According to Piagetian thinking, children move through four stages of cognitive development, acquiring new knowledge, skills, and abilities in each stage. Piaget's work introduced the notion that children think differently at different ages. His theories led to the idea that experiences in early childhood programs can promote growth within a developmental stage and support movement to a more advanced stage.

Bruner followed Piaget's work, extending the theory of cognitive development. He identified three stages of cognitive development and supported the stance that learning occurs in these stages as children make meaning of their experiences. Discovery learning, as described by Bruner, is a powerful learning model. Through discovery learning, children interact with materials or examples and draw their own conclusions or general principles based on their investigations.

Vygotsky agreed with Piaget and Bruner about the impact that a child's interaction with the environment makes in learning. His work emphasized the importance of interactions with others and the connection between language and cognitive development. Vygotsky developed the theory of the zone of proximal development (ZPD), which illustrates the zone or space within which a child is learning. With assistance from an older child or adult, a child can achieve more or accomplish higher-level skills than if working alone. Gradually, less help is needed from others (scaffolding) as the child becomes more skilled or able to complete the task independently.

In the area of social development, Erikson identified eight stages of psychosocial development. The core of a child's personality is revealed through her interpersonal relationships (Maier, 1978). A child's personality is also shaped by the crises she encounters and her reactions to each crisis. The four stages of psychosocial development in early childhood present a framework that will help you understand the actions of children at different ages and stages of social development. For example, as you observe a toddler asserting her independence, you might draw on Erikson's theory that the child is testing her autonomy. Paying attention to these stages and the behaviors associated with each stage will help you plan activities and curriculum to support social growth.

Social and emotional development are closely related. Social development can be thought of as growth in interactions with others, whereas emotional development is the growth of a sense of self. Maslow's self-actualization pyramid reminds you that a child's basic needs must be met before she is ready to learn and to interact joyfully in her environment. Children's physiological needs—such as hunger, thirst, or rest—must be attended to before they willingly engage in learning activities.

Moral development falls within both social and emotional developmental areas. An understanding of Erikson's and Maslow's theories will assist you in understanding the social and emotional nature of moral reasoning. In order to make wise decisions about what is wrong or right, a child needs a stable sense of self and the ability to interact socially with others. Kohlberg developed a stage model of moral development, where children move from moral decisions based on following the rules to moral reasoning about different situations based on the specifics of that situation. Listening to stories and having discussions about everyday events (including conflicts in the child's setting) will help children reflect on other's decisions and think about how they might respond in a similar setting.

Each theorist discusses the impact of the child's interaction with her environment as part of the learning process in each developmental area. Behaviorists propose that altering the environment can change a person's behavior. Skinner's work with operant conditioning showed that applying a reinforcement or punishment following a behavior will strengthen or extinguish the behavior. Although behaviorism is used in everyday interactions, early childhood educators are encouraged to examine the practice and make purposeful decisions about when and how to use this model of social learning.

Gardner's work in multiple intelligences presents a learning model that acknowledges and supports the growth of learning in different formats. It is easy to assume that others learn like you, which might lead you to plan most activities to emphasize this area of intelligence. Becoming familiar with the eight intelligences, however, will assist you in planning activities that support learning in each of these areas. Diversity of varied types of experiences enables the young children in your care to grow and develop in multiple intelligences.

As you read the case studies in this book, take time to come back to this chapter and revisit the developmental theories. You will want to bring your new knowledge with you into the different early childhood programs presented in the case studies. Doing so will enable you to assess your emerging philosophy of early childhood education and ground your beliefs in the work of these notable theorists. Your understanding of these developmental theories will continue to increase and expand as you work with young children and observe the theories in practice.

BECOMING AN EARLY CHILDHOOD PROFESSIONAL

Your Professional Portfolio

1. Thinking of an age group or developmental level of children that you are interested in working with, develop an activity that would address learning in four or more of the different intelligences. Identify each intelligence and discuss how the activity promotes learning in that area of intelligence. Create a chart that shows the relationship of an activity to multiple intelligences, and place it in your portfolio.
2. In a kindergarten class, children are using solid objects to explore the concept of conservation, as described by Piaget. The teacher stacked five books in one pile and the children talked about the characteristics of the books as well as the set of books. The teacher then moved the books into single spaces, essentially spreading out the five books on the rug. The children discussed what is different and what is the same between the two sets of five books. Now it's your turn to develop an activity about conservation, using solid objects. Develop a plan and use it to teach someone else in your class or a young child. The plan and your written reflection about the success and challenge of teaching this activity will become part of your portfolio.

Your Professional Library

Berk, L. (2001). *Awakening children's minds.* New York: Oxford Press.

Berk, L., & Winsler, A. (1995). *Scaffolding children's learning: Vygotsky and early childhood education.* Washington, DC: NAEYC.

DeVries, R., & Zan, B. (1994). *Moral classrooms, moral children: Creating a constructivist atmosphere in early education.* New York: Teachers College Press.

Gardner, H. (1993). *Frames of mind: The theory of multiple intelligences.* New York: Basic Books.

Hyson, M. (1994). *The emotional development of young children: Building an emotion-centered curriculum.* New York: Teachers College Press.

Katz, L., & McClellan, D. (2001). *Fostering children's social competence: The teacher's role.* Washington, DC: NAEYC.

Kohn, A. (1999). *Punished by rewards: The trouble with gold stars, incentive plans, A's, praise, and other bribes.* Boston: Houghton Mifflin.

CHAPTER 4

Children's Play
A Source of Development and Learning

CHAPTER focus:

When you finish reading and reflecting on this chapter, you will be able to:

1. Articulate the importance of play and describe the contributions that play makes to children's development.
2. Describe the differences between the play of infants, toddlers, preschoolers, and children in kindergarten and primary grades, and draw implications for curriculum from those differences.
3. Begin preparing for your adult role in children's play and contemplating the decisions you will make to prepare for, participate in, or intervene in their play activities.
4. Describe and assess children's physical, emotional, social, and cognitive development when observing their play activities.

"I think that play is the most serious thing in the world. I was playing when I invented the aqualung," said underwater pioneer Jacques Cousteau. Unfortunately, not all adults share the sentiments of Cousteau. They do not always appreciate the value of play; for example, you will hear adult comments such as:

> "They're just playing but they're not learning anything."
> "It's alright for young children to play but by kindergarten there's a lot to learn."
> "Their playtime is so free—how can you tell what they're learning?"
> "Play is a mere time filler."

Play is often regarded as unimportant. Even parents express a lack of valuing, with comments like "She's just playing" or with concerns about the amount of time children spend in "mindless play" (Hurwitz, 2003). Children appear to have picked up on this attitude and often respond to the age-old question of "What did you do in school (or preschool or child care) today?" with, "We just played," causing some parents to feel anxious or even angry. Many parents do not fully understand or value the role of play in children's development and in early childhood education's curriculum (Brewer & Kieff, 1996/1997).

In contrast to those adult observations, educators who have observed children for long periods of time can describe the serious quality of children's play and can list impressive learning outcomes from play activities. Research studies continue to document the learning that happens when children play (Berk, 1994; Isenberg & Jalongo, 1993). Recognition of the value of play isn't a new insight. In 1948, Pratt passionately defended play as she wrote about children's work:

> Children have their own meaning for the word play. To them it does not, as it does to adults, carry the ideas of idleness, purposelessness, relaxation from work. When we began our school, we had it named a "play school," as a way of saying that it was our teaching. It was the children who made us, early in the school's history, delete the word from the school's name. To them, it was not a "play school" but a school and they were working hard at their schooling. How hard

> they work, only we who have watched them really know. They do not a waste precious moment. They are going about their jobs all the time. No father in his office or mother in her home [remember—this was written in 1948] works at such a pace. For a long time I was principally afraid that they would exhaust themselves in this strenuous new kind of school. (p. 9)

Definitions and Thinking about Play

To help you begin to appreciate and understand play, we have gathered some definitions of *play*. We also describe some of the qualities to observe when you watch children at play. The thinking of theorists, researchers, and well-known early childhood educators is quite convincing regarding the importance of play in the lives of children. Here are some of their thoughts:

- "Play is the essential ingredient, the vehicle by which children communicate, socialize, learn about the world around them, understand themselves and others, deal with their problems, and practice some of the skills they will use in the future" (Hartley, 1971).
- "Play is the fundamental means by which children gather and process information, learn new skills, and practice old ones" (Spodek, 1986).
- "Play is the need of every child. . . . And when we observe children at play, we often see enjoyment and delight. Because of this fun aspect, adults sometimes think of play as a form of amusement or fun only, not as something to be taken seriously. However, play is an important childhood activity that helps children master all developmental needs" (Maxim, 1989).
- "Play is that absorbing activity in which healthy young children participate with enthusiasm and abandon" (Scales et al., 1991).
- "Through play, children learn about cultural norms and expectations, discover the workings of the world, and negotiate their way through their surroundings" (Klein, Wirth, & Linas, 2003).

Carlotta Lombroso, a prominent nineteenth-century philosopher of education, wrote in 1896, "Play is for the child an occupation as serious, as important, as study is for the adult; play is his means of development and he needs to play, just as the silkworm needs continually to eat leaves" (source unknown). Even the United Nations, in its 1948 declaration of the rights of children, identified play as a basic right of children.

Characteristics of Play

In addition to those thoughts about play, Rubin, Fein, and Vandenberg (1983) and many others in early childhood education have further refined the definition of *play*. Through their observations and studies of play, they determined that an activity can be described as play only if it contains the following essential characteristics:

1. *Play is intrinsically motivated.* Children are naturally drawn to play activities; that is, the desire to play comes from within them. The satisfaction and pleasure they derive from play is self-motivating. When you spend much time with young children, you realize that you don't have to reward them or offer any incentive to get them to play; getting them to stop playing is another matter, however.
2. *Play is freely chosen by the participants.* Often, play beckons children either through interesting materials, adult encouragement, or peer invitation, but it's the child's decision to play. If it is required, then it is not play. Many adults can relate to this quality. When you cook an elaborate meal because you feel like it, it's play, but when you cook because you have to, it's a chore. Similarly, when you work in your garden be-

cause you love to putter with plants, it's play, but when you have to weed and water the garden, it's work.

3. *Play must be pleasurable and engaging*. If play isn't pleasurable and engaging, it's unlikely that it will be freely chosen by children. If you observe children at play, those qualities are quite evident and a delight to watch. Play can also be serious and frustrating, even engaging children in fearful and violent activity, but there remains a level of satisfaction. The pleasure and satisfaction attracts children to repeat play activities over and over again.
4. *Play is nonliteral.* The best part of play for many is that it doesn't have to be real. Pretending allows one to change reality and to participate in dreams. At a young age, children begin much of their activity with, "Let's pretend. . . ." As their play expands, the pretending allows the children to experience much of the lt world in the safety of fantasy.
5. *Play is actively engaged in by the player.* As Caroline Pratt reminded us, play can be exhausting. When children have played hard, for example, invariably they will sleep well. Some of the activity may be physically engaging, whereas other activity may be mentally engaging. Again, if the play is not intrinsically motivating and pleasurable, children will not engage in it.
6. *Play is process oriented*. The process of play is what invites children. The actual activity is the motivating and sustaining aspect of play. Some play may have products or outcomes, but children are generally unconcerned with them and even forget about them. Much of young children's play is repetitious because they like the process and want to repeat it over and over again.
7. *Play is self-directed*. Play is an opportunity for the child to explore what he can do. It may be a chance to explore what he can do with a new object or with a new friend. Thus, play is a wonderful experience in learning about self. Young children have few opportunities to be in control, so play is their chance to control a situation by either manipulating an object, organizing the activity, or engaging another child.

Kostelnik, Soderman, and Whiren (1993) added more dimensions to play by calling it **episodic,** meaning that it changes as it goes along and that shifts occur as children play.

Children are attracted to play that is intrinsically motivating and pleasurable. Why are these children so engaged in their play activity?

They begin with one goal or intent, and as the play develops, the direction changes depending on the play. Recently the quality of freedom from external rules has been included as another characteristic of play (Klein et al., 2002). In their play, children set the rules about roles, acceptable behaviors, entering and exiting, and settings and structures.

Observing the Characteristics of Play

We're going to visit a family with three young children so that you can watch their play activity for the characteristics we have just described. We've been invited to the home of Francis and Akosa and their three boys, Wamalwa (2 years old), Otioli (5 years old), and Chimieti (7 years old). Francis and Akosa are from Kenya. They came to the United States to pursue education and to make their home here. They live in a spacious home in a suburban neighborhood away from the city's hectic pace and traffic. Before watching the boys' play activity, we talk about their family and how their ethnic background may influence the boys' play.

Getting to Know the Family

A Cultural Context for Play Development

Akosa tells us that she and her family continue to eat their native foods and have a hot meal together each night. Some of the most common foods are ugali, chunks of thick corn meal, and collard greens, which grow in the backyard. Francis shows us the family garden and explains to us that the boys often help him with weeding and watering. "We want the boys to fit in when we take them to Kenya, so we try to maintain important aspects of our life there." The family eats with their fingers and uses authentic food names. Francis laughs, "On Friday nights, we have pizza—delivered—and everyone gets to stay up as late as they want." Akosa tells us about how they share their cultural background with the boys: "We tell them stories about our home, like what we did when we were growing up, and about their grandparents. In Kenya, you don't put yourself first. You try to promote the common good by sharing and cooperating. We want the boys to talk about *our* not *mine,* but we have to work at it." She continues, "We don't want our children to be so self-absorbed, so we watch their play activities and their play choices. We haven't bought any video games and we don't watch much TV. When they do ask to watch, we question them with, 'How is it going to help you? What will you learn?' When they do watch TV, they see a lot of negative images of Africans and then we see them appear in their play."

We thank Francis and Akosa for sharing their ideas about raising the boys. Their comments will guide us as we record our observations of the boys at play. It's the kind of information most early childhood educators would want to learn in order to understand the children.

Observing the Children: Watching Play Characteristics

It's a warm, sunny day and the boys are playing with neighborhood friends, Brittany and Paul, in the front yard. Chimieti, who loves gymnastics, is teaching the other children how to do cartwheels. As they watch, he skillfully performs perfect cartwheels. Soon, there are children's bodies twirling all over the yard. Brittany, age 5, ends up in a kind of somersault when she attempts the cartwheel. Otioli is determined to do cartwheels and he repeats the movements over and over, trying to do as well as his big brother. Chimieti continues to coach him, "Keep your feet up" or "Keep your legs straight," but Otioli isn't coordinated enough. Wamalwa is watching the children and squealing at them. Every so often, he rolls on the grass and then looks to see if anyone is watching his performance. Paul, who is 7 years old, just watches from under a tree. When Otioli asks him to try it, he shakes his head.

Soon, everyone but Chimieti is bored or tired of the cartwheels, and the children turn their attention to the large oak tree in the front yard. Paul, Otioli, and Brittany quickly climb the tree and sit with their legs dangling. Wamalwa stands below the tree and shows us that the children are up there by pointing to them. He has a look that says, "I want to go up there, too." His oldest brother Chimieti comes over and lifts him high enough to reach a branch. He grabs the branch and swings briefly before he is lifted down. Then Chimieti jumps up and swings himself again with great agility. Before long, the three children up in the tree are pretending to be sentry guards on the lookout for the enemy. We hear:

"You look over that way and yell if you see the enemy."

"I'll look in this direction and give a signal to you if I see anything."

"We can jump down and grab the bad guys if they come by."

Chimieti joins in with, "I'll be the enemy and hide in the bushes and try to sneak up on you." In the meantime, Wamalwa is left out of the play and begins to fuss. Akosa hears him and comes to bring him into the house for a nap. As she settles him into his bed, she puts on a tape of an African children's choir. "He loves that tape. Sometimes he just sits and listens to it for a long time." Once Wamalwa is resting quietly, his mom tells me about his tree climbing: "He just loves to climb trees. I think that he watched his brothers for so long that he became determined to get into a tree. The next thing we knew, we would find him up in the tree. It was frightening, so we took the lower rungs off the tree. We had built a tree house and added rungs to the lower part of the tree. Well, taking off the rungs didn't stop him. One day, he took a little stool and climbed up, and on another day, he took a cooking pot and stood on it to climb up. Once he's up there, he's not real happy. He wants to get down and then to climb up again. If I'm outside with him, he will do it over and over again."

Francis and Akosa's children demonstrated well the characteristics of play that we listed previously. Wamalwa's play—his tree climbing—is especially illustrative of many of those qualities. Wouldn't you love to know what he's thinking each time he figures out a way to climb up that tree? Watching and listening to children like Otioli, Chimieti, and Wamalwa as they play is the best way to learn about play and its value.

The Value of Play

Those outside the early childhood profession who have little understanding of children may be wondering why we place so much emphasis on play. Why devote an entire chapter to play? As early childhood educators, we are often called on to justify scheduling two hours of play in a kindergarten program or encouraging children's play all day in a preschool. As we described earlier, many parents do not understand or appreciate the kind of outcomes that are possible with children's play. Those who have studied children's play and those educators who spend their days observing children at play can describe many rich benefits of play. Look at some of those outcomes that play accomplishes:

- *Children develop a sense of competence.* As children play with materials, they have the opportunity to make things happen or change things; thus, they experience some control over their world. Because they are in control when they play, they generally choose materials and activities for which they have some skills or interest, so they are comfortable. Their play experiences are successful, so their confidence is enhanced.

  At a time in life when they have limited control over their world, it is important for young children to experience situations that they can control. These are essential experiences for the development of self-esteem, autonomy, and responsibility. For example, let's watch 3-year-old Ibrahim as he goes to the shelf where baskets of little figures (a favorite for toddlers) are stored and chooses the basket of dinosaurs. He dumps them out on a table and sits down in front of the pile. One by one, he stands the figures up in a row in front of him. When he finishes, he begins rearranging them into two lines with dinosaurs facing each other. Then he stages little fights between each pair with the result being that one dinosaur is lying on its side after each fight. Ibrahim makes quiet noises as he manipulates the figures to fight with each other. When he finishes the line of fights, he sits back in his chair with a subtle smile on his face.

  If we could get inside of Ibrahim's head, we would probably hear his feelings of power and satisfaction. "I can do it," he may be saying to himself. He continues his play for another 15 minutes, so he obviously likes it and is accomplishing what he set out to do.

- *Children are able to practice skills.* Practice involves the repetition of both physical skills and mental skills. Almost every skill is new when you are a child, so the repetition is actually an enjoyable experience. Each practice can lead to a new or more elaborate skill, so the interest remains high for children. Only when the practice becomes involuntary, required by others, does practice lose its play quality. The best example of play as practice of physical skill is the young child's experience with a tricycle.

  For instance, when Haley first encountered a tricycle out in the play yard, she walked around it a few times before even trying to sit on it. She then got on the tricycle and got off, got on and got off, and continued a few more times. From there, Haley tried to ride the tricycle, and once she felt secure in doing so, she rode and rode and rode. She was able to increase her speed, and eventually she tried to go backwards. Each new skill was practiced.

  In the beginning of her experience with the tricycle, Haley was engaged in a type of practice called **mere practice** (Piaget, 1962). Mere practice is the kind of practice we observe in much of infant play. Another kind of practice is mental practice.

  Mental practice is something we all do when we are trying to memorize a new phone number—we say it to ourselves over and over. Mental practice can be a play activity if it's done playfully and for fun. For years, Keeley (we'll learn more about her in Chapter 10) joyfully sang the alphabet song and counted to 100 with great glee. She was accomplishing mental practice in her play.

  Children's play, then, provides practice of the simplest to the most complex skills of sensorimotor and cognitive development.

- *Children are able to develop socially.* Even though young children do not play with peers for a number of years, their early play is often with adults and with materials, and near other children. Without the opportunity to play with others, children would not have the experiences they need to build social concepts and skills. For example, when Otioli plays with his friends, Brittany and Paul, and even with his big brother, he experiences a need to share, to cooperate, to negotiate, to problem solve, and to communicate, and he gradually develops those skills.

- *Children are able to solve problems and make decisions in a safe situation.* That nonliteral quality of play—the freedom to pretend to be or do anything—provides the context for trying out adult roles, solving problems, and making decisions without any real consequences, so it's safe to take risks. Children are comfortable in those situations and can develop the skills needed when they feel safe. It's an opportunity to try out different roles and experience different situations. Elizabeth Jones (2003) describes the importance of social problem solving as a life skill that children as well as adults will be needing more and more as our world keeps changing.

- *Children gather and process information.* Through play, children interact with their world and all of its objects, processes, and events. If you watch even the youngest child with an unknown object, you will see first the process of exploration—touching, smelling, tasting, looking, and listening—followed by manipulation of the objects. Play with objects, situations, processes, and other aspects of their world is children's way of gathering information and connecting the new information with what they have previously experienced or already know.

- *Children express emotions, release tension, and explore anxiety-producing situations (Santrock, 1990).* Sometimes through vigorous physical play and sometimes through pretend play, children are able to let adults know what they are feeling. They may not be able to label or tell us about their fear of monsters, but they can show it as they pretend to be ferocious monsters or to run away from the monsters. Children can't tell us that they're frustrated, but they can express it by banging cymbals together or playing a very bossy adult to their dolls. Play allows one to express the full gamut of emotions—joy, pleasure, pain, frustration, anger, and exhilaration. The kind of rough and tumble play that we will talk about later in this chapter is a great form of release for children, as is chasing, shouting, and jumping.

DEFENDING THE VALUE OF PLAY. One of your responsibilities as an early childhood educator will probably be to defend the value of play and to communicate how play helps children develop and learn. In addition to the general benefits we just listed, there are specific learning outcomes that children achieve easily through play. Children develop their literacy understandings and skills through play, their mathematical concepts through play, and their science appreciations and processes through play. As you meet the children in this book, notice what is happening when they play. Information about developmental levels of play can guide your observations and enable you to interpret more accurately what you see children doing. Use this chapter to get ready for your professional role by becoming more knowledgeable, appreciative, and articulative about the role of play in children's development and learning.

JOURNAL 4.1: A parent of a 5-year-old comes in to talk to you about his child's learning in your classroom. "When I watch him with his friends in the neighborhood or at home, all they do is play. They play with those little cars and trucks, build things with Legos, and use a lot of cardboard and tape to make garages. I can see that it's kind of creative, but how is he learning?" Practice what you will say to this parent and to others about the value of play. ●

Play and Development: From Infants to Eight-Year-Olds

Because you will soon be meeting groups of infants, toddlers, preschoolers, and children in kindergarten and primary grades—children in play situations at home and in early childhood education programs—we will describe developmental levels of play and some typical play activities for each of those age groups. Our intent is to get you ready to be a good observer so that you can learn about and understand children's development by watching them.

Infant Play

The kind of play that occurs in the first year of life is full of discovery, repeated practice, and delight at one's own accomplishments. Watching infant play can be one of the most fascinating observational experiences. Until recently, the first month of life was considered a nonplayful time by Piaget and others, but current observations suggest that babies of this age begin using their senses for exploring their environment. That exploration is considered a kind of beginning play.

EXPLORATION AND PLAY. Some experts say that infants explore before they can play, so this is probably a good time to differentiate between *exploration* and *play*. Piaget thought that exploration preceded play in terms of the amount of time spent. **Exploration** was seen as a process to gain information, whereas **play** involved practicing and recombining the information gained through exploration. Play and exploration are highly interrelated and may not be different enough to be separated, but we think that it is important to notice the two kinds of activities when watching children. You can decide for yourself if they are different enough to make a distinction.

For many early childhood educators, the differentiation between exploration and play may help with some decisions about children's activities. We have often seen children who are not interested or ready to participate in a new form of play but who may want to manipulate the materials or playthings for a while, or watch others engage in the activity. They may be exploring and gathering information, and it may be necessary for them to do so before they engage in the play themselves. We adults make decisions about time and schedules for children, and if we appreciate exploration as an important step before play, we may schedule differently. If we observe infants, for example, we will have a real appreciation for the need to explore. Babies can explore visually, imitate facial expressions, and show preferences for faces, patterns, and things that move. Their first months are full of exciting sensorimotor development as they play with their bodies, with objects, and with people.

PRIMARY CIRCULAR REACTIONS. From about 1 to 4 months of age, the kind of playful activity seen in infants has been called **primary circular reactions** (Piaget, 1962). Those reactions are simply exercises of reflexes. Infant play continues rather simply—looking and listening. For about the first four months, babies watch faces, movement of objects and people, as well as the movement of their own body parts. They also listen to voices, music, the world around them, and themselves. During that time, they discover, quite accidentally, their ability to cause movement or sounds, if the situation is supportive. Parents or caregivers can set up situations in the baby's crib in such a way that when the baby moves, when a sound is made, or when the baby kicks, a mobile moves or a bell rings. Even during these early months, babies begin to repeat enjoyable activities.

SECONDARY CIRCULAR REACTIONS. Repetitive behaviors that cause effects are categorized as **secondary circular reactions.** This is the time when the baby is able to grasp items—rattles being a favorite. They continue to enjoy simply looking at things but now they begin to explore through manipulation. First, they hold on to the toy; next, they realize they can move it; and finally, they achieve the ultimate—they can feel it with their mouths or taste it. Babies love to put things in their mouths and experience all of the sensations of taste. Manipulation of objects and sometimes people's faces become a favorite form of play for infants.

This is an exciting time for infant play, especially when the baby can hold an object and bang it against something. A large spoon and a pot or just a rattle against the floor provide satisfying play for an infant at this stage. Adults may grow weary of the racket but the infant is completely taken by her ability to create a sound.

TERTIARY CIRCULAR REACTIONS. From ages 8 to 12 months, infants add new skills to their looking, grasping, mouthing, and hitting abilities, referred to as **tertiary circular reactions.** For example, if you watch Luke at this age, he now holds the red plastic ring well, nibbles on it occasionally, then transfers it from one hand to another repeatedly. Sometimes he holds it out in front of him, turns it over and studies it, and puts a finger inside the ring. There doesn't seem to be any end to the things he can do with the ring. Later, Luke may add another item, perhaps a rattle, and eventually bang the rattle against the ring. This is a time when the baby is repeating familiar activities with the ring but trying to change what he does with the ring instead of repeating it in exactly the same way.

When Luke gets a new toy, his dad notices that he touches it with his finger a great deal and looks at the toy from different angles. At this age, Luke is developing an interest in textures and noticing all of the new details of his object. He is also beginning to like to put objects into other objects, so a tub of his family's plastic cookie cutters is a favorite plaything.

MOBILITY. From ages 6 to 12 months, infants begin to scoot, creep, and crawl until they can navigate all over a house. Some also begin pulling themselves up on chairs or other furniture items and take their first steps. This mobility definitely enhances their play because they can get to items and materials of interest. The fringe on a tablecloth, the legs of a chair, the basket of magazines, and the plant in a pot of dirt become new playthings. You have only to watch an infant squeezing the dirt in his hands or pulling the magazines out of the basket with glee to know that play is going on.

APPROPRIATE PRACTICES FOR SUPPORTING INFANT PLAY. As you will find in Chapter 7, quality programs for infants are scarce and yet so important. Table 4.1 (Bredekamp & Copple, 1997) lists appropriate and inappropriate practices for supporting infant

TABLE 4.1 **Appropriate and Inappropriate Practices Supporting Infant Play**

Appropriate Practices	Inappropriate Practices
The play areas are comfortable; they have pillows, foam-rubber mats, and soft carpeting where babies can lie on their stomachs or backs and be held and read to. A hammock, rocking chair (preferably a glider for safety), overstuffed chair, and big cushions are available for caregivers or parents and infants to relax in together.	The play areas are sterile, designed for easy cleaning, but without the different textures, levels, colors that infants need to stimulate their senses. There is not an area where an adult can sit comfortably with an infant in her arms and read or talk to the baby.
Space is arranged so children can enjoy moments of quiet play by themselves, have ample space to roll over and move freely, and can crawl toward interesting objects. Areas for younger infants are separated from those of crawlers to promote the safe interactions of infants in similar stages of development.	Space is cramped and unsafe for children who are learning how to move their bodies.
Visual displays, such as mobiles, are oriented toward the infant's line of sight and designed so that the interesting sights and effects are clearly visible when the baby is lying on her back. Mobiles are removed when children can grasp them.	Visual displays are not in an infant's line of sight. They are often used as a substitute for appropriate social interaction of infants with adults.
Sturdy cardboard books are placed in book pockets or a sturdy book stand. Books that the adults read to the babies are on a shelf out of reach. Books show children and families of different racial and cultural backgrounds, and people of various ages and abilities.	Books are not available or are made of paper that tears easily. Books do not contain objects familiar or interesting to children.
Toys provided are responsive to the child's actions: a variety of grasping toys that require different types of manipulation; a varied selection of skill-development materials, including nesting and stacking materials, activity boxes, and containers to be filled and emptied; a variety of balls, bells, and rattles.	Toys are battery powered or windup, so the baby just watches. Toys lack a variety of texture, size, and shape.
A variety of safe household items that infants can use as play materials are available, including measuring cups, wooden spoons, nonbreakable bowls, and cardboard boxes.	Household items that help make the infant room more homelike are not available.
Toys are scaled to a size that enables infants to grasp, chew, and manipulate them (clutch balls, rattles, teethers, and soft washable dolls and other play animals).	Toys are too large to handle or so small that infants could choke on or swallow them.
Mobile infants have an open area where balls, push and pull toys, wagons, and other equipment encourage free movement and testing of large-muscle skills and coordination. Low, climbing structures, ramps, and steps are provided. Structures are well padded and safe for exploration.	Balls and other moving toys are for outdoor use only. Equipment designed for crawling up/down or under/ through is not available, or structures are safe only for older, more-mobile children.
Open shelves within infants' reach contain toys of similar type, spaced so that infants can make choices. Caregivers group materials for related activities on different shelves (e.g., fill-and-empty activities are on a shelf separate from three-piece puzzles or moving/pushing toys).	Toys are dumped in a box or kept out of children's reach, forcing them to depend on adults' selection.
There is ample, accessible storage for extra play materials of a type similar to what is already displayed and for materials with increasing challenge. Caregivers can easily rearrange their space as young infants become mobile. When an infant has explored a toy with his mouth and moved to other things, the toy is picked up for washing and disinfecting and replaced with a similar toy. Everything is nearby, so caregivers do not have to leave the space to replace a toy.	Storage closets are far from the infant space and poorly organized, making it difficult to rotate materials, bring out more complex materials, or add to the variety of activities in the space.

(continued)

TABLE 4.1 ***(continued)***

Appropriate Practices	Inappropriate Practices
Room temperature can be controlled; vents are clean and provide an even flow of air. Floors are not drafty. Windows provide natural light and fresh air. Caregivers carry infants to the windows to see outside.	The infants' environment suffers from one or more of these deficiencies: the room is either too cold and drafty or too hot; the room has little natural light; and/or the windows are not accessible so that caregivers can hold infants and they are able to look out.
Adults periodically move infants to a different spot (from the floor to an infant seat, from the seat to a stroller, etc.) to give babies differing perspectives and reasonable variety in what they are able to look at and explore.	Babies are confined to cribs, infant seats, playpens, or the floor for long periods indoors.
An outside play space adjacent to the infant area includes sunny and shaded areas. It is enclosed by protective fencing. The ground around climbing structures and in some of the open space is covered with resilient, stable surfacing for safety, making it easy for mobile infants to push wagons and ride-on toys. There are soft areas where young infants can lie on quilts.	Infants rarely go out because there is no adjacent play area, and nearby parks and playgrounds offer no shaded areas or soft surfaces for babies to lie on or crawl about freely. Large group size and inadequate staff-child ratios make outdoor play difficult.

Source: Developmentally Appropriate Practice in Early Childhood Programs (pp. 75–76) by S. Bredekamp and C. Copple, 1997, Washington, DC: NAEYC. Copyright 1997 by NAEYC. Reprinted with permission from the National Association for the Education of Young Children.

play from the National Association for the Education of Young Children (NAEYC). These practices give you a hint of how involved you will be in the play of infants. If you think that infant play is amazing and sometimes exhausting, be prepared to be overwhelmed by the play of toddlers.

Toddler Play

As we found earlier in this chapter, when we watched Wamalwa or listened to his mother (in Chapter 3), toddlerhood is an extremely active time. A lot of energy surrounds a toddler—on the part of the toddler as well as on the part of the adult who is both stimulating and supervising him. Wamalwa's climbing was only one of his favorite play activities that required close adult supervision. Another important role of his parents and his older siblings was the provision of toys—objects for play.

OBJECT PLAY. Unlike the object play of infants, the object play of toddlers involves two or more objects. Remember how Luke began to combine other toys with his favorite ring? Toddlers also use objects appropriately. Luke's red ring fits on a pole for a stacking toy, and as he progressed, he began to use it for stacking. Instead of using blocks simply to empty and fill the box or shelf, toddlers begin stacking them. Instead of mouthing the doll's head, a toddler may cuddle the doll. As toddlers play more and more with objects, their play becomes more sophisticated. A ball that has been bounced for months becomes something for the puppy to eat. This is called the **representational use of objects,** which is the beginning of make-believe or symbolic play.

For Wamalwa, the most appealing play objects are the toys of his brothers. While they build with Legos and blocks, Wamalwa uses them as furniture, guns, and fish. He does not even attempt to play with his older brothers, but he does play nearby quite happily. Most toddlers find the toys used by others most attractive, and this can be a source of frustration among toddler peers, but Wamalwa's brothers are generally kind and understanding.

MOTOR SKILLS AND PLAY. Toddlerhood is a time of great motor skill development. The small motor skills of toddlers develop well and enable them to fit puzzle pieces together, play musical toys, turn the pages in a book, scribble and draw with crayons, mold play-dough into desired shapes, and pour liquids from a small pitcher. Their large motor skills also develop well and enable them to throw a ball, push and pull toys around the house or yard, climb stairs, and run and jump. Think about the skills that Wamalwa used to climb trees. One of his favorite play activities with anyone who will join him is throwing and retrieving a ball. He isn't able to catch the ball yet, but he is deliriously happy running to retrieve it over and over.

ROUGH AND TUMBLE PLAY. Rough and tumble play occurs during this time, and is a favorite of toddlers as well as adults. Research has documented that infants and young toddlers demonstrate this kind of play independently; research has also shown that very young children see examples of this type of play all around them. Adults initiate rough and tumble play primarily with boys, and the initiation usually comes from fathers (Lamb, 1981). The purpose of rough and tumble play is a puzzle. It's definitely a form of physical exercise, but not to the extent that it is a significant source of exercise; it's a kind of play fighting. It doesn't seem to be a practice of any particular skills, but it may contribute to social skills because children have the opportunity to "read" another's actions or facial expressions. In the meantime, it is undoubtedly a favorite of children, both boys and girls.

Many adults do not enjoy or appreciate rough and tumble play, often out of worry that a child will be hurt. This sometimes does occur. When Chimieti and Otioli wrestle together, Otioli often runs crying to his parents with an arm twisted or a head bumped. So there's legitimate concern, but that concern turns to frustration when Otioli, after very little comforting, returns just as intensely as before to his wrestling match.

Smith (1989) and Pellegrini and Perlmutter (1988) studied rough and tumble play and identified differences between such play and genuine aggression. Those differences, shown in Figure 4.1, can really help you make decisions about how to respond to rough and tumble play. Knowing some of those differences will remind you to refrain from interfering with children's play fighting or at least may encourage you to observe it more closely.

Sometimes, children's rough and tumble play is a form of drama or pretend play, or at least it begins that way. Playing "bad guys" or "enemies" or "monsters" often turns into rough and tumble play, which isn't surprising, considering both forms of play are developing in children.

The "rough and tumble" play of toddlers continues to be a favorite play activity into the primary grades.

FIGURE 4.1

Differences between Rough and Tumble Play and Aggression

- Aggression may begin with or be triggered by competition for a toy, equipment, space, or friendship of a peer, but rough and tumble play is not generally related to any competition.
- Aggression is accompanied by serious facial expressions and behavior (frowning, mean talk, sneering, and crying), but rough and tumble play is usually done with smiling, laughter, and playful teasing.
- Aggression is usually between two children, but rough and tumble play can involve many children at a time. Anyone can join in.
- Aggression may result in children going their separate ways, but rough and tumble play usually attracts and keeps children together for other forms of play.
- Aggressive behavior is characterized by children using all their strength to hurt another child, but rough and tumble play is more of a mock fight with no intent to hurt.
- Aggression is accompanied by children's bodies that are taut and full of stress, but in rough and tumble play, children's bodies are relaxed.
- Aggressive behavior is characterized by displeasure, but rough and tumble play is characterized by pleasure and fun.

SYMBOLIC PLAY. Early symbolic play is done without words—it is simply using an object to represent another object. The earliest symbolic play is focused on the toddler herself—that is, on her familiar activities, such as eating, sleeping, and getting dressed. You can imagine that this is a comfortable starting point for very young children—routines that they know well. This play has been called **autosymbolic play** because children represent themselves and are beginning their symbolic play. From there, toddlers begin to use objects to represent other objects. They are able to go beyond themselves and represent the world around them.

As the child advances and begins to use language, her words represent objects or people, a higher level of representation. When Keeley was a toddler, she engaged in intense symbolic play each night as everyone finished dinner. She would place her spoon inside her cloth napkin and it would be her baby. She would go to each person at the table and ask, "Would you like to hold my baby?" Those who chose to hold the baby were expected to do so with care and love, and she would gently hand the "baby" to you. After a while, the spoon in the napkin became other things—a birthday present, a bird, jewelry, and so on.

During toddlerhood, children pretend and involve others in their pretending. Wamalwa often pretends to feed himself and has just recently begun to pretend to feed his mother. He really enjoys that kind of "first me, then you" pretending. When toddlers begin to incorporate others into a sequence of pretending, their pretend play becomes more complex. It is the beginning of a series of increasingly more complex symbolic play. From there, you will see incredible changes as children progress to preschool age, the years from ages 3 to 5, in their abilities to use actions and words to convey nonliteral meanings.

APPROPRIATE PRACTICES FOR SUPPORTING TODDLER PLAY. As you can see, the changes that occur in the development of toddlers—physically, socially, linguistically, and cognitively—will be evident in their play and supported by their play. Before we progress to preschool years, take a moment to review some appropriate and inappropriate practices from NAEYC's recommendations, presented in Table 4.2.

TABLE 4.2 Appropriate and Inappropriate Practices Supporting Toddler Play

Appropriate Practices	Inappropriate Practices
Adults engage in reciprocal play with toddlers, modeling for children how to play imaginatively, such as playing "tea party." Caregivers also support toddlers' play so that children stay interested in an object or activity for longer periods of time and their play becomes more complex, moving from simple awareness and exploration of objects to more complicated playlike pretending.	Adults do not play with toddlers because they feel self-conscious or awkward. Caregivers do not understand the importance of supporting children's play, and they control or intrude in the play.
Adults respect toddlers' solitary and parallel play. Caregivers provide several of the same popular toys for children to play with alone or near another child. Caregivers realize that having three or four of the same sought-after toy is more helpful than having one each of many different toys.	Adults do not understand the value of solitary and parallel play and try to force children to play together. Adults arbitrarily expect children to share. Popular toys are not provided in duplicate and are fought over constantly, while other toys are seldom used.
Adults frequently read to toddlers, one individually on a caregiver's lap or in groups of two or three. Caregivers sing with toddlers, do fingerplays, act out simple stories or folktales with children participating actively, or tell stories using a flannel board or magnetic board and allow children to manipulate and place figures on the boards.	Adults impose "grouptime" on toddlers, forcing a large group to listen or watch an activity without providing opportunity for children to participate.
Time schedules are flexible and smooth, dictated more by children's needs than by adults'. There is a relatively predictable sequence to the day to help children feel secure.	Activities are dictated by rigid adherence to time schedules, or the lack of a time schedule makes the day unpredictable.
Adults adapt schedules and activities to meet individual children's needs within the group setting. Recognizing toddlers' need to repeat tasks until they master the steps and skills involved, caregivers allow toddlers to go at their own pace. They have time to assist a child with special needs because the group of toddlers knows what is expected and is engaged.	Adults lose patience with toddlers' desires for repetition. Toddlers must either do things in groups according to the caregivers' plan or follow adult demands that they spend a certain amount of time at an activity. Caregivers have little time for a child with special needs.
Toddlers are given appropriate art materials, such as large crayons, watercolor markers, and large paper. Adults expect toddlers to explore and manipulate art materials and *do not* expect them to produce a finished art product. They use nontoxic materials but avoid using food for art because toddlers are developing self-regulatory skills and must learn to distinguish between food and other objects that are not to be eaten.	Toddlers are "helped" by teachers to produce a product, follow the adult-made model, or color a coloring book or ditto sheet. Because toddlers are likely to put things in their mouths, adults give them edible, often tasty, fingerpaints or playdough.
Children have daily opportunities for exploratory activity, such as water and sand play, painting, and playing with clay or playdough.	Adults do not offer water and sand play, paints, or playdough because they are messy and require supervision. Children's natural enjoyment of water play is frustrated, so children play at sinks whenever they can.
Adults respect toddlers' desires to carry favored objects around with them, to move the objects from one place to another, and to roam around or sit and parallel play with toys and objects.	Adults restrict objects to certain locations and do not tolerate children's hoarding, collecting, or carrying objects about.

Source: Developmentally Appropriate Practice in Early Childhood Programs (pp. 84–85) by S. Bredekamp and C. Copple, 1997, Washington, DC: NAEYC.

Preschool Play

The years from ages 3 to 5 are a marvelous time to sit back and watch children represent everything and anything with the greatest of imagination. You begin to get a view of their perspectives of the world, of people, of life, and of who they are. Watching their symbolic play is especially revealing of how they perceive the happenings around them, so we begin to describe preschoolers with a discussion of the changes and capacity of their symbolic play.

SYMBOLIC PRETEND PLAY. As they leave toddlerhood, young children continue to represent themselves in their pretend play, but they expand on their representation of and actions upon others (adults and objects). They pretend to comb their own hair, pretend to comb dad's hair, and pretend to comb a doll's hair. That same play begins to get more complex as the child talks for the doll or her dad, or when the child attributes feelings to a stuffed-toy dog or his mom.

Keeley often talked to her pretend baby in the napkin as if the baby had needs or likes. "You like to be rocked, don't you?" she would say. Later, she would talk for the baby: "I want a bottle," she would say in a baby voice. Keeley began to assume other roles and her symbolic pretend play began to reveal much of her life. Her favorite play was in the role of "teacher" and the adults in her family had to sit on the floor to be read to, or get ready for their naps, or wash their hands for lunch. Her words, tone of voice, and kinds of directions may tell you much about what her day was like.

The kind of symbolic pretend play in which children assume the role of another continues to gain complexity. Children usually begin with familiar roles, that of mother, father, or other relative, then to adults in their lives, such as teacher, doctor, grocery clerk, librarian, or bus driver, to name just a few. The next level of such play is when the child assumes an unfamiliar role, one about which he has little or no information. Even without experience, children roleplay astronauts, ballerinas, cowboys, and police officers. Young children of this age also often act out the roles of husband and wife.

During this time, children use objects a great deal but give them human qualities. Keeley could manage two roles—that of herself interacting with her doll and that of the doll expressing her wants. We heard her change voices for each role and it was quite impressive.

PRETEND PLAY WITH PEERS. Throughout this chapter, we have been encouraging you to observe children's play because there is so much to learn. Another interesting focus for your observations is the pattern that you can see in their processes when they engage in pretend play with other children. First, you will see an *initiation phase,* a time when a child is approaching a play activity, or deciding on with whom to play, or scanning an area to consider a play choice. Some children are quite good at initiation, and others may need your support.

The next phase of the pattern is a *negotiation phase,* when children decide the theme of their play, the roles each will play, and any kind of rules or structures. The last phase is the *enactment phase.* This is the time the children have been working up to—when they will actually pretend together. This is when they enact the scenarios that they negotiated. Watching this process gives you an insight into the potential complexity of children's pretend play.

JOURNAL 4.2: A parent approaches you with concern about her child's "pretend world": "I worry about all the pretending Lisa does. She pretends to have playmates and she plays with them. She pretends to be different characters each night at supper and insists that we go along with her. Is it possible for her to be pretending too much? What benefit could all this pretending have?" Respond to Lisa's mother. ●

You may have some ideas to share with Lisa's mother, but you may also feel that you could use more convincing information. What we have learned from observations of children's play is that we can tell so much about what they understand, what they are thinking, and their concerns and confusions. As we continue, you will learn about other ideas to comfort Lisa's mother.

COMMUNICATING UNDERSTANDINGS. When you watch preschool children, their interpretation of roles and other forms of pretend play tell you about their understandings. The way they present their understandings is called a **scheme.** Schemes are children's concepts of what is real in terms of objects, actions, and roles. A child may show you her scheme of what a cash register or a scanner is by the way she pretends to use it, or may show you her scheme of what a beach is by the way she pretends to be there. Young children begin with simple schemes, but during preschool years, they combine and carry out different levels of schemes in a sequence, and eventually have multischemes. Watch the children in the following scene and identify the schemes and look for different levels in a sequence.

Eli and Amanda: Schemes

Eli and Amanda are playing "house" (their word) at preschool. Amanda is using a duster to dust the varied furniture items in the dramatic play area. She swishes it over the top of the table and china cabinet, then pauses to appreciate her work. "I'm making the house nice and clean," she tells Eli. "I'm making a stew for us," he responds. He gathers an assortment of plastic vegetables from the refrigerator, pretends to wash them and cut them up, then puts them into a pot. He begins to stir the pot and sniffs it, saying, "Umm, it smells good."

Amanda is pushing a wheel toy and making a vacuum sound all around the area. Later, she appears with a purse over her arm and indicates that she's going to the store. "Do you want anything from the store?" she asks, but Eli shakes his head as he continues to stir. When she returns, Eli tells Amanda that the stew is ready. She sits at the table and waits to be served. Eli brings some dishes to the table and puts the pot in the center. He ladles out the pretend stew into their dishes and begins to eat.

After a minute or so, Amanda says, "I bought some ice cream for us." She goes to the refrigerator, pretends to take something out, and brings them each a dish and spoon. Both children enthusiastically eat their pretend ice cream.

Identify the schemes in the play you just observed. What kind of schemes does Amanda have? How about Eli? What schemes do both children have?

The ultimate goal of children's symbolic or pretend play is "to integrate meaning derived from their experience with knowledge and skills from all developmental domains as they create roles or scenarios" (Kostelnik, Soderman, & Whiren, 1993). What that means is that play provides an opportunity for children to pull together previously learned ideas, information, and skills, and connect new ideas, information, and skills into physical, emotional, social, and cognitive learning. Figure 4.2 shows you the kinds of progress children will make toward that goal as they pretend, taking on roles and creating scenes. Those progressions will continue as children experience kindergarten and primary grades, and their symbolic play will become more complex and exciting. The physical play of preschool-aged children changes, too, as they mature, taking on a complexity and seriousness.

PHYSICAL PLAY ACTIVITIES. Most preschool children continue to have a great deal of energy and need plenty of physical play activities during their day. Their physical play begins to change, however, as they develop during this time. What began as free and enthusiastic delight with running, jumping, and climbing frequently now has more purpose. Children at this age get a bit serious about their physical play, although rough and tumble play continues with great frequency. This is a time when children begin working on skills—aiming the ball and hitting a target, running fast, jumping high, or performing the perfect cartwheel.

FIGURE 4.2

Objectives for Children's Emotional, Physical, Social, and Cognitive Learning

As children progress toward the ultimate goal, they will:

1. Mimic in their play behaviors what they have seen or experienced.
2. Use their bodies to represent real or imaginary objects or events.
3. Assign symbolic meaning to real or imaginary objects or events.
4. Take on the role attributes of beings or objects and act out interpretations of those roles.
5. Create play themes.
6. Experiment with a variety of objects, roles (leader, follower, mediator), and characterizations (animal, mother, astronaut, etc.).
7. React to and interact with other children in make-believe situations.
8. Dramatize familiar stories, songs, poems, and past events.
9. Integrate construction into pretend play episodes.

Source: Developmentally Appropriate Programs in Early Childhood Education by M. J. Kostelnik, A. K. Soderman, and A. P. Whiren, © 1993. Reprinted by permission of Prentice-Hall, Inc., Upper Saddle River, NJ.

Some of their physical play begins to have rules and organization. Most of the early rules and organization are composed by the children themselves, and you'll hear them come up with rules as they go. Generally, when the situation arises, they make up the necessary rule. Some very simple physical games are played by children during their preschool years. Games such as Tag and Duck, Duck, Goose are simple, energetic, and have minimal rules.

ADULT ATTITUDES TOWARD PLAY. The time between toddlerhood and entry to kindergarten is eventful in children's play. Amazing changes occur as children explore, experiment, and engage in play. The major change related to children's play is the adult attitude toward its legitimacy. When children play in preschool, most adults are delighted and enjoy their play adventures. But when children enter more formal schooling, starting with kindergarten, the acceptance of play becomes limited, and adults begin to have concerns about the amount of time spent in play. The time that children spend in kindergarten and primary grades, their years between ages 5 and 8, is a time when children's play can reach its highest potential to fulfill all aspects of their development. It is a time when play can energize learning, can take symbolic representation to a sophisticated level, and can enhance all school curriculum.

Unfortunately, most adults are not aware of the ways that play helps children of this age to develop skills and concepts of literacy and math. It also builds the foundation of more general competencies that are necessary for success in school and beyond (Bodrova & Leong, 2003). A major responsibility of your future professional role will be to provide information to parents for understanding the importance of play.

Kindergarten and Primary Grades Play

Family life differences and socioeconomic and cultural backgrounds will have significant influence on children's play at this stage. When general life experiences combine with different levels of maturity, children's play will be marked with huge diversity in terms of pretend themes and content, physical skill and agility, interest and enthusiasm for varied activities, gender differences, and even the children's definitions of play. It is also a time when children are spending their days in environments that don't always support play or that try to present learning activities as play. So, children's perceptions of what is play and what is not play are important for your understanding of their play.

CHILDREN'S PERCEPTIONS OF PLAY. The research study shown in Box 4.1 (Wing, 1995) is a very meaningful portrait of children's perceptions of play. It is a good starting point for your understanding of kindergarten and primary grade children's play in the confines of many of school settings. Bergen (1988) refers to a category of play called "work disguised as play" to describe task-oriented activities that teachers attempt to transform into directed or guided play. Math and spelling games and other learning activities that promote rote learning (learning by repetition) are often presented enthusiastically as enjoyable activities, but Wing's research is a reminder that children know the difference.

BOX 4.1

Children's Perspectives on Work and Play

In 1995, to determine what children saw as play, Lisa Wing asked kindergartners, first-graders, and second-graders about their classroom activities. She thought that they could provide important information for teachers, parents, and school policymakers. Children spend the greatest part of their day involved in classroom activities and those activities communicate to children what school is about. Almost immediately in her study, Wing learned that children classified school activities as either work or play. From there, she asked how children made their distinctions, what criteria they used to interpret activities, and what messages they received from adults, peers, and the school environment.

Teachers of the children in the study described their programs as "hands on, with lots of materials, children choosing what to do, free exploration" (Wing, 1995, pp. 225–226) and summed the learning as "a process of playful exploration and discovery" (p. 226). Their classrooms were arranged in learning centers, and children spent the greater part of the day in small group or self-directed activities. Children often made choices about their learning activities and did so in cooperative groups.

"The words *work* and *play* came up repeatedly as children talked about their classroom activities, but in their minds, play was not work" (Wing, 1995, p. 226). Whether an activity was obligatory was the major element in determining the difference between work and play. Teachers' intentions and directions were central to work activities, but children's intentions were central to play. Children used the term *have to* with activities in writing, spelling, math, projects, reading, and calendar. When children talked about their play activities, the terms *get to* and *can* were used. When children were required to use materials that they typically associated with play—such as blocks, crayons, and sand—in a specific way, those activities became work.

An important insight came from observations about teachers' roles in work and play activities. The researcher noticed that teachers were usually uninvolved in those activities children classified as play, such as painting, block play, sand, and construction activities. Their involvement was quite different in those activities that children called work. Teachers remained close to the children, led them or circulated among them, or assisted and supervised them. Teachers usually gave directions for work activities but seldom for play activities.

Another area of difference for children's differentiation between work and play was seen in their perceptions about the physical and cognitive demands of their activities. Children referred to thinking, concentrating, effort, and neatness with respect to the demands of work. Listen to the children describe the differences between *work* and *play:*

> *Ted:* When you're not using your mind, that's playing. It's a big, big difference. You really try to concentrate really hard when you're working, but not when you're playing (Wing, 1995, p. 234).
>
> *Stacey:* Well, coloring isn't really playing. It's really working. When it's working, it's something to take your time on and just do your best. The difference is when you take your time and you do your best, it's called working, and when you just try to do it, do it a little fast and a little taking time, it's called playing (Wing, 1995, p. 235).

JOURNAL 4.3: Put yourself in the role of a primary grade child who has figured out the difference between work and play. Your teacher just gave directions for an activity described as "a fun math game" and it's one in which you end up practicing simple addition facts. What kind of questions might you have about math, about your teacher, and about school and learning? How might you feel about those same areas? ●

The continuum of play and work in Figure 4.3 reflects the ideas children expressed in Wing's interviews about the distinction between the two, and captures their thinking about activities that they could not classify clearly as one or the other. The continuum reflects all of the possibilities between those activities that are clearly work and those that are clearly play.

It is interesting to note in Box 4.1 the differences between the teachers' perceptions of work and play and the children's perceptions of the two. When teachers thought that children had plenty of play activities, children perceived the opposite. It was also noted that during play activities, teachers remained apart from children and clearly did not join in the play. They used that time to finish other projects or work on material preparation or bulletin boards. During work activities, the teachers were very involved, giving directions, supervising, and guiding. Their behavior clearly gave clues to children about which activities were play and which activities were work.

One conclusion you may reach from the study in Box 4.1 is that you will want to become a co-player with children during their work and play. Both Piaget and Vygotsky would

FIGURE 4.3

Children's Perceived Work: Play Continuum

PLAY		WORK
	Nature of the Activity	
Free exploration of materials Generally involves manipulatives or other objects Does not require quiet Process-oriented Does not require finishing	Activities that are teacher-designed but allow for some discovery or creativity Self-selected activities that require concentration or attention to detail Games with rules and academic content	Teacher-directed and designed activities Product-oriented Usually involving pencil and paper Sometimes requires quiet Projects (in kindergarten) Must be finished
	Child Involvement	
Children's intentions central Usually physically active Little mental concentration or cognitive activity evident to the child Can interact freely with peers Always fun	Teachers' intentions usually central but more choices available to the child Can usually interact freely with peers Usually fun	Mental concentration and cognitive activity evident to the child Can sometimes interact with peers Usually physically inactive Sometimes fun
	Teacher Involvement	
Few teacher expectations Rarely evaluated by the teacher	Generally some teacher evaluation Teachers' expectations and intentions central	Outcomes evaluated by the teacher

Source: "Play Is Not the Work of the Child" by L. A. Wing, 1995, *Early Childhood Research Quarterly, 10* (2), p. 240. Reprinted by permission of Ablex Publishing Corporation.

support those roles for teachers. If your role is to plan, organize, and encourage children's play, you will probably want to be involved in the play. Later in this chapter, we will talk more about the adult role in children's play, but for now, it appears that children expect you to be engaged in their play activities.

In addition to children's perceptions of work and play in kindergarten and primary grades, there are changes in their physical play and an upsurge of rough and tumble play. If you spend some time on the playground with first- and second-graders, you will see those changes and the frequency of their rough and tumble play.

INCREASES IN ROUGH AND TUMBLE PLAY. In studies of preschool children's play behaviors, rough and tumble play accounts for 5 percent of their free play, but in early elementary school (kindergarten through third grade), it accounts for up to 17 percent of children's free play. Pellegrini and Boyd (1993) think that the frequency can be explained by the fact that children have moved from preschools where play is valued to an institution where it is not. In many elementary schools, children have little opportunity to engage in self-directed play. When the opportunity does exist, the children are usually on the playground at recess. The researchers note that the playground is a male-preferred setting and many of the play behaviors there are typically male. They also note that as the frequency of fantasy play decreases, rough and tumble play increases.

PLAY ON THE PLAYGROUND. At the same time that teachers are concerned with the safety of children's play on playgrounds, there is a growing concern that young children's level of physical activity is not adequate for healthy living and physical fitness. As a profession, we are aware of the health benefits of physical activity, and yet, there is evidence that when children are using the playground, only a small percent of their play consists of vigorous activity (Staley & Portman, 2000). Play is the ideal context in which children can increase and maintain the appropriate level of physical fitness through movement and motor skills as recommended by the Council on Physical Education. Motor skills include locomotor activities (running, skipping, crawling, jumping, etc.), stability activities (balancing, stretching, shaking, playing Freeze, etc.), and manipulative activities (throwing, kicking, dribbling, etc.). When you look at those skills, appropriate playground activities begin to emerge but many of them require adult facilitation and supervision. It will be important for you and your parent volunteers or aides to be prepared to guide children's playground behavior and development of physical fitness with a repertoire of games and activities. You will also need to prepare to observe children's play carefully on the playground to keep the setting safe and comfortable for all children. That same watchfulness is necessary with other kinds of play for this age group, because the play of 5- to 8-year-olds has become so complex.

Playgrounds are ideal environments for simple games—games with opportunities for important social interactions, games that are content rich for kinesthetic awareness, and games that provide fun and relaxation. Kinesthetic awareness is essential in most outdoor game activities as children use their bodies to learn, to try something new, to pretend to be something, or to express something (Church, 2003). Adults can promote the awareness in the following ways:

1. Invite children to explore what their bodies can do. ("What would happen if you walked backwards in the game?")
2. Add language and vocabulary to what children are doing. ("You are swaying your shoulders as you go in and out.")
3. Reflect with children at the end of an activity. ("Let's stop for a few moments and talk about how it felt to dance like that.")

METACOMMUNICATION IN PRETEND PLAY. By age 5 or 6 through age 8, children's pretend play has the advantage of extensive experiences, a developing sense of humor, and a wide range of understandings. Along with the sophistication of their symbolism, which now extends to words and other written symbols, children engage in what is called

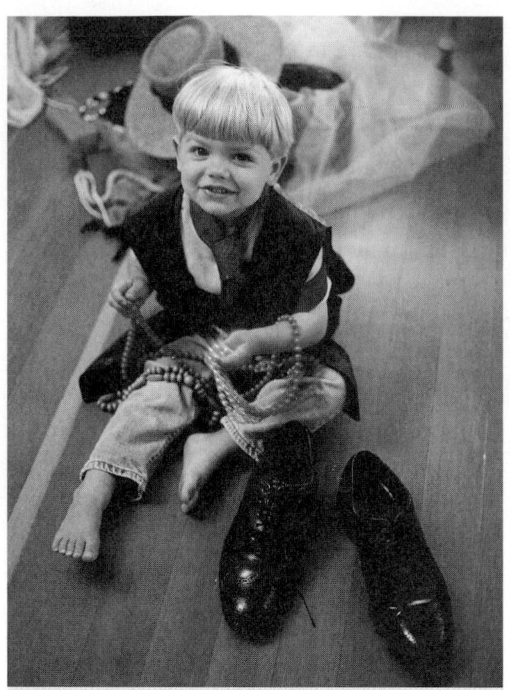

What kind of role might this child be preparing to take and what might he communicate to his peers?

metacommunication. For example, children are communicating about communicating and these metacommunications are quite complex. When children use them, they are telling their peers what is play and what is not. In fact, children communicate a whole series of messages in their pretend play through metacommunications:

- They set the stage for their play or construct a play frame. ("Let's pretend that we're taking the puppy to the vet.")
- They transform objects and settings. ("This is the puppy [pointing to a pillow] and this is the vet office [pointing to a closet].")
- They extend the play. ("Pretend that our puppy died.")
- They elaborate on character feelings or actions. ("You're very sad about our puppy and you want to buy a new one.")
- They change the role. ("Pretend that I'm in charge of the pet shop now.")
- They end the play or change the sequence. ("Pretend that we're at home and we're going to bed." "I don't want to play anymore.")

The value of metacommunication is that it communicates the information needed for a pair or small group of children to pretend play together. Metacommunication assures that everyone knows what is happening, what the roles are, what the props represent, and when things change. Like so much of children's pretend play, metacommunication provides good information about children's thinking and social concepts if we will watch and listen. In addition to the metacommunication that occurs in kindergarten and primary grades, there is an increase of problem solving in group pretend play.

PROBLEM SOLVING IN GROUP PRETEND PLAY. As children mature and gain experience, they are able to maintain pretend play in a group for longer periods of time. Those play situations begin to include problems to be solved by the players. Generally, children stay with known and comfortable settings but create stories in them to add excitement, puzzles, and complexity to their play. For instance, they may create a situation of an earthquake happening during a picnic or a mom losing her baby in the grocery store. From their scenarios, they take a consistent series of steps to solve the problem or address the dilemma they created. Here's a sample of a series of steps the children might proceed through in their pretend play:

1. "We're all at the grocery store, okay? And this is the deli, and this is the meat department, and this is the bakery. Jerlean, you're the mom and you lose your baby when you're shopping. I'm the owner of the store and Joey's the cash register guy. Pretend it's real crowded in the store." (setting the stage and describing the problem)
2. "Help, help, I've lost my baby. Somebody help me. Where's the owner?" (identifying the problem)
3. "Here I am, this is my store. We have a big store. This is a very crowded day—lots of people in the store. I don't know how we're going to find your baby. How did you lose him? Let's get the cash register guy to help." (developing of the plot)
4. "I'm the cash register guy and I can talk to people on my microphone. I'll ask all the people to look for your baby. Don't worry, Mrs. Daniels, we will find your baby." (resolving the problem)
5. "Here he is—your baby. He was playing by the cereal boxes. We found him and now everyone is happy. The end." (ending)

As children mature, these problem scenarios become more complicated and extend into unfamiliar settings and plots. This is a time when children need a supportive environment and plenty of time for practice to gain complexity in their play.

The pretend play of children this age is often referred to as *dramatic play*. It is an excellent and comfortable setting in which children can express thoughts and feelings, and work through the uncertainties of worrisome situations such as divorce, job loss, new baby, and so on. Consequently, play supports children's emotional development. The dramatic play of children in kindergarten and primary grades also stimulates language development, with the introduction and clarification of new words and concepts, practice in using language, and opportunity for verbal thinking (Vygotsky, 1962). Much of children's pretend play occurs with literacy activities in settings such as a post office, grocery store, house, train station, or airport. Again, teacher guidance and provision of materials can stimulate both variety and frequency of literacy activities. Those same literacy activities can be part of another form of play for this age group—games with rules.

GAMES WITH RULES. This is a time when children have a logical system of thinking and a passion for order, so games with rules are a good fit for this age group. The kinds of games with rules that these children enjoy may be sensorimotor in nature—such as marbles, ball games, tag, hopscotch, jacks, or hide-and-seek—or cognitive in nature—such as checkers, card games, Clue, Monopoly, or other board games. Games with rules introduce new elements into children's play. Up to now, there hasn't been much competition in their play, but games with rules involve competition between two or more players. Additionally, the games are directed by a set of rules that are agreed to in advance by all players and cannot be changed. You might recall that younger children often make rules as they go along or change them in a serendipitous way (when they feel like it). The rules of checkers and Monopoly have been around a long time, so there's not much possibility of change.

JOURNAL 4.4: We have been focusing on the benefits of play all through this chapter. When children begin playing games with rules, there continues to be benefits, but there also may be some disadvantages. Think of a familiar game, such as checkers or Clue, and list the benefits of such a game for children of this age. Then think of the disadvantages of playing the game. ●

Another development that characterizes children of this age is a concern with fairness. When his family plays games together on Friday nights, Otioli is quick to observe any infractions of the rules, especially on the part of the adults. He is also hard on himself for the least little mistake. His newly developed conscience is especially strict and doesn't tolerate accidents or errors well. The conscience of his older brother, Chimieti, has softened a bit, and he is able to emphasize with others. He will often say to Otioli, "He can't help it. It was an accident" if their friend Paul does something wrong in a game.

COMPETITIVE AND ORGANIZED SPORTS. This is also a time when children engage in competitive sports, another kind of game with rules. Even with the competitive element, children in kindergarten and primary grades can have a great time out on the soccer field or on a baseball team with their friends, especially if there isn't a great deal of interference by the adults. A friend who coaches soccer with a passion for letting it be the children's game, recalls the casual nature of his team. One child was running down the field next to another child and asked the child if he wanted to come over and spend the night. Seconds later, he ran over to his parent and asked, "Can Andrew spend the night?" in the midst of the game.

Millions of children in the United States participate in organized sports each year, with an average of three to four hours of involvement per week. In other words, sports takes up about 20 percent of the play time of children ages 6 to 8. If we go back to the benefits of play, we'll probably find that organized sports have the potential to achieve some of those benefits. If organized appropriately, children will gain self-esteem and skills of cooperation as well as get good exercise. We've all seen the opposite kind of coaching—the kind that pressures children to win above all else. When you go back to the characteristics of play, you can quickly see that it is no longer play for children on such a team.

Much of the play in kindergarten and primary grades continues through middle childhood, adolescence, and adulthood: games with rules, organized sports, and some fantasy (pretending). But much of the zest and creativity may disappear, due to society's lack of acceptance of play in its true form for children after the age of 8. One aspect of play that does carry on into adulthood very well is the social development that emerges from play. We have not really talked directly about the social aspect of play and the stages that children move through in their play. In order to see the whole picture of children's play, it is important to put that information together with the changes in sensorimotor (physical) and symbolic play that children experience.

Social Development and Play

The social development of children has been studied intensely in the context of play, probably because children's play is the best setting to observe their social development and because play contributes so much to that development. Both perspectives will be important for you to keep in mind as you watch children and plan for their play activities. Let's begin with the value of play for children's social development. The question is: How does play contribute to children's social skills and social understandings? Remember that our goal for children is social competence—that is, the ability to function effectively in society.

Play and Social Competence

To be socially competent, a person needs a number of skills or specific abilities. Sharing, cooperation, perspective taking, conceptions of friendship, interpersonal strategies, and communication skills are just some of the components of social competence. Play is a context in which children learn about their social world with "opportunities to rehearse social skills, to learn about acceptable behavior, and to develop awareness of their peers" (Klein et al., 2003). Play also offers a chance to learn sharing and cooperation, perspective taking and other interpersonal strategies, and understandings of friendship, while advancing children's communication skills. Much of the play development we have just described for infants through children in primary grades included social development aspects, but we think that you will need to be even more aware of the exciting possibilities for children when they play.

SHARING AND COOPERATION. As soon as children begin to play with toys or other materials and are in the company of other children, they have the opportunity to share. Typically, children don't share easily until about age 3, but one of our colleagues (Smith, 1997, personal communication) has videotapes of very young toddlers who respond to another toddler's stress by bringing a toy to him or her. A good early childhood setting should be equipped with enough of each material or toy so that young children do not need to share until they are ready. An example of inappropriate practice for toddlers is "Adults arbitrarily expect children to share. Popular toys are not provided in duplicate and are fought over constantly" (NAEYC, 1997a, p. 84). In Chapter 8, you will hear Darren, an early childhood educator of toddlers, talk about a decision not to force sharing and about strategies to help children begin to take turns (which is a kind of sharing).

Sharing and cooperation begin in infancy, when adults and siblings play with babies. When parents play games with babies, infants begin to learn how to wait their turn. There is also the opportunity to develop an awareness of others, which is essential for later cooperation. Although adults initiate games with infants, researchers have noted that once the game begins, babies take on an active role in keeping the game going and are very involved in the game (Ross & Lollis, 1987). As toddlers, children have endless opportunities to share and cooperate, many of which they are not ready for, but nevertheless they begin to see the possibilities and to see examples. Contemporary researchers of children's social play find that 2-year-olds will cooperate when they play with very familiar peers. By the time they are in preschool, they are better able to share and to feel quite good about doing so. You often hear a 4-year-old tell an adult, "I shared with Emily" or "I'm sharing my new puzzle." Sometimes, sharing new toys or favorite items of play is too difficult for children; in fact, some programs even have a policy that children cannot bring in playthings if they aren't able to share them. By kindergarten and primary grades, children are expected to share many materials in school and do so easily.

PERSPECTIVE TAKING. **Perspective taking** is kind of like putting yourself in another person's shoes so that you have an understanding or appreciation of that person's thinking and feelings. Rubin and Howe (1986) define it as being able to simultaneously consider one's own thoughts, feelings, and views of the world along with another's (p. 115). When young children begin to pretend play, they begin their development toward perspective taking. When they provide talk about how a doll or stuffed animal is feeling or what the doll wants, they are taking the perspective of another. As they mature and begin to talk for the doll, they continue their development. Later, as they play varying roles, they display their perspective taking of their parents, doctor, teacher, and others in their lives. Within the interactions of dramatic play, children witness and hear other perspectives. In the course of their play, they may challenge those perspectives or accept them to broaden their own perspectives. Rubin (1980) treats us to a delightful interaction between two 4-year-old boys, one of whom is playing the father and one of whom is playing the mother:

> *Father:* "So long, I'll see ya later. It's time to go to work."
> *Mother:* "Hey, wait for me. I gotta go to work, too."
> *Father:* "Moms don't work . . . my mom don't work . . . stay here."
> *Mother:* "Well my mom works . . . lots womens work ya know. My mom is a perfessor at the university."
> *Father:* "OK, then, just hurry so we won't be late. Are you sure ya wanna work?" (p. 75)

Some of the sharing we see in young children goes hand in hand with their perspective taking. We hear children say, "Josey is sad, so I gave her my doll." It's the kind of perspective taking and sharing that Smith observed in very young toddlers. Even the youngest of children are surprisingly capable of perspective taking.

CONCEPTIONS OF FRIENDSHIP. Although conceptions of friendship begin quite early when children are placed in group settings, we cannot be sure of real concepts until later when children are able to display their understanding of what friendship is or what a friend does. Often, a preschool curriculum focuses on friendship as a theme, but for many children it is simply a matter of saying the words associated with friendship rather than a true understanding. By kindergarten and primary grades, children become increasingly interested in establishing quality friendships. According to Hendrick (1990), most children by age 7 find it almost unthinkable not to have a friend. For example, Keeley and her best friend, Dani, can play for hours at a time. They prefer to play with each other over any other choices, and they truly miss each other when one of them is ill or out of town. They share, they cooperate, they take each other's perspective, and they genuinely care about each other. They experience stimulation, assistance, companionship, and affection from their friendship (Parker & Gottman, 1989). Many adults have friendships that began in first grade and have been maintained to adulthood.

INTERPERSONAL STRATEGIES. Interpersonal strategies include a wide variety of social approaches that young children are learning and practicing. Some take extensive experience and some come fairly easy. The interpersonal strategies of developing relationships with others and living within our society include:

- *Perceives, interprets, and responds to social situations appropriately.* Young children are often not skilled at judging a situation before responding. When we were observing

Francis and Akosa's children we watched an incident that we think illustrates this lack of skill. We saw the boys' friend, Brittany, ask for permission to have the children come inside her home to play. When Brittany's family said that she couldn't have the boys come in to play because one of them caused problems, Otioli announced it for the entire group in a way that embarrassed everyone concerned. His intentions were good, but he wasn't skilled at responding in a way that was socially acceptable.

- *Establishes contact with others in appropriate ways.* Toddlers make endless errors in their efforts to make contact. They may knock over another child, push a child, grab a toy, or stand nearby without saying a word. We once watched a very shy boy wanting to make contact with a group of children who were building with blocks. After days of watching, he knocked over a very elaborate building and looked surprised when the group became upset with him. After consistent teacher coaching, this child learned appropriate ways to make contact with other children and to request entry into their play.
- *Expresses needs, rights, and emotions appropriately.* It is not surprising to see a toddler bite another child to express a right or an emotion, or to witness a young preschooler throw a tantrum to express a need or an emotion. Even children in kindergarten need practice in naming their needs, rights, or emotions. One of the adult roles needed for children's social development is that of a coach. Young children respond well to the encouragement to "Tell him that you don't like to be bumped" or "Tell us that you feel angry right now." Adults can also model appropriate ways to express needs ("I need everyone to be quiet so that I can read"), rights ("It's my turn to talk"), or emotions ("I am feeling so excited today").
- *Sustains relationships.* When children are enjoyable to be with, they are able to sustain relationships. A variety of characteristics and skills makes them enjoyable—cooperation, sharing, sense of humor, helpfulness, good judgment, flexibility, and so on. In order to sustain a relationship, a child also has to care about another child or children, so it takes some maturity to sustain a relationship.
- *Flexes to accommodate others and situations.* Very young children don't flex well. They need routines, a consistent group of peers and adults, and few changes. Being flexible is just too difficult for a toddler or a young preschooler. However, as children become more sociable and have more experiences with peers, they develop the capacity to take another's perspective, to feel empathy for another, and to exhibit a strong sense of fairness. Thus, they can give up a turn, a plaything, a schedule, or a plan. When Wamalwa was injured accidentally by his brother during play, Otioli gave him his treasured Lego model to play with, even though there was a chance that it would be destroyed by the toddler. When Chimieti and Otioli wanted to go down the street to play but their parents asked them to stay home for our visit, they were agreeable about staying.
- *Negotiates conflicts.* The strategies and examples in Table 4.3 give us a sense of the abilities necessary for children to negotiate conflicts. This is a very complex aspect of developing and maintaining relationships. Some children will have had no experience in negotiation, either because of limited experience with groups of peers or because well-meaning adults solved most of their conflicts. All of the other interpersonal skills we have just described will influence how well a child is able to negotiate conflicts. Again, children will need guidance and coaching of adults to foster the strategies in Table 4.3.

COMMUNICATION SKILLS. Most play situations offer opportunities for speaking and listening. Even if children are playing alone or are not ready to interact with peers, adults can use the situation to ask questions, offer comments, and engage the child in conversation. The way an adult talks with children will send a message about how children are regarded. Children need a stress-free language environment if they are to communicate.

TABLE 4.3 Negotiating Conflicts

Strategy	Example
Expressing one's own rights, needs, or feelings	"It's my turn to use the stapler."
Listening to and acknowledging others' rights, opinions, and feelings	"Oh, you haven't finished yet."
Suggesting nonviolent solutions to conflict	"How about giving it to me in 2 minutes?"
Explaining the reasons behind the solution suggested	"That way we'll both get to use it before lunch."
Standing up against unreasonable demands	"No, it's not fair if you use it the whole time. I want it, too."
Accepting reasonable disagreement	"OK, I hadn't thought of that."
Compromising on a solution	"I can use tape now, and you can use tape later when I'm using the stapler."

Source: Developmentally Appropriate Programs in Early Childhood Education by M. J. Kostelnik, A. K. Soderman, and A. P. Whiren, © 1993. Reprinted by permission of Prentice-Hall, Inc., Upper Saddle River, NJ.

Early childhood educators are encouraged to use responsive language when speaking to children. Stone (1993) describes **responsive language** as language that "conveys a positive regard for children, and a respect for and acceptance of their individual ideas and feelings" (p. 13). Responsive language includes giving children reasons for our statements, encouraging children's choices, and making positive comments on children's efforts. Table 4.4 shows a comparison between responsive language and **restrictive language,** language that communicates disrespect and adult control.

Once children begin playing in pairs or groups, they explore vocabulary, expressive conversation, body language, and other forms of communication to interact with each other. Their play provides rich opportunities and support for developing social competence. In addition to observing the multiple benefits of play for children's social development, we know that children progress through levels of play that are indicative of their social development. One of the researchers who intensely studied children's play was Mildred Parten. In the 1930s, she observed and recorded the play of children from ages 2 to 5 and developed a framework of levels of play that continues to be used today when looking at children's social maturity in play. You will read about the framework as we describe play and assessment.

TABLE 4.4 Examples of Comparisons between Responsive Language and Restrictive Language

Responsive	Restrictive
We have to pick up all of the blocks today because tonight our carpets are being cleaned.	It doesn't matter why. We just have to clean everything off the floor.
It's choice time and there's room at the easels and at the Lego table. Which would you like?	You haven't painted all week—you need to paint today.
I need your help in getting ready for our field trip. Everyone needs to put on coats and be ready to listen.	We can't go on our field trip until everyone is ready and quiet.
We walk in our classroom so that no one gets hurt.	No running in our classroom.
You really shaped your play-dough into interesting figures. Tell me about them.	You didn't spend much time with the play-dough. Can't you make something?

Play and Assessment

It has been said that play can be called "the ultimate integrated curriculum" (VanHoorn et al., 1999, p. 265); therefore, play gives you the best possible setting to observe children's learning and development. A play-centered curriculum and a play-centered environment provide the ideal context for observing all aspects of children's development—physical, emotional, cognitive, social, and even some of their dispositions. Children's play is comfortable for them and, as such, is natural and authentic as a context for assessment. Such assessment doesn't cause the stress often observed when children are assessed with unfamilar materials, by unfamiliar personnel, or in unfamiliar settings.

Many of the observational recording forms available (and found in later chapters) provide a focus for observations of play and related assessment. However, many teachers' and caregivers' observations are recorded on Post-its whenever children's play behavior occurs. Thus, you will need to develop observational skills, techniques for recording what you see, and the capacity to make judgments about your observations. Your development will take time and practice and a real commitment to assessment of children at play. It will require "sensitivity, thoughtfulness, and a repertoire of strategies for determining when to assess by careful observation" (VanHoorn et al., 1999, p. 266).

Two play theorists who studied children's play extensively have developed classifications or systems for looking at children's play. Many educators have used these systems as an observational focus for observing play.

Smilansky's Components for Assessing the Quality of Children's Sociodramatic Play

Smilansky's (1968) observations of children's sociodramatic play yielded a set of components found in high levels or sophisticated sociodramatic play of preschool, kindergarten, and primary grade children. This type of play often occurs in areas of ECE environments specifically set up to encourage such play, such as dramatic play areas, but also occurs in areas that children create or transform into such spaces. Playgrounds, block areas, the space under a table, and tents become dramatic play areas in which children can display the following components posed by Smilansky:

- *Roleplay.* You will constantly hear children say, "I'm the dad" or "I'm the policewoman" or "I'll be the baby" as they begin to behave in ways consistent with the role just stated.
- *Use of props.* Children are wonderfully creative in using real objects (broom, wagon, etc.) or pretend replica of real objects (large wooden spoon for a microphone). It is equally important to notice how they use that prop for their play.
- *Make-believe episodes.* When children's play goes beyond simple imitation of adult action and is integrated into an elaborated episode, it is called a make-believe episode. An example is when Joellen comforted the baby doll, rocked it in her arms, and then said to Ricky, "I think that we need to take the baby to the doctor." The conversation is followed by a subway ride to the doctor's office and so on.
- *Persistence or time spent.* Children's sociodramatic play may be a brief occurrence or may go on for 30 minutes. If Joellen had comforted the baby doll with rocking, then put it in its bed and wandered off to the block area to play, Smilansky would not have considered her play at a very sophisticated level.
- *Social interaction.* When Joellen involved Ricky in her play and later Nancy as the baby doctor, the level of her dramatic play increased in terms of the cognitive and social complexity. This component refers to two or more children playing together.

 *Verbal communication.* You will see children playing together and using language simply to establish roles and to organize the environment but you will also see children using language to carry on a dialogue in their pretend roles. Joellen began her play by establishing roles and a scenario: "I'm the mommy and you're the dad, and pretend that our baby is sick." Very quickly she switched and began talking as the mommy, indicating again complexity in her play.

Smilansky's components provide a framework for your observations of children's sociodramatic play. From her components, you can see that children's play can range from simple to quite complex when they engage in sociodramatic play. Another noted observer of play, Parten, provides a second potential framework for your observations.

Parten's Levels of Play

Parten outlined levels of play that started with simple immature social play and increased in social sophistication to a complex level. Those levels or categories of play will be useful for your observations of children's play and for planning curriculum.

SOLITARY PLAY. The first level, **solitary play,** is not surprising if you have watched 2-year-olds. For example, Tony is playing with a puzzle in the midst of five other young toddlers, but he does not seem at all aware of them—the puzzle has his full attention. At times, he looks up and observes Annabella playing with play-dough, but he does not interact with her, and, after a brief look, he returns to his own play. This is called **onlooker play** and it occurs during solitary play.

PARALLEL PLAY. **Parallel play** is a common form of play in a toddler class and sometimes with young preschoolers. When we visited Ibrahim's class of toddlers (Chapter 8), we often saw four toddlers sitting at a table playing with play-dough. When we watched closely, we could see that each of the four children was playing completely independently, and generally not communicating to each other. That is, they were playing in the same place, with the same materials, but involved in separate and distinct play. That is parallel play. Parten saw parallel play as a transition for children to move from solitary play to more socially interactive play.

ASSOCIATIVE PLAY. **Associative play** is similar to parallel play in that children are focused on separate play activities, but these children interact. They talk, lend materials, share, take turns with common materials, notice each other's play, and are communicative. In Ibrahim's classroom, we often saw associative play when the easels were set up outside on the playground. Two or more children would paint their own creations, but talk about what they're doing, share the red paint, and notice each other's art. We would hear them comment, "I like your painting—it's pretty" or "Oh, that's beautiful" or "You did a good job." Much of what an observer hears will reflect adult comments because children mimic adult comments. At times, it looks like the children are more interested in the social aspects of easel painting than in the painting itself.

COOPERATIVE PLAY. Parten considered **cooperative play** the highest level of social maturity in play. It is the kind of play in which two or more children engage in a common activity and share a common goal. Sometimes the tasks of the activity are divided among the players and sometimes all of the players are doing the same activity toward the common goal. In Keeley's kindergarten classroom, many hours were spent constructing with blocks. The children's comments reflect their cooperative play: "Let's all get a bunch of blocks and pile them up as high as we can," "Dani, you get the big blocks and put them over here," and "Raul, you get those boards to put across our bridge." Children have watched adults cooperate, have had opportunities to be part of a cooperative venture, and are ready for what a cooperative group can accomplish.

As children gain experience and mature, their cooperative play skills increase. They begin working in small groups, two or three children, and advance to being able to play in groups of five or six. They are also better able to manipulate materials and their environment. They have new skills and competencies, so they are able to contribute to the group goal. Children who have reached this stage are able to elaborate on ideas and to pursue complex plans. They are gradually less dependent on toys and other materials because they can use their imaginations to change the reality of what they are doing or where they are. It is fascinating to watch a group of 5- and 6-year-olds engaged in cooperative pretend play.

Kindergartners: Cooperative Pretend Play

Their kindergarten teacher, Mr. Hardt, had read them stories of the Pilgrims coming over on the *Mayflower.* The children had intense discussions about the difficult journey and how the children on the ship must have felt. The group made lists of everything they knew about the voyage and researched for more information in the school library. One day, Mr. Hardt suggested that they dramatize the voyage on the *Mayflower.* Eight of the children very enthusiastically volunteered. They went out to the playground where a huge post was to serve as the ship's mast. The children were left on their own to plan their drama. "I have an idea," said Elena, "We can hang sheets from the pole to be sails." The other children got excited with her and continued to come up with other props and a set. From there, the children decided on roles for themselves. Two boys wanted to be the Captain, so they deliberated about another important role for themselves. Alfredo agreed to be the navigator, and Joseph smiled as the Captain. Other children took on the roles of a mother, father, child, and ship workers. Without stopping to plan their script, they began dramatizing the voyage.

Joseph: "Ahoy there, I'm the Captain and I want everyone on the deck. Where is my navigator?"
Alfredo: "Here I am, sir. I will get everyone to come on deck."
Group: "Good morning, Captain."
Joseph: "My navigator tells me that we are going to hit a storm. This could be rough. You might get sick." (Aside to his teacher: "Is it OK if someone gets sick?")
Alfredo: "There will be giant waves. Don't be scared."

The scenario continues through the storm and on to a sighting of land. The group finishes excitedly, landing in Plymouth, and is ready to perform for their classmates. Note that Mr. Hardt played a small role in their play but was available for assistance if needed. He would have stepped in if the situation had warranted it, but he observed the children's ability to manage their own drama and arrangements. The adult role in children's play is a critical one, and it will be important for you to be thinking of how you will interact with children as they play. Box 4.2 takes a closer look at children interacting at play.

Adult Roles in Children's Play

When you watch children, it may seem that adults do not and should not have any roles in children's play; however, a closer look will tell you that adults have significant roles in the play. Those roles may not be obvious because some of the adult work is a type of preparation for play. That preparation includes providing the setting and materials for play, and setting up the ground rules for a play environment. Other adult roles are obvious. When adults intervene for safety reasons, or to assist a child who doesn't have the skills needed,

BOX 4.2

Play Interactions of Children in Inclusive Settings

Researchers Hestenes and Carroll (2000) observed the play of 29 children with and without disabilities in their classroom and on the playground to better understand the experiences of inclusive preschool settings for children. Legislative mandates have required that children be placed in the least restrictive environments, resulting in a huge increase in inclusive programs for children of all ages. Even though the preschool children in the study had different levels of ability, each child engaged in all of the various types of play available. Both groups of children, those with disabilities and their typically developing peers, spent more of their time in gross and fine motor play than in sensory or dramatic play.

The observers noted that typically developing children spent less time interacting with their peers with disabilities than was expected, and that children with disabilities interacted less with their typically developing peers. When children were interviewed, there was a relationship between their understanding of disability and their preference to play with peers with disabilities, but their actual observed play behavior did not agree with their stated preferences.

In this study, teacher presence was a significant predictor of children's inclusive interactions. Previous research had suggested that teachers could initiate and facilitate play between typically developing children and children with disabilities through their modeling and supervision. Although we need to understand better how teacher interactions influence children's play in inclusive settings, this study and others make it clear that a teacher's presence and support is a key factor in the frequency of inclusive interactions. It is a reminder that we need to go beyond just placing children together; we must learn more about how to *support* them in inclusive settings.

or to facilitate more complex play, they play significant roles. What's also important when thinking of adult roles is a caution about behaviors that interfere with or stop children's play. If you don't have adequate experience or don't watch children enough, your well-meaning help may have the opposite effect on children's play. As we learned in Box 4.2, your role will be critical for the play of children with disabilities. In addition to the close observation we have urged, you may need to alter the environment or adapt the play materials. The play activity may need to be simplified and you may need the assistance of the children or another adult as you support a child with disabilities (Sandall, 2003).

As you watch the children and adults in the chapters that follow, you will begin to develop your own role for being involved in children's play. For now, we will describe some important and supportive roles while cautioning you about roles that do not contribute to children's play.

Preparing the Environment for Play

Your decisions about the play environment will depend on the age and development of the children who will use it. It is quite obvious that a play setting for 1-year-olds will be different from a play setting for 6-year-olds. We urge you to study the *Developmentally Appropriate Practice in Early Childhood Programs* (Bredekamp & Copple, 1997) guidelines for how to set up environments for each age group. We begin with a recommendation that is appropriate for all ages—provide for active experiences and for challenge.

PROVIDING FOR ACTIVE EXPERIENCES AND CHALLENGES. If the setting is for infants, the room arrangement and the kinds of toys provided will encourage the infants'

Sand play offers the opportunity for both active enjoyment and learning experiences. Why do you think that sand play is such a favorite?

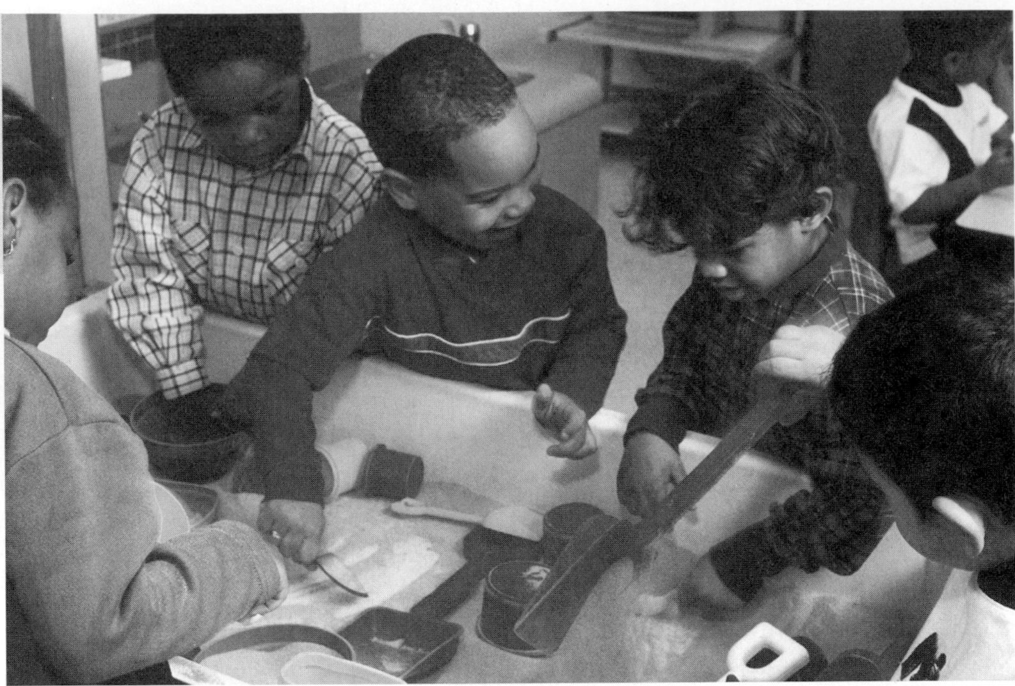

activities and challenge their newly developing skills. There will be lots of open space for rolling, crawling, and early walking without obstacles, as well as objects that can be grasped, manipulated, and enjoyed. For toddlers, the environment will include puzzles, blocks, balls, and beads to string, as well as providing housekeeping tasks that feel like play to toddlers (washing windows and tables, sweeping the floor, etc.). All of the playthings and activities are designed to challenge the children and to foster a sense of "I can do" (Wasserman, 1990). By the time children are in preschool, they need complex stimulation and changing materials to maintain learning. Many preschool programs arrange materials and equipment in centers to focus children's play. Preschool curricula often follow a project approach, so that children's play integrates all aspects of their development and builds from intense interest in a project.

SUPPORTING PRODUCTIVE PLAY. By kindergarten and primary grades, it takes a skillful adult to provide active learning experiences and challenges. Wasserman (1990) talks about "productive play activities"—activities that promote children's thinking and reasoning, and ultimately learning. Figure 4.4 describes Wasserman's criteria for productive play activities. She urges early childhood educators to adjust these guidelines to children's maturity and experience, to their independence and autonomy, and to their ability to work in groups.

BASIC CONDITIONS FOR PLAY. Bruner (1985a), another researcher of play, says that certain conditions contribute to the "richness and length of play" (p. 604). They are important conditions for you to keep in mind when you set up the environment for play and for deciding on your role. Bruner's conditions include the following:

- *A playmate.* Anyone who has watched young children at play knows that two children will play longer and engage in more complex play than one child. Many a parent will invite another child over to play because it has such a positive influence on her own child's play and it makes life easier for the parent. When there's more than one child, there is the opportunity to have conversation, to exchange materials, to get feedback on play, and to negotiate.

FIGURE 4.4

Criteria for Productive Play Activities

1. Investigative play tasks are open-ended. They do not lead students to "the answers."
2. Play tasks call for the generation of ideas, rather than the recall of specific pieces of information.
3. Play activities challenge students' thinking; indeed, they *require* thinking. Higher-order mental challenges are built into each play task.
4. Play activities are "messy." Children are, in fact, playing around. Learning through play is nonlinear, nonsequential (Wasserman, 1989).
5. Play tasks focus on "big ideas"—the important concepts of the curriculum—rather than on trivial details.
6. Each play task provides opportunities for children to grow in their conceptual understanding. When children carry out investigative play, they grow in their ability to understand larger concepts.
7. The children are the players. They are actively involved in learning. They are talking to each other, sharing ideas, speculating, laughing, and getting excited about what they have found. They are not sitting quietly, passively listening to the teacher's thinking.
8. The children are working together, in learning groups. Play is enhanced through cooperative investigations. Cooperation, rather than competitive individual work, is stressed.

Source: Reprinted by permission of the publisher from Wasserman, S., *Serious Players in the Primary Classroom: Empowering the Young Child through Active Learning Experiences* (New York: Teachers College Press, © 1990 by Teachers College, Columbia University. All rights reserved.), p. 27.

- *Appropriate play materials.* Many of the commercial play materials available today do not sustain children's attention for very long. They appear exotic and complex, but once a child has begun playing with the toy, he finds that the material is not flexible and that it can be used only in singular ways. When we visited Francis and Akosa, they lamented about the attraction of so many toys in the United States and compared those play materials with those of their childhood. "We played with simple materials—with toys that we made ourselves—and they kept us interested so much longer." They expressed regret about many of the boys' toy preferences that offered no challenge and that ended up in the toy box in a short time. They compared those choices with sets of Legos, which were a constant source of challenge as the boys constructed all kinds of things alone or together.
- *An adult nearby.* The nearby adult is not necessarily involved in the action of play, but is ready to be a buffer, a comforter, or an encourager when needed. Bruner notes that children play longer and with more complexity when an available adult is nearby. Many of us in our parenting have made the same observation and have had our children instruct us in our role. "Stay here in my room," says the child, "I just want you here while Tina and I play."

KEY ELEMENTS OF HIGH-QUALITY PLAY. In preparation for play, adults set the stage with time, space, and play materials—three key elements of high-quality play (Ward, 1996). In terms of **time,** children need long stretches of uninterrupted time to sustain different types of play, especially dramatic and constructive play. Those studying play (Johnson, Christie, & Yawkey, 1987) recommend 30- to 50-minute time blocks for free play in preschools and kindergartens in order to allow children the freedom to persist and expand on a play theme. Those observers also note that when children are repeatedly hampered by play periods that are too short, they resort to very simple forms of play.

The second key element is **space.** Children need sufficient space to play effectively. Experts believe that young children need at least 25 to 30 square feet to play well. In addition to the amount of space, the arrangement of space has an impact on children's play. Programs for young children usually avoid large open spaces because those spaces don't encourage high-quality play. In fact, those spaces often encourage running and rough and tumble play. Instead, partitioned spaces encourage focused play, especially dramatic play.

The third key element is **play materials.** Materials must be selected for appropriateness with respect to children's development. An environment with too few materials will not support children's high-quality play, but an environment with too many materials will confuse, distract, and interrupt children's high-quality play. One of the best ways to decide about play materials is to watch children use them and to consider the goals for children. Play materials must provide opportunities to experience and develop toward those goals. For example, if a goal for primary children is literacy, then plenty of literacy materials should be placed in the environment. Those materials will include typewriters, computers, paper of all kinds, a variety of writing utensils, books, games, lap pads, mailboxes, envelopes, and newspapers. If a goal for toddlers is the development of small motor skills, then the play materials should include play-dough, crayons and markers, puzzles, beads, interlocking blocks, and miniature figures.

In time, children can make many choices about their environment and can gather their own play materials. Children as young as age 3 can describe their environmental needs, can suggest ways to rearrange the environment, and are able to propose changes in play materials. In those situations, adults will serve as guides or facilitators.

Children's development advances when they have opportunities to practice newly acquired skills as well as to experience a challenge just beyond their level of present mastery. Your observation of children will be critical in determining what they are ready for, what they need to practice, and what will nudge them with a challenge. If a preschooler enjoys the puzzles currently out on the shelf, and each day appears to be assembling them with increasing ease, then it's probably time to put a few new puzzles out and to make sure that they are just slightly more difficult.

Intervening at the Right Time: Secure Play

Professionals who work with young children worry about inhibiting or disrupting children's play with interventions. There are, however, appropriate times for adult intervention—times when their role is to assist, to challenge, and to question children's play. Beyond safety issues, determining the right time to intervene and how to intervene is a critical decision for early childhood educators. We describe some of the most frequent "right times" and suggest possibilities for your intervention.

HELPING CHILDREN ENTER ONGOING PLAY. Until children develop the skills of making contact with others or of gaining access to a group situation, they may need supportive adults to assist them. This is the initiation phase we described earlier in the chapter. Ramsey (1991) encourages adults to help the child who has not been invited to join or who does not know how to make contact with those at play. "Interactions in preschool classrooms are short, so children are constantly having to gain entry into new groups. This process is made more difficult because children who are already engaged with each other tend to protect their interactive space and reject newcomers" (p. 27).

This may be true, depending on how the classroom environment has been set up. Many educators currently work to build a sense of community in classrooms, and in some programs, children take responsibility for each other and take the initiative to help each other. Early childhood educators may nevertheless need to model an entry for the child by encouraging her to say, "I want to play blocks with you" or "I would like to join your game." You may also help the child enter by taking on a new role in the ongoing play by suggesting to her, "Ring the doorbell and announce that the pizza is here." Another strategy comes from Beatty (1995), who suggests that you encourage the child to begin parallel play next to the group with the hope that the group will eventually let her in. Group or activity entry is a very important social skill and children will need your guidance, encouragement, modeling, and coaching so that they can become skilled.

> Play access struggles with other children are the most critical learning opportunities that young children must deal with. Such conflicts teach profound lessons in getting along with others: how to watch and wait, when to initiate contact, how to learn what is going on in the play, how to blend in with the group, what to say so you won't be rejected, and what to do in case you are rejected. These crucial lessons are repeated over and over as children ebb and flow during free play. (Beatty, 1995, p. 108)

Not only will you be assisting children who need your help in gaining entry to a play group but you will also be teaching crucial social skills when you assist children in those situations.

ADDRESSING UNOCCUPIED BEHAVIOR. In many classrooms and programs, a child will be seen wandering aimlessly or generally unoccupied while all around him are children intensely involved in play. There are several possibilities for a child's unoccupied behavior: boredom, overstimulation, illness, and emotional upset, to name a few. To determine the reason, you will need to have been a good observer so that you know the child well. Using your clues from previous observations, your relationship with the child will assist you in probing the reason for his behavior. If it's boredom, you have some fairly simple approaches easily available. It may be time to bring out some new play materials, adding more interest and challenge to the environment. This is an ideal time to find out what interests the child at home so that you can build on those interests. Be sure to listen to conversations to find out topics of interest that will direct some of your choices of materials.

Sometimes, overstimulation will cause children to wander. Too many choices, too much noise, too many people, or too much activity affects some children with confusion. Find a more secluded part of the room (or make one with partitions) and offer just two or three choices.

If the reason for unoccupied behavior is illness or emotional upset, then you will need to address those issues before the child can play happily. We have often found that when children who are just on the verge of being sick come to the child care center or school, they will wander aimlessly. They're just not themselves, but they don't know what to do about it.

INTERVENING TO ADD CHALLENGE OR TO STIMULATE. When you intervene to challenge or stimulate, you run the risk of turning the play into work. So we urge caution here. Here are some examples of when this intervention is warranted:

> When children are having difficulty getting along and playing together
> When children's play seems repetitious and about to dissolve
> When children do not initiate or engage in pretend play (Ward, 1996, p. 22)

You have several possibilities for intervention to address those situations. The first is a good starting point for you when you are developing experience and skill in your role as an early childhood educator.

- *Parallel play for adults.* We urge you to try parallel play for yourself. Position yourself beside the child and model the play behaviors you are encouraging. Don't try to interact or direct the child's play. This nonthreatening approach is a great way to help children extend their play with new materials and behaviors.

- *Co-playing for adults.* Another approach is to co-play. Very often, children will invite an adult to co-play with them, and it's a good opportunity to encourage and enrich their play. Children especially like their teachers to join them when they play restaurant, house, or airplane. Once on the scene, the teacher's dialogue can enhance the play. Listen:

    Child: Teacher, teacher, come to our house.
    Teacher: May I come to visit you today?

Child: Sure, come in and sit down. We're having lunch.

Teacher: Oh, I don't want to interrupt your meal. Maybe I should come back another time.

Child: Oh, no, we want you to come in. You can eat with us.

Teacher: Thanks, I would like that. What are you having for lunch?

Child: Chicken and pizza. Do you want some?

Teacher: Well I'm a vegetarian, so I eat only vegetables. Do you have any?

Child: Oh, sure, I'll fix you some. Honey (directed to second child), can you go to the store and buy some vegetables? (Other child leaves and returns with a brown paper bag.)

You get the idea. Your conversation begins to add depth and new ideas to the play. Your co-play is nonthreatening because you've established rapport by playing in their setting, one that they have established. In the process, you have the potential to help children persist in their play, to include other children in the play, and to ask higher-level questions to extend the play. Besides that, it's fun.

Other intervention strategies come from Smilansky (1968), who studied children's pretend play extensively. Her two strategies are more direct but have the potential to stimulate children who are uninvolved or playing rather listlessly.

- *Outside intervention.* With outside intervention, you make suggestions to a child or children from outside the play. You may be sitting nearby and suggest to Julia that she visit the group playing house, or that she schedule an appointment at the beauty shop, or that she apply for a job at the store.
- *Inside intervention.* Inside intervention requires you to put yourself in the middle of the children's play. It's quite intrusive but sometimes necessary. For example, let's say the children are sitting together playing with blocks and not much is happening. There is no interaction and not much construction. You go and sit in the middle, saying, "I think that I'd like to build an airport. Would anyone like to help me?" Hopefully, you will soon have an energetic group busily constructing runways and terminals all around you.

Deciding to intervene in children's play is a complex decision. Why might this adult be intervening?

A Playful Attitude: Sending a Message of Acceptance

Children watch adults every minute of the day, whether the adults are involved in play or not. What we adults say and do—even what we wear—sends messages about how we feel about play. Our attitude about events in our classrooms or programs sets a tone for the environment.

David Elkind (2003) is concerned about the pressures of society and the need for "recollections of happy moments" to comfort both children and adults. Not only does he urge us to provide support and resources for children's play but also to "adopt a playful attitude that will encourage children to do the same" (p. 50).

LAUGHING SENDS A MESSAGE. Our first recommendation for being playful is to find as many opportunities as possible to laugh. When an unexpected event happens in your class or when you're with children, try to find humor in it. It will be especially effective if you can laugh at yourself. Children can learn to do the same if they see significant adults laughing at themselves. Children are learning to tell jokes, so why not consider telling them a simple joke every day? Also, be ready for young children's jokes. They often don't make sense, but children find them hilariously funny.

When children become silly, you will need to determine whether it is an appropriate time to laugh with them, and even be silly yourself, or whether they need a focus or direction. Much will depend on the children's usual play behavior and on the situation (what other children are doing and whether the silliness will disturb the setting). If there is tension or the children are growing weary, then it may be just the right time to unwind with everyone laughing.

You might also consider doing some pretend laughing. Picture this: You are sitting with a group of children and you suggest, "Let's all laugh for one minute." Or you might set the scene—"As you are walking down the street, you see a little red and white dog with a bow on each of his ears and pretzels on his tail and . . ."—and wait for the giggles. Or you might ask each child, in turn, to "laugh like a king," "laugh like a baby," "laugh like a hyena," "laugh like a monster," and so on. Or if it's a noisy day, ask the children to laugh without making any sound.

What we are encouraging here is to communicate that the environment is safe and supportive of play. If children know that you laugh at your mistakes and that you can be silly once in a while (or more often than that), they will be secure in their play.

PARTICIPATION SENDS A MESSAGE. At times in this chapter we've urged you to enter children's play for intervention purposes. Now we suggest that you sit and play with children for no reason at all. For example, when a few children are playing with play-dough, sit with them and roll the dough and pat it and make something from it. Or when children are lying on the floor reading books, get down on the floor and read with them. Or when children are painting, get in there and paint, too. You might feel inhibited about finger painting or dancing to music, but you can get used to it well in advance of working with children. Gather a group of your friends who also want to work with young children, and plan a play party. Use the time to experience lots of the play materials and activities that you will later provide for children.

The advantages of joining the play of children are abundant. You send a message about the value of play and about your relationship with them. You also increase their comfort level for interacting with you. While playing with children, you will be able to observe information about their development, and they may tell you about themselves in ways that wouldn't ordinarily happen. They will feel increased security with you. You might also find that you have fun.

In sum, the adult role is a significant one—one of decision making at all times. An early childhood educator can never be on "remote." Constant watching, listening, interacting, and responding are required. Your role in children's play is one that can contribute to and support their learning and development, but you will make frequent decisions about that role.

PRINCIPLES AND INSIGHTS: A Summary and Reflection

A set of principles of child development and learning inform developmentally appropriate practice for working with children and families from infancy through primary grades. One of those principles clearly states the role and value of play: "Play is an important vehicle for children's social, emotional, and cognitive development, as well as a reflection of their development" (Bredekamp & Copple, 1997, p. 14). Those principles also encompass other important elements for children's development and learning:

- The importance of practice
- The need for different modes of learning
- The need for different ways for children to represent what they know
- The importance of active learning
- The need for direct physical and social knowledge

All of these elements add up to play. It is the one approach that satisfies the principles of development and learning, assuring us that children's growth is furthered and enhanced through play. Therefore, child-initiated, adult-supported play is an essential component of developmentally appropriate practice (Bredekamp & Copple, 1997, p. 14). In the chapters ahead, you will see that children from infancy through primary grades have a need for and greatly benefit from play.

In this chapter, we asked you to begin thinking about play. What does play mean? What is the value of play? What characteristics will you see in children's play? From there, we described the changes in children's play as they mature from infancy to toddlerhood to preschool and to kindergarten and primary grades. Begin watching the children in your life or the children you encounter in the grocery store or at the park so that you become more aware of different levels of play. We put emphasis on children's social development in play so that you would be especially watchful of social changes and growth. Finally, we described your role in children's play. It is a strategic role and one that demands your constant awareness of children and their play.

You are entering the early childhood education profession at a time when children's play is changing and there are many professionals who are concerned about the changes. In the last 20 or 30 years, children spent more time playing alone at home. They have graduated from educational toys to video and computer games. Their pretend play is intensely influenced by books and TV shows and they do not use their imaginations well. Children today appear to depend on concrete materials or props, and resort to repeating aggressive actions over and over again instead of developing involved play scenarios (Bodrova & Leong, 2003, pp. 10–11).

Children's play will be an essential and rewarding part of your professional life. Be ready to be open to children—their freshness, their creativity, their energy, and their seriousness. Play is truly their business—and they will want your respect, appreciation, and participation.

BECOMING AN EARLY CHILDHOOD PROFESSIONAL

Your Professional Portfolio

1. Record a series of children's play episodes in which there may be a need for adult intervention. Describe your decision about an adult's role in those episodes and give a rationale for what you prescribe.
2. Write a letter to the editor of your local newspaper, advocating better playgrounds for the children of your community. Describe the values of play and the kind of play settings that promote children's development.

Your Professional Library

Bredekamp, S., & Copple, C. (1997). *Developmentally appropriate practice in early childhood programs* (2nd ed.). Washington, DC: NAEYC.

Bronson, M. (1995). *The right stuff for children birth to 8: Selecting play materials to support development.* Washington, DC: NAEYC.

Hirsch, E. S. (Ed.). (1984). *The block book.* Washington, DC: NAEYC.

Jones, E., & Reynolds, G. (1992). *The play is the thing: Teachers' roles in children's play.* New York: Teachers College Press.

Owocki, G. (1999). *Literacy through play.* Plymouth, NH: Heinemann.

Paley, V. G. (1990). *The boy who would be helicopter.* Cambridge, MA: Harvard University Press.

Rogers, C., & Sawyer, J. (1988). *Play in the lives of children.* Washington, DC: NAEYC.

VanHoorn, J., Nourot, P., Scales, B., & Alward, K. (1999). *Play at the center of the curriculum.* Columbus, OH: Merrill.

CHAPTER 5

Early Childhood Curriculum

Thinking and Practices

CHAPTER focus:

When you finish reading and reflecting on this chapter, you will be able to:

1. Define curriculum and identify its major elements while observing an early childhood program.
2. Describe the philosophy and thinking of major early childhood education curricular approaches and list their intended outcomes for children.
3. Differentiate among programs such as Bank Street, High Scope, Waldorf, and Reggio Emilia.
4. Describe how an inclusive curriculum accommodates and promotes the success of all children.
5. Begin to embed assessment in the curricular activities of young children.
6. Begin to weave several curricular approaches into your future planning for children.

Maybe you've heard the term **curriculum** before or maybe this is your first encounter. If you're currently taking a class in early childhood education, your course syllabus is a form of curriculum. It usually has course goals or objectives, a description of the content, learning activities or an outline of course topics, and information about how your learning will be assessed. So even if you haven't heard the term before, you now have a beginning idea of what curriculum is. We'll begin this chapter with a much broader understanding of curriculum and then look at examples in early childhood education.

What Is Curriculum?

To help you think about curriculum in an expansive way, reflect on how you spend your time on an ordinary day. For example, one of your authors starts her day at 6:00 A.M. with a walk around the downtown area of the city for an hour. It's like a field trip—there are always fresh store windows, new construction, another shop opening, and unusual people watching. The walk is followed by coffee and a quick bath, then breakfast while looking at the local newspaper. Even on the dullest of days, something catches my eye in the news and I learn some new information or hear a story that leaves me thinking all day. Leaving the house for a day at the university includes a look at the calendar to organize for the scheduled events. Most days include a meeting or two, student appointments, and communicating with students, colleagues, and community members by phone or e-mail.

Teaching classes fills the late afternoon, and then catching up on paperwork finishes the day. Often, before leaving work, I reflect on the day and assess what was accomplished. I also make a plan for the next day—a "to-do" list. The evening races by—supper, a few phone calls, and reading professional journals or a good novel. Then it's off to sleep at 11:00 P.M. In a sense, that is my daily curriculum—the intent of the day, the activities, the environments, the people with whom I interact, and the assessment of the day's work. Each day, I learn from my friends and family, from the local newspaper, from a discussion at a meeting, from a cookbook, from an e-mail message, from journals or a novel, and from my students. All are sources of ideas, issues, questions, problems, insights, and stimulation. Even on my most ordinary day, the curriculum of my life is rich and full.

JOURNAL 5.1: Pause here and reflect on the curriculum of your life. What kind of ideas or insights do you gain on an ordinary day? Who are the people you learn from? Where do you learn best? What is there about the environment that helps you learn? What keeps you learning? What is the most exciting curriculum your day holds? How much of your typical day is planned and how much emerges or evolves?

After you finish reflecting on your day, see if you can develop a definition of *curriculum.* That will be our starting point as we work together on this chapter's discussion of important ideas about curriculum and significant curricular practices. What are the significant words in your definition? List them in your journal. Now that you have a bit of comfort with the term, we're going to move to an educational context for defining curriculum.

Defining Curriculum

Think of yourself as a teacher. Your definition of curriculum now becomes a kind of teaching plan that emerges from your philosophy about learning. It is influenced by what you know about child development and by your own experiences as a student. When you think about your experiences as a young 4- or 5-year-old student, what do you remember? How would you define curriculum if all you knew were those early educational experiences? Curriculum has been defined as "an organized framework that delineates the skills and content that children are to learn" (Helm, 2003, p. 6). From that framework, you make the decisions about how children are to learn. That's why we described decision making as an important quality of early childhood educators in Chapter 1.

CURRICULUM PLANS. For many teachers, their curriculum or teaching plan usually includes goals and objectives; descriptions of teaching and learning activities; lists of materials, equipment, and resources; schedules, if needed; and assessment strategies. There are year-long curriculum plans, monthly curriculum plans, and weekly curriculum plans (see Figure 5.1) as well as written and unwritten curricula (the plural of *curriculum*) and commercially developed curricula. When groups of teachers from one school district develop curriculum, such as that found in Figure 5.2, individual teachers typically use that framework to design other parts of the learning plan.

At the time of this writing, teachers at all levels are urged to attend to national standards in the disciplinary areas. In the chapter on primary grades, we discuss the standards for math, science, social studies, and literacy, and we urge you to get acquainted with those standards through their websites. The standards, much like the school district examples in Figure 5.2, provide sets of skills and understandings in a hierarchy, starting with simple concepts or abilities for young children and extending to more abstract and complex ideas and higher-level skills for older children. Whether you use the standards or a school district curriculum or that of a particular preschool, you will need to start with what you know and believe about children and learning.

The idea of curriculum being a teaching plan is interpreted in many different ways by educators. Some early childhood educators say that you should follow the children's

FIGURE 5.1

Weekly Plan from an Elementary Teacher

Sept. GRADE OR CLASS First (Robin) WEEK BEGINNING

	Before Sch.	Enter 8:40–9	Arrival (reg.) 9–9:30	Whole Group 9:30–10	Recess 10–10:15		Literacy Centers → 10:15–11:15	Clean & Inspect 11:15 to 11:25	Lunch 11:30 to 12	Quiet Reading 12–12:30	Share Books 12:20 to 12:30	Math 12:30–1	Learning Centers 1–1:40		Recess 1:50 to 2	Gathering 2:05–2:20
18 MONDAY	Ann Carstiom here PSU (new jobs) (Zaro's 1st B-day)	journals	✓ New jobs ✓ Calendar ✓ Zaro's B-day ✓ Read: Not this Bear	Writing (review use of writers' workshop boxes)			finish spelling assess.			Theme tabs Beavers & Squirrels / Ravenbooks otters & Racoons		Discovery time Ask kids rules (review) + Q + Q! Write down "Math News" (on easel chart?)		↑		Read: Buzzy Bear or The Garden / take home Zaro dittos!
19 TUESDAY		↓	Calendar Shoe patler 8 rules Read: Bledford Bear	↓	Library	Recess 10:30 to 10:45	Lit. Centers 10:45-11:15 Label room "otter clan" (make pics) Diana 10:50-11:10		↓	Ravenbooks Beavers & Squirrels / Theme tabs otters & Racoons		Pattern pages (little brown beans) (first do up real bears again)	Redo Math Assess.	↓ clean up & inspection 1:40-1:50		Read: ~~Ernest & Celestine~~ discuss care of records
20 WEDNESDAY		↓	Calendar (Dot chart patterns) (Read: Breakfast time)	↓	P.E.		Literacy Centers 10:30-11:15 (no recess on gym day a.m.) Label room "Squirrel Clan"		↓	Magazines to each clan		Discovery time see Mon.	↓			Read: Ernest & Celestine / Take home Bear note!
21 THURSDAY	get math books for Fri	↓	Calendar (Dot chart patterns) Read:	Make an award for your bear	Music	Recess 10:30 to 10:45	Lit. Centers 10:45-11:15 Meeting Note, Meagan and Matt Rewriting time expectations	Pam here	↓ Cindy here ↓	Textbooks to each clan in color tubs (New-show how to)		Bear Measuring Stations Unifix cubes scale string make booklet	↓ early clean up! do Math Assess!	ready to go home		Computer 2-2:23 (no recess and leave from comp. lab. room)
22 FRIDAY	✓ Math pages!	↓	Calendar (Dot chart patterns) Read: Who will be my friend?	↓ Write about your bear (use blank bear ditto)	Recess 10 to 10:15	Lit. Centers 10:15–10:50 → Meeting Caritza, Mario, Jesus—ABC cards	Clean time 10:50 / Entertainment time 11 to 11:25			Library books Otters & Racoons / Theme tubs Beavers & Squirrels		Math books pp. 1-16	↓ Math Assess.	clean & inspect		Outside w/ Bears (Recess & stories)

Source: Robin Lindsley, Primary Teacher, Boise-Eliot School, Portland, OR 97227. Reprinted by permission.

FIGURE 5.2
Canby School District: Mathematics

Math Awareness *(Kindergarten)*

Measurement
- Begins to understand differences in length and weight
- Begins to explore measuring using non-standard measurement

Developing Math *(First Grade)*

Measurement
- Explores the concepts of length, weight, money, temperature, and time
- Begins using non-standard measurement
- Begins to make estimates of measurement for length and weight
- Makes predictions using vocabulary: likely, unlikely, and certain

Expanding Math *(Second Grade)*

Measurement
- Uses non-standard and begins to use standard measurement
- Understands the concepts of length, weight, money, time, and temperature
- Makes estimations of measurement for length and weight

Benchmark Level I *(Third Grade)*

Measurement
- Develops understanding of length (U.S. & metric), weight, money, time, temperature, area, perimeter, volume, and angle
- Uses non-standard and standard for length, weight, money, time, temperature, area, perimeter, volume, and angle measurement
- Makes and uses estimates to measure length and weight

Source: Canby School District, Canby, OR. Reprinted by permission.

lead for your curriculum. Let's look at another way of defining curriculum to understand that notion of following the lead of the children in your care.

AUTHENTIC CURRICULUM. Another way of thinking about curriculum is what Sobel calls **authentic curriculum**—"the process of movement from the inside out, taking curriculum impulses from the inside of the child and bringing them out into the light of day, into the classroom" (1994, p. 35). Sobel's ideas are much like those of Froebel, the creator of kindergarten, who encouraged us to bring ideas out of children rather than put them in. Listen again to Sobel's words: "Authentic curriculum is what springs forth from the genuine, unmediated individual and developmental fascinations of children and teachers" (p. 33). You won't find this kind of curriculum planned out on paper; it just happens! Hawkins (1973) describes it as "some little accident" that occurs when you are not expecting it, presenting you with the opportunity to encourage a new learning or curiosity. "The bird flies in the window and that's the miracle you needed," says Hawkins (p. 499). Another term for this thinking about curriculum is **emergent curriculum.** When you visit the toddler program in Chapter 7, you will see and hear about this kind of curriculum.

The blend of planned curriculum and spontaneous curriculum is very much like our lives. Even on the most organized or tightly scheduled day, unexpected events are accommodated and often provide the real stimulation and learning of the day. For instance, when your friend calls you to meet for lunch to discuss a problem, your thinking takes off in a new direction. Or when you see an interesting new plant in the park or a striking work of art in a gallery window, your day is enriched.

The two kinds of curricula, planned and spontaneous, can comfortably work together in the way you teach children. You can begin with a well-planned curriculum that expresses your philosophy and matches what you know about child development. Then within that curriculum, you stay flexible to seize the moment when curriculum emerges from the children's interest or curiosity or from an exciting event. Contrast the following examples:

Planned versus Spontaneous

Mrs. Mahoney's first-grade children were studying the concept of size and had looked at shoes, houses in the neighborhood, cars, and themselves. They measured items in their classroom as well as on the playground. It was an interesting curriculum with lots of real examples. One day, as they were listening to a story about size, a fire drill occurred. Instead of the usual practice, there were fire trucks in the parking lot participating in the drill. When the children returned to their classroom, they could see the trucks outside their classroom window and they talked excitedly about them. Mrs. Mahoney insisted that they return to their circle and finish the story about size. The children did so reluctantly and with little enthusiasm for the concept of size at that moment.

Another group of first-graders were beginning to write about a book they had just read when it began to snow. It was the first snow of the year in a city where it seldom snowed. Needless to say, all of the attention was "out the window" and so Ms. Reeves encouraged the children, "Go and get a good look at the weather." After a few minutes when the excitement eased, she asked the children to think of words to describe the snow. She wrote the ideas on the chalkboard as the children talked about *white, pretty, cold, flakes, wet, dancing, sparkle, shiny,* and *fun,* as they continued to press their noses to the windows. Ms. Reeves then encouraged them to go to their tables and write about the snow. There was little hesitation when children sat down—their ideas seemed to flow onto their papers.

Both Ms. Reeves and Mrs. Mahoney had a curriculum plan. Like many teachers, Mrs. Mahoney felt compelled to finish what she had planned for the children. Being flexible is not easy for many of us, especially after you've spent time planning your objectives and activities. You have probably experienced situations similar to what happened in these first-grade classrooms in your role as an adult learner. One of us was teaching a course about play and its curricular implications when the Gulf War broke out. To have continued with the curriculum plan for the evening class would have been insensitive and frustrating for everyone. The students needed to talk about the war. One had a son stationed overseas and she came to class feeling weepy. Another was teaching kindergarten and wanted to get ideas about how to talk to children about war. Another came into class out of breath, telling us, "This parent stopped me as I was leaving school and she was so thrilled that we were at war. She kept talking about how it was time that we took action and let them know that they can't get away with things." Everyone processed the event in some way that evening. We actually got to the topic of war play for children and had the opportunity to talk about research and philosophy related to children's play with guns and pretend fighting. It was spontaneous and meaningful curriculum connected to the planned curriculum of the course.

Expanding the Definition

By now, you have some beginning ideas of what curriculum is and can be. We think that good teachers start with well-planned curriculum and stay open to authentic curriculum, or "teachable moments." Before exploring ideas about curriculum, we want to add a few more definitions to your picture of curriculum. Some of the more important curricular approaches or aspects of curriculum will be discussed next.

PHILOSOPHY OF CURRICULUM. Your **philosophy of curriculum** consists of your beliefs and values related to curriculum. When you have developed such a philosophy, it will be influenced by your beliefs about children and what they need to grow and learn.

It will also be influenced by your own experiences as a child—learning from your family, your community, your school situations, and your peers. In Chapter 1, we described the influence of teacher biographies on their teaching. Your philosophy will certainly be influenced by your preparation courses and the materials you read, such as this book. Visits to early childhood programs will affect your philosophy, as will conversations with your peers. If you have children of your own, your parenting role will also influence your philosophy of curriculum.

In the sections ahead, you will encounter the thinking of brilliant early childhood educators who have very distinctive philosophies of curriculum. Their philosophies directed the kind of programs they planned for the children in their care—the type of materials selected, the manner of environment arranged, the kind of adult/child interactions that occur, the way the day is scheduled, and the variety of activities provided for the children.

DEVELOPMENTALLY APPROPRIATE CURRICULUM. **Developmentally appropriate curriculum** (or **practices**) is a term for the kind of curriculum that recognizes and appreciates children's levels of development, growth, and interest. It is curriculum that accommodates a child's physical, emotional, social, and cognitive readiness. Developmentally appropriate curriculum draws in children because it appeals to their natural curiosity, it nurtures their spontaneous thinking and doing, and it encourages their creative spirit. In a program for 2-year-olds, for example, developmentally appropriate curriculum is seen in the use of low tables that are set up with play-dough, puzzles with three or four pieces, and lots of water play. Plenty of materials are available, so children don't have to share, and large blocks of time are allotted for free exploration without interruption.

Developmentally appropriate programs may look very different, but they are characterized by three common principles:

1. They take into account the educator's knowledge of how young children develop and learn in the kind of activities and outcomes that are planned for the programs.
2. Children are seen and planned for as individuals, not as groups of 4-year-olds or toddlers.
3. Children are treated with respect and understanding—with sensitivity to their changing capacities and a "faith in their continuing capacity to change" (Kostelnik, Soderman, & Whiren, 1993, pp. 32–33).

Teachers who have a strong foundation of knowledge of child development and learning are able to use developmentally appropriate practices (DAP) successfully (Snider & Fu, 1990). Regardless of the curriculum or the approaches you select, the thinking of developmentally appropriate practice can frame what you do and how you do it. We will return to DAP later in this book, but you should also know that developmentally appropriate practices and curriculum are described in a set of guidelines developed by the National Association for the Education of Young Children (Bredekamp & Copple, 1997). They are an essential to have on hand when making curricular decisions or planning curricular activities. You will find yourself using the NAEYC guidelines so frequently that the famous green book will be quite worn out when you begin to teach.

INTEGRATED CURRICULUM. The word *integrated* means interwoven like a braid. **Integrated curriculum** reflects the natural connections between school and life and promotes a meaningful and relevant learning context (Nagel, 1996). It promotes holistic learning and builds on the relationships among science, math, language, the arts, and other curricular subject areas. If the children are exploring math concepts while painting a collage to represent their neighborhood and writing labels for the buildings and streets, you have integrated curriculum with geometry, literacy, and art. While the children are constructing their pizza snacks, if you are recording each child's recipe for making pizza and will later read the recipe cards with individual children, you are integrating literacy with a cooking activity, which itself integrates math and science through measurement and combining ingredients to create a new whole (i.e., the pizza).

THEMATIC CURRICULUM. As its name implies, **thematic curriculum** is curriculum built around a theme or a project. It is an ideal approach to curriculum, especially for young learners, because all of the curricular areas (math, science, literacy, art, music, etc.) can be connected within a theme as the children work on a project. We recently observed a summer curriculum for kindergarten and first-grade children focused on *links* as a theme. During the week of activities, children studied patterns of chain link fences throughout their neighborhood, made paper links, found natural links in the environment, explored ways to link with each other in creative movement activities, and made up a song about friendship with the word *links* used repeatedly in the chorus. The *links* theme enabled the teachers and the children to connect science, math, art, music, social skills, and literacy throughout the curriculum.

You probably have begun to notice how these variations of curriculum reflect specific thinking or philosophies about how children learn. That's an important theme as we continue through this chapter.

Chapter Preview

We'll return to these definitions of curriculum later with more examples. We intend to integrate or connect them to other ideas about curriculum, and it will be helpful that you are now somewhat familiar with the terminology. You may encounter these terms as we explore ideas about curriculum from the work and writings of Maria Montessori, Sylvia Ashton-Warner, Caroline Pratt, Constance Kamii and Rheta DeVries, and Carl Bereiter and Siegfried Engelmann, and from programs such as Bank Street, High Scope, Waldorf, and Reggio Emilia. Before moving on to these ideas, take a few moments and go back to Chapter 2. Review the ideas of Froebel, Piaget, and Gardner, for their work is most significant when we talk about curriculum.

CURRICULUM IDEAS: FROM PHILOSOPHY TO PRACTICES. A number of great thinkers have spent their lives observing children, creating theories about how children develop and learn, and recommending how best to promote that development and learning. We would be negligent to approach the study of curriculum without looking at these experts' ideas to help you get the "big picture" of what curriculum is and can be. We want to do so with a critical eye, however; that is, we want you to be ready to stop and reflect about each person's ideas. As you read, try to keep your child development information at the forefront and pay attention to your intuition about children and people, in general. We agree with some of the thinking and practices discussed in this chapter, but we also disagree with some of it. We will attempt to present these ideas neutrally because this is a time for you to begin to form opinions, to critique, and to make decisions concerning your beliefs and intentions about work with children. Stop and reflect as you read. Talk about the ideas with your peers. Ask questions in your classes. Be open to many possibilities.

Ideas about Curriculum

Maria Montessori

Maria Montessori is probably the best known of the thinkers we will describe in this chapter. She was the first Italian female physician, and, years ahead of her time, was a feminist and a children's advocate. She became intrigued with the education of young children for various reasons. She did not like the rigidity of Italian public education and was concerned about the education of children who were mentally retarded or delayed.

Montessori abandoned her role in medicine at a time when Italy's economy was precarious, when many families lived in poverty and in facilities without regard to health and safety. As she pondered her concerns about the situation, a reform movement brought about programs of employment for parents. That was the good news. The bad news was that children were left alone for long days.

MONTESSORI'S THINKING. The situation of children without care attracted Montessori's attention. Influenced by what she knew as a physician and by her efforts to educate "deficient children," she developed Children's Houses *(Casas dei Bambini)*—schools for children living in the tenement apartments of Rome. Montessori's ideas were reshaped over the years as she worked with both poor and wealthy children, as society changed, and as her ideas were transported to other countries, specifically the United States. To begin to understand her ideas, it's important to look at Montessori's five dominant beliefs:

1. Her method represents a scientific approach to education.
2. The secret of childhood resides in the fact that through their spontaneous activity, children labor to "make themselves into men" [Montessori, 1964].
3. Mental development, similar to physical growth, is the result of a natural, internally regulated force.
4. Liberty is the imperative ingredient that enables education to assist the "unfolding of a child's life" [Montessori, 1964].
5. Order, most especially within the child, but also in the child's environment, is prerequisite to the child becoming an independent, autonomous, and rational individual. (Goffin, 1994, p. 49)

What do these statements mean? Basically, Montessori believed that children could grow and develop very well if left to do so without too many restrictions but with an orderly environment that promoted their efforts at being independent and critical thinkers. Her approach was scientific in that it evolved from studying children and what they could do and in that she prescribed both teaching techniques and materials for her schools.

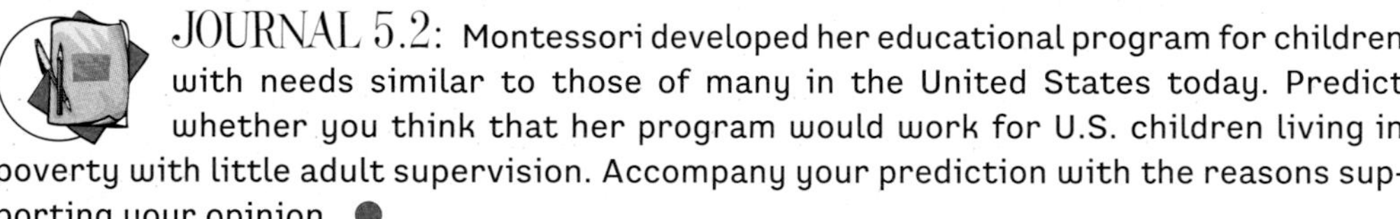

JOURNAL 5.2: Montessori developed her educational program for children with needs similar to those of many in the United States today. Predict whether you think that her program would work for U.S. children living in poverty with little adult supervision. Accompany your prediction with the reasons supporting your opinion. ●

MONTESSORI'S ADVICE IN ACTION. Montessori urged teachers to conduct naturalistic observations of children in *carefully prepared environments.* This refers to the orderly environments we talked about in Montessori's beliefs—environments planned to promote the children's freedom to take care of their own needs and freedom from dependency on others (the goals described in her beliefs). Teachers in a Montessori program are to observe and direct children's learning, so they are called directresses rather than teachers.

If you walked into a Montessori program, you would likely see several rooms for different purposes, child-sized furniture and equipment, real dishes and other items, flowers and plants, and well-organized materials with careful storage and labeling. Materials, which are a very important aspect of the curriculum, are generally carefully crafted. They are displayed in open shelves for children's independent use. Many materials are graded in difficulty; that is, they range from simple to use to very difficult or complex to use. Montessori's materials are often **autotelic,** or self-correcting, so that the child has immediate feedback.

IN A MONTESSORI CLASSROOM. Looking back at Montessori's goals for children, it's easy to understand the environment and ultimately the curriculum. As children de-

The attraction between Maria Montessori and children with whom she worked appears to be reciprocal.

velop the ability to take care of their own needs, they learn best from firsthand experience. In a Montessori classroom, they have *practical life experiences* such as gardening, polishing silver, buttoning and zipping, and flower arranging. Directresses make sure that each activity builds a foundation for a more complex and difficult activity or task, because Montessori believed that learning is cumulative. Most of the day is spent in individual tasks or activities, rather than in group activities. Children move freely about the classroom and make their own choices.

If you are comfortable with Montessori's ideas and want to see them in action, we encourage you to visit a program in your area. There are many Montessori schools and classes in the United States; there are even some Montessori classrooms in public schools. Be aware of the authenticity of the program you observe. Some programs use the Montessori name but are not faithful to her ideas. You can check with the professional associations concerned with implementing Montessori programs. One of them is the American Montessori Society (AMS) founded in 1956. That organization oversees the training of directresses and accreditation of schools in the United States.

From Montessori's advice to watch children in order to know how to teach them, we move to another woman with similar thinking.

Sylvia Ashton-Warner

If asked, Sylvia Ashton-Warner would say that the raw materials of curriculum for children are "patience, caring, listening, intuition, and the elements in nature" (Mamchur, 1983). Like Montessori, her ideas are considered creative and original; unlike Montessori, Ashton-Warner was contemporary. Her ideas originated from over 20 years, most of her adult life, of teaching Maori children and being taught by them.

IDEAS ABOUT CHILDREN. To understand Ashton-Warner's ideas about curriculum, it is essential to understand her ideas about children. They are definitely unique. Listen to her words (because we can't possibly capture the meaning without her eloquence) describing the children with whom she worked: "I see the mind of a five year old as a volcano with two vents: destructiveness and creativeness. And I see that to the extent that when we widen the creative channel, we atrophy the destructive one" (1963, p. 33).

With that thinking, it's easy to see why Ashton-Warner would emphasize creative activities and spontaneous expressions of children. Her notion of children also included an emphasis on their aggressiveness. She saw it as an instinct without which many world events would not occur. She labeled children's mental and emotional reactions as aggressive and believed them to be caused by the frustrations of childhood. When Ashton-Warner looked at the school environments of most children, she saw those drives ignored or frustrated even more. She saw children especially discouraged by the written materials used in schools because she observed that children could not relate to the "Dick and Jane" characters or actions. Using children as a source of curriculum, Ashton-Warner developed innovative approaches and materials, especially in the area of literacy.

LITERACY CURRICULUM. The main idea of Ashton-Warner's approach to literacy is her notion of key vocabulary. **Key vocabulary** are self-chosen words, determined by each child, written on little cards (the 3" × 5" size works well). Ashton-Warner considered key words to be important if they were "one-look" words; that is, the child remembers the word after only one look. As a teacher, she began the day by placing the cards of all the children together on a mat. She described (1963) the children as "making straight for them to find their own, not without quarreling and concentration and satisfaction." Once they found the cards, they would sit with a partner and hear each other's words. In a sense, they teach each other. We observed a teacher using Ashton-Warner's key words approach in a class with 3-, 4-, and 5-year-olds, and each child's words clearly gave us an indication of what was happening in his life. A 4-year-old boy had discovered a small garden snake in his backyard on the previous day, and his words relayed his excitement: *snake, green, grass, tongue, fast,* and *hiding.*

The key words become the focus for writing, reading, and spelling activities. They are important and easy to read if they've been chosen well. *Chosen well* means that the words have real meaning for the children. When the children took their turns going to Ashton-Warner to dictate their words, she found that she often needed to engage them in conversation about their lives before they could come up with meaningful words. Otherwise, the children would just say whatever came to mind simply to take their turn, but the word would be forgotten immediately. The same is true of children's writing experiences. If the story or subject is directed by an adult, it has no value to the children. They may write, but the writing will be an impersonal experience.

In addition to the rich literacy activities of her program, Ashton-Warner included regular periods for dance, art, drama, and music. The day's routine even included a designated time for daydreaming. The most impressive quality of Ashton-Warner's approach to education emerges when you read her accounts of her teaching and her children. Whenever something was not working, she immediately took responsibility. For example, when a child came up to her, wanting to go outside instead of doing his work, she thought to herself, "It's my fault that he wants to go outside. Something is wrong with my infant room" (1963).

Although you probably won't find a program in your community that is patterned after Ashton-Warner's curriculum ideas, you will see the same thinking in a classroom in which the teacher is using a **whole language approach** to teach literacy. You will see children's words valued and used as the curriculum for teaching reading and writing. You will probably be able to recognize the whole language curriculum fairly easily. We also encourage you to experience the richness of Ashton-Warner's classroom by reading her book, *Teacher* (1963). Her conversations with children and her reflections about teaching cannot be condensed well into another person's words.

Ashton-Warner developed her ideas about children while working in British schools with Maori children. Our next thinker watched children in New York City in a tiny apartment that became their first play school setting.

Caroline Pratt

Much like Ashton-Warner, Caroline Pratt spent an extensive amount of her time watching children, especially as they played with blocks. From her observations, she developed a belief in children's ability to create and test knowledge about their world through their play. She insisted on calling it their *work* because she saw that children were quite serious about their play. Listen to her passionate expression of ideas about children's work:

> Children have their own meaning for the word play. To them it does not carry the ideas of idleness, purposelessness, relaxation from work as it does to adults. When we began our school, we named it a play school, as a telegraphic way of saying that in our way of teaching, the children learned by playing. It was the children who made us, early in the school's history, delete the word from the school's name. To them it was not a play school but a school, and they were working hard at their schooling.
>
> How hard they work, only we who have watched them really know. They do not waste a precious moment. They are going about their jobs all the time. No father in his office or mother in her home [remember—this was written in 1948] work at such a pace. For a long time I was principally afraid that they would exhaust themselves in this strenuous new kind of school. (1948, p. 9)

Pratt truly modeled the phrase, *learning from children.* She noted that blocks could be used for all kinds of play and testing, so she designed the wooden unit blocks that we have today in many ECE programs. We can credit her with the fact that blocks are a mainstay of programs all over the world.

PRATT'S IDEAS IN ACTION. Pratt's ideas about curriculum can be best understood if you observe the City Country School in New York City—the school she talked about that began with the name *play school.* Children from ages 2 to 8 spend much of their day in work that centers on blocks. On the playgrounds, there are large wooden blocks, boards, and hollow boxes. Children engage in constructive and dramatic play with these materials for hours each day all year long. In the classrooms where the youngest (2 to 4 years) children work, there are multiple shelves of blocks, probably more blocks than you've seen in other programs. In a classroom for 3-year-olds, there are very few accessories—some wooden people, trains, and colorful squares of fabric. At the end of the school year (the month of May) in that same class, we observed intense block building, elaborate structures that extended over about nine feet of floor space. During the play, the teachers spend much of their time observing, recording notes, and "learning from children."

BLOCKS IN CURRICULUM. Blocks also have a central role in the classroom for 5-year-olds. These children are able to leave their block structures in place all week. There are streets painted on the floor, paths and parks drawn among the buildings, as well as many signs in children's handwriting, labeling streets and most of the structures. The block city emerges as these 5-year-olds visit buildings in their New York City community—sometimes an impromptu trip when a need arises or a planned field trip for the entire class. Every Friday, there is a routine in which the children visit each other's buildings or neighborhoods. The children conduct tours, using the wooden people as guides. When you look closely at activities such as the Friday visits, you get a sense of the integration of curriculum that takes place in the block play (or work) at City Country School. It's impossible not to wonder how many of these children become architects or builders.

Although many parents and children are completely devoted to the City and Country School, and the school's faculty is consistently committed to Caroline Pratt's ideas, it is not a curriculum that everyone appreciates.

JOURNAL 5.3: Reflect from the perspective of a parent who has toured City Country School and listened to a presentation about the philosophy of Caroline Pratt. You decide that City Country School is not for your child. What may be some of your reasons? ●

Think about the value of block play. What kind of learning do you think can occur in block play?

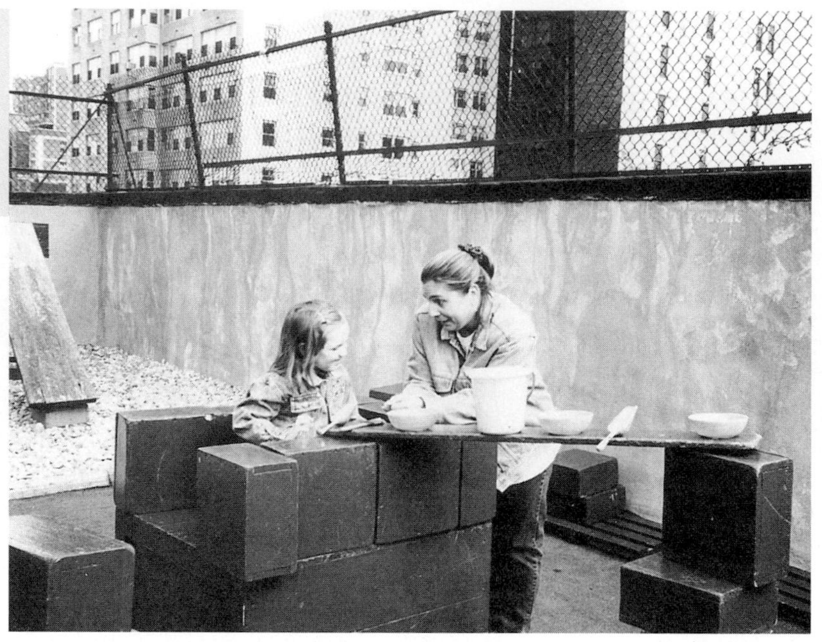

Pratt was influenced by the thinking of John Dewey, who believed that children are able to direct their own learning if adults provide the structure and opportunities and allow them to learn through real experiences. Our next pair of idea people were influenced by major theorists of early childhood education: Piaget and Kohlberg. Before reading about them, think about Piaget's theories about how children develop and learn and Kohlberg's theories about how children develop beliefs.

Constance Kamii and Rheta DeVries

With Piaget's theories as their major focus, Constance Kamii and Rheta DeVries developed many ideas about curriculum. Their ideas have been adopted mostly for preschool programming, but some of their thinking about math, reading, and writing has been extended to public school curriculum for kindergarten and primary grades. Because the thinking of both Piaget and Kohlberg are important for understanding the curriculum philosophy of Kamii and DeVries, we ask you to reflect on their theories. Review Piaget's stages of cognitive development and his concept of constructivism as well as Kohlberg's stages of moral reasoning to better understand the curricular components that follow.

CURRICULAR COMPONENTS. Some basic components of a curriculum directed to the outcomes or goals just listed are the following:

1. **Moral reasoning emphasis** evolves from a democratic classroom where teachers and children solve problems together, negotiate conflicts, collaborate in rule setting, and take responsibility for classroom life. Group games with rules, as well as discussions about hypothetical dilemmas, will give children opportunities to apply moral reasoning to real-life situation. Observe with us a classroom that uses such a curriculum:

Moral Reasoning

A class of 4- and 5-year-olds had a successful cookie sale after a week of excited baking and sign making. "Now it's time to decide how we want to spend our money," Paul reminded the children as they met in their morning circle. He asked the children to make suggestions and listed their ideas on the flip chart. "I want a Barbie house," suggested Aurelia. "I want a remote control car," shouted Ignatio. The list went on. Tessa quietly suggested, "I think that we should give the money to some poor children." Several children nodded. Many suggested, "I think that we should go on a trip with that money." When the list was full, Paul reviewed their ideas. Then he asked, "Would it be OK if we use our money to buy a Barbie house for Aurelia?" His question prompted much animated discussion about why that use of the money wasn't "right." After 20 minutes of discussion, Paul told the children, "I think that we need more time to work on this decision. Think about it some more and tomorrow we'll talk about it again and see if we can decide on one idea with which everyone can agree."

2. **Physical-knowledge activities** involve children's actions on objects and their observations of the reactions. Their observations will frequently lead to cause-and-effect understandings, to the development of relationships, and to much accommodation and assimilation. Some of the most common activities to provide such experiences for children are water play with float and sink materials, cooking, making and flying kites, mixing paint colors, and weighing and measuring items.

3. **Group games** will instill in children how to be both collaborative and independent players. With young children, you can begin with very simple games, such as Farmer in the Dell and Duck, Duck, Goose. With primary grade children, more complex games will intrigue them, such as Fruit Basket, Red Rover, and Simon Says.

4. **Logico-math activities,** especially those embedded in routine situations in which number is a natural issue, will lead to developing skills of logic and organization. Examples include division of materials to the group, keeping class records, recording the weather or the lunch count, and voting for class choices. Logico-math activities are further emphasized in group games.

To implement the ideas of Kamii and DeVries in your work with children, you will need to be an excellent observer of children and have a critical understanding of how each child thinks and understands events. Notice that these qualities keep recurring throughout this book. As you have probably figured out, once you understand children's thinking and understandings, you will be better at connecting what you know about children with the kind of activities you plan and the environment you arrange for children.

OUTCOMES FOR CHILDREN. The work of Kamii and DeVries is quite complex and it keeps changing somewhat as they continue actively to explore curricular ideas and to work with children. Here, we will provide just the general ideas and some applications of their thinking. Let's begin with curriculum for young children, directed by the following goals:

1. The children will be autonomous; that is, they will construct their own learning and develop independent thinking.
2. The children will develop according to the framework of Piaget's stages of cognitive development.
3. The children will develop cooperative relationships, reflecting both social skills and understanding the perspectives of others.
4. The children will develop moral reasoning according to the framework of Kohlberg's stages of development.

When you look at these outcomes, you can deduce that two aspects of curriculum are essential: Children must interact with their social and physical environments, and within children there must be an interaction between their current way of understanding an event or phenomenon and new information about an event or phenomenon. Remember assimilation and accommodation? These two criteria are often described in curriculum language as *hands-on learning* and *learning by doing,* or, quite simply, as *play*. Now you're probably feeling a little more comfortable about the ideas of Kamii and DeVries. Use them to help you better understand Piaget and to apply his thinking to work with young children.

INTERACTIONS WITH CHILDREN. You can use your understanding of children to know what questions to ask them, when to be quiet and listen, and when to encourage an answer. Kamii and DeVries (1978) express concern about the way we adults interact with children and especially caution us against "imposing our ideas and answers" on them because "children will soon learn not to trust their own ability to make sense of their experiences." One of us remembers a year when the arrangement of the classroom didn't feel comfortable, routines weren't running smoothly, and certain areas of the classroom were sometimes very congested. I was hesitant to ask the children, yet I knew that they were the best source of information about the room. To be honest, the other realization was that once the children gave their ideas, it would be important to respect and use their ideas. Otherwise, a lack of trust would certainly occur. We sat together and talked about the feel of the room, and the children certainly agreed that it just wasn't working. Their suggestions primarily focused on the removal of three large circular work tables, and, as a replacement for the work space, using carpet squares for floor sitting. The children, ages 3 to 5, enthusiastically moved the tables to a storage room and rearranged the space with shelves of materials and a case of carpet squares. The days then proceeded more smoothly.

By now, you may be thinking that there's a similar theme to the thinking and curriculum approaches we've been describing for you. You may be wondering if there's any alternative thinking to the theme, so we move next to two thinkers who have different ideas about children and curriculum.

Carl Bereiter and Siegfried Engelmann

Carl Bereiter and Siegfried Engelmann's ideas came from theories of behaviorism and the work of Skinner. (Do you need to return to Chapter 3?) Their thinking was based primarily on stimulus-response theory, which you have likely encountered in your psychology courses. Curriculum designed by Bereiter and Engelmann was not based on child development; instead, it was focused on learning rather than development. Their definition of *learning* will help you understand how they thought about curriculum. "Learning refers to the change in a subject's behavior to a given situation brought about by repeated experiences in that situation" (Hilgard & Bower, 1975, p. 17). They saw children as recipients of learning, not participants in learning. Today, this viewpoint is called the *banking approach* to learning—one makes regular deposits of information in students, much like one makes deposits of money in a bank.

CATCH-UP CURRICULUM. Before we go any further, it is important for you to know that Bereiter and Engelmann developed their ideas about curriculum during a time when there was concern about the learning of young children from economically disadvantaged and culturally diverse home environments. At that time, children were mistakenly labeled *culturally deprived* because they didn't have the advantages and the language of their middle-class peers. That thinking was based on the idea that White middle-class culture was the only culture, so that those who didn't experience it were deprived. Today, we call similar children *at risk,* because their home environments and experiences don't match those of their middle-class peers and because most schools are not designed to meet their needs. Many feel that it is the schools and communities that are at risk, because they don't match the needs and experiences of those children.

Bereiter and Engelmann (1966) decided to design curriculum to make sure that those children could catch up, so that they could "emerge from school with the same skills and knowledge as more privileged children" (p. 6). They created an academic curriculum to teach the skills children needed in order to succeed in school.

TEACHING WITH BEREITER AND ENGELMANN. Bereiter and Engelmann's curricular ideas primarily focused on language, reading, and arithmetic, and began with a preschool model but expanded to current use in kindergarten and primary grades. You may have heard of their programs: Direct Instruction and Distar. Their teaching approach requires that teachers work with small groups of children (5 to 15 in a group), that each subject is taught separately, and that the classroom environment is very businesslike. Much of their curriculum was programmed; that is, teachers were told what to say, how and when to say it, and what children must answer in response. Scripts with directions, structured examples, and sequences of subskills and wordings were supplied. Efficiency was very important—each minute was seen as precious for helping the children catch up. Parents were to work with their children at home, using practice books to reinforce the skills learned in class.

To help you visualize Bereiter and Engelmann's thinking applied to a program for children, listen and observe a teacher using their Distar method with first-grade children:

Distar Method

Several children are seated at their desks and working in workbooks. Another group of children is sitting at a long table at the back of the room with headphones on and listening to tapes. The rest of the children are sitting in a semi-circle facing their teacher, David. He is holding a book so that the page with large letters and symbols faces the children. David points to an individual letter on the page and asks one or more children to respond. Sometimes he says, "Everyone, what sound does this make?" The child or children respond immediately by making the sound associated with the letter to which David is pointing. We watch and hear George and Elyssa saying, "Mmmm" when David points to M, but Melaney looks confused and doesn't make a sound. After the children respond, David gives them feedback with, "Wow, you are really with it today!" Within a few minutes, each student in the group has had several turns to respond to the questions. The interactions have been rapid and the entire session has lasted about 12 minutes. At the end, the children practice writing the alphabet sounds they have been working on, and they say the sound out loud each time they write it.

Compare the learning of these children with the learning of children in a Distar classroom.

JOURNAL 5.4: Think about being a child in David's class. What does it feel like for George? For Melaney?

Summary: Stop and Catch Your Breath

We've been spending a lot of time in people's heads and you may be ready for a break. Maybe the topic of *curriculum* is making you feel overwhelmed with so many ideas and approaches. To help you keep the ideas clear, you might return to each of the professionals and make a list of their general ideas, especially those that feel comfortable with your ideas about children and learning. You might also look for common themes and unique ways of thinking about children and their development. Again, consider those themes in the context of what you believe about children. Spending some time organizing the thinking you have just read about will get you ready for the next section of this chapter. We're going to look at some programs now as a different way to explore ideas. As you read about the programs, stop and reflect on what kind of thinking and decision making is behind what the children and adults doing.

Early Childhood Education Programs

Let's return to New York City, where we met Caroline Pratt. Perhaps it is the dynamic quality of that metropolitan site and the diversity of lives that comprise the richly varied neighborhoods that prompt and promote the creative and courageous thinking and programs we are describing.

Bank Street Approach

At the same time that Caroline Pratt was developing her ideas about curriculum and starting the City Country School, other progressive educators were thinking about the "whole child" and the importance of children to a humane society. Begun as the Bureau of Educational Experiments, the Bank Street approach got its name when the Bureau moved to 69 Bank Street. Later, under the direction of Barbara Biber, the approach was named for its "essential theoretical characteristics" and called the *developmental interaction approach.* The approach was implemented at the Bank Street School for Children, a laboratory and demonstration center for the Bank Street College of Education, with preschool through eighth grade. The school served two important functions. First, it was a research center focused on the study of the application of developmental theory to classrooms. Second, it served as a teacher education center to prepare educators who would plan and implement developmentally appropriate learning environments for children.

THE BANK STREET TRADITION. Over the years, Bank Street has always been thought of as the ideal nursery school program; often, the elementary school aspect is overlooked. If you were to look at any developmentally appropriate preschool, kindergarten, or primary grade classroom in your city or your neighborhood, you would see the teaching strategies, the teacher/child relationship, and the classroom organization and materials of the developmental interaction approach. The qualities of being child centered, experience based, and process oriented appear in the handbooks of many early childhood programs, and they describe the Bank Street program well. A **child-centered curriculum** is one in which the environment, activities, materials, and adult interactions are designed to meet children's interests, needs, and abilities. That may sound familiar by now. **Experience-based curriculum** is one that emphasizes rich, appropriate experiences for children's learning. That, too, may sound familiar by now. **Process-oriented curriculum** focuses on the process rather than the product, so that adults and children will talk about the making rather than what is being made.

The uniqueness of the Bank Street approach is that its advocates insist on the experimental nature of education; that is, instead of a planned curriculum, you teach by continuously studying children and trying out ideas (activities, materials, etc.). The trial-and-error quality of the approach is difficult to imagine for many of us. The approach is such a personal approach—on the part of the teacher and on the part of the child. It depends on the "teacher's knowledge and ability to recognize and skillfully respond to the individuality of each child and his or her interests" (Franklin & Biber, 1977, p. 26). When you think about the diversity among your classmates studying early childhood education, you can imagine the wide variety of responses possible among them, even if they were all responding to the same child. Now, imagine the wide variety of children. Biber (1988) says, "The ideal teacher is aware of the differences in the social codes and styles of interaction among young children from widely different cultural groups" (p. 46). With all those variations possible, Bank Street is truly a personal approach and is intensely dynamic! It can be called individually developmentally appropriate because it doesn't depend on the kind of normative child development stages we described in Chapter 2, but instead on each child's development.

One of us visited Bank Street years ago, and the classroom scene is still vivid because of its rich activities and intense involvement of a large number of children. Somehow, the children had become involved in the study of dyes. It began with one child's curiosity about how his shirt became a certain color and it led to an in-depth project about dyes. The large room contained 3 or 4 adults and over 20 older preschoolers. One group was making dyes from vegetables (beets, carrots, and spinach), plants, and other natural materials in one area of the room. Nearby were fabrics and bits of yarn drying from the experiments with dye. Another group was weaving newly dyed strips of cloth. One of the adults was taking dictation from children who were telling stories and sharing bits of information from their library research about dyes. A testing area displayed paper samples and blots of color. Children and adults were pursuing their own interests in varied ways with activities that made sense to them.

CURRICULUM GOALS OF BANK STREET. Before moving on to another program, it would be beneficial for you to look at the goals of the Bank Street or developmental interaction approach (see Figure 5.3). They don't look vastly different from the goals of other

FIGURE 5.3

Program Goals of the Developmental-Interaction Approach

1. Opportunities for children to explore, manipulate, and make an impact on the environment
2. Opportunities for children to expand and extend knowledge of their environment
3. Opportunities for children to cognitively incorporate and order experience in play
4. Opportunities for children to develop impulse control
5. Opportunities for children to cope with and respond to conflict
6. Opportunities for children to develop self-images and feelings of competence
7. Opportunities for children to develop "mutually supporting" interaction patterns

Source: Adapted from B. Biber, 1977, "A Developmental-Interaction Approach: Bank Street College of Education" in *The Preschool in Action: Exploring Early Childhood Programs* (2nd ed.) by M. C. Day & K. Parker (Eds.). Boston: Allyn and Bacon.

curricular thinking or practices. What is different is that this approach emphasizes that these goals are not end points or outcomes. They are meant to *guide* the work of teachers and the processes of individual children. Ultimately, the developmental interaction approach is concerned with the following (Goffin, 1994, p. 88):

1. *Competence of children.* Their use of knowledge and skills will enable children to live in the environment and with others.
2. *Individuality of children.* Children's autonomy and sense of self-worth are based on knowledge and feelings of their own competence and the views of those around them.
3. *Socialization of children.* Self-regulation of behavior is necessary to participate in forms of society and in relationship with others.
4. *Integration for children.* Connecting disparate experiences and reactions will enable children to possess a "big picture" and appreciate the events of their lives.

Although the language of their program goals is different, the Bank Street approach has intentions for children that are similar to those of the next program.

High Scope Approach

The High Scope approach began as a curriculum model for preschool at the Ypsilanti Perry Preschool and was later extended to curriculum for kindergarten through third grade. The name was meant to communicate high aspirations and a broad scope of interests. David Weikart is the educator responsible for the thinking and organizing of the curriculum ideas of High Scope. Early in the development of the High Scope curriculum, the work of Piaget became influential and the curriculum was renamed the *cognitively oriented curriculum.* Many people continue to call it High Scope, however—even though the name was changed more than 20 years ago.

EMERGENCE OF THE HIGH SCOPE CURRICULUM. When High Scope programs first began, teachers were teaching with very direct methods, often instructing children in motor and perceptual skills. With the influence of Piaget's ideas, they began instructing children in Piagetian tasks because they thought that those tasks would move children to the next stage of cognitive development. As Weikart and his colleagues studied Piaget further, the curriculum was based more on the idea that children are active learners and can construct their own knowledge. Teachers stopped their direct teaching and were free to participate with the children in activities. The preschool curriculum recommends *key experiences* for the children. Those experiences are organized into three categories and within each category are types of learning experiences:

1. *Social and emotional development,* including recognition and solution of problems, understanding routines and expectations, and communicating with others
2. *Movement and physical development,* including block building, climbing, ball throwing and catching, and play with manipulatives
3. *Cognitive development,* including representation, language, classification, seriation, number, space, and time

The key experiences give structure to the curriculum while at the same time maintain a flexibility to accommodate new possibilities. Teachers can use these experiences to organize their planning of activities. They also are linked to how both children and program are assessed. Teachers use them as a framework with which to observe children.

THE PLAN-DO-REVIEW COMPONENT. In addition to the key experiences, another curriculum component is unique to High Scope. It is a sequence called *plan-do-review* and it is used frequently throughout the day. Let's look in a High Scope classroom and see what plan-do-review looks like:

Vanessa: Plan-Do-Review

It's planning time, and 4-year-old Vanessa approaches her teacher Sylvanna and describes what she is going to do during the outside play period. "I'm going to make a bakery and sell cakes," says Vanessa, pointing to the sandbox. Sylvanna asks, "What kind of cakes?" and adds, "Are you going to sell anything else?" Vanessa talks about chocolate and gingerbread cakes, and cookies and pies. She says that she will put candles in some of them for birthdays. Eagerly, Vanessa heads for the sandbox and a shelf of pails and plastic containers. She begins the "doing" phase of the sequence. After outdoor play, children engage in a recall or review of their activities. Again, their teacher Sylvanna encourages representation of their "doing"—by talking, or drawing, or pantomiming, or writing about their activities. Vanessa draws a shelf of cakes, some with candles, and price tags on each one. She is anxious to show her drawing to the group and to talk about her cakes.

If Vanessa engaged in plan-do-review inside the classroom, she would have a choice of learning centers or work areas, usually a block area, an art area, a quiet area, and a house area. During small group time, the teachers present an activity in which all the children participate—usually in key experiences. This is a time when teachers can observe children, assess their development, and guide their progress. High Scope teachers ask children a lot of questions throughout the day to extend the children's thinking and to promote problem solving and independent thinking.

We have been describing a preschool classroom and curriculum, but if you were to visit a classroom in an elementary setting—kindergarten through third grade—you would still see work areas and key experiences, but they would be related to public school elementary subjects of math, language and literacy, and science. For example, the work areas would include a reading/writing area, a math area, a computer area, an art area, and a construction area. Most teaching would take place in small groups and some cooperative work would be part of the day.

Today, there is a High Scope foundation that sponsors research, curriculum development, professional training for teachers, and public advocacy. As you will learn in Chapter 13, research on High Scope or Ypsilanti Perry Preschool has demonstrated that there are multiple long-term benefits of well-developed early childhood education programs. Through the advocacy of Weikart and his colleagues, policymakers, legislators, and the general public have been convinced of the cost effectiveness and social value of such programs.

Waldorf Approach

The Waldorf approach to education began with one school designed for the children of the workers of the Waldorf-Astoria Cigarette Company and it blossomed into a worldwide educational movement (Uhrmacher, 1993). Basically, Waldorf schools are private, nonsectarian programs with an arts-based curriculum. Children learn subjects such as literacy, math, science, and so on through artistic activities.

Waldorf schools apply the thinking of Rudolf Steiner, who developed a system of education in Germany in 1919 as an alternative to traditional education (Foster, 1984). Steiner, like many early childhood educators, believed in educating the whole child, but his interpretation of *whole* included the mind, the heart, and the will. Like so many of the thinkers you've encountered in this chapter, Steiner also believed that curriculum comes from the child. "Education does not give or take but strengthens the forces within each child" (Aeppli, 1986, p. 10). Said differently, you must know children well in order to educate them. Waldorf teachers have two major intentions as they work with children:

1. To develop subject matter through image, rhythm, movement, drawing, painting, poetry, drama, and so on;
2. To involve aesthetics in all that is done throughout the school day (aesthetic conditions) program. (Uhrmacher, 1993, p. 89)

BASIC IDEAS OF RUDOLF STEINER. Rudolf Steiner's thinking about curriculum was similar to the thinking of John Dewey. Contrary to the thinking of many educators, Steiner pointed out that teachers do not provide experiences for students. You may be startled by that idea, but his thinking was that teachers provide conditions (such as materials, space, schedule, etc.) and then each child has her own experience. So, one way of looking at Steiner's educational system is to examine some of the conditions of his schools (Uhrmacher, 1993, p. 91):

1. *Aesthetic conditions*—those conditions that enhance a child's appreciation of beauty and sensuality
2. *Social conditions*—those conditions that promote or strengthen interactions and relationships between children, and between children and adults
3. *Symbolic conditions*—those conditions such as stories, pictures, rituals, and ceremonies that will teach and influence children indirectly
4. *"Sensitive" conditions*—those conditions that enhance a child's perceptive abilities or a child's "feeling live"

Some of these conditions may sound unusual or be difficult to understand due to a translation of Steiner's ideas into English. However, when we visit a Waldorf classroom, you'll see what those conditions look like in practice.

VISITING A WALDORF SCHOOL. It would be ideal to spend a whole day in a classroom, but for the sake of brevity, we'll drop into different classes at different times of the day.

Waldorf Approach

Atlantic Monthly writer Todd Oppenheimer describes his visit to a Waldorf kindergarten class in San Francisco: "I felt my stomach relax. The lights were dim, the colors soft pastel. Intriguing materials for play were everywhere. The children had organized them into a half dozen fantasy worlds—there was a make-believe woodshop in one corner; in another, reminiscent of a farmhouse bedroom, two girls were putting a doll to bed in a cradle" (p. 73). He continues to describe other materials to include "wild hats and capes, pinecones and driftwood, bowls of nuts and other items from the natural world" and their intent to "challenge children's spatial creativity" (p. 74). Later, in a second grade, the writer observed children studying geometric progression by "creating concentric circles of times tables and musing about their similarity to planetary patterns" (p. 76). When finished, the children sang their complex multiplication drills in an exercise room and hopped and clapped in a syncopated rhythm that amazed the author.

In another class, a third grade, Mr. Stevenson places sunflowers and pumpkins on top of an orange cloth in the center of the room. He asks, "Could we please begin, everyone?" The children who are in the classroom go into the hallway and line up at the door. When the teacher is ready, the children come in one at a time to shake hands and hear, "Good morning Ethan. . . . Good morning Talya. . . ." These greeting are followed by morning circle to recite verses. The students and teacher bend down from the waist, arms stretched toward the ground and say, "The earth is firm beneath my feet." They rise and move their arms above their heads with "The sun shines bright above." They continue with the verse and body movements and recite it five more times, using quieter voices each time. When they finish, there is silence for a brief time (Uhrmacher, 1993, pp. 87, 91).

As Ms. Hernandez introduces math thinking or numeracy to young children, she takes a stick and allows the children to see and experience it as a whole. Then the stick is broken into 2, 4, and 8 pieces. "The child observes that by splitting the big 1, the smaller 2, 4, and 8 arise, and that the pieces become smaller the more the stick is broken." An alternative to the stick is to have children work with a large lump of clay and work it into 2, 4, and 8 smaller lumps. After the children have experienced numbers with varied concrete materials, they can begin to count. Counting is done with clapping or foot stamping. We hear, "Clap two times, four times, and eight times." Later, we hear children saying, "I have two eyes, two ears, two arms, two hands, two feet" (Aeppli, 1986, p. 47).

Children and family members arrived at the little preschool in Pacific Grove—such a calm and welcoming environment. "It was a little confusing, however, because the rooms were almost bare, none of the usual toys, only a child-sized lunch table and chairs, and some hand-made objects, scarves, and baskets of natural items" (K. Driscoll, 2003, personal communication). None of the adults appeared to be in a rush and there was much conversation between them and children. As the morning proceeded, children wandered in and out of the rooms, spending time in the garden or sand area, telling stories with the available objects, or sitting quietly as if in reflection. Hearing them address each other with "Dear Emily" or "Dear Alex" was unusual to hear but it was the norm in this preschool. Late in the morning, one of teachers asked the children if they would like a story. Children responded with "Yes, please," or put away their materials and approached where she was sitting. She was wearing a wide full skirt and she spread it on the floor around her and the children sat on its edge. The teacher had a felt horse and king in her pocket and she began a story about them, placing the figures on her skirt. Before long, the children added detail to the story or asked questions that took the story in another direction. It was completely interactive storytelling.

You may want to visit a Waldorf school for yourself to see more of Steiner's thinking. You will find the visit a very inspiring experience.

The next program we will talk about originated in Italy. This fairly recent discovery for U.S. early childhood educators has prompted many teachers from the United States to visit the Italian community of Reggio Emilia to get ideas. Just in case your passport isn't current, we're going to take you there for a brief visit.

Reggio Emilia Approach

More than 30 years ago, through the efforts of women advocating for children, a law established free education for children ages 3 to 6 (later adding infant/toddler centers) in Italy. The legislated free programs emphasized quality in both education and care. In Reggio Emilia, a small northern town, the programs were literally built by parents with proceeds from the sale of military equipment after the end of World War II. Professor Loris Malaguzzi guided those beginning efforts and continues to provide insightful leadership to the educational program at Reggio Emilia.

DEVELOPMENT OF THE REGGIO EMILIA APPROACH. With thinking similar to that of the Bank Street approach, the Reggio educators consider their work "an educational experience that consists of practice and careful reflection that is continuously readjusted" (Gandini, 1993, p. 13). Like so many ECE professionals, the Reggio educators have been influenced by the ideas of Dewey, Piaget, Vygotsky, and the latest research in child development. A look at how the Reggio educators describe children will tell you much about their approach. "All children have preparedness, potential, curiosity and interest in constructing their learning, in engaging in social interaction, and in negotiating with everything the environment brings to them" (p. 13). With that image of children, it is not surprising that the Reggio approach studies children as individuals and responds to them appropriately.

REGGIO CURRICULUM. Curriculum at Reggio is called *emergent,* meaning that it is not determined beforehand. The educators develop general goals and predict children's responses to activities and projects so that they can prepare the environment. Then the children take over and the curriculum emerges. Much of the curriculum at Reggio takes the form of projects, and those projects may come from children or teachers. Sometimes, an event or a problem may result in a project, such as a study of shoes that occurred when a child came to school with a new pair of shoes. The children were curious about how shoes were made and wanted to investigate the materials of shoes. Projects are actually intensive constructions of knowledge—studies conducted by children guided by adults or with adult resources. Projects can vary in length from a few days to several months. To get a sense of the richness of the Reggio emergent curriculum and the project approach, listen to Carlina Rinaldi, a *pedagogista* (educational advisor) at the school:

Reggio Emilia Approach

This project begins at the end of a school year for 4- and 5-year-olds. The teachers talked with the children about remembering their vacation and holiday experiences. The children and parents agreed to take along on their vacations a box with small compartments in which a child could save treasures. "Every fragment, every piece collected would become a memento of an experience imbued with a sense of discovery and emotion" (Edwards, Gandini, & Forman, 1995, p. 108).

In the fall, the teachers began with questions about the holidays, much like teachers do in U.S. schools. They asked, "What did your eyes see?" "What did your ears hear?" One child, Gabriele, shared an experience that prompted an adventure for the children and adults alike. He responded to the teachers' questions about his holiday: "We walked through a narrow long street, called 'the gut,' where one store is next to another and where in the evening it is full of people. There are people who go up, and people who walk down. You cannot see anything, you can only see a crowd of legs, arms, and heads" (p. 109).

The idea of "crowd" caught the teachers' attention and their questions prompted rich meanings from the children. "The teachers immediately apprehended an unusual excitement and potential in the word" (p. 109). Listen to some of the children's thinking about crowds:

Nicola: It is a bunch of people all attached and close to one another.
Luca: There are people who jump on you and push you.
Ivano: It is a bunch of people all bunched up together just like when they go to pay taxes (p. 109).

The concept of *crowd* became the focus of a series of teacher conversations, children's conversations, and then an explosion of activity—drawings, walks in the city, more drawings, and paintings. The curriculum truly emerged from Gabriele and the children's responses to his description of a crowd. From there, the children could decide to study *crowds* as a project. Later in the book, you will see toddlers in a classroom where emergent curriculum is in place, and where kindergarten children engage in the project approach.

CURRICULAR SUPPORTS AT REGGIO. There are several completely unique features of the Reggio Emilia program that deserve description. In addition to teachers and many parent participants, there is a teacher trained in visual arts who is called the *atelierista.* There is also a special space—a studio or workshop—called the *atelier.* Everyone (adults and children) uses the tools and materials of the *atelier.* Another unique feature of the program is the extensive documentation of children's thinking, discussions, work, and progress that is collected and used. The documentation takes the form of photographs, tape recordings, and other records. The Reggio educators value the documentation as a way to understand the children better and a way to assess their own work as educators.

At the same time, the process of collecting documentation communicates to children that their work and their efforts are valued.

Some of the Reggio Emilia ideas are finding their way into elementary schools in the United States today (see Box 5.1). One practice that is becoming common is the teacher and group of students staying together for more than one year. In Reggio, a pair of teachers and a group of children stay together for three years. Although their environment changes as their development progresses, the community of learners stays intact. At Reggio, teachers see themselves as researchers, continually documenting their work with children. Many U.S. elementary teachers conduct *action research* in their classrooms to find answers, to solve problems, and to guide their decision making, just as the Reggio teachers do. Finally, the Reggio approach works with the child in relation to other children, to the family, to the teachers, to the school environment, to the community, and to the wider society—and the interconnections and reciprocity are encouraged and supported. Many programs and schools in the United States have embraced those same important relationships and integrated them into preschool and elementary curriculum.

Head Start Teachers and Staff Study Reggio Emilia

Later in this chapter we describe the thinking of teachers who studied the project approach. Catherine Gillespie (2000), a university professor, conducts action research—in Head Start programs. Her most recent study was focused on 21 teachers and staff and 100 children and their families who agreed to explore the Reggio Emilia approach and be studied while doing so. Gillespie observed in the classrooms; interviewed children, teachers and staff, and families; took photos of classrooms; and collected samples of children's work. Her work reinforces a common conclusion about many of our curricular approaches—they are complex and they demand intensive study, exploration, and ongoing learning. For the Head Start teachers and staff, learning about and implementing the Reggio Emilia approach was a process without an end. The participants agreed on the importance of collaboration and their monthly study groups.

To help you understand the Reggio Emilia approach a little better, we describe some of the changes made in the Head Start classrooms as reported by Gillespie (2000). The first area of change was the classroom environment. Teachers and staff concentrated on quick, fairly easy, and "satisfying" changes, such as, "transforming one area of a classroom into an art studio" and "replacing all commercially made classroom wall decorations with beautiful creations made by children and others" (p. 22).

At Reggio Emilia, the schedule is sensitive to children's time needs and rhythm, as well as to those of the staff. Long interrupted blocks of time for in-depth work are valued. Head Start teachers made schedule changes that were directed to those blocks of time with less structure and more flexibility. Some teachers added a daily group meeting when they could talk with children about how they used their time and how they worked as a group (p. 23).

Other areas of attention and change were child-initiated projects, documentation of children's work, and collaboration among children and adults. The teachers and Gillespie noted the value of the monthly study group for both learning and support. Overall, this action research study reminds us that we need to give ourselves generous amounts of time and a learning support system to master various curricular approaches. Like the Head Start teachers and staff, you will need to take small steps and make minor changes while you continue to learn and explore. Those teachers can tell you it's worth it: "We know that our Reggio journey will be never ending, but the words and expressions of the children show us that we are on the right path" (p. 27).

Current Curriculum Guidelines and Approaches

For the last few years, our professional associations have collaborated to provide clear and definitive guidelines for the kind of curriculum that will support the development and learning of young children. Some of the work is prompted by a concern that young children will be subjected to learning approaches and pressure to achieve learning goals that are developmentally inappropriate. Other concerns emerge from current assessment practices that are being directed to younger and younger students. Reports that young children cry and experience stress-related symptoms such as stomach and headaches when required to perform on inappropriate standardized tests (Guddemi, 2002) are a source of professional concern. In addition, many of the assessments provide little helpful information to teachers or parents.

In 1990, the NAEYC and the National Association of Early Childhood Specialists in State Departments of Education collaborated to develop guidelines about appropriate curriculum content and assessment for young children. Their 20 guidelines described the importance of "relevant, engaging, and meaningful" content, of content that "reflects and is generated by the needs and interests of individual children," and of "curriculum that respects and supports individual, cultural, and linguistic diversity," of "psychological safety," and of "strengthening children's sense of competence and enjoyment of learning." The guidelines were intended for use in planning instruction, for communicating with parents and professionals, for program evaluation, and for decision making about the appropriateness of activities, curriculum, and assessment.

More recently, the two professional associations collaborated to respond to the growing pressures of national standards and those of more than 25 states to "describe desired results, outcomes and learning expectations for children below kindergarten age" (2002, p. 1). Rather than write new standards, the newest document articulates the four essential features that must characterize learning standards if they are to be developmentally effective. As stated in the position statement, "Early Learning Standards: Creating the Conditions for Success," the four essential features will assure benefits for young children and their families:

1. Effective early learning standards emphasize significant, developmentally appropriate content and outcomes.
2. Effective early learning standards are developed and reviewed through informed, inclusive processes.
3. Early learning standards gain their effectiveness through implementation and assessment practices that support all children's development in ethical, appropriate ways.
4. Effective early learning standards require a foundation of support for early childhood programs, professionals, and families.

The curricular approaches we will describe in this section respond to both the earlier guidelines and the essential features of the recent position statement. They are inclusive curriculum, multicultural curriculum, and the project approach. All three reflect contemporary issues that are being addressed in our ECE programs and practices. They also respond to a growing research base that has forced us to rethink curriculum and how we support the learning of young children. The three approaches will expand your thinking about curriculum and give you a lens with which to observe the programs and professionals in the chapters that follow.

Inclusive Curriculum

Inclusive curriculum has been defined as an approach that emphasizes the kinds of authentic experiences we described at the very start of this chapter and the kind of child-centered learning that characterizes so many of the models and thinking we described throughout these pages. Inclusive curriculum is also like emergent curriculum, which you will see in action when you meet Ibrahim in Chapter 8. His teachers respond to his choices when they plan curricular activities, or adjust the schedule, or set out new materials. As in so many models, play is the "valid context" for such authentic learning (Winter, 1999, p. 61). Play in inclusive curriculum provides all the opportunities we describe in Chapter 4—opportunities for literacy to develop, for social interaction, for the beginning of all kinds of skills. In an inclusive environment with children of all levels of development, play provides:

- A chance to vary the complexity of materials and activities
- A chance to embed various therapeutic interventions in activities
- A chance to enhance social and language skills in a natural context
- A chance to make curriculum culturally relevant for children (pp. 61–63)

While attending to age and developmentally appropriate learning experiences, inclusive curriculum focuses on individual appropriateness with differentiated experiences and adjustments to ensure each child's success. The term *accommodation* is used and it means that adjustments in curriculum are made to "help children work from their areas of strength and ability" rather than from their deficits. When "efforts to accommodate individual children occur in a learning environment that encourages successful participation of all children" (Winter, 1999, p. 165), there is a sense of equity, and that is what inclusive curriculum is all about. Inclusive curriculum provides accommodation for children with disabilities, for children who are gifted and talented, and for children who are linguistically and culturally diverse, while ensuring gender equity and focusing on the whole child. Such practices are a focus of the cases in Chapters 7 through 12. You will hear how teachers and administrators and parents define inclusion. They will also help you "spot" inclusive practices in their programs.

Providing inclusive curriculum often requires that early childhood educators work with other professionals such as early childhood special educators or health specialists, but as Bergen (2003) reminds us, "We have much to learn from each other" (p. 65). Our common values and methods as well as our belief that all children must have the opportunity to learn at their highest potential have enabled us to be effective in providing inclusive curriculum for young children. Much of that thinking is foundational to our next curricular approach—multicultural curriculum.

Multicultural Curriculum

Broadly defined, *multicultural curriculum* consists of the "methods and materials we use to generate children's cultural sensitivity" (Vold, 2003, p. 32). Over the years, our profession has developed and adopted varied approaches to help young children understand and appreciate diversity. Our curriculum has focused on heroes, holidays, and discrete cultural elements such as food, language, and so on, and it has focused on trying to help children take on the perspective of diverse groups. The human relations approach to multicultural curriculum has been most prevalent in early childhood settings—that is, an approach that works to "help children communicate with, accept, and get along with people who are different from themselves" (p. 32).

Today, with a growing awareness of the importance and appropriateness of multicultural curriculum, the approach is focused on children's moral and cognitive development. We must pay attention to how children form values and beliefs and how children process information. We also have solid research that tells us that young children notice differences, that their awareness influences how they construct their notions of the world around them, and that the significant adults in their lives influence their attitudes about diversity.

The work of Louise Derman Sparks and the antibias curriculum that you will learn about in Chapter 8 has probably been the most influential multicultural curriculum development in our profession. It focuses on helping children become aware of the connection between power and issues of race, language, and physical disabilities, and the presence of stereotypes and biases. The goals of antibias curriculum give you a good idea of how the curriculum works to create a "total environment of respect and affirmation of diversity":

1. To nurture each child's construction of a knowledgeable, confident self-concept and group identity
2. To promote each child's comfortable, empathic interaction with people from diverse backgrounds
3. To foster each child's critical thinking about bias
4. To cultivate each child's ability to stand up for him or herself and for others in the face of biasing. (Derman-Sparks, 1998, pp. 188–189)

The debate about how best to encourage and support young children to appreciate and understand the diversity that surrounds them will continue in our efforts to develop the most appropriate and effective curriculum, but in the meantime, there is something that you can work on to get yourself ready. Because you will soon be one of those influential adults in young children's lives, you are challenged to become a multicultural person yourself. Your perspectives and understandings will be powerful forces in determining the way you will work with children or the environments you will create. It is time to begin to question your beliefs, to learn about differences, to notice biases and stereotypes around you, and to find models of a multicultural perspective. We'll suggest some readings at the end of this chapter to help you get started.

The Project Approach

The third curriculum, the project approach, is not new, and it is not really a curriculum. It is an approach with the potential to offer children many opportunities to develop knowledge, skills, and dispositions, so we have included it here with curriculum. The project approach is authentic and it is a form of emergent curriculum—that is, curriculum that emerges from children's interests, curiosities, needs, and situations surrounding them, as we described in the beginning of this chapter. Many of your future colleagues have been using, experimenting, and reflecting on the project approach for many years, so there are lots of insights for you to use. First, we'll describe what it is, how it's being used, and what it looks like when children are engaged in projects.

The project approach, which is being used in classrooms all over the country, is specifically for children ages 4 through 8. During those years, the intellectual development of children progresses rapidly, quite unevenly, and with huge variance among individual children. The project approach accommodates those qualities of development by providing related alternative activities and tasks for a wide range of abilities and experiences. Some of the popularity of the project approach is due to its ease of use in mixed-aged settings. Those settings group children of different ages and ability levels, thus making the project approach a good curricular match for the diversity.

What is the project approach? Let's take a look in a classroom in which children are studying architecture. It's a mixed-aged classroom in a public school. Children of kindergarten, first grade, and second grade are engaged in building models of homes and other buildings. Some of the children are working in groups, while others are working on individual constructions. Many of them are following a sketch or design that they developed the day before. Some have even used blueprint paper. There is a great deal of labeling being done as the children write the names of rooms and discuss exteriors such as brick, wood siding, and stucco. Earlier in the week, an architect visited the class and left a display of blueprints and drawings. The children often walk over to the display to study a particular design. After their work session, the children gather with their teacher to discuss their work. They refer to a walk around the neighborhood during which they surveyed and recorded kinds of roofs, types of exteriors, number of stories, and special features. Those charts hang on the wall. Their teacher then shares a book of photographs, showing the work of Frank Lloyd Wright. The children enthusiastically talk about the designs and constructions.

During the month in which the children and their teacher studied architecture, they experienced the important components of the project approach:

- Class discussions
- Investigations
- Field trips
- Visiting an expert or having a guest speaker
- Real objects or artifacts
- Roleplay

On different days children have measured rooms, sketched more designs, developed symbols for designs, written descriptions of homes, and pretended to be realtors, architects, and interior designers. Around the room are architectural magazines and books, many blueprints and sketches, photos of homes and buildings, special measurement tools, and a drawing table with special lights.

The topics for project work usually begin with the children's immediate environment and expand outward to information not so closely related to their lives. Many teachers choose topics for their classes; others follow the children's leads for choice of topics or allow topics to emerge from everyday events. There seems to be an endless number of possible topics, but "no particular body of facts or knowledge need be covered through project work" (Katz & Chard, 1989, p. 67).

Project work offers children many choices in their tasks—what work to do, when to work, whom to work with, and where to work. The teacher is primarily a facilitator who provides materials, alternative activities, and logistical arrangements, and who supports information sharing. Project work usually follows a sequence that moves from planning to actual project work to reflection and review. Planning involves sharing information, describing experiences, and establishing common understandings. During this time, children are encouraged to bring items from home, collect materials, assist with visits and field trip arrangements, and begin their activity plans. The next phase consists of all of the experiences previously described as the main components. This is a time when children are introduced to new information through field trips, guest speakers, books, exhibits, and other forms of study. This is also a time of much drawing, writing, discussion, reading, and investigation. In the final phase, children may display what they have learned through reports, stories or books, displays, projects, plays, and other activities to summarize information. When the children finished their project work on architecture, they invited the class next door to visit their displays and conducted guided tours of their exhibits.

Teachers, consultants, administrators, and teacher educators met at a recent NAEYC conference to discuss the challenges they face in early childhood education and how the project approach can help them meet the challenges. Many of the discussions continued long after the conference, and educators Judy Helm and Sallee Beneke (2003) published the insights in one of the books we recommend at the end of this chapter. Throughout the book they recommend some practical strategies for addressing each of the following challenges:

1. Overcoming the ill effects of poverty
2. Moving children toward literacy
3. Responding to children's special needs
4. Helping children learn a second language
5. Meeting standards effectively (pp. 2–3)

Helm and Beneke also attend to current concerns about the dominant role that television plays in the lives of children, and the wide variation in the quality of child care before school entrance and of after-school care. The authors and their teacher collaborators insist that the challenges are just that—challenges, and not deficits. In Box 5.2, we list and describe some of their practical strategies to give you just a sampling of the wealth of thinking and ideas they have provided, and of their enthusiasm for meeting the challenges. We hope that it entices you to read the entire book.

We think that you will see examples of the practical strategies throughout the stories of programs in the chapters that follow. They are important strategies for all children in all programs. As Helm and Beneke (2003) conclude, children need to "construct their own learning and create their own goals and areas of investigation" (p. 33). All parents need to be involved in their children's learning in meaningful ways. Utimately, children need to see themselves as "successful learners" and they can achieve that image when they are engaged in the project approach.

In all of our curricular approaches, it is important to assess children's learning, and ideally to embed that assessment into the curricular activities. From here, we turn from the concerns about curriculum to those about assessment.

The Project Approach: Meeting the Needs of Children in Poverty

When teachers examined their use of the project approach in meeting the challenge of "overcoming the ill effects of poverty," they focused on children's verbal ability, self-images, and abilities to cope and problem solve, as well as adults as resources. They already knew that the project approach promotes the development of a good relationship between teachers and families, and that it often involves a wider community of support. They came up with eight "practical strategies" for maximizing the effectiveness of projects for children living in poverty" (p. 20). Here are a few of those strategies:

1. *Maximize opportunities for self-initiated learning.* Self-initiated learning can come from children's interests and curiosities as well as from their questions and desire to find answers for themselves. When Tomas's family was expecting a new baby, many of his peers were curious about babies and wanted to know more about what they eat, and how they talk, and how they grow. The resulting project about babies led to deeper questions, studies of the children themselves as babies, visits with parents and babies, and varied math, science, and literacy activities all focused on babies.
2. *Support children's emotional involvement in learning.* During project work, teachers encourage children to talk about how they feel as they are working and learning. Another aspect of project work is the documentation of learning. When children document their work through a series of writings, drawings, charts, and constructions, they are able to see their own progress and are encouraged to describe both pride and frustrations.
3. *Focus on the environment and culture of the child.* When children come to school with limited experiences outside their homes, it is important to encourage topics or study that focus on the children's neighborhood and community. Children and their families will be more comfortable, engaged, and familiar, and thus more likely to be curious or able to raise questions. Projects that grow from explorations of a child's neighborhood will more likely provide culturally relevant experiences and learning. Children and their families will be more likely to talk about the project—conversations that will probably continue after the project is finished.

The practical strategies continue to recommend strengthening intellectual dispositions and to encourage children to solve their own problems and practice social skills. Emphasis is on parent involvement, the role of literacy, and the maintaining of high expectations and standards.

Assessment and Curriculum

Assessment is critical to curriculum because it provides information about children that enables educators to match the child and the curriculum or to improve the curriculum to better meet the child's needs and interests. Although we have talked about assessment in previous chapters, it's probably a good idea to give it more meaning here. Simply put, *assessment* is a process for gathering information about children, and its ultimate purpose is to improve what we do to support and facilitate their learning and development. That definition describes an appropriate process for assessment in early childhood education but many people hear the word *assessment* and think only of standardized tests. Such inerpretation of assessment leads to concerns for young children. Previously in this chapter, we described the stresses of inappropriate assessment and the lack of helpful information they provide. Early childhood educators have been articulate and strong in their advocacy for young children when it comes to assessment. Their message has never been to eliminate assessment but to use it appropriately. The sections that follow describe such appropriateness in terms of making it authentic, embedding it in curriculum, and designing it to culturally responsive and ethical.

AUTHENTIC ASSESSMENT. *Authentic assessment* refers to the kinds of activities we have described as authentic curriculum—play-based, child-centered, hands-on learning. Strategies of authentic assessment involve observing children in natural settings—that is, settings in which they are comfortable and can demonstrate varied aspects of their development. Thematic curriculum, projects, cooperative learning groups, and play are ideal situations for assessment (Miller, 1996).

EMBEDDING ASSESSMENT IN CURRICULUM. You can become skilled at assessment if you practice observing children and recording what you see as often as possible. From there, as you plan curriculum, think about which activities will provide opportunities to observe what children can do and what they understand. For example, if you're planning a series of activities about winter, you might plan some of the following assessment possibilities:

1. As children are painting the giant mural about winter, capture anecdotal notes about how they interact with each other.
2. As children work on their winter books, move from child to child, asking questions about their weather understandings and recording their answers.
3. As children play the matching games about winter (appropriate clothing, animal behaviors, etc.), listen to their explanations and record their thinking.
4. As children "ice skate" with shoe boxes on their feet on the classroom lake or rink, observe their large motor skills and record them on a class checklist.

These assessment examples are the kind you embed or build into your curriculum planning. That way, you're ready to record and capture the wealth of information that is available when children are engaged in curricular activities.

CULTURALLY RESPONSIVE AND ETHICAL ASSESSMENT. In our efforts to provide inclusive curriculum, we must take care to assess children in ways that are ethical, culture fair, and gender fair (Winter, 1999, p. 177). Our observations and recording systems must be accurate and unbiased. If we are sure to collect various kinds of information about children and we do so systematically at different times and in different settings, we are more likely to be accurate in our descriptions of children's abilities. It is ideal to combine parent observations with your observations to be certain that your interpretation is culturally responsive. Parents and family members may see and interpret a child's behavior differently than you do, so it will be important to hear and understand their perspectives and values. Using children's work samples and a description of the context of the work and reasons for its selection as assessment information will again ensure accuracy and ethical assessment practices (p. 177). In Chapter 11 we describe a teacher's use of portfolios to organize and communicate assessment information. Her ideas will extend your assessment understandings further.

Putting It All Together: Weaving the Thinking and Approaches into Your Curriculum

You are probably wondering, "How do I ever begin?" Our response is to spend some time thinking about all the ideas and philosophies we have just described. Think about children and what you already know and feel about supporting their development and learning. Soon, we will ask you to watch for those curriculum ideas at work in the programs we visit together in Chapters 7 through 11. Before you do, we strongly encourage you to reflect with us in Journal 5.5 that follows.

Both children and adults learn in a classroom where there is respect for differences and a spirit of discovery.

JOURNAL 5.5: Return to the beginning of this chapter and skim the curriculum descriptions. Make a list of those ideas and approaches that feel right to you and those that don't. After making your list, ask yourself *why* some of the ideas feel right and why some don't. You might also think about being 3 or 5 years old, and think about whether those ideas would feel right at those ages. This process should begin to reveal your developing philosophy about children and their learning, your values, your comforts and discomforts for working with children, and perhaps the kind of situations in which you will be confident and those in which you will not. It would be powerful to share your list with one of your peers or a group and discuss your differences and similarities. ●

PRINCIPLES AND INSIGHTS: A Summary and Review

In sum, we encourage you to "learn from the children" as Caroline Pratt has urged, observe their development, listen to what emerges from their conversations and activities, and be flexible. Be open to that "bird flying in the window" that David Hawkins described so enthusiastically. Experiment, as Bank Street urges teachers to do, and don't be afraid to make mistakes. Heed the lessons of Sylvia Ashton-Warner and have the "patience, caring, listening, and intuition" to be creative and original with your curricular approaches. At the same time, be cautious not to impose your ideas and answers on children, as Kamii and DeVries warned. When you make mistakes, talk about them with the children. Contemplate the lives of the children and provide real-life activities and materials, as Maria Montessori did.

As we encouraged in Chapter 1 and in this chapter, continue being a learner of early childhood education. There are numerous workshops on curriculum, great books to read, and wonderful teachers all around you with ideas as rich as any we've described in this chapter. As you meet the children in the chapters that follow and observe them both at home and in early childhood programs, you will see much more curriculum. You will be anxious to finish your studies and have a classroom of your own so that you can try out some of your ideas as well as the ideas of others. Look forward to that time, for it is a time of discovery and excitement.

BECOMING AN EARLY CHILDHOOD PROFESSIONAL

Your Professional Portfolio

1. After observing a class (preschool or kindergarten) for a day, develop a one-day plan for yourself. Assume that you are the teacher and use the ideas of this chapter to plan a day for a specific group of children. Along with your plan, describe a rationale for each of the routines or activities you plan.
2. Read one of the books listed in the section that follows and write a critique of the curriculum. Describe your agreement and disagreement with the ideas of the book. In doing so, begin to develop your philosophy of curriculum.

Your Professional Library

The comprehensive nature of this chapter makes it difficult to confine this reading list to just a few books and addresses. If you want to read more, check the references at the end of the book. Don't be put off by the age of some of our recommendations—some of these curriculum books are ageless.

Ashton-Warner, S. (1963). *Teacher.* New York: Simon & Schuster.

Driscoll, A. (1995). *Cases in early childhood education: Stories of programs and practices.* Boston: Allyn and Bacon.

Edwards, C., Gandini, L., & Forman, G. (1995). *The hundred languages of children: The Reggio Emilia approach to early childhood education.* Norwood, NJ: Ablex.

Goffin, S. (1994). *Curriculum models and early childhood education.* New York: Macmillan.

Helm, J. H., & Beneke, S. (2003). *The power of projects: Meeting contemporary challenges in early childhood classrooms—Strategies and solutions.* Washington, DC: NAEYC

Helm, J. H., & Katz, L. (2001). *Young investigators: The project approach in the early years.* Washington, DC: NAEYC.

Hochman, C., Barnet, M., & Weikart, D. (1979). *Young children in action: A manual for preschool educators.* Ypsilanti, MI: High Scope Press.

Nagel, N. (1996). *Learning through real-world problem solving: The power of integrative teaching.* Thousand Oaks, CA: Corwin.

Pratt, C. (1948). *I learn from children.* New York: Harper & Row.

Winter, S. M. (1999). *The early childhood inclusion model.* Olney, MD: Association for Childhood Education International.

CHAPTER

6

Families and Communities

Context for Understanding Children

CHAPTER focus:

When you finish reading and reflecting on this chapter, you will be able to:

1. Show awareness of and be sensitive to the wide diversity of family structures, organizations, and demographics.
2. Appreciate the contemporary issues faced by families.
3. Articulate reasons for involving families in the education of young children.
4. Describe guidelines for building partnerships with families.
5. Assess communities as contexts for understanding young children and their families.

A walk through my neighborhood at about 8:00 A.M. begins to reveal the incredible diversity of families today. As we pass a small cottage-style house, we hear Keeley and her single mom, Kerry, getting ready for their days at school and work, respectively. It's typically a busy start to the day with both of them leaving at the same time.

Farther down the block in a two-story colonial house are two parents and two children who are also preparing for the day. Mom is fixing breakfast for the children while Dad walks the dog. We watch later as the father leaves for work and the mother walks the children to the nearby elementary school. An hour or so later she takes off for her part-time job at a local community agency.

Behind their house is a duplex. On one side lives a grandmother who is raising two girls, a teenager and a preschooler. It's a quiet start to their day as the soft-spoken grandmother reminds each of the girls to straighten her room before coming to breakfast. The teenager runs to catch her bus, while the preschooler remains home to be joined by two other children of similar ages from the neighborhood. Her grandmother is a home caregiver.

In the small apartment complex at the end of the street, we see a single father with his two children, getting ready to go to work. He leaves the apartment carrying his briefcase and several lunch boxes and jackets, and the children follow. He drives them to the nearby elementary school, stops in their classrooms to speak to the teachers, then heads to his office.

Families Today

The families observed on our morning walk are but a microcosm of the diversity of families that exist today. Their differences—family size, family structure, home environment, and work patterns—are a beginning look at the kinds of diversity you will encounter as an educator of their children. That diversity becomes more complex when socioeconomic differences, ethnic and cultural differences, and beliefs about child rearing expand the variation. The community context adds more dimensions to the family differences and to the lives of children. In addition, families today are faced with significant issues and stresses that influence their child-rearing practices and ultimately your educational practices.

This chapter will give you a framework for understanding much of the information of this book. Your understanding of child development theories and information cannot be removed from family and community contexts. Early childhood education curricula must be designed with understandings of and connections to families and communities. Decisions about guiding children's behavior must be made with respect for family differences and often in collaboration with families. And most important, your role as an early childhood educator includes the responsibility to partner with both families and community if you are to provide maximum support and guidance for children's learning and development.

We begin with a consideration of families and work. The escalating numbers of women in the work force have altered family dynamics and ultimately the nature of child rearing. In addition, for both men and women, careers have become intense and more demanding of time and energy, but also a source of more satisfaction, as you will see in the section that follows.

Today's Families and Home versus Work

In 1997, Hochschild interviewed 130 adults and followed them through their "typical days" of juggling families and work. He found that both parents worked more hours than ever before, more than was completely necessary, and not for the reasons we would expect. They worked more hours not for the money, or for fear of job loss, or for advancement reasons, but because they gained so much emotional and social satisfaction at work. In contrast, they found home life stressful, complex, and demanding. It appeared from Hochschild's study that work offered an escape.

The study was one of a limited group of people but it is a trend to consider because it has such huge implications for those who decide to take care of and educate children. When you consider the national statistics reported later in this chapter, you realize how important it is to develop an understanding of the complexity and stresses of family life. It is equally important for you to understand how children feel and think about family life and the effects of adult work lives. A recent study, described in Box 6.1, provides surprising insights about parental employment from children's perspectives. The study is a good reminder for you as you begin your professional preparation—keep checking with children, find out what they think, listen to their ideas, and include their perspectives in the information you use for decision making and planning.

Partnering with families is essential to good early childhood education practices, and those families will vary as widely as their individual children. You will need to have knowledge of their diverse family structures and values, an understanding of their stresses and the complexity of their lives, and an attitude of acceptance toward their diverse life-styles and priorities. At the same time, you will be working to meet their needs and collaborating with them to set common goals related to their children. If all this sounds like a call for "Super-Professional," it is! Children deserve that kind of working relationship between their early childhood educator and their families. This chapter begins to prepare you for that relationship by exploring many of the possible variations in families and communities and describing the issues of today's families.

BOX 6.1

Children's Ideas about Parents' Work and Family Life

Ellen Galinsky has long studied work and family life, but mostly from the perspective of adults. For this recent study she decided to probe for children's perspectives. Over 1,000 children and 600 parents were interviewed about their experiences with parental employment. Some of the differences in the answers of the adults and children were surprising. The most startling difference occurred when children were asked: "If you were granted one wish that would change the way that your mother's/father's work affects your life, what would that wish be?" Many parents (56 percent) guessed that their children would want more time with them. Children, however, wished that their mothers (34 percent) and their fathers (27.5 percent) would be less stressed and tired. It was equally surprising that "more time" was the wish of only 10 to 15 percent of the children.

Eight themes emerged from the data of the study *Ask the Children,* and those themes provide clear guidance for how we as professionals think and talk about work and family life, and how we behave and communicate with children (Galinsky, 2000, pp. 64–68).

1. Working is not good or bad for children; it is how children are parented that makes a difference.
2. It is not just mothering that's important; fathering is very important, too.
3. It is not quality time or quantity time; both make a difference.
4. Parents' jobs affect how they parent.
5. Children are worried about parents because of the stress parents bring home.
6. Children aren't aware that their parents like their jobs as much as parents actually do.
7. It is not child care *or* parent care; child care does not supplant parent care—it is a support to the family and children.
8. A number of parents don't know what goes on in their children's lives.

Ask the Children: What America's Children Really Think about Working Parents (Galinsky, 1999) is worth reading in its entirety and we recommend it for your Professional Library at the end of this chapter. The insights from children around each of the eight themes will give you information for how to work with children, families, and communities. Most importantly, the study reinforces the importance of really listening to children.

Families and Communities: Significant Understandings

Today's television shows, even with their diverse portrayals of families, are but a microcosm of the complexity of families in the twenty-first century. Not only are families organized differently but the roles within families are also vastly different. Families today are characterized by changes from traditional patterns and issues that were never talked about or addressed openly even when they existed. No matter what ECE role you pursue, your interactions with children will need to be sensitive to the complexity and changes in families.

In addition to the individual variation of each family unit, you will also need to consider the community in which children live. Ozzie and Harriet and the Brady Bunch lived in neighborhoods where everyone knew each other and looked out for each other, which was the norm in many communities. Today, such a neighborhood is a rarity! Our communities are vastly different from each other—socioeconomically, geographically, politically, and in the subtleties of relationships, values, communication, and so on. Children will arrive in your classroom, influenced by both their families and their communities, with experiences, values, attitudes, socialization, and motivations.

In a great many situations, early childhood professionals, especially teachers, come from backgrounds that are quite different from the children they teach. It is most unlikely that you will work in the same community in which you live. In Ozzie and Harriet's day, the boys' teachers probably lived a few blocks away. Harriet may have encountered the school principal and his wife in the grocery store on Saturdays. Many teachers today have never seen the neighborhoods in which the children in their classrooms live, and may not have much understanding of their lives.

Our experiences in education and related professions have confirmed the importance of families and communities—of knowing them, involving them, and viewing them as partners, resources, and advocates. Project Head Start has provided excellent leadership for many years in how to involve families and communities. Its programs have demonstrated how to integrate the diversity of families and communities in curriculum, how to respect the variation in family life-styles, and how to work in partnership with communities to better serve the needs of children and families. In addition, research (Epstein, Jansorn, Salinas, Sanders, Simon, & VanVoorhis, 2002; DiNatale, 2002) has shown that when families are involved in children's education through partnerships with schools and other programs, children are more successful and families and educators experience positive gains—everybody wins.

In this chapter, we will guide you in your development of understandings and sensitivities regarding the diversity of families and communities, and we will demonstrate the skills you will need to involve and work in partnership with them. We'll begin by looking at the nature and functions of families today. We will explore the contemporary changes in families that may help you understand why the families of today's children may be different from the families you may have experienced. We will also look at some of the stresses and issues that families face. Child-rearing differences will help explain some of the variations in children with whom you work, and we'll describe those differences with examples that may be familiar.

Personal Assessment for Awareness

Before beginning, you'll find it helpful to assess your own family and community. It's a comfortable starting point for thinking about the differences and influences of family and community.

JOURNAL 6.1: Reflect on your childhood and analyze your family and community at the time when you were young. We've developed a framework (see Figure 6.1) for you to record your impressions—it will prompt you to think about influences that may not come immediately to the surface. The major ideas in the framework are important concepts of this chapter. When you finish reflecting on your childhood, take a break. After a few days, reflect again. This second time, analyze your current living situation—your family and community today. ●

The framework in Figure 6.1 easily converted to a set of questions to pose to families. Their answers will be one source of information to help you get to know the children and their families. It is possible that families will pause and reflect on their own situations as they answer your questions. As we continue throughout this chapter, you may come up with additional questions. While you are reading, think about what kind of information will help you better understand children and families and meet their needs.

As people go through life, they are socialized by everyone and everything they encounter. Socialization begins with one's family and the communities in which one lives. It doesn't stop when one reaches adulthood. People continue to be socialized and to change as a result. Today, as we write this chapter, a list of possibilities has affected who we are. Early this morning, a newspaper story of a 90-year-old who wrote her first book stirred up our enthusiasm and energy to write. A colleague at work has been diagnosed with can-

FIGURE 6.1
Framework for Reflection

Family Reflection

1. List the members of your family (with names, ages, and relation to you).
2. What is the educational background of the adults?
3. What is the employment of the adults?
4. Describe the decision-making process of the family.
5. What are the recreational activities of the family when they are together?
6. How are the household chores distributed?
7. Describe the home.
8. What are the family values or priorities?
9. What kind of support do the adults provide to the children?
10. Who and what are the important influences (people, events, etc.)?

Community Reflection

1. Define your community.
2. Describe the demographics of your community (urban/rural, size, socioeconomics, etc.).
3. List your community's resources.
4. What are the common community meeting places?
5. What kind of attention and support are given to children and families?
6. What are the community issues?
7. What are the advantages of your community? The disadvantages of your community?
8. What are the important influences in the community?

cer, and we think about immortality and become philosophical about our lives. Later, we meet with teachers and listen to their experiences with children who face issues that none of us is prepared to address. We pause and question our approaches to teaching. Some of these experiences may be only fleeting influences but others stay with us and affect our thinking and behavior for years. That process, called **socialization,** is a powerful lens through which to observe children. We begin this section on families with descriptions of how families socialize children, because it helps us convince you of the importance of studying families while studying children.

Family Socialization

Family socialization begins a process through which humans learn and develop to be the adult persons they become. Has this happened to you? You have a close friend, Joan, whom you've known for many years, and finally you meet her family and think to yourself, "Now I understand where Joan gets those habits and behaviors from." For some, the effects of family socialization are very evident and long lasting; for others, there is not much obvious effect; and for still others, it looks like there's no relationship at all. If you look closely, you'll see that some adults choose to adopt behaviors and values that are completely opposite from those of their families. For those individuals, you might also say, "Now I understand why Allan is that way." The socialization is just as strong, but it has a different effect.

For some adults, their interactions with family continues in such a close relationship that the family maintains a dominant role in their ongoing socialization. You probably know some friends in that kind of situation. When you used Figure 6.1 to reflect on your family, did you find different influences during your childhood and your current situation?

EFFECTS OF FAMILY SOCIALIZATION. In Chapters 2 and 3, we described Erikson's stages of development. Those stages offer another model for understanding socialization. In each stage there are influences or agents of socialization who have an impact on the

Family socialization occurs through daily interactions between adults and children. What socialization messages might this child be learning?

child and the messages of socialization being received. As the child develops and advances in psychosocial development, the agents become stronger or weaker in their capacity for influence. Early in a child's development, the family is, of course, the strongest agent, but as the child advances to preschool age, programs or schools begin to exert influence. At school age, peers are active socialization agents. For the first eight years, family, school, community, and peers play a role in the following aspects of a child's socialization:

- The development of trust
- The development of independence
- The tendency to take initiative
- The sense of competence and ambition
- Decisions about who one is
- Relationships with others
- Decisions about future generations
- Reflections on one's life

INTENTIONAL AND UNINTENTIONAL SOCIALIZATION. Some of the influence of families is intentional and some of it is unintentional, a result of some spontaneous interaction. Watch Keeley and her mom and see if you can pick out the intentional and unintentional socialization.

Keeley: Socialization

Kerry, Keeley's mom, is getting ready for work. She stands in front of the mirror and spends a long time putting on makeup. Keeley is sitting near her on the floor playing, but she mostly watches her mom's makeup routine. Then Kerry fixes her hair, pushing it over her ears a certain way and checking her reflection in the mirror frequently. "It's your turn," she says to Keeley and she begins to brush Keeley's hair. "I want a French braid," Keeley says to her mom in a demanding tone. "Is that the way you ask for things?" her mom asks. Keeley gets quiet and says, "Mom, would you fix my hair in a French braid, please?" Her mom smiles and responds lovingly, and immediately starts forming the braid.

The intentional lesson Kerry was trying to teach Keeley is pretty obvious. But what was Keeley learning without Kerry intending to teach it to her? This may take some discussion and there may be some disagreement among your classmates about the unintentional socialization occurring for Keeley. The important idea is that Kerry is not even thinking about teaching Keeley anything in particular. She is simply going about the process of getting herself ready for work, but socialization is occurring.

Family Structures, Organizational Patterns, and Functions

Using the language of the U.S. Bureau of the Census, *families* are defined as "two or more related people living in a household." That sounds like a fairly generic definition, but it is a bit confining for today's families. Some families don't live together in a household but they are families, and two people living together don't have to be related but they can still be a family. If you were to survey your peers and list the variations in family structures, you would probably find the following:

- Two married adults living together
- Two unmarried adults living together
- One adult and a child or children
- Two married adults and a child or children
- Two unmarried adults and a child or children
- One adult and one adult child
- Two married adults, a child or children, and a parent of one of the adults
- Two adults with a child or children from other marriages
- One adult with a child or children and a grandchild or grandchildren.

The list goes on, and with every possible variation. Within family structures, you find more complex differences, such as foster parents, gay or lesbian parents, stepchildren, adopted children, and so on. The structure of the family is one of several factors that influences its ability to feel comfortable in participating in educational settings, thus it will be important for you to know families well as you plan programs for children. An important first step in building a bridge between the culture at home and the one at early childhood educational settings is for educators to talk with families often so that both get to know and understand each other's perspectives and behaviors (DiNatale, 2002).

ORGANIZATIONAL PATTERNS. The possible variation within family structures contributes some information about a child's socialization but from there, the organization of families complicates the socialization process. When we talk about family organization, we are referring to three basic emphases in the way a family handles responsibilities and decision making. Those organizational emphases may be culturally influenced, a family tradition, or a response to societal conditions:

1. **Matriarchal organizations** are those families in which the mother is the primary adult with responsibility for socialization of the children. The mother has the authority to make the family decisions and usually controls the resources for carrying out the responsibilities and decisions.
2. **Patriarchal organizations** are those families in which the father is the primary adult with those same responsibilities, authority, and resources.
3. **Egalitarian organizations** are those families in which the responsibilities, authority, and resources are shared by the adults and the children. It's a family structure in which there is a lot of shared decision making.

FAMILY FUNCTIONS. In addition to the organizational differences, there are three major functions of families: economic functions, socialization functions, and support functions. Those functions serve both families and society. They are essential for our survival.

Some families carry out the *economic function* with one adult working outside the home to earn an income and the other adult taking care of the home and family. Some carry it out with two adults earning incomes and sharing the home responsibilities. One of your authors had a grandmother who was widowed and left with 13 children. While Grandma baked bread to sell and took in ironing, the six oldest children worked at odd jobs around the neighborhood to earn money to help support the family. There are families in which one of the children supports the entire family. There are also families in which the family works together raising crops to earn the family income. Those are but a few examples, but already you can appreciate the huge variation in families' economic functions.

The second function is one you have already encountered in this chapter. Another way of thinking of the *socialization function* of the family is through the teaching or lessons learned in the family context. The most basic lessons are related to values and beliefs, but the family is also a major educator of children's knowledge and understandings, skills, and attitudes. In the early days of this country's history, families were the main educators, but today, the function is been shared between home and school. However, some families feel too busy and stressed to deal with the ever extending issues and lessons that children need. On the other hand, some families are hesitant about turning this important function to others. As a future early childhood professional, you will need to check in with families about your curriculum and be aware of the influence of your own attitudes and beliefs on what you teach children.

The third function is about the *emotional and social support* that every human needs. Children who are developing emotional security and social skills need to be surrounded and cared for by nurturing adults. This function is especially important during early childhood, illness, and old age. This nurturance function is augmented for many families by child care providers of all kinds as more and more parents work to fulfill the economic functions.

An additional function of families for the survival of society is the *reproduction function.* The attitude toward this function has changed over the last 30 years and many adults are making the decision not to have children. Some of the pressure for this decision has come from the economics of society, and some from the professional opportunities expanded for women. There also appears to be less pressure placed on those adults who decide not to have children.

Although all families fulfill the basic functions just described, they prioritize them differently. Some families place their economic function as their highest priority, making money to provide for the family as most important. Others, not as concerned about financial matters, make the support or socialization of their children a priority. Many families balance the functions. It's actually quite a complicated balance and is dependent on a wide range of other circumstances. What is important is to realize that families are struggling to handle multiple functions in the midst of multiple challenges. Those challenges faced by today's families will require your study and sensitivity.

Contemporary Challenges Faced by Families

Entire books are devoted to the topic of challenges faced by families. Each time you open a newspaper, there's a human-interest story of a new challenge faced by families in the midst of rapidly changing federal and state policies and programs. These challenges include poverty, homelessness, divorce, single parenting, and stress, to name just a few. We'll begin with the stresses faced by today's families, and how they affect young children.

Stress in Families

Stress is not a new challenge for families. Life must have been quite stressful for the early pioneer families with the many dangers, the harsh weather and living conditions, and the transition from living in other countries. Today, families, including children, appear to face more stress and to create more stress. The traditional **stressors** (conditions or situations that cause stress) for children include separation anxiety, sibling rivalry, transition to child care or school, peer pressure, and developing independence. For adults, too, the traditional stressors continue—economic pressures, crime, traffic, crowded conditions, and the responsibility of raising a child. The less predictive nature of family life has become a stressor for both adults and children. Even the youngest of children knows of someone whose spouse or parent has left the home. With the doubling of the divorce rate since 1965, both adults and children worry about the possibility or face the feelings of "being abandoned" or the guilt that the divorce is their fault.

Stress in Children

We are just now beginning to learn about stress in the children themselves. Researchers suggest that children under the age of 6 are developmentally less able to cope with stress (Allen & Marotz, 2003). They typically cannot separate their own feelings from what is happening, or choose an appropriate behavior to respond to a new or anxiety-inducing event, or modify their physical reactions in response to stress. The younger the child, the greater the impact of new events and the more powerful and potentially negative stress becomes (Jewett & Peterson, 2003). It will be important to understand children's lives in order to prevent and reduce stress as you provide for their care and development.

WORK STRESS. The work life of most adults has become more complicated and stressful, and with it comes another list of stressors. In some working situations, there is a constant threat of job loss due to technological change and management reorganization. Even for those employees who learn new skills and embrace new technology, there are no guarantees. All of us know someone who has become suddenly unemployed after years of steady work and who is experiencing difficulty finding new employment.

In addition to the insecurities and pressures of today's fast-paced work world, many parents come home to additional pressures and insecurities. At the end of a typical long day, Kerry feels guilty because she is often too tired to play with Keeley. She has barely enough energy to feed her and get her to bed. Sometimes she is not as patient as she would like to be, and that realization is stressful. There's also the stress of taking care of their home in the few hours that are available. There's little chance for a social life—an evening out with a friend, or a late movie once in a while—and that's another source of stress. As you learned earlier in this chapter, children are very concerned about the stress and fatigue adults bring home from work (Galinsky, 1999).

CHILD CARE STRESS. The need for child care adds to the stresses of young families. Issues of availability, quality, cost, and scheduling complicate the situation. Even with the best care at an affordable price in a convenient location with a schedule that accommodates one's work life, many families still feel guilty about not spending time with their children. The most recent statistics at the time of this writing show that every day, "13 million preschoolers, including 6 million infants and toddlers, are in child care" (Children's Defense Fund, 2002). Those numbers represent three out of five young children and do not include after-school or summer activities for school-aged children. Full-day child care easily costs $4,000 to $10,000 per year, which is at least as much as tuition at a public university. This is especially distressing when you realize that one out of four families with young children earns less than $25,000 per year.

In addition to the cost issues with child care is the even more stressful issue of quality. Recent reports indicate that much of child care in the United States is poor to mediocre. Patterns of inadequate care have been reported for infant care, child care centers, and family day care to the extent that children's health, safety, and development are in jeopardy (Children's Defense Fund, 2002). A look at data about the number of children in care, the cost of care, and the quality of care makes it easy to understand why finding child care is such a major problem and cause of stress for families.

In some families, children are cared for by alternating parents working opposing shifts so that one is home while the other is at work. This is referred to as *tag-team care.* No child care option is ideal. Much center care is of uneven quality, with frequent changes in caregivers. Low-income families, who spend almost a quarter of their total income on child care, cannot afford good-quality centers. Many of the informal home care arrangements are not licensed and may have too many children or unsafe conditions. Even relatives may not be ideal caregivers if they are doing it only to earn money. Many relatives are grandparents, and, as we describe later in this chapter, they are worn out by child care responsibilities. Tag-team care by two parents is also wearing on the adults' relationship and well-being. In the next chapter, you will meet three families who are struggling with child care issues and experiencing the stresses and discomfort associated with not being completely satisfied and secure with their infant care arrangements. Their stress is common among today's families.

STRESS FROM WITHIN. Some of the stresses in family life originate within the family. The perfectionist adult and the high-achieving child, for example, can bring stress to all family members. Many of us have observed the stress in a family when one parent is determined to have a baseball champion or a star pianist in the family. The pressure for straight As will also be felt by all members of the family.

SYMPTOMS OF A STRESSFUL FAMILY. Curran's (1985, pp. 8–10) symptoms of a stressful family provide a vignette of many of today's families struggling with the pressures of careers, child raising, and living conditions that do not support families. As you read the following list, think of how the symptoms will affect the relationships within a family and think about the unintended socialization the symptoms will pass on to children. The symptoms, which are familiar enough to be worrisome and remain current today, include the following:

1. Constant sense of tension and urgency; no time to relax
2. Short tempers; sharp words; siblings fighting; misunderstandings
3. Mania to escape (to work, to one's room, to the television)
4. Feelings of frustration over not getting things done

JOURNAL 6.2: Select two or three of the preceding symptoms and reflect on the short-term effects and the long-term effects on children and adults. What will happen to the families if the symptoms persist over a long period of time?

You could probably predict the kinds of stressors that cause the preceding symptoms because you have probably observed or experienced them yourself. They include economics, children's behavior, insufficient adult time, lack of shared responsibility in the family, and communication with children.

Although many families take great pride in their ability to juggle demanding careers, a beautiful home, community involvement, and a calendar overflowing with children's dance classes and soccer games, doctor and dentist appointments, adult time for aerobics and golf, birthday parties, dinner parties, volunteering at the schools, and time with grandparents, one wonders about the cost of such a pace. As you watch a group of children, see if you can determine how their home life may look and sound.

Four-Year-Old Adults

Jonathan, Erika, and Manny (all 4 years old) are in the dramatic play center one morning. Jonathan says, "I'll be the dad and you be the mom, Erika." "OK, let's pretend that we're going to brunch," says Erika. Jonathan objects, "No, I will cook." Erika insists, "No, I want to go out." "Too spensive," Jonathan says, "I want to stay home." Erika pouts and says nothing. "OK, you get the baby ready," says Jonathan, pointing to Manny. Manny quickly gets down on the floor and cries like a baby. Erika talks to him softly and brings a jacket to put on him. "Here, baby, we're going out to eat now." "Hurry up, dear," Jonathan says. Erika responds, "I can't do everything—I need help." Jonathan shrugs his shoulders and says, "OK, I'll help with the baby."

As the three children continue to play, they pretend to take the subway and discuss getting off at 45th street. Erika shouts to Darcy across the room, "Wanna be our waitress?" Darcy rushes over to the area, begins pulling out dishes from the cupboard, and says, "We don't have menus." Erika assures her that it's okay, and that she can just tell them what the "specials" are today. Conversations abound concerning cereal, eggs, sausage, orange juice, and bananas. Erika asks, "Do you have waffles today?" Darcy answers that there are two kinds of waffles: blueberry and chocolate. Erika tells Jonathan and Manny that the waffles are low fat and "very healthy." "No fat for me," she said. Jonathan nags, "Hurry. I have a meeting soon."

Can you begin to predict what you would encounter if you were to visit Erika's home? What information have you gathered in your very brief observation?

As we talk about the common issues facing families today, you will get a preview of scenarios played out in children's interactions with each other or with adults. Children portray what they see in the lives around them, playing roles that are significant in the world around them. For many young children, a common happening in their lives or the lives of their friends is divorce.

Divorce and Single Parenting

The stresses of the divorce process and the obstacles facing single-parent families are many and sometimes formidable. The process begins with a negative public image, even though the number of divorced parents and single-parent households is undeniably significant. The general public still regards divorced parents as being defective and views the adults as failures. The term *broken homes* continues to reinforce the negative stereotype associated with single parents and their children.

As an early childhood educator, you will undoubtedly experience large numbers of children from divorced or separated parents, and children from single nonmarried parents. The reality of American families is seen in the predictions that one-half of all U.S. children will experience the marital breakup of their parents, and of those children, nearly one-half will experience the dissolution of their parents' second marriages (Gasden & Ray, 2002).

ECONOMICS OF DIVORCE. Divorce often begins with a costly financial and intensely emotional legal process. Even with the ease with which divorces are granted under no-fault divorce laws and the lack of assigning blame, there are significant and immediate consequences for the family. Divorce continues to reduce the economic position of women and children more so than that of men. Men typically earn larger salaries, so they continue to increase their standard of living as time goes on. In addition, when the family's assets are divided, it usually is an equal division between the parents, so the parent who has custody of the children then divides his or her half with the children.

The parent who has custody of the children now faces the functions of a family (economic, socialization, and support) alone. For many of those parents, there is a need to work outside of the home, so that the time available for family functions is diminished. In addition to society's tendency to treat the single parent as deviant or abnormal, their families suffer discrimination when they are held to the same expectations to which two-parent families are held.

EFFECTS ON CHILDREN. Before looking more closely at single-parent families, we need to look at what has been learned about the impact divorce has on children. Many studies have been conducted to learn about the effects of family dissolution. In your future work with young children, you will encounter those whose parents have been divorced for a long time and those whose parents have just finished divorce proceedings. You will probably experience a divorce in progress while working with children and parents. One of your authors worked in a large child care facility for several years and regularly experienced a visit from a parent that started with, "I want you to watch Erin closely for the next few months. Her father and I are getting a divorce and I'm worried about how it is affecting her." The details varied in each case, but the parents were always genuinely concerned about their children. In most cases, the adult sitting in that office was in need of comfort and support just like her or his child.

The period during and immediately following divorce is often a disruptive one. There are usually changes in the parents' work habits. Many parents have to seek employment for the first time, or have to work more hours, or change jobs. Divorce may precipitate a move to a different home. Our experiences and that of many early childhood educators tell us that during and after divorce, children often show changes in behavior. Young children experience new fears, sadness, anger, and heightened anxiety. They may act out and become aggressive, perhaps taking responsibility for the divorce, thinking that it was something they did or didn't do. For a short time after the divorce, these young children will be on their best behavior, thinking that their change will bring the other parent back. We've often heard parents say with great relief that their child didn't show any effect of the divorce, and then, months later, be amazed when the child displays very contradictory behavior or becomes aggressive and miserable. Lizzy's story (see Box 6.2) illustrates a common occurrence for children whose parents are separated or divorced. It is very likely that you will meet Lizzy in your future role as an early childhood educator, so her story and the perspectives of her parent and teacher are important to hear.

Some studies have found children of divorce to be more dependent, demanding, unaffectionate, and disobedient in behavior than children from intact families (Hetheringron, Cox, & Cox, 1976). The children in the studies feared abandonment, harm, and loss of love. So much of children's responses depend on the way the parents handle the divorce. Custody battles take a huge toll on the children, and those parents who continue their divorce battles over time will usually raise children with more problems than those who maintain a good relationship.

Depending on the availability of the two parents, children are often without the live-in father role model. Some experts see a serious long-range effect of divorce as the removal of marriage models. They express concern about children growing up without realistic expectations of relationships and future mates as a result. Simons and Associates (1996), however, offer a different look at families of divorce. In some situations, the extended family of the single parent may provide attention and assistance to the family. Often, a close support of friends becomes an extended family. One of your authors was a single parent with four young children. Several of the older couples in our neighborhood became "grandma" and "grandpa" to the children and provided generous support to them.

JOURNAL 6.3: From whom or what do you think children acquire their expectations of relationships? If they don't have models in their families, what other sources do they have? Reflect on the potential for those influences.

All in all, children face significant adjustment even in the most amiable of divorces. Berns (2004) describes a set of important tasks that children must master before they can truly adjust to the divorce of their parents (see Figure 6.2). Without the accomplishment of the those tasks, children continue to face the problems often seen in the families of divorce. From there, the effects of divorce on children are mediated by the kind of family configurations in which they live.

FAMILY CONFIGURATIONS AFTER DIVORCE. Divorce has led to several configurations of families: single-parent mothers, single-parent fathers, joint custody arrangements, and the emergence of stepparents. These configurations are not exclusive, just the most common. A brief look at each of these and how they might influence children will extend your understandings of families and your ability to address family differences. Table 6.1 provides a profile of the kind of family organizations in which children live, as well as information about the employment, economics, parent educational levels, health and nutritional

BOX 6.2

Lizzy's Story

The Parent's Story

I expected Lizzy to be very excited about visiting her dad for Thanksgiving. But she seems glum and worried about her visit.

Lizzy's father and I have been separated for several months now, and I guess the changes haven't been easy for my daughter. She and her dad were always close. So when my husband moved out, Lizzy became clingy, whiny, and angry. She asked question after question. "When is Daddy coming back? Are you going to go away too? Did I do something bad?" I was miserable myself at the time, and it took a lot of effort to comfort my little girl.

Lately, things have been much better. Lizzy loves school. She speaks to her father on the phone regularly, and they see each other at least twice a week. Yet Lizzy still gets upset if her dad is just a few minutes late picking her up. I've noticed, too, that she's a little shy and on her best behavior when her dad is around.

Since every moment with her dad seems very precious to her, I was really surprised that she was upset about going to her father's for Thanksgiving. For the last few nights, Lizzy's had bad dreams. She also found her old security blanket and is sucking her thumb again. It's hard to know how to reassure her, especially since I'm a little nervous myself about spending this first holiday away from my child.

The Teacher's Story

When I greeted Lizzy this morning, I noticed that she looked awfully sullen. I made a mental note to be especially alert to her needs.

Later, Lizzy volunteered what was on her mind: "On Thanksgiving, my dad is taking me to the parade and we're going to my aunt's house. In the nighttime, I'm sleeping over at my dad's house—for my first vacation."

I tried to reassure her as best I could. "Sometimes it's hard to do new things," I said, "but I bet you'll have fun, and you'll be able to tell your mom all about it when you get back."

In spite of my pep talk, Lizzy didn't seem particularly reassured.

Dr. Brodkin's Assessment

Young children often grieve over the breakup of their parents' marriage. Among other things, the departure of a parent exaggerates an underlying fear of abandonment. Lizzy is convinced that because Dad left home, Mom might leave too.

Lizzy's concern about spending this first holiday with only one parent is understandable for another reason: Preschoolers in this situation often comfort themselves by denying that their parents' separation is permanent. However, Thanksgiving spent alone with Dad and Dad's side of the family will dash Lizzy's hopes for the family to be reunited.

What Can the Teacher Do?

The support of this caring teacher is very important to Lizzy right now. The teacher's pep talk was very valuable, even though the child didn't respond to it.

Preschoolers whose parents are separated often rely on their teachers' constancy and reassurance. Just a few moments spent alone with her teacher and a special cheerful word from her each day will help Lizzy continue to adapt to the changes in her life.

The teacher should continue listening to Lizzy's concerns. Later, when Lizzy is ready, the teacher can introduce her to some new activities she might enjoy. Whatever helps Lizzy to feel worthy of love is worth doing, and chatting with her mom will enable the teacher to find the best way of accomplishing that.

What Can the Parents Do?

Fortunately for Lizzy, her parents are not feuding over her. Her mother respects the child's relationship with her father and may sense that this separate holiday will help Lizzy gradually accept the impending divorce. Of course, Lizzy and her mother will miss each other. Lizzy's mom should acknowledge that and continue to reassure her daughter that she'll be there when Lizzy gets back. She could point out that Lizzy can speak to her on the phone when she's away, just like she speaks to Dad.

Gentle corrections of the child's misconceptions, along with acceptance of her feelings, will

(continued)

BOX 6.2 **continued**

bolster Lizzy's self-esteem. In time, Lizzy will realize that the breakup of the marriage is not her fault. And with such understanding parents, one day she is likely to see that she is loved by both her mom and her dad—and that she will never lose either one of them.

Resources on Divorce

How to Help Your Child Overcome Your Divorce by Elissa P. Benedek, M.D., and Catherine F. Brown. Washington, D.C.: American Psychiatric Press, Inc., 1995.

How to Win as a Stepfamily by Emily B. Visher, Ph.D. & John S. Visher, M.D.; 2nd edition, New York: Brunner-Mazel, 1982.

Source: From "I'm Going to My Dad's for Thanksgiving" by Adele M. Brodkin from *Scholastic Parent & Child* magazine.

support, and benefits to children of each of the major ethnic groups in the United States. It gives you a current preview of the home situations you can expect for the children with whom you will work.

Single-parent mothers are the most frequent configurations after divorce. The latest predictions are that at least 50 percent of all children born today will spend some part of their childhood living in single-parent families, generally headed by women (Gadsden & Ray, 2002). In many female-headed families, poverty or reduced income results from divorce. Women typically earn less than men, so the family economics are seriously affected when the mother is awarded custody of the children. The resulting poverty can be associated with more than half of the disadvantages of single-parent families.

FIGURE 6.2

Adjustment Tasks Faced by Children of Divorce

1. Acknowledgment of the reality of the marriage break-up. Many children cannot face the fact that their parents have split and that they are not living together anymore. They hold on to the hope that everything will get fixed eventually.
2. Detach from any parental conflict and focus on usual pursuits. Most children have their own agenda of interest and needs and under ordinary circumstances focus on themselves and their friends. For a time they will focus on the divorce, their parents, and any conflict that is occurring, rather than their own pursuits.
3. Adapt to the loss. For a while children will be absorbed with their sense of loss. Many experience feelings of rejection and disappointment, and will need time to get over those feelings.
4. Resolve anger and self-blame. Children need to get over their self-blame and blaming their parents, and come to terms with the situation without the aspect of blame. They also need to express and let go of the anger they feel toward their parents and the situation.
5. Accept the permanence of divorce. For a long time children hold on to the hope that their parents will get back together. It is an important task for them to accept the idea that their parents will never be together again.
6. Achieve realistic hopes about human relationships. This may take a lifetime and lots of experience, but it is contingent upon completion of the other tasks.

Source: Excerpt from *Child, Family, and Community,* 3rd edition by Roberta M. Berns. © 1993. Reprinted with permission of Wadsworth, a division of Thomson Learning: www.thomsonrights.com. Fax 800-730-2215.

TABLE 6.1 A Profile of America's Children (March 1996)

Percent of Children under 18	Total	White	Black	American Indian	Asian Americans	Hispanic
Living with both parents	71.6%	78.0%	38.7%	57.1%	84.0%	67.2%
Living with only a father	3.4	3.3	3.9	6.0	3.1	3.2
Living with only a mother	24.2	17.9	56.9	36.5	12.5	28.6
Living with grandparents only	2.0	1.4	5.4	3.5	0.9	2.4
Who are foster children	0.6	0.5	1.3	1.1	0.2	0.7
With a grandparent in the home	8.0	6.1	15.7	11.9	13.4	10.2
Received some child support in 1995	12.5	12.4	14.4	15.6	4.7	7.9
Parents own their home	56.9	63.4	28.2	35.9	50.3	33.4
Family had earnings in 1995	92.1	94.7	80.7	85.5	88.8	86.4
At least one parent at work	84.1	88.5	64.9	73.5	79.7	75.4
A parent unemployed	6.5	5.8	9.4	12.9	6.0	10.5
Whose mother works	59.6	61.1	53.7	54.1	55.9	43.3
Father works, mother at home	20.4	23.2	7.7	12.4	20.4	27.4
A parent completed college	27.7	30.0	13.2	15.2	45.2	8.1
Neither parent is a HS graduate	14.7	12.6	23.9	23.4	16.2	43.9
Child is not a citizen	3.4	2.8	1.9	1.2	21.3	12.1
Living below poverty	20.5	16.0	41.3	41.4	19.2	39.5
Living above poverty and below 4 times poverty	56.8	58.8	49.4	48.4	51.3	53.9
Living over 4 times poverty	22.6	25.2	9.3	10.1	29.4	6.6
Living in central city	24.7	19.1	48.1	27.5	38.1	40.0
Covered by private health insurance	66.1	71.0	43.9	44.6	67.2	38.3
Covered by employer-provided health insurance	61.6	66.0	41.6	42.9	61.3	36.7
Covered by Medicaid	23.2	18.3	45.4	51.8	21.9	37.4
Covered by any health insurance	86.2	86.6	84.7	86.3	86.0	73.2
Without health insurance	13.8	13.4	15.3	13.7	14.0	26.8
Family received food stamps in 1995	18.1	13.5	40.3	33.2	14.8	31.6
Family received SSI benefits in 1995	4.2	2.8	9.5	5.1	8.9	4.8
Family received AFDC/General Assistance in 1995	12.6	8.7	30.5	24.6	12.9	21.5

Source: Children's Defense Fund, *The State of Children in America's Union,* 2002, Washington, DC. Reprinted by permission.

The absence of a father may also contribute to the development of children. For years after a divorce, boys may have trouble concentrating and may interact aggressively with their mothers, teachers, and other boys (Hetherington, Cox, & Cox, 1985). Girls are also influenced by the father's absence, displaying one of two possible patterns. The first pattern is behavior characterized by passiveness, withdrawal, and shyness with males; the other pattern is aggressiveness, overt activity, and flirtatiousness with males (Hetherington, 1972).

Many variables determine what happens to both boys and girls: their age when the father leaves, the quality of the mother/father relationship before the divorce, the length of the father's absence, the availability of other male models, and the emotional state of the mother during and after the divorce. So much is dependent on the role of the nonresidential father and how he interacts with children. The effects of divorce and single parents are influenced by a wide range of complex factors, so we urge you to use caution in generalizing about what happens to children.

It is interesting to note that current studies have documented that mothers in divorced families spend more time on homework projects with their children than do married women working. It has also been noted that single parents (mothers or fathers) are more likely to praise good grades and are more likely to get upset and angry when their children receive bad grades. Recent studies documented a noteworthy pattern: Single parents spend more time talking with their children than do married parents (Morrison, 1995; Richards & Schmiege, 1993).

Single-parent fathers are a second configuration. As you can see from Table 6.1, only 3.4 percent of all children live with a single-parent father. Consequently, little has been written about them and few research studies have been conducted. Until recently, it was an automatic decision that children would live with their mother, but now the courts are taking into consideration the actual needs of the children and specific situations, so fathers are beginning to get custody.

When fathers do get custody of children, much of the child raising is done by others—caregivers, grandparents, other relatives, and friends—more so than with single-parent mothers. Thus, children with single-parent fathers do usually have contact with female role models. Research has also shown that children living with a single-parent father have more contact with their mothers than children living with a single-parent mother have with their fathers.

Single-parent fathers appear to have more of a struggle balancing employment, housework, and child rearing. Society doesn't prepare boys for those roles very well, so assuming domestic tasks and parenting are often more difficult for men than women. Support groups for men have sprung up to assist with the isolation men have felt in those roles. As you can see from the statements in Figure 6.3, attention to fathers, married or divorced or single, has become critical to quality early childhood education programs and practices. The insights remind us that we will need to develop new understandings of families in general, and of fathers in particular if we are to develop good relations with fathers and engage them in our programs. The research indicates that higher levels of father involvement in children's typical routines and activities are associated with fewer behavior problems and higher levels of sociability (Gadsden & Ray, 2002, p. 38). There is much indication that father involvement influences children's school success. "Fathers can ensure that their children are exposed to the best environmental stimuli by participating at home and in early childhood settings" and early childhood educators can provide both encouragement and support for their participation (pp. 39–40).

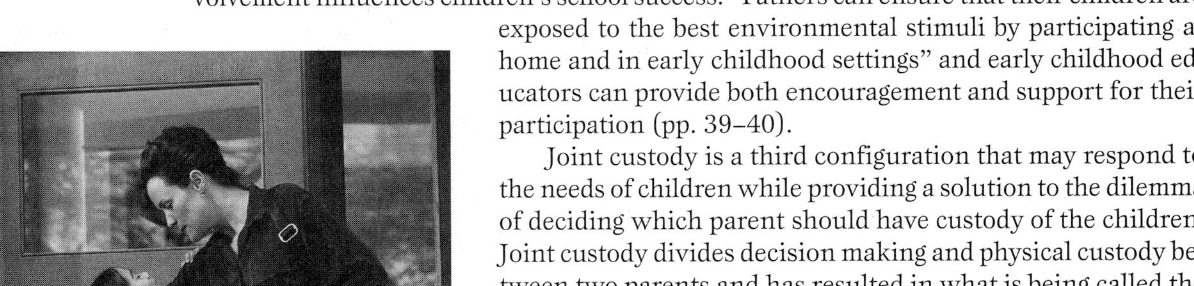

Single parents often struggle to balance employment, housework, and child rearing. It's often difficult to maintain children's needs as a priority.

Joint custody is a third configuration that may respond to the needs of children while providing a solution to the dilemma of deciding which parent should have custody of the children. Joint custody divides decision making and physical custody between two parents and has resulted in what is being called the *binuclear family.* In general, children do not feel abandoned, for they are part of two homes and two family groups. The real advantage of joint custody is the necessity for both parents to put aside their differences and focus on the children, if this arrangement is to succeed. Joint custody requires real cooperation and communication to work well. There are issues of scheduling, agreement on decisions, consistency of discipline, and, for some children, the stress of continual separation and reattachment. This configuration is too new to know the long range effects of this arrangement.

Families with stepparents are a fourth configuration. With approximately 1.5 million adults remarrying each year, and most of them with children, there are many stepparents to be considered when we look at the whole picture of children's families. The biggest issue for stepparents is the lack of legal rights. Many stepparents share in the parenting and support of children but have no rights.

The new family that forms when two adults with children from other marriages get together is called a *blended family.* In

FIGURE 6.3

Insights for Early Childhood Educators to Engage Fathers: Key Ideas

- Federally funded early childhood programs such as Head Start and other child-family programs have been mandated to become "father friendly"—welcoming and inviting fathers to participate.
- Typically, early childhood educators tend to engage more with mothers than with fathers because mothers typically have been the primary providers of child rearing, caregiving, and socialization.
- Research needs to more precisely define *father* and *family involvement* and examine the culturally rich dimensions of children's early care and education experiences in order to guide programs in their involvement of fathers.
- The more hours mothers work and the more children in the household, the greater the likelihood that fathers will provide caregiving.
- Father involvement is influenced by a father's willingness to engage as an equal partner in family life, child care, and child socialization. That willingness may be influenced by cultural norms and expectations.
- The likelihood that a father's presence will result in a positive interaction with his child increases if he can accept and work with other caregivers for the child's welfare, even when the nature of his relationship and residence with the child has changes.

Source: Based on Gadsden and Ray (2000, pp. 33–37).

many cases, the remarriage process is almost as traumatic to the family as divorce. The adjustments that go with forming a blended family are significant:

- New roles and relationships
- New rules and values
- Less family cohesion
- Newly defined family communication
- Loyalty dilemmas for children
- Competition for attention
- Hostility toward the new parent and new siblings

In the first few years of the remarriage, every decision is a complex process with new relationships and roles. Those first few years are difficult and require understanding, patience, consistent communication, and positive working processes. Groups such as the Stepfamily Association can be helpful to blended families. If a child in your preschool or kindergarten is in a newly blended family, you may want to stay in close contact with the family, knowing that a huge transition is taking place.

A final configuration that has followed divorce is that of grandparents as parents. The *new nuclear family,* or *skipped generational parenting,* is becoming a prominent alternative family structure that continues to increase at a rapid pace. Over three million children live in households where their grandparents are present, and, according to the 1990 Census, in more than one-third of the homes, grandparents are the sole caregivers of the children (Nelson, 1997). Although grandparents as parents is not a completely new phenomenon, the contributing factors for such family structures today are different from the past. The major causes are teen pregnancy, high divorce rates, domestic violence, incarceration of parents, substance abuse, and AIDS. The rise in skipped generational parenting is prevalent in all ethnic and socioeconomic groups, but a large percentage (46 percent) of all children being raised exclusively by grandparents are African American. Many of those grandparents (61 percent) live on fixed incomes, so the issues of poverty, health care, and sometimes homelessness add challenges to the already challenging task of raising grandchildren.

Although most grandparents are quite experienced in child raising, becoming a parent again brings on a sudden life-style change for most grandparents. Many of the children turned over to their care are emotionally and/or physically impaired. The older adults are often impaired themselves, so the parenting role and related responsibilities are doubly challenging. An additional stress in the relationship comes from guilt and a need to come to terms with the situation that is keeping the children's natural parents from handling their own child-rearing responsibilities. Many of the grandparents blame themselves for the situation in which their son or daughter becomes a drug addict, or abuses a child, or needs to work long hours due to financial difficulties associated with divorce.

As an early childhood educator, it will be important for you to develop new understandings and sensitivities with respect to this family structure. Some of you may have been raised by grandparents, and you will have some good insights about what issues are faced by this new nuclear family. For those of you who were not raised by grandparents, it is important for you to reflect on this issue.

JOURNAL 6.4: It's the end of the day in your preschool program or first-grade class and one of the children in your care, Tomas, is being picked up by grandparents who are his sole caregivers. In addition to the sensitivities you would have for parents, in general, at the end of the day, what would you keep in mind as you greet Tomas's grandparents?

The configurations that we have described may follow divorce or they may result from choices made by adults to embrace alternative parenting and family configurations. What is important for your professional role is your awareness of these configurations. That awareness, accompanied by frequent and sensitive communication, will support your capacity to respond to the diversity of young children and their families.

Poverty

A few key points about children and poverty will provide a picture of how many young children live:

- More than 1 in 6 children nationwide live below the poverty line (U.S. Census Bureau, 2000).
- The poverty rate is highest for young children (U.S. Census Bureau, 2000).
- The child poverty rate in the United States is two to three times higher than that of most major industrialized nations (National Center for Children in Poverty, 2001).
- When family income is below the poverty level, young children are at risk of infant mortality or health problems that affect learning and development.
- Children are more at risk when poverty occurs early in life (Helm & Lang, 2003).
- Living in poverty may involve homelessness or living in an unsafe neighborhood.
- Parenting, caregiving, and interactions with children may be jeopardized by the stresses of poverty.

Added to that overwhelmingly worrisome data are the direct effects of today's economy on children and families in poverty:

- The median income of families with children has not kept up with inflation. The difference between families with and without children represents a growing generational divide. Young workers in their child-bearing years are suffering most of the brunt of economic losses.
- It takes two earners to support children. Millions of families have been forced to send a second parent into the work force to compensate for the lower wages now earned by one worker. Even with those two parents working, declining wages have meant that family incomes don't keep up with the cost of living.
- Child care expenses and other work-related costs reduce the new lower incomes even further.
- Job-related benefits are shrinking. Fewer and fewer employers are providing essential fringe benefits.

EFFECTS ON CHILDREN. For children of all ages, poverty has some devastating effects. Figure 6.4 displays some of the demographics related to poverty. Poor children are two times more likely than nonpoor children to have stunted growth, iron deficiency, and severe asthma. A government study in 1996 showed that poverty placed children at greater risk of dying before their first birthdays than did a mother's smoking during pregnancy. Another study conducted by the U.S. Department of Education found that for every year a child spends in poverty, there is the chance that the child will fall behind grade level by age 18. In the 1994 book, *Wasting America's Future,* the Children's Defense Fund estimates that every year of child poverty at current levels will cost the nation at least $36 billion in lost future productivity alone, because poor children will be less educated and less effective workers.

For parents struggling to raise a child, poverty adds extensive stress to the family. McLoyd (1990) states that economic hardship experienced by lower-class families is associated with anxiety, depression, and irritability. With those qualities may come a tendency on the part of parents to be punitive, inconsistent, authoritarian, and generally nonsupportive of their children. The strain of poverty may also promote the use of disciplinary approaches that take less time and effort than approaches such as reasoning and negotiating. Spanking and forms of physical punishment are quick; they may relieve frustration and they don't demand much thinking in the midst of multiple worries and stress.

EFFECTS ON PARENTS. Families in poverty, when parents are working, are influenced by the kind of occupations in which the parents work. Kohn (1977) has found that lower-class parents look at their children's behavior with a focus on its immediate consequences and its external characteristics, whereas middle-class parents explore their children's motives and the attitudes expressed by their behavior. Kohn interpreted these differences as connected to the characteristics associated with the level of occupation. Bronfenbrenner and Crouter (1982) concur that parents' workplaces affect their perceptions of life and the way they interact with family members. Consequently, their parenting styles reflect aspects of their work life. Again, as you watch children play, you will see indications of these influences in their conversations, roleplaying, interactions, vocabulary, and perspectives.

It is possible that parents from higher socioeconomic statuses—parents with enough money to be comfortable while raising their families—are more likely to show more warmth and affection, talk to their children more, be more democratic, be receptive to

FIGURE 6.4

Key Facts and Significant Moments: A Look at America's Children

- 3 in 5 preschoolers have mothers in the labor force.
- 1 in 4 children lives with only one parent.
- 1 in 5 children is born to a mother who did not graduate from high school.
- 1 in 8 children has no health insurance.
- 1 in 3 children is behind a year or more in school.
- 1 in 8 children is born to a teen-age mother.
- 1 in 8 children lives in a family receiving food stamps.

Every 11 seconds	a child is reported abused or neglected
Every 43 seconds	a baby is born into poverty
Every minute	a baby is born to a teen mother
Every minute	a baby is born without health insurance
Every 19 minutes	a baby dies

Source: Compiled from Children's Defense Fund, *The State of Children in America's Union,* 2002, Washington, DC. Reprinted by permission.

their children's opinions, and stress creativity, independence, curiosity, ambition, and self-control. When you put yourself in the shoes of parents from lower socioeconomic statuses—parents without enough money to be comfortable while raising their families, with constant worries about how to feed, clothe, and shelter their children—you can begin to understand why their behavior might differ significantly from the behavior of parents from higher socioeconomic statuses.

POVERTY AND HOUSING. The information on poverty previously described looks even more bleak when reviewed in the context of housing costs. Rent increases have exceeded inflation and much low-income housing has been lost to decay, gentrification, and urban development. The National Low-Income Housing Coalition reported in 1996 that a full-time minimum-wage income is now inadequate to afford moderate-cost, moderate-quality housing in every one of the 404 metropolitan areas that were studied (Bernstine, 1997). At the same time, the federal government is cutting back on housing assistance for low- and moderate-income families, slashing its support for both public housing and assisted housing. In cities where housing assistance is available, waiting periods for housing averages 19 months for public housing and 31 months for housing certificates. Some of this information on housing costs helps explain the prominence of another challenge to families—homelessness.

Homelessness

Each family's experience of being homeless is different. Much depends on why the family is homeless—loss of job, substance abuse, psychiatric disability, divorce, recent immigration, illness, runaway situations, or poverty. That experience is also filtered through a range of temporary homes—a safe and clean family shelter, a welfare hotel/motel, a large crowded gymnasium-type shelter, the family car, or a make-shift tent along the highway. The information on the costs and lack of housing described in the previous section has been cited most frequently as a major cause of homelessness. Much about the experience also depends on what kind of services are available to the family from federal, state, and local sources.

The McKinney Act of 1987 was recently reauthorized as part of the No Child Left Behind Act of 2001 with a specific definition of *homelessness* as living in motels, cars, or campgrounds, and possibly extended to families that are "doubled up" with another family in an apartment. The new act eases the intimidating barriers of enrollment policies and procedures, and makes school attendance for homeless children a priority. School districts must appoint a liaison to communicate with homeless families and must ensure that homeless students are not separated or segregated based on their housing status (Berliner, 2002). Both elementary and early childhood educators will need new understandings and alternative ways of addressing the needs of homeless children with respect to their homework, attendance, food and sleep needs, social experiences, and family communication.

The composition of homeless families (now one-third of all homeless people) includes the full range of kinds of families. Every possible family structure is present, from two-parent families with an unemployed breadwinner to a single mom who is fleeing with her children from domestic violence. Homelessness puts families, and especially young children, in environments that often feel chaotic and disorganized. There is little of the security and comfort that young children need for their healthy development. Childhood is a time when young children are working toward a sense of self, autonomy, and trust in their world, and it's difficult to do so in some of the shelter situations or in a daily move from place to place.

The problem of homeless young children has become so significant that two trends have occurred: Research has focused on these children to determine the effects of homelessness, and early childhood programs (schools and child care centers) have been developed to meet the needs of these children (McCall, 1990). The research is important because of its implications for policymakers, educators, and service providers. You will get some idea of what these young children need by looking at the studies that have been done.

RESEARCH ON HOMELESS YOUNG CHILDREN. In general, research has documented widespread developmental delays and emotional disturbances in young children who are homeless (Bassuk & Rosenberg, 1990; Grant, 1990). Studies of the effects of homelessness have documented poor health status, higher-than-expected developmental delays, and emotional and behavioral problems exhibited by the children (Molnar, Rath, & Klein, 1990; Rafferty & Shinn, 1991). Educators and caregivers report short attention span, withdrawal, aggression, speech delays, sleep disorders, difficulty in organizing behavior, regressive behaviors, awkward motor behavior, and immature social skills (Klein, Bittle, & Molnar, 1993). Many of these behaviors can interfere with a child's healthy development and self-esteem.

Parents describe a number of issues that could easily explain the observations of educators:

- "Since we first applied for shelter, my kids have changed schools eight or nine times."
- "It's not fair to make us wait so late to take us into the shelter and then get us up so early. My kids don't want to get up after five or six hours of sleep."
- "We don't have enough clothing and I can't get what we have washed so they can go to school." (Children's Defense Fund, 2002)

Some researchers, however, interpret quite differently what the studies show. They see the behaviors as coping mechanisms, or "highly developed inner strengths" (Douglass, 1996). Douglass and colleagues intensely studied individual young children in an urban family shelter with an on-site early childhood education program. The researchers saw deficiencies in coping strategies, or ways of managing and mediating stressful events. We are going to look at one of the children in that early childhood program to see what the researchers noticed.

Keisha

Four-year-old Keisha lived in the shelter for one year and attended the ECE program during that time. During her first four weeks in the program, she showed almost no attention span or ability to focus on a task or activity. Her standard greeting to others was a rude "shut up" or "get away from me." She was aggressive, she bit others, and she spit. According to her mother, these behaviors began shortly after the family lost their apartment and became homeless. An assessment of Keisha during this initial period found her to be angry, defensive, unable to form meaningful or supportive relationships with peers or adults, unable to focus on a task, aggressive with her peers, and lacking in verbal skills.

By her fifth week in the shelter and the ECE program, Keisha had begun to settle in. She began to smile, to speak, and to carry on elaborate conversations with both children and adults. She tentatively developed friendships, reaching out to children and teachers. She sought attention from teachers by using positive behaviors, rather than by negative behaviors. She seemed to magically transform into a loving, warm, happy child who dived into projects and activities with depth, understanding, a readiness to learn, and enthusiasm. Feeling safe, loved, "at home," and adjusted to her new home and school, Keisha was able to leave behind her reactions to the stress of moving and to continue meeting the developmental challenges and milestones of a typical four year old. (Douglass, 1996, pp. 747–748)

CONSIDERATIONS OF HOMELESS YOUNG CHILDREN. If in the future you were to work with a homeless family, what could you expect? Even the simplest of registration forms and other kinds of data are problematic for homeless families. They have no permanent address or telephone number, nor do they generally have records on the children. Basic essentials such as clothing and food may also be issues for the homeless families.

In working with the child of a homeless family, you may need to address issues of cleanliness and health. Children may be tired, hungry, or ill. In spite of homeless families' best efforts, there may not be adequate facilities to care for their children. If the children have been homeless for a long period, a room full of play materials may be overwhelming to them. You will need to provide extensive support to the child and to the family.

A major issue for homeless families is health. Their living conditions are not very supportive of good health habits, and they seldom have health care benefits. It is one more source of stress in their lives and the lives of many families.

Health

The dilemma surrounding health insurance and benefits for families is much like that of housing costs and availability. The Children's Defense Fund 1997 Yearbook describes the situation for children and families: "The erosion of private, employer-based insurance coverage for American children of working parents is threatening their chances of getting a healthy start in life. . . . As a result, the number of uninsured children has risen from 8.2 million in 1987 to 12 million in 2000" (2000, p. 26). Many of those children have one or more working parents but the parents' incomes are too high to qualify for Medicaid, and their jobs don't provide employer-paid insurance coverage for their families. Seldom can they afford the high cost of premiums for family health insurance coverage.

LACK OF HEALTH COVERAGE: EFFECTS ON CHILDREN AND FAMILIES. The human costs of children's and families' lack of health coverage are fairly predictable. Those families are more likely to report poorer health, see doctors less often, and be without preventive care. A decision these families frequently face is whether to spend their money on prescriptions or food. Most children in these families have ear infections and asthma that go untreated, miss school more often due to illness, and seldom have regular checkups. These same children often were born to women who did not have prenatal care. Figure 6.5 reveals information about children without health coverage.

GOOD NEWS ABOUT CHILDREN'S HEALTH. The good news with respect to children's health is that many states have taken the initiative to fund programs that support the families who need health coverage and services. For example, New York funded a Child Health Plus program that helps working families buy private health insurance for children. Massachusetts has passed legislation to extend health coverage to at least 125,000 of the state's 160,000 previously uninsured children.

The other good news can be seen in improved immunization rates (a record level of 80 percent). Congress and the states have expanded efforts toward this end, and the ef-

FIGURE 6.5
Who Are the Uninsured Children?

Race and Ethnicity

43.8 percent are White.
30.6 percent are Hispanic.
19.8 percent are Black.
4.6 percent are Asian or Pacific Islander.
1.3 percent are American Indian or Alaskan Natives.

Family Structure

87.3 percent have at least one working parent.
64.6 percent have at least one parent who works full-time throughout the year.
66.3 percent live in families with incomes above poverty.
53.6 percent live in a two-parent household.

Note: Children are younger than 19. Children of Hispanic origin are excluded from the other racial and ethnic categories. Insurance, income, and employment information are for 1998; all other information is for March 1999.

Source: Children's Defense Fund, *The State of Children in America's Union,* 2002, Washington, DC. Reprinted by permission.

forts have paid off: The rate of common children's diseases has decreased significantly and in 1996 were the lowest ever reported. There is, however, an alarming number of children who have died (roughly 1,000 each year) and who have been diagnosed (roughly 30,000 since 1981) with AIDS and HIV infection. This is another health battle to be waged with respect to young children.

Interracial Marriages and Biracial Children

Children of mixed parentage account for a growing population in early childhood programs. The National Center for Health Statistics (NCHS) reported 620,000 births of children with one Black and one White parent in 1990 and predicted a continuing increase. A similar pattern is seen for marriages between other races and for the birth of children with other dual heritages. Much like divorce, the stress related to interracial marriages comes from society's disapproval of the unions of two people of different races. The stress for children comes from a kind of ambiguous ethnicity or conflicts about their dual ethnic identity.

Early childhood educators are aware of the connection between a child's success and his or her racial/ethnic self-esteem. As we have described in Chapter 2, identity is an emerging concept for young children. For young biracial or bicultural children it is a fluid or changing identity, depending on the child's development and environment (California Child Care Health program, 2000). It will be important for children to process their dual identities, and early childhood educators will need to provide support to both children and families during those times.

SOCIALIZATION OF BIRACIAL CHILDREN. What typically happens to **biracial and bicultural children** is that they are socialized much more in one culture than the other. "The child of dual heritage is not likely to have equal exposure to both of her cultural heritages" (Morrison & Rogers, 1996, p. 30). At the same time, the biracial child is aware of the values, perceptions, and typical behaviors of the two cultural systems. Very early in these children's lives, they become aware of being different. Whether it be in child care or preschool, or in the community, the biracial child may experience the social pressure that is often directed to someone who is different.

When parents are asked about the racial or cultural identity of their biracial child, their responses vary significantly. Those responses indicate their uncertainty about the dual heritage or their discouragement with societal pressure. The variation in parents' responses is one indication of the stress that is experienced by families of dual races or cultures. Biracial children experience the feeling of not "fitting in" anywhere during their childhood and it becomes a serious source of conflict for many biracial adolescents (Gibbs, 1989). One of those socialization messages that we talked about earlier in this chapter comes from society and it tells children that everyone belongs in a group. From there, children develop their identities within a group. The situation is further complicated because children need to identify themselves with their parents, and each of the parents has a different ethnic identity. Ideally, biracial children need to identify with both of their parents, but society and the parents themselves don't support such development.

MAINTAINING LANGUAGES AND CULTURES. In Chapter 8, you will meet Ibrahim, his brother Muhammed, and the boys' parents, Faridah and Amr. They talk about the difficulties of keeping both parent languages available to their children and describe their awareness of Ibrahim and Muhammed becoming part of the dominant White culture. Faridah tells us that the common language of the two adults is English because neither of them speaks the other's language. "When we talk with the boys, however, we each use our own language, so that they are becoming fluent in both languages—Malay and Arabic." We realized as we listened to Muhammed's excellent English that the boys are trilingual. Faridah moves smoothly from speaking with us in English to speaking with her sons in Malay, and Amr did the same.

When we ask Faridah about how she and Amr work to keep the two cultures part of their family and the boys' heritage, she describes her role as one of acquainting the boys with foods and home traditions from her country. "The way we furnish our home also reflects our cultures," she states as she describes the lack of items hanging on the walls. She laments that her husband has many books and materials from his country to use with the boys because his friends send packages to him regularly, and that most of her materials have been translated into English. "What we have most in common is our religion," Faridah tells us. That common culture is their Muslim religion, and it influences their eating habits, their social life, and their support network, which is primarily composed of friends who attend the same mosque.

When you get to know parents like Faridah and Amr, you realize the complexity of raising biracial or, in their case, tricultural children. During our conversation, we realized the importance of the information they were sharing for the early childhood educators who work with their children.

Summary of Contemporary Challenges

You may be wondering how you can use this information if you are a teacher or a caregiver. After reading about divorce and poverty, you may be also be feeling overwhelmed by the enormity of family issues. Before talking about how to work in partnership with families, we think that it's important to reflect on those issues, to talk about how you are feeling, and to plan to use some of those new awarenesses.

Family Involvement in Early Childhood Education

Before reading this chapter, you may not have thought much about families and the role they will play in your future work in early childhood education. We have all been very focused on the children and their development and their play up to this point, so it's not surprising that parents and families have not been a major consideration. Stop and think about your own experience as a learner and about how your family was involved in your education.

New Thinking about Family Involvement

How many of you remember your parents going to conferences or to Open House nights? How many of you remember your parent serving as a driver or chaperone for field trips or other events? Those are fairly common experiences. As you will read in the next part of this chapter, educators now think much more holistically about family involvement. There's compelling information from research about the importance of that involvement, and there are both state and national policies recognizing and recommending that involvement. As you read about the children in Chapters 7 through 11, you will see their families involved in their early childhood programs and classes in a wide variety of ways. Before you observe those involvement strategies and approaches, let's talk about why family involvement is important and how to develop a philosophy about family involvement.

When families are involved, there is a communication to children about the value of their families. Sometimes, that value may not be what is intended. When Keeley's mom, Kerry, assists in the computer lab at her school, Keeley may think that the school believes that her mom is smart and that Keeley's teacher appreciates her mom. However, if Keeley only observes her teacher communicating with her mom to talk about Keeley's problems in class, there is another message. If the only request for help is to bake a cake for the school fair, there is yet another message.

All children want to feel pride in their families, and that pride will probably influence how the child feels about herself. Extensive research, much of it very current, shows that families are critical to children's success. We think that the findings of some of those studies are an important foundation to your philosophy about family involvement and to your decisions about the role families will play in your future work.

Research on Family Involvement

In 1981, when *The Evidence Grows* (Henderson, 1981) was published (a first report on parent involvement), there were only 35 studies. It was a time when it was not generally recognized that involving parents (not families) would influence children's success. In 1987, when *The Evidence Continues to Grow* (Henderson, 1987) was released, the number of studies increased and so did the awareness of the importance of families. No longer was the vocabulary limited to parent involvement.

NEW EMPHASIS. In the latest edition of the report, *The Family Is Critical to Student Achievement: A New Generation of Evidence* (Henderson & Berla, 1996), there are 66 studies, and the range of involvement goes far beyond parent involvement to family/school partnerships, community-based programs, and family literacy programs, and to topics such as changes in family structure and status and the contributions of families to children's general development. One important change is the emphasis on families, consistent with the focus of this chapter. Henderson and Berla describe their reasons for the term *family* rather than *parents:* "In many communities, children are raised by adults who are not their parents, or by older siblings. For many, this provides an extended support system and those who are responsible for the children and who function effectively as their family deserve recognition" (p. x).

A look at the summary of the findings will give you a sense of the specific recommendations that emerged from those 66 studies. The authors are quite enthusiastic: "The evidence is now beyond dispute: When schools and families work together, children have a much better chance for success, not just in school, but throughout life" (Henderson & Berla, 1996, p. 1). What's also exciting about the findings is that the impact of family involvement in children's education goes beyond children's success. There are benefits for everyone. Let's look briefly at those outcomes.

BENEFITS FOR CHILDREN AS STUDENTS. The benefits for children may look like they are too broad for your thinking about young children because they generalize across a wide age span (ECE to high school). If you keep in mind that the patterns for success begin in early childhood, then the benefits have much relevance for work with young children. Those benefits of family involvement include:

- Higher grades and test scores
- Better attendance and more homework done
- Fewer placements in special education
- More positive attitudes and behavior
- Greater enrollment in postsecondary education

These benefits are very much in parallel with the kind of results reported for high-quality early childhood programs such as Head Start and the Perry Preschool Project (Schweinhart, Barnes, & Weikart, 1993). Although few studies have followed young children to adulthood, those that have done so have similar findings. Many of the dispositions, feelings about learning and school, and commitment to study begin at home. The development of attitudes, values, and lifelong habits calls for a partnership between you, the early childhood educator, and the families of your children. What about the families? What happens to them when they are involved with schools or programs?

BENEFITS FOR FAMILIES. The benefits to families are encouraging, and especially critical when you think about the difficult issues that today's families face while raising children. The major benefit to families is that they experience an increase of confidence in themselves and in their child's educational program. Because they feel valued by the educators working with their children, they see themselves as more capable of assisting those educators, but, even more importantly, they see themselves as more capable of helping their children at home. That kind of confidence is bound to increase the levels of involvement of families in children's education, and ultimately children's success in school.

One of the additional benefits that often accompanies family involvement is the increase in the number of parents who, themselves, pursue additional education. Head Start has consistently demonstrated this benefit. Although it has not been well documented, there are countless stories of parents and other family members who have experienced success as family participants in the Head Start programs. From there, many of those family members progress to workshops and training sessions, and again experience success. Once they complete this step, postsecondary education (community colleges and universities) doesn't look so daunting. In our travels to Head Start centers around the country, many an early childhood educator talks about how she or he started as a parent volunteer or a member of the advisory board. Those stories are definitely enough to encourage our work toward family involvement. But how about our programs and schools? What kind of benefits can we expect from family involvement?

BENEFITS FOR SCHOOLS AND COMMUNITIES. The kind of benefits that schools gain include improved teacher morale and higher ratings of teachers by parents. It follows that if teachers are feeling valued and there is a culture of energy and positive thinking, children will be affected and learning will be enhanced. Other benefits include the kind of assistance and support families can provide to programs. Sometimes, it's an extra pair of hands; sometimes, it's resources from a parent's hobby, career, experiences, or travels. That support and help again influence the quality of educational opportunities that are offered to children. Ultimately, those schools have students with higher achievement, and everyone feels good about that kind of benefit. It makes sense that those schools would also have better reputations in the community. Most communities care about the education of the children who live in them. Those schools that produce high achievement will naturally be valued and supported by community members.

The research on family involvement leaves little doubt about the importance and the benefits of families' participation in children's education. Early childhood educators have traditionally encouraged parent involvement, so the transition may not be so difficult to involve families. Understanding families and communities is the starting point, and the goal of this chapter. From that understanding, it will be important to develop a philosophy about families. One of the basic tenets of successful family involvement approaches is that families are seen as the child's first teacher and are valued for their support and caring of their children. Think of families as learning environments for the children you meet.

Families as Learning Environments

As you continue to develop your philosophy for working with families, we suggest that you consider the findings of studies that looked at families with high-achieving students and those with low-achieving students. When you think about how much time children spend with their families, a consideration of how that time is used is critical. As you get to know the families of the children with whom you work, an important question to ask is: How does your family spend time together? Rather than ask about how much time families spend together, which may be threatening to already stressed parents, a question about family activities will be comfortable and will give you a picture of the child's home life.

RESEARCH ON EVERYDAY FAMILY ACTIVITIES. Studies (Henderson & Berla, 1996; Moles, 1992) of families whose children experience success in school found the following aspects in their home life:

- A daily family routine that includes a sharing of household chores, consistent bedtimes and times to get up, meals together, and quiet places and time for study or reading
- Monitoring of children's activities, including TV watching, neighborhood play, and arrangements for child care, especially care before and after school
- Modeling the value of learning, self-discipline, and hard work through family conversations and adult modeling and demonstrations that success comes from working hard, studying, and using the library
- Setting high but reasonable expectations for achievement with goals that are appropriate for the children's age and development, as well as recognition of talents and achievements
- Encouraging children's efforts and progress in school, including a relationship with teachers and other staff, communication about the importance of education, and provision of support and interest in schoolwork
- Reading, writing, and discussions among family members so that literacy, in all its forms, is part of the daily family interactions
- Using community resources for family needs, including sports and recreational opportunities, instruction and entertainment related to the arts, inclusion of other role models and mentors, and access to libraries and museums

When parents interact with their children, such as spending time together in activities on the weekend or socializing together at mealtimes, they can significantly influence the learning of their children. Knowing how difficult it is for many contemporary families to have that kind of time together adds a challenge to our multiple roles as early childhood educators. As family advocates and educators, we need to share the research information. As child advocates and educators, we want to support the family's efforts and be sensitive to the diversity of their situations. The research confirms the critical role of families in the growth and development of children, which says to us that we need to do all we can to learn about families and to work in partnership with them. The new generation of evidence about the family's importance will remind us over and over that we need to understand today's families—their stresses, their organizations, their issues, and their strengths. The more we can support families in their roles in children's lives, the better the lives of children will be.

COMMUNITY CONTEXT FOR FAMILIES. We have tried to show and highlight the ethnic, cultural, and socioeconomic diversity of the national community in which children live, and the diversity of family structures and organizations from which children come to early childhood education programs. Differences in cultural values or expectations for members of communities can lead to differences in the socialization goals and strategies parents adopt for their children (Okagaki & Diamond, 2000, p. 74). For children to develop and learn optimally, you will need to understand and be able to respond to children's diverse developmental, cultural, linguistic, and educational needs. That understanding and ability to respond will require your knowledge and acceptance of children's diverse family units with a broad range of values, experiences, socialization, and environments. In their recommendations for working with families, the NAEYC guidelines urge us to "actively involve parents and families in the early learning program and settings" and to "recognize that parents and families must rely on caregivers and educators to honor and support their children in the cultural values and norms of the home" (1996b).

Much of what we have said about families can be applied to communities. There is a growing awareness that communities contribute significantly to children's growth and development. The complexity of society demands the involvement of all the individuals and organizations that can possibly have an impact on one's life. In a later chapter, you will meet Angela Russo and all of the community members who influence her life and that of her mom, Marie. She is an example of the importance of understanding the context in which families live if you are to understand the children and families. That understanding is a first step to the goal of building partnerships with families.

Building Partnerships with Families

The NAEYC guidelines for developmentally appropriate practice (Bredekamp & Copple, 1997) are a good beginning for your thinking about building partnerships with families. The guidelines talk about programs in which "professionals and parents work together to achieve shared goals for children."

DEVELOPMENTALLY APPROPRIATE PRACTICE: INVOLVING FAMILIES. The NAEYC guidelines recommend the following:

1. Reciprocal relationships between teachers and families require mutual respect, cooperation, shared responsibility, and negotiation of conflicts toward achievement of shared goals.

   This guideline means that there must be some opportunities for cooperation, shared responsibility, and negotiation. Some of the basic parent conferences or Open Houses don't really provide those opportunities. Even the development of mutual trust requires enough interaction to get to know the families and to make sincere efforts to understand each perspective. One early childhood program scheduled evening sessions called Family Story Time, in which family members and educators sat in comfortably small circles and shared family stories—sometimes funny stories, sometimes sad stories, and sometimes stories of unique family traditions. Although the Family Story Time sessions were slow starting, in time, family members and educators bonded through their stories and became much more comfortable with each other. Bruner (1990) confirmed the use of stories to help people understand each other's cultures and to build relationships. When you meet the children and families in Chapters 7 through 11, you will observe and hear about other approaches to build trust and to prepare for cooperation and shared responsibility. One very important reminder here is that you can't very well negotiate with families if you haven't developed a relationship first. Negotiation is not a healthy starting point for partnerships.

2. Early childhood educators work in collaborative partnerships with families, establishing and maintaining regular, frequent two-way communication with children's parents.

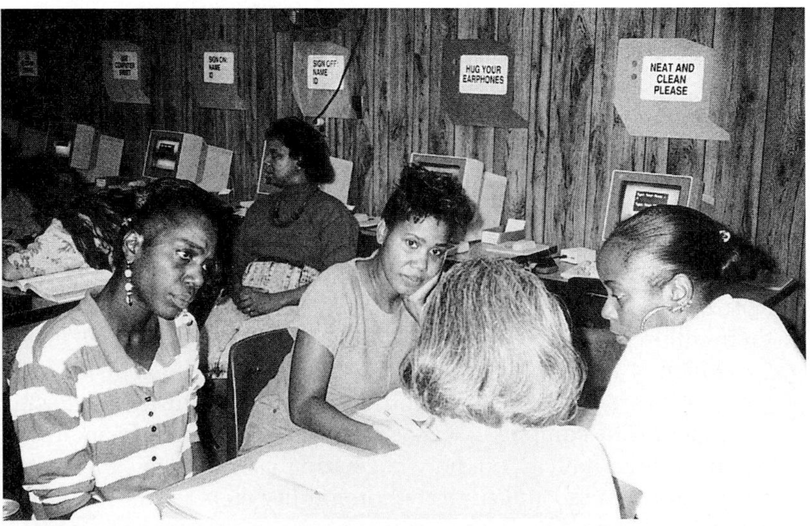

Authentic involvement of families in program decisions may require many discussions and preparation.

If we begin with real respect for families, we will seek and support two-way communication. Much of the communication has been one way, from the educator to the parent. Following this guideline begins with an attitude of respect for families. The tenets of successful family involvement programs in Figure 6.6 offer a foundation the communication of partnerships.

3. Parents are welcome in the program and participate in the decisions about their children's care and education. Parents observe, participate, and serve in decision-making roles in the program.

    Many programs have successfully involved families in making significant decisions. Head Start has parents and other family members serve on hiring committees, curriculum committees, and a range of policy committees. This kind of involvement means that educators have to assure families that they have a real voice in the decisions, not just token representation on committees without real impact on decisions. Authentic involvement also may require preparation. One of your authors worked with a program in which parents were involved in major hiring and curricular decisions, and I quickly learned that parents needed a great deal of information and discussion before they could actively engage in important decisions. Their preparation empowered them to be decision makers.

4. Early childhood educators acknowledge parents' choices and goals for children and respond with sensitivity and respect to parents' preferences and concerns without abdicating professional responsibility to children.

    One of the most common situations in which parents' preferences present a dilemma for early childhood educators is related to children's naps. For a variety of reasons, parents will ask the teachers or caregivers to "not let Emily sleep too long at naptime" or to "wake Eli after one hour of nap." The difficulty arises when Emily or Eli is then grouchy, tired, or listless for the rest of the day or appears to need more sleep and even asks to sleep some more. Many early childhood educators have had intense negotiations with parents or family members over this issue, usually with a balance between parent needs and child needs.

    Darren, the educator in the toddler program in Chapter 8, talks about the goals of many parents of toddlers: "So often, they want their toddler to be able to share." He tells us about the conversations with parents in which he describes the needs of toddlers to become independent and to establish identity, and his assurance to parents that their children will eventually be able to share but that it will probably take all year. "I talk a lot about not insisting on sharing or forcing children to do so," says Darren, and he describes for parents the possible outcomes of forced sharing. Darren

FIGURE 6.6

Basic Tenets of Successful Programs

- The first and most basic tenet is that parents are their children's first teachers and have a lifelong influence on their children's values, attitudes, and aspirations.
- Children's educational success requires congruence between the values that are taught at school and the values expressed in the home.
- Most parents, regardless of their level of education, economic status, or cultural background, care deeply about their children's education and can provide substantial support if given specific opportunities and knowledge.
- Schools must take the lead in eliminating, or at least reducing, traditional barriers to parental involvement.

Source: Working Respectfully with Families: A Practical Guide for Educators and Human Service Workers by C. Connard, R. Novick, and H. Nissani, 1996, Portland, OR: Northwest Regional Educational Laboratory. Reprinted by permission.

really models the guideline of respecting parents while keeping the integrity of his responsibility to children.

5. Teachers and parents share their knowledge of the child and understanding of children's development and learning as part of day-to-day communication and planned conferences. Teachers support families in ways that maximally promote family decision making capabilities and competence.

   Recently, one of your authors asked a group of families and teachers to make two lists. The first list consisted of all the kinds of information that families could contribute to programs or schools to help make a child's experience successful. With no hesitation, families and teachers came up with the following examples:

   - Interests
   - Fears
   - Play activities
   - Eating habits
   - Family experiences (travel, recreation, etc.)
   - Previous educational or child care experiences
   - Kinds of playthings
   - Responses to stress
   - Difficulties
   - Health
   - Family reading patterns
   - Home guidance/disciplines
   - TV watching habits
   - Influence of extended family

   Their lists continued to fill several large sheets of chart paper. The group sat back and studied their lists and sighed, then responded to a second question. What kinds of information can teachers provide to families to help them understand their child's experiences outside of the home? Again, the hesitation was brief, and the following are some of their examples:

   - Interactions with peers
   - Strengths and limitations
   - Favorite activities
   - Responses to success and failure
   - Memory
   - Persistence at tasks
   - Leadership/follower roles
   - Contributions to the group

   The outcome of this list-making activity was a wonderfully mutual appreciation for the wealth of information available when there is two-way communication about children. That very comprehensive picture of children is essential to the ability of teachers and caregivers and families to work together to understand children and to support their development.

6. To ensure more accurate and complete information, the program involves families in assessing and planning for individual children.

   Many programs are using a variety of strategies to involve families in both assessment and planning processes. Elementary schools have initiated goal-setting conferences for teachers, parents, and children, and are experimenting with children-led teacher/family conferences. Parents are often asked to contribute to and comment on children's work in portfolios. Darren (in Chapter 8) works with parents during his first home visit to set goals for the year for children, and later refers to those goals when he meets with parents for conferences. When communication is consistent and comfortable, families feel secure about suggesting curriculum topics or activities for their children.

   The NAEYC Standards for Early Childhood Professional Preparation (2002) describe the need for teachers to know about and understand why and how to use assessment that is developmentally appropriate and effective, in partnership with families to positively influence children's development and learning. Many aspects of assessment can be shared with families. For example, parents or family members can be involved in observing and assessing children's strengths and needs. Assessment of young children is certainly seen as best done in partnership with families.

7. The program links families with a range of services, based on identified resources, priorities, and concerns.

Information sharing between educators and families takes different forms. Many families appreciate informal conversations that take place in the classroom.

Although this guideline expands the responsibilities of the early childhood educator, the challenges for today's families and children that we have described in this chapter remind us that educational programs cannot exist in isolation of other services for families. The kind of programs that truly meet family needs have libraries of resources (parenting books and magazines), information about community services, knowledge of and networks with health agencies, and economic support. An exceptional program in Gainesville, Florida, has what they call *one-stop shopping* for families—a facility with preschool and child care programs, library extensions, parenting classes, adult education courses, a medical clinic, and a social service center (Driscoll, 1995). The program communicates sensitivity to the stresses of family lives and challenges of supporting family needs.

8. Teachers, parents, programs, social service and health agencies, and consultants who may have educational responsibility for the child at different times should, with family participation, share developmental information about children as they pass from one level or program to another.

Information sharing takes different forms, depending on the programs involved, the purpose of the information sharing, and the kinds of responsibilities participants have for the child. One very important reminder for such sharing is the need for clear language. Educators are known for using a great deal of jargon in their work, and studies have shown that parents especially are put off by such talk (Buskin, 1975).

The impression with which you may be left after considering the guidelines for developmentally appropriate practice is that family involvement and partnerships are hard work. Yes, it does take an attitude of respect for families, planning for consistent two-way communication, negotiation between family preferences and developmental decisions, and ongoing attention to the relationship with families. With all of the effort needed to build and maintain partnerships, you may be asking: Why?

To add further complexity to family involvement, let's return to the ecological perspective we proposed when we began this chapter. Today, when we build partnerships, we need to consider both families and communities.

Linking Families, Communities, and Early Childhood Programs

In her work to promote family involvement, Epstein and colleagues (2002) has posed three important attributes to successful family involvement. The attributes are appropriate, even when, they are extended to include communities. Remember the basic tenets of Figure 6.6 for successful family involvement programs. From there, the list proceeds to Epstein's attributes:

1. Effective partnership practices are developmental. The interests and needs of families are in flux as their children grow and develop, so relationships must accommodate the changes. Healthy partnerships also grow, develop, and require nurturance for development, just as children and families do.
2. Effective partnership practices must be responsive to both common and unique family needs. This attribute rests on one of the main ideas of this chapter: the diversity of families and communities. There is no "one size fits all" for partnerships between families and communities.
3. Children must be key participants (Heleen, 1992, p. 6). Whatever direction partnerships take and whatever activities are planned, the focus must be on children. Goals for children are the heart of successful partnerships.

As part of her work with the Center on Families, Communities, Schools, and Children's Learning, Epstein has categorized the major types of activities that are found in successful involvement programs. Figure 6.7 displays those categories and sample activities. Some of them are traditional; in fact, your own parents probably engaged in some of the activities. Some of the activities are innovative and will require significant changes in the way educators work with families and communities. Figure 6.8 describes the challenges and redefinitions of the categories if educators truly want to work collaboratively with families and communities.

You will need to spend some time studying the challenges and redefinitions of the categories if you intend to truly respect and work in partnership with all families and communities. Return to the figures as you meet families in the chapters ahead. Here are a few additional sensitivities for your future work with today's diverse families and communities:

1. Assess your language when addressing families. If the notes or letters sent home begin with "Dear Parents," you are eliminating a number of family members from involvement.
2. Check your scheduling of activities to be sure that you accommodate the diversity of families' schedules. Some can attend daytime events; others can attend only evening events.
3. Be sure that communication is sent in languages that reflect the demographics of the families and community. Provide an interpreter for events so that all families can understand the messages.

In addition to the time and language barriers to family involvement, early childhood educators often suggest that transportation, child care, expenses, food, and a variety of misunderstandings may prohibit or discourage families.

Those are some basic starting points. Remember that this is a *developing* process—don't become overwhelmed by the enormity of possibilities for family and community partnerships. You won't be alone in your efforts. Early childhood programs have traditionally been oriented to parent involvement, and current efforts are expanding the concept to families and communities.

PRINCIPLES AND INSIGHTS: A Summary and Review

This chapter has been packed with facts and figures, as well as guidelines, suggestions, and examples to illustrate the diversity of families and communities. As you meet the children and families in the chapters that follow, you will be even more aware of that diversity and what it means for you as an early childhood educator.

FIGURE 6.7

Epstein's Framework of Six Types of Involvement and Sample Practices

Type 1	Type 2	Type 3	Type 4	Type 5	Type 6
Parenting	**Communicating**	**Volunteering**	**Learning at Home**	**Decision Making**	**Collaborating with Community**
Help all families establish home environments to support children as students.	Design effective forms of school-to-home and home-to-school communications about school programs and children's progress.	Recruit and organize parent help and support.	Provide information and ideas to families about how to help students at home with homework and other curriculum-related activities, decisions, and planning.	Include parents in school decisions, developing parent leaders and representatives.	Identify and integrate resources and services from the community to strengthen school programs, family practices, and student learning and development.
Sample Practices	**Sample Practices**	**Sample Practices**	**Sample Practices**	**Sample Practices**	**Sample Practices**
Suggestions for home conditions that support learning at each grade level. Workshops, videotapes, computerized phone messages on parenting and child rearing at each age and level. Parent education and other courses or training for parents (e.g., GED, college credit, family literacy). Family support programs to assist families with health, nutrition, and other services. Home visits at transition points to preschool, elementary, middle, and high school. Neighborhood meetings to help families understand schools and to help schools understand families.	Conferences with every parent at least once a year, with follow-ups as needed. Language translators to assist families as needed. Weekly or monthly folders of student work sent home for review and comments. Parent/student pickup of report card, with conferences on improving grades. Regular schedule of useful notices, memos, phone calls, newsletters, and other communications. Clear information on choosing schools or courses, programs, and activities within schools. Clear information on all school policies, programs, reforms, and transitions.	School and classroom volunteer program to help teachers, administrators, students, and other parents. Parent room or family center for volunteer work, meetings, resources for families. Annual postcard survey to identify all available talents, times, and locations of volunteers. Class parent, telephone tree, or other structures to provide all families with needed information. Parent patrols or other activities to aid safety and operation of school programs.	Information for families on skills required for students in all subjects at each grade. Information on homework policies and how to monitor and discuss schoolwork at home. Information an how to assist students to improve skills on various class and school assessments. Regular schedule of homework that requires students to discuss and interact with families on what they are learning in class. Calendars with activities for parents and students at home. Family math, science, and reading activities at school. Summer learning packets or activities. Family participation in setting student goals each year and in planning for college or work.	Active PTA/PTO or other parent organizations, advisory councils, or committees (e.g., curriculum, safety personnel) for parent leadership and participation. Independent advocacy groups to lobby and work for school reform and improvements. District level councils, and committees for family and community involvement. Information on school or local elections for school representatives. Networks to link all families with parent representatives.	Information for students and families on community health, cultural, recreational, social support, and other programs or services. Information on community activities that link to learning skills and talents, including summer programs for students. Service integration through partnerships involving school, civic, counseling, cultural, health, recreation and other agencies and organizations, and businesses. Service to the community by students, families, and schools (e.g., recycling, art, music, drama, and other activities for seniors or others). Participation of alumni in school programs for students.

Source: "School/Family/Community Partnerships: Caring for the Children We Share" by J. L. Epstein, May 1995. *Phi Delta Kappan,* pp. 701–712. Reprinted by permission.

FIGURE 6.8

Challenges and Redefinitions for the Six Types of Involvement

Type 1	Type 2	Type 3	Type 4	Type 5	Type 6
Parenting Challenges	**Communicating Challenges**	**Volunteering Challenges**	**Learning at Home Challenges**	**Decision Making Challenges**	**Collaborating with Community Challenges**
Provide information to *all* families who want it or who need it, not just to the few who can attend workshops or meetings at the school building. Enable families to share information with schools about culture, background, children's talents and needs. Make sure that all information for and from families is clear, usable and linked to children's success in school.	Review the readability, clarity, form, and frequency of all memos, notices, and other print and nonprint communications. Consider parents who do not speak English well, do not read well, or need large type. Review the quality of major communications (newsletters, report cards, conference schedules, and so on). Establish clear two-way channels for communications from home to school and from school to home.	Recruit volunteers widely so that *all* families know that their time and talents are welcome. Make flexible schedules for volunteers, assemblies, and events to enable parents who work to participate. Organize volunteer work; provide training; match time and talent with school, teacher, and student needs; and recognize efforts so that participants are productive.	Design and organize a regular schedule of interactive homework (e.g., weekly or bimonthly) that gives *students* responsibility for discussing important things they are learning and helps families stay aware of the content of their children's classwork. Coordinate family-linked homework activities, if students have several teachers. Involve families and their children in all important curriculum-related decisions.	Include parent leaders from all racial, ethnic, socioeconomic, and other groups in the school. Offer training to enable leaders to serve as representatives of other families, with input from and return of information to all parents. Include students (alone with parent) in decision-making groups.	Solve turf problems of responsibilities, funds, staff, and locations for collaborative activities. Inform families of community programs for students, such as mentoring, tutoring, business partnerships. Assure equity of opportunities for students and families to participate in community programs or to obtain services. Match community contributions with school goals; integrate child and family services with education.
Redefinitions	**Redefinitions**	**Redefinitions**	**Redefinitions**	**Redefinitions**	**Redefinitions**
"Workshop" to mean more than a *meeting* about a topic held at the school building at a particular time. "Workshop" may also mean making information about a topic available in a variety of forms that can be viewed, heard, or read anywhere, anytime, in varied forms.	"Communications about school programs and student progress" to mean two-way, three-way, and many-way channels of communication that connect schools, families, students, and the community.	"Volunteer" to mean anyone who supports school goals and children's learning, or development in any way, in any place, and at any time—not just during the school day and at the school building	"Homework" to mean not only work done alone, but also interactive activities shared with others at home or in the community, linking schoolwork to real life. "Help" at home to mean encouraging, listening, reacting, praising, guiding, monitoring, and discussing—not "teaching" school subjects.	"Decision making" to mean a process of partnership, of shared views and actions toward shared goals, not just a power struggle between conflicting ideas. Parent "leader" to mean a real representative, with opportunities and support to hear from and communicate with other families.	"Community" to mean not only the neighborhoods where students' homes and schools are located but also any neighborhoods that influence their learning and development. "Community" rated not only by low or high social or economic qualities, but by strengths and talents to support students, families, and schools. "Community" means all who are interested in and affected by the quality of education, not just those with children in schools.

Source: "School/Family/Community Partnerships: Caring for the Children We Share" by J. L. Epstein, May 1995. *Phi Delta Kappan,* pp. 701–712. Reprinted by permission.

Our best advice is to notice those differences in your everyday life. Observe families in grocery stores, in libraries, in restaurants, on buses and trains, and as you walk through your town or city. Begin to take note of family structures and organizations. Be aware of how families socialize children—the messages that are communicated. Listen to the issues and challenges faced by families.

As you prepare to be an early childhood educator, get to know your community better. Perhaps you could assemble a scrapbook or album about your community. This is called *advancework* (Frieberg & Driscoll, 1996). It's what a company does when there is a move planned and employees will be transferred to a different community. The company sends in an advance person to study the new community. Put yourself in that role. Here are some possibilities for your advancework:

- Interview some parents and business owners in the community.
- Take photos of key facilities.
- Walk through major neighborhoods.
- Take an inventory of recreational facilities.
- Visit the Chamber of Commerce.
- Read local newspapers.
- Visit the community's website.
- Scan local bulletin boards (often found in grocery stores).
- Check on adult education programs.
- Inventory the child care and early childhood programs.
- Check the library use by families.
- Attend a city council meeting or a school board meeting.
- Inventory the churches of the community.
- Observe families as they use community facilities.

That's just a beginning! As you study your community and its families, you will extend that list to all kinds of interesting and informative aspects of the place where you live. As you do so, be open to the richness of the diversity of today's families and communities. There are some Ozzie and Harriet families left, and there's also Keeley and her single mom, Kerry; Faridah and Amr and their sons Ibrahim and Muhammed; Felipe and his mom and grandmother; Erin Cheyenne and her two working parents; and there's a whole village helping Marie Russo raise her daughter Angela. Celebrate their differences as you join us to meet and observe the children and families.

BECOMING AN EARLY CHILDHOOD PROFESSIONAL

Your Professional Portfolio

1. The advancework we described in the chapter summary is an ideal entry for your portfolio. Be sure to describe the importance of each of the contents of your advancework for understanding children and families.
2. Volunteer to assist with a family event in your community or at an agency that provides services to families. Document that participation and keep a journal of your insights and concerns.

Your Professional Library

Appalachia Educational Laboratory. (2000). *Family connections handbook 1, 2, 3.* Charleston, WV: Author.

Diffily, D., & Morrisson, K. (Eds.). (1996). *Family-friendly communication for early childhood programs.* Washington, DC: NAEYC.

DiNatale, L. (2002). Developing high quality family involvement programs in early childhood settings, *Young Children, 57* (5), 90–95.

Epstein, J., Sanders, M., Simon, B., Salinas, K., Jansorn, N., & Voorhis, F. (2002). *School, Family, and Community Partnerships: Your Handbook for Action* (2nd ed.). Thousand Oaks, CA: Corwin.

Espinosa, L. (1995). *Hispanic parent involvement in early childhood programs.* ERIC EDO-PS 95-3.

Galinsky, E. (1999). *Ask the children: What America's children really think about working parents.* New York: Families & Work Institute.

Henderson, A. T., & Berla, N. (1996). *The family is critical to student achievement.* Washington, DC: Center for Law and Education.

Lee, F. Y. (1995). Asian parents as partners. *Young Children, 50* (3), 4–9.

CHAPTER

7

Infant Care Programs and Practices

Luke's Story

CHAPTER focus:

When you finish reading and reflecting on this chapter, you will be able to:

1. Discuss the 10 principles of infant caregiving.
2. Describe caregiving and play as curriculum with infants.
3. Define the role of the primary caregiver in an infant care setting.
4. Explain the rationale for individualized curriculum in infant care programs.
5. List and explain several reasons why a caregiver would work toward establishing a close connection with an infant's family.

Approximately 67 percent of mothers with children under 12 months of age currently leave their child in the care of someone other than the infant's parents (Ehrle, Adams, & Tout, 2001). Who is caring for these infants? What options are available for infant care? As you think about these questions, consider the dilemmas and anxiety that many parents face as they begin their search for infant care. We will briefly introduce you to three families who are experiencing concerns about infant care. You will then meet a family who feels secure and involved in their child care situation.

Finding Good Infant Care

Child care for infants is such a juggling act—trying to find the right balance and the optimal place for an infant during the important first year of life.

Mei-Ling: Grandparent as Caregiver

Mei-Ling has been worried for the past few months. It is difficult for her to feel right about her decision. Vivian, her infant daughter, is only four weeks old, and Mei-Ling finds herself constantly worrying about her plans for Vivian's care. During her pregnancy, Mei-Ling began searching for infant care options, knowing she would return to work when her baby was eight weeks old. After many discussions with her husband and friends, she began visiting recommended child care centers. Those visits were discouraging—she could not see herself putting Vivian in these settings. It seemed that several centers operated with an assembly-line format. Certain infants were placed in cribs at established times; other infants were placed in a row of six high chairs and being fed. Mei-Ling was distressed with the thought of leaving Vivian in a setting that did not appear to meet the individual needs of infants.

After discussing her observations, Mei-Ling and Jeff made a decision to ask Jeff's mother if she would be willing to care for Vivian for her first year. Jeff's mother, Grace, had previously offered to care for her granddaughter, so it seemed the best option for all involved. Mei-Ling and Jeff wanted Vivian to be loved and safe while they are at work, and they knew that Grace would attend to Vivian's needs.

Three months later, Mei-Ling and Jeff have new concerns—not so much about Vivian, but about taking time and energy away from Grace's normal routine. When they pick up Vivian in the evening, it appears that Grace is often exhausted from her day. She isn't able to meet friends for outings, as she did in the past. Now, Mei-Ling and Jeff feel guilty about taking up her time, yet they want to keep Vivian with a family member until she is one year old. Grace has agreed to continue, but Mei-Ling can't help but wonder if she should try to come up with a different plan or perhaps work four longer days so Grace could have one weekday off.

Brynna: Family Home Care

Brynna, a single mother, questioned friends about child care arrangements when she decided to return to work when Carl, her son, was four months old. While talking with friends, she found out that a neighbor, Summer, cares for toddlers in her home. Brynna decides to go to Summer's apartment to discuss the possibility of Carl being cared for by Summer. Carl is younger than the toddlers Summer takes care of along with her own daughter. Summer agrees to include Carl in her home care program, but she wants Brynna to understand that, with four toddlers in her care, she won't have much time to play with Carl.

Brynna feels a family home care situation is the best option for her. Summer is a creative, high-energy woman, and having Carl in a home nearby will help with commuting time. Sometimes it seems that Summer's home is in need of cleaning, but that is a compromise Brynna will make to find nearby care for Carl. Right now, Brynna hopes that this arrangement will work for Carl and Summer. It's not the same as staying home with Carl, but Brynna knows she needs to return to work to keep her position in the company.

Neil and Karen: Child Care Center

Neil and Karen work at a company that assembles parts for large trucks. Near their plant is a child care center. Neil drops by to visit and finds the infant and toddler room to be a busy place. He notices on the daily schedule that there are activities scheduled for the mornings, but mostly free choice for toddlers and caring for infants in the afternoon. The infants appear clean and have a lot to watch with the toddler activity going on around them. There is an opening for an infant, so Neil decides to enroll Katy, their five-month-old daughter, in this day care center. The center has a sliding scale for monthly costs, which means that their income level qualifies them for a discount on the monthly cost of infant care. Neil and Karen are pleased about the costs but feel a little insecure about the center and the large number of infants and toddlers in one room. Their friends reassure them and remind them that they are lucky to have found affordable care for Katy.

Selecting Child Care

You have just read about three different options for families with infants. Each family had similar struggles and worries when looking for quality infant care. Studies conducted by the National Institute of Child Health and Human Development (1997, 2002) found that high-quality child care is associated with positive outcomes for young children (see Box 7.1).

BOX 7.1

Results of the NICHD Study of Mother/Child Interactions and Cognitive Outcomes Associated with Early Child Care

The National Institute of Child Health and Human Development (NICHD) investigated the impact of child care on two different domains: mother/child interactions and cognitive and language development in the first three years of life. A frequent, yet difficult, question to answer regarding child care is the effect of child care on infants' and toddlers' development. To answer this question, over 1,360 children participated in the study conducted at 10 different sites.

Assessments included observations of mother/child interactions, observations of the child's child care environment, observations of the child in his or her home, and standardized measures of the child's cognitive and language development. Children were assessed at the ages of 6, 15, 24, and 36 months.

Study results found that although family, maternal, and child characteristics contributed greatly to social and cognitive development, early child care provided small, yet significant, influences on the qualities of mother/child interaction and on children's cognitive and language development. For example, more hours of child care related to less sensitive interactions between a mother and her child during the child's first three years of life. At the same time, it was found that more hours of child care was not related to the child's cognitive or language development (NICHD, 1997).

In further study, researchers reported that higher-quality child care and experience in a center-type arrangement led to better preacademic skills and language performance at age 4½ years (2002).

Although family, maternal, and child characteristics are attributed with a larger proportion of the total variance in findings of the study, results did show contributions made by child care to a child's cognitive and language development and in mother/child interactions. These results emphasize the importance of *quality* child care, as well as help answer the question of what impact early child care has on child development and mother/child interactions.

How do parents determine if an infant care program is of high quality? Although there are specific indicators that help determine the quality of a program, parents must take the time to observe, watch caregiver and infant interactions, and interview the director or responsible adult about the program, his or her qualifications, and references. Ultimately, the parent is responsible for making the final decision about the infant care program.

With the lack of quality care and the lack of infant programs, in general, many parents feel they have to compromise their standards. As a nation, the difficult issue of ensuring that all families have access to quality child care during this critical period of development—the first year of life—has not been resolved. In contrast to these three families faced with compromises in finding ideal infant care, you will now meet a family that feels they have the best possible infant care for their son, Luke, and visit his infant care program.

Visiting the Infant Care Program: A Corporate Child Development Center

Winding through the large complex of red brick buildings of Mentor Graphics, you look around for the Child Development Center (CDC). There it is! You don't need a sign to tell you this brightly colored building is the Child Development Center.

You have heard about the Mentor Graphics Infant Care Program and read that Mentor Graphics has been named one of the "100 Best Companies to Work For" by *Working Mother Magazine.*

Entering the building, you are met by Sue, coordinator of the infant care program. Sue greets you warmly. "We are glad to have you visit us today. Why don't we go directly to the Infant Suite, and then meet later to discuss the infant care program and any questions you might have."

Your First Impression

Interactions between Caregivers and Infants. As you walk inside the door of the Infant Suite, you see two infants on the floor with a caregiver. She is talking with them, sharing her thoughts about their movements and interactions. "You seem to be enjoying the sunshine coming in the window, Amil." He responds to her talk by kicking his legs and moving his arms. She continues, "Look at how you can reach the mirror, Emory." Emory smiles and continues to stretch her arms toward the mirror. There seems to be ongoing interaction between the infants and their caregiver, and you sense a special connection between them.

In a small room adjacent to the large area is a changing room, where an infant and her caregiver are cheerfully engaged in a diaper change. On the wall above this area is an organization system holding a tub labeled with the name of each infant, containing diapers, supplies, and extra clothes. A caregiver and infant are in the changing room, where you listen to their conversation. "Now we are going to put on the clean diaper," says Caryl, the caregiver, in an encouraging and inviting tone. The infant seems familiar with the routine and reaches to feel the clean diaper. They seem to be in partnership in the process of changing the diaper. This is not a task *done to* the child, but rather a **caregiving activity** that is accomplished *with* the child. Each step was explained and shared out loud. As they finish up and Caryl washes her hands, she says, "Marta, now we are finished and will go back to the floor where you were visiting with Emory."

Homelike Environment: Supporting Infant Development. You follow Caryl and Marta to the floor area, noticing that this room is like an apartment or small home. There is a kitchen off to the right side with a refrigerator, microwave, stove, and dishwasher. On the other side of the room is a living room area, with pillows and pads on the floor and a couch. The sleeping area has a door and is similar to a separate bedroom. There are also several other sleeping areas or nooks for infants within the large room, with mats for infants. Each door in this room has a window near the bottom, so when infants are crawling they can look through these windows, either into the toddler room or outside. The light airy atmosphere is inviting. It is easy to appreciate the windows and the connection with the outdoors. The backyard is landscaped with grass and trees. The whole area, both inside and outside, seems comforting and comfortable.

Each infant has her or his own storage bin for clothing and diaper supplies in the changing room.

JOURNAL 7.1: What are the benefits for infants, families, and caregivers in the infant room environment?

Attention to Infant as Individual. You sense a calm atmosphere in this setting, with caregivers very attentive and tuned in to the infants. Sandy, one of the caregivers, is feeding Oliver a bottle while sitting on the couch. She talks softly to him, "You look like you're enjoying this bottle and this time to rest," while he snuggles close to her. He has her full attention while he is being held and fed. You again observe that the caregivers have special relationships with the infants and seem to be tuned in to their needs and personalities.

Near the back of the room you notice Caryl coming out of the separate sleeping room. As you walk over to the room, you see a chart on the wall, with the names of the infants and times recorded near the names. You ask Caryl about the chart. She explains that caregivers check infants while they are sleeping every 10 minutes or so. They then record the activity and position of the infant on the chart next to the time of the "sleeping room check." You peek in the window and see there are three infants in cribs in the room. There are eight cribs in the room. Caryl also tells you that each child has her or his own crib and has an individual routine for help getting to sleep. Some infants like to be left in the crib with a soft pat on the back; others like to have their caregiver talk or sing to them for a few minutes; and still others relax with a back rub.

Arrival Routine: Welcoming Infants and Parents

The door to the hall opens and Ingrid arrives with her mother, Sharon. Sharon checks in at the door by signing in and bringing the **Daily Log** up to date (see Figure 7.1). After filling in the log, Sharon

FIGURE 7.1
Daily Log

Infant Room Notes

Name *Luke* Date *12/17*

My Child woke up at *5:30*

My Child last ate at *6:45*

Have you given your child any medication today?

Y (N)

What kind ______

Anticipated time of pick-up: *5:30*

Is there any other information about your child that would be helpful to us?

______

______

Feedings:

Time	Food/amount	Liquids
9:05	*cereal/ 1/2 banana*	
9:35		*4 oz bottle*
11:40	*cereal*	*milk in cup*
2:15	*cracker*	*2 oz apple juice*
4:30		*5 oz bottle*

Diapers:

9:15	*12:45*	*3:15 (B.M.)*	
10:40	*2:10*	*4:15*	*(5:00)*

Naps:

9:45 to *10:35* ______ to ______ *12:55* to *2:05*

Anecdotal Notes:

Luke was very snuggly today. He also used a lot of chewies to help his teeth.

Source: Mentor Graphics Child Development Center. Reprinted with permission.

brings Ingrid into the room. Caryl, Ingrid's caregiver, greets them, "I knew it was about time for Ingrid to arrive. I am so glad to see you. We have lots of great things planned, including outdoor time today." Ingrid's face lights up and she smiles as Caryl talks with her. Sharon changes Ingrid's diaper and places the clothing supplies in her storage tub. They then come back into the main room, "Let's put your lunch and snacks in Ingrid's space in the refrigerator." Ingrid is 11 months old and beginning to walk. She heads over to the table where several toddlers are finishing up their morning snack. Sharon walks over with her, sharing, "Honey, I have two meetings to go to today," as she says good-bye to Ingrid. Ingrid doesn't respond, so Sharon gently touches her shoulder saying, "I am leaving for my work now and will be back later for you. Have fun with your good friends today." Caryl goes over to the table and sits near Ingrid, placing some cereal in her bowl as she responds to Sharon, "We'll see you later."

Infant and Parent Routine: Transition to Caregiver. You notice that each time a parent and infant arrive, the parent changes the baby's diaper and spends some time with the infant before leaving for work. Being curious about this interchange, you check with Caryl. Caryl explains that each family develops a Good-Bye Plan that they follow when they bring their child to infant care. The staff feels that it is important for each family to develop a comfortable routine, similar to a bedtime ritual. This might include looking around the room while visiting with their infant, diapering the infant into a "center" diaper, or simply sitting with the child for a few minutes. The infant care **Good-bye Plan** follows one developed by NAEYC (see Figure 7.2). Each family creates their own routine and shares this with the staff. Some families have more time at the end of the workday or come for a visit during the day, which allows them to make a connection with their infant and their infant's caregiver in the setting of the care center.

Now that you have had a chance to become familiar with the setting in the Infant Suite, it's time to meet Luke.

Meeting Luke

Responding to Individual Interests. Over by the sleeping room is a window that is about one foot from the floor and goes up about three feet. There is Luke! He is watching the toddlers outside in the

FIGURE 7.2

Good-Bye Plan

Saying "Good-bye" is a very hard thing to do for both parents and children. Children may scream, cry, or cling when you attempt to leave. This behavior is called separation anxiety and it is a normal part of growing up. It is important to acknowledge that it is not easy for parents to leave their child with someone else for long periods of time. Separation evokes strong feelings in us all—guilt, sadness, anger.

There are some things that can help make the process a little easier for parents and children. We ask parents to establish a written arrival plan for their child. These routines, like bedtime stories, add predictability and are comforting. Elements of an arrival plan include such things as consistency, giving your child your full and focused attention during brief play time, simple caregiving routines like changing a diaper, and always saying good-bye. We ask that parents always tell their children "good-bye" before they go. This enables the child to play freely without worrying when the parent might disappear and also forms the very basis of their ability to trust you.

It is our hope that parents and teachers be supportive of one another in this good-bye process. We can do this by consistently following a departure plan and working together on this ongoing process of saying "good-bye."

Child's name: *Luke*
Date: *September*

Approximate length of time I can spend with my child each day:

5-10 mins., plus occasionally come by during lunch hour

The routine I plan to follow:

Bring Luke to Infant room.
Drop Luke off after a smooch and a few minutes of play. Arrive between 8:15 & 8:45.

What things can the teachers do to support your plan?

Notice Luke's mood when I leave and remind him I will be back after his afternoon snack.

Source: Mentor Graphics Child Development Center. Reprinted by permission. Adapted from *So Many Goodbyes,* 1990, Washington, DC: NAEYC.

play yard. Luke taps on the window. Kristine, his caregiver, walks over to him and sits down next to him. She says, "Oh, look, there's your brother, Isaac. We will go visit him in his room later today." Kristine turns to you and explains, "We take the infants to the other rooms, especially to visit siblings. We want them to interact with other children, feel at home, and spend time with family members. It's an important part of our day."

Luke has a smile for anyone who comes near him. He is nine months old and recently learned to stand by pulling himself up on furniture or windowsills. When Kristine notices that he's no longer looking out the window, she asks, "Would you like to hear a story?" She carries him over to a sitting area and pulls several small books from a shelf. Luke taps one about ducks and Kristine starts reading to him. She makes duck noises and Luke nods his head with her quack sounds, making small grunt sounds of his own. It appears that this is a familiar story and routine to him. He smiles each time she quacks.

Connections between Home and Infant Program. When they finish the story, Luke and Kristine notice Emory has crawled over to visit. She looks at the mobile hanging near the window. Next to the mobile is a display with photographs of Luke and his family. You look around this part of the room and see similar displays, all at floor level. A sheet of Plexiglas covers a 3' × 4' display of family photographs—another homelike touch! Kristine, Luke, and Emory look at the photographs of Luke's family. Kristine points out, "Look, here's Luke and his brother all wet and soapy in the bathtub." The infants are looking at the photographs and seem to enjoy her story about Luke's family.

Providing Guidance for Infant Behavior. Just then, Emory reaches out and bumps Luke with her head. Luke is startled and begins to cry. Kristine pats Luke on the back, telling him, "I know that surprised you and hurt. Emory, it is important to be careful with people. If you want to play with Luke, you must be gentle." Kristine provided attention to both infants while responding to Emory's behavior. Kristine tells you, "We need to interrupt situations that could cause injury and give immediate feedback to both infants. It's my role to provide guidance. Emory might want extra attention or might be hungry, but she also needs to respect Luke's personal space. I have to make a quick decision about stopping any physical harm." After this interaction, Luke appears calm again and crawls toward the climbing stairs.

If you were observing in a classroom with older children, Kristine's interactions with Luke and Emory in this situation might be viewed as classroom management. With young infants, a primary goal is for each infant to learn to respect himself and others. Setting clear boundaries about appropriate behavior and building on positive interactions helps infants learn to interact with others in a supportive, healthy environment.

Emory's caregiver, Caryl, comes over to pick Emory up for a bottle and diaper change. "Hello there, Emory. I think you're feeling a bit hungry. Am I right?" Kristine tells you, "You've probably noticed that we always give individual attention during bottle feeding and diapering. We continually talk with our infants and engage them in whatever we are doing with them. It is important for them to feel safe and respected."

Lunchtime: Respecting Diversity of Families. Luke begins to make whining noises and Kristine asks him if he is getting hungry. By now, it's late morning. She brings him over to the table and helps him sit in one of the special wooden chairs made for the infants ready to support themselves in a sitting position. She helps him into the chair and allows him to make as many of the movements himself without her help. "Look, here's a bib with Luke's name on it," she tells Luke as she puts the bib on him. Then Kristine looks in the refrigerator on the shelf marked with Luke's name. "Your father brought a rice and squash lunch for you." Kristine tells you, "Since the infants are on an individual plan, their families provide meals until they are 1 year old and then they can choose to eat the center meals or continue with food from home. This way, we make sure each infant has the food the family wishes him to eat at this young age."

Conversing and Socialization. During lunch, Luke and Kristine engage in a conversation. She asks him, "Do you want more squash or banana?" He picks up a piece of banana and she says to him, "Oh, so you are hungry for banana." They continue their conversation. Luke notices what other children are eating and points at the applesauce that Emory is eating. Kristine asks him, "Do you want some of your pears?" He looks at her and opens his mouth, waiting for the pears. The infants who are able to pick up small pieces of food are busy feeding themselves. No one seems to worry about spilled food or messy faces—it's all part of learning how to feed yourself! The atmosphere is pleasant, similar to a family dinner together, with conversation and encouraging words.

Afternoon Nap: Individual Preferences. Luke prefers to sleep for short periods of time, and one of his nap times is right after lunch. He typically has three short naps (about one hour long) during his day at the center. His after-lunch routine includes a diaper change, drinking a bottle while cradled by Kristine, and falling asleep soon after being placed in his crib. When he wakes up, he is ready for more exploring. Kristine says, "If he hasn't had enough sleep, he'll be grouchy, which is not like Luke. When this happens, we place him back in his crib to sleep some more. He most often wakes up ready to play again."

Luke's Favorite Activities and Explorations. Figuring out Luke's favorite activities is difficult. He seems to enjoy exploring everything in the room. Now that he is pulling himself up, he looks for furniture to stand near so he can pull himself upright. Kristine tells you, "Luke never seems bored. He loves to play with everything he finds." Right now, Luke likes to touch faces and hair. He will play with most any toy he finds. Perhaps he does have a favorite, though. One of Luke's favorite activities is outdoor time. He notices when the stroller is brought into the room and the caregivers begin getting children ready for outdoor time.

Discovering the World Outdoors. Each day, caregivers take the children outside. Parents bring warm coats, hats, and mittens for their children during the cooler months of the year. Kristine tells you, "The world outdoors is an important part of children's development and learning. We want them to experience and enjoy the outside air, sounds, and smells."

Looking out the window, you notice a low fence between the infant and toddler play yards and the yards where the older children play. You also notice that there are no typical playground structures, such as swings or slides, but there are trees, grass, toys, and two covered play areas. Kristine says, "I enjoy time outside myself. Since this is early winter, many days are rainy or damp, so we take the infants outside in strollers or buggies. Luke enjoys these buggy rides. During the drier days last fall, Luke spent time exploring the play yard. He liked to pull the grass and grab handfuls of grass." Kristine continues, "I find it relaxing to spend time visiting with the infants outside. There is a lot to see when you slow down and look around from an infant's perspective." You've already noticed that Luke will often crawl over to the window to look out on the play yard. He does seem to find the out of doors interesting.

JOURNAL 7.2: Why might outdoor time be an important part of a day for infants?

Visiting Brother: Attention to Siblings. Several times a week, Kristine and Luke go down the hall to the preschool room to visit Isaac. She tells you, "Sometimes Luke just watches Isaac play and other times Isaac will come over and sit near Luke and tell him what the other kids have been doing." Isaac greets Luke when they arrive, saying, "Luke is here! Look, Luke, I made this little snake today. When it's dry, I can take it home." Luke responds by smiling and pointing to the snake. After 15 minutes of visiting, Kristine says, "Good-bye, Isaac. We're headed back for Luke's nap." Isaac comes over and hugs his brother, then rushes off to play with blocks. Both brothers seem to enjoy the visit.

Dad Arrives: Communicating about Luke's Day. Luke wakes up from his last nap around 5:00, rested and ready

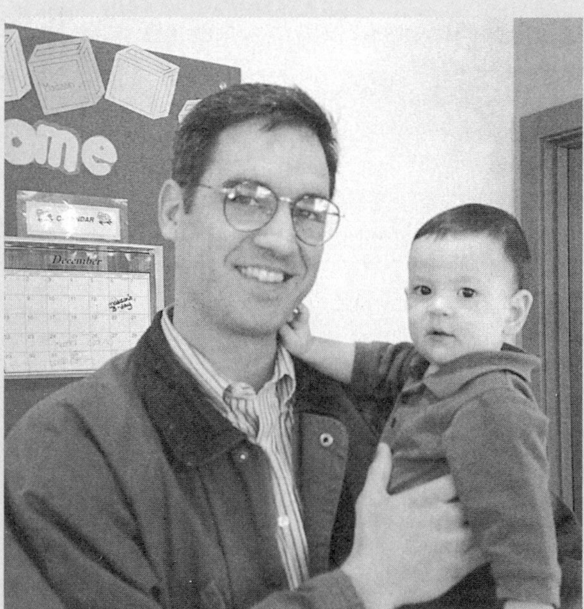

Both Luke and George look forward to their time together. Parents and families are an important component of the infant care program.

to greet Dad. George arrives about 5:45. Several parents have already arrived to pick up their infants, so Luke senses it must be about time for his Dad to arrive. When George comes in the door, he walks over to the rug area where Luke is holding a play telephone. "So, are you calling Dad to come pick you up?" asks George. Luke smiles. George picks up Luke and carries him over to Kristine. "Well, how was today?" Kristine is filling out Luke's Daily Log for George to take home with him. "Luke had a busy day, with three naps and time to go outside and ride around in the buggy and look for birds. We also went to visit Isaac."

Kristine asks if George has noticed Luke being fussy or pulling his ear the past day or so at home. She tells him, "Today, I noticed Luke touching his right ear several times, so I wondered if he might be getting another ear infection." George thanks her for the observation and says, "Julie and I will watch and let you know if we notice anything tonight or in the morning." With Luke still in his arm, George checks the Daily Log, picks up Luke's dirty clothes and food containers, and heads for the door. "Thanks, Kristine. We'll see you tomorrow." And off they go.

What an interesting day! Infants are absorbing so much while responding to the warmth and interactions with a caring adult. Luke and Kristine seem so comfortable with each other. Kristine recognizes Luke's individuality and works hard at creating a day that meets his developmental needs and his style of interacting with his environment. Luke's day at infant care is certainly a symbol of the investment that his father's company is making through their support of employer-sponsored infant care program.

A Conversation with Luke's Dad

A visit has been arranged with Luke's father, who works at Mentor Graphics and is usually the parent who brings Luke to the center and picks him up in the evening. You will enjoy meeting George, who is enthusiastic about the Child Development Center and the philosophy of the center. Both of his children have spent their weekdays at the center since they were several months old.

George arrives in the early afternoon. He begins the conversation by stating, "The Child Development Center here at Mentor Graphics allows our family to feel guilt free about working. It's provided peace of mind for us." George is an accountant with Mentor Graphics and Julie is an engineer at a nearby firm.

Benefits of an Employer-Sponsored Child Development Center

When George and Julie were married, they became curious about the on-site, **employer-sponsored child care program.** George appreciates the stance his employer has taken in sponsoring the center and the benefits provided through employer-sponsored child care. In fact, when George recruits new employees with young children, he discusses the important benefit of the employer-sponsored Child Development Center at Mentor Graphics. George feels that the CDC affects loyalty and employee commitment to the company. He definitely sees the CDC as a "world-class" child care program and promotes the center as a recruiting tool and important employee benefit.

Impact of the Infant Care Program on Family Life

When asked about the effect of the infant care program on family life, George responds, "I feel our children are the most needy in their first 12 months of life, and without the quality of this program, I am not sure we both would have continued working. We would have had to consider a different style of caring for our infants or a different life-style."

George also talks about the impact the program philosophy has made on his family life. He feels that he has learned a great deal about parenting from the caregivers at the center. Many of their approaches to infant care have been adopted by George and Julie in their own home. For example, George says, "Both of our children have learned to entertain themselves as floor babies. They don't expect to be put in swings or bouncy chairs. They seem to be quite content moving around the floor and looking around." You certainly noticed this when observing Luke. He was often engaged in exploring his environment.

Communication between Families and the Center

Luke's family finds that **communication** is essential between families and caregivers. The infant care center has established several different formats for communication and actively invites frequent input and feedback from families. Some of the formats for communication include conferences, which are scheduled on a regular basis and as needed, e-mail, voice mail, phone calls, portfolios developed by each caregiver, drop-in visits by parents, and the Daily Log. Kristine and Luke send George or Julie e-mail messages several times a week. Sometimes Kristine might write about something Luke is doing, and often Luke will tap the computer keys to add his own message. George appreciates the connections and feels part of Luke's day.

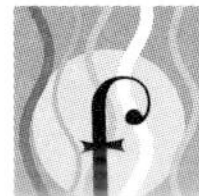

DAILY LOG: A FAMILY-CENTERED RECORD. When George "signs in" Luke in the morning, he fills out information about Luke's wake-up time, meals, diaper changes, and other facets of his morning. Kristine reads the log and continues to complete the log as the day goes on. At the end of the day, Kristine adds a brief note about a highlight of the day or a concern she wants to discuss with George. Often, the end of the day can become quite busy and the Daily Log helps Kristine and George note information about Luke that they want to share. George finds that he looks over the Daily Log during the evenings when Luke seems to be fussy or tired. He can check when Luke last slept, how long his naps were, or if he might be hungry. Kristine also writes down times when she thinks Luke might be getting a cold or feeling ill. Then George and Julie watch for similar symptoms

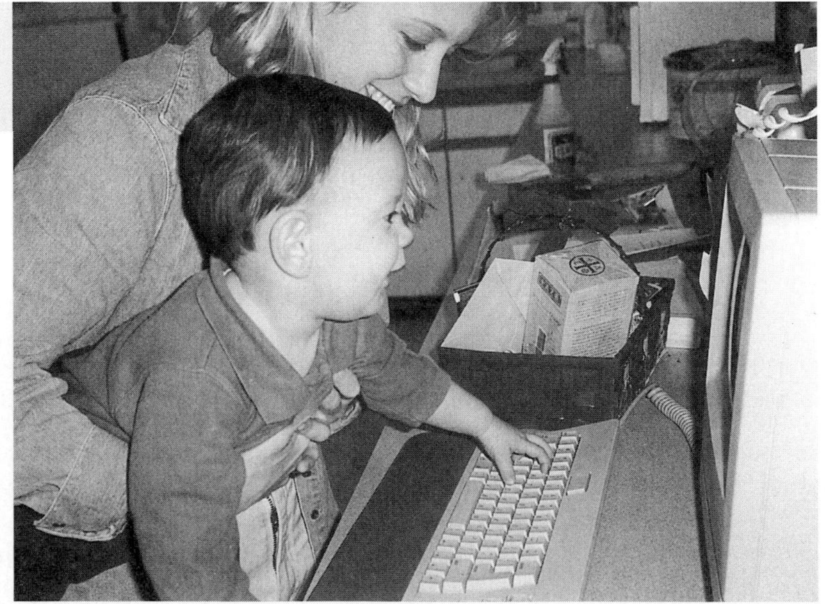

Luke is sending an e-mail message to Dad—in code?

in the evening and the next morning. The log serves as a communication tool for everyone who interacts with Luke and it keeps information flowing to help Luke's transition from home to the center and back home again.

PORTFOLIOS: AUTHENTIC ASSESSMENT. Kristine developed a **portfolio** for each of the three children for whom she is the primary caregiver. George shared how impressed he was with Luke's portfolio (see Figure 7.3). He felt that Kristine captured the last five months of Luke's development and growth through the photographs and journal entries she entered in the portfolio. Kristine adds to the portfolio over the two-year period that she is caregiver with each child, and then presents it to the family at the final conference.

USE OF TECHNOLOGY FOR COMMUNICATION. George greatly appreciates Kristine's use of technology in their communication. For example, last week he received a photograph on his e-mail a few minutes after Luke and Issac had been playing together in the toddler room. Kristine used the digital camera to take a photo of the two boys as they greeted each other with a hug. She used the computer to send the photo off to George. "This helps me feel connected to the kids, and I look forward to checking e-mail," shares George. Kristine also uses the camcorder to record major developmental milestones as Luke begins to grasp toys, crawl, sit up, and maneuver the stair structure. She finds these technology tools helpful in providing documentation in the portfolio as well as providing visual communication with the family.

FIGURE 7.3
Portfolio Entry

October 7
Two bottom teeth have been spotted!

October 16
You inch-worm across the floor!

October 24
You hold your own cup of formula but you can't quite tip it up to drink yet!

October 25
You pull yourself up to your knees and are able to get back down!

WHAT A BUSY MONTH!

Source: Mentor Graphics Child Development Center. Reprinted by permission.

Final Thoughts: Benefits of Employer-Sponsored Child Care

George summed up his thoughts about employer-sponsored child care by expressing, "The center seems to make the company more family friendly. It feels like the company is taking care of things in our life that are important. And, of course, it helps to have your child in the 'Ivy League' of child care programs." The program and the company yield stability and a strong commitment to the importance of children and families. As you end your visit with George, he reminds you, "I look forward to your visit at our home next week with Kristine and our family. But be forewarned—it's likely to be a whirlwind with our two young children!"

George provided valuable insights into infant care from a parent's perspective. He also shared thoughts about working for an employer that sponsors an excellent child development center.

Visiting Luke's Home with Kristine

Kristine will be taking you to Luke's home as she visits the family. She was also the primary caregiver for Isaac, Luke's older brother, and has been to their home several times. You soon see Luke's home, which has many windows. Maybe that's why he enjoys standing at windows at the center. He has already learned that he can see a lot of action when looking outdoors.

Luke's Home: Understanding Family Values

George and Julie greet you at the door, along with Luke and Isaac. You go into the family room, where the coffee table is immediately put to use, as Luke pulls himself up to be part of the group. Outside the window you notice the backyard has several plastic cars, a "short" basketball hoop, and some riding toys. Julie tells you, "When we're home on weekends, we enjoy having neighborhood children visit and play in the yard." This reminds you of your conversation with George. The family places a special priority on the children.

A Typical Family Evening

Kristine thinks it might be helpful to you to hear about a "typical" family evening. Julie and George groan, and George says, "Well, as soon as we arrive home, we seem to be on fast forward. I bring home the boys and Julie starts dinner. We try to eat by 6:30 and spend dinnertime talking about our days. We encourage the boys to share their days. Having the Daily Log from the infant center helps us talk about Luke's day and include him in the conversation." Julie continues, "By 7:30, we start the bedtime routine with baths. The boys have lots of floating toys for the tub and this is a 'wind-down' time for us. Next is storytime. We all pile onto the bed and read one or two stories. By then, Isaac and Luke are ready to sleep."

George again brings up the Daily Log from the infant center. "We know how long Luke's naps were for the day, so we can pretty much predict his bedtime." After the boys are asleep, George and Julie visit with each other and get ready for the next day. George tells Kristine, "Knowing you will be there for Luke is important to us. The infant center makes it possible for us to feel positive about where Luke is each day while we're at work."

Thanking the family for the visit and saying good-bye, you turn to Kristine and thank her for inviting you. Kristine replies, "Visiting the family at home is how I learn more about their routines and it also helps the child feel more comfortable with me, knowing that I have been to their home."

Visiting with Sue, the Infant Care Coordinator

Some of your first questions are about the employer-sponsored Child Development Center, program philosophy, and curriculum. You wonder about the program and employer-sponsored child care. Sue, the infant care program coordinator, responds to your first question about employer-sponsored child care by describing Mentor Graphics Corporation's involvement in developing and implementing the Child Development Center.

Mentor Graphics Corporation-Sponsored Child Care

Mentor Graphics Corporation is known as a "leading manufacturer of software used by semi-conductor and circuit board designers" (Crockett, 1997, p. C1). In the late 1980s, the corporation made a decision to build a new campus to serve as corporate headquarters. At this time, the company's Facilities Department surveyed employees about desired facilities at the new site. Many employees requested on-site day care. The Human Resources Division formed a committee to study the feasibility of developing such a center. The committee explored different child care options and made the decision to go forward with the development of a quality, on-site Child Development Center to serve the children of its employees. The program at the Child Development Center would also be congruent with company beliefs—stressing the importance of education for its employees and the community, and if it is worth doing, it is worth doing right.

Consequently, the Mentor Graphics Child Development Center is a model early childhood and family support program. The center has three main purposes: to facilitate the development of young children and their families; to enhance the ability of employee-parents at Mentor Graphics to be productive by supporting them in their work/family roles; and to make a contribution to the community by providing a high-quality model of care and education for young children. The center serves 123 children each day in the main 12,000-square-foot building and a new building for children from birth to age 3 (3,680 square feet) located at corporate headquarters.

Now that you have a basic understanding of the role of the corporation in supporting this child care program, you are probably interested in learning more about the infant program itself.

Philosophy of Care: Respecting Children and Parents

Sue suggests a good overview and starting place for you might be with the *Mentor Graphics Parent Handbook* that the center developed. In the Philosophy of Care section, you read:

> Parents are respected as the most important people in a child's life. . . . Goals for infants and toddlers in our care include: respecting each child as a unique and special person; attending to each child's physical and psychological needs; fostering and developing a relationship with a caregiver the child can trust; providing a safe, healthy and developmentally appropriate environment; creating opportunities to interact with other infants and toddlers; and supporting each child in their exploration and use of all their senses. (Mentor Graphics Child Development Center, 1996, p. 15)

As you continue to read the *Handbook,* you notice the program goals are designed to create an environment that promotes the development of a healthy and curious child. Sue shares that the philosophy of care was developed over a period of time by a group of caregivers, teachers, and parents. Everyone read pertinent articles and discussed their vision for the Child Development Center, which was translated into a philosophy of care.

Infant Care Program: Individually Appropriate Practice

The infant care program includes children from age 6 weeks to approximately 18 months of age. Sue explains, "In the infant care program, each child has a different routine and caregivers are very aware of **individual routines.** We establish the day for each child based on her particular needs, interests, and personality. The program is developed around the child, which is why we consider it to be an **individual program.**" This means that feeding, sleeping, playing, diapering, and other activities are developed around the needs and developmental levels of each infant. In contrast, due to inadequate staffing or lack of knowledge about infant development, some centers feed all infants at the same time or put them down for naps at the same time. (Remember the places that Mei-Ling visited?) Another feature in the Mentor Graphics infant program is that each caregiver (infant specialist) is assigned three infants and develops daily programs around the needs and desires of each infant in her care.

The caregiver remains the **primary caregiver** for the infant throughout the infant's program. Caregivers start out with infants when they enter the program at 6 weeks of age (or older) and continue with them through the toddler program, until they are close to 3 years old and enter the preschool program.

JOURNAL 7.3: Why would the center have a caregiver work with the same child for a two- to three-year period? What might be some benefits of this arrangement? Can you think of some disadvantages?

Kristine, Luke's caregiver, expressed the importance of the individual schedule when she shared her thoughts about working with three infants as a primary caregiver. "Being responsible for the primary care for three infants ensures that no child gets lost in the shuffle. We learn each infant's schedule, personality, and preferences and are able to respond to them as individuals." The role of primary caregiver with infants is one that requires knowledge, skills, and dedication to the development and uniqueness of each child. An important benefit of primary caregiving is the bond that forms between the child and adult. Another benefit is found in the "positive effect on the caregiver's sense of value" (Bernhardt, 2000).

Although each caregiver is the primary caregiver for three infants, the caregivers also attend to each other's infants when the need arises. Remember when Luke visited his brother? Caryl then assumed care for the other two infants until Kristine returned. The quality of infant care is indeed dependent on the quality of the staff, as you have heard from parents, educators, and researchers. Also, quality infant programs embrace curriculum that is developmentally appropriate for the needs of each infant.

CURRICULUM OF INFANT PROGRAM. Sue is clear that the two major components of the infant curriculum are caregiving and play. When a caregiver is providing care for an infant, her attention is focused fully on that infant. She explains, "Caregiving interactions provide for social, language, and self-help skills. Each time an infant is fed or diapered, we talk with her and tell her what we are doing. We want the infant to feel respected and part of the caregiver interaction."

The second component Sue mentioned was play, and she shares, "The importance of **infant play** cannot be emphasized enough. You'll notice we don't have bouncy chairs or playpens or any mechanical infant devices. We want infants to feel empowered in their own environment. Our infants spend a lot of time each day on the floor. They learn to

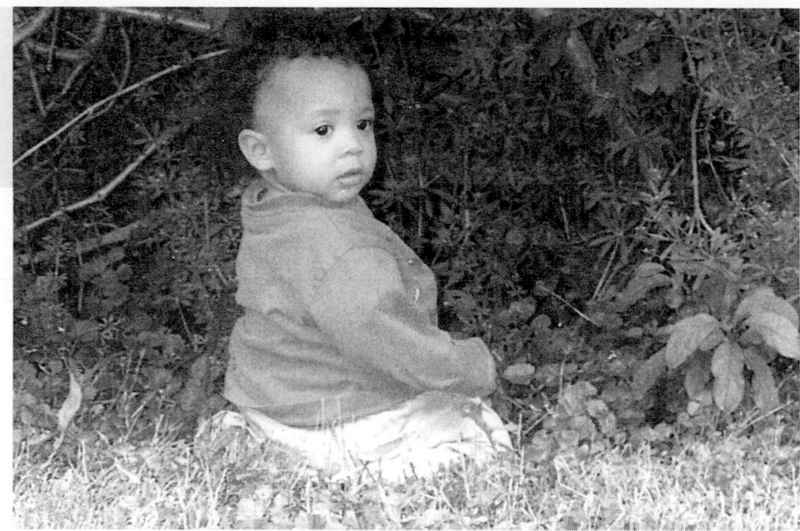

Sebastian is engaged in exploring his environment. Which senses might he be using?

roll over, move their necks and heads, reach for objects with their hands, and scoot around when they are developmentally ready."

While you observed the program, you rarely saw infants being "entertained." Much of the time, infants are busy on the floor with toys, engaging with other infants (closely monitored by a caregiver), interacting with a caregiver, or having their caregiving needs met. So this is what is meant by play! The infants actually "learn about themselves, other people and the world around them" (Mentor Graphics Child Development Center, 1996) by interacting within a safe and comfortable environment.

The curriculum in the infant care program at Mentor Graphics is consistent with **developmentally appropriate practice** for infants. Activities, toys and other objects, interactions, and program guidelines are created using the knowledge base of child development during infancy along with strengths, needs, and interests of specific children and families. **Development** is viewed as a continual process, with each child reaching milestones at various ages. For example, most children learn to walk without assistance between the ages of 9 and 17 months. Understanding that there is a wide range of time when children accomplish certain developmental skills helps caregivers provide different activities and learn to have different expectations for individual children.

Many early childhood educators consider Magda Gerber's contributions to be the most influential on infant care philosophy and practice. Gerber worked with infants in Hungary at Loczy, an institution for children from birth to age 3. In her subsequent work with caregivers of infants, Gerber emphasized an infant's need for respect, individualized caregiving, and a connection with a constant person (1979). These needs should be reflected in the everyday curriculum and practices with infants. This approach to infant care is called *Resources for Infant Educarers (RIE),* co-founded by Magda Gerber and Tom Forrest, M. D. Gerber's teachings are apparent in Mentor Graphics Infant Care Program.

ASSESSMENT AND INFANTS. Assessment in the infant care program is individualized for each infant, with the curriculum responding to this assessment. Sue finds a purposeful observation of a child to be a helpful format for assessing. The use of the portfolio to document growth is a partner to actual observations and serves as visual documentation. Sue adds, "Of course we only assess within the context of what the child is doing and describe the actions of the child. For instance, when a child begins rocking back and forth on her arms and legs as a initial stage of crawling, we note the child's actions through descriptive data. We would never force the child to move to crawling—just note the actions and provide opportunities for the child to progress." The assessment "reflects progress toward important learning and developmental goals" (Bredekamp & Copple, 1997, p. 21).

As you observed in Luke's infant care, activities and schedules are planned for the infants on an individual basis, which promotes developmentally appropriate practices. Remember Luke's desire to pull himself up on objects so he could be standing? Kristine made sure that Luke had opportunities to be near stable objects so he could use his muscles and coordination to pull himself upright. Through observations, she was aware of and able to assess his developmental level and incorporate appropriate activities into his curriculum.

INFANTS WITH SPECIAL NEEDS. When asked about including children with special needs in the Mentor Graphics Infant Care Program, Sue shared, "All of our children have differing needs. Because the curriculum in the infant care program is individualized and developmentally appropriate, we are able to provide caregiving that responds to a child's individual social, language, cognitive, and physical development."

While you observed in the infant care program, you might have met Emily, an 11-month-old infant. Emily's curriculum is planned to meet her special needs, as her physical development is delayed. She receives special education services from Ryka, a physical therapist. Ryka works with Emily from 2:00 to 3:00 on Wednesdays and Fridays. Most of the time is spent increasing Emily's muscle strength, so she can sustain a sitting position for longer time periods. Emily is now able to sit without support for several minutes. Ryka also meets with Emily's family and caregiver to discuss activities they can be working on with Emily. Emily participates in most of the same activities as the other infants, with planned attention and efforts made to assist her in her physical development. Emily is included in all aspects of the infant program. Planning developmentally appropriate curriculum also requires knowledge and respect of the child's family and culture.

RESPECTING THE DIVERSITY OF INFANTS AND THEIR FAMILIES. Sue continues, "Another important belief of our program is respect for the child and family. While you observed, did you notice how caregivers interacted with parents and how the center welcomes input from the family about their child?" This is all part of the Child Development Center's philosophy in action. The open communication and request for individual family and child information and preferences allow the caregivers to create an individualized program for each infant. Input provided by the family is an important component in the development of each individual plan. Parents are also welcome at the center at any time. The caregivers want to provide the best care they can and do so in a way that supports the family's preferences and honors the diversity of our families and children." Gonzalez-Mena

A Conversation about Inclusion

According to Sue at Mentor Graphics Child Development Center, "Our philosophy about inclusion is based on respect for one another—our differences as well as our similarities. In a culturally diverse community like ours, teachers need to be thoughtful, willing to listen and learn from families. We have found that families are our best source of information about their children, their unique family customs and culture.

"It's the job of the center's staff to do the groundwork which supports inclusion. A shared philosophy and a commitment to providing high-quality care and education for every child and the ability to work together help us reach our common goal. The practices of primary caregiving and continuity of care in our infant program support relationships between a teacher and families over time. Families recognize our professionalism and learn to trust that we will use shared information to take good care of their children and create an environment that welcomes families and to the best of our ability reflects their child's home culture. When we have a child with special needs, we partner with the family to find the most appropriate resources within the center and the community. We work with parents to be advocates for the child. We have found that we need to learn from the child, the parents, the experts, and from our own experiences."

and Bhavnagri (2002) recommend that caregivers receive diversity training to help them provide quality care in culturally relevant contexts.

When you observed Luke's lunchtime, you saw each infant eating food provided by his family. Sue notes, "We have learned that our families' cultures are often expressed in their food and food preparation. Several of our children continue bringing food from home so that their family's preferences continue throughout their time in the Child Development Center." For example, Marta often has beans and rice with her lunch, following a custom of her family. Knowing the family preference enables the caregivers to respect the family culture.

"Learning about the infant program before the child enters is important to the continuity of our program philosophy and characteristics, such as our curriculum and our belief about respecting infants." Sue has developed a procedure to help orient "new" families.

ORIENTATION FOR NEW FAMILIES: COLLABORATIVE PLANNING. Before enrolling an infant in the center, parents meet with Sue for an hour-long orientation and discussion of the center's philosophy and activities. Parents then arrange to visit the center. Three weeks after their visit, they make a final decision about enrolling their infant in the care center. After this time, the primary caregiver makes a home visit, with the purpose of easing the transition from home to the center for the infant and family. Following the home visit, the family writes a letter to the caregiver about their infant's typical schedule, routine, and particular needs and comforts (see Figure 7.4). The letter informs the caregivers about any specific wishes of the family. Sue wants her families to feel welcome and to spend time with their infant at the center. She finds this connection helps both parents and infants understand the role of the center in their lives.

Once the parents decide to enroll their child in the infant program, they set up a **"starting schedule"** with Sue. Each schedule varies according to the infant's needs and acclimation to the infant center. Infants might begin coming to the center for several mornings a week, then gradually move to full days once the infant seems comfortable with her caregiver and the surroundings.

Sue shares, "Often, I spend more time helping the parents adjust to the center and being separated from their child. We try to learn the best routine or schedule for each infant, based on individual needs and personalities. But sometimes it is harder for the parents.

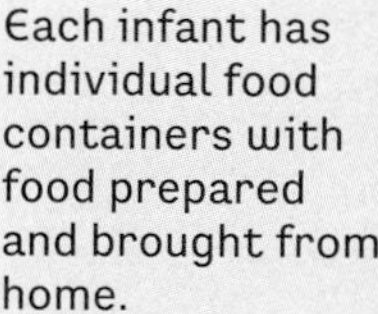

Each infant has individual food containers with food prepared and brought from home.

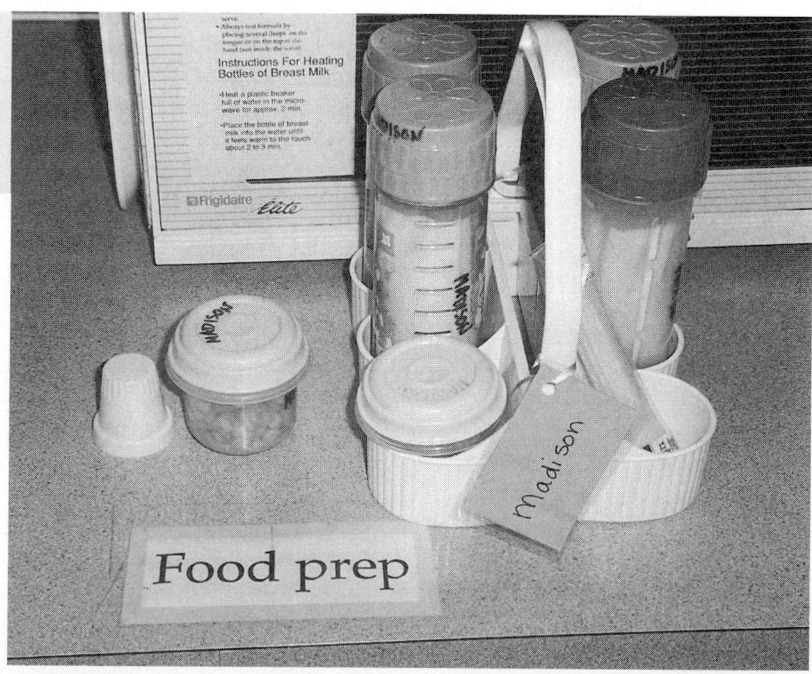

FIGURE 7.4
Letter from Family

Date: January 2
To: Caryl and Infant Room Care Givers:

We'd like to introduce our daughter, Ingrid. Born on September 12, she is a pretty little girl with lots of hair—that is usually what people comment on first when meeting her. Ingrid lives with her Mom and Dad, and big brother James (18 months her senior). Mom is looking forward to visiting Ingrid at lunchtime, when time permits, sometime between noon and 1 p.m. Ingrid will spend Monday–Friday from 8:00 a.m. to 5:30 p.m. in the CDC. Mom will normally do drop off and pick up.

Ingrid generally has a happy and laid-back personality when she is not bored or hungry or tired or in need of a new diaper. Ingrid will let you know when she needs service by crying. In time, you'll be able to guess what she needs by the time of day in her schedule or, when you really get to know her, by the type of cry. Ingrid will reflect your mood—if you have a happy smile, Ingrid will be happy to give you one in return. If you are stressed or hurried, Ingrid will become anxious as well.

Ingrid loves to be talked to as well as talk herself. She can babble on and on about whatever. Her Mom and Dad "talk" with her to encourage vocalization. Mom and Dad also read and sing to Ingrid. It has a great calming effect. Ingrid LOVES music, musical mobiles, toys, and singing. She has a musical bear in her crib that you can pull to help calm her to sleep. Please bring music to Ingrid each and every day if you can. You don't have to have a good voice (as Mom knows) to sing to Ingrid—she loves to watch facial expressions—the more animated, the more she likes it.

Ingrid has been used to one-on-one care with Mommy at home. Full-time group care will be new for her. If you cannot attend to her needs immediately when she sends out her usual distress signal (a cry), please respond to her verbally to let her know she has been heard and you are on the way. Mom and Dad have been using this technique at home successfully. Especially when big brother James is around.

Ingrid loves motion. She will be a big fan of stroller rides, both indoors and outdoors. There should be a pink fuzzy suit in her day bag for outdoor rides. Let us know when you have a hard time getting her into it. It fits her right now. Ingrid also loves to be held and cuddled. When all her obvious needs are met and she is still in distress, she is calmed by being held and walked. We offer her a pacifier at these times as well but she is finding her thumb more now.

Ingrid is a very sweet girl and learning to give lots of smiles. She's starting to coo and really interact. I find that when she is overstimulated and ready to stop eye to eye contact, she really looks away and sometimes starts to fuss a bit. She gives pretty clear messages.

Let's see, I guess there's not much else. I look forward to getting to know all of you better. Please don't hesitate to ask questions or let me know if there is something else you need.

Thank you,

Bonnie & Erik

Source: Mentor Graphics Child Development Center. Reprinted by permission.

They feel torn about leaving their infant in child care." Sue has found several books that are helpful for parents to read. She also introduces families to each other. Often it helps "new" parents to talk with other families who have made this transition. It seems that establishing a planned routine helps both the infant and the parent in their separation each morning.

JOURNAL 7.4: What are some of the ways in which this infant care program involves families? Describe one of these ways in detail, stating why this involvement might be important from the family perspective.

COMMITMENT TO A QUALITY PROGRAM. As you may have noted through your conversation with Sue, there is a strong commitment to a quality program shown by the corporation, CDC staff, and families. The staff understands the role of the primary caregiver and how important this person is to the infant and to the infant's family. Frequent communication, parent education, visits and conferences at the center, and a sharing of the goals of the Child Development Center lead to a common vision for child care. Families, staff, and management work together to create an employer-sponsored child care program that is viewed as a program that supports the growth and development of healthy children, healthy employees, and healthy families.

Now that you have visited the Mentor Graphics Infant Care Program and have had an introduction to the philosophy and curriculum of its infant care program, let's take a closer look at infant care programs, in general.

A Closer Look at Infant Care Programs

Infancy is a special time when caregivers and parents have the opportunity to nourish a child while he is most dependent on adults to meet his needs. Infants need adults to feed, clothe, clean, and care for them. They also need a safe, stimulating environment in which to grow. There is a rapidly increasing need for infant care, and, unfortunately, a lack of quality care available for infants and toddlers (Cost, Quality, and Child Outcomes Study, 1995, NICHD, 2002).

Children might begin child care as early as 6 weeks of age. Infant care programs differ on the age that they accept infants and also on the age for transition to the toddler program. Some programs make the change to toddler programs near 12 months of age, when many infants begin walking. Other programs continue the child in the infant program until they reach 18 to 24 months, adjusting the curriculum for young infants (2 to 10 months) and older infants (11 to 24 months). As more mothers of infants return to work, families are faced with the dilemma of finding the right care for their infant. Let's take a look at the basic needs of infants, a general overview or description of quality infant care programs, and current issues and trends relevant to infant care.

Programs and Infant Needs

All infants have similar needs in the first months of life. They share a common need for "good health and safety; warm, loving relationships with their primary caregivers; and care that is responsive to their individual differences" (Lally et al., 1995). Infant care programs that recognize the importance of close relationships to an infant's development address this need by designating one primary caregiver for each infant.

Recent research on brain growth during the first years of life helps caregivers recognize the importance of talking with infants, encouraging movement and social interactions, and providing stimulating curriculum throughout the day (see Box 7.2).

ROLE OF THE PRIMARY CAREGIVER. The primary caregiver learns the unique needs, moods, characteristics, and biological rhythms of an infant in her care. An infant caregiver must be nurturing and possess **keen observational skills** (Honig, 1985, p. 40). These observational skills are necessary to know when and how to respond effectively with an infant. Infants have different responses to stimuli, such as light, noise, activities, or smell. Some infants delight in loud music, whereas others cry and prefer quieter music. It takes time to

BOX 7.2 A Closer Look

What Researchers Say about Brain Development during Infancy

The human brain begins forming while still in the womb. In early infancy and through the first three years of life, brain connections develop in response to stimulation (Newberger, 1997). At birth, an infant brain has approximately 100 billion neurons. These neurons form over 50 trillion connections, known as *synapses.* In the first months of life, the brain connections continue to grow rapidly. This means that the experiences an infant encounters will have an impact on the growth of her brain. Contrary to prior beliefs, infants do not enter the world with a fully formed brain. The brain is still growing and receiving connections in response to interactions and stimulation from the infant's environment.

The infant's environment exerts a tremendous impact on how the circuits or wiring of the brain are formed (Newberger, 1997). Children who have opportunities for warm interactions and stimulating experiences will tend to strengthen the synapses (connections) in the brain. Children learn best when provided with choices and with meaningful learning experiences (Rushton & Larkin, 2001). In their study of brain development and the early years, the National Research Council and Institute of Medicine (2000) presented the following themes as recommendations drawn from their research: "All children are wired for feelings and ready to learn, and early environments matter and nurturing relationships are essential" (p. 4).

These recent findings hold great importance for early childhood educators, particularly those who work with the youngest children. Rich interactive environments, both at home and in infant care programs, will help children develop their mental and emotional capacities to their fullest potential. Developmentally appropriate activities are essential to the promotion of healthy growth in infants. Interacting with an infant by playing games such as peek-a-boo or hide-and-seek, talking about ordinary objects in the grocery store, and going on walks in the woods or neighborhood are activities that affect an infant's development (Jabs, 1996). Just as most parents and early childhood educators have long believed, positive and stimulating experiences in infancy do create a foundation that continues to affect learning throughout the child's life.

learn to observe and honor preferences while also trying to balance the need for stimulation and a variety of experiences in the curriculum. Since infants are not talking and expressing their thoughts through verbal language, the caregiver learns to watch their faces and body language. Does the infant tighten her fists and start taking shallow breaths? This might mean she wants out of a situation. Does a gentle rub on the back produce a small smile and relaxed posture? Back rubs might be an effective way to help this infant relax.

It is the role of the primary caregiver to recognize the specific signals that an infant is sending. When Luke was making little whining sounds late in the morning, Kristine recognized he was communicating his desire for food. He was hungry and ready to eat lunch. She was in tune with Luke's signals and able to respond to his needs. Luke was learning that he had the ability to influence his environment and receive food when he was hungry. The first step in guiding infants toward healthy independence is to address bodily needs promptly (Honig, 2003a). This interaction helps build security in the infant's life through the realization that his signals or communications lead to a response from a person he trusts—his primary caregiver.

PRINCIPLES OF CAREGIVING. Beyond recognizing Luke's needs, Kristine involves him in each **caregiving interaction.** A caregiving interaction takes place each time the caregiver connects, communicates, responds, or relates with an infant. Gonzalez-Mena and Eyer (2003) emphasize the importance of developing a relationship between a caregiver and an infant, and have outlined 10 principles of care giving, as shown in Figure 7.5.

FIGURE 7.5
Principles of Care Giving

Principle 1:	Involve infants and toddlers in things that concern them.
Principle 2:	Invest in quality time.
Principle 3:	Learn each child's unique ways of communicating and teach him or her yours.
Principle 4:	Invest in time and energy to build a total person.
Principle 5:	Respect infants and toddlers as worthy people.
Principle 6:	Be honest about your feelings.
Principle 7:	Model the behavior you want to teach.
Principle 8:	Recognize problems as learning opportunities and let infants and toddlers try to solve their own.
Principle 9:	Build security by teaching trust.
Principle 10:	Be concerned about the quality of development in each stage.

Source: Based on Gonzalez-Mena and Eyer (2003, pp. 9–23).

Involving infants and toddlers in things that concern them is the first principle of care giving described by Gonzalez-Mena and Eyer (2003). In their work, they have found it important to engage and involve infants in the "ordinary" events of the day, such as diapering, feeding, and playing. Keeping the infant's attention and describing the actions includes the child in "what is being done to her" and makes her a partner in activities that concern her.

This intense involvement can also be characterized as quality time, the second principle of caregiving. Remember when Luke was eating lunch and Kristine carried on a conversation with him? She was fully engaged in his activity and gave him her attention. It is an expectation of the infant care program at Mentor Graphics that caregivers help each other when they are aware that one caregiver is engaged in quality time with an infant and another child in their care needs attention. The contrast to this would be a situation where a caregiver was feeding three infants lined up in front of her in infant seats.

When you first met Luke, he was standing at the window and watching his brother outside in the play yard. He was banging on the window and intent on watching Isaac. Kristine talked to Luke about his brother and told him that they would visit Isaac later in the day. She recognized his banging on the window and his attentiveness to watching Isaac at play. She also verbalized descriptions of Luke's actions. This interaction is an example of the third principle: learning a child's individual communication patterns and teaching him your communication style. Kristine shared her thoughts with Luke, "We will go visit Isaac this afternoon after lunch. You'll like that, won't you? I feel ready for a visit myself."

Throughout the day, there are numerous opportunities to engage infants in learning about their environment, which contributes to their development. During outside play, Kristine described the environment around Luke. She told him, "If we listen carefully, we can hear the birds that you like to hear. And look, you are pulling the green grass. Doesn't it feel slippery today?" She purposely communicates about everyday events and activities and pays attention to experiences that foster Luke's social, emotional, physical, and intellectual development. While playing on the grass, Luke was using fine motor skills, learning the names of objects, sharing a social time, and having his emotional needs met. All developmental areas were engaged. These discussions are based on the fourth principle of caregiving: expending the time and energy to assist an infant in his development.

If Luke wakes up from his nap a bit early and seems grumpy, Kristine talks to him and says, "You seem to be feeling grumpy and need a bit more sleep. Let's take you back to your crib and let you get the rest you need." Using her observational skills and her knowledge of Luke's unique signals, she communicates to him what she sees, what Luke will be doing next, and where she is taking him. This is far different from picking up an infant and carrying him back to the crib without talking to him. The difference is called **respect** for the infant, which is the fifth principle of caregiving.

Respect for an infant also means allowing the infant to work things out for herself. For example, 10-month-old Emory was attempting to crawl toward a soft ball on the carpet. She seemed to go backwards with her efforts and began to fuss. Instead of rescuing her immediately, Caryl, her caregiver, waited to see if Emory would be able to change her direction and head toward the ball. Caryl then talked soothingly to Emory, "Look where the ball is Emory. You are close." Emory laid down her head and was quiet for a moment. She then rolled over and reached out with her arm and touched the ball. Instead of interrupting the learning at the first sign of frustration, Caryl respected the infant's learning and encouraged her to keep trying.

JOURNAL 7.5: *Liking* infants is different from *respecting* infants. Describe a basic difference between these two actions or beliefs.

The sixth principle recommends that caregivers recognize their own feelings and be honest about feelings. It is also important to learn to express feelings in a safe and healthy manner.

Modeling behavior you want infants to learn is the seventh principle, which is related to expressing feelings in a healthy format. Young children learn a great deal from their observations. When an infant sees a caregiver respond in a comforting way to a child who is crying, the infant begins to learn to connect comforting from a caregiver as an empathetic behavior.

The next principle is viewing problems as learning situations and allowing infants to attempt to solve their own problems when feasible. Remember Bruner's and Vygotsky's discussion about scaffolding, where the adult provides the structure or assistance to enable the child to accomplish a task or activity? This principle builds on this concept. It is tempting to "rescue" an infant and hurry and move a toy into his grasping range. On the other hand, if you want the child to develop the motor skills to reach the toy, allowing him to make attempts to do so is helping him learn to solve his own problem.

Being dependable so an infant learns to trust in a secure environment is the ninth principle. The Good-Bye Plan at Mentor Graphics highlights this principle. The adult is asked to let his infant know that he is leaving and have an established routine so the child begins to trust that his parent will return. This is vastly different from sneaking out of the room while the child is involved in an activity and later notices he is abandoned.

The tenth principle is providing for each stage of infant development. Knowledge of child development is critical to this stage, as is awareness of the infant's individual development in the various developmental domains. Appreciating the infant's current level of development and allowing time for the infant to explore and grow in this area is showing respect and encouragement for what the infant can do.

Did you notice that Kristine, Luke's caregiver, follows these 10 principles in her work with infants? She has developed a close, respectful relationship with each of the three infants in her care.

PHYSICAL ENVIRONMENT OF AN INFANT CARE PROGRAM. The day in infant care is constructed around caregiving and caregiving routines. A typical infant care program would ensure there was a safe, clean environment for the caregiving activities of diapering, eating, sleeping, and playing. In the Mentor Graphics Infant Care Program, you saw a designated area for each of these activities. Supplies are stored so caregivers can access them easily, yet the items are out of reach of older infants who are mobile. Caregivers wash their hands frequently throughout the day and always after diaper changes and before meals and bottle times.

Toys and other objects for play are placed in spots that infants can reach, whether on a low bookshelf or on the floor. Since infants learn much from sensory interactions, a va-

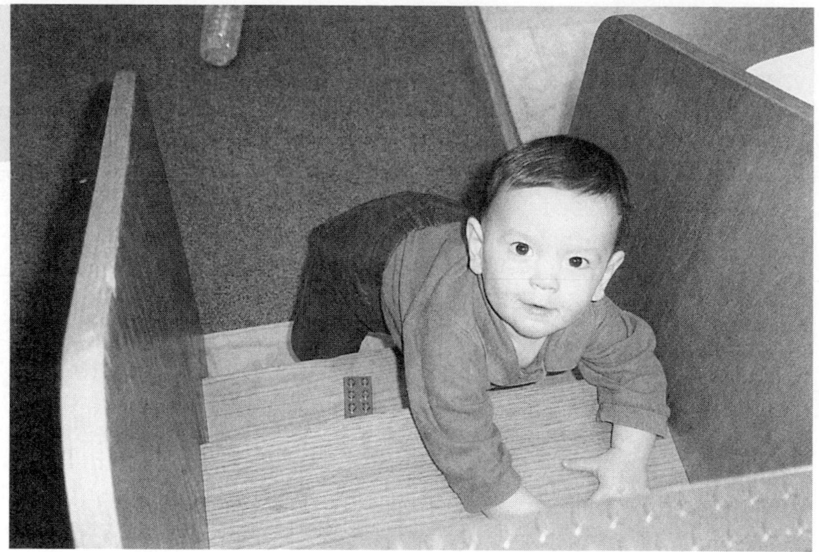

Luke has learned to go up the stairs but is cautious about going back down.

riety of tactile, visual, and motor experiences should be available. Within the infant play room, various textures should be available for infant touching. For example, a rough texture from a Berber-type rug contrasts with a spongy texture from foam rubber balls. Infants need opportunities to touch, crawl on, and walk on many surfaces. Different textures within their environment provides for a variety of touch sensations.

Toys and furniture should provide for a variety of uses and be selected for durability, ease of cleaning, and interest to infants. Homemade toys can create as much interest as expensive toys. Kristine shared, "The clear plastic pop bottle half-filled with oil, colored water, and large buttons is a favorite of some of our infants. They can hold on to the bottle, bump it to make it roll, or grab it and shake it. Just make sure to check the tape around the lid often during the day!" Some toys are left in the closed cupboard and exchanged with other toys periodically. Sue explains, "Too many toys are overstimulating. It's better to have a few available at a time and rotate them every week."

In the play area, Luke enjoys the climbing ramp, which has three stair steps enclosed in a wooden structure. He likes to climb and crawl on this, as he attempts to reach the top step. Another favorite object is a long mirror placed low on the wall. An infant can lay on the pad in front of the mirror and watch himself. This provides visual and motor stimulation, as older infants attempt to touch the mirror when they recognize body parts such as their faces. Infants also respond to auditory stimuli. A tape of music or a caregiver singing a song provides an enjoyable experience. Some caregivers like to play quiet music to calm an infant or rhythmic music when the infant is alert and playful. Singing can be reassuring and soothing to an infant, as he listens to melodies and familiar words (Honig, 1995) sung by his caregiver. A variety of objects, such as soft balls, wooden blocks, rolling bottles, and larger play structures, encourage the infant to explore and learn within an interesting environment.

Just as a variety of objects within the infant care room create interest, so do a variety of surfaces. Different tactile surfaces, which might include smooth, hard surfaces (perhaps a tile floor) and soft surfaces (such as a pad where the infant lies when she watches herself in the mirror) provide variety. The quiet area might have dim lights, whereas the kitchen is bright. These differences in the infant's environment provide a range of texture, size, brightness, and color that stimulates sensory experiences.

Goals for Infant Care Programs

The primary goal of quality infant care programs is to provide a healthy, safe, and caring environment. Within this environment, another goal is the development of an appropriate individual program for each infant, based on the caregiver's knowledge of infant development, her observations of the infant, and input from the infant's family.

While parents are at work, they want to know that their infant is safe, secure, and being cared for by someone who understands infant development and is committed to a special relationship with their infant. A program goal that focuses on nurturing a respectful relationship between an infant and her caregiver would meet these parental expectations, along with viewing families as the primary caregivers in the infant's life. Program goals are reflected in the curriculum of an infant care program.

Curriculum for Infants

Curriculum, or the schedule of activities and events, varies greatly among ages and developmental levels of young children. Infants have needs that are very different from the needs of preschool-aged children, and would be frustrated in an atmosphere where they were expected to eat, sleep, play, and be diapered on a group schedule. Infant care programs create individual plans around the needs, family wishes, and personality of each child. Caregiving, play, and quiet time compose the curriculum in infant care.

CURRICULUM AND DIFFERENT DEVELOPMENTAL AREAS. Each day, an infant learns and grows. As discussed earlier, an infant does not need to be directly taught specific skills. Infants learn when they are in a safe, secure atmosphere, with multiple opportunities to interact with others and with their environment. Growth is occurring in each of the developmental domains. **Developmental milestones** are found in Table 7.1, which provides a guideline of when infants acquire certain behaviors or skills. This guideline assists caregivers in creating curriculum to meet the needs of infants in their care. Kristine finds it helpful to refer to these milestones when she plans activities. The guidelines help her assess whether the curriculum is appropriate for an infant's development, as well as provide a check to be sure that she has planned for each of the different developmental areas.

Very young infants begin to recognize the sight and smell of their primary caregiver within a few weeks of birth. By several months of age, the infant will imitate facial expressions, such as opening her mouth wide or smiling. When she reaches 1 year of age, she tends to be quite interested in her peers. These are representations of **social interactions** (interest in others) that start at birth. Curriculum planning for the social domain would include a warm relationship with the primary caregiver along with opportunities for exploring and interacting with peers.

If you observe a young infant, from 2 to 4 months old, you might notice the infant sucking his fingers or gazing at his hands. He is beginning to learn to distinguish himself from the rest of his environment. As he grows in **self-awareness,** he begins to respond to his name and identify his body parts. Infant caregivers plan many activities that help infants identify themselves. You might observe games with infants, such as "Where is Manuel?" Manuel will hide behind an object and peek out and respond, "Manuel here." Infants from 6 to 18 months old enjoy games of naming and touching their body parts. Emory will respond to "Where is your nose?" by touching her nose. The next step for older infants would be for the caregiver to ask, "Where is my nose?" They are now ready to distinguish between their own selves and another person as they grow in self-awareness.

Infants learn a great deal from being touched and touching objects. A young infant finds that moving her arms can expand her immediate environment as she reaches for and touches things around her. As she grows older and her motor and physical skills expand, she is able to sit in chairs, walk, and build with blocks. Assessment of an infant's **physical development** provides direction for curriculum planning. The infant care environment must also be assessed for safety reasons. As an infant becomes mobile, her environment must reflect her range of accessibility. For example, wall sockets should be covered with safety plugs, cords should be placed out of reach, cupboards should contain "safe" items only, and large objects that could be pulled over or dropped should be moved out of the way. These safety precautions allow the infant to move more freely within her environment, building her motor and physical skills as she learns to roll over, crawl, sit up, walk, and climb.

The environment of the infant becomes more interesting as he learns to use tools and move. For instance, a 2-month-old might discover that jiggling in his crib causes a mobile to move slightly. As he grows older, he is able to make more **purposeful movements** to reach particular results. Scott found that he could push a stool over to the counter and climb on the stool to see what was on the counter. He was able to use tools and movements to accomplish his goals. When an infant has developed eye-hand coordination and small muscle coordination to the point where he can grasp a spoon and begin to control arm movement, he is ready to learn to use a spoon (a tool). Eating applesauce or other semi-solid foods is great practice for learning to coordinate a spoon. Gradually, the infant learns that the tool (spoon) allows him to eat faster and to end up with more food in his mouth. Be prepared with bibs, cloths, and plenty of trial and error learning!

Infants learn through language (cognitive and language development) as they make sounds, listen, and respond to others (see Box 7.3). Communication starts on the first day of life. An infant learns to distinguish familiar voices and to discriminate between happy and not as happy sounds at a young age. By the time he is a year old, he begins to babble and combine babbles to create his own words. He also begins to look at objects that are named out loud. For instance, when Amil hears someone say "ball," he looks toward the ball storage basket and often will start crawling in that direction. He connects the word with an object. His curriculum includes making frequent conversations, listening to books read to him, playing games that name objects, and hearing responses from his caregiver to his use of language. Infants are continually developing language during this period of their lives.

Responding to sounds and use of language also affects an infant's **emotional development.** He learns what creates or causes pleasure or displeasure and how to obtain comfort. Infants also learn how to express feelings. Remember when Luke knocked on the window while his brother was playing outside? He had learned that this gesture would catch someone's attention and he might be able to interact with his brother. A major curriculum goal includes responding to an infant's feelings. This response helps him feel more secure and understand that he is empowered to interact with and have an impact on his own environment.

CAREGIVING AS CURRICULUM. Since caregiving routines are designed for an individual infant, the curriculum or daily schedule of activities differs for each child. Luke prefers three short naps each day, whereas Emory has a morning and afternoon nap. Emory arrives earlier in the morning than Luke and leaves by 4:00 P.M. Her individual plan is adjusted to meet her needs. Her caregiver, Caryl, pays attention to changes in her routine and notes these on her Daily Log. Diapering and eating times are accommodated on each individual schedule. Caregivers learn when their infants need snacks, or seem to want early or late lunches. Of course, such schedules are adjusted daily to meet infant needs.

Looking back at the role of a caregiver and the 10 principles of caregiving that Gonzalez-Mena and Eyer developed, can you see the curriculum for infants embedded within these principles? The exchange between the caregiver and the infant during lunch becomes a learning situation for the infant. Kristine talks about bananas with Luke, naming the fruit as she talks about his action of picking up a banana. She asks, "Would you like another piece of this yellow banana?" The language she uses is rich and descriptive, and her tone is calm and conversational.

Kristine also gives Luke her full attention as she communicates with him. When she is feeding Luke his bottle, Kristine often sits on the couch in the living room area. She talks quietly with Luke, talking about his family, their day together, or planned activities. **Caregiving interactions** are opportunities to enhance the healthy development of infants. Kristine continually involves Luke in each caregiving activity. She is not doing something *to* him, but *with* him. This philosophy of caregiving empowers Luke to become an active participant in his care, learning about himself and his world in the process.

TABLE 7.1 Developmental Milestones of Children from Birth to 18 Months

	Interest in Others	Self-Awareness	Motor Milestones and Eye-Hand Skills
The early months (birth through 8 months)	• Newborns prefer the human face and human sound. Within the first two weeks, they recognize and prefer the sight, smell, and sound of the principal caregiver. • Social smile and mutual gazing is evidence of early social interaction. The infant can initiate and terminate the interactions. • Anticipates being lifted or fed and moves body to participate. • Sees adults as objects of interest and novelty. Seeks out adults for play. Stretches arms to be taken.	• Sucks fingers or hand fortuitously. • Observes own hands. • Raises hands as if to protect self when object comes close to face. • Looks to the place on body where being touched. • Reaches for and grasps toys. • Clasps hands together and fingers them. • Tries to cause things to happen. • Begins to distinguish friends from strangers. Shows preference for being held by familiar people.	• The young infant uses many complex reflexes: searches for something to suck; holds on when falling; turns head to avoid obstruction of breathing; avoids brightness, strong smells, and pain. • Puts hand or object in mouth. • Begins reaching towards interesting objects. • Grasps, releases, regrasps, and releases object again. • Lifts head. Holds head up. Sits up without support. Rolls over. Transfers and manipulates objects with hands. Crawls.
Crawlers and walkers (8 to 18 months)	• Exhibits anxious behavior around unfamiliar adults. • Enjoys exploring objects with another as the basis for establishing relationships. • Gets others to do things for child's pleasure (wind-up toys, read books, get dolls). • Shows considerable interest in peers. • Demonstrates intense attention to adult language.	• Knows own name. • Smiles or plays with self in mirror. • Uses large and small muscles to explore confidently when a sense of security is offered by presence of caregiver. Frequently checks for caregiver's presence. • Has heightened awareness of opportunities to make things happen, yet limited awareness of responsibility for own actions. • Indicates strong sense of self through assertiveness. Directs action of others (e.g., "Sit there!"). • Identifies one or more body parts. • Begins to use *me, you, I.*	• Sits well in chairs. • Pulls self up, stands holding furniture. • Walks when led. Walks alone. • Throws objects. • Climbs stairs. • Uses marker on paper. • Stoops, trots, walks backward a few steps.

Note: This list is not intended to be exhaustive. Many of the behaviors indicated here will happen earlier or later for individual infants. The chart suggests an approximate time when a behavior might appear, but it should not be rigidly interpreted. Often, but not always, the behaviors appear in the order in which they emerge. Particularly for younger infants, the behaviors listed in one domain overlap considerably with several other developmental domains. Some behaviors are placed under more than one category to emphasize this interrelationship.

TABLE 7.1 *(continued)*

Language Development/ Communication	Physical, Spatial, and Temporal Awareness	Purposeful Action and Use of Tools	Expression of Feelings
• Cries to signal pain or distress. • Smiles or vocalizes to initiate social contact. • Responds to human voices. Gazes at faces. • Uses vocal and nonvocal communication to express interest and to exert influence. • Babbles using all types of sounds. Engages in private conversations when alone. • Combines babbles. Understands names of familiar people and objects. Laughs. Listens to conversations.	• Comforts self by sucking thumb or finding pacifier. • Follows a slowly moving object with eyes. • Reaches and grasps toys. • Looks for dropped toy. • Identifies objects from various viewpoints. Finds a toy hidden under a blanket when placed there while watching.	• Observes own hands. • Grasps rattle when hand and rattle are both in view. • Hits or kicks an object to make a pleasing sight or sound continue. • Tries to resume a knee ride by bouncing to get adult started again.	• Expresses discomfort and comfort/pleasure unambiguously. • Responds with more animation and pleasure to primary caregiver than to others. • Can usually be comforted by familiar adult when distressed. • Smiles and activates the obvious pleasure in response to social stimulation. Very interested in people. Shows displeasure at loss of social contact. • Laughs aloud (belly laugh). • Shows displeasure of disappointment at loss of toy. • Expresses several clearly differentiated emotions: pleasure, anger, anxiety or fear, sadness, joy, excitement, disappointment, exuberance. • Reacts to strangers with soberness or anxiety.
• Understands many more words than can say. Looks toward 20 or more objects when named. • Creates long, babbled sentences. • Shakes head no. Says two or three clear words. • Looks at picture books with interest, points to objects. • Uses vocal signals other than crying to gain assistance. • Begins to use *me, you, I.*	• Tries to build with blocks. • If toy is hidden under one of three cloths while child watches, looks under the right cloth for the toy. • Persists in a search for a desired toy even when toy is hidden under a distracting object, such as pillows. • When chasing a ball that has rolled under the sofa and out the other side, will make a detour around sofa to get ball. • Pushes foot into shoe, arm into sleeve.	• When a toy winds down, continues the activity manually. • Uses a stick as a tool to obtain a toy. • When music box winds down, searches for the key to wind it up again. • Brings a stool to use for reaching for something. • Pushes away someone or something not wanted. • Creeps or walks to get something or to avoid unpleasantness. • Pushes foot into shoe, arm into sleeve. • Feeds self finger food (bits of fruit, crackers). • Partially feeds self with fingers or spoon. • Handles cup well with minimal spilling. • Handles spoon well for self-feeding.	• Actively shows affection for familiar person: hugs, smiles at, runs toward, leans against, and so forth. • Shows anxiety at separation from primary caregiver. • Shows anger focused on people or objects. • Expresses negative feelings. • Shows pride and pleasure in new accomplishments. • Shows intense feelings for parents. • Continues to show pleasure in mastery. • Asserts self, indicating strong sense of self.

Source: Reprinted with permission from *Caring for Infants and Toddlers in Groups: Developmentally Appropriate Practice,* ZERO TO THREE: National Center for Infants, Toddlers, and Famlies, 1995.

BOX 7.3 A Closer Look

When Does Language Development Begin?

> Language is a complex, specialized skill, which develops in the child spontaneously, without conscious effort or formal instruction, is deployed without awareness of its underlying logic, is qualitatively the same in every individual, and is distinct from more general abilities to process information or behave intelligently. (Pinker, 1994, p. 18)

The development of language in infants occurs on approximately the same time line across different cultures. Newborns are sensitive to nuances in language and begin to discriminate the speech sounds that are part of the language spoken in their environments. By the time an infant reaches 3 months of age, she has already focused on the speech sounds she hears, including the patterns of accents, syllables, rhythms, and intonations of language. Jusczyk (1997) has reviewed research conducted on language development and states that these studies indicate that infants have the capacity or ability to "discriminate many different kinds of speech contrasts" (p. 56).

Kuhl (1992) has found that infants' brains create auditory maps of the phonemes (small units of sound) that they hear. By 6 months of age, English-speaking infants have developed a different auditory map in their brain than infants in Swedish-speaking homes. Familiar sounds (phonemes) now form the infant's spoken language. When a child reaches 12 months of age, her auditory map is formed. As people age, it becomes increasingly difficult to learn new sounds that are unfamiliar. This, in part, explains why adults have more difficulty learning a foreign language than young children. The young infant's brain is considered more "plastic" and able to respond to and imitate sounds.

Studies have also shown that there is a clear relationship between the amount of parent speech the child hears and the child's vocabulary growth (Huttenlocher et al., 1991). The more sounds a child hears, the larger her vocabulary. The sounds of words builds up neural circuitry for learning more words and new sounds (Begley, 1996). By 1 year of age, most children are connecting words with meaning, knowing that *puppy* refers to their dog, *ice cream* is something good to eat, and *bottle* holds something to drink.

The implications of these findings of language development support what many early childhood educators have long practiced—talking with an infant is important to her development. Babbling and cooing as forms of communication encourage adult interaction and shape language development. Object-naming by adults, an infant's ability to study and understand objects, and social interactions contribute to an infant's ability to learn words (Hollich et al., 2000). During the early months of life, auditory connections are formed in the brain and they affect language development, vocabulary, and use of language for the child's entire life.

JOURNAL 7.6: Describe an interaction between Kristine and Luke that represents the philosophy that caregiving is curriculum. What might Luke be learning in this interaction? ●

PLAY AS CURRICULUM. Play is an integral component of curriculum in early childhood programs, including infant care programs. When you observed the Mentor Graphics Infant Care Program, you saw that infants did not require highly stimulating toys, bouncy chairs, or other apparatus to learn. They do need a close relationship with a nurturing, observant caregiver. Infants learn best when they feel safe and trust the person caring for them. They also learn through interacting with objects in their environment. An infant might pick up a block and try to place it in his other hand. During this action, he is learning to transfer an object using eye-hand coordination and small muscle control. Doing these actions *for* the child does not help his growth and development. He must have

Meagan notices a lot going on around her from a safe viewpoint.

the opportunity to physically go through these motions at his own speed and for as long as he is satisfied and interested in the learning. When an infant learns on his own, he is adding to "his emerging sense of positive self-esteem and love of learning" (Greenberg, 1993, p. 108).

The environment or setting of the play area affects the learning that takes place through infant play. Dramatic play and other creative arts such as art and music are also part of the curriculum for infants. Appropriate art activities might include "dancing, singing, clapping and moving to chants and rhythms" (Honig, 2003b). Infants take pleasure from hearing familiar songs and music. Chants such as pat-a-cake and dramatic play with peek-a-boo are familiar to many of us and have been enjoyed by generations of children. Each of these activities includes active experience and use of multiple senses as they lay the foundation for creative expression. Infants need a protected place, free from older children running through the area, dropping toys, or otherwise placing the infant in danger. Infants who are not yet walking are safest on the floor or carpet, where they can begin to learn to roll over, creep, crawl, and pull up on nearby furniture. When the infant play area is safe and free of obstacles, adults have more time to spend observing or interacting with infants, assuming a less directive role in the infant's play.

QUIET TIME AS CURRICULUM. Infants also need **quiet time** during the day. With other infants and caregivers in one setting, naturally, there is a lot of activity and stimulation. Quiet time provides an opportunity for an infant to regroup. Some infants wake up from their naps and seem to be thinking while laying in their cribs until a caregiver arrives. This might be their quiet time. Other infants might like to spend some time in a quiet part of the care center, where they relax and look around for a few minutes. Again, this is an individual need. Some infants like several quiet breaks each day, whereas others seem to be able to find their own quiet time within the day.

Caregiving, play, and quiet time form the curriculum in an infant care program. The curriculum also reflects the philosophy and goals of the program. In Luke's infant care program, each caregiver worked with three infants and their families. Kristine learned the priorities and needs of her three families and planned curriculum accordingly. She also developed close, nurturing relationships with each infant. These relationships reflect the philosophy of the Mentor Graphics Child Development Center and were evident when analyzing the curriculum of the infant care program. Curriculum for any program must be based on developmentally appropriate practices and on the philosophy and goals of the program. Appropriate curriculum for infants "should be built into the infant's every experience" (Gerber, 1981, p. 84).

Curriculum development and curriculum implementation are responsibilities of each caregiver. Now let's explore the different roles of staff who work in infant care programs and their preparation or education.

Infant Care Programs and Staff

Programs for infants require a special type of teacher or caregiver. Knowledge of infant development, interest in working closely with families, and understanding the importance of nurturing while providing opportunities for exploration are essential requirements for the position of infant caregiver. Let's look at some of the different positions that might be available in an infant care program, along with the training or education needed for each position.

INFANT CARE PROGRAM DIRECTOR OR COORDINATOR. Depending on the size of the program, there is a program director or coordinator who is responsible for administrative duties. That individual might also be a caregiver part of the day. The director is responsible for program budget, facilities, communicating with parents and the community, supervising staff, enrolling children, meeting codes established by state and local agencies, and preserving continuity of the program philosophy and curriculum. Although requirements vary, most programs require that the director has a bachelor's or master's degree in early childhood education, coursework in program administration, and three or more years of caregiving or teaching in a similar program. The program director sets the tone for the program and is the liaison between parents, caregivers, and the community.

INFANT CAREGIVER. Since the caregiver is directly responsible for a small group of infants, she must have a solid understanding of infant development and be able to translate this knowledge into appropriate caregiving and play experiences. She must also have the "ability to work with infants warmly, calmly, and in an unhurried way" (Gordon, 1988, p. 47). Most programs expect their caregivers to have an associate degree with coursework in child development or early childhood education, along with experience working with infants.

INFANT CAREGIVER ASSISTANT. The caregiver assistant is also responsible for a small group of infants. A characteristic of quality caregiver assistants is continued interest in learning about infant care and early childhood education. Most assistants have completed high school and several courses or workshops in child development. A program director would be more likely to hire candidates who had prior experience in early childhood education and a commitment to reading and learning more about infancy and child development.

One of the best ways that a center can ensure that their staff keeps current with the best practices in infant care is to encourage caregivers to attend workshops or courses in early childhood education, specifically those focused on infant care. All staff should participate in professional development in order to continue to build their knowledge base in infant care practices.

Professional Development

Many centers find that continuing education plays a key role in keeping staff knowledgeable of infant care practices. Continuing education provides opportunities for staff to improve and expand their knowledge base. Continuing education or professional development also assists staff to reflect on and shape their program philosophy as they consider curriculum and activities appropriate for infants.

Examples of professional development activities include participating in workshops, courses, a planned degree program, or professional conferences on early childhood education. In addition to outside resources, on-site staff may have expertise in a specific area and might share this expertise with the rest of the staff. Some infant care programs find that setting aside one afternoon a month to work together on professional development greatly improves their shared knowledge.

Early childhood educators recognize that the knowledge in their field is expanding rapidly. Continuing education is required to keep up with the latest research findings. For example, the prior discussion on brain research with infants translates into the need to provide rich, stimulating experiences for all infants. Nurturing interactions influence the development of an infant's brain. Attending workshops or courses that help caregivers plan curriculum for their infants based on new knowledge in brain research will affect the learning environment of the infants.

As recent as 10 years ago, there was little knowledge about working with infants who had prenatal exposure to drugs or other substances. Caregivers can learn a repertoire of ways to comfort and help these infants in their early developmental years. Prenatal exposure to drugs, alcohol, and other substances places children at risk for adverse behavioral outcomes (Chatterji & Markowitz, 2000). Participating in courses or workshops about caring for substance-impacted infants is another example of professional development,

Many caregivers assess their own professional knowledge base and seek continuing education to expand their learning. Some centers choose an annual theme for professional development, such as working with families or language development, and offer to pay for workshops and programs that support these themes. Providing funds for continued education is one of the most cost-effective ways that a center can ensure continual professional growth of their staff.

Having discussed infant care programs, curriculum of these programs, and the staff preparation and roles of infant programs, let's turn to some current issues and trends in infant care. These issues are in the midst of much debate and discussion. As you read this section, think about your personal stance or views on these issues.

Current Issues and Trends in Infant Care Programs

Changing Roles: Families as Partners

Children, families, and caregivers benefit from family participation in the care and education of young children (Gestwicki, 2000). A family brings extensive knowledge of their infant to the caregiver. Partnerships between infant caregivers and families "build bridges for children between their worlds of home and child care, helping them feel safe, secure, and happy in both places" (Dombro, 1995, p. 22).

JOURNAL 7.7: What were some communication formats that George and Kristine used to bridge the worlds of home and child care for Luke? Briefly describe two different formats you might select to use.

Parents are experts about their child's particular needs, dislikes, and preferences. Caregivers have worked with different infants over a period of time and have gained a perspective of child development that can help the family "understand their child in terms of a broad spectrum of development" (Dombro, 1995, p. 23). By working as a team with families and by consulting frequently with the family, caregivers learn more about both the expectations and the culture of the family, which leads to a better environment for the infant (Szanton, 2001).

As more is learned from research conducted by those who study infant care programs, more support is given to actively involving families in infant care and the program. Families are the primary nurturers and teachers of young children (DiNatale, 2002). By discussing and sharing the culture of home and the one at the infant center, families and caregivers are more likely to understand each other's perspectives and behaviors. Communication via the Daily Log and a brief chat with the caregiver and family member supports continuity in the infant's life.

Curriculum Issues and Infant Care Programs

The issue of curriculum resurfaces with the push to increase academics in early childhood programs. It seems that curriculum for each age group is sometimes being pushed to the next lowest age group, creating the "hurried child" (Elkind, 1981). Although the model of individual programs for infants is accepted as the "best" model, financial concerns may overrule this priority, creating programs more group oriented and increasing the ratio of children to caregiver.

You may have seen advertisements for reading programs for infants, or programs that expectant mothers can purchase that will supposedly raise their child's IQ while still in the womb. In contrast, Elkind (1981) has an important message about infancy. He feels that this is the time when children develop their basic concepts about the world and "form their most critical attachments and social orientations" (p. 100). This learning and development takes "time and effort and cannot be rushed" (p. 100). Infants who feel safe and secure are ready to explore their world and learn through these explorations. The curriculum should fit the child, rather than the infant fit an established curriculum or expectations beyond his developmental level.

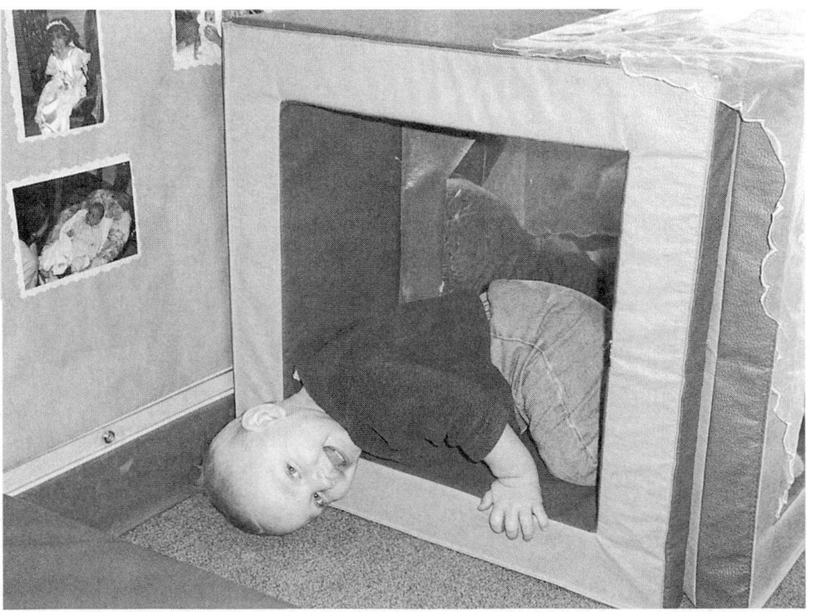

Courtney is busily exploring different perspectives from her cube. This corner of the room has a padded mat to ensure safety for infants.

Should Companies Sponsor or Support Infant Care Programs?

Each morning, George arrives at work with his two sons. His first stop is the Child Development Center. Then off George goes to his job, knowing that his children are nearby and in an optimal child care environment. His employer, Mentor Graphics Corporation, is dedicated to providing benefits to employees that help them in the workplace, whether this means professional development opportunities, an on-site gym and trails for exercising, or sponsoring a quality child care program.

Neugebauer (2002) has studied employer-sponsored child care for over a decade. He notes that as America's businesses have accepted employer child care as a valued benefit, employers are now beginning to seek various options in child care, such as resource and referral programs, summer camps, or back-up care for ill children. Friedman (2001) proposes that providing a range of initiatives (e.g., flexible work schedules, financial assistance benefits, paid leave, on- or near-site child care, and information and counseling services) lead to a family-friendly work culture. Establishing a family-friendly work culture improves employee recruitment and retention.

Neugebauer also finds that the economy of the United States impacts the growth of employer child care, with businesses more reluctant to move forward in support of child care in times of a struggling economy. Faced with challenges with the economy, businesses that provide on-site child care do so more as a matter of corporate ethics than as financial self-interest (Siegel, 2002).

Social Issues and Policies in Infant Care

Major social issues directly related to infant care programs include the growing number of mothers of infants entering the work force, an increased recognition of the need for quality programs for infants, and equal access to quality programs for all families. In Chapter 13, you will read about social influences on early childhood, so the discussion in this section will briefly focus on issues pertinent to infant care. You have been reading about the importance of quality care for infants and factors that contribute to a high-quality infant care program. How does a family find a program that meets their needs and expectations? This is a dilemma faced by many parents as they search for good programs for their infants.

Cultural sensitivity is an urgent need with the increasing number of families representing greater racial and ethnic diversity. Caregiving practices that meet individual family needs must take into account the family's culture. Caregivers must receive diversity training so they can provide quality care in a culturally relevant context (Gonzalez-Mena & Bhavnagri, 2000). Through frequent communication between caregivers and families, decisions about culturally responsive and developmentally appropriate practices can be implemented in a thoughtful and mutually agreed upon approach.

Over half of all infants in the United States are in some type of infant care, whether the program is in a family home, a relative's home, or an infant care center. The number of infants expected to need infant care continues to increase. This trend translates into a considerable need for infant care programs. Throughout this chapter, you have read about the importance of the relationship between an infant and his primary caregiver, and how critical this bond is in creating a rich environment for the infant. The establishment of standards and government funding for infant programs are ways that society can influence the quality and availability of programs. Needs for infant programs vary in the staffing ratio and in the type of structure and setting for the infant. These needs must be addressed in the standards that are developed and reflected in the design of quality infant care programs.

Development during infancy affects a child for the rest of his life. All children in infant care should have access to quality infant care. This is the responsibility of the community, both in terms of the local community and the broader community of the nation.

Legislature, funding, and establishment of standards that promote both quality infant care programs and access to infant care programs address social issues and the development of policy affecting infant care.

PRINCIPLES AND INSIGHTS: A Summary and Review

The more one learns about infant care, the more one comes to understand the importance of a quality care program. Infant caregivers are important professionals who contribute greatly to the well-being and growth of infants and to the needs of young families. As you continue in your early childhood studies, you will undoubtedly be asked for recommendations of high-quality infant programs. Knowledge gained from this chapter will help you answer this question as you apply your knowledge to local programs.

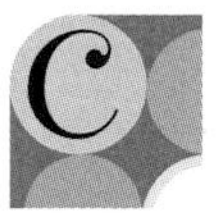

In discussions with others about infant care programs, you will likely bring up the critical role of the infant caregiver. The interaction or relationship between the infant and the caregiver forms the foundation of an individually designed program for each infant, based on her needs and those of her family. Besides the individual design of each infant's program, the caregiver also looks to developmentally appropriate activities and experiences for infants. Understanding infant development and application of infant development into curriculum is a key responsibility of each caregiver. Curriculum for infants is a combination of caregiving and play, based on each infant's individual needs.

Another point you are likely to share is the family's role in infant care programs and the partnership between families and the caregivers. Frequent communication between the family and caregiver help each of them do a better job. You have learned several formats for communication from Luke's caregiver and have seen how these worked with his family and Kristine. Caregivers learn much from each family about working with their infant, and families learn more about this special developmental period from the caregiver.

We asked you to think about the larger issue of availability of infant care programs. Luke was participating in his father's employer-sponsored child care program. This is one approach to the growing need for child care programs. As more parents with young children enter the work force, the demand for infant care programs increases greatly. Who will care for these children and how will the quality of these programs be assured? Later in this book, you will read about becoming an advocate for young children, which is essential to the development of quality early childhood programs.

Infancy is a time of enormous learning and development. Special people are needed to provide interactions that create safe, nurturing environments for infants, whether these people are parents or caregivers. Remember Mei-Ling and Jeff, Brynna, and Neil and Karen? They are the parents of the infants you met in the beginning of this chapter. Think how they might have felt if they had located infant care with a caregiver whose primary role was to create an individualized infant care program for their infant. Although the infant care they found was adequate, did it meet your criteria for a high-quality infant care program? Our hope is that all families will have access to state-of-the-art infant care, whether it be with relatives, child care centers, or family home care.

BECOMING AN EARLY CHILDHOOD PROFESSIONAL

Your Professional Portfolio

1. Expand on Journal Entry 7.5. How does a caregiver show respect for an infant? Do you think an infant knows if she is respected? Put your thoughts about this topic in your portfolio.
2. Imagine you are the parent of an infant and develop a Good-Bye Plan for your family. What might be a good routine when you leave your infant in the care of someone else? When finished, share your plan with someone else in your class and place it in your portfolio.

Your Professional Library

Brazelton, T. B., & Greenspan, S. (2000). *The irreducible needs of children: What every child must have to grow, learn and flourish.* Cambridge, MA: Perseus.

Dombro, A., Colker, L., & Dodge, D. (1999). *The creative curriculum for infants and toddlers.* Washington, DC: Teaching Strategies.

Gerber, M. (Ed.). (1979). *Resources for infant educarers: A manual for parents and professionals.* Los Angeles: Resources for Infant Educators.

Gonzalez-Mena, J., & Eyer, D. (2003). *Infant, toddlers, and caregivers: A curriculum of respectful, responsive care and education* (6th ed.). New York: McGraw-Hill.

Honig, Alice. (2002). *Secure relationships: Nurturing infant-toddler attachment in early care settings.* Washington, DC: National Association for the Education of Young Children.

Mangione, P. L. (Ed.). (1995). *Infant/toddler caregiving: A guide to culturally sensitive care.* Sacramento: California State Department of Education.

CHAPTER 8

Toddler Care

Ibrahim's Story

CHAPTER focus:

When you finish reading and reflecting on this chapter, you will be able to:

1. Describe the concept of *emergent curriculum* and why it is appropriate for toddlers.
2. Use your understanding of toddler development to assess the appropriateness of materials and equipment, curricula, activities, environments, and adult interactions for toddlers.
3. Plan appropriate activities and select materials for toddler play.
4. Develop awareness of bias and stereotypes and understand the role of antibias curricula.
5. Interpret a toddler's needs, interests, and interactions.

In Chapter 2, we promised that you would never get bored around a toddler, and here's a chance to prove it. Gather your energy and concentration! You are about to join four other adults and a room full of toddlers. The location is a toddler program at a university laboratory school.

Visiting the Helen Gordon Child Development Center

The expression *the calm before the storm* needs to be reversed to describe the situation into which we are entering. It's truly "the storm before the calm" and anyone who has been around a toddler or a group of toddlers when they are tired knows what we mean.

Meeting Ibrahim and His Peers: A Look at Toddler Development

It's 12:35 P.M., and at first glance it looks like bedlam in this room full of toddlers. Amidst the noise and movement, however, everyone seems comfortable and engrossed in their routines. There's soft music playing in the background. At one rectangular table, Harry eats two peanut butter sandwiches, one in each hand. He's completely focused on the sandwiches, and stops only to pour himself a glass of juice. When he finishes, another toddler, Ibrahim, reaches for the pitcher and spills the small amount of remaining juice. He becomes upset, but is quickly assured by Cindy, one of the adults, that it is not a problem: "It's OK, Ibrahim. You can wipe it up." She hands him a sponge, but he continues to fuss. Cindy, realizing that he is upset about his shirt sleeve being wet, responds with, "Let's go get another shirt out of your cubbie, and we'll hang this one up so that it can dry while you're resting." Ibrahim takes her hand and looks more relaxed about the situation.

At the table in a nearby chair is Ruth, repeating whenever an adult is near, "More watermelon." Occasionally, one of the early childhood teachers reminds her that there isn't any more, but Ruth is determined. Haley, with her wide face and blunt cut bangs of auburn hair, is walking around with her pacifier in her mouth, dragging her blanket, and whining a little to herself. In an adjacent room leading to the bathroom, two children struggle to remove their slacks and underwear. One of them, Andy, shouts, "I need my diaper, Darren," and he is assured from across the room by Darren, "I'll be right there to help you." Several toddlers are placing their plates in the tub of water and suds, and some are settling onto cots that have been placed around the two rooms that make up the toddler area. Everyone appears to have a routine and there's plenty of adult support.

Suddenly, Rikku cries out and Jennifer tries to comfort him, asking, "What's wrong?" He sobs loudly that his blanket is gone, and she takes his hand, saying softly, "Let's go and look for it together." They look around the room and in all of the cubbies. In a nearby room, Alex is sound asleep. He went to sleep as soon as he and his friends came in from the play yard. "Alex was too tired to eat," Jennifer tells Rikku as they walk by the sleeping child. "Me, too," sniffs Rikku.

With his blanket found and under his arm, Rikku heads for one of the cots. Jennifer tells him and Anita, who is already resting on the next cot, "I'll get you two some books to read while you relax." She returns and sits between the children. "Which book would you like me to read?" she asks. Anita points to the animal book and Rikku says, "Me, too." She begins to read softly to the two children. On the other side of the room, Heather is rubbing the backs of children who are just starting to rest. The room is beginning to quiet, but we still hear Ruth asking for more watermelon and from the bathroom there's one last request for a diaper.

Meeting Individual Needs

Assured that most of the children are starting to sleep, Jennifer goes to Ruth and sits next to her at the table. "You really liked that watermelon, didn't you?" she asks Ruth. With the beginning of a whine, Ruth talks about wanting more. Jennifer explains again that there isn't any more watermelon, "But I have an idea for you," she gently tells Ruth. "Before you go to sleep, let's write a note to your dad and ask him to buy you some watermelon at the store after work today. Then you can have some for supper. Would you like that?" Ruth nods, and Jennifer brings a piece of paper to her and they begin to write the note.

We see that Darren is wrapping up a lunch for Alex so that when he wakes up, he will be able to eat. The other early childhood teachers are still rubbing backs or reading softly, and soon most of the toddlers are asleep. Ruth is feeling better and ready to rest, too. Jennifer takes her hand and walks to Ruth's cot with her.

We're at the Helen Gordon Child Development Center, a university lab school in the heart of the city. We stopped here in Chapter 1, as we acquainted you with the range of options in the early childhood profession. The Center is 23 years old, is nationally accredited, and is a pride of the university and the community. The center staff works hard to attract a diverse group of children and to hire a diverse staff. The program has featured an antibias curriculum for about five years and the staff continues to study and assess their practices to assure that children are not learning bias in their classrooms as they learn about their world. You will see evidence of their commitment to antibias curriculum as we spend time with the toddlers. Many parents are very involved in the Helen Gordon Center. The staff values their participation and pursues it in varied ways. We will talk to some of the staff and get to know one set of parents later, but for now, it's back to the toddler room.

Remember that your observations of children are intended to help you learn about their development and the characteristics of their age. Your observations of the interactions between adults and children will provide models for you of good practices in terms of curriculum, guidance and discipline, materials and equipment, and parent involvement. Look around the room, listen to the conversations, and watch the children and adults for ideas about how to work with toddlers.

Getting to Know Toddlers

Meeting the Physical Needs of Toddlers

If you had been here in the toddler room at 8:40 A.M., you would have seen the children arrive with their parents. Darren and Jennifer are the early childhood educators in this toddler program and they're both working in an area near the door. As children come in, they stop and greet each child and adult. We hear: "What a bright yellow jacket you are wearing today, Haley! How are you feeling?" "Rikku, you and your dad look like you got a good rest last night." "Good morning, Ibrahim. Good morning, Faridah. How are you this morning?"

A Little More Sleep. One of the children, Bryanna, arrived exhausted. "She just didn't sleep well. I could barely get her up, but I have to get to class," sighed her mom. "Bryanna, would you like to rest a little more?" Darren asks. She nods her head wearily and walks to a little adjoining room with two cots. "I sleepy" she says, with a little whine in her voice. Within minutes, she is sound asleep. Some of the toddlers are clinging to parents and others have forsaken their parents and are happily engaged in play. Audrey and Melissa are already sitting at a table with play-dough and accessories, and other children are climbing in and out of a wooden structure.

A Quick Breakfast. Ruth arrives with her dad, carrying a tiny paper bag. "Ruthie is going to eat her breakfast for a few minutes," her dad tells the two early childhood educators. "It was a hectic morning at home, so we went to the bakery on our way. Ruthie, tell them what you picked out, honey," her dad asks. Ruth opens the little bag and pulls out a croissant. She looks at her dad and says sadly, "I forget." He hugs her and says. "That's OK. It's a croissant." He pulls a bagel out of his bag and Ruth shouts, "Bagel." "Yes, a bagel is dad's favorite," her dad responds. They eat together until Ruth appears to be satisfied and ready to play.

Curriculum and Guidance with Toddlers

Soon, there are 16 children present. Two early childhood student teachers, Heather and Cindy, have arrived, making the ratio 4 children to 1 adult. We watch and note that children do not have to do much waiting for attention or for assistance. The adults move about, making themselves available to facilitate problem solving or to guide behavior whenever necessary. When Kim and Dion squabble over a favorite toy, Darren approaches them. "Kim, I know that you want that camera, but Dion had it first. While you wait, would you like to help me check the play yard to see if everything is in order?" Kim appears happy to join Darren. Once outside, Kim notices a puddle and crouches down to touch the water. Darren immediately walks over to her and watches. Kim proceeds to pat the water and watch the ripples. Darren waits and then says, "You're making ripples. When you pat the water, you're making ripples." We hear Kim say softly to herself, "Ripples . . . ripples . . . ripples."

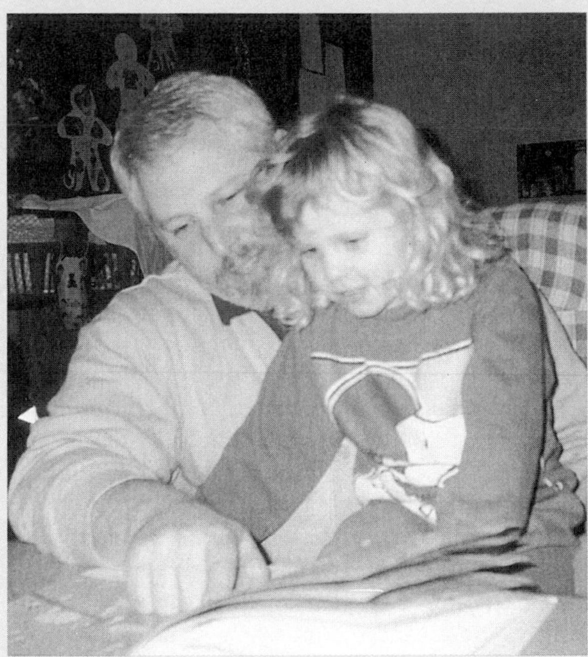

Ruth and her dad spend time together before he leaves her at the center. How does this help Ruth make the transition into her day away from home?

Beginning Literacy. On the other side of the room, Cindy, one of the student teachers, is reading *The Very Hungry Caterpillar* to two children who are sitting near her legs and listening quietly. Another child stands next to her, rubbing her hair. "Let's read it together," suggests Cindy. The children obviously know the story, because they join in the familiar phrases. As Cindy reads each phrase of the book, the toddlers finish each page with, "But he was still hungry." As we listen, we can feel the children's excitement as they continue filling in the words. They are experiencing reading and there's a thrill that accompanies their sense of accomplishment. We hear Cindy affirm their efforts with, "You really know how to read *The Very Hungry Caterpillar!*"

Essential Limits: Guidance for Toddlers. While they were reading, Rikku climbed up the adjacent bookshelf and now he looks like he's about to jump. Cindy turns to him, saying, "You can sit up there, and you can climb up and down, but you can't jump." Rikku sits and watches the children's activities in the nearby house center. Cindy remains on the floor near him and waits. "Would you read me a story?" Rikku asks. "Sure," Cindy answers. "Come and pick out a book that you would like to hear." He climbs down from the shelf and looks at the book selection.

Diversity in the Environment. As Rikku studies the book possibilities, we move near him and observe the choices for toddlers. We see that there is a variety of books with fairly simple text and lots of excellent illustrations or photos. We also see different cultures represented in the book selections, such as

A Is for Aloha by S. Feeney (University of Hawaii Press, 1985)
Hello Amigos by T. Brown (Henry Holt & Co., 1986)
A Place for Grace by Jean Okimoto (Sasquatch, 1996)
Round Is a Mooncake: A Book of Shapes by Roseanne Thong (Chronicle, 2000)
Willie Was Different by Norman Rockwell (Random House, 1997)
Do You Know What I'll Do? By Charlotte Zolotow (HarperCollins, 2000)
Baby Rattlesnake by Te Ata (Children's Book Press, 1989)
All the Colors We Are by K. Kissinger (Redleaf Press, 1994)
Animales Marinos (Marine Animals) by Violeta Denou (Teo Descubre series, 1997)

As we walk through the room, we note the various posters and artwork hanging on the walls. There's a Persian Alphabet Tree and a colorful poster of a preschool classroom with the title El Espuerzo Bien Vale la Pena Lleva a Tus Hijos a Vacunar. We also see a measuring chart with photos of children from four different cultures. Pictures of families decorate all the walls, and we review them to see what kinds of families are represented: an African American couple, a Hispanic dad and baby, two Anglo girls, an African American mom holding a briefcase and hugging her son, and a Chinese toddler with two adults. The diversity represented in this toddler environment makes us want to learn more about the antibias curriculum emphasis of this center.

A table of art materials catches our eye. There are many kinds of paper—foil, cellophane, gift wrap in prints and stripes, paper towel and tissue, and colored and white drawing paper. Nearby are scissors, paste jars, crayons, and markers.

In the small adjoining playroom, we see large graphs drawn on chart paper: one is titled Our Eye Colors and the other is called Our Hair Colors. There are also collections of photos of the children on field trips. In both rooms, we notice that there are labels on items in the room—clock, window, door, books, and so on.

In the bathroom is a shelf full of boxes of disposable diapers. Each box is labeled with a child's name. There are two small sinks and toilets close to the floor, all with the label *sink* or *toilet.* We notice a large box of extra clothes and bottles of sunscreen on the shelf. There's also posters urging children to wash their hands.

Safety with Toddlers. As we look across the room, we see that Ibrahim has put a pail on his head and is pretending to be a monster. He tries to walk around but bumps into shelves and the wall and almost knocks himself over. Jennifer is watching and decides that Ibrahim is going to get hurt. She stops him by putting her arms around his waist and says, "Listen to my words, please. I don't want you to get hurt, and when you can't see where you are going, you could get hurt. You've been bumping into things and I'd like you to wear the pail in a way that lets you see." Ibrahim looks at her, takes off the pail and places it on a shelf, and runs off to the table where he left his helicopter. He brings it back, saying, "It go round and round." "Yes, it spins," says Jennifer. "No, it go round and round." He continues to turn the

wheels, making the propeller spin. "Have you been on a helicopter?" asks Jennifer. Ibrahim just looks at her, offering no answer. "Have you been on an airplane?" she asks. "Yes," he says, "I go with my father." He goes and gets an airplane off the shelf and shows Jennifer that it doesn't have a propeller. He sits down at the table and plays with the helicopter, but he becomes distracted by the group of children at the other side of the room who are doing a finger-play. We hear:

"Rolly Polly up up up. Rolly Polly up up up.
Rolly Polly out out out. Rolly Polly out out out.
Rolly Polly clap clap clap. Rolly Polly clap clap clap.
Rolly Polly roll to your lap."

Participation from a Distance: Using Anecdotal Information. Ibrahim stays at his table but he begins to do the motions to the finger-play and his mouth is moving with the words. Another toddler sits across from him and we notice that he, too, is mouthing the words. When the group finishes the finger-play, Ibrahim goes back to his helicopter, saying, "Round and round."

We notice that Jennifer has been writing notes on Post-its ever since she chatted with Ibrahim. When we look over her shoulder, we see that she has noted that Ibrahim appears to know the words of specific finger-plays and that she has recorded Ibrahim's comments about the helicopter. During this same time, several of the children have gone outside with Darren. Earlier, he set up some learning activities to encourage children to practice throwing. There's a tire and a set of bean bags, a poster with holes and more bean bags, a low basketball hoop and rubber balls, and several large balls. Darren has obviously designed activities that will support children's achievement and enthusiasm. Sanders (2002) recommends designing physical tasks that all children can successfully accomplish 80 percent of the time. Darren also provides feedback as children throw the balls and bean bags, as well as encouraging their exploration. "Can you throw any other way . . . or dribble differently?"

Toddler Persistence and Supportive Guidance. Ibrahim has gone outside, and soon we see him opening the door and trying to bring a rolling cart into the classroom. Another educator, Bob, stops Ibrahim and says, "The cart stays outside." Ibrahim continues to push it through the doorway, as if he didn't hear. Bob repeats, "It stays outside." As Ibrahim continues to push it in, Bob takes the handle from Ibrahim's hands and turns it around, saying, "It needs to stay outside and I'm going to push it out." Ibrahim shows no response and runs outside to join a group of children. We see Bob jotting a note on a Post-it.

If we had been watching these toddlers in September or October, soon after they began coming to this program, several of the incidents like the one between Ibrahim and Bob may have resulted in a temper tantrum, or with Ibrahim protesting loudly, "No," or holding tightly to the cart and refusing to let go. As 2-year-olds, many of these children were asserting themselves and doing so at every opportunity. It's May, however, and most of these children have celebrated their third birthday and have begun to develop some social maturity. The tenacity and the "nos" remain, along with an occasional temper tantrum, but, in general, these children are exhibiting a willingness to conform to the expectations of others.

Taking Turns: Toddler Social Development. Throughout the morning, individual children have been painting at the easels set up along the wall. Now, the easels are empty, and we hear Darren going around the room, asking children, "Would you like a turn at the easel?" Most of the children are very involved in another activity, but Melissa nods her head to indicate that she would like a turn. Haley is watching and shouts, "Me, too. My turn at the easel." Darren walks with the girls over to the easels and they begin to paint. He tells us, "We keep a list each day of the activities for which children have to wait for a turn." He adds, "We don't like to have children waiting, but with

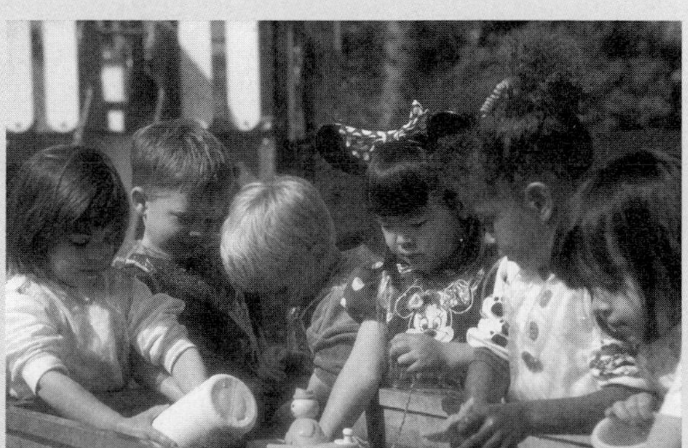

Each toddler is experimenting with water in unique ways.

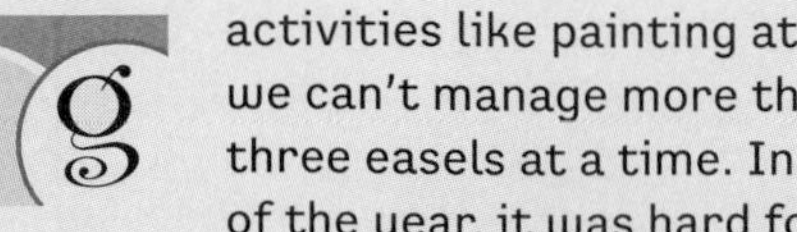

activities like painting at the easels, we can't manage more than these three easels at a time. In the beginning of the year, it was hard for the children to wait. They would hang around the easels because they weren't certain that they would really get a turn. But now, they go off to other activities; they know that we keep a list so that we remember to find them and offer a turn. We also assure them with information such as 'Ned is having a turn, and you will follow him.' "

Darren continues, "We also discovered that our lists provide good assessment information about children's play preferences. We noticed that Haley is on a list almost every day, but that Ibrahim is almost never on a list for the easel. We mentioned it to his mother and she agreed that he doesn't seem to like to paint." Darren tells us that the educators won't insist that Ibrahim paint but will look for ways to connect painting to the kinds of activities that he likes.

Reviewing Our Observations: Informing Guidance

Soon, the group will be getting ready for lunch and Ruth will want her watermelon. We're going to stop and reflect for a few minutes about what you have seen in the toddler classroom. Remember: Your observations are a source of information about the children and their programs. We think that you can come up with sound ideas about early childhood programs for toddlers from even a brief morning of observations.

JOURNAL 8.1: What characteristics of toddlers' development became apparent as you watched their play and interactions with people and objects? Consider their motor development, their social development, their emotional development, and their language. What are they able to do?

JOURNAL 8.2: What kind of guidance strategies did you see as you watched the early childhood educators handle problems or situations that could turn into problems? For example, recall when Ruth insisted on more watermelon, or when Kim and Dion were struggling over a camera, or when there was the potential for Ibrahim to hurt himself.

Accommodating toddler development and using appropriate guidance strategies are the heart of a good program for toddlers. Attending to the developmental characteristics of toddlers is first and foremost in terms of programming for them. Because they are active explorers developing autonomy, the kind of guidance strategies adults use with toddlers will determine whether they develop a sense of doubt and shame or a sense of autonomy. As you noticed, the few simple rules of Jennifer and Darren's classroom had to be repeated clearly and consistently. Honig (2002) reminds us that toddlers are learning social rules and values as we interact with them, and that classroom rules will help their process of socialization.

Toddler Development: Responding with Curriculum and Guidance

We hope that your observations of toddlers prompted your awareness of what toddlers are like and what their needs and interests are. Before we start, let's go back to our definition of *toddlers* from Chapter 2. We said that toddlerhood begins when a child starts walking and talking, somewhere around 12 months. Toddlerhood has been called a transition between infancy and childhood. Some educators think in terms of young toddlers, ranging from 12 months to 24 months, and older toddlers, ranging from 24 months to 36 months. Darren and Jennifer are really experts when it comes to toddler development and their ideas about curriculum and guidance will further your understanding of toddlers, in general.

Conversations with Darren and Jennifer: Their Responsibilities

Darren arrives in plaid shorts, a T-shirt, and tennis shoes, a little breathless from his run from the kitchen. "I had to bake the children's cookies while they're resting," he tells us. He is the head teacher of the toddler room and he describes his responsibility as one of "keeping the room flowing so that all children have the opportunity to take advantage of all the materials/activities." He says that the most difficult part of his role is delegating to other staff and "helping them to see the big picture behind decisions." Jennifer arrives and is also dressed casually in slacks and a T-shirt. She is a mother of a young child (3 years old) herself and she feels that her role is ideal for blending career and parenting. Both Darren and Jennifer have degrees in early childhood education and have worked at the Helen Gordon Center for several years.

TALKING ABOUT CURRICULUM. We ask about the curriculum in the toddler program, and Jennifer immediately uses the term *emergent curriculum* (Jones & Nimmo, 1994). She expands with, "We build off of the children's interests or curiosities and develop materials and activities." Darren adds, "We spend a great deal of our time getting to know each child's strengths, interests, and experiences so that we can plan from the child." (Remember that the idea of curriculum originating with children was pioneered by early educators Maria Montessori and Friedrich Froebel. Both educators were avid observers of children and used their observational information to design play materials and activities).

Recalling the busy quality of the toddler room and the many interactions between adults and children, we ask about how these two educators maintain their information about the children. "We keep written notes about our observations of the children's interests, especially our conversations with individual children," Jennifer responds. Darren jumps in, "Bugs, caterpillars, worms, birds, animals, flowers—they're really into nature, the world around them."

From there, the two educators describe their efforts to integrate basic concepts of math, science, language, and other curricular areas. "It's pretty easy," Darren says, "Most of their interests lend themselves easily to curriculum planning." Darren describes a recent interest in trucks and the ease with which they were able to focus all kinds of activities around trucks. He sheepishly admits, "Occasionally, some of the curriculum comes from us. I wanted to plant a garden, so I asked if any of the children would like to help me get a garden ready." Not surprisingly, the children were quite enthused about the garden and all of the related activities. Jones and Nimmo's (1994, p. 127) sources of emergent curriculum confirm using children's interests and teachers' interests as sources. Other sources include things in the physical environment, people in the social environment, curriculum resource materials, serendipity (that is, unexpected events), the daily tasks of living together, and values of the school, community, families, and cultures. If we were to observe for months, we would probably see all of those sources reflected in Darren and Jennifer's emergent curriculum.

Jennifer tells us that they repeat activities that they know the toddlers enjoy. Toddlers like repetition, so it makes sense. She says, "For example, they have consistent interest in play-dough—it's a security for them. They know it's there and they can always go to it."

TALKING ABOUT GUIDANCE. Although we observed numerous guidance strategies when we visited their classroom, guidance is such a prominent part of their work with toddlers that we wanted to discuss it further with Darren and Jennifer. "We try not to step in unless someone's having a really hard time or is affecting the other children." They describe their efforts to model language for the toddlers, knowing that many of their inappropriate behaviors come from the inability to express what they want or their lack of social skills. "When Rikku hurts Ibrahim, we encourage Ibrahim to tell Rikku how it feels," explains Darren, "And we encourage Rikku to talk about what he was trying to say or do when he hurt Ibrahim." The other response made by the educators is to look at the environment and remove something or change it to be sure that it supports the children's development. They talk about wanting to be certain that they are not contributing to the child's inappropriate behavior.

When all else fails, their final response in certain situations is to remove children from the group for a brief time period. That removal is often necessary for children to "settle down" and regain their composure. "We mostly talk with them about whatever happened and try to get them to talk about it," adds Jennifer.

Darren shows us a list called Helpful Practices for Guiding Toddlers that he and the other educators use as a regular reminder of how to help toddlers gain control of their behaviors. The list includes the following:

1. Use clear language when explaining limits and expectations to toddlers. [Remember when Bob said, "The cart stays outside" and Jennifer said, "Listen to my words"?]
2. Be consistent with limits and expectations.
3. Be sure that the expectations are age appropriate. [Expecting toddlers to sit still or wait for long periods of time would just be asking for misbehavior.]
4. Take children's conflicts seriously. [Darren and Jennifer just described for you how they spend time talking with children during and after a conflict.]
5. Describe positive behavior or expectations. [Telling children "We walk in the classroom" rather than "Don't run in the classroom" teaches rather than controls.]
6. Give children enough time to process your message and use it to change their behavior.
7. Model the behavior you expect so that children can witness what the behavior looks like rather than just hear about it. (Schreiber, 1999, p. 25)

It's almost impossible to separate the elements of programs for toddlers—development, guidance, and curriculum. In fact, another major source of emergent curriculum are the developmental tasks of the children. Toddlers are exploring every moment, and their exploration demands boundaries to keep them safe and to teach the rules of life. You will find that when we talk about an aspect of toddler motor development, we immediately connect that development with curriculum—an activity or kind of equipment that is appropriate to promote that aspect of development—and at the same time we remind you of the guidance needed for that development.

TALKING ABOUT ENVIRONMENTS. Descriptions of "best practices with toddlers" refer to an environment with plenty of multisensory play materials that use large and small muscles, and that encourage exploration and language (McMullen, 1999). Jennifer tells us that they can get quite creative in the way they set up the environment, but they must always pause and consider the health and safety of the children. "We want them to be active and independent," she says. Darren adds, "We also want them to be problem solvers and explorers." Balancing those goals with the safety of toddlers is quite a challenge. The other challenge is accommodating the very diverse needs and interests as well as the many levels of development observed in this toddler class. "I guess that one of our rules for ourselves is to be flexible," Darren adds. He tells us that they change the environment frequently—always trying to find a room arrangement and materials that stimulate toddlers while not disrupting their comfortable routines.

Observing Ibrahim in His Family Context

"Toddlers are concerned about who they are and who is in charge" (Bredekamp & Copple, 1997). This is a time of "me do it," yet it is also a time when lots of security, comforting, and limits are needed from the adults in their lives. Many of the new adventures for toddlers are related to human interactions and to interactions with the world around them. A major part of the toddlers' world is their families. It is important to consider the context of family when observing children, so we visited Ibrahim's family in order to better understand his development and his activities at the center.

VISITING IBRAHIM AT HOME: UNDERSTANDING HIS SOCIALIZATION. Ibrahim and his parents, Faridah and Amr, and his brother, Muhammed, live in a small apartment on campus. Their home is simply furnished and absent of much decoration. Faridah explains, "We can't put figures on the walls due to religious beliefs—besides, I prefer this spartan look." There is one mirror and children's drawings on the door. Each parent has a computer, one in the living room and one in the dining room. The boys have a closet for their belongings and some shelves for books, paper, and crayons.

The family is preparing to move because Faridah has taken a teaching position at a university in Malaysia. Faridah speaks Malay and Amr speaks Arabic. He teaches Arabic to adults and children, and consults with small businesses. English is the common language for the two parents.

The family has a flexible schedule in order to spend time with the boys. After Faridah, Muhammed, and Ibrahim leave the center each day, they go home for supper. Some nights she eats with the boys, and on other nights, Amr eats with the boys. "We sit on the floor around a piece of oilcloth to catch the crumbs," Faridah describes for us when we ask about their family meals. The family observes some dietary rules of their Muslim religion and prays five times daily.

Muhammed describes the boys' favorite activity as one of jumping and flying around the living room. He tells us, "Sometimes we put stickers all over us like feathers, but we never fly from the window—only from the couch." Faridah describes the boys' use of the couch pillows for dramatic play: "One day, they were pretending to be frogs, and they told me that the pillows were lilypads." The boys also play with large Legos and toy guns and cars. Both parents read to the boys each night. Muhammed interrupts to tell us, "Our father reads usually one book when he puts us to bed." He says, "This one or this one and we have to pick." He continues with, "Our mom reads one or two or three books."

Our home visit to Ibrahim's family really helps us interpret his behavior at the center. A look at the physical, social, emotional, and cognitive aspects of toddler development in the context of individual families will help you understand what we observed in Ibrahim's classroom and will give you the skills to predict what will happen in his class on other days or when he is at home with his family.

Physical Development: Curriculum and Guidance

Physical development includes extensive and expanding motor abilities, nutritional issues and eating habits, and highly individualized needs for sleep and rest. The changing quality of toddlers' physical development directs major components of an early childhood program—schedule, environment, number of adults, activities, and materials and equipment.

MOTOR DEVELOPMENT: LARGE MOTOR CONTROL. Toddlers (approximately 2 years and older) not only like to roll and jump and climb and run but they also are fairly good at those motor skills. They take great pride in pushing and pulling wheel toys and can steer well. The outdoor play space at the Helen Gordon Center has a variety of wheel toys as well as structures for climbing and jumping. Toddlers are not especially skilled at watching for others when jumping or steering, so they need constant supervision and occasional reminders to be careful of other children. We heard Jennifer frequently say, "When you get ready to jump, look around the ground to see if anyone else is there, so you are a careful jumper." A few of the children have begun to hang from the parallel bars, but they like to have Darren and Jennifer next to them. "It's scary," says Rikku, but his face is full of delight with his new skill.

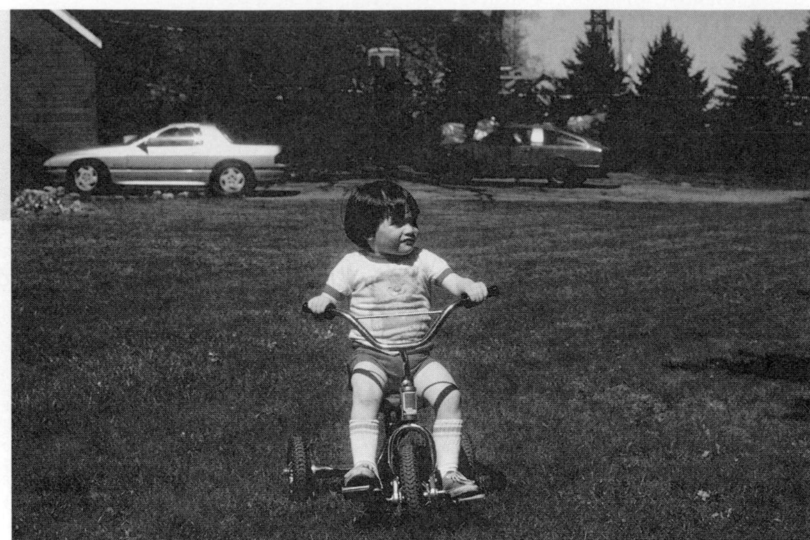

Toddlers are not especially skilled at steering their toys, but their attempts are intense and a source of pride.

Throwing and retrieving (sometimes catching) objects is a never-ending favorite activity for toddlers. A box near the door to the outdoor play space is full of all kinds of items to throw—basketballs, foam balls, rubber balls, bean bags, and plastic darts. Again, toddlers need reminders about appropriate places to throw balls and about being careful of others. As you observed, various receptacles for throwing balls and bean bags are both inside and outside. What we did not see and hear was how Darren varied his encouragement of children's use of the throwing activities depending on their physical development. For some children, he simply affirmed their exploration of throwing balls or bean bags. For others, he offered *cues,* words, or phrases that help children learn or perform a skill better (Sanders, 2002, p. 54). After watching Louis experiment, struggle, and explore how to throw a ball into a hoop, Darren makes suggestions or asks Louis what would happen if he stood a certain way.

Most toddlers have learned to stand on one foot, and you will observe them experimenting with that skill as they watch other children playing. Toddlers have also become quite skilled at walking on tiptoes. "Sometimes when we walk to the library or the grocery story, it takes a long time," describes Jennifer. She adds, "They're always experimenting with new ways to move, so we have to give ourselves plenty of time to get places, rather than rush them. I guess it's our own doing. We are always asking them questions like, 'How many ways can you walk, or move backwards, or use your feet?' "

MOTOR DEVELOPMENT: FINE MOTOR CONTROL. By age 2½, toddlers have good hand and finger coordination and enjoy playing with small objects and manipulating their small parts. The play-dough trays and accessories are out on a table almost everyday in the toddler room, and there's a huge collection of plastic figures—zoo and farm animals, dinosaurs, cars and trucks, airplanes and helicopters, and people. They are also quite possessive of the figures, so there's potential for conflict. "It's one of the reasons why we have so many bins and pails of figures," Darren explains. If you were to watch the toddlers over a period of time, you would see that they enjoy putting many items in their mouths, so early childhood educators need to be watchful of these materials. Those situations offer an opportunity to teach toddlers about safety issues.

Their fine motor control also encourages toddlers to draw, paint, and enjoy other creative activities. The large colored markers are their favorite, but they also use crayons, colored chalk, tempera paint with brushes, finger paint, and blunt scissors. Early in the year, most of their drawing with markers and crayons was of scribble quality, but now many toddlers are making deliberate strokes, circles, and figures. They are frequently intrigued with drawing on themselves, on walls, or on unintended surfaces, so again, you will need to provide guidance for their artistic tendencies.

The finger-plays like "Rolly Polly" that we heard the toddlers chanting when Ibrahim decided to participate from a distance are another favorite activity to develop the small muscles of the hands as well as coordination. Finger-plays are a good example of activities that integrate many aspects of development simultaneously. In Figure 8.1, Diffily and Morrison (1996) offer their description and use of finger-plays for the development of communication with parents. It is an example of the kind of information that the educators at the center often send home to help parents understand the value of simple activities and to share some of the curriculum for use at home.

Speaking of tiny items, toddlers are able to thread beads and can enjoy the activity for brief time periods. If you watch toddlers in an activity such as threading beads, you will see intense concentration and will also notice that most toddlers can't sustain the concentration for long periods. So, bead work is usually a brief activity, and, depending on bead size, one that probably should have close supervision.

Many of the materials and the kinds of equipment needed to stimulate and support toddlers' motor development will require close supervision. Environments for toddlers will also require careful maintenance to keep them safe in the midst of the children's very active play. Figure 8.2 displays a basic safety checklist that you could use to set up a classroom for toddlers. It can also be used for daily checking of the condition of equipment and materials.

NEED FOR REST AND SLEEP. Toddlers have a great amount of energy, but most of them also require a significant amount of rest and sleep. As you observed in the toddler classroom, they can't keep going when they get tired—they just have to sleep. The sounds in the classroom just before naps reminded us of their need for sleep—whining, crying, demands for diapers, pacifiers in mouth—they seemed to be quite aware of their need and

FIGURE 8.1

Finger-Plays and Action Songs

Rhymes and movements for the hands and fingers, some of which date back almost 2,000 years, are still used in early childhood classrooms, as well as the more modern action songs that involve the whole body.

As children learn fingerplays and action songs, they learn the names of body parts, numbers, and shapes. They also learn other concepts and skills, including

- manual dexterity and muscle control;
- sense of rhythm of speech and music;
- new vocabulary;
- ability to follow directions;
- grasp of order and sequence;
- increased attention spans; and
- listening skills.

Fingerplays and action songs are a fun way to learn. They are a great way to pass a few minutes of transition time—while you are waiting in the car, in line at the grocery store, before or after dinner.

Children love repeating familiar rhymes, so come back to the same songs often enough that your child can learn the words of the rhyme and the movements that accompany the words.

Perhaps you remember a fingerplay from your childhood that you can share with us. If you would like to learn more fingerplays or action songs that are hits with kids of your child's age, just ask us—we'll be happy to share some great ones.

Source: Family-Friendly Communication for Early Children Programs (p. 48) by D. Diffily and K. Morrison, 1996, Washington, DC: NAEYC. Copyright 1996 by NAEYC. Reprinted with permission from the National Association for the Education of Young Children.

FIGURE 8.2

Classroom Safety Checklist

Art Area

____ Scissors use supervised
____ Water spills cleaned up
____ Hazardous materials eliminated (sprays, solvents, glazes, permanent markers)

Block-Building Area

____ Building space adequate
____ Blocks free from splinters
____ Construction height within limits
____ Toy accessories free from sharp edges, broken parts

Book Area

____ Floor area covered
____ Heating vents, pipes covered
____ Rocking chairs away from children on floor

Computer Area

____ Electric cords, plugs out of children's reach
____ Location away from water
____ Children seated with computer on low table or stand

Cooking Area

____ Cooking appliances in compliance with local safety codes
____ Electric appliances, microwave ovens controlled by adult
____ Sharp implement use supervised by adult
____ Number of children in area limited

Dramatic Play Area

____ Clothes hooks away from eye level
____ Plastic dishes, cutlery unbroken
____ Play jewelry, earrings, beads unbroken
____ Dolls, toys with no small removable parts (e.g., buttons)

Large Motor Area

____ Climbing, sliding equipment cushioned
____ Wheeled vehicle use controlled
____ Safety rules established and enforced by adult

Manipulative Area

____ Tiny beads, counters eliminated
____ Sharp or pointed objects eliminated
____ Objects with splinters, peeling paint, broken parts discarded

Music Area

____ Cords on record players, radios, tape recorders out of reach
____ Equipment using small batteries eliminated

Sand/Water Area

____ Sand or water spills cleaned up
____ Broken, rusty, or sharp-edged toys removed
____ Glass implements eliminated
____ Safety goggles used at sand table

Science/Math Area

____ Aquarium and incubator wires out of reach
____ Houseplants nonpoisonous

Woodworking Area

____ Adult-size tools supervised
____ Safety goggles used
____ Safety rules established and enforced by adult
____ Number of children limited

General Room Conditions

____ Floor covering smooth, unbroken, and untorn
____ Traffic patterns between areas clear
____ Heaters, pipes, vents covered and sectioned off
____ Electric cords, wires, plugs out of children's reach
____ Electric outlets covered
____ Smoke detectors in appropriate locations
____ Fire extinguishers accessible
____ Peeling paint removed, refinished
____ Broken furniture, toys removed, repaired
____ Sharp corners of room dividers padded
____ Emergency procedures, phone numbers, clearly posted

Bathroom

____ Sinks, toilets child-size
____ Stands, stools sturdy
____ Slippery floors cleaned up
____ Cleaning and disinfecting materials locked up
____ First-aid kit out of children's reach; accessible to adults

Stairs/Exits

____ Exits clearly labeled
____ Stair steps smooth, unbroken, of nonskid material
____ Carpeting, mats smooth, untorn, not slippery
____ Stair railings reachable by children
____ Two exits in every classroom
____ Stairs well lighted

Outdoor Playground

____ Playground enclosed with fence
____ Debris, broken glass removed
____ Cushioning under climbers, slides
____ Large equipment anchored in ground
____ Swings of safe material (belts, tires)
____ Young-child-size equipment used
____ Railings around high platforms, on steps
____ Sharp edges, missing or loose parts, splinters on equipment corrected
____ Adequate supervision when in use

Source: Skills for Preschool Teachers, 5th ed. by J. J. Beatty, © 1996. Reprinted by permission of Prentice-Hall, Inc., Upper Saddle River, NJ.

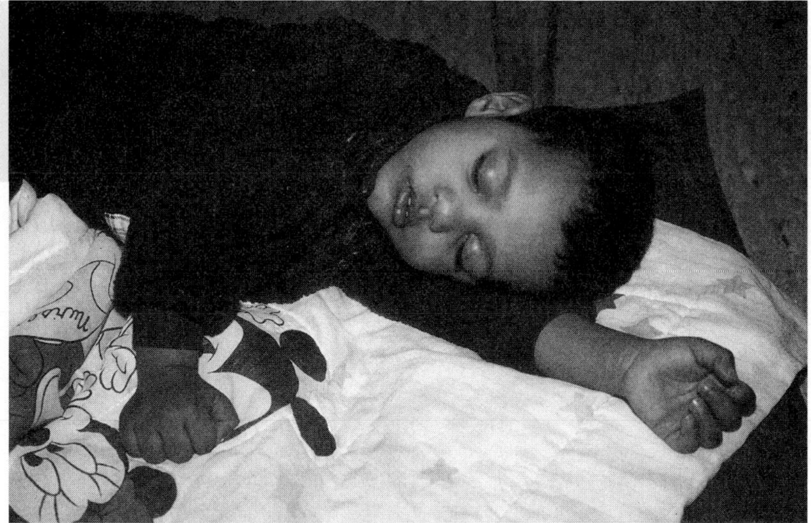

Toddlers are often exhausted from their exploration, successes, curiosity, and creativity.

ready to give in to their exhaustion. Similar to the flexibility accommodating toddler appetites was the flexibility accommodating toddler fatigue levels. Remember how Bryanna went right to sleep as soon as she arrived in the toddler room one morning? She hadn't slept well the night before, so it was important to respond to her fatigue. Remember when Alex couldn't even make it to lunch because he was so tired from his morning of play? These two children needed long sleep periods, whereas other children in the room may take very brief naps and be ready to play again. Some of the variation in children's need for sleep and rest is due to individual development and some is due to family scheduling. Notice that not only were the adults at the Helen Gordon Center flexible about the toddlers' need for sleep but there was also a small area out of the traffic where one or two toddlers could rest undisturbed. Both scheduling and the environment responded to the toddlers' individual variations in their rest and sleep patterns.

EATING AND NUTRITION. The eating habits of toddlers vary significantly from one to another, but also for individual toddlers from one day to the next. Jennifer noted that Harry was eating twice as much as anyone else for about a week now, but a month ago, he would barely eat anything. Most toddlers eat small amounts and need frequent snacks to support their energetic routines during the day. At the Helen Gordon Center, there is a morning snack, lunch, and an afternoon snack. Fruit or crackers are also available for those times when toddlers get hungry between snacks and lunch.

Toddlers' food preferences vary so much that meal planning for them is a challenge. Some of their preferences are influenced by their families and meals at home, but much of what looks like food preferences is a part of their development of who they are. You will see some toddlers ready to try anything as a kind of adventure, and then brag about it to all who will listen. You will also see some toddlers hesitant to try anything that looks different or that they haven't tried before. If you observe in the toddler room for a couple of weeks at the Helen Gordon Center, you will see a fairly basic menu with the same foods repeated and occasional seasonal additions such as watermelon. The research on young children's food acceptance patterns has demonstrated that repeated exposures to specific foods increase children's acceptance of them (Birch, Johnson, & Fisher, 1995). The research also recommends getting children to taste new food with encouragement but not manipulation. Figure 8.3 provides useful information for feeding toddlers.

Toddlers are also refining their abilities for feeding themselves (Poulton & Sexton, 1995/96) and are especially interested in serving themselves and pouring their own drinks. Spills are frequent and are generally not an issue for the children or adults. Did you notice that the adults barely responded to Ibrahim's spilled milk? Even the process

FIGURE 8.3
Tips for Menu Planning

- Offer a variety of colors, textures, temperatures, and flavors that encourage children to eat more and to try new foods. *Examples:* raw vegetables, applesauce, macaroni and cheese
- Prepare foods so that they retain natural flavors, aromas, and nutrients. Children may like raw fruits and vegetables better than cooked ones. *Examples:* raw broccoli, cauliflower, yams, green beans (especially with a dip)
- Serve children what they generally prefer—plain, identifiable foods. Casseroles and other combined foods are not typically appealing to children. *Examples:* potatoes and chicken bits, hamburger patties and noodles, ham slice and rice
- Offer choices to help ensure that children eat from each of the meal components. *Examples:* carrot and celery sticks, apple and pear slices

of wiping up a spill is a motor activity and a move toward independence for the toddler. If you were to observe the toddler class for an extended time period, you would see that mealtimes offer very important learning opportunities for every aspect of development for toddlers.

FLEXING FOR INDIVIDUALLY APPROPRIATE PRACTICE. When you look at the big picture of toddler physical development, you can see that they have developed both fine and large motor skills, so your program will provide a variety of opportunities, space, and equipment for them to use those skills. When you watch toddlers, you also see that their appetites and sleep habits are very much in flux, so your program will need to provide the flexibility and space arrangements to meet those needs. Bredekamp and Copple (1997) recommend the following practices for that flexibility:

- Time schedules are flexible and smooth, dictated more by children's needs than by adults'. There is a relatively predictable sequence to the day to help children feel secure. (p. 84)
- Adults respect children's schedules with regard to eating and sleeping. Toddlers are provided snacks more frequently and in smaller portions than older children. For example, two morning snacks are offered at earlier hours than the usual snack time for preschoolers. Liquids are provided frequently. Children's food preferences are respected. (p. 85)

Throughout our description of the physical development of toddlers and appropriate curriculum and guidance, the key words are *active* and *flexibility*. What we saw in Darren and Jennifer's room and have discussed in the pages you just completed is *individually appropriate practice*. Bryanna's needs were met, and Rikku's needs were met, and the two children are quite different. You will note the same individuality with respect to social development, described in the next section.

Social Development: Curriculum and Guidance

Here are some familiar scenes in the toddler room at the Helen Gordon Center:

- Haley comes up to Ruth and puts her arms around her and hugs tightly. Ruth objects and squeals, "No!" On another day, when Haley hugs her, Ruth may hug back, and the two girls will stand there for a time hugging and giggling.
- Ibrahim is playing with the plastic dinosaurs and Rikku sits at the table next to him and watches. Without a word being said, Ibrahim hands one of the dinosaurs to Rikku, and the two of them play side by side.

- At the play-dough table, Melissa and Ned are sitting next to each other. Each child is intensely working with play-dough, molding it with their hands, and only occasionally looking at the other child. There is no conversation. On other days, Ned may hand Melissa a piece of dough.

What we see in these scenarios is that toddlers are beginning to develop social maturity as they show affection for others, share occasionally, communicate with peers, and begin to play cooperatively. "Social contact among two-year-olds is brief and fleeting," but three-year-olds "seek out social interaction and want to be part of a group" (Hughes, 1991). They have also learned acceptable ways to express their feelings when they want something or when others hurt them (Hill, Strommel, & Wu, 2002, p. 40). People are more important to these toddlers than they were a year ago, and their increasing social skills have much to say to their early childhood educators about appropriate curriculum and guidance.

SHARING. The ability to share is emerging in the toddler room, but it's difficult for Ned some days and easy for Ibrahim some days. That ability to share applies to toys, friends, the adults in the room, and attention. Depending on how they're feeling, toddlers can even take pleasure in sharing, but much depends on their levels of security and their experiences with sharing (Wittmer, 1996).

As in so many aspects of the toddler program, the adults are key to the development of sharing. First, they, along with each child's family members, are models of sharing. In the toddler room, we often hear Darren say, "I'd love to share my crayons with you. Let's color together" or "Would anyone like to share the play-dough with me?" The guidance used by the adults will also teach sharing. Although it's not always possible and not consistently a good idea, it is appropriate at times to encourage sharing. For example, when Ned pulls all of the animals toward him to shut out Rikku and keep him from taking one of the toys, Cindy notices that Rikku is just sitting and so she might urge Ned with, "It looks like Rikku would like to play with you," followed by, "Would you share a few animals with him?" Depending on the kind of day Ned is having, how he is feeling, and what kind of experiences he has had with sharing, he may say, "Sure" or "No" with great emphasis. As Hughes (1991) reminds us, "Toddlers enjoy being near other children, but they are still limited in their ability to share and to cooperate."

When we talked with Darren, he told us that many of the toddlers' parents wanted them to learn to share. "It's taken all year for most of the children to share some of the time. We think that forced sharing interferes with security, so we don't insist—we just encourage." So much of the toddlers' sharing is related to their simultaneous development of autonomy and identity that they must retain some control of that behavior. As they become more social, people matter more than objects and it becomes easier to give up that truck, or doll, or dinosaur.

JOURNAL 8.3: **Sharing is apparently quite important to parents and to educators. Reflect on why parents emphasize sharing to such an extent. Write a note to a parent who inquires about his toddler child's progress toward being able to share and explain why it's taking a long time to develop.**

THE IMPORTANCE OF OTHERS. Sharing is but one aspect of the social development of a toddler. Other social milestones include:

- Shows increased awareness of being seen and evaluated by others
- Sees others as a barrier to immediate gratification
- Begins to realize that others have rights and privileges
- Gains greater enjoyment from peer play and joint exploration
- Begins to see benefits of cooperation
- Identifies self with children of same age and sex
- Is more aware of the feelings of others
- Exhibits more impulse control and self-regulation in relation to others
- Enjoys small group activities (Bredekamp & Copple, 1997, p. 70)

Those milestones are not exhaustive and should probably all contain the word *sometimes.* They are written with attention to the changes from infancy, so when the milestone is "exhibits more impulse control," we are talking about them in comparison to their impulse control during infancy. Toddlers are changing so rapidly—progressing and regressing—that the milestones have a tentative quality.

Zeavin (1997) says that the critical factor in programs for toddlers is the *human environment*—other toddlers who are experiencing similar social development and adults who understand that development and respond to their "trial and error" with sensitivity and guidance. Every issue for toddlers is a relationship issue. Throughout their day, they express their relationships with materials, with adults, with peers, and with themselves.

Early childhood educators who work with toddlers are very loved by them—verbally and physically. Toddlers are fascinated with their caregiver adults and other adults in their lives. This is a time when they begin to project to their own future, to being in adult roles. Consequently, toddlers are very good at "being the teacher"—Darren may hear himself in the script as Rikku plays him, or as Haley plays Jennifer. Not only are they trying out adult roles but toddlers also use pretend play to expand their social understandings.

SOCIAL UNDERSTANDINGS. One of the favorite activities of toddlers that develops social understandings and extends their interactions with others and their world is dramatic play. The toddler room at the Helen Gordon Center has extensive materials and equipment for pretend play—for example:

- Dolls of all sizes and colors
- Child-sized furniture
- Telephones
- Dress-up clothes (shoes, purses, jackets, long skirts, and hats)
- Dishes, pots and pans, and plastic food
- Blankets
- Suitcases
- Broom and dustpan

Notice how basic these materials are and how many ways children play with them. Toddlers do not need extensive accessories for their pretend play. (Check Tables 8.1 and 8.2, pages 261–264, for examples.) Be creative. Use your imagination and add five more items to the list of items for pretend play. Keep in mind simplicity and safety.

We did notice a large number of dolls in the toddler room—realistic dolls, dolls of different colors, large dolls, durable dolls, and more—all unclothed and most looking like they had been bathed many times. Some early childhood educators see toddlerhood as the beginning of true doll play. The children give more meaning and characteristics to the doll, and the doll takes on more complex roles in pretend play. One day in the toddler room, Ruth had two of the dolls propped in chairs, one on each side of her. She had named them and they were her "babies." She had a dish and utensil in front of each and was encouraging them to "eat your supper all up." Ruth's mom would probably hear herself in that role—her expressions, her tone of voice, and her mannerisms.

Toddlers also begin to use materials to represent objects or props for their pretend play. One morning, Ned brought a tube of Chapstick to school and it became his "bone" as he played dog for part of the morning. Sometimes the large wheel toys became a bus or train for pretend play on the playground, or a bucket of sand became soup or a grocery item. Toddlers have begun to use their immediate world at preschool and at home to explore and make sense of their lives. Pretending with an adult is especially appealing to toddlers. Research has shown that 2- and 3-year-olds will sustain their pretend play much longer with an adult roleplaying with them than when they are pretending alone (Haight & Miller, 1993). Ned often says to one of the adults at the center, "Pretend I'm your dog" and they do. It's a pretend situation that he repeats almost daily, so it's comfortable for him. Research also shows that pretending with adults leads to pretending with peers. Pretending with a mom or an uncle provides practice and vocabulary, so that a child can get ready for playing and pretending with others.

EARLY COOPERATION. In a few years, the toddlers we observed will be able to engage in cooperative play and participate in games with rules, but for now, most children play alone. Occasionally, you will see scenes like the one that follows:

Rikku

Rikku has a drum and stick and begins marching in the open space in the toddler room. He marches around the tables and weaves around the room. Ibrahim watches briefly, then goes to the basket of instruments, takes a drum and stick, and follows Rikku. Haley looks up from her play with dolls, hurries to the basket, gets another drum and stick, and joins in the march. The marching pace has picked up and the three children are quite tickled with themselves and their small parade. Ned goes over to the basket and gets out a xylophone and sits at the table and plays it, watching the three marchers as he does so. Rikku speeds up his marching and the other two follow. When he slows down, they do, too. When he yells, "Stop," the others get quiet and stop their movement. He marches again and they follow.

Zeavin (1997) calls this "gleeful and exuberantly contagious" play that indicates the beginning of cooperation and even early stages of a game with rules. Haley and Ibrahim were cooperating with Rikku in his marching game, and Ned followed to a lesser degree. We've seen similar scenes on the playground with the wheel toys in which one child establishes a kind of routine, and one or more toddlers will follow. Because toddlers are usually isolated or engaged in parallel play, the incidents of cooperation are fairly limited. Most social interactions by toddlers are with adults. Their teachers and caregivers are the focal point of their conversations, their interactions, and even much of their pretend play.

When Darren and Jennifer talk about the rewards of working with toddlers, they both describe social development. If you were able to observe their toddlers throughout the year, you would be as impressed as they are. Children accomplish incredible growth toward very complex social understandings and skills during toddlerhood. The curriculum and guidance provided in the toddler room supports that growth by providing and guiding countless interactions each day. Many of those same interactions nurture emotional development, which is described in the next section.

Emotional Development: Curriculum and Guidance

Toddlers are making rapid advances in the area of emotional development, and it is a time for very sensitive support and guidance from adults. A major focus of development is identity formation accompanied by emotional thinking and ideas, and the ability to express feelings. Observing toddlers at play will provide extensive information about their emotional development. From there, guidance strategies will play a prominent role in nurturing the development.

IDENTITY FORMATION. Toddlers are working hard to develop a sense of self. Much of their resistance to adult limits, or their "no" responses to requests, are attempts to establish themselves as individuals. When you watch them, you see other signs of this development; for example, they talk about themselves, assign characteristics to themselves, and evaluate themselves. As toddlers explore their room at the Helen Gordon Center, we see them work hard to master a variety of tasks, such as assembling puzzles, forming the play-dough into a specific shape, or arranging the animals in a line. Most of these efforts are accompanied by an acknowledgment of "I can do it" to themselves or to a caregiver or teacher. These toddlers are feeling some power and establishing themselves as capable of doing things.

As children go about their business of play in the toddler room, everything going on about them is contributing to their sense of self. The conversations in the room, the actions and interactions of adults and other children, and the materials and activities are all incorporated into lessons that toddlers integrate into their developing identity formation. Lally (1995) suggests that some of these lessons can include:

- What to fear
- Which of one's behaviors are seen as appropriate
- How one's messages are received and acted upon

- How successful one is at getting one's needs met by others
- What emotions and intensity level of emotions one can safely display
- How interesting one is (p. 61)

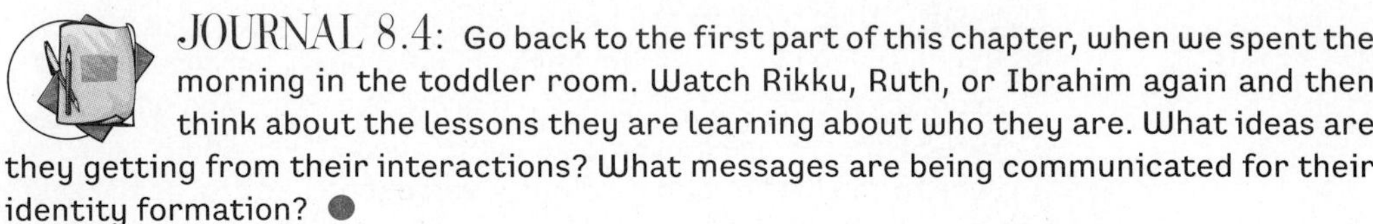

JOURNAL 8.4: Go back to the first part of this chapter, when we spent the morning in the toddler room. Watch Rikku, Ruth, or Ibrahim again and then think about the lessons they are learning about who they are. What ideas are they getting from their interactions? What messages are being communicated for their identity formation?

The importance of both curriculum and guidance is that they are sending key messages to the children. Toddlers are learning that they are capable, that they are respected, and that they are enjoyable. They are learning that they have choices and that others like to be with them. The next time you see an adult and a child in a grocery store, observe them to determine what messages are being communicated to the child about himself. Do the same as you watch children and adults on the bus, or at the library, or walking down the street. Those messages contribute significantly to the child's overall emotional development and specifically to her identity formation. Equally important are the opportunities for toddlers to try out all kinds of roles and to experiment with their own potential. Toddlers need to build a sense of themselves from their own efforts.

EMOTIONAL THINKING AND IDEAS. Greenspan (1995), who describes stages of emotional development, sees toddlers experiencing stages of emotional ideas at about age 18 months and emotional thinking at about age 30 months. Around 18 to 24 months, toddlers create images in their minds and begin to play those images out with make-believe or pretend play. This is the beginning of their ability to put labels on their feelings through gestures or words. Some toddlers are quite expressive and play out aggression, violence, separation, anger, and fears. This is where the adult role is critical. Toddlers need acceptance of what they express, and guidance in their expression. When Haley makes monster sounds and faces, says "I scare you," and gets louder and more fierce in her gestures, your response will teach her about the feelings and ideas she is expressing. Sometimes, the tendency is to ignore or to humor such play, or even to stop it because of feelings of discomfort. Instead, when Haley hears, "It really is scary to see a monster, isn't it?" she will probably expand on her feelings or she will process something that's been bothering her. We may hear "I don't like monsters" or "There's a monster in my bedroom" or "My brother makes monsters and he chases me." Toddlers' imaginations can create fears and their explorations of the world can contribute new concerns. This is an important time for them to express those fears and to know that they will receive support, assurance, and sometimes clarification.

Since toddlers do not have the language to express many of the feelings they have, they need other outlets for their emotions. Music and movement activities are excellent for expressing feelings. Toddlers really like upbeat rhythms and respond naturally through simple movement (Wittmer, 1996). Darren and Jennifer often have this kind of music playing in their classroom in the mornings. Painting to music is a favorite activity. A recording of *Fantasia* or the *Grand Canyon Suite* will provide stimulating background for painting. The toddlers also enjoy percussion instruments, as you observed earlier, and they do a lot of experimenting with different sounds. Toddlers can also get overstimulated by some kinds of music, however, so it's important to provide a variety of rhythms. Remember that during lunch and preparation for naps, there was soft music playing in the toddler room. Toddlers do well with music to calm them at different times of day.

ESTABLISHING INDEPENDENCE. Early in the year, as Darren and Jennifer reminded us, the toddlers were asserting their independence by being stubborn or rigid and sometimes negative. "No" was heard throughout the room. Many of their activities were repeated over and over and usually in the exact same way. Any adult who has read and reread a favorite story to a child knows that you don't dare skip a page or change a word, or you will hear vehement complaints. Recently, one of your authors read a book to her granddaughter and was told, "You didn't finish! You forgot to say who wrote it."

Young toddlers often object to routines and requests simply on principle. If you ask them to go outside, they will want to stay in. If you ask them to stay in, they will want to go outside. They are often expressing their developing need for autonomy. Older toddlers continue their expression but in much more enjoyable ways. They want to show what they created or what they can do. As Hughes (1991) describes it, "There is a joy in accomplishment and an interest in showing off one's creations and talents" (p. 75). Ibrahim often approaches Jennifer with, "Teacher, I made a building" or "Look at my snake."

This period of accomplishment is a time when early childhood educators and caregivers may feel compelled to lavish praise on the toddlers: "What a great job you did!" "That's a beautiful painting!" "I like the way you cleaned up all the animals." Recently, however, early childhood educators have begun to examine those responses and the idea of frequently praising children's accomplishments. Marshall (1995) says, "If we look closely at our children taking a new step or seeing their progress or success at a task, their facial expressions will tell us that they are pleased even before we have a chance to spout a word of praise" (p. 27).

Children need encouragement and acknowledgment of their accomplishments (Hitz & Driscoll, 1988) rather than adult approval. At the same time, the adults can help the children begin to evaluate themselves. Instead of praise, toddlers will hear, "You painted a colorful picture. Tell me about it" or "You have picked up all the animals. What do you think of the job you've done?" As children develop their abilities, they need to express their feelings about those abilities. Rather than establishing the need for adult praise or rewards, it is an important time to acknowledge and support their efforts while helping them develop independence from adult evaluation. Figure 8.4 provides examples of encouraging responses.

The emotional development of toddlers is also complex and not always visible. It takes consistent observations and good listening to maintain awareness of toddlers' emotional needs. Again, the curriculum and kind of guidance approaches with which you respond to them will promote their emotional health, just as you promote their physical and social health. You will see in the section that follows that cognitive development requires the same kind of respectful and nurturing response that is needed during emotional development.

Cognitive Development: Curriculum and Guidance

The lives of toddlers are full of exploration, questioning, discovery, and determination to understand events, objects, and words. This is a time of exciting new mental activity. Toddlers are fascinated by language. Remember Haley repeating "Dinosaur" to herself, and Kim saying "Ripple" over and over? Toddlers are discovering the power of words and they use them for every possible function. Along with their language development is the beginning of literacy development. The period from ages 16 to 36 months are full of new awarenesses: perceptual, temporal, and spatial. Sensory materials continue to be very important to toddlers and they use a great number of tools. They are interested in the effects of their behaviors on the world around them. Once again, all of these developments have many implications for curriculum and guidance in a toddler program.

EXPLORATION AND DISCOVERY. The kinds of materials and the arrangement of the environment will certainly determine the depth of toddlers' exploration and discovery. Check the examples in Tables 8.1 and 8.2, pages 261–264, for their potential to stimulate such toddler play. Guidance strategies will communicate how much freedom they will have to conduct their study of the world. If materials can be used in only one way, then the potential to explore will be limited. In some classes, you will hear that the dolls must stay in the house center. In Jennifer and Darren's class, the dolls are taken all over the room, they are bathed, they are transported in wagons, and they sit in chairs to hear stories. Remember when Rikku was not discouraged from climbing? This gave him the opportunity

FIGURE 8.4
Examples of Encouragement

Setting 1
Carmen helped set the table for snack.
Encouraging Statements
Thank you for helping us set the table.
You put a spoon by every bowl.

Setting 2
Tommy helped to pick up the blocks in the block corner.
Encouraging Statements
You picked up many more blocks than you have ever picked up before.
When you help us pick up the blocks we all get finished much sooner.

Setting 3
Jaci listened intently during storytime.
Encouraging Statements
I could tell by the look on your face that you really enjoyed listening to the story today.
I noticed that you listened very carefully to the story.

Setting 4
Denise played with Jimmy at the sand table. They experimented with funnels for more than 20 minutes.
Encouraging Statements
You and Jimmy played together for a long time at the sand table.
You were able to share with Jimmy at the sand table today.

Setting 5
Marc needed help with a project and Ben helped him.
Encouraging Statements
It looks like Marc really appreciates the way you helped him with his work.
Thank you for helping Marc.
You noticed that Marc was having a problem and you gave him some help with his project.

Setting 6
Sue seldom talks in the group but today she told a short story about Halloween.
Encouraging Statements
That was a very scary story you told.
When you told that story I could just picture ghosts in our classroom. It gave me goosebumps.

Setting 7
Daniel just finished a painting. He comes to you, the teacher, and says, "Look at my painting, isn't it beautiful!"
Encouraging Statements
You look happy about your painting.
Look at all the colors you used.

Setting 8
Michele completed an assignment all by herself.
Encouraging Statements
It must feel good to you to be finished. You must be very pleased that you were able to do that all by yourself.

Setting 9
Matthew says, "Look how fast I can run!"
Encouraging Statements
You are running much faster than you used to run.
You must feel excited when you run that fast.

Source: "Praise or Encouragement? New Insights into Praise Implications for Early Childhood Teachers" by R. Hitz and A. Driscoll, 1988, *Young Children, 43*(5), p. 12. Washington, DC: NAEYC. Copyright 1988 by NAEYC. Reprinted with permission from the National Association for the Education of Young Children.

to experience the classroom from another height. Educators of toddlers have the challenge once again of balancing safety and stimulation, and every situation may be different, just as each child is unique.

In the process of exploring, children discover that objects are different colors, different sizes and shapes, and different textures. Remember the art table with the varied kinds of paper? It is set up to encourage the kind of discovery approach that is being recommended for children's development in art. It builds on children's natural inclination to manipulate objects with their early investigation of art media and exploration of ways to express themselves with art (Althouse, Johnson, & Mitchell, 2003, pp. 41–43). Jennifer often sits at the table with several children, using both language and modeling to initiate their exploration. We might hear, "How does the tissue paper look when you squish it?" or "What kind of paper makes the most noise when you hold it?" Equipment and materials such as water tables, play-dough, finger paints, sand and dirt, and fabric also encourage those discoveries. Those endless collections of plastic figures (animals, cars, and so on) and blocks encourage discoveries daily. Most child development experts describe toddlers' ability to go from simple stacking of blocks to elaborate and interesting structures that represent their world (a garage, the zoo, a bridge, and so on).

Although the toddler room at the Helen Gordon Center was well equipped with blocks, we saw little use of blocks during our observations. We decided to ask Jennifer about this. She commented, "They don't use them unless you sit down with them and encourage with something like 'Let's build a garage.' " This is a bit strange, because we can't ever remember an early childhood program in which the blocks were not used extensively. In fact, our observations of the Town and Country School in New York City considered blocks the major focus of their curriculum for 3-year-olds (Driscoll, 1995). Jennifer expressed the same puzzlement we were feeling. We begin to question this issue together.

One possibility for the lack of block play is the location of the blocks. This may be a good time to look at the floor plan of Darren and Jennifer's room for toddlers (see Figure 8.5). Our observations told us that most of the activity took place in the large main room and the outdoor area. Children had the freedom to go outside at any time and they did so. Most of our observations of children in the smaller room consisted of one-on-one interactions with adults and saying good-bye to parents and family members. This may be an example of the environment sending a message about specific materials (the blocks).

FIGURE 8.5
Floor Plan of the Toddler Rooms

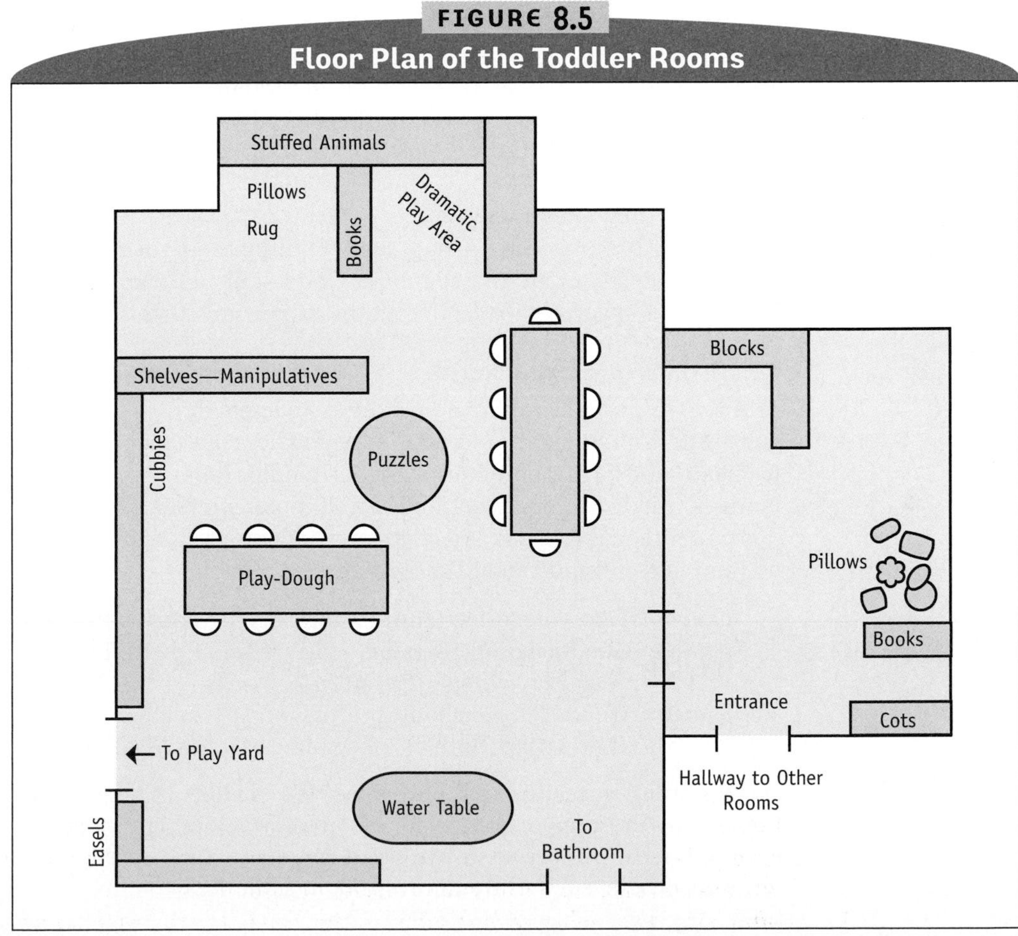

As you can see from this section, the environment is very much a curriculum for toddlers who are exploring and discovering their world. The materials and equipment that Darren and Jennifer provide throughout their room motivate and encourage those activities. The way the room is arranged continues to nurture the toddlers' desire to explore, yet keeps them safe from themselves and others. It's a "balancing act" of providing limits that don't inhibit exploration while keeping this lively age group safe.

PERCEPTUAL AWARENESS. Toddlers show much interest in the attributes of objects. They enjoy matching a group of similar objects and even sequencing items in order of size. Their discovery of shapes, colors, sizes, and textures now leads to sorting and grouping. Remember Piaget's classification and seriation skills discussed in Chapter 3? All those plastic figures that end up everywhere are essential materials for the sorting and classifying that toddlers are learning. Many commercially developed materials with shape, color, and size differences are enjoyed over and over by toddlers who sort and resort them. Teacher-made materials and items from home are ideal for children to sort. Some of the simplest materials engage children in these new awarenesses: leaves in the summer and fall, cloth scraps, large shells and rocks, and so on.

Can you add to the list? The possibilities are endless. Toddlers will develop patterns with these items, and will enjoy creating their own matching games: texture matching games, color matching games, and the like. You will hear them begin to count as they manipulate their plastic figures or other items. They will also display a beginning understanding of quantity. You will hear Haley ask, "How big?" or "How little?" Her understanding of quantity is not systematic but it is beginning. When you plan and use items for perceptual awareness, remember that close supervision will be important.

Toddlers are also attracted to puzzles with four to eight pieces. When you watch the children, you will begin to notice that they are starting to work out problems mentally, rather than always using trial and error. Toddlers talk to themselves a great deal because there is so much going on in their heads. Piaget called this talk "egocentric speech" and Vygotsky called it "inner speech." The research on the connection between thought and language refers to the talk as "private speech" (Berk, 1992) and has demonstrated that children who talk to themselves have higher rates of social participation and are more socially competent than children who do less talking to themselves (Berk, 1984, 1985).

As children manipulate objects—sorting and classifying them as big and small, or hard and soft, or dark and light—they are extending their vocabulary at the same time. Their language development and communication skills are expanding as rapidly as their discoveries and awarenesses, and with the expansion comes the beginning of literacy.

LANGUAGE AND LITERACY. Everything in the toddler environment and every encounter with another child or an adult is an opportunity for toddlers to develop their language and communication skills. Young toddlers put together two-word sentences, which we heard during our observations in the toddler room. As they gain new experiences and maturity, their sentences get longer and more complex. Most 3-year-olds speak in compound sentences and use adjectives and adverbs well. Listen to some of Ibrahim's talk as he interacts with his mom, Faridah, and Jennifer:

Faridah: Good morning, Jennifer. Ibrahim has something exciting to tell you.
Jennifer: Good morning, Faridah and Ibrahim. I'm anxious to hear your news.
Ibrahim: Yesterday we see "Hercules."
Jennifer: Wow! Tell me about it.
Ibrahim: It was scary and lots of swords. Me and Muhammed play Hercules.

Ibrahim's speech is well developed. It's obvious that there is much conversation at home and lots of opportunities for language development. Some of the other toddlers are speaking more simply with two-word sentences such as, "Me sleepy" or "I swinging," whereas others, such as Ibrahim, speak in sentences.

This is a time for *approximations,* which are children's attempts at adult or conventional language. They are listening to adults all the time, so it's not surprising that they would attempt to sound like them. When Haley says "I goed there," she is approximating adult talk. This is also a time for *overextensions,* which are young children's use of a word for similar but different objects, situations, or categories. When Ned learned the word *plant,* he called everything with leaves a plant—trees, bushes, artificial flower arrangements, and so on. This is a time for *creative vocabulary,* as well. When Rikku doesn't have a word for what he wants to say, he creates one. A common example of creative vocabulary is the word *cooker* to refer to the person who cooks.

Toddlers learn how to ask questions, and the adults who work with them can tell you that this new skill is used constantly. From 18 months to 3 years of age, toddlers are developing vocabulary, using every experience, every object, and every conversation they hear. Well aware of this rapid development, Darren and Jennifer have been experimenting with occasional small group time with question sessions. Church (2003) encourages early childhood educators to promote children's natural curiosity with such sessions and to use children's own questions as guides to their interests and curiosities about the world (p. 44). Ibrihim's question, "Why is the play area wet in the morning?" prompted three of his peers to suggest all kinds of possibilities—some creative, some intriguing, and some real. Church also suggests using unusual or unfamiliar objects, photos, stories, and other prompts for interesting question sessions. As the educators experimented with question sessions, it became apparent that toddlers were rapidly developing language and that development was accompanied by beginning literacy.

Toddlers are very interested in print. They frequently ask, "What does this say?" When they see adults writing, they are curious about the content. Some toddlers recognize familiar words such as *stop, McDonalds,* and *exit.* They see words and expressions all around them, so it is not surprising that they are interested and that they begin to "read." They also begin to write. You will occasionally see a toddler with a pencil or crayon and paper "writing note my mom." Ruth sat and watched as Jennifer wrote a note to Ruth's dad. Ruth felt satisfied that the note (which Jennifer read aloud to her) would help her get more watermelon.

Studies of early readers and their families reveal some interesting insights about children's early literacy. The behaviors displayed by parents that seemed to facilitate early reading in children are actually appropriate for early childhood programs. They can be translated into basic guidelines for a classroom for young children, and are quite relevant for toddler programs. These include (Durkin, 1966):

- Adults read to children on a consistent and regular basis.
- Adults provide children with access to a wide range of print materials.
- Adults read and interact with print.
- Adults respond to children's questions about print.
- Adults make writing and drawing tools and paper available to children.

SECOND LANGUAGE ACQUISITION. In the toddler room at the Helen Gordon Center, several children are learning two languages at the same time. They are referred to as *simultaneous bilingual*—their dual language development began at birth. Ibrahim is becoming trilingual. His mother speaks Malay, his father speaks Arabic, and he is learning English at the preschool. Many young children are growing up in homes in which other languages are spoken and are attending programs in which English is spoken. Box 8.1 shares some insights from research and suggestions for supporting the language development of bilingual children.

Professionals who work with young children will be experiencing an increasing number of bilingual learners in the coming years. It will be important for you to understand more about language development as you continue your professional preparation, so that you can respond to the complexity of children's language development and to the possibilities of second language learning.

BOX 8.1

Language Development of Bilingual Children: Insights for Teachers and Caregivers

In her studies of the developmental path of preschoolers who are learning a second language, Espiritu and colleagues (2002) identified three stages that children go through in second language learning. She also described teacher supports for each of the stages.

1. In the first stage, children are quiet. They may limit their play and conversation to children who speak their home language. During this stage, early childhood educators are urged to build relationships with the child and family and to provide materials, books, and conversation in the child's home language.
2. In the second stage, children display limited use of the second language. Teachers will need to work patiently with the children to understand their early communications in the second language. At the same time, the children will need interactions with others who speak the second language, materials and books in the second language, and adults whose first language is not the same as the child's to provide major interactions and responses to the child's needs.
3. In the third stage, children are demonstrating "selected use of the second language." It will be important to continue to use the child's home language, and provide activities and interactions that use both languages. The educator's modeling of the second language will be critical to the child's development in that same language.

Summary and Additional Insights

One conclusion you may have reached after observing in the toddler room and then thinking about curriculum is that materials and equipment (toys) are really a major part of the curriculum. They promote all aspects of development—physical, social, emotional, and cognitive. Toddlers interact with materials and equipment (play materials) from morning until night, as they explore, develop new language, experiment with relationships, and communicate feelings. The match between their play materials and toddler development is essential for feelings of success, interest and curiosity, and exploration and creativity.

Tables 8.1 and 8.2 give an overview of play materials for young toddlers and older toddlers. If we had observed in Darren and Jennifer's room early in the year, we might have seen more of the play materials listed in Table 8.1. Some centers do not have the budget to have a vast array of play materials like we've seen in our observations. The Helen Gordon Center is a university laboratory school, so it has support for maintaining the latest equipment and materials. We'll discuss other elements of the uniqueness of a laboratory school or program next.

The Helen Gordon Child Development Center: A University Laboratory School

As you learned in Chapter 1, laboratory nursery schools or preschools have been an important institution in early childhood education for many years. They have a long and rich history and have provided leadership models to the early childhood education profession since the early 1900s.

TABLE 8.1 Overview of Play Materials for Young Toddlers: One Year Old

Social and Fantasy Play Materials	Exploration and Mastery Play Materials
Mirrors Well-secured wall mirrors (rounded edges, unbreakable) Full-length (upright), unbreakable mirror, firmly mounted or in nontippable stand Hand mirrors (light, sturdy, unbreakable) **Dolls** Soft-bodied or washable rubber/vinyl baby dolls Simple accessories for caregiving: bottle, blanket Simple doll clothes—need not be detachable (lightweight; painted, stitched, or molded hair and features; no moving eyes or articulated limbs; sized to fit easily in child's arms: 6 or 8–13 inches) *(from about 18 months)* Small peg people (not swallowable) **Role-Play Materials** Play telephone Simple housekeeping and work-role equipment Simple doll equipment—bed, baby carriage (sturdy and large enough to hold child) **Puppets** Puppets operated by adult *(from about 18 months)* Small hand puppets, sized to fit child's hand **Stuffed Toys/Play Animals** Washable, soft animals (simple in design, with bright colors, contrasting features that are painted, stitched, or molded) Soft rubber or vinyl animals (6–8 inches)—a few for exploring and beginning pretend play **Play Scenes** *(from about 18 months)* Small people/animal figures, with simple supporting materials (vehicle, barn) to make familiar scenes **Transportation Toys** Simple, lightweight vehicles (6–8 inches, with large wheels or rollers; lightweight; rounded/molded appearance, may make noise when pushed) First train—1–2 cars, no tracks, simple or no coupling system *(from about 18 months)* More detailed vehicles—can have a few simple, sturdy moving parts (doors or hoods that open) Trains with simple coupling system (wood link, large blunt hook, magnet)	**Grasping Toys** (toddlers are losing interest in the small, hand-held manipulables enjoyed by infants) **Sand/Water Play Materials** Simple floating objects, easily grasped in one hand Small shovel and pail *(from about 18 months)* Nesting materials useful for pouring Funnels, colanders Water activity centers Small sand tools (container with shovel or scoop; rake with blunt teeth) **Construction Materials** Light blocks (soft cloth, rubber, rounded plastic, or wood cubes for grasping and stacking, 2–4 inches on a side)—15–25 pieces *(from about 18 months)* Unit blocks (suggested by some experts and teachers)—20–40 pieces Large plastic bricks (2–4 inches, press-together type) **Puzzles** Simple prepuzzles or form boards, 2–3 pieces, in familiar shapes *(from about 18 months)* 3–5-piece fit-in puzzles (knobs make them easier to use but must be very firmly attached) **Dressing, Lacing, Stringing Materials** Large, colored beads (fewer than 10) *(from about 18 months)* Lacing cubes or board with thick, blunt spindle **Specific Skill-Development Materials** Pop-up boxes (easy operation) Simple activity boxes/cubes (with doors, lids, switches) Nesting cups (with round shapes, few pieces) Simple stacking materials—no order necessary *(from about 18 months)* Activity boxes with more complex mechanisms (turning knob or dial or simple key) Simple lock boxes Nesting materials of more complex shapes (square) Objects in closed containers that may be opened (by simple screwing action) 4–5-piece stacking materials Cylinder blocks Pegboards (with a few large pegs) Simple matching and lotto materials **Books** Cloth, plastic, or cardboard picture books Simple picture and rhyme books with repetition for lap reading *(from about 18 months)* Touch-me or tactile books

(continued)

TABLE 8.1 ***(continued)***

Music, Art, and Movement Play Materials	Gross Motor Play Materials
Art and Craft Materials Few large, nontoxic crayons Large paper taped to surface **Musical Instruments** Rhythm instruments for shaking—bells, rattles *(from about 18 months)* Rhythm instruments for banging—cymbals, drums **Audiovisual Materials** Adult-operated players and records, tapes, CDs, etc., with simple repeating rhythms, rhymes, and songs *(from about 14 months)* Music to "dance" (bounce) to *(from about 18 months)* Simple "point to" and finger-play games and songs	**Push and Pull Toys** Push toys with rods (rods with large handles on ends) Toys to push along the floor—simple cars, animals on large wheels or rollers For steady walkers, pull toys on short strings (broad based to tip less easily) *(from about 18 months)* Simple doll carriages and wagons (low, open, big enough for child to get into) Push/pull toys filled with multiple objects **Balls and Sports Equipment** Soft, lightweight balls, especially those with interesting audio or visual effects (noises, unpredictable movement) Larger balls, including beach ball size *(from about 18 months)* Balls for beginning throwing and kicking **Ride-On Equipment** Stable ride-ons propelled by pushing with feet (no pedals; no steering mechanism; four or more wheels spaced wide apart for stability; child's feet flat on floor when seated) Ride-ons with storage bins *(from about 18 months)* Bouncing or rocking ride-ons (with confined rocking arc and gentle bounce for toddlers; child's feet touch floor when seated) **Outdoor and Gym Equipment** Low, soft or padded climbing platforms Tunnels for crawling through Swings (pushed and monitored by adult), with seats curved or body shaped, front closing, and made of energy-absorbing materials *(from about 18 months)* Low toddler stairs with handrail

Note: Although the four categories provide a useful classification, play materials can typically be used in more than one way and could be listed under more than one of the categories.

Source: *The Right Stuff: Selecting Play Materials to Support Development* by M. B. Bronson (pp. 60–61), 1995, Washington, DC: NAEYC. Copyright 1995 by NAEYC. Reprinted with permission from the National Association for the Education of Young Children.

The History and Role of Laboratory Schools

The early laboratory schools were sites of teacher training and research, much like the Helen Gordon Center is today. The research focus has helped maintain the role of lab school programs in times of shrinking resources on campuses nationwide (McBride & Lee, 1995). Early in their history, lab schools were the site of research that manipulated the environment or activities to study various aspects of children's development. Today, you will find much more naturalistic research being conducted—that is, observational studies of children as they work and play together in the usual settings.

The use of the Helen Gordon Center for both research and professional preparation has had an impact on the quality of the program. As you observed in the toddler room, college students such as Cindy and Heather practice by working with the children, under the guidance of the early childhood educators. Administration and staff are constantly assessing the practices at the center in order to model the best practices. Because the staff interacts with teachers-in-training, who question early childhood practices, the staff consistently

TABLE 8.2 Overview of Play Materials for Older Toddlers: Two Years Old

Social and Fantasy Play Materials

Mirrors
Full-length unbreakable mirror firmly mounted or in nontippable stand
Hand mirrors (light, sturdy, unbreakable)

Dolls
Soft-bodied or washable rubber/vinyl baby dolls (12–15 inches)
Simple accessories for caretaking-feeding, diapering, and sleeping
Simple, removable doll clothes (closed by Velcro, large hook and loop, or snap; 12–15 inches)
Small peg or other people figures (not swallowable) for fantasy scenes

Role-Play Materials
Dress-up materials
Housekeeping equipment—stove, refrigerator, ironing board and iron, telephone, pots and pans, cleaning equipment
Simple doll equipments, baby carriage (sturdy and large enough to hold child)

Puppets
Small hand puppets sized to fit child's hand (that represent familiar human and animal figures and community diversity)

Stuffed Toys/Play Animals
Soft rubber, wood, or vinyl animals (6–8 inches) for exploration and pretend play
Mother and baby animals

Play Scenes
Small people/animal figures, with simple supporting materials (vehicle, barn) or unit blocks to make familiar scenes

Transportation Toys
Small cars and vehicles to use with unit blocks (4–5 inches; sturdy wood or plastic)
Larger vehicles for pushing and fantasy play
Large wood trucks to ride on
Trains with simple coupling system and no tracks (for use with unit blocks)

Exploration and Mastery Play Materials

Sand/Water Play Materials
People, animals, vehicles for fantasy play in sand/water
Nesting materials useful for pouring
Funnels, colanders, sprinklers, sand/water mills
Small sand tools—container with shovel or scoop; rake with blunt teeth

Construction Materials
Wooden unit blocks (50–60 pieces)—no need for specialized forms (arches, curves)
Large plastic bricks (2–4 inches; press-together)
Large nuts and bolts

Puzzles
(from about 24 months)
4–5-piece fit-in puzzles
(from about 30 months)
6–12-piece fit-in puzzles (knobs make them easier to use but must be firmly attached)

Pattern-Making Materials
Pegboards with large pegs
Color cubes
Magnetic boards with forms

Dressing, Lacing, Stringing Materials
Large beads for stringing
Cards or wooden shoe for lacing
Dressing frames and materials

Specific Skill-Development Materials
5–10 pieces to nest/stack
One turn screw-on (barrel) nesting
Simple lock boxes
Hidden-object pop-up boxes (with lids, doors, dials, switches, knobs)
Safe pounding/hammering toys
Cylinder blocks
Shape sorters with common shapes
Simple matching and lotto materials
Color/picture dominoes
Feel bag/box, smell jars

Books
Sturdy books with heavy paper or cardboard pages (short, simple stories or rhymes with repetition and familiar subjects; simple, clear pictures and colors)
Tactile/touch-me, pop-up, hidden-picture, and dressing books

(continued)

TABLE 8.2 *(continued)*

Music, Art, and Movement Play Materials	Gross Motor Play Materials
Art and Craft Materials Large, nontoxic crayons Large, nontoxic markers Adjustable easel Large, blunt paintbrushes Nontoxic paint and fingerpaint Large paper for drawing, painting, fingerpaints Colored construction paper Easy-to-use, blunt-ended scissors Chalkboard and large chalk **Musical Instruments** Rhythm instruments operated by shaking (bells, rattles) or banging (cymbals, drums) and more complex instruments (tambourine, sand blocks, triangle, rhythm sticks) **Audiovisual Materials** Adult-oriented players and records, tapes, CDs, etc. Music with repeating rhythms—for rhythm instruments Music to "dance" (bounce) to Simple point-to and finger-play games and songs Short films and videos of familiar objects and activities	**Push and Pull Toys** Simple doll carriages and wagons (low, open, big enough for child to get inside) Push toys that look like adult equipment (vacuum cleaner, lawn mower, shopping cart) **Balls and Sports Equipment** Balls of all shapes and sizes, especially 10–12-inch balls for kicking and throwing **Ride-On Equipment** Stable ride-ons propelled by pushing with feet (steering devices but no pedals; wheels spaced wide apart for stability; child's feet flat on floor when seated) Bouncing or rocking ride-ons (with confined rocking arc and gentle bounce for toddlers; child's feet touch floor. when seated) *(as child nears age 3)* Small tricycles (with 10-inch wheels) **Outdoor and Gym Equipment** Tunnels Swings with seats curved or body shaped and made of energy-absorbing materials Low climbing structures and slides, with soft material underneath

Note: Although the four categories provide a useful classification, play materials can typically be used in more than one way and could be listed under more than one of the categories.

Source: *The Right Stuff: Selecting Play Materials to Support Development* by M. B. Bronson (pp. 76–77), 1995, Washington, DC: NAEYC. Copyright 1995 by NAEYC. Reprinted with permission from the National Association for the Education of Young Children.

reflects on their decisions. Consequently, the staff at the lab schools are thoughtful and clear about their reasons for why they interact with children the way they do. Our conversations with Darren and Jennifer demonstrated their commitments to children's development as the first consideration for what they do. Those conversations also illustrated the high level of professionalism found in the staff of the center. We have a few questions left, so let's have one last discussion with Darren and Jennifer.

A Conversation about Assessment of Toddlers

We've learned a lot about curriculum and guidance from our observations and previous conversations with these two early childhood educators, but we have some questions about assessment. With their emphasis on knowing the children in order to make decisions so that curriculum emerges from them, we're curious about how Darren and Jennifer learn about and keep track of all the toddlers. Darren describes their initial information gathering with a family history form (see Figure 8.6): "We encourage families to provide as

FIGURE 8.6

Helen Gordon Child Development Center: Child History Form

We would like to find out about your child before she/he enters the program. The information provided to us on this form will assist with your child's transition to the program and allow us to provide the best possible care for your child and support for your family. Thank you for taking the time to fill out this form.

Name/Nickname ______________________ Birth date __________ Sex ________________

Who are the important people in your child's life? ________________________________

____

____

What are your child's special interests? ____

____

____

What should we know about her/his personal habits (eating, sleeping, toilet, dressing)? __________

____

____

What are your child's fears or dislikes (e.g., people, places, activities, or routines)? __________

____

____

Have there been any changes in your child's life recently that might impact her/his adjustment to this program (a birth, death, separation, etc.)? ________________________________

____

____

Has your child had previous experience with child care? What kind? How many hours? How did she/he adjust? ____

____

____

Has your child experienced any recent developmental milestones (physical, cognitive, or emotional struggles or accomplishments, such as toilet training, language)? ______________________

____

____

(continued)

FIGURE 8.6
(continued)

What language does your child speak at home? ______________________

____

What can you tell us about your family culture, values, traditions, or routines that will better enable us to build connections for your child between home and school and help her/him to feel comfortable in this program? ______________________

____

____

____

____

How does your child express emotions (joy, tension, anger, fear, etc.)? ______________________

____

____

Does your child have any dietary restrictions or health considerations that we should be aware of?

____

____

What are your expectations for your child this year at HGCDC? ______________________

____

____

____

____

In what way can we provide extra support to you in your relationship with your child? ______________________

____

____

____

Source: Helen Gordon Child Development Center staff. Reprinted by permission.

much detail as they are comfortable with and explain how the information will help us plan for their children." He tells us that during the home visits "we don't have any agenda. We try to follow the child's lead, play with the child, and visit with the parent. Primarily, we want them to be comfortable with us before they come to the center." The home visit information is usually extensive and the recordings begin the process of information gathering for each child. Darren adds emphatically, "We learn so much in the home visits."

Once children enter the toddler program, as we observed, Darren and Jennifer keep anecdotal records on each child. "By the first parent conference, I usually have at least 60 anecdotal notes on each child, and can put together a profile—my picture of the child—for the parents and family members." Darren describes a process for assessment that begins with the home visit: "During our first home visit, we work with the parents and other family members to develop goals for their child. From there, I have those goals in mind as I observe the child and keep notes. Sometimes, I develop a checklist based on specific goals or an aspect of development, and I often keep frequency counts on each child's play choices. There are so many adults in the room that it's easy to gather information on each child. At intervals during the year, I am able to provide a kind of narrative report card with that profile of each child."

It's clear when talking to Darren and Jennifer that observation is key to assessment of young children, especially active and changing toddlers. Figure 8.7 provides some beginning guidelines for observations. It's also clear that there must be a commitment to be consistent in recording what the toddlers are doing and saying in order to develop a holistic and authentic picture of each child. Those pictures of children are important for the kind of planning that Darren and Jennifer do and for communicating with parents about children's progress.

Our conversations with Darren and Jennifer have given you a snapshot of the thinking and experience you will encounter at the Helen Gordon Center and in laboratory

FIGURE 8.7

Suggestions for Classroom Observations

1. Begin by recording the date, time, location, and activity that is occurring. Note the length of observation.
2. Focus the observation as much as possible on what the child or children are doing and saying. (Record quotes whenever possible.)
3. Develop a shorthand or abbreviation system for efficient recording (for example, initials for children, *T* for table, *Bl* for blocks, *PD* for play-dough, etc.).
4. Consider occasional use of a floor plan to record a child's use of the environment by tracking with symbols or arrows where he or she spends time.
5. Make note of unusual circumstances (for example, child's health, weather, changes in routine, etc.).
6. Be sensitive to issues of confidentiality by maintaining records in secure cabinets.
7. Include a variety of settings (group times, outdoor play, center time, etc.), times of day, and other variations in your observations to obtain an authentic profile.
8. As much as possible, hold your judgments while recording an observation. When finished, read your notes and then add your impressions or an evaluation of what you observed. Another possibility is to wait until you have a series of observations before making judgments.
9. For ideal observations, ask another adult to be in charge of supervising the children, so that you can observe without distractions. You may even want to let children know that you cannot be interrupted for a particular time frame.

schools in general. Antibias thinking and curriculum is a kind of expertise for which the entire staff is known and it is an important topic for you to explore before you leave the center. We scheduled time with the director of the center in the hope that her insight will help you understand and begin to develop awareness of bias in yourself.

Antibias Curriculum

Ellie Nolan is the director of the Helen Gordon Child Development Center and we meet with her to learn about how the staff began their study and their efforts to assure an antibias curriculum for the center. Ellie describes the early work originating from her own interest in multicultural education during her graduate studies. She is passionate about the staff's commitment. "We began questioning how well we were representing cultures, race, and values in our curriculum, how race and culture issues influence interactions between children, between children and teachers, between teachers and teachers, and between parents and the center." From there, the center moved to a self-assessment focused on antibias curriculum. Their work was inspired and guided by NAEYC's *Anti-Bias Curriculum: Tools for Empowering Young Children* (Derman-Sparks, 1989).

ANTIBIAS CURRICULAR GOALS FOR CHILDREN. **Antibias curriculum** "enables children to comfortably explore the differences and similarities that make up our individual and group identities, and to develop skills for identifying and countering the hurtful impact of bias on themselves and their peers" (Derman-Sparks, 1992, p. 3). "Antibias curriculum aims at promoting a strong sense of pride in self and family, and a respect for other people as individuals and as members of social groups" (Corson, 2000, p. 386). When teachers who have embraced antibias curriculum were asked to discuss their goals for children, their responses included phrases such as "to become tolerant, understanding, and compassionate," "to be able to make judgments about what's fair and what's not," "to sort out what they have the power to change and what they can't do anything about," and "to become effective thinkers and problem solvers, not accepters of dogma" (Derman-Sparks, 1992, pp. 2–3).

Both Derman-Sparks and Corson have documented examples of young children making biased comments, such as "Girls can't be bus drivers" and "You can't play with us, you Chinese" (while pulling on their eyes to make them slant), so antibias curriculum and practices are important for even the youngest of the children at the Helen Gordon Center. Those educators who have explored antibias curriculum have discovered that they were not just embracing new methods, but that their thinking also had to change. As the educators at the Helen Gordon Center discovered, the process takes time and it demands ongoing attention. We asked Ellie Nolan about the beginnings.

"We started very simply by assessing our environment and our materials for varied kinds of bias." Ellie describes careful assessment of books, posters, dolls, songs, and music for cultural values. "If everything in the environment is about White people, what does that tell children?" Derman-Sparks (2003) describes these kinds of environmental checks for diversity as "first steps" or markers of a program that is well on its way to quality multicultural/antibias education (p. 43). At the Helen Gordon Center, the staff didn't stop at those "first steps." They went beyond race and considered diversity of family structures and family traditions. Gender stereotypes became an additional focus as the staff examined their classroom resources. The criteria for the selection of books and materials in Figure 8.8 will give you an idea of the kinds of questions and thinking you need to use when you have your own classroom. Although the criteria were designed for books and toys, they can be used to help you examine the many sources of messages for children. Those messages come "through our words and actions and silences" and you need to be vigilant about checking that the messages are what you intend for children to hear and learn (Neugebauer, 1992).

FIGURE 8.8

Criteria for the Selection of Books and Materials: Look for the Messages in Children's Books

Evaluate the Characters

Yes	No	
❒	❒	Do the characters in the story have personalities like real people?
❒	❒	Do they seem authentic in the way they act and react?
❒	❒	Do they speak in a style and language that fits their situation?
❒	❒	Are they real people with strengths and weaknesses rather than stereotypes?
❒	❒	Are characters allowed to learn and grow?
❒	❒	Is their lifestyle represented fairly and respectfully?

Evaluate the Situation

❒ ❒ Do the characters have power over their own lives?
❒ ❒ Do they resolve their own problems and reap their own rewards?
❒ ❒ Are human qualities emphasized?

Evaluate the Illustrations

❒ ❒ Do the illustrations respectfully depict ethnic, age, cultural, economic, ability, and sexual differences? (Illustrations can be humorous, but they must fit the context of the story line and be consistent in portrayal.)
❒ ❒ Do the illustrations and the text work well together to communicate the story?
❒ ❒ Is the style of illustration appropriate to the story?

Evaluate the Messages

❒ ❒ Do the messages conveyed, both directly and indirectly, respectfully and accurately portray the human condition?
❒ ❒ Are there hidden messages that are demeaning in any way or that reinforce stereotypes?

Evaluate the Author/Illustrator's Credibility

❒ ❒ Does the author/illustrator's background and training prepare her or him to present this story? (Do not disregard, but do consider carefully, stories about women written by men, stories about people with handicaps written by people without handicaps, and stories about one ethnic group written by another.)

Consider Your Selections as a Whole

It is not possible for any one book to portray all that we want to say to children, so it is important to look at your whole library:

❒ ❒ Are there stories about the contemporary life of a given ethnic group, as well as tales and legends?
❒ ❒ Do the cultures represented in your library at least cover (and, optimally, extend well beyond) those cultures represented by the families in your program?
❒ ❒ Are there books in which the disability or racial or economic difference is just part of the context for a story about people's lives, as well as books that focus on that particular difference?

Look for the Messages in Materials and Equipment

❒ ❒ Does this toy stereotype people by sex, race, age, family situation, physical skills, or intellectual skills?
❒ ❒ Does the selection of materials as a whole represent the diversity of humankind?
❒ ❒ How long will this toy hold a child's interest?
❒ ❒ Can the toy be adapted or used in different ways to change with different interests and ages of children?
❒ ❒ Can the toy be combined with other play materials to extend its possibilities?
❒ ❒ Is the toy safe, sturdy, and appealing?
❒ ❒ Does the packaging of the toy reflect diversity? (If not, throw it away or use it for discussion, and write to the manufacturer.)
❒ ❒ Is the way in which children play with these materials consistent with your program's philosophy and goals?

Source: "What Are We Really Saying to Children? Criteria for the Selection of Books and Materials" by B. Neugebauer from *Alike and Different: Exploring Our Humanity with Young Children* by B. Neugebauer (Ed.) (pp. 160–162), 1992, Washington, DC: NAEYC.

JOURNAL 8.5: Review the criteria given in Figure 8.8. Which of the questions caused you to pause? Why? Did any of them surprise you? Why? Select a toy or a book and use the criteria to assess it. Keep the criteria in mind as you watch television, browse through a magazine, or notice advertising.

You might think that bias is not relevant for work with toddlers, but research shows that by age 2, children have begun to develop their own gender and racial identities and are influenced by the stereotypes and prejudices around them (Derman-Sparks, 1992). You only have to listen to young children to know that bias is already part of their thinking and attitudes. You might see very young African American children reject their own skin color as "dirty" or "not pretty" or 3-year-old girls put themselves in the role of making dinner while the boys go off to work. The goal of antibias curriculum is for children "to become tolerant, understanding, and compassionate by the time they are five" (Derman-Sparks, 1992, p. 3). That goal is integral to the goals of effective early childhood education programs, but it takes concerted effort and study on the part of the educators to truly achieve that goal.

ANTIBIAS PHILOSOPHY AND THINKING. Returning to our discussion with Ellie, we ask about what followed the review of materials and assessment of the environment. "We wanted antibias thinking to become part of our thinking, we wanted to be proactive about bias, and we wanted to be truly different in our practices, not just look different." At this point, she used the term "questioned our assumptions," and we asked for an example. She laughs a bit uncomfortably and describes an example with which many of us with a history in early childhood education could identify: "Well, we had always been concerned with children getting to the center at a specific time each morning because we began routines and activities at 9:00 A.M. We disliked having children miss the opening exercises. We used very strong language in our parent handbook about being on time: Children *must* arrive at 9:00 A.M. We were judgmental of those tardy families. Some of our thoughts included: They must not value education or That parent is irresponsible. I know that in classrooms when a family was late, there were looks directed to them and attitudes directed to them. We even went so far as to say that parents had to get permission to bring children in late."

Ellie continues, "Well, when we began examining our assumptions, we stopped short. This whole issue of time being so important is a White cultural value. It doesn't have the same meaning for other cultures. We were communicating that other cultural values didn't count—were not good. We were reinforcing stereotypes about other cultures always being late. We went back to our handbook and softened the wording. We wanted to acknowledge the importance of family's individual schedules and time priorities." Ellie shares a section of the parent handbook to illustrate the changes in wording that resulted from their realization:

> Teachers need a stable, consistent group of children and block of time to successfully meet their curriculum goals. Therefore, we suggest that your child be here by 9:00 A.M. Children who arrive late often have a difficult time adjusting to the day or separating from their parent(s) as they are not familiar with the day's plans. Children need time to greet friends and "settle in." We recognize that it is impossible not to be late once in a while! If you are going to be late, please make arrangements with the teachers in advance, and if that is not possible, call the Center so that they know when to expect your child. It may be that the class is going on a field trip or has made other special plans that you will need to know about. (Helen Gordon Child Development Center, 1996–97, p. 11)

ONGOING PROFESSIONAL DEVELOPMENT FOR ANTIBIAS CURRICULUM. Ellie acknowledges that the time example is but one in a long series of realizations. The staff begins each year with an intense awareness workshop, with readings, guest speakers, reflections, and self-assessment. There is an aggressive recruitment and hiring process to maintain diversity in staff.

In addition to the staff diversity, the center has truly achieved a set of "quality markers"—benchmarks that indicate staff is "well on the way" to quality multicultural/ antibias education:

1. Staff actively incorporate children's daily life experiences into the daily curriculum.
2. Curriculum and interactions are tailored to meet cultural as well as individual needs of children.
3. Daily classroom life and curriculum integrate diversity and justice issues.
4. Families are actively involved in the program, with provisions for language other than English.
5. There is intentional encouragement of children's development of critical thinking and strategies for resisting prejudice and unfair behaviors.
6. There is ongoing, collaborative, and intentional reflection on practices and the influences of the staff's cultural backgrounds. (Derman-Sparks, 2003, p. 173)

Derman-Sparks (2003) talks about finding staff that "reflect the cultural and language diversity of the children and families they serve and the communities of their centers and schools" as a "quality marker," an indication that the program has gone beyond the "first steps" (p. 173). "We attract diverse families now," Ellie explains, "because of what we stand for, because of what we value." She adds, "Families talk to each other, they share their impressions and their experiences with other families, so we attract families that want this kind of environment for their children." An example is a message in the gay and lesbian community that the center is a "safe place for all families." Recommendations and opinions given among families is a strong force for recruiting diverse families and children. The center is an ideal place to talk about inclusion after hearing about the antibias thinking of the staff.

The diversity of children, families, and staff at the Helen Gordon Center is definitely an attraction for those families who choose the program for their young children, but there are other program qualities that families list when describing the reasons for their choice. Many of the families value their involvement in the center. Ellie and the staff make family involvement a high priority right alongside antibias curriculum. It's part of their thinking about how to provide the best environment for the children who walk through the doors each day. The center's family involvement approach is another model for you as a future teacher and caregiver.

Family Involvement

As you can tell from listening to Ellie, as well as Darren and Jennifer, families of the children at the Helen Gordon Center are very important and their involvement is a critical component of the center. Like the antibias curriculum, it's not so much the strategies of involving the families as it is the thinking of the staff and administration that makes a difference. High levels of family involvement begin with respect and trust, and those messages are communicated directly and, more importantly, subtly through so many means.

DAILY COMMUNICATION AND INTERACTIONS WITH FAMILIES. Ellie says, "There aren't necessarily formal mechanisms for family involvement, but we think about the families in all of the decisions we make." She describes the center's staffing as being at a level that allows for daily quality interactions with parents or family members. Remember Darren and Jennifer's conversations with the toddlers' parents as the children arrived? There wasn't that rushed feeling experienced at some centers when children are "dropped off" or gently pushed into the room by a fleeting adult. Many parents barely get a "Good-bye, have a nice day," because teachers or caregivers are busy taking care of a group of children. There's enough staff in the toddler room that either Darren or Jennifer or both can take the time to discuss Bryanna's lack of sleep or listen to Faridah and Ibrahim's news.

A Conversation about Inclusion

We looked forward to talking about inclusion with Ellie Nolan because we were sure that she and her staff had reflected a great deal about the topic. Her definition of *inclusion* is one of "welcoming whoever comes to our program—making space, adjustments, accommodations, and bringing them into the community." Ellie described the center's population as a range of children all over the developmental continuum and affirmed that "we would never divide or separate children because of differences." When asked for evidence of inclusion in an early childhood program, she described some of the practices of the Helen Gordon Center:

- A range of children with different developmental levels, needs, and experiences
- Families with different backgrounds and traditions
- Play materials (books, puzzles, dolls, pictures, games) that reflect the diversity of children and families in the center
- Different ways of communicating—in print and orally
- Individual responses to every child and family
- A focus on children's strengths and potential (an assets-based approach)

Ellie described the center's recent use of a digital camera to display the children and their families in prominent places in the center. It's a way of saying "This is who we are." She also described a practice of "catching" those children with challenges in displays of their strengths, a good day, and when they're at their best. "We take photos of those times and display them to counteract negative impressions that originate with their challenges. We want others to see them at their best."

Limited time for communication was listed as the most common barrier to parent involvement (Swap, 1987). Those time limits are true for both educators and family members. "Most often, parents and teachers interpret the other's lack of availability as a signal of their lack of concern for the child" (p. 8). Staff at the center have found a mutually convenient time for consistent availability that seems to work for both educators and families. Those morning conversations are important, and when combined with home visits and several conferences, they can contribute to a relationship of trust and respect.

When descriptions of "best practice" in toddler care are summarized from the past decade of research, one very important practice that emerges is that the staff facilitates positive communication with each other and with parents and families (McMullen, 1999). The Helen Gordon Center demonstrates that kind of communication in the daily interactions with families and in the strategies used to give families a voice in the decisions of the program.

Remember how Ruth's dad came in and had breakfast with her before leaving for the day? It was obvious that it was not an unusual occurrence. Ellie tells us, "Many parents or family members come in and have lunch with their children on a regular basis." She explains, "Some of that is the ease of our location—middle of the campus and middle of downtown." She adds that it is greatly encouraged. Family members hear the message all the time: We need you, your presence is valued, come in and read a story, go with us on a field trip. "Those are pretty traditional, but they're comfortable and both adults and children are happy."

GIVING FAMILIES A VOICE. Besides home visits, parent conferences, and newsletters from each class to keep families informed about curriculum, there's also a Parent Advisory Board, which is a formal structure to involve parents in the decisions and policies of the center. "The board provides feedback to the Center and advises on such matters as budget, and the board acts as an advocacy group on behalf of the Center when necessary" (Helen Gordon Child Development Center, 1996–97, p. 10). Ellie tells us, "When we an-

FIGURE 8.9
Example of Parent Bulletin Board: Encouraging Input to Playground Redesign

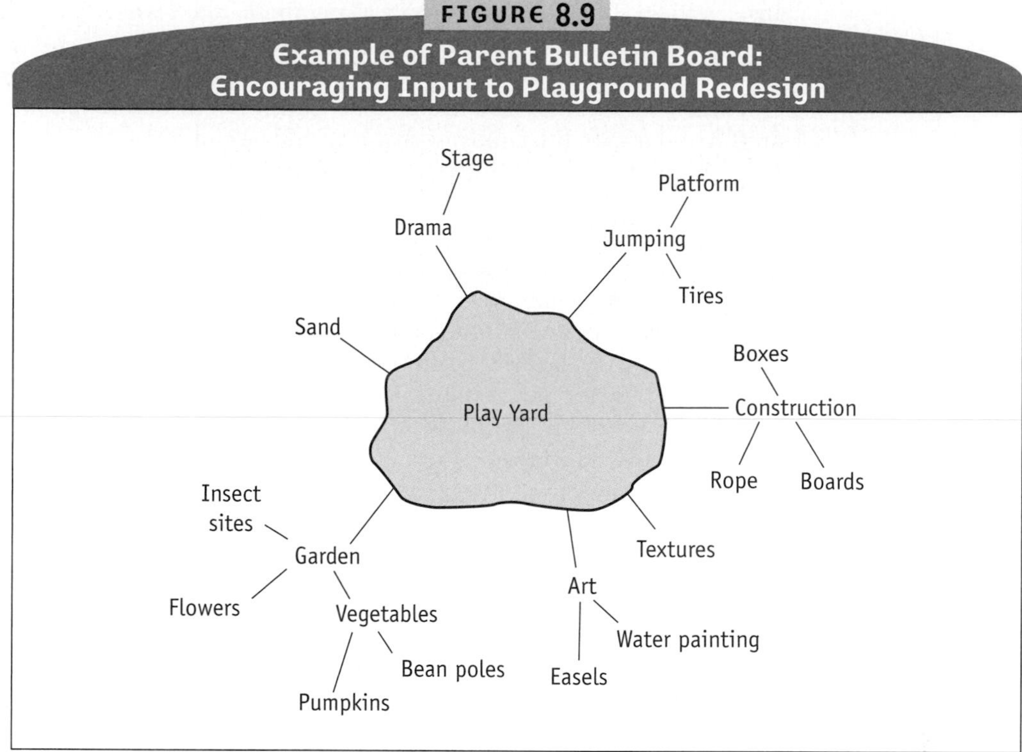

ticipate major changes, especially those that influence all of the children, we try to involve all of the families, not just those on the advisory board." She describes a recent bulletin board that was designed to encourage and stimulate family contributions to plans for restructuring the playground area. Figure 8.9 shows the "web" of thinking about playgrounds that appeared on the bulletin board after the following note went home to parents and family members:

> We are planning to make some changes in our playground and we need your ideas. In the lobby you will find a bulletin board labeled "Playground Ideas." Think back to when you were a child. . . . What kind of games, activities, and materials did you use for playing outside? What do you feel would be important for your child to experience here at the Center?
>
> We are using a brainstorming method called "webbing," which is one of the ways we plan curriculum and build on the ideas of children and teachers. Our web theme is outdoor play, and the bulletin board displays the beginning of the web. Please contribute to the web with your ideas—new ones or ones that build or connect to another. We will also have a notebook available for you to share pictures of play yards that you have seen or for additional comments you want to share. The webbing process will continue through March 7th.
>
> Thank you for your time and interest. More information will be coming your way soon.

The strategy of involving families communicates a value for families' ideas and input that goes beyond most involvement approaches. Family members have a voice in what happens at the center. Involvement empowers parents; they consider themselves as partners with staff in the education of their children. We scheduled some time with Ibrahim's parents to ask how they feel about their son's experiences at the center. We're especially interested in their ideas because Ibrahim is one of the many biracial children at the center, and we wonder about the impact of the center's curriculum on his development. Talking with his parents will also give us more insights about toddlers and their needs.

A CONVERSATION WITH FARIDAH AND AMR: PARENTS' PERCEPTIONS AND VALUES. Faridah and Amr's first interaction with the staff of the Helen Gordon Center occurred when Muhammed attended the program. Faridah described her fears and insecurities: "It was difficult—he was my first child. I was not familiar with child care—had never used a program—and the media examples of what can happen were frightening." Amr commented that he was surprised at the level of accommodation they received from the staff. Muhammed had unusual eating habits and required a special diet, and the staff worked with the family so that he could be comfortable. "They reported so carefully to us about his daily activities—always so much information about his interests, his mood, his feelings," he added.

Faridah admitted, "I learned a lot from watching in the classrooms and from parent conferences." She continued, "I began seeing different parts of my children, and my parenting skills have changed since the boys came here." She laughed when she told us about how her friends noticed Muhammed's maturity and his language development and that they decided to send their children to school, too. Amr summarized the effects of the boys' experience: "They taught my children to make choices (not what I would have thought of doing in my culture) and they've become independent."

Our conversation with Faridah and Amr added to our understanding of their family and of Ibrahim's development. It also provided insight into parents' perceptions. Those perceptions can be attributed to the intense efforts made to respond to family differences, to understand cultural variations in child rearing, and to work toward creative solutions that incorporate both parents' and educators' concerns through dialogue and reflective thinking (Gonzales-Mena & Bhavnagri, 2003, p. 37).

PRINCIPLES AND INSIGHTS: A Summary and Review

Remember how we promised that you would not get bored spending time with toddlers? The same is true for those families and early childhood professionals who surround toddlers. There is an energy and vitality to their conversations and interactions. Perhaps you are now thinking about toddlers and feeling attracted to working with them. Maybe you are thinking that toddlers are not for you. Regardless of your decision, it will be important to understand their development as part of your knowledge base of human development and child development. We urge you to extend your observational experience from this chapter by spending time in other classes for toddlers. Listen to educators like Darren and Jennifer. Meet with parents like Faridah and Amr to understand toddlers and, more importantly, to see them in the context of their families and their culture.

As part of your professional development, you have observed a university laboratory school in this chapter and have been introduced to antibias curriculum. As you continue your studies and other professional experiences, we urge you to expand your awareness of and sensitivity to bias by reading more about the topic, by attending workshops about antibias curriculum and teaching approaches, and by discussing the topic with educators who are committed to the concept.

BECOMING AN EARLY CHILDHOOD PROFESSIONAL

Your Professional Portfolio

1. Your observational data will be a good entry in your portfolio, but be sure to accompany the recordings with a summary and reflection on what you learned about toddlers and the effect of their settings, curriculum, and adult interactions.
2. Develop a floor plan for a developmentally appropriate program for toddlers. You might want to consult *Developmentally Appropriate Practice in Early Childhood Education Programs* (Bredekamp & Copple, 1997).

Your Professional Library

Copple, C. (Ed.). (2003). *A world of difference: Readings on teaching young children in a diverse society.* Washington, DC: NAEYC.

Greenberg, P. (1991). *Character development: Encouraging self-esteem and self-discipline in infants, toddlers, and two year olds.* Washington, DC: NAEYC.

Jones, E., & Nimmo, J. (1994). *Emergent curriculum.* Washington, DC: NAEYC.

Miller, K. (1988). *More things to do with toddlers and twos.* Mt. Ranier, MD: Gryphon House.

Neugebauer, B. (1992). *Alike and different: Exploring our humanity with young children.* Washington, DC: NAEYC.

Sanders, S. W. (2002). *Active for life: Developmentally appropriate movement programs for young children.* Washington, DC: NAEYC.

Segal, M. (1998). *Your child at play: Two to three years—Growing up, language, and the imagination.* Washington, DC: Zero to Three Project.

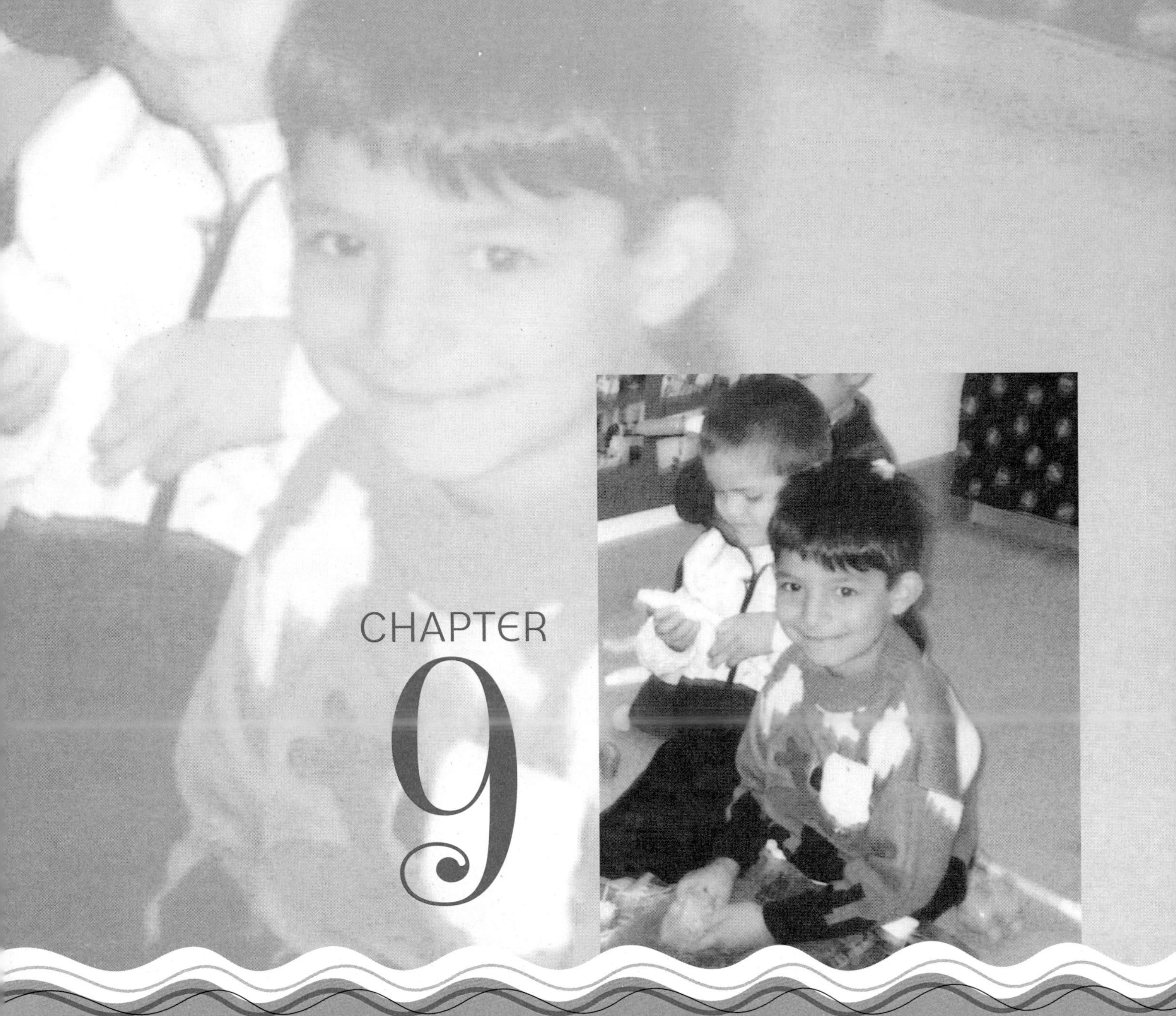

CHAPTER

9

Head Start

Felipe's Story

CHAPTER focus:

When you finish reading and reflecting on this chapter, you will be able to:

1. Outline different curricular activities planned for a preschool setting.
2. Describe the history of and need for Head Start programs.
3. Summarize several recommendations for or indicators of a quality preschool.
4. Describe strategies to support cultural and linguistic diversity with young children.

In 1965, Head Start began as a federally funded comprehensive preschool program designed to break the cycle of intergenerational poverty. Initially, Head Start consisted of summer programs, focused on preparing 5-year-olds to succeed in kindergarten. The program has gone through numerous changes over the years, yet continues to assist young children and their families gain access to education, health care, and social services. Let's join Felipe as he begins his morning at Washington County Head Start.

Washington County Head Start

It's 8:15 in the morning and the Head Start minibuses are arriving. About 8 to 10 children and several adults step out of each bus. With the morning rain, everyone hurries into the Community Action Building and heads for different classrooms. The children, 3 and 4 years old, hang up their coats and go to the sinks to wash their hands in the common area. Susana, the teacher in Felipe's classroom, greets her 20 students (all 4-year-olds) as they enter the room.

Breakfast: Nutrition and Socialization

The children find a place to sit at the tables, which are already set with dishes and food. Each morning, they begin their day with breakfast. "Es tan bueno comer con amigos (It's so nice to eat with friends)," the children say together before eating. Food is served family style, with children passing bowls of cereal, pouring milk, and helping themselves to bananas. Susana, Rita (the teaching assistant), and Rosa (a parent volunteer) sit with the children and join in the morning conversation. "Bananas taste good," says Madalena. "Whoops," announces Isabella as she spills her milk. She quickly picks up the dishcloth and cleans up her milk. The conversation and eating continues. You observe that many children are speaking Spanish, with some English words mixed in their sentences.

As the children finish breakfast, they carry their dishes to the dish-washing area, where a parent volunteer helps them. Estella scrapes her leftovers into a tub and rinses her plate. She shows you how to clean your dishes, "Put your glass over here and leave the banana peels in the garbage."

Raul leaves his dishes on the table as he heads for the blocks. Susana walks over to Raul and quietly reminds him, "Remember, we clean up our own dishes. Then you play." Raul heads back to the

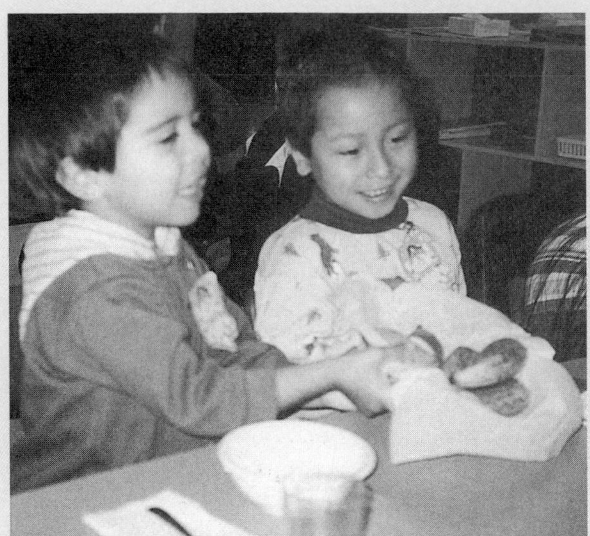

Valentin begins breakfast by sharing the fruit basket. The children enjoy making their own decisions about their food.

table and picks up his bowl, spoon, and cup. "Now I play," he announces. Susana tells you, "We prefer gentle reminders to provide **guidance.** It is like 'reading' the environment, always keeping an eye on what is going on and being ready to step in to help the children choose an appropriate action." You admit it didn't seem punishing, merely helpful, when she provided direction to assist Raul.

The Playground: An Environment for Physical Development

After the children clear their spots at the tables, they put on coats for outside play. There are two outside times each morning. Today, they have a choice of playing a game called Red Light, Green Light, playing with balls, or choosing other activities. Pepe and Ramon eagerly climb the climbing structure, which looks like a fort with ladders and slides. Part of the outside area is covered, so children play here without getting wet. Everywhere you look, you see children moving around, some individually and others playing together. You are reminded of the physical development of 4-year-olds and their need for activities that involve the use of large muscles. With the space and equipment outside, these children are developing coordination and balance through the games and activities, promoting the use of their large muscles. Rita, Jessica, and Eduardo are drawing enormous pictures with sidewalk chalk. "Look at the giant man I made," exclaims Jessica. Indeed, it is huge—at least eight feet tall. Rosa is with Felipe and Estella, playing some type of tag game, running and skipping along the edge of the play area.

Providing Guidance. Thinking about Susana's comment about reading or scanning the environment, you watch Rita and Rosa who, although involved with activities with children, scan the entire play area continually. Just as Ramon starts to jump from the perch of the fort, Rosa walks over and asks him, "How are you supposed to get down from the fort, Ramon?" Ramon looks at her and moves off the perch and starts to climb down the ladder. So, this is why people say teachers have eyes in the back of their heads. These teachers seem to process what is going on around them and make good predictions about what might happen next. They also know when to step in to help the children problem solve. For example, after Rosa asked Ramon how to get down from the fort, she waited until he moved toward the ladder. She seemed to know that prompting with a brief question was enough to change Ramon's activity.

After 15 minutes, Rita calls to the children, "Time to go inside. Think about what you might like to do today during choice time."

Learning Centers

Today, children are busy with puzzles, books, blocks, the dramatic play and kitchen area, or working at a gardening table with plastic plants and real garden tools such as trowels and gardening gloves. There are many choices in the classroom. Eduardo shows you how to plant. "Put on your gloves first. See, this is the dirt. Put that in the pot and then put a flower in to grow. And here is the water." Susana tells you that sometimes this is a sand table or a water table, but right now, it's the gardening table. The activities planned for this week revolve around the theme of spring, and the gardening table fits right in with this theme.

You notice that besides the gardening area, there are several different centers set up around the room: a reading center, mail center, puzzle table, and a blocks and transportation center. A **center** (also called *learning center, activity center,* or *interest center*) is an area with materials that support active learning and typically include activities planned around children's interests, individual and small group learning, and developmentally appropriate learning. Near the rug is the reading center, with large pillows, a couch, and a cart with books (some written in Spanish and some in English). On one of the tables are puzzles, with Isabella and José working with these. "Look, I found the piece to fit here!" At another table, Rita has placed a typewriter, paper, envelopes, stamps, pencils, and crayons. Three children are talking about mailing letters: "We better get our letters ready before the mail leaves." In the back of the room are two different areas. In one area are clothes for dramatic play and a small kitchen with real pots and pans, where Miguel, Esteban, and Floranna are "making a huge cake for everybody." The other area has blocks, cars, trucks, and traffic signs. Felipe, Eduardo, Berenise, and Deanna are building a town. "Let's make this the store and the school goes here. Put the stop sign near the school, OK?" It appears that learning centers offer lots of choices for the children.

Carolyne, the program coordinator, comes to the door of the classroom. She asks, "Would you like to talk about our program? We have about 20 minutes before their next activity." Sounds great—you have observed just enough to have even more questions than when you first arrived this morning.

Community Action Organization

Walking down the hallway toward Carolyne's office, you wonder, "Is this a new building?" "Yes, it's several years old. We are housed within the Community Action Organization Building," replies Carolyne. "We had a 10-year building drive to raise the funds for this building. This was truly a collaborative effort, with block grants, fund raising, and donations from local businesses and donors supporting the Community Action Building." Other Community Action programs are housed in the adjacent wing of the building. The programs range from social services, emergency housing assistance, to skills training for adults. Head Start is viewed as a branch of these resources, as children and families receive education and social services to support family needs.

The New Community Action Organization Building

Overview of Washington County Head Start Program

Carolyne suggests that she start with a brief overview of their Head Start program. "We are a countywide program, with about 350 children and their families. Our overall purpose is to increase the social competence of children from low-income families by providing 'developmentally appropriate education and care for children, involve and support their parents, and offer early childhood services that meet family needs' " (Washington County Community Action Organization, 1996). At each of the centers, the staff includes a center coordinator, one teacher/home visitor per class, and one or more assistant teachers. In addition, consulting staff includes mental health consultants, early childhood special education consultants, and family workers. "We work together toward our goal of increasing social competence of our children, and we meet frequently to accomplish this goal."

Head Start Services and Eligibility. In order to enroll in Head Start, families must meet certain criteria, as the program is established to provide services for children and families with low-income levels. Figure 9.1 describes the services provided by this particular Head Start program. Families who qualify (are below a certain income level) are able to participate in the program without any fees. In this center, Carolyne explains, "We reserve approximately 10 percent of our program enrollment for children with special needs. Unfortunately, only about one-third of children who qualify are able to attend Head Start. We do not have enough funding to provide services for the other two-thirds of eligible children." Hopefully, this situation will change as more legislators support an increased budget for Head Start.

Hispanic Population of Children in Washington County Head Start

Many children in Washington County's Head Start Program are of Hispanic descent. In fact, in Felipe's classroom, all 20 children are Hispanic. The teachers acknowledge and celebrate the different cultures of the children and include many activities to promote cultural awareness and appreciation.

The largest number of culturally and linguistically diverse children enrolled in Head Start across the nation are Spanish speaking, with many other language groups represented in increasing numbers (U.S. Department of Health

FIGURE 9.1

Washington County Head Start: Community Action Organization

To Enroll:

- Call office nearest your home. Make an appointment to visit the office for intake.

  Office hours are Monday–Friday, 8:30 a.m.–5 p.m.

- Prepare to bring the following:
  Income information
  Immunization record
  Birth certificate (child must be 3 or 4 by September 1 of the school year)
  Information about your child's disability, if he or she has one
- There are ten Head Start Centers in Washington County serving 346 children.
- Head Start has limited enrollment; children are enrolled as space becomes available.
- Children are enrolled in the site nearest their home that offers the services they need.
- Enrollment opportunities for children with disabilities are available.

Options:

- Head Start preschool (no cost to income-eligible families)
- Paid preschool and full child care, before and after school care, available in Gaston only

Head Start Services:

- Quality preschool, focus on constructive play, cultural diversity, personal safety/abuse prevention, social skills
- Individualized education plan and ongoing assessment for every child
- Comprehensive screening including vision, hearing, nutrition, height/weight, developmental, speech/language, assessment of physical and dental exams
- Social services—family worker available to assess family needs, follow up as indicated
- In-home visits by teacher support parent as educator and home as learning environment
- Transportation provided by Head Start in some areas
- Parent involvement opportunities include Policy Council, parent committees, classroom volunteering, employment, and training

Source: Community Action Organization Head Start. Reprinted by permission.

and Human Services, 2003a). In 1999, the Head Start Bureau identified specific steps to include more children and families from the growing Hispanic population in Head Start programs. Currently, Hispanic children represent 30 percent of those enrolled in such programs (U.S. Department of Health and Human Services, 2003a).

All teachers at this Washington County Head Start Center speak Spanish and English, which reflects the importance of communicating and learning in a child's and family's first language. When you visit Felipe's classroom and later meet with Susana, Felipe's teacher, she will share her thoughts about bilingual and bicultural education.

Importance of Families in Head Start

Families are an integral component of Head Start. Family involvement includes volunteer work in classrooms or the school, serving as a representative on the Policy Council (each classroom elects one parent representative), or participating in parenting classes. There is a **Family Services Staff** at the center that provides social services through a coordinated model. This model identifies and supports the strengths, needs, and interests of each family through accessing social services (such as medical services or housing programs), providing educational training, or linking parents with employment programs.

Home Visits. In addition to support through social services, Head Start teachers visit each family in their home a minimum of five times each year. These home visits are seen as "the most effective way to produce changes in the child's long-term dispositions toward learning. The parent who understands the school program and who sees the child as a learner is better equipped to advocate for the child. Home visits also enable us to reach out to the parent . . . so we can build parent self-esteem and help families reach their goals" (Washington County Community Action Organization, 1996). Later, Susana will share the format and themes of the home visits with you.

Parent/Teacher Conferences. Teachers also hold two parent/teacher conferences during the school year to focus on goals for each child and to provide support needed for the child to reach these goals. Teachers make phone calls home and send frequent notes to keep in contact with families. Carolyne finds, "All of these different communication formats are essential to involving families in Head Start." Another way families are involved is through adult education. A classroom for adult education is located in the Washington County Community Action Building. Families also are a key partner in the development and implementation of programs for children with special needs.

Adult Education Program. Passing classrooms as you walk back down the hall toward Felipe's classroom, Carolyne points out the five classrooms in this section of the building. Four of them house Head Start classes and one is for an adult education program. "Each morning, parents of Head Start children who are interested in pursuing a GED (Graduate Equivalency Diploma), job training, or improving their English language competency spend time in this classroom. Tutors and volunteers assist parents in achieving educational goals." Carolyne continues, "Parents are welcome to ride the school bus, volunteer in the classroom, attend adult education classes, and share meals with their children." Helping parents improve their education is a goal of Head Start. "It's important to meet both the child's and parent's educational needs. Their learning is woven together. For example, many children are being introduced to the English language in their Head Start classrooms. At the same time, their mother and/or father might be learning English in the adult literacy program. They can share and practice their new language skills together at home." You glance in the adult education classroom and see several people at computers and two small groups in conversation. This does seem to be a logical place for an adult education program, right next door to their child's classroom.

JOURNAL 9.1: How might educational opportunities for parents at the Head Start center relate to their child's learning? ●

With this brief introduction to Washington County's Head Start Program, you head back to the classroom, eager to observe Felipe, his classmates, and Susana in action. Curious about the curriculum and the bilingual nature of this classroom, you enter the room just as the children begin circle time.

Felipe's Morning

Circle Time: Building a Community of Learners

Circle time follows breakfast, outside play, and choice time. Susana turns to José and says, "It's your turn to ring the bell." José rushes over to the counter, picks up the bell, and rings it, saying, "Time to go to circle!" The children clean up the areas where they have been playing, with parent volunteers and teacher assistants helping them. Susana is seated on the large rug near the front of the classroom. Children begin to join her there. Rita, the teacher assistant, is helping Manuel put puzzles away. Each time Rita looks away, Manuel

A Conversation about Inclusion

Talking with Carolyne about inclusion reveals how the staff in this Head Start program develops and implements programs that reflect inclusive practices. Carolyne states, "We interpret inclusion as placing a child with special needs in a classroom with her or his typical developing peers, working toward the goal of enabling the child to experience the same opportunities as all children."

In discussing the program at Community Action Head Start, Carolyne explains, "Services are responsive to each child's individual needs. Communication is maintained with each family, particularly during the process of assessment and in the writing of the learning goals for each child. Continuous communication is also maintained with early intervention support staff, resulting in a collaborative working team. Our staff is trained to recognize when to intervene and help a child or when to allow a child to complete a task independently. Curriculum and routines are adapted for each child, with programs planned on an individual level. The classroom environment is set up with each child's learning needs taken into consideration."

dumps the puzzle out again. Rita notices what Manuel is doing and provides guidance by saying, "This time we will put the pieces in, leave them in, and then go to the rug." Together, they finish the puzzle and walk over to the circle.

When the children are settled at the circle, Susana puts a tape in the tape player. The music starts and Susana begins singing, "We all go around walking together." The children stand up and start walking around the circle, joining in the song. The first verse is in English, the second verse in Spanish. Julio and Isauro hold hands with Rita, as they walk along. Julio has some difficulty with his balance, so Rita is nearby to provide support as needed. "Not too much," she says, "Only enough to make it safe for him." Julio has motor challenges, sometimes bumping into objects or falling down. Susana referred him for further testing and diagnosis, as she wanted him to receive support services to help him in his development. She shares, "I'm glad he's in our class. I want him to have the support he needs to help him with his physical coordination and development."

As the song ends, the children stop walking. Several children bump into each other, which causes some giggles. Susana requests, "Sit down, please, and let's think about our job chart." You've noticed that she starts many of the activities with a brief overview about the activity. This must help the children focus on what is going to happen next and know what Susana expects of them. Felipe points to the job chart, "Today, I want to check for the bus." Susana holds up cards with names and asks Rosina to pick five cards. "These are today's workers: Marcos, Gerardo, Francisco, Julio, and Jenesis." The five children come up to the pocket chart and each places his or her name card into a pocket with a picture of a job on the outside. Two children will wash tables after lunch, one child will inform Susana when the bus arrives, and Julio and Jenesis will choose a book for story time. Felipe laments, "I wanted a job, teacher." Susana reminds him, "You had a job yesterday and we have to take turns. But you can ring the bell for outside play today." That brings a smile to Felipe's face.

Susana finds circle time to be a format for her to convey the daily jobs and to communicate her respect for the children's needs to play, pretend, and choose activities (Stone, 2001). By noting that Felipe wanted a job and finding one for him, she was communicating her acknowledgment of his desire to have an assigned duty. Susana also finds circle time as a way to model respect as she listens to the children and their thoughts each day. She models with words and respectful behavior. These are important ingredients in creating community.

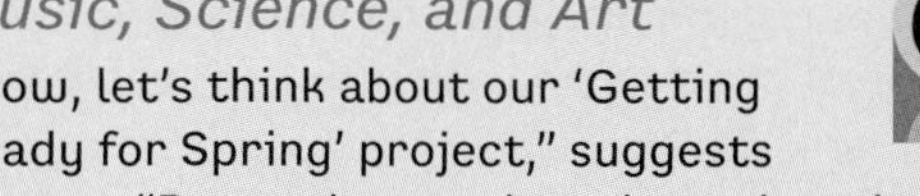

Project Time: Integrating Music, Science, and Art

"Now, let's think about our 'Getting Ready for Spring' project," suggests Susana. "Remember, we have been dressing the dolls the past few days. What did we want them to wear to be ready for spring weather?" Teresa smiles, "I put boots on the little boy and made an umbrella for him." Rita holds up the doll wearing a raincoat, boots, and holding an umbrella made from fabric and a pipe cleaner. "Look at him. He's ready for the weather now," shares Rita. Felipe says, "Just like today—rain, rain, rain." Susana holds up a handful of pipe cleaners and a basket of fabric. "Today, when you go to one of the centers, you may choose to make a rainy-day picture with umbrellas, or paint a picture about any ideas you have about rainy spring days, or make rainy-day things."

Rita has already prepared paint and placed brushes at two of the tables. The third table has scissors, glue, fabric pieces, pipe cleaners, and construction paper on it. "You may choose to paint first and then add decorations, or make decorations and then paint the picture," says Rita. The children go to the tables, picking up paint smocks placed over the back of chairs. Rita and Susana help the children get started. Rita also turns on the tape player, so they can sing along with rainy-day songs.

During these different activities, children make choices about their projects. Some children use paints, others use construction paper or fabric. Isuaro finds the glue stick and is gluing clouds all over his paper. At another table, Marcos and Berenise are making lots of colorful boots. At the painting easels, Jessica is painting large circles. She says, "These are suns trying to come out today."

At the construction table, Rosa, the parent volunteer, is helping children cut out fabric for umbrellas. Felipe wants to "make lots and lots of raindrops." He likes to add extra details to his pictures, and he's excited about the idea of shiny raindrops. Felipe finds some aluminum foil for his rain drops. "Wow, everyone will see my rain now!" Next to him, Madalena is cutting out little boots. She wants to make "a whole page of boots so kids can keep their feet dry." Sounds like a good idea, as you notice rain is still falling outside.

Trying to scan the entire classroom, you see an adult with each of the three groups of children at the different activity tables or centers. The children have choices about their projects, with adult supervision and assistance nearby. The activities or choices are designed to be developmentally appropriate for 4-year-olds, including large pieces of paper for paintings, glue sticks instead of large bottles of glue (it's difficult for 4-year-olds to control the amount of glue on their project), fabric already cut in small pieces, and paints in stable containers to reduce spills.

While the children work on activities, adults are engaged in conversation with the children about their creative work without directing their work. You hear Lucero exclaim, "Oh, look at the raindrops. They keep moving down your page." Ruben explains, "Sí, I want a rainy, rainy picture." They both seem pleased with Ruben's work.

Susana explains, "I integrated art, music, and science into our Spring Project theme. I think it

helps the children understand the season better when they connect with lots of different subjects and real occurrences in their life. So talking about weather in relation to what to wear in this season is important for them to learn."

The children work on their projects for about 40 minutes. At this point, Rita and Susana remind the children, "Clean your hands first, then take off your paint smocks. We will let your paintings dry while you are outside playing." After washing their hands, the children head for the coat racks, pull on their coats, and go out to play.

The painting easels are a popular spot in this classroom. What do you notice about the paint supplies, materials, and related equipment?

Measurement: Active Mathematics

During this second outside play, Susana brings out three pairs of boots and a tub of water. Several children pull on a boot, put their foot in the colored water, and make a footprint on the playground. "Look," exclaims Susana, "Your foot is really big." Estella and Roberto begin measuring their boot prints and try to decide who has the biggest boot. Susana provided time for students to explore the concepts of measurement as she encouraged inquiry and use of the language in mathematics. She was following the recommendations from the NAEYC/NCTM Joint Position Statement on Early Childhood Mathematics (2002), considered by many early childhood educators to provide early learning standards in mathematics. After a few more minutes spent measuring boot prints, Felipe asks, "Teacher, is it time for me to ring the bell yet?" "Sure," says Rita. Felipe reaches for the bell and reminds everyone, "Time to wash your hands for lunch."

Lunchtime: Nurturing Language

Again, the children start their meal by saying, "Es tan bueno comer con amigos." Conversations are about rainy-day pictures, boot prints, and plans for their afternoon. Ruben remembers, "Today, we are going to my friend's house and see his new kittens." That starts a string of stories about cats and kittens. You hear Susana asking Teresa, "What is your favorite fruit?" Several conversations are about the food the children are eating. You think of the Head Start Parent Handbook you saw in Carolyne's office and recall that nutrition was a program goal. This might be why the children and adults are discussing food and food groups. Rita is sitting near Felipe and Marcos as they discuss pizza. Felipe says, "Next to ice cream, pizza is my favorite." Rita asks him, "What is on top of pizza?" He says, "Ketchup and cheese." "This red sauce is made out of tomatoes, just like ketchup," notes Rita. "Well, I like tomatoes," agrees Felipe.

Soon, the meal is ending. Children follow the same routine, bringing dishes to the cleaning cart, scraping food, and sorting dishes, glasses, and silverware into appropriate soaking containers. They then head for a story on the rug before going home. Rosa, the parent volunteer, reads the story in Spanish, chosen by Julio. Just as she finishes, Marcos looks out the door and announces, "I see buses!" Susana walks toward the door with the children. They begin singing, "Adios amigos, es hora a partir (Good-bye my friends, it's time to go)." Susana, Rita, and Rosa help with coats and walk with them to the door. "See you mañana, and remember to tell your family about your rainy-day painting and boot prints."

Susana turns to you and says, "I need to make a quick phone call to Jessica's mother. Let's meet in the classroom for a visit about our program." You help Rita hang up the rainy-day paintings. The paintings are all different and quite colorful.

A Visit with Susana

Susana's Philosophy: Working with Families to Support Learning

You ask Susana to tell you how she came to work at Head Start. She responds, "My college work was in psychology and I began working in a child care center following graduation. After a year at that center, I heard about an opening in Head Start. I started five years ago as an assistant teacher and two years ago was promoted to lead teacher."

Knowing that a teacher with five years of experience has a rationale or a philosophy for what happens in her classroom, you ask Susana about her philosophy of teaching. She tells you, "In my classroom, my major goal is to help children become the best that they can. By this, I want children to learn social skills and learn how to solve problems in getting along with each other as well as academic skills to help them in their development. I also spend part of each school day working with families. I teach from 8:30 to 12:00 and then spend from 12:30 to 4:00 meeting with parents, talking on the phone with families, or planning for or going on a home visit, along with my curriculum planning. So my philosophy of teaching also includes working with families to help them support their child's learning."

When you observed the children in Felipe's classroom, you saw that many activities were designed to allow for student-centered learning. You ask Susana why she plans for choice and free-play time for the children. She explains, "We have a 45-minute block planned each day for free-play or choice time. Although there may be a theme connected with a project we are working on, we want children to choose their activities and friends to play with. Children learn so much from play. At 4 years of age, they are ready to spend time negotiating activities and making choices. Did you notice the children working with the typewriter?" she asks. "Some of them are typing their names with the typewriter. They are learning to use a keyboard and to put letters together. The children are successful, whether they type their name or make up pretend words. They can finish the activity with a stamped letter, perhaps draw a picture on it, and we send it to their home or a friend's home. All of this is developmentally appropriate for this age child. It also fits with my philosophy of teaching—structuring or planning activities that have an **expected outcome or objective,** such as learning about letters and about the mail system, yet is open ended enough to allow children from differing ability levels to be successful learners. The children have freedom to choose which activities they want to be involved in during this free-play period."

STUDENT-CENTERED LEARNING: PLANNING FOR THE WHOLE CHILD. Another aspect of Susana's philosophy is revealed when reviewing her **written plans.** When you look at her planning book, you see that she has a system to check if each of the developmental areas (cognitive, social, emotional, and physical) are incorporated in activities

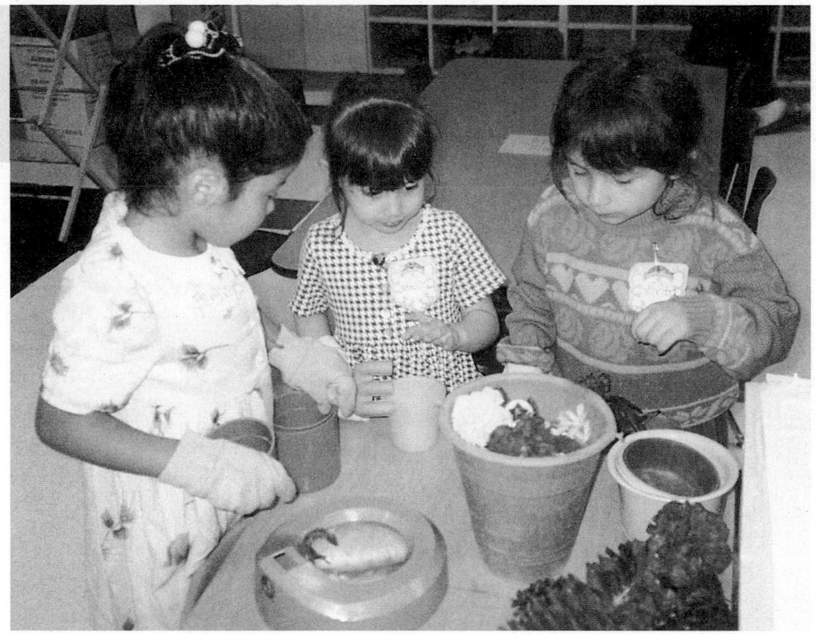

What might these girls be talking about in this gardening activity?

throughout the day. Remember the children working in the gardening table? They were talking about what plants need to grow (cognitive development), planning their garden together (social development), expressing satisfaction and delight with their planting skills (emotional development), and using small muscles and eye-hand coordination skills (physical development) to place the dirt in the pot with garden scoops. This was a developmentally appropriate activity for 4-year-old children, as it incorporated activities at their level as well as extended the skills and knowledge they were learning in class.

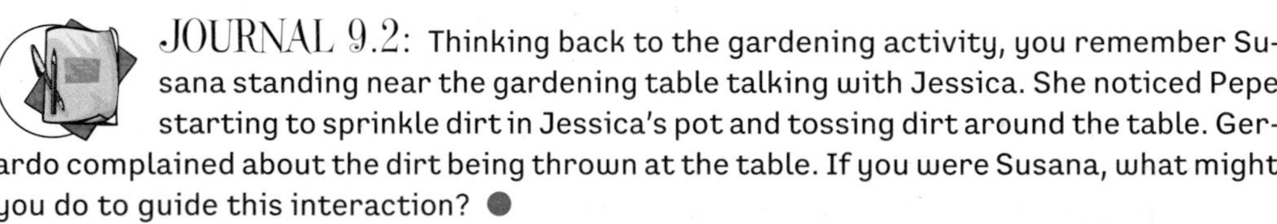

JOURNAL 9.2: Thinking back to the gardening activity, you remember Susana standing near the gardening table talking with Jessica. She noticed Pepe starting to sprinkle dirt in Jessica's pot and tossing dirt around the table. Gerardo complained about the dirt being thrown at the table. If you were Susana, what might you do to guide this interaction? ●

As Susana translates her philosophy of education into practice, she considers the children's learning needs and goals. In order to develop these goals, a screening assessment is conducted in the early part of the school year that helps her develop appropriate learning goals.

Screening: Assessment for Curricular Decisions

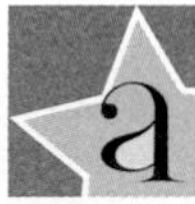

During the fall, each new student entering Head Start is administered the Early Screening Inventory (ESI). The ESI is an individual developmental screening assessment designed for use with children from 3 to 6 years of age. The ESI takes 15 to 20 minutes to administer and is composed of 25 items that are scored from 0 to 3 points, according to the child's response. The purpose of the ESI is to provide staff and family with information about the child's functioning in three major developmental areas:

1. *Visual-Motor.* Includes a Draw-a-Person task and items that examine fine-motor control, eye-hand coordination, and ability to remember visual sequences and to reproduce two and three dimensional visual tasks
2. *Language and cognition.* Includes items that examine language comprehension and verbal expression, and ability to reason, count, and remember auditory sequences

3. *Gross motor/Body awareness.* Includes items that evaluate a child's large muscle coordination, balance, ability to hop, skip, and imitate body positions from verbal cues. (C. Westlake, personal communication, July 3, 1997)

The ESI is administered in the child's primary language. As in most developmental screening assessments, different developmental areas are broken into observable tasks, which the child performs during the individual assessment session. Tasks are sequenced on a developmental continuum and linked to an age at which a child should typically be able to perform the task. The results of the assessment show significant developmental delays or areas where children are more advanced.

Children are not "screened out" of the program; rather, the purpose of the screening is to develop individual educational plans for the child, based on her current level of development. When Julio was screened, it was found that he had developmental motor delays. The result of the screening led to a referral for further testing and diagnosis, in the process of securing special education services to support and assist Julio in his development. Approximately 10 percent of the enrollment in Head Start programs is designated for children with special needs. These children are included in their classroom with their peers, with special education services coming to the program.

Susana explains, "Since screening is administered early in the school year, I can discuss the strengths and needs of each child with his or her parents. We then work together to develop each child's educational plan to reflect goals drawn from this assessment."

You ask Susana about the controversy regarding the use of screening inventories. You've heard that some educators feel that screening children leads to categorizing them and looking at their weaknesses more than at each child as a whole. Susana tells you, "We think of the screening inventory as one piece of information about a child. The screening helps us see if there are areas we should focus on to help the child learn. And if the child knows more than was shown on the inventory, we move to other areas in his or her education plan." Her comments help you see that in this Head Start program, the screening inventory is used for information purposes and not as the sole representation of what a child knows or can do.

Now that you have learned more about the educational philosophy that Susana works from, let's look at the curriculum in her classroom, which is grounded in her philosophy of teaching.

Curriculum Planning for Preschool Children

When asked about curriculum, Susana shares, "My curriculum comes mainly from the learning needs of my students and my knowledge of developmentally appropriate learning activities for 4-year-olds. Also, many of the major ideas for projects and themes come from ideas shared by the teachers in our center. We plan together in the beginning of the year and then make many changes according to the children's learning needs and interests that emerge during the year. We also look at individual education plans for each child and make sure this is incorporated in our day-to-day curriculum. And, of course, since all of my children are Hispanic and speak Spanish, we work with a bilingual and bicultural curriculum." These areas of curriculum will be explored in this section.

TEACHERS' SHARED PLANNING TIME. At this Head Start center, teachers have a shared planning time on Mondays. They plan several large projects for the month and make more specific plans for the week. Susana finds she gets great ideas from other teachers. "It seems we each have special interests or talents and share these with each other. One of the teachers is an artist and we really appreciate her ideas about painting and drawing."

An example of shared planning is evident in the current project theme of spring. One teacher owns a nursery and brings in seeds and soil for other teachers to use in their classrooms. She also donated gardening tools. The children will take a field trip to the nursery. Working together has brought expertise and additional resources into the classrooms and benefited both teachers and children. Susana reflects, "When I first started here, I had no experience in curriculum planning. I relish the ideas and the sharing among the teachers here and have learned a lot about curriculum and teaching from working together."

EDUCATION PLAN. Each child in the Washington County Head Start Program has an individualized **education plan** developed between the family and the teacher. During an early fall visit, the teacher makes a home visit to each child's family with the goal to develop the education plan for the school year (see Figure 9.2). Parents discuss what they

FIGURE 9.2
The Education Plan

The Teacher and Parent will develop an Individualized Education Plan for each child in the program. The Plan will describe educational goals for the child based on family goals as well as the results of comprehensive screening and assessment. It will form the basis for individualized educational activities throughout the year. The child's progress will be tracked and goals adjusted as circumstances change or goals are achieved.

For children starting in September or October, the Plan must be complete and in the child's file before the Winter break. For children starting after October, the Plan must be complete within 6 weeks of the child's first attendance. If this is the child's second year in the program, a new Education Plan should be written based on this year's Assessments.

One week prior to Ed Plan home visit send home *Parent IEP Questionnaire* to be filled out by parent. Be sure to have extra copies at the conference for parents who forgot. Just looking at the questions ahead of time helps get the parents thinking, even if they don't write anything down.

Children who were three on September 1st should have the Education Plan for Three Year Olds; children who were four on September 1st should have the Education Plan for Fours.

Assessment Tools to Take to the Education Plan Conference

Refer to Screenings and Assessments to identify the child's Strengths and Goals (Needs).

- Early Screening Inventory
- Health and Developmental Assessment
- Classroom and home visit observations
- Home Visit Plan and Record
- Oregon Assessment

Parent Involvement

As you review the *IEP Questionnaire,* invite parents to discuss what they hope their child will learn at Head Start. Be aware that parents have probably been conveying their goals all along, but in different words. (Example: "He has nobody to play with" is a way of saying, "I hope my child will make friends at Head Start.") The teacher can reflect the goals s/he believes the parent has been communicating rather than asking the intimidating question, "What are your goals?"

Writing and Goals

"What do we want the child to learn by the end of this school year?" Your goals for the child will relate mostly to the child's functioning in an educational environment. The family goals will be broader, looking at the child's functioning at home, in the neighborhood, and at school. Both are valuable.

Source: Community Action Organization Head Start. Reprinted by permission.

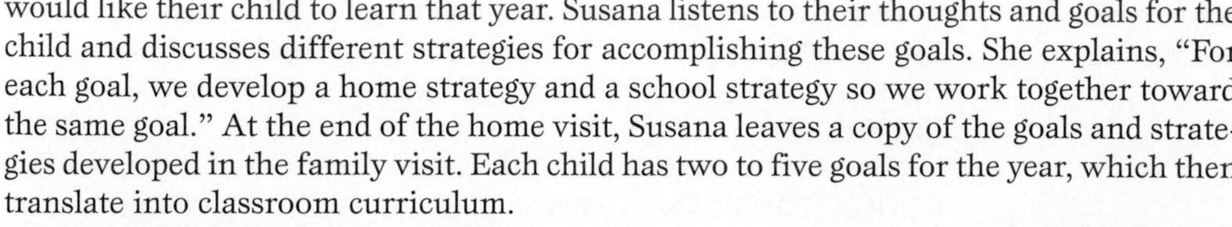

would like their child to learn that year. Susana listens to their thoughts and goals for the child and discusses different strategies for accomplishing these goals. She explains, "For each goal, we develop a home strategy and a school strategy so we work together toward the same goal." At the end of the home visit, Susana leaves a copy of the goals and strategies developed in the family visit. Each child has two to five goals for the year, which then translate into classroom curriculum.

For example, Manuel's parents expressed concern about his language development. "Manuel mostly uses two- or three-word phrases when he talks with us," they explain. "It seems like his brother was using more words when he was age 4." Susana assures them that Manuel's language is within the normal range of development for his age, but she agrees that focusing on this would be a good idea, especially through spontaneous play and conversational activities. Manuel's family and Susana developed a goal that would encourage Manuel to use four- and five-word phrases and respond back to him with full sentences. Each day, Susana plans time for Manuel to spend in an activity that encourages conversation, such as sharing about the calendar or events at home. She records his progress each week and shares this with Manuel's family (see Figure 9.3). His mother is also encouraging longer phrases and sentences in her interactions with Manuel. By learning what each family considers important for their child's learning, Susana finds, "I am able to plan curriculum that incorporates these individual education plans in our time at school."

INDIVIDUAL EDUCATIONAL PLANS AND CHILDREN WITH SPECIAL NEEDS. Individual educational plans assist students with special needs to receive appropriate education and services through Head Start. In Susana's classroom, three children were

FIGURE 9.3
Note Home to Manuel's Family

Dear Inez and Ramon:

Several times this week Manuel spoke in four or five word phrases! He was very interested in our gardening table. When I worked near him, I asked him to tell me about planting. He said, "Put lots of dirt here." You might want to talk about planting with him. He has some great ideas.

See you at our home visit next Thursday.

Susana

identified as having special needs as a result of the developmental screening in September. Julio is now participating in physical therapy to improve his motor skill development. The physical therapist comes to the classroom and works with Julio one morning each week and then meets once a month with Susana to discuss Julio's progress and ways to integrate physical therapy in his classroom activities. The speech and language therapist meets with two children in the classroom on a weekly basis. Her recommendations for the children are included in their individual education plans, so the families and Susana work together to meet the child's needs. The early childhood special education specialist is a consultant who works with the specialists and with teachers and families to develop and monitor individual family service plans (IFSP). These plans are developed to assist the child in improving in specific areas that were identified as needing special attention. In most cases, the goals in the IFSP are also included in the child's individual education plan.

ASSESSMENT OF PRESCHOOL CHILDREN. Susana finds the guidelines in the NAEYC publication, *Developmentally Appropriate Practice in Early Childhood Programs* (Bredekamp & Copple, 1997) to be a good resource for her to use in designing assessment of the children in her program. "When the family and I plan the educational goals for the year, we need some marker for where the child is now and a way to note the child's progress during the year. With children who are 4 years old, I wouldn't give tests all year to check their progress. I want to assess them in a way that is appropriate to their age and experiences here in the program and at home." The assessment that Susana finds the most useful is ongoing, purposeful, and helpful to her in adapting curriculum and teaching to meet the developmental and learning needs of the children (Bredekamp & Copple, 1997).

Susana finds that observations and interviews are the two most useful types of assessment with 4-year-olds. But before an observation, she plans the intent of her observation and develops a form to record key points. For example, a recent focus was on children's social interactions during choice time or outdoor play. Using a chart listing the names of her students, Susana recorded the type of activity a child was involved in and the role of the child in the social interaction. Sample questions she used for the focus included: Is the child a leader or a follower or does the child change from one to the other? Did the child share materials or equipment? Did the child resolve conflict if it arose? Did the child alternate between group play, partner play, and individual play? By keeping these questions in mind, she narrowed her focus during the observation, which made this a valuable observation rather than just "watching." Susana also stressed the importance of recording the information. "By the time the day ends, I easily forget exactly what I observed. And I find that the sheet with the class names helps me remember to observe each child."

Findings from the observations are helpful in looking at learning patterns of a child and noting growth or changes over a period of time. The observations are made in relation to the individual education plans developed by the family and Susana, and provide helpful information about the progress the child is making on the individual goals.

BILINGUAL CURRICULUM. Throughout the morning, Susana most often speaks in Spanish for instructional purposes and other times in English during conversations with the children. Most of her students' first language is Spanish. Susana's intent in using Spanish for instruction is to ensure that the children's learning is comprehensible, which requires use of the child's primary language. **Bilingual education** is interpreted differently by many educators. We will refer to bilingual education as the presentation of curriculum in two languages—the home or primary language of the child for acquisition of new knowledge and English for learning the dominant language. In this model of bilingual education, the teacher consciously organizes instruction so that the primary language is used for learning. The purpose of using the second language, English, is to promote second-language development. Susana has had her own experiences with learning a new language and culture as a child. She tells us, "I came to America from Peru when I was 14 years old. I did not know English and wanted to make new friends. I was so lonely. It is very important to me to find a way to honor the language the child speaks and also to help that child learn English so he or she can be successful in school. And for the children who primarily speak English, I think it's important for them to learn Spanish. Most of them have relatives who speak Spanish only. If these children learn Spanish, they can communicate with their grandparents and learn more about their heritage and culture. One language or culture should not be discarded for another. Both should be honored."

JOURNAL 9.3: Susana shared some of her struggles with learning English and living in a new culture. How might these experiences affect her belief about bilingualism and biculturalism in her classroom? ●

CULTURAL AND LINGUISTIC DIVERSITY. Susana's comments about bilingualism and biculturalism are similar to those made by the NAEYC in its position statement on linguistic and cultural diversity and by other prominent educators (Garcia, 2002) and sociologists. Garcia (2002) encourages early childhood educators to view cultural and linguistic diversity as an asset and a resource that children and their families bring to the school. Susana acknowledges and celebrates the cultural diversity of her students, while providing the educational experiences necessary to help prepare them for their future schooling.

One of Susana's professional development goals is to learn more about language development for children coming from a monolingual home. She wants to help Spanish-speaking parents understand the importance of communicating in the language in which they are strongest at home. She wants the children to have rich conversations with their families, which Susana feels occur more often when families, use the language in which they are most familiar.

To meet her goal of increased competence in bilingual education, Susana feels, "I need to take some courses and workshops about bilingual education in early childhood and supporting families to retain their primary language and culture. I have much to learn about current research and findings about best practices to support linguistic and cultural diversity." You appreciate Susana's interest in continuing her learning in this area and you know her students and their families will benefit from her drive to learn more. Later in this chapter, you will read about supporting linguistic and cultural diversity.

Families are such an important component of Head Start, as you will experience when going to Felipe's home with Susana.

HOME VISITS: CONNECTING HOME AND SCHOOL. Susana visits each family at their home five times a year. Every visit has a focus, as well as time to talk about the child's progress and any questions or concerns the family might raise. Home visits support the connection between home and school and improve communication. Figure 9.4 shows an overview of the home visits and parent/teacher conferences.

Prior to the visit, Susana calls the family to schedule a time to meet and to share the primary reason for the visit. "I want them to have time to think about the topic so we can share ideas during the discussion," she explains. The five topics for this year include:

- Orientation to the program, including completing any paperwork or forms
- Developing the educational plan
- Educational projects (includes projects that support the child's educational plan)
- Poster project (All about Me)
- Transition to kindergarten plan (reviews what the child has learned and goals to work on over the summer; the plan is sent to the kindergarten program)

Since you and Susana have an appointment with Felipe's family, it's time to leave. Today, the focus is making a poster about Felipe.

FIGURE 9.4

Education Home Visits and Parent/Teacher Conferences

Washington County Head Start
POLICY

Teacher home visits are the most effective way to produce changes in the child's long-term disposition toward learning. The parent who understands the school program and who sees the child as a learner is better equipped to advocate for the child, to seek out growthful experiences for the child, and to make sure the child gets to school. Home visits also enable us to reach out to the parent in a personal and supportive way, so we can build parent self-esteem and help families reach their goals.

Home Visits

Each enrolled family will be visited in their home by the lead teacher within two weeks of the child's first attendance. Families remaining in the program more than 3 months will have a second home visit. Families participating for more than 5 months will have a third home visit.

Home visits must be scheduled by the teacher two to seven days in advance of the visit. The Center Coordinator must be informed in advance of the home visit schedule of the teacher. The teacher uses the Parent Participation Record form to record the date, time, and content of the home visit. The parent initials this record.

Home visits cannot be conducted with daytime caregivers in lieu of parents. Caregivers may be included in home visits if the parent desires. It is acceptable to conduct home visits with another adult relative who lives with the child provided the parent who enrolled the child agrees.

Parent-Teacher Conferences

The teacher will meet with the parent(s) to review the child's status, needs, progress, and goals twice during the program year. Conferences are held at the center unless the parent needs to meet somewhere else (place of employment, home).

For children who enroll before Thanksgiving, the fall conference will be held before the Winter Holiday. For children enrolling later, the first conference will be held within 45 days of first attendance. The Individual Education Plan will be completed and approved by the parent at this conference. For children receiving Early Childhood Special Education services, the teacher should participate in the IFSP meeting in lieu of writing a separate Individual Education Plan. The teacher should assess the parent's need for support in preparing for the IFSP and serve as the parent's advocate.

The final conference is held upon withdrawal from the program or in May. The child's progress on Education Plan goals is reviewed and the parent and teacher write the Transition Plan, looking forward to the child's next educational placement.

Source: Community Action Organization Head Start. Reprinted by permission.

A Home Visit with Felipe's Family

This is Susana's fourth visit of the year to Felipe's home. She sent home a note to remind Felipe's family about materials they might want to have ready for the poster—perhaps photographs and ideas about favorite foods, friends, or places. Susana brings a basket of ribbons, glue, scissors, and fabric scraps for decorating the poster.

Felipe's Family

You drive with Susana and arrive at the apartment complex where Felipe lives with his mother, brother Antonio, and grandmother. Susana tells you, "Our conversation will be in Spanish if the grandmother is home. If she is not there, we will converse in English. Felipe's mother is fluent in both English and Spanish. I always ask the family the first time I meet them if we should talk in Spanish or English. It is most important for us to have a good discussion in the strongest language of the family." Felipe and Antonio are waiting outside the door. "Hello. Here we are." calls Felipe. Felipe's mother, Anna, is standing at the door. "Welcome and come inside, please," greets Anna. Anna shares, "My mother is at church, making projects for the upcoming church bazaar. She said to tell you hello and hopes to be here for our next home visit."

POSTER PROJECT: FOCUS ON FELIPE'S IDENTITY. After greetings are exchanged and Anna serves coffee, Susana starts unpacking her basket. "Well, everyone, I hope you will enjoy this project as much as I do," shares Susana. She pulls out a questionnaire to get the conversation about Felipe started. "Let's talk about Felipe's favorite things, and then he can make some pictures and glue them on the poster." Felipe says, "I like Street Sharks and dinosaurs. Can I start making them for the poster?" "Yes, go ahead and start drawing," responds Susana. "What about favorite foods?" "Oh, ice cream, always more ice cream." Susana writes Felipe's name at the top of the poster and leaves room for a photograph. She then writes *Favorite Food: Ice Cream* below his name. Felipe says, "Here are the Street Sharks." Susana writes *Favorite Toy: Street Sharks* on the poster. Susana asks Felipe if he and Antonio would like to make some ice-cream cones with the construction paper. "Sure, we can make different colors," replies Felipe.

They look at the photographs that Anna has on the table. Anna tells about Felipe as a toddler. "See him riding his truck with Antonio? He always loved to be moving." Felipe chooses that photograph to put on his poster, "Oh, I want the one with the truck and Antonio." Antonio asks, "Can I glue this on?" Felipe helps him use the glue stick and says, "You did a good job, Antonio." After adding his favorite color (red) and his favorite friend (Miguel), the poster is finished. Susana asks the family, "Doesn't this look wonderful? We will bring this to school for a few days to share. Felipe, you can tell your friends at school about the pictures on your poster. Then you will bring this home to keep."

ANNA'S JOB. With the poster project finished, Felipe and Antonio leave the table to play. Susana asks Anna to tell you about her job at Pine Hill Elementary School. "I am a teacher's assistant working with younger children and helping them with their reading and English. In first grade, many of the children learn to read in Spanish. Over half of the children speak Spanish as their first language. As they get older, more of their instruction and assignments are in English. I feel fortunate to be able to use my Spanish to help the children. School is important and they must learn as much as they can. Felipe will start kindergarten there next year. I am very proud of him." Anna has worked at the school for two years. She was divorced from Felipe's father several years ago. His father is involved in Felipe's Head Start program and assisted on the last field trip. Anna adds, "I want the best possible for my two sons. We will work hard together to help them do well in school."

ANNA'S HOPES FOR HER SONS: DEVELOPING IN TWO CULTURES AND LANGUAGES. Anna's work at the elementary school provides her with a larger view of the complexity of bilingualism and biculturalism. Being raised in a country different from where one's parents were raised and learning a new language different from the home language has both benefits and challenges for families. Anna shares her belief about preserving the family's Hispanic heritage: "Felipe was born here, but my parents are from Mexico. My mother lives with us and helps a lot with the boys. She does not speak much English, so it is good for Felipe and Antonio to talk with her in Spanish. I try to have them teach her some English, too. She helps me cook meals and watches the boys if I have errands or appointments. Sometimes I cook American-type food, while other times we might have tortillas, beans, and rice. I want the boys to learn about both cultures and languages."

Susana compliments Anna on her thoughtfulness in continuing the boys' culture. "It's important for them to learn about their heritage and customs in Mexico. You are doing a wonderful job teaching them about Hispanic ways while also preparing them for school."

PARENT INVOLVEMENT. Anna serves on the Policy Council at Head Start. She shares, "I learn a lot about schools at work that I can share with other parents. At Head Start, the parents work together with the teachers. I think it is important for parents to learn to be involved in their children's school. When we learn this at Head Start, then we can continue our involvement when our children start kindergarten in the public schools. Many Hispanic parents feel that they cannot go to the school because their English is not good enough or that they do not know enough to ask questions. At Head Start, we learn that we do have good questions and that our children learn better when we know what is going on at school."

You think about the long-term impact made by involving parents during the preschool years, and realize that Anna has shared some insightful knowledge. All parents need to feel welcome at schools, and learning this through Head Start involvement helps parents continue to interact with their children's schools.

JOURNAL 9.4: If you were the teacher in a program with children and their families speaking languages other than English, how might you encourage parents to become involved in their child's education and related activities? ●

SAYING GOOD-BYE. Susana notes the time. The visit was scheduled for one hour. First, Susana tells Felipe, "You have been working very hard in school—I want to share that with you and your family. And also to let everyone know how helpful you are with the other children. I know you always try to help others work out problems." Then Susana thanks Anna: "We appreciate your time with us this afternoon and your work on the Policy Council. You have a lot of important knowledge and insights to share with parents." Anna calls the boys over: "Let's say good-bye to teacher Susana and her guest." Felipe says, "Thank you for helping me make the pictures, teacher Susana." Antonio adds, "When I get bigger, can we make one for me, too?" Susana assures Antonio, "Yes, when you are 4 we will make your poster!"

Susana reminds Anna, "Our next home visit is in five weeks and we will talk about Felipe's transition to kindergarten. Please think of any questions you have and we can talk about those. Also, remember you can call me any afternoon." Anna shares, "I have been thinking about kindergarten, so I'm glad that's our next topic. Thank you, Susana." You also thank Felipe, Anna, and Antonio for the enjoyable and informative visit.

With this introduction to Felipe and his family's experience with Head Start, let's take a closer look at Head Start and other preschool programs.

What Is Head Start?

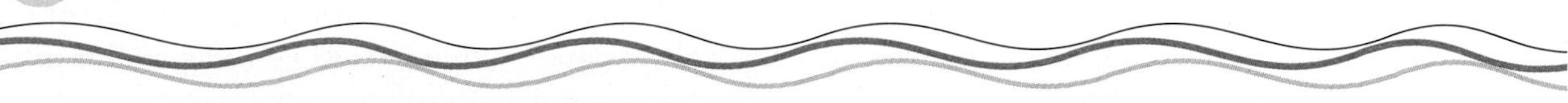

History of Head Start

Head Start was implemented in 1965 as a comprehensive program to help children from low-income families gain access to educational, social, and health services prior to entering kindergarten. It was viewed as a transition program to prepare children to be successful in their initial public school experience. In the memo shown in Figure 9.5, you can capture some of the excitement and energy behind the beginning of Head Start.

FIGURE 9.5
Project Head Start Memo

EXECUTIVE OFFICE OF THE PRESIDENT
WASHINGTON, D.C. 20506

OFFICE OF ECONOMIC
OPPORTUNITY

February 12, 1965

MEMORANDUM

TO: All CAP Staff

FROM: Jule Sugarman

SUBJECT: Project Head-Start

OEO will be announcing this weekend the initiation of Project Head-Start. This program is focused on providing federal assistance to communities for the establishment of child development programs during this coming summer. These programs will involve health, social services and educational activities for children who are to enter school in the fall. Tentatively, it is planned to finance these programs under Section 207 although there is a possibility that at least some of them will be financed under Section 205. Fiscal Year 1965 funds will be used. The summer program will no doubt lead to increased community interest in similar programs beginning in September.

A special staff is being assembled in Washington to handle Project Head-Start. It will be headed by Dr. Julius Richmond who is currently Dean of the Medical School at the State Medical College of New York (Syracuse). Ben Tryck is Administrative Officer for the group and should be the point of liaison for CAP personnel. Mrs. Lyndon Johnson will be honorary chairman of the national committee supporting the program.

Mr. Shriver is sending letters to community leaders throughout the nation which will call their attention to Project Head-Start. His letter will include a registration card which can be returned to OEO indicating that the community is interested.

Source: Memo from the Office of Economic Opportunity, Executive Office of the President, Washington, DC.

During the 1960s, there was a heightened awareness of the effects of children living in poverty on their later education and life success. As a nation, there was concern about these young children, which prompted development of a program to help break the cycle of failure. Head Start was part of the War on Poverty. Because the recipients were young children, it was supported by many legislators, including President Lyndon B. Johnson and much of the general public. Sargent Shriver was a chief supporter of Head Start, viewing it as an opportunity to support the victims of poverty—young children. Shriver had been discussing programs for young children with experts in the fields of medicine, child development, psychology, and education. Richard Boone, director of the Office of Economic Opportunity, made the suggestion that Shriver consider adding medical screening, nutrition components, and hiring of paraprofessionals (primarily parents of Head Start children) as one-fourth of the staff (Zigler & Muenchow, 1992).

In the summer of 1965, Head Start was launched as a national program under the direction of Dr. Julius Richmond, a pediatrician, and Jule Sugarman. Nearly half a million children enrolled in Head Start that first summer, receiving educational programs, medical and dental attention, social services, and nutritious meals. The program soon evolved into a nine-month program, continuing an emphasis on education, social services, and family involvement. Through the history and evolution of Head Start, there have been many program changes with much of the original philosophy in place. Head Start is considered the "nation's most successful educational and social experiment" (Zigler & Muenchow, 1992, p. 244).

Program Goals

Although changes have occurred in Head Start over the past 40 years, many of the current program goals are similar to those you would have seen in the early years of the program. The overall goal of Head Start is to provide comprehensive services that "foster healthy development in low-income children" leading to an increase in school readiness (U.S. Department of Health and Human Services, 2003a).

In each state and community, Head Start looks slightly different. Some programs find their community health or social services offer adequate resources for their families, and view the role of Head Start as helping families access existing services. Programs are allowed flexibility within the structure of federal guidelines, which enables local communities to develop programs to reflect their needs.

To meet the major program goals, assessment of activities and accomplishments within the areas of education, social services, and family involvement is required to determine if goals have been met. The next section looks at each of these areas and discusses how these components support the child and family.

EDUCATION: CURRICULUM FOR THE WHOLE CHILD. As you saw in Felipe's classroom, the school day includes activities to support learning in each developmental area. There is a commitment to developmentally appropriate curriculum in Head Start programs. Curriculum is planned to meet the current needs of 3- and 4-year-old children and to help children be successful in kindergarten and school in general. The curriculum includes lessons and activities that promote cognitive, social, emotional, and physical development. The goals from each child's individual education plan influence the curriculum. Attention in the curriculum is also given to the cultural background of the families in the program and of the larger community.

A parent volunteer works with four children as they cut and glue during choice time.

The curriculum that Susana developed includes many activities that encourage active play and social interactions. During the morning, children are involved in large group activities (circle time) and in small groups (choice and project time). She alternates activities that are teacher directed with activities that allow for more individual choice. Most 4-year-olds are beginning to be able to stay with an interesting project for an extended time period, so Susana plans some longer time blocks (45 minutes) for projects. Not only does this allow children to explore and create projects but it also helps them stay focused on an activity, which is a skill they will need in kindergarten the following year. Many of the activities that you saw in Felipe's class would be found in other preschool programs for 3- and 4-year-old children, as well.

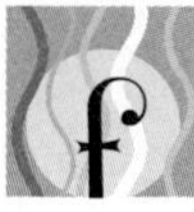

SOCIAL SERVICES AND RESOURCES FOR FAMILIES. Head Start programs are an important resource for many low-income families. Although families may have accessed different social services prior to their child's enrollment in Head Start, this is often the first time these services are coordinated, with assistance available to help strengthen the entire family. Figure 9.6 discusses some of the family services available at Felipe's Head Start program.

Through support of the entire family and their needs, a child is more likely to experience a healthier home environment, leading to improved learning. For example, in times

FIGURE 9.6
Family Services

Head Start believes that supporting a family's development also supports the child's development. Every center has staff who work with parents at home and in the center to solve problems and utilize resources identified through a family strengths assessment and plan. The program is using two models this year:

- The coordinated model which has a Family Service Specialist providing social services as assigned to approximately 60 families in one or two sites.
- The integrated model in which the Center Coordinator and Lead Teacher teach the class cooperatively and each provides social services and home visits to about 10 families.

Family Services Staff Can Help by:

Identifying strengths, needs, and interests.
Finding resources and services.
Working with parents in times of crisis.
Advocating with Welfare, Housing, Food Stamps and other agencies.
Providing assistance to parents seeking a GED, education or training.
Linking parents with employment programs.

Getting Ready for Head Start: Family Strengths Assessment

What are the strengths and challenges your family is facing today?
Do you feel safe and secure in your home?
Do you have access to health care for yourself and children?
Do you have enough food each month?

Source: Community Action Organization Head Start. Reprinted by permission.

of monetary crisis, Head Start staffs are able to refer parents to the appropriate agency to access food stamps, thus ensuring that the family is able to obtain food.

Medical and dental screenings and follow-up services are also provided through Head Start. Prior to enrollment, a child has a physical examination and must be current with immunizations. If parents are unable to pay for these services, Head Start will assist them in obtaining medical services, and, in some programs, Head Start will pay for necessary medical care.

Another social service focuses on nutrition. A nutrition assessment is conducted with each family. Children and their families receive nutritional counseling during the year, with specific outcomes established for each family based on the nutritional assessment. Children also eat two meals during their day at Head Start, which are planned to meet the federal guidelines for nutritional requirements.

FAMILY INVOLVEMENT. Each Head Start program offers various opportunities for family involvement. As you learned earlier, Felipe's mother, Anna, serves on the Policy Council, which works with Head Start administration to make program decisions. Other parent options include volunteering in or preparing materials for the classroom, attending parenting classes, helping on field trips or projects, and assisting in fund-raising activities or special events. In many programs, family events are planned throughout the year to encourage interactions between families.

Besides these activities, parents are involved in the program through their role in developing their child's education plan, and by participating in parent/teacher conferences and home visits. Family involvement is clearly a priority in all Head Start programs.

HEAD START AND PRESCHOOL. Head Start programs and preschool programs serve children of the same age—3- and 4-year-olds. Head Start was selected for this chapter in this book for several reasons. It is far more comprehensive than many preschool programs. Few preschools have the funding to support parental involvement and social services in the capacity that Head Start does. Highlighting Head Start in this chapter enables you to observe a broad, comprehensive program for children of preschool age. The curriculum of many preschool programs is similar to Felipe's program. Thus, you are gaining knowledge about quality programs for 3- and 4-year-olds while also learning about support services for children and their families associated with Head Start. A look at preschool programs and at some general commonalties between preschool and Head Start will help describe a variety of programs available for this age group.

Preschool Programs

Preschools of Yesterday and Today

Preschools were called *nursery schools* in the early 1900s. Rachel and Margaret McMillan are considered to be pioneers in education for young children. These sisters were concerned about the health and development of children in England and consequently established a "nurture school" in the slums of London in 1911. The program in these schools included preventive health care (bathing, dressing in clean clothes, nutritious meals, and rest) and outdoor play. The goal of these activities was to nurture the child and to address the needs of children living in poverty. Some of these same goals are seen in preschool and Head Start programs today.

THE BEGINNING OF PRESCHOOL: A BRIEF HISTORY. In the United States, Abigail Eliot began the nursery school movement in 1922. Eliot had worked in England with the McMillan sisters as they developed the first nursery schools. Many of the early nursery schools in the United States were connected to colleges or universities and were viewed as a rich setting for teacher preparation and research. Eliot emphasized the need for a program to be established at nursery schools, with activities planned each day as part of this program. A major interest of Eliot's was the involvement of parents in their child's education. Her background was in social work and she viewed the relationship between parents and children as an important component of nursery school programs. Many people attribute the focus on parental involvement in early childhood to this emphasis initiated by Abigail Eliot.

In the 1930s, during the Depression, a large number of public school teachers found themselves out of work. Under the Works Project Administration (WPA), unemployed teachers were hired to work in nursery schools. Because of government funding for these unemployed teachers, the number of nursery schools increased significantly. As the Depression ended and World War II began, federal funding was no longer available for the WPA nursery schools. Child care programs were developed during World War II for the children of mothers working in war-related industry through the Lanham Act.

At the end of World War II, government funding for child care programs stopped. Program support now came from tuition fees paid by families. In the early 1950s, parent-cooperative nursery schools began to spring up around the country. Cooperative nursery schools provided child care and education at reasonable costs, with parents involved in the school administration and the day-to-day running of the school. Because many nursery schools required tuition or time commitments from parents, nursery school education was primarily available for children from middle-class families. With this change, less emphasis was given to health care and the school day was shortened, often with 3-year-olds attending a program two mornings a week and 4-year-olds attending nursery school three mornings each week. Parent-cooperative preschools are still in existence today, as you saw when you visited the preschool in Chapter 3.

PRESCHOOLS OF TODAY. Parents looking for a preschool for their child have many different options available. Preschool programs are now part of the day at most child care centers and home care centers. The preschool portion of the day might be a half-day or full-day program. Parent-cooperative preschools are often half-day programs, several days per week, although some are on a full-day schedule. Another type of preschool program is connected to universities. These programs, which are often called *laboratory schools,* serve as a site for research and the study of child development and education. Some churches provide preschool programs, as well, with financial support subsidized by the church.

As you can see, there are many options for parents to examine as they select a preschool program for their child. Parents would want to observe at the preschool and discuss program goals, schedules, priorities, and family involvement with the program director and caregivers before making a decision about enrolling their child. The curriculum and day-to-day activities differ widely at these preschools.

PRESCHOOL CURRICULUM. Some preschools might focus on art, music, and movement, whereas others may have a strong academic focus. When selecting a preschool program, parents should be knowledgeable about early childhood education—for example, it would be important for parents to assure that the curriculum content is designed to be developmentally and individually appropriate. *Developmentally appropriate* includes age appropriateness (based on what is determined to be appropriate for this age group), and *individually appropriate* accounts for the staff's knowledge of individual needs and interests. Bredekamp and Copple (1997) describe components of a preschool program that is developmentally appropriate practice. Examples include:

- Daily opportunities exist for aesthetic expression in a variety of forms and media.
- Learning environment encourages children's initiative, exploration, and interactions with other children.
- Teachers bring child's home culture and language into the shared culture of the preschool.

- Children have opportunities to plan, think about, reflect on, and revisit their own experiences.
- Children have choices and options in their selection of learning experiences.

Preschool curriculum also includes experiences that promote learning in each area of development (i.e., physical, emotional, social, and cognitive). Remember how Susana plans for her students? She uses a format that reminds her to include each of these developmental areas throughout the morning. Susana also sets up centers around the room, and checks to make sure the centers include activities in each of the developmental areas, as well as encourage active engagement in learning and with other children.

Many preschool programs approach cognitive learning through inquiry and exploration. Rather than being told information or completing worksheets, preschoolers are experimenting and testing theories such as plant growth through a gardening center and later observation and discussion of these plants. This approach to learning enables children to construct their own understandings as they explore, interact, and actively engage in learning.

EARLY LITERACY. The International Reading Association and the National Association for the Education of Young Children (1998) developed a position statement on early literacy development that provides guidance to those who work with young children. Many educators view the position statements as standards for best practice. With preschool-aged children, experiences that support literacy learning would include the following:

- Print-rich environments with opportunities for children to see and use written language
- Adult reading of high-quality children's literature on a daily basis
- Experiences that encourage children to talk about books and focus on the sounds and parts of language as well as the meaning
- Activities that incorporate literacy tools, such as writing notes to each other or making signs for a building
- Experiences that expand the child's vocabulary, such as trips in the community and introduction to a variety of materials and resources

CREATIVE ARTS IN PRESCHOOL. The creative arts hold an important place in preschool curriculum, including drawing, painting, music, storytelling, and dramatic play. Preschoolers enjoy using novel materials to create projects. Miller (2003) recommends the following:

- Prepare materials so children have options and choices of open-ended projects.
- Arrange materials for easy access.
- Provide enough time for children to explore without rushing.
- Encourage children to initiate their own ideas.
- Express your own interest and enthusiasm for creative activities with the children.

Purposeful planning on the teacher's part enables children to be creative and experience the joy of discovery in the arts. Art is integral to life itself, and an integral component of early childhood curriculum (Althouse, Johnson, & Mitchell, 2003).

JOURNAL 9.5: Think of a creative art activity appropriate for preschool-aged children. Sketch a center to support this activity. What materials would you have available? What would be the purpose of the activity or learning gained by the preschool children? ●

MOVEMENT FOR PHYSICAL DEVELOPMENT. Play can enhance movement programs and provide children opportunities to develop physical skills. However, movement programs must be planned around the developmental needs of each child and the group as a whole. Including daily developmentally appropriate movement experiences has the potential to help children become physically active and healthy throughout their lives (Sanders, 2002). Young children who learn foundational motor skills (throwing, catching, kicking, skipping, running, etc.) are more likely to continue to participate in physical activities. The preschool curriculum should include time for choice of physical activities, as well as planning developmentally appropriate physical activities. Some educators might choose to use a checklist of motor skills to assist in curriculum planning, noting when specific skills might be used in a game or recess activity, and when it might be appropriate to plan an activity when the skill will be practiced.

TECHNOLOGY IN THE PRESCHOOL. In Felipe's classroom, there were two computers available for student use. Software that encouraged creativity through drawing and problem solving were the most frequently used programs. Susana had set up icons on the screen that connected with the project theme students were exploring. While studying plants, the children were able to click on a plant icon and select different programs that included drawing plants, arranging the order of the life cycles of plants, and simple problem solving with plants. When using the programs, the children were able to store and retrieve their work and return to the problem for further investigation. These programs help children move toward symbolic thinking and engage in more advanced problem solving, which are appropriate uses of technology with young children (Swaminathan & Wright, 2003).

Figure 9.7 presents several questions to assist a preschool teacher in setting up a computer center and considering best practices in use of the computer and software. For further information about supporting early childhood curriculum with technology, an excellent source is the Center for Best Practices in Early Childhood Education at Western Illinois University.

SIMILARITIES AND DIFFERENCES BETWEEN HEAD START AND OTHER PRESCHOOL PROGRAMS. It is difficult to make specific comparisons between Head Start and all other preschool programs. Head Start programs around the country differ from each other, as do preschool programs. There are several commonalties that most programs for 3- and 4-year-olds share, however. Most all Head Start and preschool programs include art, music, and movement activities. Play is another common aspect, as play provides for many enjoyable learning experiences appropriate for this age group. Listening to stories read by adults is another favorite activity of children this age.

FIGURE 9.7

Supporting Best Practices in the Preschool Classroom Computer Center

- Is your computer center accessible to all children and in a safe place for children to learn, with electrical cords out of the way of traffic?
- Are multiple child-sized chairs available for the children at the computer center to encourage cooperative learning, language, and social development?
- Is the computer monitor placed at an appropriate level so children do not have to strain to view the screen?
- Are children allowed to use the computer independently, with adults facilitating learning experiences?
- Are toys, games, or books related to the software located near the computer center to extend activities and provide for further exploration?
- Are classroom CD-ROMs easily accessible so children can make their own choices?
- Do you use *KidDesk* (Family Edition and/or Internet Safe) or another desktop management program to protect the hard drive and to allow children to safely and independently navigate through programs?

Source: Adapted from *Your Preschool Classroom Computer Center: How Does It Measure Up?* (Macomb, IL: Center for Best Practices in Early Childhood, Western Illinois University, 2001). Reprinted by permission.

The emphasis on beginning academics varies widely among preschools. Most preschools leave these skills for later years, although a few schools do begin teaching the alphabet and printing letters and numbers. In the move toward a developmentally appropriate curriculum, there is increased emphasis on creating a balance in cognitive, language, social, and emotional development, with free-play and project-based learning important parts of the curriculum.

As mentioned earlier, a major difference between preschools and Head Start is found in the support for families and access to social and health services. Head Start is highly regarded for its comprehensive program, which attends to social, educational, and family services in order to support the development of the whole child. Although some preschools have lists of community resources and local agencies, they typically have less connection to social services as in Head Start programs.

Research conducted on Head Start programs has provided a wealth of information about best practices in early childhood education. Two critical learnings gained from Head Start experiences are the importance of involving parents in the child's education and the need for the preschool curriculum to address individual education plans. Incorporating these two program components as goals of any preschool program strengthen the overall program, regardless of the family income level. The knowledge gained from studying Head Start programs has been disseminated to early childhood educators, which has led to benefits in other programs for young children and their families. A priority of both Head Start and high-quality preschool programs is the importance of qualified and prepared staff. Although there are guidelines established in each state and by the NAEYC, some programs might adapt these requirements to meet local needs, such as staff having competence in the home language of the children in the program.

Preschool Staff

Staffing patterns vary from program to program, often based on the number of children enrolled. According to standards, in 2003, at least half of the Head Start teachers are to hold an associate, baccalaureate, or advanced degree in early childhood. Another option is to hold a child development associate (CDA) credential. The CDA credential means an individual has documented his or her training and experience in the early childhood profession and has met established criteria.

To meet these requirements, some programs developed flexible learning options to enable current teacher assistants to receive their associate degree. Sixteen tribal colleges have partnered with American Indian Programs Branch of the Head Start Bureau to develop early childhood associate degree programs for Head Start teachers and staff. Nearly 400 students were to graduate from the tribal college Head Start programs by 2004. This program has had a positive impact on the local communities and the future of these tribes (Wesit, 2002).

Three positions are common at most preschool programs: program director, teacher, and teacher assistant. In Head Start Programs, federal guidelines require additional positions, mainly to support families and ensure all educational, social, and health needs of the child and family are met. In many centers, parents are hired in paraprofessional roles.

PROGRAM DIRECTOR. The program director assumes responsibility for administration of the program. She has training or experience in administration and is responsible for administrative decisions. For example, when a staff position is open, the program director would work with an advisory group to conduct interviews and make a decision about hiring new staff. If the program director is an early childhood specialist, she would likely assume the role of directing the educational component of the program.

TEACHER. Since you spent time talking with and observing Susana, you are aware of her professional responsibilities. She plans and carries out the curriculum, makes home visits, conducts parent/teacher conferences, and records the progress and development of the children. Teachers are expected to hold a degree in early childhood education or child development, or have extensive experience or training that qualifies them for the position of teacher.

TEACHER ASSISTANT. Teacher assistants work under the direct supervision of the teacher and usually have a high school diploma or equivalent, experience working with young children, and some training in early childhood. The teacher assistant works closely with the teacher, children, and families. Rita is familiar with Susana's curriculum and her guidance procedures and follows these in her interactions with the children.

Quality of and access to preschool and Head Start programs are current issues and concerns at the local, state, and national levels.

Current Issues in Preschool and Head Start Programs

Many of the issues and trends in preschools and Head Start relate to the need for high-quality programs. Research has provided evidence that high-quality preschool programs "contribute to children's readiness to enter school and remain on grade" (Schweinhart, 2001).

HIGH-QUALITY PRESCHOOL. How does one determine if a preschool program is of high quality? Currently, fewer than half of the programs in early education earn a "good" or "high" rating (Espinosa, 2002). The quality of early education and care has a significant influence on a child's social and academic development, and children at risk for school failure are more strongly influenced by the quality of their preschool (Espinosa, 2002). With these findings in mind, it is apparent that not only the program, but the quality of the program impacts a child.

What are the recommendations to create preschool programs that are considered to be of high quality? Espinosa (2002) makes the following five policy recommendations:

1. Develop state standards that address preschool teacher qualifications, group size, and class ratios. The National Association for the Education of Young Children has created standards for preschool programs that can be adopted at state levels and provide the framework and expectations for quality programs.
2. Improve teacher salaries and benefits to the levels of comparably qualified K–12 teachers. Many preschool teachers make approximately one-half of the salary that a public school teacher earns per year. Quality programs require quality staff, and improving salaries for preschool teachers is an issue that requires attention.
3. Develop measures of early educational quality that include recent research findings on early literacy, mathematical, scientific, and social-emotional learning. With a wealth of research in early childhood education available, it is critical for program developers to review the research and literature and to implement program curriculum built on this knowledge base.
4. Provide continuous education and improvement efforts for preschool teachers and programs. Related to efforts to implement program curriculum and components based on research findings is the need to provide professional development opportunities for preschool teachers and other professionals involved in early childhood education. Dissemination through training and workshops will enable those in the field to make changes consistent with the current knowledge base in early childhood education.
5. Collaborate at the federal, state, and local levels to establish a coordinated system of high-quality education and care for all 3- and 4-year-olds. Rather than independent efforts to improve programs, a coordinated effort (of both program design and financial aspects) will lead to a stronger and more consistent system for change.

Head Start programs are designed to be of high quality and to meet federal program standards. Currently, there are changes to the program requirements that impact Head Start Programs.

CHANGES IN HEAD START. Following the 1998 reauthorization of Head Start, Congress mandated that Head Start programs implement standards leading to increased attention in the Head Start curriculum to early literacy, numeracy, and language. All Head Start programs must comply with the Program Performance Standards, which are designed to ensure that Head Start goals and objectives are implemented and that all programs and agencies provide the highest quality services (U.S. Department of Health & Human Services, 2003a). The Head Start Bureau worked with early childhood experts to develop assessment formats, resulting in the Head Start Child Outcomes Framework. Children are assessed three times a year on the mandated items, as well as other areas that the program determines. Each program then utilizes this data to make continual improvements in their program (U.S. Department of Health and Human Services, 2003a).

EARLY HEAD START FOR INFANTS AND TODDLERS. When you read about infant development and infant care programs in Chapter 7, you were presented with current research about infant brain growth and the need for stimulation in the early years, particularly from birth to age 3. Early Head Start was established under the Head Start Act Amendments of 1994, with the purpose of expanding the benefits of early childhood development to low-income families with infants and toddlers, and to pregnant woman. This program draws from the research findings that early intervention through high-quality programs can enhance a child's social, physical, emotional, and cognitive development; assist parents to be better caregivers; and help parents reach their own goals, including further education and economic independence (U.S. Department of Health and Human Services, 1999).

Early Head Start must also met Head Start Performance Standards by providing early, individualized child development and parent education services through a combination of home visits and experiences in other settings, such as family or center care. An important goal of Early Head Start is to connect families with other services available in the local community to access health care, nutritional assistance, and social services. In 2002, more than 62,000 children under the age of 3 were served through Early Head Start Programs (U.S. Department of Health and Human Services, 2003a).

RESEARCH AND EVALUATION OF PROGRAMS FOR PRESCHOOL CHILDREN. Early research focused on evaluating the effects of Head Start on children and their learning. There was an eagerness to predict that Head Start would significantly affect a child's development. The early research looked for intellectual gains, as measured by IQ increases. After conflicting findings and concern that intelligence was a narrow measure of gains from participating in Head Start programs, the research agenda shifted to a more qualitative or holistic view of Head Start's benefits (Zigler, Styfco, & Gilman, 1993).

A major research project began in 1997, called the Head Start Family and Child Experiences Study. Early findings report that from the 3,200 children studied, Head Start classroom quality is good; Head Start children are acquiring early literacy, numeracy, and social skills; and program quality is connected to children's performance (U.S. Department of Health and Human Services, 2000). This longitudinal study will be continued for several years. At the same time, the study group is piloting new approaches to measure and collect data in Head Start programs.

Demonstration projects, where successful programs disseminate information about their program, would help other programs that are struggling with quality issues. Observing "best practices" in a classroom of children is a format that would assist other teachers in learning about curriculum and instruction. There is much to learn through research on different components of preschool programs. Dissemination of these findings will help early childhood programs make improvements based on research findings.

Another important issue in preschool programs is the need to develop responsive environments to support the rapidly increasing number of culturally and linguistically diverse children and families.

Supporting Cultural and Linguistic Diversity

The term *cultural diversity* refers to the unique collection of beliefs, practices, traditions, and worldviews that characterize a particular group of people (Trawick-Smith, 2003), with respect toward the variances represented by different cultures. Linguistic diversity, or language minority students, are children who participate in a non-English-speaking environment and are exposed to an English-speaking environment in the school setting (Garcia, 2002). In the broader picture, children and their families may be considered linguistically or culturally diverse although they speak English. For example, a child might be a third-generation member of a family speaking English, yet "maintain the dominant accent of [his or her] heritage language" (NAEYC, 1996a, p. 7), or cultural values, beliefs, or customs. As the number of young children who are culturally and linguistically diverse increases, early childhood educators are attempting to meet the challenge of providing programs to meet the needs of these children and their families.

Cultural Diversity of Young Children

The demographics of the population making up the United States is changing rapidly. Children in early childhood programs today represent different cultural and linguistic backgrounds than the children of 10 years ago and the children you will be working with in the future. Predictions of the number of children from culturally and linguistically diverse homes is expected to increase through the next two decades. As Table 9.1 shows, the number of non-White and Hispanic children will increase and the percentage of White children enrolled in schools will decrease. In fact, in six states and most large cities, the number of non-Hispanic Whites in the public schools are now in the minority (NCES, 2003). This is called the *minority majority*. These changing demographics present important data to early childhood educators, who are attempting to learn what is involved in becoming responsive educators for children from diverse cultures. Let's look at teaching strategies and practices, as well as basic understandings, that support culturally and linguistically diverse children.

TABLE 9.1 Number and Percentage Distribution of Children under Age 18 by Race/Ethnicity: 1990, 2000, and Projected 2020

	Percentage Distribution			Percent Change	Percent Change
Race/Ethnicity	**1990**	**2000**	**2020**	**1990 to 2000**	**2000 to 2020**
Total	100	100	100	10	10
White/non-Hispanic	69	64	55	2	−5
Black/non-Hispanic	15	15	14	8	6
Hispanic	12	16	23	43	58
Asian/Pacific Islander	3	4	6	48	60
American Indian/Alaska Native	1	1	1	7	8

Note: Detail may not add to totals due to rounding.

Source: U.S. Department of Commerce, Bureau of Census, *Statistical Abstract of the United States: 2000*, based on Population Estimates Program.

Creating an Environment Responsive to Diversity

In the past, the quickest route to success for immigrants arriving in the United States was to learn basic English and fit in with the dominant culture. High levels of English were not needed to earn a living. This is no longer the dominant view in education. Development of language is closely connected to cognitive development. Learning in the first language helps a young child gain knowledge (NAEYC, 1996a) more than attempting to learn the same knowledge in a language in which the child has little comprehension. NAEYC's recommendations for early childhood education for cultural and linguistic diversity include the following:

- Recognize that all children are cognitively, linguistically, and emotionally connected to the language and culture of their home.
- Acknowledge that children can demonstrate their knowledge and capabilities in many ways.
- Understand that without comprehensible input, second-language learning can be difficult.

These recommendations help create a learning environment that supports continued growth in the child's first language as she learns English, while also supporting and honoring the language and culture in her home (see Box 9.1).

BILINGUALISM. Learning a new language (English) while continuing to develop the home language (also called the *first* or *primary* language) can create the gift of **bilingualism.** Educators are cautioned to use the term *bilingualism* judiciously. Students whose first language is strong, but who are still catching up to native speakers in English, are not yet fully bilingual. That is, although the child may begin to appear fluent, educators cannot assume that this child can be taught in English without extra support (Reer, 2004).

When Susana presents new information, she speaks in Spanish to assist children in gaining new knowledge in their home language. She wants the children to learn new concepts in their primary language, rather than learn new language and new concepts at the

BOX 9.1

What Are Some Practices Implemented in Culturally Responsive Communities?

The literature in teacher education has examined different teaching practices that contribute to student learning. These educational practices are often termed *effective instructional or teaching strategies* (Freiburg & Driscoll, 2000). Many of these strategies are also effective for learners in culturally and linguistically diverse classrooms. Villegas (1991) adds to the list of effective teaching strategies by emphasizing that effectiveness in these settings is "defined primarily by the ability to create meaningful classroom activities that take into account students' background experiences" (p. 18). The students' background experiences reflect their cultural experiences. Acknowledgment and incorporation of these experiences into the child's curriculum and instruction in the classroom helps students bridge the cultural gap between home and school.

Garcia (2002) recommends that teachers implement the following practices to create a culturally responsive learning community:

1. Bilingual/bicultural knowledge
2. High expectations of diverse students
3. Diversity viewed as an asset
4. Ongoing professional development on issues of cultural and linguistic diversity that address both instructional and curriculum development

Susana is reading in Spanish, the first language of these three children.

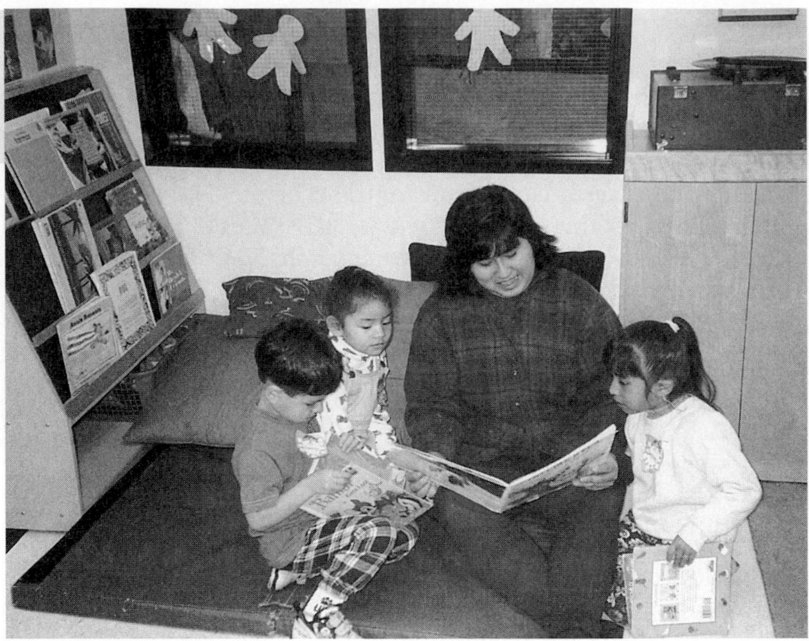

same time. Susana's active encouragement of families to continue speaking Spanish with their young children supports the cognitive development of the children. The continued use of the primary language at home also facilitates the family's ability to communicate with each other.

JOURNAL 9.6: Describe an activity that might be done at home with a 4-year-old child to reinforce learning in the first or home language.

The continued presence of both languages in this Head Start classroom promotes learning in the primary language and retention of the primary language while learning a second language. Susana's teaching follows recommendations made by Krashen (1996):

1. Comprehensible input is provided in English, as long as students understand the subject matter (often music, art, or physical education) when it is presented in English (the second language).
2. New subject matter is taught in primary or first language, without translation.
3. Literacy development is presented in the first language.

All written material in Felipe's classroom is displayed in Spanish and in English. For example, the job chart is written in Spanish, with English "subtitles" listed below each job. Developing literacy in the first language facilitates literacy development in a second language (Krashen, 1999). Students progress more quickly in learning to read when they do not make continual translations to understand written material.

Wong Fillmore and Snow (2002) raise concerns about possible problems that might occur when the expectation is that all children are to use the school's language (English), even in their early transition into the school setting. If the home language is not English, the message conveyed to children and parents is that their home language has little role or value in the school. The process of socialization into the school culture can be made more positive when a teacher respects the students' home languages and cultures, and acknowledges the critical role these play in the lives of the child and family.

It becomes more complicated when several different home or first languages are spoken by children in the classroom and the teacher does not speak these languages. Recommendations for a multilingual situation include:

- Learn to speak several words in each of the children's home language.
- Group children who speak the same language together at least once each day to help them continue language development.
- Arrange for an interpreter to assist in parent conferences and home visits.
- Include books, music, and games representative of each child's cultural heritage in the classroom.

In addition to these recommendations, educators who incorporate project-based learning (such as the projects around the theme of spring in Felipe's classroom) and cooperative learning (students working together in small groups) are building an environment that supports cultural and linguistic diversity. Children have opportunities to work together, share ideas, talk with each other, and learn to cooperate with others.

VALUING CULTURAL DIVERSITY. Creating a learning environment responsive to cultural and linguistic diversity is an important goal and challenge for each early childhood professional. Preserving and continuing the child's first or home language and culture while learning English and the "school culture" supports an environment that honors and respects each child and family as well as helps the child develop to his fullest potential. Garcia (1997) challenges early childhood educators to

> care about and be an advocate for our linguistically and culturally diverse children and families by nurturing, celebrating, and challenging them. They do not need our pity or remorse for what they do not have; they, like any individual and family, require our respect and the use of what they bring as a resource. (p. 13)

As our classrooms and centers become increasingly diverse, it is nearly impossible to be knowledgeable about each cultural group and its beliefs and attitudes about child development, education, and parenting. Although we may know about several different aspects or beliefs within a cultural group, there is great variation among individual beliefs within any group. Those who work with young children can learn from listening to parents and sharing personal perspectives as we come to understand our individual families' goals for their children. Involving families is critical to the educational success of all children. Early childhood educators must find ways to support family involvement (Lundgren & Morrison, 2003). Possibilities include asking families to share photographs, music, traditions, or family activities with the other children. Considering these suggestions and the importance of honoring each of our families and their cultures enables us to honor the diversity of our communities.

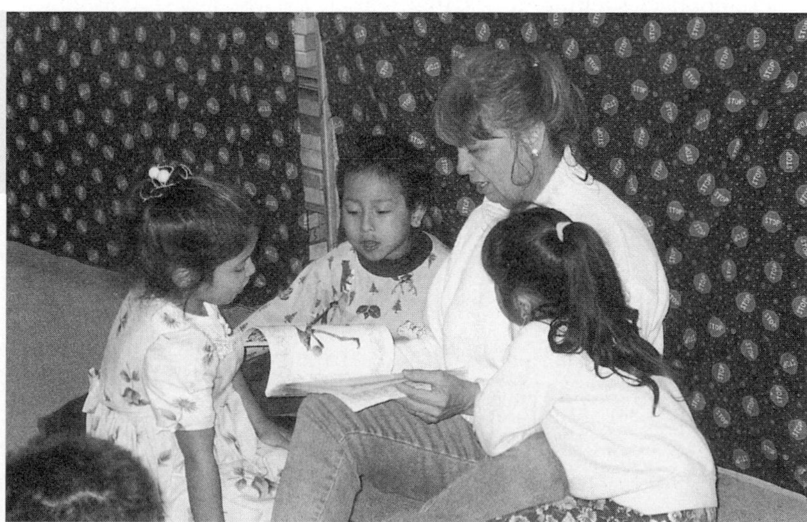

Children share their thoughts about the story, recognizing their ideas are valued by Carolyne.

PRINCIPLES AND INSIGHTS: A Summary and Review

Your visit to Felipe's Head Start program highlighted Head Start's focus on children and families. You saw children and several parents arriving on the bus together. The children went to their classrooms, while the parents headed for the adult education classroom or volunteered at the center. Through education, social services, and other family services, the child and family are supported in their development.

Your morning proved to be a busy one. Children were involved in projects, interactions, and activities that encouraged their learning in each developmental area. Felipe and the other children in Susana's class worked on several different activities related to the topic of spring, through art, music, listening to stories, expressing ideas, and connecting clothing and weather to spring. You observed many activities you might see in other preschool programs.

Felipe's mother, Anna, serves on the Policy Council. His father often goes on field trips with the class. All parents participate in home visits and parent/teacher conferences, along with establishing educational goals for their child. Families are an integral component of the program, with the belief that helping the family is helping the child.

Susana is aware of the challenges of working with children speaking languages other than English. One of her priorities in teaching is to help parents understand the importance of bilingualism and biculturalism. Susana discusses the importance of maintaining the child's home language with families. She also follows specific recommendations for creating a responsive environment for culturally and linguistically diverse children, communicating her respect for and appreciation of the richness children bring to the classroom.

Changes are needed in preschool and Head Start programs. Some of these changes include increasing staff salaries, making curricular changes that reflect developmentally appropriate practices and responsiveness to cultural and linguistic diversity, acknowledging and adapting to needs of families, and ensuring quality in all programs. Research and evaluation of existing programs provide data to make improvements that promote successful early childhood practices.

By observing Felipe in his Head Start program and meeting with his family and teacher, you had the opportunity to see why this program is considered the nation's greatest educational experiment (Zigler & Muenchow, 1992). The mission of Washington County Head Start (Figure 9.8) does, indeed, provide a framework for the holistic emphasis of education, social services, and family involvement woven together to create a quality program for preschool-aged children.

FIGURE 9.8

Washington County Head Start Mission Statement

Our Mission:

We will provide developmentally appropriate education and care for

children,

involve and support

parents,

and offer early childhood services that meet

family needs.

Source: Community Action Organization Head Start. Reprinted by permission.

BECOMING AN EARLY CHILDHOOD PROFESSIONAL

Your Professional Portfolio

1. After observing a preschool, draw a diagram of the setting. What types of activities occur in different areas of the room? How is the space designed to encourage children to take initiative in projects and activities (e.g., sinks and faucets at a child's level for independent use). Label the areas, furniture, and fixtures in the room and place the diagram in your portfolio.

2. In Felipe's program, you observed his involvement in a project about springtime. If you were teaching 4-year-olds, what project might you like to incorporate into the curriculum? Develop your project idea in an outline form, including some major themes and resources you would want to make available for the children.

Your Professional Library

Beaty, J. (2004). *Skills for preschool teachers.* Upper Saddle River, NJ: Pearson Education.

Davies, B. (2003). *Frogs and snails and feminist tales: Preschool children and gender.* Cresskill, NJ: Hampton Press.

Garcia, E. (2002). *Student cultural diversity* (3rd ed.). Boston: Houghton Mifflin.

Hildebrand, V., Phenice, L., Gray, M., & Hines, R. (2000). *Knowing and serving diverse families.* Upper Saddle River, NJ: Prentice-Hall.

Taylor, B. (2005). *A child goes forth: A curriculum guide for preschool children.* Upper Saddle River, NJ: Merrill/Prentice-Hall.

U.S. Department of Education and U.S. Department of Health and Human Services, Early Childhood-Head Start Task Force. (2002). *Teaching our youngest.* Washington, DC: Author.

CHAPTER 10

Kindergarten

Keeley's Story

CHAPTER focus:

When you finish reading and reflecting on this chapter, you will be able to:

1. Describe the curriculum in a developmentally appropriate kindergarten program.
2. Summarize a philosophy of classroom management for kindergarten-aged children.
3. Justify the appropriate use of technology with young children.
4. Discuss the content of and need for after-school care programs.

Keeley and her mother, Kerry, live in a rented house that needs paint, but is brightened with flowers, a birdhouse, and decorations made by Keeley. Keeley is waiting on the porch. She opens the front door as Kerry welcomes you and shows you a project the two of them have been working on recently. On the kitchen table are some clay figures waiting to dry. Keeley is anxious to show you around the house, so you begin her tour.

Visiting Keeley

The rooms in Keeley and Kerry's home are comfortably furnished with lots of evidence of Keeley's activities. In the kitchen is an easel with paints. A large dollhouse is in the dining room. It's definitely their home and Keeley shares some housekeeping chores. "I empty the little trash cans," she tells you proudly. "And I set the table," she adds. Kerry and Keeley plan menus for the week each Sunday, and often cook ahead for lunchboxes and dinners.

In spite of working long hours at her job, Kerry spends a large amount of quality time with Keeley. They read for hours, have tea parties, and plant a garden. Every year, Keeley plants sunflower seeds and cares for the plants. Kerry tells the story of their first sunflower garden: "The plants had grown to a height of 4 feet—they towered above Keeley and she loved them. Every day she would water them. One morning, we saw that someone had cut most of the sunflowers down. Keeley was devastated. We both cried and made plans to paint a giant sign for the garden. The sign read 'ME AND MY MOMMY LOVE THESE SUNFLOWERS. PLEASE DON'T TAKE ANY MORE. KEELEY.' "

Kerry has dedicated herself to raising Keeley. She faces many struggles as a single parent but is mindful of providing a wonderful, rich home and childhood for Keeley.

Selecting Kindergarten: One Parent's View

When it came time for kindergarten, Kerry sought advice from the early childhood staff at the preschool that Keeley attended. They recommended a neighborhood public elementary school, Eliot School, which has a high level of parent involvement and a focus on the arts. Kerry and Keeley visited the school and the kindergarten classrooms and both felt enthusiastic about what they observed. "It felt right—we both knew it was the place for Keeley," says Kerry.

By September and the start of kindergarten, Keeley could read a number of her books and frequently wrote notes to others. She approached Eliot School with great enthusiasm. Like many parents at Keeley's school, Kerry volunteers two days each month. She takes these afternoons off from her job and works at night to make up the hours. She is determined to be involved in Keeley's school. "I want her to be successful in school—she is so smart."

In kindergarten, Keeley has made new friends easily, is invited to other children's homes, and loves to invite others to her home. Her best friend Daniella often spends the night. Both girls go to the after-school program at Eliot School. When Kerry or Oma (Keeley's grandmother) pick Keeley up at 5:30 P.M., they often find her listening to a story with a small group of friends, playing a game, or drawing with markers. She is content, hungry, and ready to be with her family. She signs herself out, and skips to the car.

Learning about Keeley, her prior school experiences, and her family helps you understand why Kerry selected the kindergarten program she did for Keeley. Kerry knew that a nearby school was noted for a strong academic program. When she visited this school, she observed children sitting at their desks and spending blocks of time on worksheets. It was often quiet in the classroom, which seemed odd to Kerry after her experiences with the busy atmosphere in Keeley's preschool.

Although Kerry wanted Keeley to learn all she could, she sensed that the classroom atmosphere affected how a kindergarten child experienced learning. Kerry discussed learning environments with her family and with the preschool teachers and felt confident that Eliot School's kindergarten was the right choice for Keeley. The kindergarten teachers were committed to providing a curriculum based on the learning needs of 5-year-olds within a developmentally appropriate curriculum. In fact, on the day that Keeley and Kerry visited Eliot's kindergarten, they observed the children in water play with bubbles, building structures with blocks, and engaged in different choice activities.

Soon you will have the opportunity to observe this kindergarten and meet the school principal and teacher. As you visit, think about the difference between a classroom where children are expected to work while sitting at their desks in quiet concentration and a classroom where children are moving about, talking, exploring, and engaged in active learning.

Kindergarten: Its Position in the School System

Kindergarten is placed in a unique position within the schooling system. Children entering kindergarten typically have had preschool experience and will move to more formal schooling the year following kindergarten. This places kindergarten in between preschool and the primary grades. Is it the bridge between preschool and first grade? Should kindergarten be more like preschool or more like the primary grades? Or can kindergarten be a special experience that helps young children learn social and beginning academic skills?

Kerry faced these questions as she selected a kindergarten program for Keeley. When she visited the kindergarten at Eliot School, she saw children painting, reading, working on computers, building with blocks, and making snacks. In the second kindergarten program Kerry visited, the children were also busy, but were working at their desks in workbooks. Children were writing letters of the alphabet and drawing pictures of objects that began with that alphabet letter. Kerry noticed painting easels in the room, a reading corner with books at a table, and blocks on the rug. She learned that these activities were available after children finished their work. Kerry thought, "It seems like the activities that children this age should be involved in are available only after a child finishes work. This seems strange, because the real work and learning is with painting, blocks, and books." Kerry did, indeed, encounter the controversy of defining what makes a good kindergarten.

From the earliest beginnings of public kindergarten, these questions and controversies have been discussed and debated by early childhood educators, parents, and the general public. Keeley's teacher, Jim, addresses some of these questions as he describes the kindergarten program and his philosophy of appropriate curriculum for 5-year-olds. You will meet him soon.

The term **kindergarten** is derived from the German translation meaning *children's garden.* Visualizing a children's garden brings to mind many bright colors and a cheerful environment. What do you visualize when you think of a children's garden? We'll explore a kindergarten where the teacher has developed a program that is considered developmentally appropriate for 5- and 6-year-olds. **Developmentally appropriate curriculum** is built around knowledge of child development and learning in conjunction with knowledge of individual children's variations, needs, and interests (Bredekamp & Copple, 1997). Table 10.1 lists developmental highlights of kindergarten-aged children, while recognizing that each child progresses at her own rate. You will be observing examples of each developmental highlight in Keeley's kindergarten.

The program you are about to visit includes many components that support and nourish growing children, similar to the care of a special garden. In Keeley's kindergarten, you will see children engaged in a wide variety of play activities while gaining knowledge and skills. You will also notice a strong focus on technology in this classroom. The children are computer literate and spend time each day accessing the Internet and checking features on their website. You might wonder: Is it appropriate for children this young to spend time on computers? This question is a focus of discussion and some controversy. Keep the question about technology in mind as you observe the children and teacher in the kindergarten at Eliot School.

TABLE 10.1 Developmental Highlights in 5- and 6-Year-Old Children

Cognitive	Social	Emotional	Physical
Beginning organization patterns *Example:* Patterning (such as the calendar patterns)	Playing/interacting with a group of children for increasing time periods *Example:* Planning for and playing a game during a 15- to 20-minute time period	Expressing feelings in words *Example:* Telling another child "I was sad when you were sick"	Refining use of large muscles *Example:* Running, hopping, beginning to skip, and throwing and catching a ball
Connecting symbols to representations *Example:* The numeral 3 refers to an amount of 3 objects	Having a "special" friend, although these may change suddenly and/or frequently *Example:* Sharing a computer program each day with one friend, then tiring of the program and shifting to another special friend interested in building blocks	Learning to interpret emotional expressions of others *Example:* Consoling a friend who feels sad or upset	Using small muscles *Example:* Painting, drawing, cutting with scissors, and printing letters/numerals

Kindergarten at Eliot School

Driving up to Eliot School, you notice that the school is located in a residential/business area. Although there are houses and trees lining the nearby streets, the school is a block away from a busy intersection. Eliot School is located in a 40-year-old brick building. Currently, 542 students are attending the school in kindergarten through fifth grade. Approximately half of the school population resides in the school boundary; the other half of the students applied to the school because of the emphasis on fine arts. This school is part of an urban school district and designated as an "arts magnet school." You will learn more about the fine arts program when you meet the principal.

After checking in at the office, you pick up your name badge, identifying you as a visitor. The principal greets you and invites you into her office.

Visiting the Principal

Pam Bradley has been principal at Eliot School for six years. She tells you, "I feel fortunate to be working with such an active volunteer group of parents and community members. Last year, they helped with performances, art projects, working with students in reading, and numerous other activities. This is impressive, considering the large number of working families in our school." Most of the volunteers are parents, but others are artists from the community.

Eliot School's Magnet Arts Program. You ask Pam about the arts program as a context for the kindergarten program. She is delighted to talk about this topic. "Right now, we have three full-time and one half-time art specialists at Eliot School. These specialists represent dance, drama, visual arts, and music, which supports our focus as an arts magnet school. She continues, "Children from kindergarten through fifth grade participate in each of these arts. The schedule is set up to allow students to participate in two art programs each semester. This is in addition to their regular curriculum." Sounds like a busy schedule, but one that certainly offers rich learning opportunities!

The purpose of your visit is to learn about the kindergarten program and the context of kindergarten within the larger school setting. You are curious about gathering more information about kindergarten at Eliot School.

Kindergarten Curriculum. Kindergarten programs reflect differences in philosophies and practice. When you ask Pam how the kindergarten curriculum is established in this district, she responds, "Most of our school curriculum is guided by state standards and the curriculum set by the Department of Education. Within this framework, kindergarten teachers develop programs to meet the needs of our students."

Pam confides, "I think there is much more pressure to include academics in kindergarten now than 5 to 10 years ago." Her advice to you is to educate parents about the importance of providing appropriate education for young children, which includes play and exploratory activities. "Let parents know that play and learning can be synonymous in a rich early childhood environment. This helps them understand the rationale of our kindergarten curriculum." This education process is part of Pam's job as well as that of the kindergarten teacher.

Qualities of Kindergarten Teachers. The teacher is ultimately responsible for the learning and activities in her classroom. You ask Pam what she looks for when she hires a kindergarten teacher. Her response to your question about qualities of a good kindergarten teacher is enlightening: "I look for someone who genuinely enjoys children and has the flexibility to work with a large number of parent volunteers and specialists. Whoever teaches in this school must be a collegial worker and willing to collaborate with others. I also want someone with an understanding of early childhood and with the ability to articulate their philosophy of kindergarten. We believe in developmentally appropriate activities and learning for this age child, and we want our kindergarten teachers to take a leadership role in promoting developmentally appropriate learning." Pam's description of a kindergarten teacher emphasizes the importance of the decisions a teacher makes about the activities and learning in a classroom, along with the ability to explain a personal philosophy of kindergarten and kindergarten curriculum.

JOURNAL 10.1: When you read the description of the "future" kindergarten teacher, what qualities do you have that match the ones described? What might you do to continue to develop other characteristics or qualities of a kindergarten teacher as described by Pam?

A First Look at Kindergarten

Leaving the office, the secretary points you toward the kindergarten classrooms. The children are arriving for the morning with a buzz of excitement. You listen to their conversations and learn that last night's snowfall is the topic of most of their talk. One girl exclaims, "We stayed up late and made a huge snowball last night. We rolled it over and over until it was huge." The children are dressed in warm coats, with scarves, mittens, boots, and hats. It takes a bit of time for everyone to hang up all this winter clothing, but you notice several children helping each other with buckles, buttons, and untying scarves and hats. You overhear, "Wow, I looked like a snowman with all that stuff on me!" The first snow of the winter is certainly greeted with enthusiasm by these children!

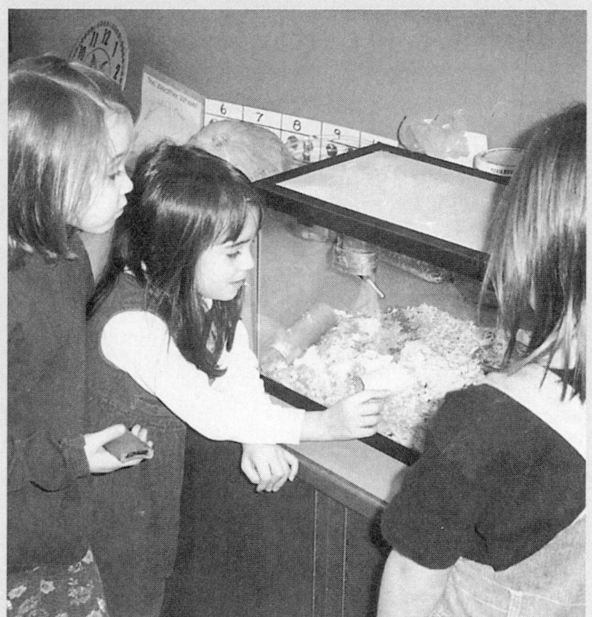

These three girls are interested in the mouse and her new babies. In what ways are they showing respect for the needs of the mother mouse?

Starting the Day: Morning Routines. After hanging up their coats, each child walks over to a sheet of paper placed on a desk near the door. You ask 5-year-old Macy what everyone is writing on the paper. She tells you, "We write our name next to the line that has our name on it. Then Jim knows who is here today. See, this is my name—Macy." After signing in, the children head toward any center or activity of their choice. There is Keeley! She has a huge purple scarf wrapped around her neck and head, and exclaims, "My mom gave me her scarf today." After she signs in, she goes to look at the mice in a glass terrarium. The mother mouse had several babies two days ago, and the children are watching her care for the babies. They are quiet and whisper as they watch, reminding each other, "Remember to use our eyes and our quiet voice near the new babies."

During the 10 minutes that children are involved in their activities, you notice that Jim, the teacher, greets each child. He has wandered to each of the activity areas and interacted with each child. When Jim stops at the mouse terrarium, Keeley tells him, "Mom and I went out in the snow and made a big snow-lady last night. She has my scarf on her neck." Jim says, "I imagine she is one fancy snow-lady. You and your mom make great projects."

Jim tells you, "You're in for a busy morning. After the first snowstorm, the children are excited to talk about the snow angels, forts, and snowmen they made at home." Jim lets you know that during calendar and weather time, the children will be discussing this topic. He also informs you that other exciting events are planned for today—a folktale told by a haiku artist and a performance by the kindergartners for Grandparents' and Other Special Friends' Day. This will be an interesting morning to observe! He also introduces you to Becky, a student teacher in this classroom.

Later, you learn from Jim that he starts the morning with time for the children to greet each other, share news, and get settled into the new day. He finds this important to the children's social development. They are learning to get along with a group of children as well as play with a "special friend." Starting the morning this way helps children make the transition from home to school and allows for social interactions.

Opening: Science and Math. You watch the children gather on the rug in front of their calendar. They talk about the date and day of the week. Meredith places an orange leaf on the November 19 space on the calendar. She followed a pattern on the calendar, with two brown leaves followed by two orange leaves. She leads the class in reading the color pattern, "Brown, brown, orange, orange." Next, Hawthorne checks the thermometer. He has some difficulty reading the numbers, so Becky, the intern teacher in the classroom this year, helps him. Together, they decide that it is 39 degrees outside. Tyson looks out the window. He sees clouds and says, "We have a cloudy day, so I will put this cloud on our weather board."

The children then burst into talk about the snow on the ground and what they did in the snow. Hawthorne shared, "My dad and I made snow angels by laying in the snow. I rolled over and my angel got flatter." When they finished sharing their snow experiences, the children picked up their weather journals and recorded the date and daily weather, and colored a picture to represent today's weather. Keeley's weather picture showed her snow-lady. When she finished drawing, she asked Jim to write *snow-lady* in her journal.

Haiku Art. As they returned their journals to the weather journal box, the haiku artist arrived. She is part of the Community–Eliot School Partnership, which is composed of artists who share their work with the children. Today, she tells a Japanese folktale. She describes a mountain that is thought to have magical powers. The children are enchanted with the tale and listen intently. When she finishes the tale, the children move back to their tables with boxes of chalk and crayons. The children illustrate the magical mountain they heard described in the folktale. There is a quiet hum of conversation as the children work on their drawings. Some of the children are talking about their drawings, while others quietly concentrate on their art.

As they finish their work, they join a circle on the floor near the side of the room and discuss their drawings with the other children and Jim. Becky collects the drawings and assures the students she will be hanging them on the bulletin board after school. She tells them, "Be sure to come and look at your drawings tomorrow and see all the different illustrations for the folktale."

Performance for Grandparents' and Special Friends' Day: Music and Dance. Just then, Becky looks at the clock and reminds the class that this is Grandparents' and Special Friends' Day and it is time to go to the auditorium. The class has been practicing a dance for the presentation. The children helped with the choreography and are ready to go! As they take off their shoes and prepare to head for the stage, Isaac decides he is too nervous to dance. Becky talks to him about all of his practice time and what a great dancer he is, but he refuses to go on stage. Hearing this exchange, Isaac's friend Bradley says, "I feel worried, too, and won't dance." Becky helps the rest of the children start their performance, while Isaac and Bradley sit with her. As the music and dancing begin, Isaac starts crying. "I really did want to dance with the kids." Becky places her arm on his shoulder and he settles in to watch the dance. At the end of their dance, the children grab their shoes and head back to the classroom.

JOURNAL 10.2: Before the performance, Becky suggested to Isaac that he might want to go up on the stage for the dance. After his third refusal, she suggested he sit in the audience and watch. What might have happened if she insisted he dance? What might Isaac learn from making his own choice?

Becky was aware of the **emotional developmental level** typical of most kindergarten-aged children. Children are beginning to express their feelings through words (verbally). It is important for adults to recognize a child's feelings and respond to his needs. This does not mean that the child always "gets his way" but it does mean that the child receives a reply or feedback. Knowing that some children are fearful of performing in front of others, Becky recognized Isaac's emotions and let him make his own choice. She responded in a developmentally appropriate way to his emotional needs.

Now that the children are back in the classroom, they are preparing for the arrival of their guests.

Sharing the Classroom Environment. Along come the grandparents and special friends, just in time to help buckle and tie shoes! Jim and Becky welcome everyone as they serve juice and cookies. The children show their grandparents and friends their work around the room. Tyson brings his father over to the mice. "Look, dad, see all the babies in here. We can watch them change. This one has hair on it now!"

Many of the children are clustered around the computer center, which has eight computers. Keeley is showing her grandmother how to access the Internet. She exclaims, "See, Oma, here is our website. It has my sunflower on it. Remember when I cut it down to take to school?" Jim has made it simple for the children to find certain programs or sites by using "bookmarks" that the children locate with symbols.

On their website, the kindergarten class has a photograph of a sunflower head taken with a

digital camera. Hawthorne says, "We asked people to guess the number of sunflower seeds in our sunflower head. There are a lot of seeds." Replies are coming in from all around the world. Meanwhile, the kindergarten students have counted the seeds by counting and placing them in little cups with 10 seeds in each cup. The older students at the school will be coming in to help the kindergartners chart the total number of seeds before they respond to the people who sent in estimates.

Jim and Becky are now walking around the room, thanking everyone for their part in making a good morning. The children begin getting ready for lunch. There's Keeley with her grandmother, who is encouraging her to pull her boots on. Keeley wants to make sure she has her cold weather clothes together for recess. You can't help but think that it was a good thing there were guests here today to help the children with coats, boots, mittens, and hats. The snowy day and the Grandparents' and Special Friends' Day worked well together.

As the classroom empties, Jim and Becky ask if you would like to come back in a week or so and observe a more typical day. Jim says, "This morning has been very interesting, but it might be helpful to see more of the 'regular' curriculum in action." He adds, "We never have a typical day, but that's what makes teaching kindergarten so interesting." Jim's outlook on teaching is engaging and you look forward to another visit.

A Full Day at Kindergarten

Today, you arrive with the children at 8:30. You watch them sign in and check the mice and their babies. Wow! The babies doubled in size. Eli and Paul head straight for the Legos. Eli states, "I want all the wheels at the Lego table. I'm going to build a dune buggy." A group of children settle in at the computers. Though one child is using a keyboard, at least three others are at the computer, discussing the game or graphics. Keeley is with another group at the computers, checking their website. This the last day of their sunflower seed guessing contest. Keeley wonders, "Will anyone get the right number? There are so many seeds in our sunflower!" The fourth-graders are coming to the kindergarten class tomorrow to help count the cups of sunflower seeds that were counted into groups of 10.

Opening Circle: Calendar with Math and Science. At 8:50, Jim calls the children over to the rug facing their calendar. It is a new month today. Maria looks at the new calendar and exclaims, "Look at the icicles that we get to use for our calendar. Some are short and fat and others are long and skinny." The children are already thinking of patterns. Jim asks Maria if she wants to put up the first icicle. She chooses a short fat icicle. "I am thinking about an ABBB pattern, I can see a short icicle and then 3 long ones. That will make a good pattern." They talk about other possible patterns for the coming month.

Next is a discussion about today's weather. Pedro goes to the window and tells the class, "It's cloudy again. It is 43 degrees outside." The children then pick up their weather journals and draw the daily weather. Jim reminds them, "Use lots of colors in your pictures." Also near the calendar is the schedule for today (see Figure 10.1). You glance at this to see what will be going on today.

***The Gingerbread Man:* Literacy (9:05–9:40).** When the children finish their weather journals, they gather on the rug for a story. Today, Jim reads *The Gingerbread Man.* Throughout the story, he asks the children to predict what might happen next. Some of the children are familiar with the story and seem to wait for the next sentence. When the old woman gets ready to open the oven, Hawthorne says, "Oh, I think the Gingerbread Man might be able to run away now that he is finished baking." Jim responds, "What makes you think he can run?" Jim poses questions that require his students to infer meaning that is not necessarily in the text, which is a key

FIGURE 10.1

Kindergarten Schedule

8:30	Arrival and Choice Time
8:50	Calendar Time
9:05	Literacy/*Gingerbread Man*
9:40	Snack
10:00	P.E.
10:30	Learning Centers
11:20	Lunch and Recess
12:00	Quiet Time
12:20	Math/Graphing
1:00	Art
1:50	Project Time
2:25	Closing Circle

comprehension skill for young children to grasp (Miller, 2002). The children enjoy coming up with reasons to support their predictions. You notice that there aren't any "right" or "wrong" answers—just interesting predictions.

Jim asks some children to pretend they are one of the characters and repeat the lines from the story. They certainly enjoy this story. When the story ends, Jim asks them to think of each of the characters in this story, starting with the first person they met. They name a character and then describe the character to Jim so he can draw it on the board. When he draws the Gingerbread Man, Eli said, "Make sure he has buttons on his tummy." When they remember the wolf, Keeley wants Jim to make huge teeth. After they list all the characters, Jim gives them a large piece of paper folded into eight sections. They are to draw one character in each section.

When the pictures are finished, Jim asks the children to tell a short story about their pictures to a neighbor and then listen to their neighbor's short story. Each child seems to give the story a different twist. Pedro shows the Gingerbread Man running to school and turning into a boy who loves to build with blocks. Jeremiah says, "Re tons." Pedro turns to him and looks at his picture. "Oh, yeah! I see red buttons on your gingerbread man." Jeremiah had just finished working with Mariko, the speech and language specialist. Mariko comes into the kindergarten room and works with Jeremiah and Sheila three times a week for 30 minutes. The goal is to help Jeremiah improve his language and pronunciation, as his language is developmentally similar to that of a 3-year-old child. Most of the children now understand Jeremiah's language, as demonstrated by Pedro's response. Jim makes sure that Jeremiah has opportunities during the day to speak with him and the children. Mariko suggested that communication within the context of activities in the classroom would contribute to Jeremiah's learning. Since Jeremiah is involved in speech and language activities within the classroom, Mariko tailors the activities to correspond to the curriculum in the classroom. Jim is also able to note what Mariko is working on with Jeremiah and Sheila and incorporate these sounds, words, and phrases into his communication with the children.

The children finish sharing their creative pictures and stories. Jim suggests the children share their pictures and stories at home with their families. He announces, "Your stories are better than television. I bet your families will enjoy these!"

For the activities Jim planned around the story of *The Gingerbread Man,* he purposely included the use of language and sequencing of events in the story. He knows that kindergarten children rely on language to connect the story events and characters. By encouraging the children to talk with each other and share their stories, he is incorporating developmentally appropriate learning in the realm of cognitive development for 5-year-old children (Cunningham & Shagoury, 2004). He is also aware of the language needs of the two children receiving special education services from Mariko, and includes these goals into the lesson through the story sharing on an individual level.

After a long work session developing the story characters and telling stories, it's time for a break. The children are going to eat a snack and then have some free-time.

Snack: Nutrition and Socialization. It's now 9:40, time for snack. Most of the children brought a snack from home, although Jim put out a box of crackers for anyone who was hungry. Jim sits down with Marietta, Pedro, and Keeley as he eats his apple. As the children finish their snacks, they move to different play areas and centers. Jim lets them know that they have 15 minutes until 10:00, when they leave for their P.E. (physical education) time.

Physical Education (10:00–10:30). Right next door to the kindergarten class is a large multipurpose room. In the morning, this room is used for physical education classes; during lunch, it becomes a cafeteria; and when school ends, it's the room for the after-school care program. Sabrina, the physical education teacher, is waiting for the kindergartners. They soon find their "spots" to sit on, which are numbers painted on the floor throughout the room. While waiting for each child to find his or her number, Sabrina notices Hawthorne sliding onto his number from a run. She quietly asks him to come over to her and asks him if he remembers how to find his number. He nods and walks to his number and sits down.

Sabrina begins talking about the first part of their class today. The children will be skipping, jogging, and hopping on the large circle around the perimeter of the room. Sabrina tells you, "We start with the same type of activity to warm up and also to let them move around some before we move into our major activity. This helps them get some wiggles out and then they are more ready to follow instructions for the activity."

When their movement time ends, the children go back to their numbered spots and wait for the next activity. Sabrina tells them that today they are using the parachute. "Yea," says Keeley. "I love to see the colors and dance around with the big parachute." There is a lot of agreement with that comment. Sabrina asks the children if they remember how to hold the parachute and Pedro reminds the class, "Fold the outside over, one, two, three, and hold on tight." "Right," agrees Sabrina. "Then we walk around the circle, carrying the parachute and make it go up and down."

The children gather around the parachute and fold over the edges and hang on. Cheri says, "When you pull really hard, the parachute gets straight and then it won't go up. I think we should pull out and then raise our arms when we want the parachute to go up." "Yep," says Pedro, "When our arms go up, it will go up, too." They continue with the parachute activity for another 10 minutes. Sabrina asks them what they would like to do for the last 5 minutes of class. They decide to get out the large foam balls and play catch or roll the balls to hit the wall on the far side of the room.

By then, it's time to go back to the classroom. Sabrina asks them, "How do you make a parachute go up?" Marie responds, "Make your arms go up high, but we all have to do it together." "You are so right," says Sabrina, "and during our next class, we will put some little ping pong balls on the parachute and see what we can make them do."

The activities the children were involved in during P.E. relate to the motor development for children of 5 and 6 years of age. The sequence of learning and practicing catching and throwing balls, skipping, and combining the use of large and small muscles (Sanders, 2002) is part of the movement program. When playing with the parachute, their large and small muscles are in use as they pull the parachute with their fingers and lift it up with the arms. This is an example of a developmentally appropriate activity for children of kindergarten age.

It takes group collaboration and the ability to follow instructions to make the parachute move up and down.

Learning Centers (10:30–11:10). "Yes, yes, yes!" Keeley sees that the paint supplies are in place at the easels. "I have been wanting to paint all day." Jim asks the children to name the different choices available today. Hawthorne looks around the classroom and says, "We can go to the Legos, the building blocks, the dramatic play corner, the painting corner, the computers, or the science table." "And also the reading corner," adds Paul. Keeley remembers, "Oh, we take our name card over to the place we want to go, and then take it with us if we change. But if the spaces are full, we find another place to go." Jim nods and gives a brief introduction to the different activities. Two parent helpers are here for the center time and are helping the children set up.

Before any activity begins, Jim ensures that the children have directions and **clear expectations,** whether he states these or has a child explain the steps or process of the next activity. Jim shares part of his classroom management plan: "When everyone is clear on the expectations, there is less confusion and need for me to interrupt and get children back on task. I guess this is preventive classroom management, by planning ahead."

Keeley heads for the painting corner. She places her name card in the pocket and finds a paint apron. Examining the colors and brushes that are out, she decides, "Today I will paint a dancing snow-lady to send to my Aunt Kelly. I'm going to be an artist like her when I grow up." She begins to paint, visiting with other children at the easels. The 40 minutes pass quickly. Some children stay at their first choice activity the entire time, while others make several moves.

Over at the blocks, Marietta and Bradley are making a tall tower. "I like to see if we can make it as high as we are," shares Marietta. "Watch out for the blue blocks, though, they make it tip too much," offers Bradley. Just then, Cheri walks over and stands very close to the tower. Sensing there might be a negative interaction about to occur, Jim provides **guidance** and encourages Cheri, "Let's find some blocks to help place on the tower. What about this red one?" Cheri then picks up a large block and asks Marietta, "Will this one work?" All three children cooperate and share blocks, continuing to encourage each other "to make it taller and taller."

Jim seems to keep track of who is at which activity and helps some of the children who appear minimally interested in their current activity. Sometimes he asks them questions about their plans and other times he makes suggestions or talks about what he sees them doing. One parent is helping at the block center, while another parent helps with the paints and hangs up finished pictures to dry.

Jim heads to the computer station, clearly one of his favorite activities. He is demonstrating a new science program to a group of four students. Jim tells you, "The intent of the program is to help young children express their categorization and classification strategies, along with sharpening their observation skills." On the computer, you see three fish and two trees in random order. The children are to identify which objects seem to go together by clicking on the similar objects. The computer then talks to them, "You show the two trees go together. Tell your partner why you decided the trees go together." The children giggle and talk to each other about their reasons for grouping the trees. This activity continues, with different objects and increasingly difficult categorizations. Jim tells you, "I am asked to preview different software, and the only way it makes sense to me to find out if it is any good is to have the children use the programs. Some of my personal rules for selecting good software are that it must interest the children, not contain any violence, and really teach them something that they might not experience otherwise."

The children work together on the activity. Maria tells Keeley, "Look, I can put these trees here and then move the fish over there and then they look like each other." "But what if we put all the big trees and big fish together and then the little trees and little fish are here?" asks Keeley. "I like groups of bigs and littles." They continue discussing their categorization or classification strategies, thinking up lots of possibilities and moving the objects into groups. The program also allows them to correct errors or move ahead to more difficult strategies, so it appears that learning is paced for individual learning levels.

This reminds you of an earlier question: How would technology look in a developmentally appropriate curriculum? You note that the children are engaged and able to navigate through the programs. They can also make choices and move to more advanced levels. You see lots of interaction. Jim will share more tips and thoughts about technology in his classroom when you visit him later.

Cleanup: Shared Routine. The next few minutes are spent cleaning up the classroom, putting supplies and materials away, and then washing hands in the classroom sink. Occasionally, you hear Becky or Jim remind someone to help clean an area where he had been playing. You can tell that the children must be hungry. They finish cleaning and hand washing rather quickly.

Lunch and Recess (11:20–12:00). The cafeteria is across the hall from the kindergarten classroom, and the smell of pizza has been drifting through the room for the last few minutes. The children find their lunch tickets in their name pockets (decorated by each child with designs and stickers) and head for the cafeteria. This is a time that Jim gets a break. He tells you, "After lunch, the teacher on duty dismisses the students for recess, on the playground outside the cafeteria door." So that's why they all wear their coats to lunch!

Quiet Time (12:00–12:20). When the children enter their classroom after the noon recess, the lights are off and a tape of classical music is playing softly. Jim and Becky greet the children as they enter, and invite them to find their quiet place. Pedro and Eli go over to the rug and lay down, as do several other children. Keeley and Marie each find a book and sit at a table together. They whisper quietly as they share their books. Some of the children fall asleep after a few minutes, while others are involved in a quiet activity. Cheri begins to talk loudly to a child near her. Jim walks over to her and reminds her that this is the time for everyone to rest quietly. He asks her if she would like to find another quiet activity. She goes over to the mouse terrarium and sits quietly on the floor, watching the mice.

JOURNAL 10.3: Why do you think Jim asked Cheri if she would like to find another quiet time activity instead of asking her to be quiet?

When quiet time ends, Becky turns the lights on. In a whisper, she asks the children to go sit on the rug. "While you are sitting on the rug, close your eyes and picture our mice in the terrarium." You wonder what this visualization is leading to.

Graphing Mice: Relevant Mathematics (12:20–1:00). Before the next activity, Jim tells you, "You will notice one of the ways I try to ensure that the curriculum is relevant and meaningful for these 5- and 6-year-olds." The graphing activity the children work on today is about something with which they are familiar—the mice in their classroom terrarium. Jim has a tub of small toy figures that represent the seven mice in the terrarium. He asks the children to think of what is different and what is the same about the mice. As they talk, children come to the tub and pick up one or more mice figures and tell something that they noticed about the mice or group of mice. They also walk over to the terrarium and check for characteristics that they could use for sorting, grouping, or categorization (Andrews & Trafton, 2002).

After 10 minutes of discussion, Jim asks the children to think of how they might make up a group of mice. Pedro says, "Let's see how many baby mice there are." The children check in the terrarium and count the babies. They decide they see six baby mice. So Jim asks Marie to find six baby mice figures. She counts the six mice. Jim then places one of the mice figures on the graph paper and asks Keeley to decide where the next baby mouse figure should go. She places it above the first one and then places three more mice on the paper. "Look, we have five baby mice on our paper." "Yes," says Jim, "Do we need more to show how many are in our terrarium?" "I want to count now," says Eli. "Now it's six!" "Wow," responds Jim, "You ended up with six mice on our graph paper." "And that's the same as in our mice house," says Marie.

Throughout this activity, the children were comparing the number of mice figures to the actual mice in their terrarium. They were using language that described the size of the mice, the color of the mice, and the number of mice. The focus of the graphing activity was mathematics, but the children were also developing vocabulary and an understanding of terminology used in mathematics.

Jim listened to the student responses and watched their manipulation of the mice as they formed the mathematical problem. He recorded his observations on a class sheet, as he found it helpful to have a written record of his assessment of student performance with the graphing.

After the group made a graph together, Jim explains that they are going to make their own graphs with mice figures. The children may use the mice figures on the graph paper to tell a story about mice. Kerry, Keeley's mother, is helping in the classroom during this activity. Jim, Becky, and Kerry work with different groups of children and record their stories about the mice. Watching Kerry, it is apparent that she has spent time in this classroom. She knows the children's names and seems comfortable interacting with them as she records their mice stories. At Isaac's table, the children decide to make two groups according to the color of the mice. The children nod in agreement as Kerry writes their story on a large sheet of paper. She leaves the paper on the table so the children can illustrate their story or graph. "I'll be back to see your illustrations and then we can share your story." She then goes to another table of children and talks with them about their graph.

Throughout the graphing activity, the children are learning mathematics and the nature of mathematics as a sense-making experience (Andrews & Trafton, 2002). Jim suggests that they think of what they might want to group and graph next, perhaps bringing a collection of something from home. This sets the children off to discussing their ideas.

Jim reminds the children that today they are working on their pottery puppets in art class. He walks down the hall with the children and watches as they enter the studio.

Studio Art (1:00–1:45). During the past two weeks, the kindergartners have been making clay puppets. The art teacher has three parent helpers today, who help students find their supplies and their own projects. Some of the children are ready to paint their puppets, while others are still working on the final shaping of the puppet. You peek in for a minute and notice conversation going on about the puppets. The studio is set up with low tables, so children are able to stand as they work on their projects. The room arrangement has been created so children move freely around the room, selecting paints and materials for their art projects (Althouse, Johnson, & Mitchell, 2003).

Thinking this might be a good time to visit with Jim, you leave the art room and go back to the classroom. Jim is getting ready for project time in the classroom, and you help him prepare materials for project time. The children have studio art and then recess, and since there's a lot to learn from Jim, you appreciate the time he spends with you.

Homeless Pets: Integrated Curriculum Project (1:50–2:25). **Project time** is planned for three afternoons a week, projects last for two to three weeks. Jim and Becky work with the children to develop projects that are of high interest, often finding that projects change direction once the children become involved in their work. Following the model of projects developed by Katz and Chard (2000), a project in this kindergarten is an "in-depth study of a particular topic" (p. 2). Children are involved in the development of the project, and as the project progresses, children "interact with people, objects, and the environment in ways that have personal meaning to them" (Katz & Chard, 2000, p. 3). The project approach refers to a way of teaching and learning that emphasizes the child's active participation in meaningful activities. With the model of project learning, children's intellectual and social development is stimulated as they learn through their involvement in an interesting project.

Remember our conversation about integrated curriculum and projects that include multiple curricular areas? This is what happens during project time in this kindergarten. New ideas and directions emerge, drawing from different areas of the curriculum as needed for exploration and solving the problem (Nagel, 1996). Jim explains to you, "It's important to allow for changes based on what the children are learning and where their interests lie. When we studied plants, student interest was very high in the sunflower heads that Keeley brought to class. I assessed their interests by listening and ended up with a webpage highlighting our largest sunflower head and a contest to guess how many seeds were in the head. Throughout the plant project, the children were involved in art (when they painted and drew plants), math (when they counted plants, measured plants that they were growing, and grouped seeds by tens), literature (when they listened to stories about plants), and science (when they learned more about the life cycle of plants). Being aware of their interests helps me keep the projects flowing in a child-centered direction."

Right now the children are considering how to solve the problem of homeless dogs and cats that live in the school neighborhood. The problem came about through a discussion that several children were having about a dog they had seen for several days outside the school. Marietta and Bradley worried about a brown dog that they had seen on their walk to school. Marietta speculated, "I don't think he has a home. He looks so sad." Bradley thought, "Where does he go at night and what does he eat?" Becky and Jim overheard the conversation and decided this would be a good topic for their next class project.

Becky is responsible for this unit of study. She began the project by reading newspaper stories about homelessness and animals and asking the children what they think this means. Becky wanted to make sure that the unit began with the current knowledge level of each child, so she spent time discussing this topic with small groups and individual children. Based on their input, she then planned activities.

Each project incorporates community involvement and is linked to the children's neighborhood in some way. In their current project, they have visited the local veterinarian, who talked about the problem of homeless animals and about the care of animals. The children are also making comparisons between human needs and animal needs, seeing that both humans and animals need food, water, shelter, and medical care. "I think we should try to help other people know that they need to take care of their pets," shares Hawthorne. "We can paint posters and hang them in the stores near here," suggests Keeley. Several students agree and are ready to start the posters. Each child will make a poster with a message to people in the neighborhood. Becky finds that the link to the community is important. "I notice that the children feel that they have something to offer to others when they learn in these projects. This is a powerful message for me to remember."

Today is the first day the class works on their posters. Some children are using paint, others opt for chalk or crayons. Several children are working together and drawing different parts of their pictures. Another group is cutting out magazine pictures for their posters. Jim, Becky, and the parent volunteer circulate around the room to record the child's message on the poster. Next week, they will go on a walk and ask local stores and businesses if they can put a poster up in their business.

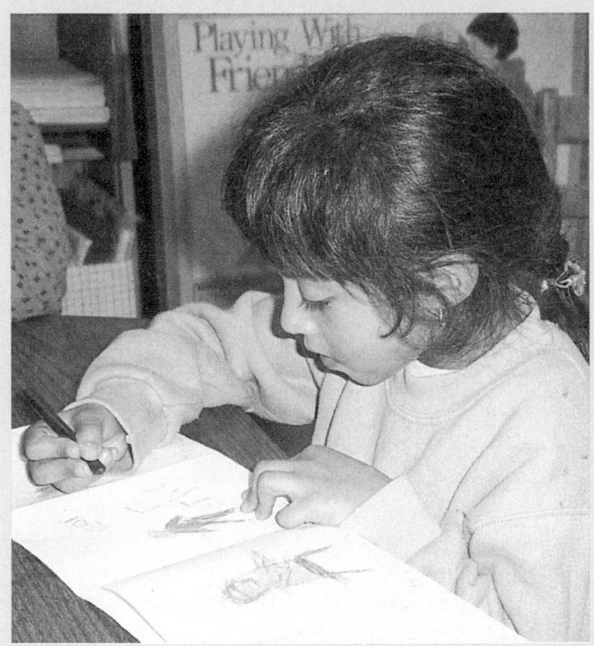

Norma is thinking intently about her drawing for the poster.

Becky was concerned that this problem might cause anxiety or concern for the children, but she now feels assured. "The children are committed to finding a way to help these animals and to try to help others learn that they should take good care of their animals." Looking at the posters, you realize that the topic matters to the children and that they do want to help the animals. You see messages such as "Please take care of your cat," "Every dog and puppy needs a good home," and "Keep your animal safe." This is an important issue that these children have chosen to help solve for their community.

Assessment of Student Learning. As in most kindergartens, **assessment** occurs on a continuous basis. With young children, it is important to look at their learning and development over a period of time. In the NAEYC Position Statement on Developmentally Appropriate Practice in Early Childhood Programs (Bredekamp & Copple, 1997), it is recommended that assessment of young children rely "heavily on the results of observations of children's development, descriptive data, collections of representative work by children, and demonstrated performance during authentic, not contrived, activities" (p. 21). Jim followed these recommendations, by incorporating observations on a regular basis and having the children develop portfolios of their work.

A **portfolio,** or a collection of important documents, of each child's work is kept throughout projects. During the first days of the project, Becky and Jim talk to each child individually and record the child's observations about the topic. This is helpful as a beginning point for the current knowledge level of the child and it also helps guide the direction of the project. Drawings, activities, and photographs of the children involved in the activities are added to the portfolio. At the end of the project, a photograph of the child's culminating activity (such as the animal poster or the flower planted in the milk carton) is placed in the portfolio. Jim and Becky make notes on much of the portfolio content, describing progress, learning of new skills, understandings that the child demonstrated, and specific interests the child had with the project. A final addition is the child's review of what they learned during the project, which is a summary dictated to the teacher or parent volunteer and added to the portfolio.

Comparing the beginning discussion of a topic to the final summary several weeks later provides insights into each child's learning throughout the unit or project. For instance, in the plant project, Marie began by saying, "Plants are green and are in the dirt." At the end of the project, she talked about seeds, light, water, and growing, along with other terms that indicated a growth in language and knowledge of plants. The portfolio also provides a visual documentation of the activities and involvement of each child in learning. Kerry looks forward to seeing the portfolios, as it keeps her informed of the curriculum and Keeley's activities in kindergarten. She has saved all of the portfolios that Keeley has brought home this year.

JOURNAL 10.4: Have you ever developed a portfolio? Perhaps you saved some papers you have written for school over a period of time or your art projects from elementary school. What can you learn by looking over this documentation of your learning and progression? Why might parents of young children enjoy viewing their child's portfolio? ●

Class Meeting (2:25–2:45). When the project areas have been cleaned up and the projects stored for the next work session, the children gather on the rug. There are about 15 minutes left to talk about their day and their plans for tomorrow. Jim asks Eli to sit in the "leader's chair" and help with the discussion. Jim recognizes that student-led class meetings help promote a positive classroom culture (Leachman & Victor, 2003). Eli eagerly sits in the chair and asks the children to close their eyes and think of their special times today. Keeley has her arm up high. "I loved painting. My mom and Aunt Kelly will really like my dancing snow-lady picture. This was a super day for me." Several other children add their thoughts of the day, as do Jim and Becky. Then it is time to find coats, boots, and papers to take home. Some of the children will be going next door to after-school care, while others will head for home or other child care arrangement. About one-third of the class does attend the after-school care program here at Eliot School, where you will visit later.

Saying good-bye to the children and the teachers, you start down the hall. Looking back, you see Keeley as she goes into the after-school care room. She is carrying her dancing snow-lady picture very carefully and telling her friend that she is going to mail it to Aunt Kelly in New York!

Learning from Jim

Jim has been teaching for 15 years. All but one year have been at the kindergarten level. He began college in the midwest at a large university, majoring in elementary education. "I always wanted to be a teacher, so I knew this would be my major even before I began college," he says. His student teaching took place in a first-and second-grade blended classroom. After graduation, his first job was at the kindergarten level. Although his college work focused on elementary-aged children, he says, "I was interested in the kindergarten position, and eager to teach at this level. During the past 15 years, I have taken many courses and attended workshops about early childhood education. I knew I needed to continue my own education." Similar to Jim's preparation, 79 percent of kindergarten teachers hold elementary certificates, and 50 percent have had preparation specific to kindergarten or the early primary years (Early, Pianta, & Cox, 1999).

Jim's Interest in the Use of Technology by Young Children

Once Jim started teaching, he saw the need to become more versed in education for young children, and has continued to learn more each year. An interest has been technology and early childhood education, which he has pursued for the past seven years. He finds, **"Technology** is an amazing tool in the classroom. My students are learning incredible things as they search the Internet, use software programs, or create presentations with the digital camera and computer." Jim is regarded as a leader in technology education and has been active in helping other teachers gain knowledge and experience in this field. Technology is truly an integral part of his classroom, as you saw when you visited for the day.

Jim states, "I'm picky about the software in our classroom. Most of the programs I prefer are open ended. I want the children to find out things on the computer that they can't learn through hands-on experiences." Jim searches for developmentally appropriate software that is "open ended and exploratory" (Haugland & Wright, 1997).

Another priority is to integrate technology throughout the curriculum to allow for its most powerful capability, that of engaging in problem solving, inquiry, and developing ideas (Clements & Sarama, 2002). Jim also recognizes the need for hands-on experiences. "I would never substitute a software program for playing with blocks. The tactile and spatial senses need to develop through three-dimensional play. Yet the computer serves as a wonderful communication tool." When you ask Jim for an example, he tells you, "For Valentine's Day, the class list was on the computer. Five-year-olds would have a difficult

The Eliot School Home Page is being investigated by this young child.

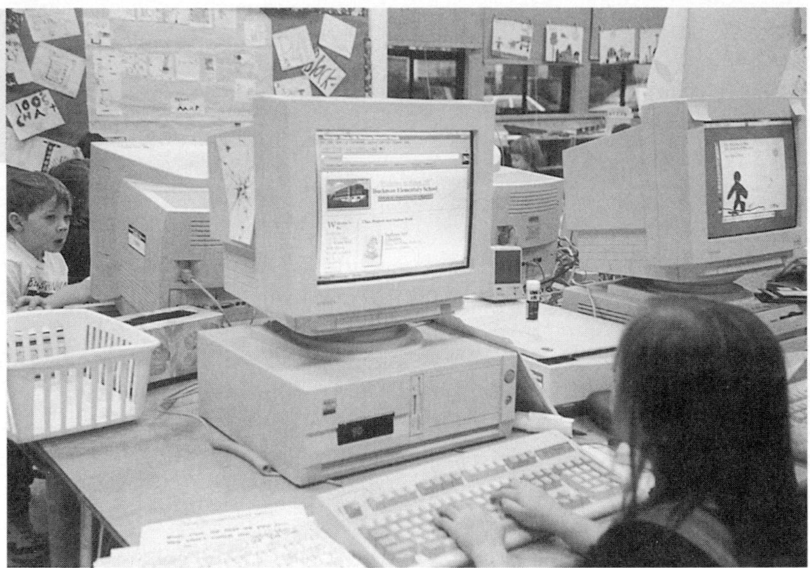

time writing our 26 names for valentines. But with the computer, they can print the names, then cut and glue or tape the names on valentines." The computer becomes a tool that helps them in their learning.

Jim also asks you to note how students work together at the computers. "See each computer has three or so students involved in the activity and in discussing the options on the program? This is typical in our classroom." Haugland and Wright (1997) discovered that young children interacted with either a peer or the teacher 80 percent of their time at the computer. This finding supports the work of Fischer and Gillespie (2003), who, through review of research and observations in classrooms, found technology to stimulate cooperation and that children often work in pairs to share feedback and assignments.

Jim's Philosophy of Classroom Management and Community Building

"You might have noticed how we work together in our classroom. My **classroom management plan** includes helping children learn to become a community and negotiate problems," shares Jim. When he begins an activity, Jim explains the steps or asks a child to explain the process, in order to ensure clear expectations of the process and children's behavior throughout the process. Consistent with current research in classroom management (Jones & Jones, 2004), Jim and his students work collaboratively to develop agreed upon behavior norms for their classroom. "We have situations each day where we need to discuss behavior and remind ourselves of our class rules. In the fall, we decided that we needed rules to make our classroom work for us, and we look back to our rules when needed." Students are expected to talk over problems and go to adults when they need help solving a problem. For instance, when Brandy and Chantel both wanted to use a new bottle of glue, they had to negotiate whether to take turns, find another bottle of glue, or use tape or paste instead. They ended up sharing the glue and sitting at the same table. Becky noticed the situation early enough and stayed nearby in case the girls needed an adult to help in their negotiation. This time, they figured out what to do and continued their work. After several months in the classroom, Jim finds, "With practice, they are learning to express their feelings and work things out. It takes continual practice and reminders, but I think it is worth the effort." Jim finds community to be essential in working with children with special needs.

A Conversation about Inclusion

In a discussion about inclusion, Jim shares how the community of his classroom accepts all children. "As a kindergarten teacher, any child that comes to my room is part of our classroom. You have children come in that do not speak English; they are part of the classroom. Some children arrive and are reading fluently; they are part of the classroom. All children come in to the classroom at different levels, varying in many ways, not just in cognitive abilities.

"Kids come in from all over the map. This has taught me to look at the child first. If a child happens to have a disability, then it is my job to find a way for the child to be successful. Teachers make accommodations every day for children. At the same time, I expect support and resources to help me and the child be successful. Furthermore, I think my attitude toward accepting all learners where they are sets the tone for inclusion in my classroom.

"I am proud of the diversity of our children. I think the attitude of acceptance and taking all children where they are when they come to us supports inclusion. I value each child and his family. Each child brings something for our community to learn from. I think it is essential to see past any label that might be put on a child and really see the child for who she is first and find ways to help her be successful in learning."

Jim also finds his role to be one of **facilitator of learning** in the classroom. Offering children choices in their learning and listening to their interests places him in the role of a facilitator. He says, "I instructor is not for me. It just doesn't fit with my picture of kindergarten." He sees kindergarten as a time of transition for most children. "I want them to be excited about school and learning. Kindergarten is that special year. My program is flexible and takes kids from where they are. Remember Keeley's interest in sunflowers? We were able to expand that and really explore sunflowers." As you observed, the kindergarten program is an active, hands-on experience. It is also based on student interests and provides a solid foundation for future learning. After thanking Jim for sharing his students and his classroom today, you realize you have much to think about in terms of kindergarten programs. It truly is a special year of learning, and Keeley's attitudes toward school and learning have certainly helped you recognize the impact of a developmentally appropriate program.

After-School Care Program

As the kindergarten children left school, Jim pointed out where children were headed. About eight children walk home, where a parent, older sibling, or neighbor will care for them. There were several parents waiting outside the school, ready to take their child home or to a family home care situation. Bradley, Marietta, and Paul got on a van to go to a for-profit child care center, which is part of a large national chain. Jim related, "A few children will be heading home alone, waiting until a parent or older sibling arrives." These children are in a self-care situation. With growing "evidence that self-care can pose risks for children, it is not surprising that parents, policymakers, and educators have turned to formal programs as one way to meet needs for after-school care" (Vandell & Su, 1999, p. 64). For this important reason, and to address the needs of families who may not be able to afford after-school care, Eliot School made an arrangement with an after-school care program to be offered at the school.

The program at Eliot School offers financial assistance to families needing a reduced rate. Keeley, Pedro, Brandy, Macy, and Hawthorne join the other children in the after-school care program at Eliot School, Fremont Hills Child Care. This program is run by a non-profit agency. Several elementary schools in this city offer after-school programs run by this child care company.

Fremont Hills After-School Program

At Eliot School, 75 children attend the after-school program. Parents may register their child on a full-time or part-time basis. Fremont Hills programs are built on the philosophy that providing a secure and warm environment promotes the self-esteem of children and supports the family. **After-school care** refers to programs in family day care homes, centers, or schools that provide supervision and activities for young children after school. The programs differ from those during the school day, with a more relaxed schedule and pacing for after school. As soon as Kerry learned that Keeley was accepted at Eliot School, she visited the after-school care program and made arrangements for Keeley to attend four afternoons a week. One afternoon a week Keeley goes to a friend's home. Kerry knew that the staff at the after-school care program received training and staff development before the program began as well as throughout the school year. She wanted Keeley in a setting where she was comfortable and where Keeley could make choices about her late afternoon activities (see Box 10.1).

CURRICULUM IN THE AFTER-SCHOOL CARE PROGRAM. A monthly curriculum plan is developed by the teachers at each site, with teachers from all of the Fremont Hills Centers sharing and exchanging ideas through a monthly newsletter. There is a monthly theme with activities related to this theme. This month, children at Eliot School were involved in creating a calendar of events and activities around the theme of tall tales. Activities included writing and illustrating stories, acting out plays, and making puppets for the tall tales.

It's now time to visit the after-school care program. Let's see what Keeley is doing now!

What Are Some Issues of After-School Care?

Two major issues of after-school care are quality of the programs and availability of care for school-age children. A prominent research study, conducted for over 10 years by the Cost, Quality, and Child Outcomes Study Team (1995) provides information about the impact of child care on children and their learning. *Quality child care* is defined "as that which is most likely to support children's positive development" (p. 1). Findings from this study indicate that quality of child care is related to the staff-to-child ratio, the education of the staff, and the prior experience of the administrator(s). In high-quality programs, more staff are available to interact frequently with children, changing the environment to an enriching learning setting. Parents should be provided with indicators of quality child care, as they are responsible for making child care decisions. At the same time, standards for high-quality child care must be enforced in each state to help eliminate poor-quality child care. A more recent study by the National Institute of Child Health and Human Development (2002) supports these findings and the need for quality child care.

With the increasing number of parents working outside of the home comes a growing need for child care. Availability of affordable after-school care remains a constant worry for parents. Families do not want to leave a young child at home alone after school, but with financial considerations, after-school care may be too costly. Families with low incomes, particularly the working poor, have the lowest access to quality early childhood services (*Education Week,* 2002). With the majority of young children in the United States in child care for a substantial number of hours (West, Denton, & Germino-Housken, 2000), there is a critical need for access to high-quality child care. Increasing the number of after-school care programs that provide financial assistance for families will enable more young children to access the care they need.

Keeley's After-School Care

Literacy, Art, and Drama

As you enter the room that serves as the after-school care room, you notice bins of tissue paper and construction paper on the tables. Several children are talking about the different colors and what they need for their puppets. Chantel sees black strips of paper and announces, "This is perfect for the straight hair on my mother puppet." She is making a mother puppet for the story *Jack and the Beanstalk.* Jon is looking for green paper, as he is working on a giant with Keeley. They talk about "huge green boots, because he has the biggest feet you ever did see."

Miss Teresa, the caregiver, had read the story several times to the children, who are now telling parts of the story to each other as they explained the role of the puppet. You wish you would be here next week to see the puppet show. These children, from kindergarten through third grade, work together in a productive and fun way. Miss Teresa and the other caregivers are sitting with groups of children and making their own puppets. The plays will have lots of colorful characters.

Over in the corner is a book cart and several tape players with headsets. One of the caregivers is sitting on the floor with four children. Some are listening to him read, while others are listening to tapes on the headset. After observing the busy day at kindergarten, you understand that sometimes children need a quiet place to relax and unwind, and may choose this type of activity to balance their day. Choices are important, and honoring differences in needs for stimulation and quiet time is essential for young children.

You ask Keeley what she will be doing after she finishes her giant puppet this afternoon. Keeley tells you, "Well, we just ate our snack, then we had project time. Next is outdoor time and we can choose games or just play if we want. After that, we come inside and have games. Today, I will ask if we can play Hokey-Pokey because I like to sing that song. And then we have choosing time until we go home. I don't know what I will choose yet, but I want to play with Pedro, so I will see what he wants to do today." Looking over at the schedule on the wall, you note that Keeley described the entire afternoon. She is certainly familiar with the daily schedule, and seems to be looking forward to her choices for the afternoon.

Family Involvement in the Program

Several parents appear at the door, reading the notices on the bulletin board as they enter. You wander over to this area and also read the notices. There is an announcement about plans for activities during winter vacation in two weeks, as well as an invitation to families to join in the monthly staff development activity on outside games and activities.

Chantel sees her dad, "Oh, Dad, come here and see my mother puppet." He walks over and she shares the new additions to her puppet, "Look at all the hair she has now. Tomorrow I want to finish her face and then make a dress for her. Can you come to our puppet show next week?" Miss Teresa has planned several different times for the puppet shows, so that families could attend. She explains, "It's important for the families to be involved in after-school care, also. We are definitely not a babysitting service, but a place where children continue to learn at their own paces and developmental levels. See the differences in the puppets? We try to incorporate projects where many different ages and developmental levels of children can work together and be successful. When they leave after-school care each evening, we want them to think about their afternoon and feel that they were engaged in interesting activities. We try to check in with families each day and have notices on the board of upcoming events. Families also receive a monthly newsletter and we hold bimonthly meetings to encourage family involvement in program planning."

Watching parents arrive to pick up their children, you think about the afternoon and the interactions between the caregivers and children and between the families and caregivers. The philosophy of Fremont Hills is apparent in the way the staff includes families and children in developing and implementing the program. You watched Keeley and her friends make choices throughout the afternoon, occasionally with guidance from Miss Teresa or other caregivers. The staff noticed if children were tired or hungry and responded to those needs. Jon spent an hour sitting with books on the large pillows, quietly looking at the books and resting. His need for quiet time was honored. Miss Teresa told his father that Jon seemed tired today and wondered if he might be getting sick. His dad thanked her for noticing and said they would try to get him to bed early tonight. You also noted that caregivers tried to check in with families to share something about their child as they left for the evening.

As you think back over the after-school program you have just visited, you realize how fortunate Keeley and her friends are to be in a safe and enriching program after they finish school each day. Keeley can make choices about how she spends her afternoon, just as she might at home. She also has a caring adult to talk with and her friends to play with. Kerry fully appreciates the quality of the program, as well as the reduced cost of the program based on her salary. She says, "It is such a welcome relief knowing that Keeley is at Fremont Hills after school. I don't worry about her and I also know she will enjoy her afternoon."

A Closer Look at Kindergarten

Common Themes in Today's Kindergartens

Nearly all children in the United States—98 percent—attend kindergarten prior to first grade. In 1998, approximately 4 million children attended kindergarten in the United States. Of these children, 85 percent were in public school and 15 percent in private school; 55 percent attended a full-day program and 45 percent were in part-day programs (U.S. Department of Education, 2000). Although kindergartens have been in existence for 150 years, it is difficult to define precisely the kindergarten of today. Most kindergartens provide experiences in art, music, and children's literature, while also planning time for play and for activities that promote physical and motor development.

How children experience these activities reflects the philosophy of a kindergarten program. In some programs, children might choose their own activities and spend much of their time socializing and in play. In other programs, the teacher may **direct** more of the learning, planning activities that all children are expected to complete, perhaps incorporating beginning reading skills into the program. In the kindergarten that you observed, Jim planned many **free choice** activities throughout each day. He believes that children learn most from participating in a few structured activities, such as a weather discussion each morning, and then moving to activities of their own choice. Some days, the children's activities have a theme, such as friends. When there is a theme, it is woven throughout their day, including art, singing, dance, literacy, science, and play time.

Schools define their own kindergarten programs, based on national, state, and district guidelines. This definition may vary according to current pressures or beliefs within the district and from national organizations representing early childhood education. There might even be two kindergarten teachers working in the same school with different programs. Do you recall the two very different kindergarten programs that Kerry visited prior to selecting Eliot School for Keeley? Differences and contrasts between programs such as these make it difficult to provide one specific definition of kindergarten.

Kindergartens began in the 1850s as learning experiences for children from age 3 to 6. They evolved into programs in the public schools for children prior to the first grade, although kindergartens are also found in private schools, churches, and child care centers. Today's kindergartens have retained some components or features from the earliest programs, as you will notice in Box 10.2, which describes the beginning of kindergarten.

JOURNAL 10.5: When reading about Froebel's kindergarten programs in Box 10.2, what do you notice that has been carried from his time period into Keeley's kindergarten class?

INCREASED PRESSURE FOR ACADEMICS. During the past 20 years, there has been renewed interest and debate about the role of kindergarten in the educational system. Remember Pam, the principal at Keeley's school, discussing the pressure for increased academics in her district's kindergarten? Pam's response was to hire teachers who understood

BOX 10.2

A Brief History of Kindergarten

In the early part of the nineteenth century in Germany, Friedrich Froebel developed the first kindergarten program, centered on the religious philosophy of nature, God, and humanity. Froebel believed that God was of central importance and that each individual has a specific role or purpose to accomplish. He felt that young children need a rich learning environment provided by teachers who understand how to implement the Froebelian philosophy with children from age 3 to 6. Certain types of play and materials were essential to this learning environment. Learning rhymes with hand or body actions is an example of Froebel's approach to kindergarten.

Froebel established training programs for future kindergarten teachers. Teachers learned how to incorporate the tools of learning in kindergarten, called the "gifts," which were the first educational materials developed for young children. These gifts were materials that reflected forms found in nature, such as squares, circles, triangles, or cylinders. Through play with these materials, children would come to understand relationships in nature.

During the mid-1850s, German immigration to the United States brought many young women with kindergarten training to this country. In 1856, Margarethe Schurz taught her children and those of her relatives in her home in Watertown, Wisconsin. This became the first kindergarten established in the United States.

Froebel's influence is still in place in U.S. kindergartens today. When you observe an environment where children are nourished and cared for, and provided with learning activities that include blocks, plants, pets, and finger-plays, you are seeing the influence of Friedrich Froebel, the father of kindergarten.

the importance of a developmentally appropriate program, and who also could educate parents about the best learning environment for young children. Some early childhood educators, such as Pam and Jim, reconfirm their interest and support of kindergarten programs that reflect children's developmental levels, whereas other educators push for an increased emphasis on academics and preparation for first grade. The controversy continues.

Are programs from each of these two stances mutually exclusive? Or could developmentally appropriate learning also include academic learning or preparation for some 5- and 6-year-olds? Take the opportunity to consider these questions as you read about and observe kindergartens, watching how children respond to different curricula. Drawing from your reading, your experiences with younger and older children, and your personal philosophy of early childhood education will help you develop your position in this current debate. Later in this chapter, you will return to this issue, but first, let's take a closer look at kindergarten programs.

KINDERGARTEN CONTENT AND PROGRAM FORMATS. When attempting to define kindergarten, the content of the program must be analyzed. Understanding the developmental stages of children at this age will help you realize how children learn best in kindergarten. Beliefs about the best learning environment for 5- and 6-year-olds should guide educators to develop programs that view the young child as an active learner, curious about her world, and ready to explore and discover (McLean, Haas, & Butler, 1994). These beliefs were certainly important to Kerry as she thought about the type of kindergarten program she wanted for Keeley.

Program formats vary widely. Some children attend an all-day kindergarten, others attend a half-day kindergarten, and still others attend full days every other day (alternate-days program). In some schools, enrichment kindergartens are offered for part of a day in addition to the regular kindergarten program.

More important than the format of the program is the *content* of each program. A kindergarten program that is individually and culturally developmentally appropriate would adhere to the following (Moyer, 2001):

- Recognition of individual differences in children's growth patterns and rates
- Education of the whole child, with attention to individual physical, social, emotional, and intellectual developmental interests
- Provision of a variety of activities and materials to encourage active participation, large blocks of time to explore interests, and time to reflect on learning
- Acknowledgment that play is fundamental to children's learning, growth, and development
- Allowing children to make choices and decisions within the class setting

In a kindergarten classroom based on these beliefs, there is room for the large range of developmental levels and activities that promotes success in learning for all children.

As an early childhood educator, you will want to be able to articulate the content of your program as well as be able to explain why you include certain content. Knowing why you incorporate certain activities and topics in your classroom helps you recognize the philosophical influence on your program content.

Kindergarten Curriculum

The traditional curriculum of a **developmentally appropriate kindergarten program** is grounded in child development theory and research (Bredekamp & Copple, 1997). The child's learning occurs throughout the entire day, with play as a primary learning activity. Children learn from doing and being involved in real experiences, whether composing a song with a friend or busily finger painting. At 5 and 6 years of age, children generally want to learn and are eager to gain knowledge and explore new places.

When Hawthorne plans his morning snack and fixes apple slices with peanut butter, he is also developing his fine motor skills as he spreads the peanut butter. His language and cognitive abilities are engaged when he explains to a friend that they will soon be eating fruit with protein for snack. He starts talking about fruit and different fruits he has

Norma shares her thoughts about the characters in *The Gingerbread Man* as she draws and visits.

eaten. His ability to sort and label demonstrates his **classification strategy,** which is important to cognitive development.

His teacher made sure that Hawthorne had a choice for snack and that he took an active role in preparing his food. A teacher's assistant was working with the children in the kitchen area and encouraged conversation throughout their snack preparation. Hawthorne was learning through this purposeful activity. This is very different from a scenario where a child might practice spreading "play clay" on a play apple or being asked questions about a snack already prepared for her. Meaningful activities help children feel that their work is important, and eating the delicious apple snack is a great way to end the important activity of meal preparation.

CURRICULUM CONTENT. All areas of child development should be included within the kindergarten curriculum. Attention to including activities that foster the development of intellectual, social, emotional, and physical development will be part of the curriculum planning process. Children who are 5 and 6 years old are growing in each of these areas and need the stimulation and learning from engaging across all of the developmental areas.

A **developmentally appropriate curriculum** purposely includes experiences throughout each of the developmental areas and at the developmental levels that match the range of a particular age group of children. In following the examples of appropriate practice outlined in *Developmentally Appropriate Practice in Early Childhood Programs* (Bredekamp & Copple, 1997), Jim attempted to create a "learning environment that fosters children's initiative, active exploration of materials, and sustained engagement with other children, adults, and activities" (p. 125).

Throughout your visits to Jim's kindergarten class, you saw a typical kindergarten day. Children were involved in learning in many different curricular areas, as well as in the various developmental domains. Lessons in literacy evolved from the story of *The Gingerbread Man.* The children were working with their comprehension of the story, the sequence, and the role of the main characters. Included in each day were experiences of being read to and independent reading, along with opportunities to write for many different purposes in both nonconventional forms and over time to conventional forms of writing (IRA & NAEYC, 1998). These experiences were planned with Jim's knowledge of the joint position statement created by the International Reading Association and the National Association for the Education of Young Children, which Jim considers the standards for teaching and learning in the early years.

Motor development (or physical education) activities included warming up with the use of large muscles and an activity that included all children in their use of small and large muscle coordination as they worked together to raise and lower the parachute.

During learning center time, the choice of activities included creative arts (painting, building with blocks, or drama) or a science table activity. Jim includes a learning center time each day to provide the children with opportunities for choice and self-directed learning.

The math lesson encouraged the children to continue developing their ability to represent amounts with a numeral. The children graphed the number of mice in different categories, which provided time and experience for deeper understanding of mathematical relationships (Andrews & Trafton, 2002). In this lesson, Jim was following the guidelines established in the joint position statement on early childhood mathematics, by providing for ample time and materials for children to engage in exploration of mathematics ideas (NAEYC & NCTM, 2002).

During the art lesson (puppet making), the children created puppets within the context of folktales they had been listening to in class. Art was a media to support their learning and was connected to learning in other areas of the curriculum (Althouse, Johnson, & Mitchell, 2003).

The integrated project the students were involved in, helping homeless pets, was an example of project work that facilitates construction of knowledge, social learning, and cultural relevance (Katz & Chard, 2000). The young children were committed to helping their community find ways to reduce the number of homeless animals while raising their own awareness of the treatment of animals. Jim believes the children learn far more when activities are meaningful and relevant, which often leads to integrated learning experiences.

When Keeley showed her grandmother the class's website and the sunflower project the students had put on the Web, you observed how these different subject areas blended to create an integrated curriculum. The students used math to count the seeds and group them into cups representing 10 seeds. Their science came into play when they found the sunflower head molding. This led to a discussion on decomposing and discussions about garbage. The children used literacy skills to read the responses and record them in their sunflower data books. They also listened to stories about sunflowers. Several of the children painted pictures and dictated short stories about sunflowers and made a sunflower book for the school library. When studying the use of sunflowers, the children were interested to learn that sunflower seeds in the grocery store were once seeds in a sunflower plant.

Because Jim was aware of the children's interests, he was able to create a project and curriculum that moved in the direction of their interests. This is also called **learner-centered curriculum**—curriculum that is determined by children's needs and interests.

JOURNAL 10.6: In your own words, describe the commonalities between project-based learning, integrated curriculum, and learner-centered curriculum.

When you become a teacher, you will find ways to weave some of your interests and expertise into the curriculum. This helps you share your interests with the children. Since Jim is highly interested in computers and technology, this is a daily part of his kindergarten program. Keep in mind some of the examples of computer learning that occurred in Keeley's kindergarten as we explore technology in the kindergarten curriculum.

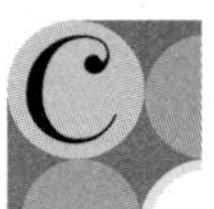

TECHNOLOGY AND CURRICULUM. Young children can use technology in a variety of ways. Some are beneficial to learning, while others might be considered a waste of time or even harmful to a child's development. Children see the use of computers on a daily basis. Whether they are at a bank, grocery store, gas station, or library, computers are part of the operation of most enterprises today (see Box 10.3).

Keeley is quite interested in her kindergarten's webpage and checks daily for responses to the question about how many sunflower seeds are in the class sunflower. This is an example of extending the classroom experience to a wider audience, yet keeping the use of technology in a meaningful context. The use of technology is integrated into her regular learning environment and is one option to support her learning (NAEYC, 1996a).

BOX 10.3

Technology and Young Children: What Is Appropriate?

Many young children have access to computers in their homes and/or child care or school settings. What computer activities are developmentally appropriate for a young child? Two major points to consider in answering this question include the following:

1. Is the activity consistent with this child's developmental stage and interests?
2. Does the activity provide a benefit to the child or does it replace a more meaningful learning opportunity?

(continued)

BOX 10.3 continued

Although research indicates there are positive effects of technology on children's learning (Clements & Samura, 2002), computers cannot replace learning from and through the important early childhood materials such as blocks, sand, water, books, and dramatic play. Computer use can be developmentally appropriate or can be misused. The NAEYC Position Statement: Technology and Young Children—Ages Three through Eight (1996a) directs early childhood educators to "take responsibility to influence events that are transforming the daily lives of children and families." This statement addresses several issues related to technology's use with young children: (1) the essential role of the teacher in evaluating appropriate uses of technology; (2) the potential benefits of appropriate use of technology in early childhood programs; (3) the integration of technology into the typical learning environment; (4) equitable access to technology, including children with special needs; (5) stereotyping and violence in software; (6) the role of teachers and parents as advocates; and (7) the implications of technology for professional development.

Children as young as 3 years of age are able to manipulate a mouse and work with software or websites. The child becomes aware of the cause and effect of moving a mouse and seeing actions on the computer screen. Most children at this age do not recognize letters or numbers, so would not use the keyboard. Although many programs indicate they are aimed at the 3-year-old, you might decide that the actual use of blocks, paints, or other objects is more appropriate than the computer.

During the kindergarten period, children are beginning to recognize letters and numbers and would find exploring with the keyboard and pressing a letter on the key and see it displayed on the computer screen as a format to reinforce letter recognition. Another use for kindergartners would be in creative areas, such as drawing, painting, or building onscreen. Of course these activities would not replace the actual painting and drawing, but be an additional resource for creativity. Think about mixing soap and water to make a bubble mixture and then twirling the bubble ring through the mixture until you are ready to blow a bubble. When you lift the bubble ring, you blow carefully until you have a large, colorful bubble. This experience is impossible to duplicate with a computer. The bubble experience involves smell, touch, and visual pleasure. A computer might duplicate the color and allow the child to draw a picture of the bubble, but the exposure to the bubble experience will help a child create meaning from the computer once she has had the actual experience. Children at this age also enjoy interactive sites, as long as they are simple to open and follow.

In the early elementary years, a first- or second-grader is able to turn the computer on and off and to locate simple bookmarks for websites as well as icons for software programs. Programs should encourage exploration and experimentation. Children of this age might use the computer to write stories and to record data in the classroom, such as the number of children in the class today, the temperature, the lunch count, and so on. Using a digital camera in the classroom and on field trips and then displaying the photographs on the computer would provide an opportunity for children to view places they have just visited and to write stories or draw pictures to illustrate their experiences that accompany the photographs. Problem solving is another skill that is enhanced with appropriate software or websites, as children make choices that lead to various outcomes or solutions. It is important that these programs also allow children to make changes and to repeat various steps as they work toward solutions.

With the magnitude of websites and software available for young children, it continues to require teacher decision making about the appropriateness of these programs. Haugland (2000) suggests there are four major types of websites that can facilitate learning with young children: (1) information, (2) communication, (3) interaction, and (4) publication.

Use of software or website scales (e.g., Haugland and Gerzog's [1998] *The Developmental Software Scale for Web Sites*) and recommendations for software or websites made by recognized organizations is helpful to those responsible for evaluating software or websites. These tools assist educators in making informed decisions about the developmental appropriateness, individual appropriateness, and cultural appropriateness of the learning resources that technology can provide for young children.

Jim worked with several parents in reviewing and selecting software. He is concerned about the number of children's software programs that focus on violent activity, even within an educational game. He finds that some software encourages interactions and collaboration and this appeals to him, as he builds a community with his students. Technology is another tool in his classroom, serving as an inviting way to learn more with and from others (Thouvenelle & Bewick, 2003).

Now that you have read about kindergarten curriculum, let's look at the preparation of people who implement the curriculum—the kindergarten staff. The current trend is a move toward a national level certification, but at this time, each state has different preparation requirements.

Preparation of Kindergarten Staff

Kindergarten teachers complete different types of preparation programs according to specific program requirements for certification established by each state. In some states, preparation for kindergarten certification for teachers is located within a university's elementary education program. This structure means that a teacher preparing to teach kindergarten completes coursework focused on teaching children who range in age from 5 through 12 years or older. Other states have specific early childhood certification requirements, with the early grades seen as a separate preparation program. Certification requirements change rapidly. If you are interested in teaching kindergarten, contact someone in the certification office at a local university or your state's Department of Education for current requirements.

KINDERGARTEN TEACHERS. Keeley's teacher, Jim, completed an elementary education program. When he started teaching kindergarten, he enrolled in workshops and continuing education courses. He recognized the special needs of kindergarten-aged students. He also observed different kindergarten programs and decided that he wanted to acquire the skills and knowledge needed to create an interactive and developmentally appropriate learning environment. He states, "There is more to kindergarten than 'watering down' the academic requirements expected in many first through third grades. I have observed several public and private kindergartens and have always been impressed with a focus on child-directed learning, free play, and project-based learning. I knew this was the type of program I wanted to develop."

Remember our brief discussion on integrated curriculum (the project time in Keeley's kindergarten) in Chapter 5? Jim knew that these projects were the right approach for his curriculum. "In fact, the projects are actually the foundation for my entire kindergarten program," he says. Think back to the discussions about the plant projects and homeless cats and dogs near the school. These were projects that were important to the students and mattered to their local community. Jim shares, "The projects help students recognize that their learning is meaningful and connected to the real world." This curriculum interest of Jim's led to his taking more workshops and courses in curriculum integration.

Some kindergarten teachers have had experience with preschool teaching prior to entering a teacher preparation program. Their experiences might become part of their certification program in early childhood, with their work experience with families and young children recognized as practicum experience. Although many states do not require certification to teach preschool children, almost all states require kindergarten teachers to have a teaching certificate. Professional organizations are pushing states to recognize the specialization of early childhood philosophy and child development and to separate early childhood education programs and certificates from elementary education. Quality kindergarten programs are staffed by teachers who understand and implement developmentally appropriate curriculum that leads to successful learning of each child (Moyer, 2001).

TEACHER ASSISTANTS. Teacher assistants are typically called *classified personnel* in school districts. The kindergarten teacher assistant may or may not have preparation in early childhood education. Many school districts offer workshops or other education opportunities for teacher assistants, which supports the professional growth and development of these important personnel.

THE NEED FOR QUALIFIED STAFF. Quality teaching staff is essential to a quality kindergarten program. In the NAEYC's list of indicators for quality early childhood programs, the caliber and competence of the staff are considered to be important indicators of the quality of an early childhood program. The education, training, and experience of the staff are reflected throughout each hour of each day. You see this in how the staff works with children, what activities are planned in the curriculum by the staff, and the staff's communication with parents, families, and colleagues. The preparation of early childhood professionals translates directly into the quality of early childhood programs.

Teacher preparation and teacher certification are definitely current issues in early childhood education. Let's examine some other important issues, as well as current trends surrounding kindergarten programs.

Current Issues and Trends Surrounding Kindergarten

As you read current articles about kindergartens, you will notice the appearance of several dominant issues or themes. Educators and parents seem to wonder about the curriculum of kindergarten and how to determine if a child is ready for kindergarten. Actually, these two issues are closely connected. If the curriculum becomes increasingly academic, one will find fewer 5-year-old children "ready" for this type of kindergarten. When the kindergarten curriculum truly focuses on the developmental levels and needs of 5- and 6-year-old children, then the issue of being "ready" for kindergarten changes substantially.

ACADEMICS AND KINDERGARTEN. Here, we'll take a closer look at the question of academics within the kindergarten curriculum. Curriculum that was formerly taught in first grade is now expected in some kindergartens.

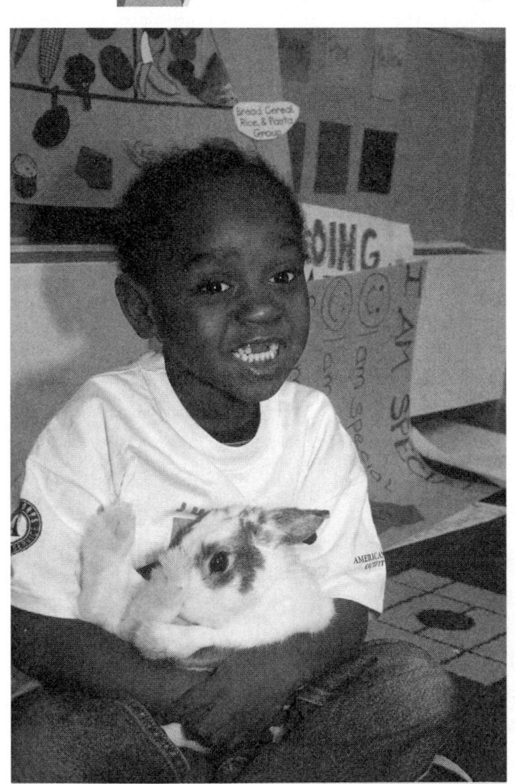

Creating a habitat is an important learning activity.

The National Association of Early Childhood Specialists in State Departments of Education (NAESC/SDE) developed a position paper in 2000 on unacceptable trends in kindergarten (the document was endorsed by NAEYC in 2001). This association became concerned with the narrowing of curriculum in kindergarten and the increasing pressure to enforce academic standards without regard to what is known about young children's development and learning (NAESC/SDE 2000). External pressures have changed the kindergarten curriculum so that it is often indistinguishable from those of the early primary grades.

According to Bredekamp and Copple (1997), curriculum content should reflect social or cultural values, parental input, and "consideration of age and experience of the learners" (p. 20). Kindergarten curriculum focused on learning rote skills and memorization is considered narrow and inappropriate for most 5-year-olds. Rather, a curriculum that promotes successful learning in a challenging and active learning environment while also providing for growth in each of the developmental areas could be labeled developmentally appropriate. Kindergarten curriculum should also include activities that encourage creativity, curiosity, play, and building of self-esteem and interest (Moyer, 2001).

Thinking of the developmental domains discussed in Chapter 3, you will recall discussions about cognitive, physical, emotional, and social growth. Learning within each of these areas would be incorporated in a developmentally appropriate curriculum, with balance sought among the domains. A strong focus on academics would skew this balance and provide fewer experiences in other developmental areas.

Perhaps this is one of the more important roles of a kindergarten—that of creating a curriculum balance among the developmental areas and looking for ways to blend activities to create a holistic program. Academics does not mean always sitting at a desk and working on a worksheet alone. Children are learning when they explore their environment, draw pictures of their observations, and share these interpretations with others. Keeley learned new classification skills when she was grouping the mice figures. This activity was different from completing a worksheet about mice. She was able to tell her own story about her classification process and the rationale for her work.

When the kindergarten program is clear about the content of its curriculum and the *why, what,* and *how* of teaching and learning, there is room to begin academic foundations within a creative, active learning environment. While Keeley and her classmates studied sunflowers, they were engaged in singing, painting, listening to stories, writing their own stories, and counting sunflower seeds. These are all beginning academic skills, yet they were woven into a project that was interesting to this group of children. Children are so curious at this age and truly want to learn. The key is to watch and learn from each child and to help all children construct their knowledge within a supportive, balanced learning environment.

The answer to the issue of increased academics within the kindergarten has not been reached yet. You will provide insights and input into this discussion as you learn more about early childhood education and visit kindergarten classrooms. Remembering the importance of developmentally appropriate curriculum provides a context for this issue. Combining a child-centered developmental philosophy that supports the foundations of academic skills and knowledge when appropriate might be one answer to this issue.

An issue closely related to the curriculum of kindergarten is readiness for kindergarten. How is it determined when a child is ready for kindergarten? Does a child have to demonstrate specific knowledge to be ready for kindergarten? These questions are part of the kindergarten debate taking place right now. Different states have different mandates or requirements for entrance to kindergarten. What is the answer to these questions? Or are there any "right" answers?

READINESS FOR KINDERGARTEN. Being ready for kindergarten brings many assumptions into the picture. Is the child supposed to be ready for kindergarten or is the school supposed to have a kindergarten program that is ready for each child? You can see how framing this issue shapes the question. Some states are pushing back the entrance age for kindergarten to reaching age 5 in the fall or even in the summer in order to enroll in kindergarten. Other states are requiring children to take placement or screening tests to determine readiness.

The NAEYC strongly opposes the use of testing to determine eligibility or readiness for kindergarten. The NAEYC-endorsed position statement on Unacceptable Trends in Kindergarten Entry and Placement (NAECS/SDE, 2000) states that all children are to be welcomed *as they are* into heterogeneous kindergarten settings. With growing concerns about the number of failing students and failing schools, there has been increased attention to "readiness" in early childhood education. Unfortunately, this forces children to be "ready" for inappropriate learning environments. By instituting testing and requirements, some children most in need of kindergarten experiences might be the ones denied entry. These children then lose a year of early childhood education that is important to their development (see Box 10.4). Children are ready for kindergarten when it is an early childhood environment that is engaging, is age appropriate, provides for individual learning, and provides knowledgeable teachers (Cassidy et al., 2003). A responsive, success-oriented kindergarten curriculum and a well-trained teacher have enormous influence on a young child's learning (NAECS/SDE, 2000).

While the debate about readiness for kindergarten continues, a connected issue, length of the school day, is also a topic of intense discussion. Some educators feel that extending

BOX 10.4 A Closer Look

What Is the Ready School?

Kagan (1994) uses the term *ready school* to describe a school where the responsibilities for children are shared across the community. She proposes that families are involved as active partners and decision makers with community programs that support early childhood education. All too often, the burden of becoming "ready" is placed on young children and their families (Cassidy et al., 2003). Shifting the focus to making schools ready for children helps share the responsibility for early childhood education. **Readying schools** means making them accessible and supportive of learning for each child in the community. The readiness debate shifts from readying each child to ensuring the school program is committed to working with families and children and that the community is actively involved in developing the optimal learning environment for young children.

the school day will improve the learning of kindergarten-aged children, but others contend that the content of the program is the factor that most affects the learning.

LENGTH OF SCHOOL DAY. There has a been a trend away from partial day or alternate-day kindergarten to full-day kindergarten in many school districts, with 55 percent of kindergartners now attending a full-day program (West et al., 2000). Perhaps the two most pressing reasons for extending the school day for kindergartners are the need for child care and the previous experiences in preschool for the majority of these children. With rising numbers of parents in the work force, young children are increasingly in need of child care. According to the U.S. Bureau of Labor, in 2000, 73 percent of mothers with children were in the labor force (U.S. Department of Labor, 2001). If a kindergarten is a half-day program, children are often bused to other centers for after-school care programs. With this approach to kindergarten and child care, children experience discontinuity in their day.

Children who have already spent full days in preschool and care centers are often ready for a full-day experience in kindergarten. Children could expand their half-day learning experiences throughout the day, having time to explore all of the centers in the room and choose more activities in their play. In Keeley's kindergarten, the full day allows for more time in project-based learning and more time to participate in the art program at the school.

Full-day kindergarten allows children and teachers more time to explore projects in depth, provides for more continuity in day-to-day activities, and provides a learning environment that lends itself to a more developmentally appropriate curriculum (Miller, 2003). Research studies conclude that full-day kindergarten is advantageous to all children (Clark & Kirk, 2000) and results in higher academic achievement and promotion of good relationships with peers (Vecchiotti, 2001). When a school district reviews its policy regarding the amount of time allocated for kindergarten, it is imperative that these discussions include the importance of program options for young children and their families. Kerry had decided that Keeley was ready for a full-day kindergarten program because she had spent several years in preschool on a full-day basis. Kerry appreciated the option of selecting a program that met Keeley's needs and her own as a single parent who works full time.

Providing quality programs and options for schedules based on a child's and family's needs, in both kindergarten and child care, should be a consideration when school districts and school boards review their kindergarten programs. Merely increasing the amount of hours does not lead to positive benefits in a full-day kindergarten. It is what children *experience* during the kindergarten program that promotes young children's exploration and learning (Vecchiotti, 2001).

PRINCIPLES AND INSIGHTS: A Summary and Review

After reading about kindergarten and the different types of programs offered at the kindergarten level, you are now more aware of the changes and pressures that early childhood educators are facing. When examining the debate about the goals for kindergarten, it is helpful to keep in mind that the purpose of the kindergarten year is to promote the learning and development of each child. Pushing children through escalated academics in kindergarten will not be beneficial to their overall development. The more the curriculum is rushed, the more children are sorted and short changed.

When you think about a quality kindergarten program, you know that it is important that the program philosophy be developed around the needs of a particular community. The families and culture of the community must be an integral part of early childhood programs. Effective kindergarten programs are built around *readying the school* for the children and including developmentally appropriate curriculum based on these children's developmental levels, learning needs, and interests.

Technology provided for enhanced learning opportunities for Keeley and her classmates. They enjoyed communicating with people around the world as well as accessing resources for projects. Jim found that websites allowed children to tap into current information as they developed questions or needed answers and information.

Keeley's kindergarten year provided her with rich, diverse experiences in each of the developmental areas. By the end of the year, she was drawing pictures and writing short stories with invented spelling. She could count by 10s to 100 and was eager to learn more about addition. Along with her classmates, she was an active participant in art and drama activities. She was pleased with her work and looking forward to spending time with her friends at school, both in the classroom and at after-school day care. Keeley is a curious learner with many questions and multiple interests. She also is confident about her work and her contributions to her class. What better way to spend this very important year in her life?

BECOMING AN EARLY CHILDHOOD PROFESSIONAL

Your Professional Portfolio

1. Visit a nearby elementary school and talk with the media specialist about software for young children. How does she make decisions about software purchases for her school? How do children access these programs? What guidelines does the school have for access to the Internet? Record your findings in a short paper for your portfolio.
2. Describe two activities that you consider to be developmentally appropriate for a 5- or 6-year-old child. Why are these activities developmentally appropriate? How did you make this determination?

Your Professional Library

Jones, E., Evans, K., & Rencken, K. (2001). *The lively kindergarten: Emergent curriculum in action.* Washington, DC: NAEYC.

Katz, L., & Chard, S. (2000). *Engaging children's minds: The project approach.* Stamford, CT: Ablex.

Lombardi, J. (2002). *Time to care: Redesigning child care to promote education, support families, and build communities.* Chicago: Temple University Press.

Pianta, R., & Kraft-Sayre, M. (2003). *Successful kindergarten transition: Your guide to connecting children, families, and schools.* Baltimore: Brookes.

Richgels, D. (2003). *Going to kindergarten: A year with an outstanding teacher.* Landham, MD: Scarecrow.

Thouvenelle, S., & Bewick, C. (2003). *Completing the computer puzzle: A guide for early childhood educators.* Boston: Allyn and Bacon.

CHAPTER

11

The Primary Grades

Erin Cheyenne's Story

CHAPTER focus:

When you finish reading and reflecting on this chapter, you will be able to:

1. Describe the important components of a daily schedule for a developmentally appropriate primary grade classroom.
2. Describe the characteristics of an active learning environment for primary grade children.
3. Plan and use classroom management and guidance strategies that support a caring classroom community and are appropriate for primary grades.
4. Develop a set of curricular approaches for primary grade literacy, math, science, and social studies, with attention to national standards.
5. Outline a plan for assessing children in primary grades—a plan that captures many dimensions of development, focuses on children's strengths, and helps children assume responsibility for their own learning.

In this chapter you will encounter Erin Cheyenne, who has already developed the capacity to think critically, to solve problems, and to make thoughtful decisions. As you meet her parents and observe her primary grade teacher, you will understand how Erin Cheyenne's capacities are being nurtured.

Meet Erin Cheyenne and Her Family

Erin Cheyenne is a bright, outspoken 7-year-old—the daughter of two university faculty members who teach courses in multicultural literature. They live in a newly purchased home on the campus where Herb and Terri work. Both parents spend all of their nonworking time with Erin Cheyenne and have schooled her at home until now. In the past, Herb and Terri arranged their teaching schedules so that one of them would always be at home with Erin. This year, they have found a primary grade classroom that has the qualities that they look for in educational settings, so they are trying it out for her. They are especially pleased about the teacher's use of cooperative learning, class meetings, and integrated art. Both parents are articulate, determined, and committed to a set of values focused on diversity. You can already see many of their qualities in Erin Cheyenne. The parents have also instilled in her their love of literature and their deep appreciation of legends and myths. Erin's writing and reading choices reflect subjects not typical of 7-year-olds.

Reasons for Educating at Home

To better understand Erin Cheyenne and her family, it's important to understand Herb and Terri's decision to school her at home. Some of their explanations include:

> We think that learning styles are important. She learns best by talking and interacting, by making up a story and acting it out. We were doubtful that this style would be supported in a classroom with 30 other students.
>
> We want a multicultural education for her—one that focuses on critical thinking, social justice, and societal reform. We want our values taught and do not want our spiritual traditions, cultures, and ethnicities negated by the school with a curriculum that is focused on Eurocentric, Judeo Christian traditions.
>
> We want her to be able to learn skills through content *she* finds interesting. We teach her using an interdisciplinary approach—for example, teaching language arts, math, science, social studies, the arts, and physical education through her study of animal habitats, dinosaurs, African and Celtic mythology (just to mention a few examples from her first-grade work).
>
> We want her to go at her own pace and to be able to "follow her bliss."
>
> We thought she would learn more, enjoy learning, and her spirit would flourish if she were loved and respected in her learning environment. We recognize that the affective component of the learning experience is paramount. Much learning is dependent on the relationship between the teacher and learner.
>
> We want a safe learning environment—by safe, we mean spiritually, emotionally, and physically. (Wheeler & Martin, 2000)

Lessons from Parents' Thinking

We think that there is much to learn from Terri and Herb's reasons for home schooling. First, you can get a sense of why parents make that choice. Second, you get an impression of some parents' perceptions of schools and what they are like. And most important, you learn about values that parents have for their children and you can integrate those priorities in your classroom and curriculum.

Erin Cheyenne's new teacher, Paula, has described her use of class meetings to Terri and Herb. Her goals for the meetings—problem solving, negotiating, appreciating others' perspectives, and building a caring classroom community (Vance & Jiménez Weaver, 2002, pp. 8–9)—are a good match with their goals for Erin Cheyenne. Paula says, "I want the children to learn how to handle issues in their school world so that they will be able to handle them in life."

Erin Cheyenne's Classroom

On the right-hand side of the pod of four classrooms, you see Erin Cheyenne's classroom. As you enter, you notice murals on one of the walls; tables clustered around the room; several bookcases; lots of tubs of assorted blocks, tiles, and wooden cubes; and colorful pillows spread out in one corner of the room. Near the library area is a wall of paintings, sketches, and collages with the children's signatures on them next to a display of Picasso, Miro, and Kandinsky. There are also quotes attached to the children's work and that of the more famous artists—"geometric shapes," "freeform shapes," "thin lines," "curved lines," and "symmetrical balance." Some of their work appears to have been produced with a computer program.

The children are reading silently—sitting, reclining, and standing all over the room. Paula, their teacher, is also reading, sitting on a bench next to Jordan. Erin Cheyenne is this week's "greeter" and she comes to you whispering, "This is our quiet reading time. Would you like a book?" She points to a basket near the door and returns to her pillow and book—*Sophie* by Aminah Brenda Lynn Robinson.

Today's Schedule

As you glance about the room, you notice today's schedule (see Figure 11.1) on the chalkboard and see that the quiet reading time is about to end. It's almost 8:45 and the next activity is class meeting.

Class Meeting. "Time for our class meeting—please put away your books," announces Anthony. He is this week's "schedule keeper" and takes his role very seriously. You observe him moving about the room, urging his friends to "stop reading" and "come to the circle for class meeting." Soon, he tells Paula, "We're almost ready." She agrees and begins the class meeting with, "Get ready to sing and sign with me." She hums a tune as she waits. Once she sees everyone is with her, she stops and signs the word *you* and begins to sing "You Light Up My Life." She and the children sing the entire song and sign the words. Some of the children sign very confidently and others need to check with their classmates or Paula. When the song is finished, Paula approaches each child, acknowledges her or him by name and some kind of greeting ("You look well rested today," or "I'm glad to see you," or "I hope you can read to me this morning"), and rubs a tiny drop of hand lotion into each pair of hands. Soon, the circle of children feel calm, hands are being rubbed, and

FIGURE 11.1
Daily Classroom Schedule

8:15–8:30	Quiet Reading
8:30–9:00	Class meeting
9:00–9:50	Math
9:50–10:30	Writers' Workshop
10:30–10:45	Recess
10:45–11:45	Reading and Language Arts
11:45–12:15	Lunch
12:15–12:45	Social Studies
12:45–1:20	Projects—Science
1:20–1:45	Music
1:45–2:45	Choice Time
2:45–3:00	Reflection Circle and Good-Bye

Paula asks, "Are there any appreciations or resentments?" She moves around the circle again, looking at each child until Natasha says, "I appreciate Jodie because she helped me clean up the pegs yesterday." Jodie smiles and says, "Thank you." Jordan says, "I appreciate William because he invited me to his house today." William also says, "Thank you." More children express appreciations until Erin Cheyenne says, "I felt frustrated when Paula stopped our project work yesterday because I didn't get to finish." Paula responds, "Thank you" in an accepting voice.

Several children express similar frustrations. Paula stops the appreciations and resentments and tells the class, "It sounds like we need to do some problem solving about our project work." Erin Cheyenne agrees, "I feel frustrated when that happens," and William adds, "I feel disappointed when I can't finish." Paula defines the problem for the group, "It sounds like we don't have enough time for our project work." "Is that the problem?" Heads nod. "Let's think of how we could solve the problem." She hangs a large sheet of paper and records the children's suggestions:

A longer time to work
Work faster
Skip recess
Come back from lunch earlier
Smaller projects

When the suggestions stop, Paula says to the children, "These are good ideas. I would like all of us to think about this for a day or two. But in the meantime, would you check on your work habits—see if you are using your time well—and I will check our weekly schedule to see where there might be more time. How does that sound?" The children agree and the class meeting comes to an end with the song, "The More We Get Together."

Math/Calendar Time. Some of the 25 children are standing in front of the calendar projected onto a screen from Paula's computer. They are discussing today's date—October 24th. Erin Cheyenne describes the pattern she found with the pumpkins marking the days of the month to date on the October calendar: "I found an ABBA pattern. See, there is a big pumpkin first, then two little pumpkins, and today has a big pumpkin again." Paula asks, "So, if we go big, little, little, big, we have an ABBA pattern? Erin and her friends nod. Jordan says, "If we put a little pumpkin on October 24th, we would have an ABBB pattern. Paula asks the group, "What do you think?" Jordan places the little pumpkin on the calendar and looks at his friends. "It's an ABBB." The children look at the rest of the October calendar for other patterns of 4 and Paula records them on chart paper. After a few minutes, she directs the children to go to their tables and make different combinations of patterns and equations using the number 4, reminding them, "If you need help, check with one of your neighbors."

For a brief time, Paula chats with us about how she adapts the curriculum to meet the learning needs of this diverse class of children. In math, the common element is calendar math with patterns and combinations of numbers that make 4. "You see that some of the children use manipulatives and visual representations of numbers, while others can handle written symbols and rhythmic patterns." She notes for us that there are both concrete experiences as well as very abstract work. She draws our attention to Jodi, who can sometimes name the pattern she is making with the plastic pumpkins. We later learn that Jodie has Down syndrome and needs to work with manipulatives and that Paula and the resource teacher find many ways to modify the curriculum for her. During that same math activity, Natasha is subtracting 6 pumpkins from 10 pumpkins and drawing an equation to display her expression of 4. Children in this first/second-grade class are engaged in learning mathematics at many different levels.

Writers' Workshop Time. Holding a red file folder, Anthony takes a seat in the Author's Chair surrounded by eight of his friends. In other parts of the room are similar groups, some at tables with hard copies of their writing and some at computer stations. Anthony pulls his story out of the folder and begins reading about bugs from another planet that he found in his backyard. The bugs are psychedelic colors and move backwards. He has illustrated the bugs with glowing colors and he reads with much animation. When he finishes, he asks his classmates to critique his story. Erin Cheyenne is the first to comment, "You made up a scarey story, Anthony—you made the bugs seem real." Another classmate comments, "I wasn't bored." After other comments, Anthony asks if there any questions about his story, and again Erin jumps in with, "I want to know how the bug goes backward." Paula is standing nearby listening and she expresses the same curiosity as Erin did. Anthony has obviously thought about the question and responds with, "Where the bugs come from, everything goes backwards and they do, too." His friends nod with understanding.

After one more child shares her story, it is time to work quietly on additional writing. All the children pull file folders from the writing center tub and go to work. Some are editing reports at the computer while others are illustrating stories. Some children are working with partners, reading their stories out loud and asking for feedback on their writing. Paula explains that they are involved in the peer edit/review process of writer's workshop. We notice that those children who have finished writing stories are working with word cards and idea files to explore topics for future writing. One small group of three second-grade children is writing a collaborative poem on the computer, and is enthusiastically coming up with words to end a rhyme.

Anthony announces that there are two minutes left before recess, so we see children finishing their work and putting materials away. The writing center has an ample supply of paper, pencils, crayons, tape, staplers, colored paper, crayons, and charcoal, as well as several typewriters and three computers. There is a display of multiple forms of text: letters to the editor, recipes, plans for a group project, captions with a photo, brochures, and school and community announcements, as well as book covers.

Recess Time. As the children gather at the classroom door, Paula describes the play choices for the playground today and hands out equipment to the children—jump ropes, colored chalk, bean bags, and hoops. "For those of you who don't want to play with the equipment, I'm going to play Statues with a group near the climbing structure." As the children are heading out, Paula tells us that once a week, the class has a class meeting to discuss playground behavior and issues that have arisen. "They work out very good strategies to handle the usual recess problems."

Paula describes how recess is a time for children to practice the problem solving, negotiating, and community building that they are developing in the classroom. When we ask if she will consider the children's suggestion to "skip recess" in order to have more time for projects, she reflects before answering. When she does, it is clear that she, like so many teachers, values recess for its "unstructured time with plenty of physical and psychological roaming space and lack of imposed rules" and its support for "children's self expression in ways that no other setting can provide" (O'Brien, 2003, p. 165).

Reading and Language Arts Time. Before we know it, Anthony is leading the children back into the classroom and announcing that it is time for reading. Another teacher has joined the class—Marty, the resource teacher, who comes in and works with Jodie and other children according to their learning needs. She also works with the classroom teachers to discuss curriculum and modifications or accommodations to the learning activities that will help children be successful. Today, Jodie approaches Marty with a smile, saying, "I remember my words that we wrote. Can I read them?" Marty is carrying boxes of cards belonging to Jodie and six other children as well as a stack of books. She and Jodie sit at a small table and Jodie immediately gets her cards out of the box and spreads them out on the table. She

quickly picks up *bug* and appears to be looking for another word. "It has squiggly marks at the end that go *ssss,* so here it is." She picks up the word *grass* and smiles. Marty engages her in conversation about each of her word cards then spends time developing two new word cards that are Jodie's choice. Jodie draws a picture on the back of each card to represent the word.

When Jodie finishes, she goes to another part of the room where several children are reading to each other. She spots Erin Cheyenne, who has brought from home a book of Native American legends for children. Jodie asks Erin to read to her and hears, "I will read you just one story, that's all." Jodie listens intently to Erin's reading and claps when the story ends. Jodi then gets a book from the shelf and begins to read. It's a book of familiar signs—McDonalds, Safeway, Stop, Baskin Robbins, and so on. Erin Cheyenne looks up from her own reading and says, "That's good reading, Jodie."

We see that Paula has a group of children with her at a storyboard. They are reading a class letter aloud together and she stops at the end of each sentence to draw the children's attention to words or letters: "You notice that this sentence has lots of words that start with *g.* Let's say them together—*gate, good, going.*" She and the children say the words and she asks them to make the *g* sound and to think of other *g* words. At other sentences, Paula points to the ending sounds or to the vowels. When they finish reading the letter a second time, Paula asks the children questions about the letter's meaning: "How do you think the writers feel when they are writing this letter? What makes you think of that feeling?'

As we get close to Paula, we see that she is noting children's initials on a checklist-type sheet all during the letter-reading activity. She comments that the checklist is a summary of "the skills and behaviors we're working on during this time." Throughout the morning, we saw Paula writing notes on Post-its and sticking them on a clipboard (see Figure 11.2). "I try to capture brief anecdotes whenever I can, whenever I see one of the children doing something or saying something that tells me that they are learning and progressing." Later, Paula places those notes in the children's folders so that in time she has lots of information about each child.

Cooperative Learning in Primary Grades. While the children are at lunch, we spend a few minutes talking with Paula. "I really want the children to learn from each other, so much of the work in the classroom is structured in a **cooperative learning** format, with small groups of children working together toward a shared learning goal. Much of what we are trying to do in cooperative learning is supported by our class meetings and some other management strategies." Paula talks about a workshop on cooperative learning and describes some of the strategies she learned for maximizing individual learning in small groups (Bolenbaugh, 2000). "The cooperative learning approach allows me to work on many social skills

FIGURE 11.2

Post-it of Anecdotal Information

11-30-2004

Erin Cheyenne read a chapter of legends book with fluency—accuracy—difficult volcabulary. Used expression (literacy).

Later demonstrated sensitivity—complimented Jodie (social skills).

and understandings at the same time children are working on math or writing or science." She describes how important it is to check in with the

groups to assess how well each student understands the work and how well the children are working as a group. Paula shows us one of several recording forms that she uses as she moves from group to group. She also explains her use of Post-its: "I used to watch and later think about a child and her learning but I learned that I need to record what I see at the time it happens." Paula admits that such documentation is more accurate and helpful in making changes in curriculum and children's learning goals.

As the children return, Paula reminds Anthony that today's schedule had to be changed because a guest is coming to show his bug collection. "In some ways, we are combining science and social studies in our project time, but I try to have such integration all the time." She

tells us that the class has been engaged in a study of bugs and that when they were collecting bugs, some children expressed concern. Erin Cheyenne was the most articulate: "I don't think it's right to take bugs out of their environment—they don't belong in jars." A serious discussion followed and the children went home to discuss the issue with their families. The next day at their class meeting, the children expressed continuing interest in the issue. When asked what they would like to do, several children, including Erin Cheyenne, suggested that a study group could do some research and report back to the class. Four children volunteered to form the group and to share what they learned with the class.

Science/Social Studies Time. Graphic designer Michael Kippenhan has come to class today. Michael's hobby is the study of bugs, and he has brought cases of bug collections to show the class. Like many teachers who use the project approach, Paula values "the kind of dialogues children can have with an expert as a way of enhancing the learning environment" (Capezzuto & Da Ros-Voseles, 2001, p. 84). Later she tells us that the class has also had guest speakers via videoconferences. "We're going to try a virtual field trip one of these days," she adds enthusiastically.

Paula has prepared their expert in advance of the visit by sharing her curriculum and describing some of the children's activities, curiosities, and concerns. The children gather around him as he opens his cases, puts up the displays, and sets out photographs and books. Jodie asks Michael if he would like to look at their drawings of the bugs they've seen and collected, to which he responds enthusiastically, taking Jodie's hand and following her lead. As the other children gather around, Paula encourages them to take turns telling Michael something they know about the bugs in their display. When it's Jodie's turn, she hesitates, "I don't know more about this bug." Erin prompts her with, "What color is that bug, Jodie?" and she responds, "Green, green—this bug is green."

After touring the children's photos, drawings, papier-mache bugs, and jars with bugs, twigs, and grass, Michael asks the children to join him to view his collection. He describes how he got interested in bugs, what he learns from studying bugs, and his care in the collection process. He shows a video of one of his trips to look for rare beetles and passes around cases of his collections. Michael tells the children that he understands their concern about collecting bugs and he shares his feelings about the issue. Paula joins him and reminds the class, "A group of you worked on a report about taking bugs out of their environment and keeping them on display. Michael asked if he could stay to hear your report—is that alright?" Erin Cheyenne looks slightly puzzled by Paula's question, shrugs her shoulders, and says, "Sure; why wouldn't it be?" Paula suggests that she check with her committee to see how they feel and Erin looks at Natasha, Myisha, and Roland. They all comment positively and Erin turns back to Paula for direction.

Paula gathers the class near the display area again and introduces Erin Cheyenne's committee to report what they have learned about the issue of collecting bugs. The committee has posters and a written report to read to the class. Erin reads quite fluently, pausing for only a few words—*protection, environment,* and *policy.* Paula asks the committee to explain what *policy* means and the other children look at Erin. "It's like rules, I think," she explains, "that's what my dad told me." When she finishes reading, the other committee members show their posters and explain the information displayed visually. Paula asks, "Does anyone have a question or a comment for the committee?" Anthony asks, "Is this the same as when people get mad about animals being caged?" Erin Cheyenne nods firmly, "Yes; that's not right either." Michael raises his hand, "I would like to know where the committee got their information." Erin mentions her family, several faculty members at the university, and some written materials that her mom read to her. Myisha said that her aunt works for animal rights and gave her some brochures.

"It's time to stop for music," Paula announces, and Anthony jumps up to say, "Get ready for music." Several of the children thank Michael for coming and Paula tells him and the class, "We will be writing to you about this visit—we will write about what we learned—and we appreciate your time." Paula invites Michael to return when the children have finished their study. "We will have a display, a book, and a little drama about bugs for the kindergarten class."

As the children leave to go to their music class, Jodie shouts, "Music, music, I love music." Paula nods and tells us, "Music really engages all of the children so well." Children can participate in varied ways, with varied skills, and at their own level of comfort, and music is noncompetitive, nonjudgmental, and so joyful for all (Humpal & Wolf, 2003, p. 104).

JOURNAL 11.1: What is the value of bringing in a community guest to interact with the children?

Choice Time. After the children go to their music class, they participate in "choice time" with a partner. Anthony announces the choices for this day as he reads from colorful cards with both words and pictures, "Today we have sewing center, table games, construction, Pictionary, watercolor painting, and clay.

Children immediately choose a partner and an activity. We hear negotiations over what the chosen activity will be: "Last time we played what you wanted; today it's my turn" and "I really want to play with dominos today, please." Soon, the group is scattered around the room. A large group is playing table games—Candyland, Dominos, Mankala, Clue, and Junior Scrabble. At the construction center, three sets of partners are building with a wide array of recycled materials (boxes, straws, lids, cups, etc.). The hour flies by and children are intensely engaged in play activities that continue to develop their literacy, math, and motor skills. Anthony gives the class a five-minute warning, "In five minutes we will begin cleanup" and then rushes back to his Clue game, "Hurry up, you guys, we have to figure out who did it."

JOURNAL 11.2: Some primary grade teachers do not offer children a "choice time" because they need all of their class time for curriculum (reading, math, etc.). After your brief observation of Paula's "choice time," how would you defend that use of time?

Reflection Circle and Good-Bye. There's a flurry of cleanup and gathering of backpacks and other belongings before children gather in a circle with Paula. In a very quiet voice, Paula begins, "This was an amazing day of learning for us—my head is full of information and new ideas." She continues, "Let's be still for a minute and think about what we learned and thought about today." The children get quiet and Paula waits for almost a minute before proceeding, "Who would like to share what he or she learned today?" Many hands go up and Paula says, "It looks like we need to go around our circle and give everyone a chance." One by one, the children describe their learning experiences:

- "I learned about very rare bugs and how hard it is to find them." (Natasha)
- "Now I know what an entomologist is. I'm going to see if my dad knows." (Erin Cheyenne)
- "I read about legends today and I will tell the class one of them tomorrow." (Roland)
- "I learned about those rules that protect animals and insects." (Michael)

Erin responds to the last description with, "He means policies, doesn't he, Paula?" Paula nods and Alex says, "Yes, policies to protect animals and insects." Paula moves from child to child, saying, "It was good to spend the day with you today," and "We really learned together today," and "I will enjoy seeing you again tomorrow." As she pats their hands, the children move to the door for departure to their buses. We hear them say good-bye to each other and to Paula.

JOURNAL 11.3: When you listen and observe what the children are doing in Paula's classroom, what can you picture in the classroom environment? How is it furnished and arranged? How does the environment feel?

Learning from Paula: Meeting Diverse Needs and Providing Guidance

Paula begins by telling us, "This is such a great group of individuals—so many unique children. Having Jodie in our class is good for all of us. Her involvement in the classroom is going smoothly now. At first, she wanted my attention a lot, but now she seems familiar with our routine. I talked with the kindergarten teacher and paired Jodie with two favorite friends from last year to help her feel more secure and comfortable in our class. Because much of our classroom instruction is in small groups or individual sessions, Jodie progresses at her own level and interacts with other students." From our brief time in the class, it was easy to see what Paula is describing. It did seem that all of the children worked together cooperatively but at their own levels and they truly helped each other. It truly feels like her "caring classroom community."

Explicit Instructions

Paula continues, "One thing I have learned is to be explicit in my instructions, whether talking about curriculum or behavior expectations. That helps Jodie and really all of the students and eliminates a lot of the usual classroom disruptions. It is amazing to see the difference when students work in their groups with clear directions. For some of the children, I give several small steps for a task rather than describe the entire task at once. Jodie is much more successful when she can complete a few tasks at a time."

Consistency and Routines

Another important aspect that provides guidance for students is maintaining consistency and routines in the classroom. Paula has noticed that creating routines "not only helped Jodie navigate through the school day, but it also helped the class as a whole operate more smoothly. We talk about our schedule, activities, jobs, and expectations for behavior in ongoing regular discussions. We hold class meetings about those topics so that we can adjust a routine that isn't working or add a job that we suddenly need."

Paula has created a positive learning atmosphere in the classroom. The room is arranged for comfort and for work. Materials are very accessible and interesting. The levels of engagement all day tell us that children were interested and challenged. The routines were planned to eliminate waiting or "down time" as well as to build a community.

A Caring and Supportive Setting

Paula feels strongly about creating a caring and supportive environment in which children take care of and respect each other. Her commitment was so evident in the circle times, the group work, and the way she spoke to the children. She admits to us, "I used to do a fairly traditional circle time with lots of class routines—attendance, calendar, weather, and a review of the day's activities. It felt pretty rote and I began to feel that it needed to be more meaningful. Through my reading and conversations with other teachers, I learned that I wasn't alone in wanting circle time to be more personal and productive (Harris & Fuqua, 2000). I decided that it is a time to promote the class community and that the children and I could interact in a more supportive and productive way. I studied the use of class meetings and began slowly introducing the children to the processes. They understand that it is a safe and positive time when we respect and listen to each other. Everyone's ideas and opinions are valued. They are really learning to be socially competent. We practiced the steps of problem solving and they learned how to make 'I feel statements' so that they can skillfully participate in the meeting." She shares the book, *Class Meetings: Young Children Solving Problems Together* (Vance & Jiménez Weaver, 2002), with us, saying, "It's from NAEYC and I reread it for new ideas now and then."

JOURNAL 11.4: After observing and listening, identify two or three strategies that Paula used to help children take responsibility for their own learning.

Primary Grades Curriculum

Spending time in a primary grade classroom with Erin Cheyenne enabled us to see almost all of the curricular areas in one day's schedule. Often, these areas are integrated, as we saw with science and social studies, for lots of good reasons and to make the best use of a very fast-paced day.

Primary Grades Literacy Curriculum

A major curricular focus in most primary grades is **literacy**—reading, spelling, writing, and communication in general. Large blocks of time focus on literacy as well as much of the environment is designed to contribute to children's development in reading and writing.

A Conversation about Inclusion

When we asked Herb and Terri to talk about inclusion, they were passionate and direct in their thoughts about inclusion, especially in reference to Erin Cheyenne's education. Their definition included phrases such as "no one perspective should ever dominate," "thinking and approaches should be holistic," and "includes nonmainstream thinking and perspectives." With respect to Erin Cheyenne, inclusion means that she will be aware of multiple identities and their traditions, and multiple ways of knowing. When Herb and Terri looked for an inclusive educational setting for Erin Cheyenne, their list of what would assure them of its inclusivity tells you much about their values (Wheeler & Martin, 2000):

- There would be multiple historical perspectives instead of only a Eurocentric perspective.
- There would be evidence in the classroom, in the learning materials, in the teaching style, and in the school's philosophy of a multicultural education approach that builds cross-cultural competencies, is sensitive to inequities and power relationships, builds on the principles of democracy, and seeks to change society.
- Children's literature would be ethnically, culturally, and gender balanced and include representation of societies, including those with physical differences, and gay and lesbian people.
- Children's literature would reflect environmental reverence and spiritual connectedness to her soul (nature/spirit helper) and animals in general.
- Cooperation and collaboration would be encouraged.
- Multiple learning styles would be addressed.
- Her voice would be heard as she is encouraged to question and think critically.
- Bias would be acknowledged in books and other materials, and solutions would be suggested for combating and resolving past injustices for the future (especially what she might do to effect change).

An important recommendation from the American Federation of Teachers (AFT, 1999) is to stimulate children's interest in reading through regular exposure to interesting books and through discussions in which children respond to many texts.

Most teachers have good collections of storybooks and other narrative texts, typically fiction, but hesitate to use informational texts or nonfiction books. They are concerned that informational books may not be appropriate, or may be too difficult, or won't interest children. Research has shown that young children need and enjoy frequent exposure to many and varied forms of literacy, including nonfiction or informational texts (Walker et al., 2003, p. 153). Children will need opportunities to explore informational texts as well as opportunities to learn strategies for reading those texts. In the activities that are described in the next section, you will see how varied forms of text can be used throughout the literacy curriculum.

In addition to informational texts, Paula encourages the development of vocabulary associated with the content of class projects, with their class meetings, with community events, and with the children's art. Box 11.1 describes Art Talk, an innovative approach Paula is using to integrate visual arts with other aspects of her curriculum.

One of the major outcomes of instruction in reading and writing in primary grades is for children to become "independent and productive readers" (International Reading Association and the National Association for the Education of Young Children, 2000, p. 13). With such a broad and important goal and the complexity of successful reading instruction comes the need for consistent and accurate assessment of each child's ongoing development of reading and writing knowledge, skills, and dispositions. Experts are clear that such assessment must be "anchored in real-life writing and reading tasks and continuously chronicle a wide range of children's literacy activities in different situations" (p. 13).

Research Findings: Art Talk in Early Childhood Education

In collaboration with five early childhood teachers, Rosemary Althouse, Margaret Johnson, and Sharon Mitchell (2003) studied children's art experiences for three years. They watched children's progress and documented their learning using art portfolios of both verbal and artistic expression. One of the unique aspects of their portfolios was a section on "Art Talk," a focus on artistic vocabulary and concepts. Art Talk was the language used by teachers in talking with young children about their artwork and was heard in the children's spontaneous talk about art.

Paula, like many educators, had limited preparation and little confidence in the visual arts. When she read about Art Talk, she wanted to promote the vocabulary but needed to learn it herself. She practices by commenting on children's artwork both verbally and in written form. She occasionally uses the Art Talk Checklist to capture children's growth in using artistic vocabulary.

Art Talk allows children to "express the quality of their marks, ideas, feelings, efforts, and inventiveness," and promotes an "understanding of the basic elements and principles of design" (p. 130). Children are encouraged to talk about *line, hue* and *value* of color, *shape, form, texture,* and *composition.* Also explored are children's stories about their artwork, the discoveries they make while creating art, specific media and special techniques, and planning for artwork.

Some suggestions for talking with children about their art include (pp. 136–137):

1. Use correct terms when commenting on children's artwork.
2. Encourage children to verbalize about their artwork.
3. Focus children's attention on the way they use art media.
4. Connect art with other curricular areas or learning experiences.
5. Introduce children to a variety of artists.
6. Refer to children as artists.

CURRICULAR COMPONENTS OF LITERACY INSTRUCTION. In the primary grades, we will typically see both reading and writing approached more formally than in kindergarten or preschool classrooms. We may see the use of a commercially published product, such as a basal reader, or a literature anthology series, or a set of informational texts. We see some of each in Paula's classroom. Varied forms of text support both the needs and the interests of children from different backgrounds. When teachers encourage multiple forms of communication involving reading, writing, and talking throughout the curriculum, children's literacy interests increase and they learn content and language (Donovan, Milewicz, & Smolkin, 2003, pp. 31–35).

In Paula's classroom we also see a variety of literacy activities and materials to support the children's development:

- Multiple kinds of reading events with all types of materials in varied settings—the class library and other activity centers (science, art, etc.)—as part of project work, in class meetings, and in the community (quiet reading time, independent reading in the library, reading the report on bugs, etc.)
- Read-alouds with all types of written material (newspapers, magazines, letters, postcards, books, maps, e-mails, etc.)
- Modeling varied written and oral texts (reports, letters, lists, stories) with individual children or small groups or the entire class (making a list at the class meeting, writing impressions after a field trip, making a chart for activity planning)
- Independent or small group composition of texts as children label drawings, write directions, develop reports, write letters, or record data
- Integration of reading, writing, and talking (Writers' Workshop processes, science reports and discussions, etc.) and with other curricular areas (art displays, projects, etc.)
- Informal handwriting and spelling instruction

Paula is committed to the goals of the joint position statement of the International Reading Association and the National Association for the Education of Young Children (2000), especially "fostering and sustaining the interest and disposition to read and write for their own enjoyment, information, and communication" (p. 2). Thus, she finds as many "real-world" situations for reading and writing as possible.

Most of the children in the class we visited are using invented spelling for their story writing but some of the more mature children, such as Erin Cheyenne, have begun to insist on "spelling it right." She and others frequently ask for help, or check their spelling, and in the process, Paula provides informal spelling instruction. The same opportunities present themselves for instruction in letter formation.

What advantages do you see in Erin Cheyenne's home environment that will support her literacy development?

RESPONDING TO CHILDREN'S DIFFERENCES WITH LITERACY INSTRUCTION. Just as we saw in Paula's classroom, children bring a wide range of diverse abilities and come from different oral and written language experiences before they come to school. Some of the children, such as Erin Cheyenne, have been surrounded by a range of writing and reading materials, have observed their parents reading and writing frequently, and have even had formal and informal instruction in reading and writing. Other children have not had access to many reading and writing experiences, materials, models, or instruction. All of these differences have prompted reading experts to reach the conclusion that "no one teaching method or approach is likely to be the most effective for all children"

(Strickland, 1994). Like Paula, good teachers use a rich repertoire of teaching strategies and materials to meet the diversity of learners. With 25 children, that takes careful thinking about curriculum and intense assessment of children's learning and progress. Without the notes Paula keeps on each child, she can't possibly know how to plan for the diverse needs and levels of readiness of her class.

JOURNAL 11.5: After reading about the complexity of literacy instruction, what are some things you can do to prepare yourself for teaching primary grades? ●

Primary Grade Mathematics Curriculum

When a child enters the primary grades, she brings with her numerous mathematical experiences. She has counted buttons, ordered objects from largest to smallest, talked about the concept of *more,* and taken a whole object and broken it into smaller objects (e.g., cookies or crackers). Mathematics is part of her everyday life.

CONSTRUCTING MATHEMATICAL MEANINGS. The task for the teacher is to encourage each child's enthusiasm for learning mathematics in such a way that children retain their enjoyment of, and curiosity about, mathematics. Young children gain meaningful understanding when involved in constructing mathematical meaning from their personal experiences (Nagel & Swingen, 1998).

The joint position statement of the National Association for the Education of Young Children and the National Council of Teachers of Mathematics (2002, p. 1) describes the importance of children's early encounters with mathematics in terms of how those experiences will shape children's attitudes, confidence, and disposition to use math. Classroom experiences in math must build on children's experience and knowledge, including their family, linguistic, cultural, and community backgrounds. Within those experiential contexts, math curriculum can focus on problem solving and reasoning, communication, connections, and representation. Mathematics learning must start with play and be extended by discussion for understanding to occur. Children need time to explore with manipulatives, handling concrete materials prior to working with pencils and paper. The work with concrete materials enables children to discover mathematical relationships and to think analytically about mathematical ideas.

MATHEMATICAL CONTENT. Following are the five major content areas in mathematics for primary age children. We give you an example of a lesson within each of the content areas.

1. *Numbers and operations.* Number sense is the foundation for later work in computations. In the primary years, children spend time developing the concept of recognizing an amount of objects and combining this amount with additional objects for beginning addition. For example, Erin Cheyenne holds up six crayons and asks those around her, "How many is this?" Her teacher watches and after children say "Six," she places three more crayons in Erin's hand and asks, "How many crayons do we have all together?" Paula recognizes the importance of working with operations using real objects. By the end of second grade, children experience working with larger numbers, becoming knowledgeable about combinations that represent amounts with two or three digits as they move toward a sum of 100 or larger.
2. *Geometry.* Prior to coming to school, Erin Cheyenne began to recognize and describe the physical attributes of two- and three-dimensional shapes. She also looked with her mom at the spatial relationship between objects as she worked with puzzles, wooden shapes, and her drawings. When Paula brought out familiar objects on a tray (a cereal box, a ball, a triangular box, an egg), Erin jumped up from her play to come

over and name the objects. Paula listened and then began asking questions: "What is the same and what is different between these two objects?" and "What other objects in our room look like the cereal box?" The discussion that followed included terminology useful in geometry as children extended their understanding of characteristics of shapes.

3. *Algebraic relationships and patterning.* Patterning is emphasized in the primary grades. Children of this age learn to sort, classify, and order objects according to attributes of shape, size, color, and other characteristics. Patterning also includes extending pattern sequences and developing patterns with physical objects and on paper, as you heard Erin Cheyenne and her friends do. In the first grade, a teacher might also work with her students to discover patterns with the first 100 counting numbers. By examining the pattern of numbers, children discover the repetition of certain digits in a certain order (e.g., after 20 follows 21, after 30 is 31, etc.). Children delight in finding patterns in the world around them.

4. *Mathematics.* In the early grades, children are expected to describe measurable attributes of objects and to compare and order objects according to the attributes. In addition, they learn to use appropriate standards and tools for measuring. Early lessons focus on comparison of objects and use of measurement vocabulary, such as *longer, shorter, wider,* and so on. By second grade, Erin and her friends use rulers and record measurement in inches and feet.

5. *Data analysis and probability.* By second grade, children should have experiences with collecting and sorting data, and making inferences from these data. One day, Paula had the children wash and cut up raw vegetables for a snack to be served with a dip. As the children served themselves their snack, they also recorded their choices on a chart of the available vegetables. After eating, they looked at the chart (see Figure 11.3) and determined which was the most popular vegetable and dips. They had begun to learn how to organize data and to interpret what data can mean.

The National Standards for School Mathematics recommends that teachers, parents, and caregivers of young children (prekindergarten through grade 2) "need to be knowledgeable about the many ways students learn mathematics, and they need to have high expectations for what can be learned during these early years" (NCTM, 2000, p. 75). The report emphasizes the importance of a solid mathematical foundation and of supporting children's efforts and confidence in their own math learning. The standards emphasize problem solving, communication, reasoning, and representation to extend the content areas previously described. As an early childhood educator, you will need to set high expectations for yourself as a math teacher. The standards urge you to "seek, if necessary, the new knowledge and skills you need to guide and nurture all students" (p. 76).

Primary Grades Science Curriculum

Paula builds on the children's curiosity as a natural foundation for learning science. She believes that a scientist is one who is "involved in the process of inquiry—raising questions and trying to answer questions about the world in which we live" (Chaille & Britain, 1997). She regards the scientific process as a process of inquiry through problem solving, creativity, and experimentation. As we watch Latoya, you will see that process in action.

CHILD-CENTERED SCIENCE. Latoya and others are getting ready for lunch recess. She turns to Erin Cheyenne, and says, "Guess what? I have a new friend on the playground. Do you want to see her?" Erin is, of course, enthusiastic and curious, as is Paula, her teacher. Paula follows as the girls go out to the playground. Latoya points, "Here she is—look on the ground. But she is little now." She turns to Paula, "What happened?" Paula responds, "She's smaller than she was this morning—is that what happened?" "Way

FIGURE 11.3
Mathematics Chart: Vegetable Choices

Our Vegetable Choices — Oct. 6

beets	celery	carrots	tomato	pepper	yam	radish	cucumber
Roland	Roland	Erin C	Roland	Rueben	Michael	Roland	Michael
Michael	Paula	Roland	Jodie	Erin C	Jodie	Jodie	Erin C
Paula	Jodie	Paula	Natasha	Jodie	Paula	Paula	Roland
	Rueben	Jodie	Paula	Paula	Joseph		Natasha
	Michael	Rueben	Joseph				Jodie
	Natasha	Michael					Paula
		Natasha					Joseph
		Joseph					

Which is our favorite vegetable?
Which vegetable do the fewest children like?

smaller," says Latoya. With questions from Paula, Latoya and Erin talk about shadows, how they are made, and what they might do to find out when the shadow is bigger and when it is smaller. Erin comes up with idea to trace around Latoya's feet with chalk, and then trace her shadow right now at 12:15 p.m. Then they will check after school and see if the shadow size has changed, and then check again in the morning.

In the scene on the playground, Latoya and Erin Cheyenne became involved in a science investigation. Their curiosity led them to question the reason shadows change size. Their observations and comparisons will help them draw inferences about the position of the sun and its effect on the size of shadows.

SCIENCE CONTENT. A primary focus of science for a child of primary age should be science as inquiry in the content areas of physical science, life science, and earth and space science. *Physical science* is the study of properties of objects, motion of objects, and the phenomenon of light, heat, electricity, and magnetism. In *earth and space science,* young children study the properties of earth and objects and changes in the earth and sky. The emphasis in *life science* is on the characteristics and life cycles of organisms and the relationship between organisms and environments. The content areas also include *science and technology, science in personal and social perspectives,* and *history and nature of science,* and they are described in the National Science Standards (NRC, 1996).

SCIENCE LITERACY. Science literacy emerges from a child's investigations of situations encountered in life and the use of science processes to make sense of and enjoy those encounters (Owens, 1999). The primary science tools that should be incorporated in science investigations are observing, comparing, classifying, communicating, hypothesizing, predicting, testing, and experimenting.

Just as important as introducing those tools and providing many opportunities to practice with them will be your documentation of the science understandings children develop. Good advice for how to record the learning comes from a collaboration of teachers (Jones & Courtney, 2002, pp. 34–36). They encourage you to:

- Collect a variety of forms of evidence of children's learning (drawings, dictations, photographs, language records, journals, etc.).
- Collect the evidence over a period of time.
- Record the understandings of the group as well as the individual (group reflections, stories, murals, questions, etc.).

Your careful documentation of children's science learning will inform your ongoing planning, new learning activities for children, and reports for parents.

Primary Grades Social Studies Curriculum

Early childhood educators encourage teachers to provide an experiential curriculum in social studies—with experiences that are ongoing and full of learning.

CURRICULAR EXPERIENCES. Some of the qualities of those experiences that foster learning of young children include the following:

1. Experiences with deep, personal meaning for children, firsthand experiences with their world, initiated by children, and age appropriate
2. Experiences with meaning and integrity and emerging from concepts of a disciplinary area
3. Experiences that involve children in group work and interactions with others with the skills needed to perpetuate our democratic society
4. Experiences with continuity, building on other experiences, forming a complete, coherent, whole, and integrated curriculum
5. Experiences with time and opportunity for children to reflect, think, and learn (Seefeldt & Galper, 2000, p. 4)

SOCIAL STUDIES CONTENT. Social studies draws on many diverse disciplines, including anthropology, archaeology, economics, geography, history, philosophy, political science, psychology, religion, sociology, humanities, mathematics, and the natural sciences. The primary purpose of social studies is to help children develop the ability to make informed and reasoned decisions for the public good as citizens of a culturally diverse democratic society and an interdependent world (National Council for the Social Studies [NCSS], 1998). The National Council for the Social Studies has identified four themes for the content of social studies and they are appropriate for primary grades:

1. *Time, continuity, and change.* Paula's class is making a book about themselves—recording what they were like early in the year, their changes, what they are like midway through the year, and of course, again at the end of the year.
2. *People, places, and environments.* Some of the children are already studying about the work of an entomologist, as you heard when their visitor came to class.
3. *Production, distribution, and consumption.* The class visited a farm to observe the production of vegetables and fruits, saw them loaded on trucks for distribution to markets, and later observed them for sale in their local grocery story.
4. *Civic ideals and practices.* At election time, the class read about and visited campaign headquarters and voting booths. They held their own elections.

As with all of the other curricular areas, it is critical to start social studies curriculum development with a sound knowledge of the children—their experiential background, their family culture, and their learning approaches. Before providing social studies experiences, Paula interviewed children, surveyed families, and toured the children's neighborhood to see what the children may have already experienced. Assessment is always an important starting point for curriculum development.

The National Curriculum Standards for Social Studies (NCSS, 1994) are an excellent resource for your own professional preparation and for future curriculum planning.

JOURNAL 11.6: After reading about math, science, and social studies for primary grades, what kind of learning experiences will you be planning for children?

Assessment in the Primary Grades

Remember the portfolios that Keeley's kindergarten teacher kept with the children's work from their project activities? Portfolios are organized and purposeful collection of student work and self-assessments collected over time to demonstrate student learning (Early Childhood Assessments Resource Group, 1998, p. 38). Paula thinks that portfolios are well suited to the needs of primary grade children and to the curricular approaches she uses in her classroom.

Portfolios

There are many reasons why portfolios are ideal for primary grades and for use with integrated curriculum, project approaches, and emergent curriculum, all of which are part of Erin Cheyenne's learning. **Portfolios** provide authentic assessment by allowing children to show how they understand and use what they have learned in an organized collection of materials (Wortham, 2003, pp. 107–110). Other reasons for their use include:

1. Portfolios are flexible and adaptable (adjust to various curricular domains, different developmental levels of children).
2. Portfolios capture many dimensions of children's development and learning.
3. Portfolios focus on children's strengths—what they can do.
4. Portfolios help children assume responsibility for their own learning. (McAfee & Leong, 1997, p. 101)

With what you know about Paula's philosophy and her goals for children, you can see why portfolios are right for her classroom. She adds, "I can have some common items in all children's portfolios and then some unique items that are different for Jodie and for Erin Cheyenne." Those anecdotal notes that we saw Paula recording go into the portfolio as well as children's work samples. Jodie's portfolio has lots of drawings and transcribed sentences, whereas Erin's portfolio has many written work samples. Paula uses the portfolios for several purposes: to communicate with parents and families, to encourage children to self-assess and plan for their own learning, and for her own reflection and assessment of student progress.

COMMUNICATING WITH PARENTS USING PORTFOLIOS. When Herb and Terri come in for a conference with Paula, Erin Cheyenne is part of that conference. She takes her parents through her portfolio, describing her various work samples. Paula prompts with, "Tell us what you did" and "Why did you decide to display your work that way?" and "What did you learn when you did that graph?" Herb and Terri ask questions, and Erin confidently describes her work and her learning. She is also able to talk about those areas in which she will work harder or "concentrate more." She then describes what she plans to do in the coming weeks.

PORTFOLIOS TO ENCOURAGE CHILDREN'S SELF-ASSESSMENT AND PLANNING. As Erin Cheyenne selects items for her portfolio, she is asked the reason for her selection. She often must choose between several items for the "best example of what you have learned." Throughout the year, Paula has taught the children some criteria to use in judging their work. She suggests criteria such as *complete, creative,* and *thoughtful,* and you can often hear the children use those terms as they make decisions about the contents of their portfolios. They are actually experiencing the beginnings of rubrics, or guidelines, for assessing the quality of their work. Wortham (2003, p. 110) encourages the use of rubrics with all kinds of student work because they ultimately motivate children to improve their own work.

PORTFOLIOS FOR TEACHERS' REFLECTION AND ASSESSMENT OF STUDENT PROGRESS. Paula works carefully to identify and annotate each item in the portfolios with dates and settings. She uses a rubber stamp with the date on all of the children's work and usually has them copy the setting information in their own writing. Sometimes children write their own reasons for including an item in their portfolios; other times, Paula writes the reason children dictate to her. Along with children's work, she includes observational data from her Post-its, checklists, and other recording forms. She then has an ongoing profile of each child and can check the portfolio for all kinds of information. Often, her first question is: What don't I know about Erin Cheyenne? She looks for progress and lack of progress, and from the portfolio information makes decisions about curricular activities that each child or all of the children need.

Paula's assessment demonstrates well the complexity of the professional role of a teacher of primary grades. Managing multiple curricular domains, a wide range of individual development, guidance directed to self-respect and independent learners, and assessment of rapid and varied learning demands specialized preparation and ongoing learning.

JOURNAL 11.7: After hearing about Paula's assessment practices, what advantages did you see for Erin Cheyenne and her friends having an active role in assessment? ●

Professional Preparation of Primary Grade Teachers

Every state requires different preparation and certification for those teachers who will teach first- and second-grade children. Unfortunately, those standards of preparation often do not include any specialized early childhood education coursework or requirements.

In 2001, the National Association for the Education of Young Children developed and approved *NAEYC Standards for Early Childhood Professional Preparation at Initial Licensure Level,* or certification level (usually a baccalaureate degree or master's degree). They are relevant for many different educational settings. The standards are part of a "larger set of expectations that form an image of what is required if all young children are to receive the kind of early education they need and deserve" (p. 2).

The standards represent a revision of the 1996 *Guidelines for Preparation of Early Childhood Professionals* prompted by changes in both the knowledge base of our field and in educational contexts or programs. The standards are especially relevant in a time of changing demographics and an increasingly diverse group of young children and families to be served. Changes in general standards for teacher education are also reflected in the new standards.

Within the *NAEYC Standards for Early Childhood Professional Preparation* is an enhanced emphasis on linguistic and cultural diversity, on inclusion, on subject matter, on communities in which children live, and on the complexity of assessment issues in today's educational settings. The standards emphasize the importance of varied teaching approaches and encourage you to develop a broad repertoire of "strategies and tools to support the learning and development of all children" (p. 8). The *Standards Summary* shown in Figure 11.4 gives you an overview of what will be expected of you (the candidate) as you complete your professional preparation. A complete description of each standard is available on the NAEYC website. It will be a good resource to guide your studies and experiences.

FIGURE 11.4
Standards Summary

1. Promoting child development and learning
Candidates use their understanding of young children's characteristics and needs, and of multiple interacting influences on children's development and learning, to create environments that are healthy, respectful, supportive, and challenging for all children.

2. Building family and community relationships
Candidates know about, understand, and value the importance and complex characteristics of children's families and communities. They use this understanding to create respectful, reciprocal relationships that support and empower families, and to involve all families in their children's development and learning.

3. Observing, documenting, and assessing to support young children and families
Candidates know about and understand the goals, benefits, and uses of assessment. They know about and use systematic observations, documentation, and other effective assessment strategies in a responsible way, in partnership with families and other professionals, to positively influence children's development and learning.

4. Teaching and learning
Candidates integrate their understanding of and relationships with children and families; their understanding of developmentally effective approaches to teaching and learning; and their knowledge of academic disciplines, to design, implement, and evaluate experiences that promote positive development and learning for all children.

4a. Connecting with children and families
Candidates know, understand, and use positive relationships and supportive interactions as the foundation for their work with young children.

4b. Using developmentally effective approaches
Candidates know, understand, and use a wide array of effective approaches, strategies, and tools to positively influence children's development and learning.

4c. Understanding content knowledge in early education
Candidates understand the importance of each content area in young children's learning. They know the essential concepts, inquiry tools, and structure of content areas including academic subjects and can identify resources to deepen their understanding.

4d. Building meaningful curriculum
Candidates use their own knowledge and other resources to design, implement, and evaluate meaningful, challenging curriculum that promotes comprehensive developmental and learning outcomes for all young children.

5. Becoming a professional
Candidates identify and conduct themselves as members of the early childhood profession. They know and use ethical guidelines and other professional standards related to early childhood practice. They are continuous, collaborative learners who demonstrate knowledgeable, reflective, and critical perspectives on their work, making informed decisions that integrate knowledge from a variety of sources. They are informed advocates for sound educational practices and policies.

Source: NAEYC Standards for Early Childhood Professional Preparation. Washington, DC: NAEYC. Copyright 2001 by NAEYC. Reprinted with permission from the National Association for the Education of Young Children.

With the new emphasis on subject matter, the national standards for all of the curriculum areas found in the list of websites in Appendix A at the back of our book will be invaluable resources for your current preparation and for your future role as an early childhood educator (Wheatley, 2003). Reading them in their entirety is probably not appealing but it will be useful to skim each set of standards and become familiar with them for curriculum planning. They will be important resources for your professional preparation.

PRINCIPLES AND INSIGHTS: A Summary and Review

After observing Paula and her diverse group of first- and second-grade children, you have a good sense of the knowledge and skills you need to teach primary grades. It is a challenging but exciting role and you learn every day with your students.

Much of the primary grade curriculum focuses on literacy with attention to reading, writing, speaking, and listening. Mathematics and science build on years of exploration and concrete experiences. In the primary grades, children work toward the development of concepts and skills along with the language associated with math or science. An integrated curricular approach or the use of projects allows educators to weave together art, music, social studies, science, math, and other curricular areas with literacy to maximize the daily schedule. Guidance considers the schedule, relevance of curriculum, the setting, and the individuality of group members. Primary grade children are ready for group work and collaboration.

Finally, assessment of student learning in the primary grades must capture the complexity of the curriculum as well as the wide variation in the learners themselves. Portfolios are an ideal approach for assessment of primary grade learning with multiple uses of the information.

BECOMING AN EARLY CHILDHOOD PROFESSIONAL

Your Professional Portfolio

1. As you observe primary grade classes, take photographs (if permissible) of class settings to save ideas about environments, materials, and activities. To each photo, add a description and reflect on your potential use.
2. Develop your own personal resource list for future projects, thematic studies, and other curricular approaches. Review the appropriate national standards for the curriculum area of interest. Include individuals you know who would be interesting guests, collections and materials you have saved, resources, hobbies, travel experiences, and so on.

Your Professional Library

Copley, J. V. (2000). *The young child and mathematics.* Washington, DC: NAEYC.

Helm, J., & Katz, L. (2001). *Young investigators: The project approach in the early Years.* Washington, DC: NAEYC.

McCracken, J. B. (1993). *Valuing diversity: The primary years.* Washington, DC: NAEYC.

Owocki, G. (2001). *Make way for literacy: Teaching the way young children learn.* Washington, DC: NAEYC.

Seefeldt, C., & Galper, A. (2000). *Active experiences for active children: Social Studies.* Columbus, OH: Merrill.

Vance, E., & Jiménez Weaver, P. (2002). *Class meetings: Young children solving problems together.* Washington, DC: NAEYC.

CHAPTER 12

Special Education

Jodie and Her Family's Story

CHAPTER focus:

When you finish reading and reflecting on this chapter, you will be able to:

1. Describe the role of an early childhood education specialist.
2. Summarize the legislation affecting the education of children with special needs.
3. Discuss the primary purposes of an IFSP and an IEP.
4. Outline several instructional strategies and curriculum modifications that support learning for children with special needs.

You are about to visit Jodie and her family. She is a delightful 7-year-old with light brown hair, brown eyes, a frequent smile, and the wonderful ability to make a positive impact on others. In fact, as you become acquainted with Jodie, you will clearly see that her primary interest lies in interacting with those around her. She was diagnosed with **Down syndrome** at birth, a chromosomal abnormality that affects her intellectual capability and her physical health but most definitely does not limit her ability to care about people.

A Home Visit with Jodie and Her Family

Jodie lives in a neighborhood selected by her parents because of the local school district's strong reputation. They learned that this school district is committed to including children with disabilities in their neighborhood schools to the fullest extent possible. Including children in classrooms with their peers matches Jodie's parents' belief regarding the importance of planned participation between children with and without disabilities (Guralnick, 2001).

As you turn down Jodie's street, you see bicycles in several driveways, basketball hoops above garage doors, and children playing across the way in the park. It looks like Jodie's parents were not alone in their choice of neighborhoods. You knock on the door just as Jodie and her mother, Lynn, open the door to welcome you.

Jodie begins talking about school and enthusiastically tells you about her teacher and her friends at school. "My favorite time is reading, but I like painting and recess, too." Jodie points to the refrigerator. "Look at my rainbow painting and my school papers. These are mine and these are Tracy's and these are made by my brother, Kurt." Jodie is pleased with her accomplishments and those of her siblings.

Jodie's Tour

Lynn turns to Jodie, saying, "OK, now it's time for you to show our guest your room." Jodie starts in the family room, where you notice photographs on the wall. Jodie points out, "That's my grandma, my sister, my mom and dad, and my brother." You then head upstairs.

Jodie opens her door and points to her collection of dolls. As she shows you her favorite, she explains, "This is Anna. She sleeps in my bed and goes in the car with me." It looks like Anna is well loved. On the bookshelf are many books and CDs. Jodie says, "I like to play CDs with songs and stories when I go to bed." She adds, "I had to help Mom clean my room after school." "Right," says Lynn, "You like it clean, but you don't like to clean it." Off to the side, Lynn says, "Jodie has a tendency to pretend she can't do something in order to enlist the help of someone else, but I am usually on to her scheme and work with her to finish tasks."

Ending Your Visit

You head downstairs just as the rest of the family comes home. Jerry is home from work early and all three children greet him enthusiastically. Tracy and Kurt were dropped off from soccer practice. Jerry says hello and, with everyone talking, Jerry tells us laughingly, "Seems like you visited us on a typical afternoon!"

Heading out the door, you thank the family for their hospitality. You now have a better understanding of Jodie after visiting her family and home and from your prior observation of Jodie's school (Chapter 11). Lynn invites you back for another conversation about Jodie's early childhood. You take her up on the offer and make a date for two weeks from now.

Walking back to the car, you think how fortunate Jodie is to have such a warm, caring family. She is fully accepted as a family member, with responsibilities and expectations like those of the other children. You look forward to your return visit.

Visiting with Jodie's Parents

Two weeks later, you visit at Jodie's house with Lynn and Jerry, this time while Jodie is at school. Lynn opens the conversation: "For me, it is important to share our family story and our early childhood experiences with Jodie. I want others to come to know Jodie and understand that Jodie is a member of our family and she also happens to have challenges. I had a normal pregnancy and was shocked when the doctor told us that our baby was born with Down syndrome. We knew very little about Down syndrome and had no idea what to expect. Maybe some of what we have experienced and learned will be helpful to people considering working with young children." Lynn then shared about Jodie's infancy and childhood.

Jodie's Infant Years

When Jodie was a few weeks old, Lynn received a phone call from Sue, also a mother of a child with Down syndrome. While at the hospital, a nurse had asked Lynn and Jerry if they would be interested in connecting with a family who also had a young child with Down syndrome.

Support from Others: Resources for Families. Sue invited Lynn and Jerry to join a support group of parents to learn more from these parents who have children with similar developmental delays. She suggested, "Their stories might be helpful to you as you hear how families coped with problems and experiences that your family might encounter." Sue also offered to visit Lynn. "She prepared me for the roller coaster of emotions associated with learning your child has Down syndrome." Lynn adds, "This was the first of many visits with Sue, who has become a close friend." Jerry then offers, "Both Lynn and I had a lot of difficulty accepting the fact that our child would have limitations and was not the perfect baby we had dreamed of for many months. We were physically and emotionally exhausted with the efforts and energy needed to care for an infant. Added to that was the stress of trying to learn about Down syndrome and what it meant for our daughter. I had recently completed law school and was beginning my career in a law firm. I worked long hours, often into the evening. Fortunately, Lynn's mother lived nearby and visited several times a week, helping Lynn with caring for Jodie and supporting her during this time. We are really grateful for her support." Lynn agrees that she is thankful for the frequent help from her mother and from the support group.

Infancy and Early Intervention Specialists. Lynn and Jerry learned about early intervention services from other members of the parent support group. They contacted their local Family Services office and Jodie began participating in **early intervention services** when she was a few months old. Until she was 2 years old, Jodie was visited weekly by an early intervention specialist who worked with her and her parents on developmental skills.

Jerry remembers those sessions with the early intervention specialist and recalls, "We had so many questions. It was helpful to know that there would be another session coming and a time and place to get answers to our questions." The specialist also used each session as a time to catch up on new skills Jodie was learning and any special challenges Jodie or the family were having. During the early months (until Jodie was 1 year old), many sessions were spent encouraging Jodie to reach for objects, drop objects, roll over, sit with support, and learn to balance herself in an upright position.

Through direct teaching, practice, and lots of encouragement, by the time she was age 2, Jodie was able to accomplish most of the large motor skills of a 2-year-old at a slightly delayed time frame. Fine motor skills, such as using a spoon, seemed more difficult for Jodie, and took much practice. Jerry recalls, "Tracy, who is a year younger, was also learning many of the same skills at the same time, so both girls would mirror each other. It seemed that the interaction with her sister encouraged Jodie to keep trying. We were discouraged sometimes, but the interaction with the early intervention specialist helped us see the progress that Jodie was making and gave us a plan and ways to help Jodie."

Toddler Time: Interacting with Peers

At age 2, Jodie started attending a community play group one morning each week. This provided her with a time to be with other children and to learn in an inclusive setting. The early intervention specialist continued to visit the home twice a month. She also met with the person coordinating the play group, assisting her in modifying activities so Jodie would be included and successful in interacting with her peers.

Modifying Play Group Activities. Lynn recalls, "Jodie loved music, singing, and moving to music with the other 2-year-olds." During play group, Jodie would sing a word or two in each song. She was encouraged to clap with the music. An example of **modifying activities** to meet Jodie's learning needs occurred while other children were learning the words to entire songs and Jodie was expected to learn one or two words as she participated in the singing. Lynn says, "Jodie seemed to enjoy her morning at the community play group and made progress with her language development." Unfortunately, it was not always as easy to make modifications in public situations.

Reactions from the Public. When Jodie was 2 years old, the family became aware of others looking at them. Lynn and Jerry talked about the obvious stares they received when they were at restaurants, stores, or events with Jodie. Jerry explains, "Some people look at us with pity or sympathy in their eyes; others walk far around us to avoid our family; and others come up to us and tell us how sorry they are about our little girl." These interchanges have been awkward for Lynn and Jerry, especially as Jodie began to

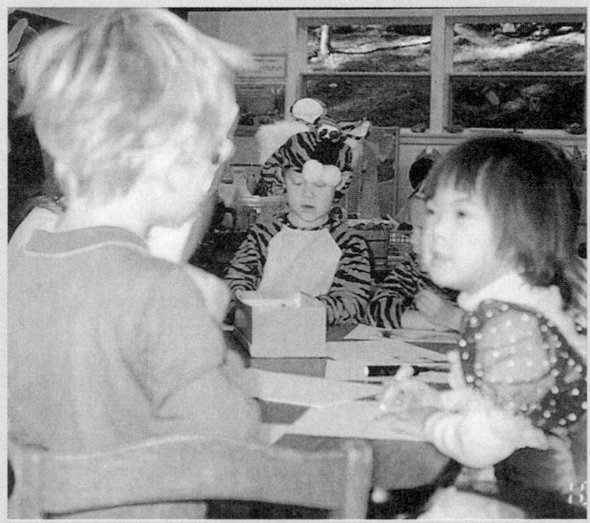

What might be possible benefits Jodie would gain by participating in a community play group?

understand what strangers were saying. Lynn decided to be proactive and tell strangers who approach them, "We are a happy, active family." She believes it is important to send a clear positive message to people about Jodie.

Lynn and Jerry acknowledge that people might not know what it is like to have a child with special needs. "Often, others don't realize that this child brings many gifts to our family. One of the reasons we pursue Jodie's education at our neighborhood school is to help others around Jodie accept her and appreciate her for who she is." They feel that once other children spend time with Jodie, the focus is less on what she can't do and more on what she can do.

JOURNAL 12.1: The experiences that Jodie's family shared have implications for a classroom teacher and the children in the class. If you were Jodie's teacher and you were planning a field trip to a grocery store, how might you handle stares and comments from strangers?

The Three's Class: Starting Preschool

When Jodie turned 3 years old, she started preschool. She received early childhood special education services, which were integrated into her day at the preschool. Her early childhood special education specialist worked with the preschool teacher and with Jodie's parents to develop an individualized family services plan (IFSP). The IFSP is a written plan for services for children with disabilities who are birth through 2 years old, and is required by law. Each IFSP must include present levels of functioning, statement of family strengths and needs, expected outcomes, services to be provided, dates for initiation and duration of services, coordinator of services, and steps to be taken to support transition to the preschool program (Lerner, Lowenthal, & Egan, 2003). Children from ages 3 to 5 might have an IFSP (as allowed by state and regional policy) or an individualized education plan (IEP). When the child begins kindergarten, the local school district is then responsible for providing special education services and uses an IEP. In most states, an IEP is implemented at age 3.

Individualized Family Services Plan. Jodie's IFSP outlined goals that the family, teacher, and specialist felt were important to focus on for the year. Several goals focused on communication skills, such as responding when asked a question and using complete sentences when talking with others. Jodie made progress with her goals, supported by her parents' work with her at home and her teacher, Karla, at preschool.

An **IFSP** reflects the individual learning goals of a child, based on her current level of functioning and on learning considered important by the family, early childhood special educator, and other specialists involved on the team. Figure 12.1 provides an example of an IFSP.

Being Part of the Group: Inclusion. There were 12 children in Jodie's class, with one other child receiving early childhood special education services for language development. Jodie often invited other children to come home with her for lunch and to play. "We were relieved that Jodie was 'part' of the group," said Lynn and Jerry, "But then we would feel guilty for being relieved. There's that roller coaster again. Parenting a child with special needs can be overwhelming. You want your child to have as full a life as possible, yet you aren't sure what is possible."

The Four's Class: Accommodating Individual Needs

At 4 years of age, Jodie remained at the same preschool, moving into the "Four's Class" with her group of friends. She attended school each weekday morning. An early childhood special educator visited the school weekly to meet with Karla, the teacher. She also participated in bimonthly meetings with Lynn, Jerry, and Karla. Box 12.1 highlights the role of an early childhood special education specialist.

By the spring of her Four's Class, most of the children were drawing symbols or primitive objects, while Jodie was still learning to hold the crayon or paintbrush and move it around on the paper. She was making progress on her IFSP goals; her sentence phrases had increased to three to four words in length. Karla, Lynn, Jerry, and the early childhood special educator met to discuss Lynn and Jerry's concerns about Jodie's transition to kindergarten. Jerry said, "I was reluctant to move Jodie into a large elementary school for kindergarten until she acquired more communication skills." The team of specialists discussed with Lynn and Jerry the benefits of Jodie learning from her chronological age peers. This discussion helped Lynn and Jerry understand the

FIGURE 12.1
Individualized Family Service Plan (IFSP) (Portion of an Example)

Child's Name Carmen Martinez Birthdate 11-5-02 Identification # ______

Parent(s)/Guardian Miguel and Anna Martinez Home Phone 321-8712

Address 527 East Street Westin, Arizona Work Phone 321-0050

Service Coordinator Janice Lacey

Resident School District Mountain

IFSP Date 11-18-04
Eligibility Date 11-24-04
Review Date(s) 5-20-05
Annual Review Date 11-24-05

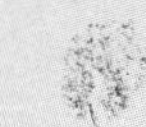

EI/ECSE Services	Method	How Often?	Location	Who Will Do This?	Who Will Pay?	Start Date	Stop Date
Communication Skill Training	One-on-one instruction	2x week 30 min. each	Home	Early Childhood Special Educator	Early Childhood Special Ed Program	11/24/04	11/24/05
Communication consultation to familiy & special educator	Meeting with family	1x month 60 min	Home	Speech therapist	Early Childhood Special Ed Program	11/30/04	11/30/05
Other (non EI/ECSE) Services							
Respite Services	Babysitting	2x month	Home	Mom and service coordinator will work on this	No cost	1/05	11/05

Are **EI** services in the child's natural environment? Yes If not, please explain: ______

Are all **ESCE** services provided with typical peers? NA If not, please explain to what extent and why: ______

Parents will be informed of the child's progress toward annual goals. Review schedule: ☒ Six month and annual review ☐ Other review schedule: ______ How will progress be reported to parents? meeting with child's parents

Parents or any IFSP member may request an IFSP meeting at any time, regardless of when the most recent IFSP occurred.

FIGURE 12.1
(continued)

Individualized Family Service Plan Participants

Child's Name: Carmen Martinez Date of Birth 11-5-02 Date 11-18-04

This plan was developed on 11-18-04 List all participants in the meeting:

Subcontractor Representative:	Service Coordinator: Janice Lacey	Preschool Teacher, if applicable:	Other:
Parent: Anna Martinez	School District Representative: Jane Johnston	Other:	Other:
EI/ECSE Specialist: Janice Lacey	Evaluator:	Other:	Other:

I participated in the development of this plan and understand the content. I consent to the *Early Intervention* services in this plan.

Parent Signature	Parent Signature	Date
Anna Martinez		11/18/04

I have participated in the development of this plan for *Early Childhood Special Education* services for my child.

Parent Signature	Parent Signature	Date
Anna Martinez		11/18/04

Present Level of Development

Child's strengths and interests:

Carmen loves music, likes to explore, and to snuggle with her parents.

How the child's disability affects participation in appropriate activities:

Communicating with peers is difficult with her speech challenges.

Information considered in developing the IFSP:

- ☒ Parent input and observations
- ☒ Staff input and observations
- ☒ Most recent evaluation dated 10-04
- ☐ Other (specify):

Health Status: Healthy, Doctor Report 10/04

Vision Screening: Passed 10/12/04

Hearing Screening: Passed 10/12/04

FIGURE 12.1
(continued)

Present Levels of Development

Child's Name: Carmen Date of Birth 11-5-02 Date 11-18-04

Can Do	*Needs to Learn	Can Do	Needs to Learn*
Cognitive: Pretend plays with toys Knows body parts Adaptive: Will use fingers to eat Will drink out of tipper cup Participates in dressing and undressing Social or Emotional: Plays with toys Interested in other children	Use spoon	Physical (gross motor): Runs Climbs up stairs Physical (fine motor): Stacks blocks Communication (receptive): Follows directions Understands "no" Communication (expressive): Uses two one-words, "dad" "pop" Beginning questions (inflection)	Work on fine motor skills—in natural setting—to play with toys Expand prelanguage use Use words

Goals and Objectives

What we want to happen (Long-Term Goal)	Criteria	Evaluation Procedure	Review Date: 5/20/04	Annual Review Date: 5/20/05
Carmen will use words spontaneously to express her needs and interests	at least 10 times daily	family and staff observation	Progress made toward goal (based on the criteria and evaluation): Is the progress sufficient for the child to meet this goal? If not, what changes are planned?	Progress made toward goal (based on the criteria and evaluation):

What the child will learn (Short-Term Objectives):

1. Carmen will indicate her needs by pointing to a picture and imitate the word represented 5x day

2. Carmen will call her mom (moma) 2x day

3. Carmen will wave "bye bye" and say words spontaneously 2x day

Note: Missing from this IFSP are the Family Outcomes/Transition page and the Placement Decision page.

Source: Form is from Oregon Department of Education, Office of Special Education.

BOX 12.1 A Closer Look

What Is the Role of an Early Childhood Special Educator?

Staff who provide developmental and educational services for children from birth to age 5 and their families are referred to as *early childhood special educators.* The role of the early childhood special educator varies across states and programs. The following is a general description of services provided by a professional who implements or coordinates the implementation of services for young children (birth to age 5) with disabilities. In your state or local program, a person providing these services may be referred to as *an early interventionist, a case manager, a service coordinator,* or *a family interventionist.*

The early childhood special educator meets the family and child as soon as the child is referred to the program, perhaps by a pediatrician, caregiver, or social worker. One of the early childhood special educator's first jobs with the family is to assist the family through the evaluation process and to link the family with other community resources. If the child is eligible for services as a child with a disability, the early childhood special educator organizes a meeting to plan services for the child and family. This is called the *individualized family service plan (IFSP).* The early childhood special educator is the lead person of the child's team to whom the family directs their questions and or concerns. This means that he or she is responsible for finding answers to the family's concerns about the child's development education and/or other services that may be available for the family.

Another responsibility of the early childhood special educator is to provide developmental or educational services to the child. These services are provided in supportive environments where the child usually spends his or her day. Very young or medically vulnerable children typically receive services at home. Children 3 and 4 years of age may receive services at home, preschool, or day care. Service delivery methods vary from program to program, depending on the needs of the child and family.

The early childhood special educator typically teaches others (parents, child care providers, teachers, etc.) in the child's setting ways to teach the child new skills and to encourage the child's development. For example, the early childhood special educator may work with a child's mother to teach the child how to hold a spoon and scoop from a bowl. Another example is an early childhood special educator who works with a preschool teacher on techniques for promoting language skills from a 4-year-old with language delays.

Early childhood special educators also may provide services by directly teaching a child new skills. This usually occurs when the early childhood special educator sees a child two or more times a week. What, how, and who teaches the child is determined by the child's team at the child's IFSP meeting. The IFSP is reviewed at least every six months for children under age 3. For children age 3 and older, the law requires that progress is reported as least as often as for children with no disabilities. Parents or any IFSP member may request an IFSP review at any time. The early childhood special educator plays an essential role in monitoring the child's development and learning, working with the family, and ensuring the child has access to community resources and support services.

Source: Nancy Johnson-Dorn, Education Program Specialist, Oregon Department of Education. Reprinted by permission.

reasons for keeping Jodie with children her age to help her social and communication skills. During the meeting, the team agreed that the most appropriate placement for Jodie would be in kindergarten.

Lynn, Jerry, Karla, and the early childhood special educator also decided to involve Jodie in summer activities. Jerry suggested gymnastics, in which Jodie showed interest. She had recently watched the Olympic Games and was intrigued with the floor exercises. Her involvement in gymnastics held potential for work on communication skills in another setting. Jerry recalls, "I met with the gymnastics coach to discuss different ways Jodie might be encouraged to talk with other children." It was important for Jodie to continue her language development and Jerry and Lynn wanted the coach to be aware of this goal.

Transition to Kindergarten

By the end of the Four's Class school year, Jerry, Lynn, and Jodie were looking forward to Jodie's transition to elementary school for her kindergarten experience. The early childhood special educator arranged a transition meeting with a special educator from the school district, the family, and Karla.

Transition Meeting. The purpose of a **transition meeting** is to discuss a child's current levels of functioning and the support and resources she would need to be successful as she moves into a new setting. At the meeting, it was suggested that the parents and Jodie call the school and visit the kindergarten. They did go to Forest Hills Elementary School and met the principal and Janis, the kindergarten teacher that the principal had selected as Jodie's teacher. The early childhood special educator also attended the school meeting. Jerry and Lynn remember, "Having someone we knew at the meeting made us feel much more comfortable. We knew she would advocate for Jodie's inclusion in the school."

The principal, Carol, talked with Jerry and Lynn about the goals of the kindergarten teachers, who place emphasis on social development through learning to work with others and on a developmentally appropriate curriculum. There were several other children with special needs also entering kindergarten that fall. For example, several children would be entering kindergarten in September with English as their second language. Carol felt that placing no more than two or three children with special needs in each class would help the teacher develop activities and lessons that would allow them to reach these children on an individual level.

Janis had worked with several children with special needs. Carol suggested, "With her experience, I feel Janis would be an excellent teacher for Jodie." Carol took Lynn, Jerry, and Jodie to the kindergarten area to observe the classes. Jerry says, "I really enjoyed watching the children and having a brief chat with Janis. She came over to say hello to Jodie and see if she wanted to look at the gerbils." On their way back to the office, Lynn and Jerry agreed that Janis seemed to be a good choice for Jodie's kindergarten teacher. Lynn recalls, "It was helpful to visit the school and classroom and meet the teacher in the spring. I was less anxious about Jodie's transition to elementary school after our visit."

Challenges for Jodie: Monitoring Progress. Kindergarten was challenging for Jodie. It was an adjustment to be in a class of 24 students, along with so much movement and noise. Jodie enjoyed music and art and loved listening to stories. Her educational goals again focused on communication skills, fine motor skills, and beginning numeracy and literacy development. She also had to work on not being the center of attention and sharing toys and materials with other students.

During the winter, Jodie had several colds and was home for a week three different times. Jerry thought, "Jodie's language skills, particularly her sentence length, seemed to decrease when she was home for long periods of time. I think her interaction with other children was an important factor in her development of language." Lynn and Jerry met with the kindergarten teacher and Marty, the special educator at the school, three times during the school year. Janis was open to their concerns and opinions and incorporated their ideas into Jodie's individual learning goals. Kindergarten was an important year for Jodie. Lynn says, "Jodie matured and learned many new skills in getting along with others during her kindergarten experience. We all felt she was ready for first grade."

First Grade

At the end of the kindergarten year, a meeting was held with the special education resource teacher, Janis, Jerry, and Lynn. They met to discuss goals for Jodie's first-grade school year. After discussion of the various classroom settings, and on the suggestion of the team of specialists, it was agreed that a multiage classroom would be an ideal setting for Jodie. Much of the day in these classrooms is spent in small group learning time or with the teacher in individual sessions. Students also stay with the teacher for two years. Lynn says, "The benefit of being with the same teacher and group of students for two years would help Jodie, who is reluctant to make large changes and feels more comfortable with a familiar adult."

Developing Learning Goals for Jodie. Paula, Jodie's first-grade teacher, and Jodie's parents had a conference early in the school year to set learning goals

A Conversation about Inclusion

Inclusion means different things to different people. As a parent, I have heard educators and legislators search for the perfect term to define the idea of placing children with special needs in "regular" settings or classrooms and supposedly treating them like any other child. We used to say *mainstream,* but that was offensive to some, so the term changed to *inclusion.* In an attempt to further define what we mean, the term *full inclusion* is often used. When done correctly, inclusion should be tailored to each child's individual situation. This requires educators and parents to look carefully at the needs of each child. What makes a child different from the majority of his peers? Aren't all children different? Don't they all have "special needs" of one sort or another? Ideally, a teacher should make her program suitable to each of her students. We know that, in reality, this is difficult.

When I speak of inclusion, I mean placing a child with significantly different needs from the group in a classroom and providing what is needed to allow that child to benefit from the experience. Sometimes this is successful without any special supports other than the teacher's awareness of that child's individual needs or some sort of technology that the student requires because of a physical difference. Most of the time, the situation is more complex. For example, when my daughter, who has Down syndrome and is mentally retarded, was in preschool, she was able to participate fully in a regular community preschool that happened to have a very knowledgeable and flexible teacher. My daughter learned from observing and interacting with the other children as much as she did from structured lessons. Placing her in a class with her peers continued to work for her through the third grade, when the curriculum became too abstract. At this point, she benefited from a classroom assistant helping her with academics while she remained in the same class, doing similar work.

As my daughter progresses through the grades, she will continue to need more individualized help, but hopefully will remain in the "mainstream" part of the time because of the support she receives. In my view, she will no longer be "fully included" in the upper grades as she was in preschool and the primary grades, but she is still in an "inclusive" setting and it works for her.

I see an inclusive setting as one that is designed primarily for the majority of students and is considered the norm, but in which children with varying needs and learning styles are able to participate. Teaching methods are adapted to meet the learning needs of each child. This could mean individualizing the curriculum for some students, or using technological supports, teaching assistants, or peer tutors. It does not mean throwing a child with special needs in a regular classroom without support and hoping for the best.

So, from my experiences as a parent, I would say my definition of *inclusion* is placing a child with special needs in an educational setting which is the norm for most students and providing that child with support so she can fully benefit in that setting, both *academically* and *socially.*

Note: This Conversation about Inclusion was written by Joy Lee, a mother of a child with Down syndrome.

for Jodie. An area of importance to Jodie's family and to Paula was learning appropriate social skills. They felt that Jodie's academic areas would progress at a steady rate, but it was very important to Lynn and Jerry that Jodie get along with others and learn socially acceptable behaviors.

Jodie enjoys interacting with others but she has a tendency to become the "baby" in a group, and her parents are concerned with the long-term effects of this role. They realize that as she matures, she needs to become more independent. Paula agrees and looks for ways to help Jodie assume leadership roles in the classroom. For the past month, Jodie has been responsible for taking notes to the office and delivering messages to the office staff. She has enjoyed this responsibility and has been a great messenger.

Other goals for Jodie include beginning literacy and numeracy skills and improving her verbal communication. Do you see a connection between Jodie's messenger position and the goal of verbal communication? This is one example of how Paula builds real-life contexts for Jodie's learning, such as assuming the role of messenger. Paula says,

"Some of these ideas are mine; others come from Marty, the resource teacher. Marty meets with me on a weekly basis and we look at upcoming lessons and projects and find ways to ensure Jodie is fully included and challenged in her learning. Marty often brings books and materials for me to use with Jodie and other students." The frequent contact with a special educator brings curriculum and instruction support for Jodie and for Paula, as well as assists Paula in assessing Jodie's learning and planning future learning needs. Including Jodie in the multiage classroom—relying on support from Marty and curriculum changes made by Paula—creates a positive learning environment for Jodie in her neighborhood school.

At this point of the conversation, you are up to date on events in Jodie's life and her schooling. Thanking Jerry and Lynn for sharing so much of their story, you express admiration of their warm supportive family and their advocacy for Jodie.

Reflecting on Jodie's Experiences

Jodie shares many characteristics similar with other 7-year-olds, while also displaying academic and fine motor skills of a child two years younger than her chronological age. Remember her interests in painting and storytelling? Many other 7-year-olds would also say that these are favorite activities. When you visited Jodie at her home, you found her to be an active member of her family. She is included in the busy family schedule, as well as participating in activities of her own choice, such as gymnastics, just like other 7-year-olds.

Jodie looks forward to going to school each day and to being with her teacher and classmates. Although Jodie is not working at the same level academically as other children in her classroom, her work is challenging to her and she is showing progress in many areas. She is included in her neighborhood school, the natural learning environment for the other children in her family (Lerner, Lowenthal, & Egan, 2003). Here, she is accepted as a contributing member of her peer group (Sandall, McLean, & Smith, 2000). Her current teacher, Paula, attributes Jodie's success in school to her earlier school experiences, her parents' support and encouragement, and her friendly nature that draws others to her. Her best friend, Tonya, enjoys playing with Jodie at school and after school. This friendship really supports Jodie's development.

Jodie's early childhood experiences have shaped her development and growth and have been enhanced by teachers, specialists, friends, and her family. You realize that she has many challenges ahead, but from your visits, you see Jodie as an eager, active member of her family, school, and community.

In the next section of this chapter, you will look at special education legislation, services, and programs. Keep in mind the different programs and services that Jodie and her family were involved with as you learn what prompted the development and continuation of early childhood special education services.

Special Education for Young Children

What Is Special Education?

As you read about Jodie, you may have wondered about the source of services she receives. The array of services and support for young children with special needs and for their families has increased significantly in both quantity and quality in the past 25 years. Legislation now provides funding for programs and mandates services to meet the needs of children from birth through age 21. These programs for children with special needs are typically called *special education programs.*

When discussing **special education,** the focus is on programs that meet the special learning needs of children. As the learning needs of each child vary, so does special education. For one child, inclusion on a full-time basis in a regular preschool, along with weekly sessions with a physical therapist for large muscle motor development (hopping, jumping, and running), would be special education. In the same preschool, another child might be attending preschool for two hours a week and spending the rest of his time in a special education classroom for children with hearing loss. In such a special education classroom, the emphasis is on assisting children learn sign language and **speech reading** (understanding spoken language by watching the speaker's face). Yet another type of special education program would be in a hospital, where a child with chronic health problems receives special education services appropriate to her developmental level and learning needs. Recognizing that the educational and related services support the individual learning needs of the child helps you understand that special education is developed around the specific needs of a child rather than around a set curriculum or program.

Who Are the Children Receiving Special Education?

Children with special needs include children with disabilities or developmental delays whose learning and development will be compromised if they do not receive special and expert attention in their early education. Legislators are recognizing the special needs of young children and have passed laws designed to ensure early intervention services for these children (Lerner, Lowenthal, & Egan, 2003). When describing children with special needs, a distinction has been made in discussing their disability by using the term *children* first and then adding the disability, such as *children with visual impairments.* This terminology reminds us to focus on the child as a child who happens to have a disability or developmental delay.

CATEGORIES OF CHILDREN WITH DISABILITIES. In the *Twenty-Third Annual Report to Congress on the Implementation of IDEA* (U.S. Department of Education Office of Special Education, 2002), the federal government recognizes 13 different categories of disabilities. Table 12.1 shows the number and percentage of students ages 6 through 11 who received special education services during the 1999–2000 school year in each of the 13 categories.

Specific learning disabilities are often not identified until a child enters school and it becomes evident that she needs special assistance to achieve her potential. In the 1999–2000 school year, 11.4 percent of the total student population were children with disabilities who received special education in the public schools (U.S. Department of Education, Office of Special Education Programs, 2002). The percentage of younger children receiving special education services is lower than for school-aged children for several reasons. As you read the following story about Jackson, consider why it is often difficult to identify some children with special needs prior to kindergarten.

TABLE 12.1 Number and Percentage of Students Ages 6 to 11 Receiving Special Education by Disability: 1999–2000

Disability	Number	Percentage of Total
Specific learning disabilities	1,118,152	39.90
Speech or language impairments	958,182	34.19
Mental retardation	238,714	8.52
Emotional disturbance	159,879	5.71
Multiple disabilities	51,312	1.83
Hearing impairments	33,847	1.21
Orthopedic impairments	36,811	1.31
Other health impairments	124,464	4.44
Visual impairments	12,558	.45
Autism	43,039	1.54
Deaf-blindness	904	.03
Traumatic brain injury	5,219	.19
Developmental delay	19,304	.68
All disabilities	**2,802,385**	**100.00**

Note: Developmental delay is applicable only to children through age 9.

Source: Twenty-Third Annual Report to Congress on the Implementation of the Individuals with Disabilities Education Act, U.S. Department of Education, 2002, pp. A5–7.

Jackson: A Child with Attention-Deficit Disorder

Jackson is a 5-year-old in the kindergarten class next to Jodie's classroom. If you had a chance to observe in his kindergarten while you were at the school, you would have noticed the children building a city with milk cartons. Several centers are set up around Jackson's classroom, with parent volunteers helping the children decorate their milk cartons and construct buildings, trees, cars, and people for their city. You would have seen Jackson at the back center: He picks up the scissors and loudly says, "Now cut paper." Jackson then makes several quick cuts in the paper, drops the paper and scissors, and hurries over to another center, where he grabs a glue bottle and starts squeezing glue on the table. Saul, the kindergarten teacher, approaches Jackson and quietly tells him, "It's time to go over to the couch and take a few deep breaths. Let's talk about your plans for building your store for the city."

Saul takes Jackson's hand as they walk together to the couch. Once seated, Saul asks Jackson, "What are your plans for making your store?" Jackson replies, "I want a big store." "So, how will you make it and what supplies do you need?" After a few minutes of conversation, Saul asks Jackson, "What are your next two steps?" Jackson thinks about this and says, "First, I will get my milk carton and then I will cut paper to glue on it for the store." "Great, then come find me and we will do the next two steps together, OK?" Jackson nods and goes back to the first center where he picks up scissors and paper and begins cutting, at a much slower pace than before.

Jackson has recently been identified as having **attention-deficit disorder (ADD)**, which is characterized by a "persistent pattern of inattention and/or hyperactivity-impulsivity" than is typically seen in children at a similar level of development (American Psychiatric Association, 1994, p. 78). Attention-deficit disorder or attention-deficit/hyperactivity disorder (ADHD) is not currently recognized as a disability category unless the child's behavior difficulty negatively affects academic performance. Saul decided

Sometimes one-on-one attention helps a child make the transition to a positive activity.

to implement a strategy for Jackson based on his prior experiences in working with children with special needs. Saul found that breaking activities into small segments helps Jackson be more successful in his learning, along with asking him to verbalize his plans to Saul. You listened to the conversation between Jackson and Saul, where Jackson was thinking through his next two steps in an activity. At that time, Saul might decide Jackson is ready for a "quiet break" with the headphones and some calming music or to continue with the building activity. Saul is working with Jackson to self-monitor his behavior and to be successful with each small step.

When Jackson was in preschool, his teacher thought he had a short attention span and that he was a "talkative" child. At that time, however, and with that age group, his behavior did not seem vastly different from the other children. Jackson attended preschool three mornings a week for two hours. There was a lot of activity going on, as well as outdoor play, which he enjoyed. When Jackson entered kindergarten, Saul noticed that he often made impulsive comments, darted around the classroom, and seemed to have difficulty staying with a project for more than a few minutes. Saul began charting Jackson's "time on an activity" and soon found that he was staying with one activity for 2 to 3 minutes and then moving to another area of the room. The other children were spending 10 to 20 minutes at centers before they moved to another activity.

Saul met with Jackson's father and a decision was made to begin a program both at school and at home to help Jackson create his own structure in his activities. In the past two months, both Saul and Jackson's father agree that Jackson is responding to the program, as he now spends 5 to 10 minutes on an activity before moving to something else.

When you think about child development and children of preschool age, you realize that many of Jackson's behaviors appeared similar to and within the range of other preschoolers. When he entered kindergarten and it was apparent he was not able to attend to one activity for an extended time, Jackson's learning needs became more obvious. It has been estimated that in most classrooms, there will be from one to three children who have behaviors typically associated with ADD or ADHD. Teachers and caregivers will want to know how to recognize the behaviors of children with ADD or ADHD, such as inattention, hyperactivity, or impulsivity that seems to be beyond the norm for this developmental level. If it is determined that a child does have ADD or ADHD, the teacher and family would develop strategies to help these children have positive learning experiences in the classroom and at home, similar to the program Saul and Jackson's father implemented to help Jackson.

UNIQUENESS OF EACH CHILD. Jackson and Jodie serve as good reminders that children with special needs are very different from each other. It is a misnomer to assume all children with special needs should be treated the same way or have the same program. Jodie is working on increasing her sentence length, whereas Jackson is working on not talking out as often in the classroom. Their programs are different and are developed to meet their individual learning needs. Just as all children differ from each other, so do children with special needs.

CHILDREN WHO ARE GIFTED AND TALENTED. Another group of children who have special learning needs are children who are gifted and talented. These children may exhibit outstanding abilities in a variety of areas, including high levels of creativity, intellect, academic ability, and motivation to succeed. The Association for the Gifted (2001) expanded the definition of *giftedness* to include attention to the child's culture, exceptionalities, and language. Special education for these children is not required by federal law, although many individual states have legislation requiring educational experiences that meet learning needs of gifted and talented children. Box 12.2 provides an overview of educational practices for gifted and talented children.

Now that you have looked at what special education is and who is served by special education, let's examine how special education has evolved over the past several decades. Some of the earliest programs for young children with special needs were implemented when the Handicapped Children's Early Education Assistance Act was enacted in 1968. Legislation at the federal government level has had a tremendous impact on the implementation and funding for special education programs and services across our nation. This legislation affects the kind of services Jodie and her family receive.

What Are Some Educational Approaches for Children Who Are Gifted and Talented?

How is it determined if a child is talented and gifted? A current definition of *talented children* was outlined in the government report *National Excellence: A Case for Developing America's Talent* (U.S. Department of Education, 1993). According to this definition, children with exceptional talent "exhibit high performance capability in intellectual, creative, and/or artistic areas, possess an unusual leadership capacity, or excel in specific academic fields" (p. 26). Students who are talented are often identified through IQ tests or from results on a standard achievement test. More recently, a combination of test scores as well as input from teachers and parents is used to identify children with exceptional talent.

Three common educational approaches for working with talented children are ability grouping, acceleration, and enrichment (Heward, 1996). With *ability grouping,* children with similar high levels of talent are grouped together for advanced courses, special classes, or enrichment activities. At the elementary school level, this might consist of a pull-out program, with children identified as talented meeting together two or three times a week for special classes. *Acceleration* is used to move a child through the curriculum at a faster pace, with options such as moving ahead a grade or more in school, testing out of courses, or earning college credit through advanced placement tests. *Enrichment* provides for more depth in learning, allowing children who are talented to explore learning outside the typical curriculum. These three educational approaches facilitate the development of a child with talented and gifted abilities, providing a rich and stimulating learning environment.

Public Law 94-142: Education for All Handicapped Children Act

In 1975, **P.L. 94-142 (Education for All Handicapped Children Act)** was established. The law stated that every child with a handicap is entitled to a free appropriate public education (FAPE), and that this education will take place in the least restrictive environment (LRE) for that child. Remember when Jodie was entering the public school district? The philosophy of her school district was to think of special education programs on a continuum, with placement in a regular classroom in the child's neighborhood school as the first choice of a least restrictive environment. P.L. 94-142 assumed a preference for teaching the child in a regular educational environment to the extent possible, using resources to support the child within the setting that is least restrictive. Figure 12.2 displays a continuum of educational settings from least restrictive (regular class) to most restrictive (homebound/hospital).

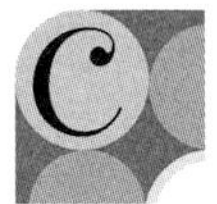

INDIVIDUALIZED EDUCATION PROGRAM. P.L. 94-142 required that an individualized education program (IEP) is designed for each child, with parents participating on the planning team. The law directed educators to create an IEP for each child and use the IEP to make educational decisions regarding what is taught to the child and where the child is taught on an individual basis. An educational plan must be developed for each child by the teacher or a teacher and several specialists and with parental input. The IEP includes current level of educational functioning, annual learning goals, short-term instructional goals, evaluation criteria to determine when goals are met, educational services and support required to reach the goals, and instructional and service provision schedule. The child's parents must be regularly informed of their child's progress toward annual goals and the extent to which that progress is sufficient to enable the child to achieve the goals by the annual review date. Formats of IEPs differ between school districts and states. Changes have been made to IEP requirements over the years, with Figure 12.3 reflecting an IEP based on reauthorization and amendments implemented in 1997.

FIGURE 12.2

Continuum of Educational Environments for Students with Disabilities

Least Restrictive ↑	*Regular class* includes students who receive the majority of their education program in a regular classroom and receive special education and related services outside the regular classroom for less than 21 percent of the school day.
	Resource room includes students who receive special education and related services outside of the regular classroom for at least 21 percent but no more than 60 percent of the school day.
	Separate class includes students who receive special education and related services outside the regular class for more than 60 percent of the school day.
	Separate school includes students who receive special education and related services in a public or private separate day school for students with disabilities, at public expense, and more than 50 percent of the school day.
	Residential facility includes students who receive special education in a public or private residential facility, at public expense, for more than 50 percent of the school day.
↓ **More Restrictive**	*Homebound/hospital* environment includes students placed in and receiving special education in a hospital or homebound program.

Source: U.S. Department of Education, 1996, *Eighteenth Annual Report to Congress on the Implementation of the Individuals with Disabilities Education Act,* p. 69.

FIGURE 12.3

Individualized Education Program (IEP) (Portion of an Example)

Student's Name: John Aaron Wright	Identifying Number: 38291-1923	Attending School/District: same	IEP Meeting Date: 3/15/04
Gender: M	District: Lakeview	Disability Code: SLD	Reevaluation Due: 3/15/05
Date of Birth (month/day/year): 5/3/97	Home School: Elm Creek Elementary	Grade: 1	Case Manager: Sara Rameriz

IEP Meeting Participants

Parent(s): Marty Wright	Regular Education Teacher: Lori Sterling	Other:
Special Education Teacher/Provider: Geoff Creston, Resource Teacher	Student:	Other:
District Representative:	Individual Interpreting Evaluations:	Other:

Service Summary (continue on next page if necessary)

Specially Designed Instruction	Anticipated Amount/Frequency	Anticipated Location	Starting Date	Ending Date	Provider: (e.g., LEA, ESD, Regional)
Specially Designed Instruction (SDI) Reading and Written Language	120 minutes/week of direct instruction in strategies for reading and written language	small group setting in classroom	3/20/04	3/20/05	LEA

Related Services	Anticipated Amount/Frequency	Anticipated Location	Starting Date	Ending Date	Provider:
None at this time					

Supplementary Aids/Services: Modifications & Accommodations	Anticipated Amount/Frequency	Anticipated Location	Starting Date	Ending Date	Provider:
Classroom modifications: Assess John's current interest in topics/subjects and provide for this choice in reading	Daily in reading and writing	classroom	3/20/04	3/20/05	Classroom teacher

Support for School Personnel	Anticipated Amount/Frequency	Anticipated Location	Starting Date	Ending Date	Provider:
Training/support for curriculum modification in reading/writing	2 x month 30 min each	classroom	3/18/04	3/20/05	Resource teacher

(continued)

FIGURE 12.3
(continued)

Student's Name: John Aaron Wright   Date: 3/15/04   School District: Lakeview

Consideration of Special Factors

Does the student need assistive technology devices or services?

__ Yes, services/devices addressed in IEP   X No

Does the student have communication needs?

__ Yes, addressed in IEP   X No

Does the student exhibit behavior that impedes his/her learning or the learning of others?

__ Yes   X No

(If yes, the IEP Team must consider strategies/ positive behavioral interventions, and supports to address the behavior(s))

Does the student have limited English proficiency

__ Yes   X No

(If yes, the IEP team must consider the language needs of the student as those needs related to the IEP)

Is the student blind or visually impaired?

__ Yes   X No

(If yes, Braille needs are addressed in the IEP, or evaluation of reading/writing needs is completed and a determination is made that Braille is not appropriate)

Is the student deaf or hard of hearing?

__ Yes   X No

(If yes, the IEP addresses the student's language and communication needs, opportunities for direct communication mode, academic level, and full range of needs, including opportunities for direct instruction in the student's language and communication mode)

Nonparticipation Justification

Does the student need to be removed from participating with nondisabled students in general education classes, extracurricular activities, and nonacademic activities?

__ Yes   X No

If yes, describe the extent of the removal and provide justification:

____

Extended School Year (ESY) Services

ESY services will be provided for this student:

__ Yes   __ No

X to be considered:

Will meet to consider ESY by 5/30/04 (date).

If yes, ESY services to be provided must be included in the Services Summary of the IEP.

Goals Objectives: FOR STUDENTS THROUGH AGE 15

Measurable Annual Goal:	Progress will be measured as indicated below: Criteria	Evaluation Procedures	How will progress be reported to parents?
John will read a late 1st-level story with 75% comprehension	50% of the time with a text at his reading level	Reading miscue samples	Through quarterly progress reports and parent conferences (2x yr)

Measurable Short-Term Objectives

Given instruction, John will use effective strategies to decode or make a meaningful substitution for an unknown word 50% of the time

PROGRESS NOTES

Note: Pages missing: Present Level of Functioning, Participation in Statewide/Districtwide Assessment, and Special Education Placement Determination.

Source: Form is from Oregon Department of Education, Office of Special Education.

P.L. 94-142 also directed federal funding to states and local education agencies for the education of children and young adults requiring special education between the ages of 3 to 21 (McCollum & Maude, 1993). Prior to P.L. 94-142, many children with special needs were denied an education. Their options included institutionalization, private schools for children with handicaps, special schools or special classrooms, or exclusion to any schooling. Each of these options led to segregation of children with special needs from the general population. Although P.L. 94-142 opened the door to education within the regular school setting for school-aged children, it did not specifically include services for younger children. Each state had the option to decide if it would offer programs for children from ages 3 to 5. This option left many young children unserved.

Another area important to early childhood education is the focus on family-centered programs. P.L. 94-142 did include parents in the IEP planning meetings, but the parents' role was often minimal. With the 1997 reauthorization, parents are invited to all meetings having to do with their child's special education. The jargon of special education can be confusing and intimidating, leaving parents with varying levels of success in providing direction and input in their child's learning program. If you are feeling some of the same frustration in trying to understand the various terms and practices of special education, you can well imagine what parents might experience.

CATEGORIZING OR LABELING DISABILITIES. P.L. 94-142 also required that a child fit within a specific category of eligibility, such as severe emotional disorder or communication disorder, in order to obtain services. This requirement introduces some challenges. First, assessment must consist of more than a test or a single measure of the young child's ability or developmental level. Including multiple sources of information and observations of the young child will yield information valuable for making evaluative decisions (Greenspan & Meisels, 1996). Second, there is a cultural and social affect that occurs from labeling a child. Again, as you recognize and appreciate the positive changes made in education for school-aged children with special needs, you see that there are several areas of the law that need modification.

Public Law 99-457: Support for Early Childhood Intervention

In 1986, P.L. 99-457, an amendment to P.L. 94-142, was enacted. P.L. 99-457 extended federal funding to serving children with disabilities from birth to age 5, while also eliminating the specific categories of disability. This law made special education services mandatory for children from ages 3 to 5. It established a new part of the law, Part H, which covers services from birth to age 3. This amendment also allowed states to add a new category, that of developmentally delayed, which encompasses many different areas of need. The term **developmentally delayed** refers to children who exhibit delays in their development, with or without a specific diagnosis (Lerner, Lowenthal, & Egan, 2003). The developmental delay is determined by comparison with age-appropriate performance. This term opened up the identification and labeling process by connoting a more general delay of development rather than a specific deficit, handicap, or disability.

Depending on available services within her particular community, Jodie most likely would not have worked with an early intervention specialist as an infant and toddler if she had been born prior to 1986. She benefited from the legislature that provided funding for early intervention services to young children and their families from birth.

STATE-LEVEL RESPONSIBILITY. By 1991–92, educational programs for children ages 3 to 21 became the responsibility of each state's department of education within the special education system (McCollum & Maude, 1993). For children from birth through age 3, it was not mandatory for the state to provide services, but funding was available for services and programs for children with special needs at this age, and for their families.

Each state differs in the lead agency and responsibilities for early special education services for infants with special needs and their families.

Jodie and her family received support and services from the time she was 3 months old. Lynn and Jerry were partners in developing and assessing the individualized family services plan and had input in the developmental goals established for Jodie. They also were involved in parent education, both in small groups and in individual settings. The parent education helped them as Jodie developed throughout her childhood. Lynn and Jerry learned many different strategies to encourage Jodie at home along with ways to stimulate her and involve her in as many typical activities as possible.

INTERAGENCY COLLABORATION. One of the important strands of P.L. 94-457—for Part H, which affects children from birth through age 3—is an emphasis placed on interagency collaboration. **Interagency collaboration** is the coordination of services from different agencies; it helps families access services and reduce the fragmentation between programs. Although services might have been available prior to this law, there was minimal connection between agencies or services. Interagency collaboration is required to provide the best possible services and resources for families of young children with special needs (Lerner, Lowenthal, & Egan, 2003). Prior to P.L. 94-457, parents had to learn how to access different agencies to find programs for their child and for the family. For example, an education program for infants might be run by the local university, whereas family services were available through the state's social services. When the child was ready to move to a toddler program, the parent then had to locate this program, and yet another agency might then be responsible for parent education.

SUPPORT FOR FAMILIES. Another strength found in P.L. 94-457 is the importance given to families of young children with special needs. The intent of P.L. 94-457 is to recognize the central role families play in the development of young children. Young children spend a majority of their time with their families. Supporting families of young children with special needs can lead to improved learning environments for children during crucial developmental periods of their lives. Lynn confirms this: "The services and resources we accessed during Jodie's early years were invaluable. I am sure that Jodie would not have reached her same level of development and learned so many essential skills before entering school." The early intervention specialist provided comprehensive services and coordination of resources for Jodie. Lynn and Jerry were active partners in decisions about Jodie and her education: "We were able to make informed decisions from the knowledge gained in parent education classes, workshops, and individual sessions." Jodie and her entire family benefited from enactment of P.L. 99-457, which is the true intent of this legislature.

JOURNAL 12.2: Briefly discuss an important benefit that Jodie and her family gained from P.L. 99-457.

Individuals with Disabilities Education Act (IDEA)

In 1990, the **Individuals with Disabilities Education Act (IDEA)** replaced the Education of the Handicapped Act (P.L. 94-142 and P.L. 99-457). IDEA (P.L. 105-17) states that children with disabilities are entitled to a free appropriate public education and that each child's education will be planned and monitored with an individualized education program or an individualized family service plan. Section 612 of IDEA states:

> to the maximum extent appropriate, children with disabilities, including children in public or private institutions or other care facilities, are educated with children, who are not disabled, and that special classes, separate schooling, or other removal of children with disabilities from the regular educational environment occurs only when the nature or severity of the disability is such that education in regular classes with the use of supplementary aids and services cannot be achieved satisfactorily. (Individual with Disabilities Education Act, 1990)

When IDEA replaced prior legislature, the age range mandated in P.L. 94-142 (6 through 21 years) and in P.L. 99-457 (ages 3 through 6) was combined to promote the involvement of the family and to offer a wide range of services and specialists to support the child in a least restrictive environment. IDEA also changed the language of the law, focusing more on the individual with disabilities rather than on handicapped children. This new terminology focuses attention to the individual, not to the label or condition. Categories of eligibility for special education services are included in IDEA.

IDEA 1997. The Individuals with Disabilities Education Act Amendments of 1997 shifted the focus of IDEA to improve teaching and learning through emphasizing the individual educational plan as a primary tool for educational planning, increasing the role of parents in educational decision making and promoting meaningful access to the general curriculum. IDEA 1997 reflects a strengthened "preference for children with disabilities to be educated and receive services with their non-disabled age-mates in typical early childhood settings" (Smith & Rapport, 1999). Part B of this law provides resources and services for children ages 3 through 5 with developmental delays or those with an identified disability. The child's learning needs are outlined on either an IEP or IFSP, with the major focus on providing support and resources for developmental learning. The use of a noncategorical classification, such as development delay, is permitted for children ages 3 through 9.

Part C of IDEA 1997 authorizes financial assistance to the states through grants to support the needs of infants and toddlers with disabilities and the needs of their families. Agencies are to provide comprehensive early intervention services that focus on the child's developmental and medical needs as well as family needs. Services and progress are documented on the IFSP and are to be provided in the natural environment, which is often the home with infants and toddlers. Infants and toddlers must be classified under a noncategorical term, such as developmental delay. Under Part C, each state has the option to include children who are at risk of developmental delays.

SUPPORT SERVICES. To early childhood professionals, IDEA means that more children with special needs are now eligible for programs, with services and resources available to support the child, family, and teacher in providing education for the child. The

What structural changes that support physical accessibility do you see in this photograph?

requirement of appropriate services to support the child in her learning through IDEA brings early childhood professionals into a team of specialists working together in planning, implementing, and assessing a child's learning. The child with special needs is granted access to the programs, but there is also the requirement of **support services** accompanying the child. These support services, such as occupational therapy or speech therapy, are critical to the child's development and to her success in a least restrictive setting.

MULTIDISCIPLINARY TEAM. When Jodie required the help of an occupational therapist to develop programs to help her with eating skills and fine motor development, the occupational therapist went to Jodie's preschool and provided the services at that site. She communicated with Karla (Jodie's preschool teacher), the speech/language therapist, the early intervention specialist, and Lynn and Jerry. Together, this team of specialists designed an educational plan for Jodie and shared her learning and her challenges. This is an example of a **multidisciplinary** or **transdisciplinary team**—that is, a group of specialists working together across areas of expertise.

American Disabilities Act (ADA)

The **American Disabilities Act (ADA)** ensures that all people with disabilities have equal rights in employment, public services, and public accommodations. ADA is a federal civil rights law that has been in effect since 1990. Young children with special needs have a right to participate in child care centers, preschool programs, or family child care homes, as these are considered public accommodations. Physical and other types of barriers must be removed to enable these children to participate fully in programs.

In early childhood education, most professionals already focus on meeting the needs of each individual child and his family, making this law an extension of existing practice. Changes may be needed in admission policies, employment practices, physical accessibility, or accommodations to meet the needs of children, staff, or families with disabilities. Reasonable changes or program modifications generally will meet the child, staff member, or family member's special need.

Importance of These Laws

Each of these laws has considerably shaped programs and services for young children with special needs. It is essential for you to be knowledgeable of the laws and to have an understanding of the support and services they provide for young children. You will also want to follow the laws and their intent in your program. Jodie's parents learned about their rights and about available programs through their parent support group and from the early intervention specialist who helped coordinate services for Jodie.

As an early childhood professional, you will want to provide the best learning environment possible. It is reassuring to know that you will have the help of specialists when working with children with special needs. Now, let's take a closer look at early childhood special education.

Early Childhood Special Education

In the previous section, the focus was on legislation that has affected special education services for all children with special needs from birth through age 21. Now, you will examine programs, settings, and services that are the outcome of this legislation.

What Is Early Childhood Special Education?

The term *early childhood special education* describes a multitude of services and programs for young children and their families. A child might be attending a day care center, involved in a toddler class at a preschool, receiving home visits, or enrolled in a public school kindergarten program. Special education refers to the specially designed instruction or services that are not available to children with special needs in a typical education program (Kirk, Gallagher, & Anastasiow, 2003), not the setting of the child's placement. With the successful inclusion of many children with special needs, most children are involved in learning for some or all of the time in a typical early childhood setting. When you visited Jodie at her school, you saw her learning about insects with other children. You also learned that she worked with Marty, the resource teacher, several times a week. The support from Marty to Jodie and to Paula, her teacher, was important in helping Jodie learn within the regular classroom setting.

The focus of special education is on developing a program or plan to meet the individual needs of the child, with changes or modifications made to the curriculum. An important element of curriculum content and design for children with special needs is age appropriateness. When you design curriculum for a child with special needs, you want to take into consideration the age of the child and the usefulness of the activity in everyday life. Does this remind you of Jodie's assignment as the messenger to the school office? She was learning skills and acquiring knowledge applicable to school and to settings outside of school.

Early Childhood Special Education Services

With these descriptions of special education in mind, you can see that a child with special needs might be attending any of the early childhood settings described throughout this book. An infant might be in her own home, a home care center, or an employer-sponsored infant care program; a toddler might go to a play group or be in child care; 3- and 4-year-olds might be in a preschool setting, a child care center, or a home care center. No matter what the setting, the caregiver or teacher will likely need to learn some general adaptation strategies to help a child with special needs succeed.

INCLUSIVE PROGRAMS. When caregivers and teachers believe that all children are entitled to a program that supports their learning in a setting with their peers, true inclusion is more likely to take place.

> Inclusion, as a value, supports the right of all children, regardless of abilities, to participate actively in natural settings within their communities. Natural settings are those in which the child would spend time had he or she not had a disability. These settings include, but are not limited to home, preschool, nursery schools, Head Start programs, kindergartens, neighborhood school classrooms, child care, places of worship, recreational (such as community playgrounds and community events) and other settings that all children and families enjoy. (Division of Early Childhood Council for Exceptional Children, 2000)

In the Early Childhood Inclusion Model (ECI model), described by Suzanne Winter (1999), an inclusive program is designed from the following three premises: each child is unique, group diversity is valued as a strength, and all children are capable of learning. An ECI model program "seeks to maximize each child's potential by focusing on strengths and abilities" (p. 54). The programs and classrooms highlighted in the case studies in Chapters 7 through 12 are inclusive programs, where all children are provided with "equitable opportunities to grow, develop, and learn within heterogeneous groups of their peers" (p. 17).

INSTRUCTIONAL STRATEGIES. Good instructional strategies, guidance, curriculum modifications or adaptations, and modifying the classroom and/or schedule are practices that work together to create a successful inclusion program. *Cooperative learning* (sometimes called *collaborative learning, peer teaching,* or *group projects*) is an instructional strategy that has proven successful in inclusive classrooms. Students teach each other and assume responsibility for the learning of others. Cooperative learning captures the affective and social aspects of learning, along with academic learning. In **cooperative learning,** students communicate with each other and become members of a group working toward the common goal of accomplishing a task or gaining knowledge. Many teachers find it useful to take workshops or courses on cooperative learning to help them understand how to teach the process of group work and create a community of learners.

Direct instruction is an instructional strategy that assists children in learning specific information or knowledge, often basic skills in reading or mathematics, or life skills. Direct instruction includes step-by-step learning, mastery of each step before moving to the next level, practice with several examples, movement toward independent work, and review of learned skills and concepts (Kavale & Forness, 2000). For example, a 2-year-old with physical challenges might have difficulty using a spoon without spilling the contents. While other children are involved in various activities, the child care provider might help the child practice using a spoon for a favorite snack of pudding. This extra time and practice helps the child learn the skill as she works toward gaining the fine motor coordination needed to master the spoon. In this situation, the adult provides direct instruction, focuses on a specific skill, and gives frequent feedback to the child, helping her learn a useful life skill.

Whatever program is used or adaptations made, the goal should be to promote learning based on knowledge and skills identified in a child's individual education program.

CURRICULUM MODIFICATIONS OR ADAPTATIONS. In Jodie's classroom, Marty, the resource teacher, assisted Paula in making curriculum modifications to match Jodie's learning needs. Earlier, when you observed Jodie working on her number facts, you saw that she was making combinations of objects to find a total of 4. Other children were involved in double-digit addition and subtraction. Paula had modified the curriculum so Jodie could be successful in learning the numeracy skills that she needed before moving to higher-level skills. Because Jodie's individual education program specified the skills she was working on in mathematics, it was fairly simple to modify the curriculum and provide differentiated instruction to meet her needs.

Curriculum adaptations often reflect an accommodation of the quantity of the curriculum a child with special needs is expected to learn. When Jodie's class was studying insects, Jodie was expected to learn the colors of her insect and what her insect liked to eat. Other children were learning about the life cycle of insects and the body parts of insects. Jodie was participating in the same curriculum at the same time, but with different expectations for the amount of knowledge she was to learn.

Since many general education teachers have not had coursework in special education, frameworks for learning to plan for inclusion have been developed. The SMART model (Winter, 1997) is an acronym for **S**elect curriculum and approaches, **M**atch instruction to the child, **A**dapt when necessary, **R**elevant skills are targeted, and **T**est to inform instruction. These five steps were designed to help teachers plan and modify instruction to meet the learning needs of individual children.

Other modifications to a program are time and schedule changes. Some children with special needs may need to have a schedule that allows for frequent breaks or time to choose low-key activities balanced with intensive learning time. Time modifications might also include lengthening the time for practicing a skill and preparing home activity packets to allow the child to continue an activity at his own pace after school. Most of the modification or adaptation techniques discussed in this chapter are helpful to other children, as well. Learning to implement these strategies helps teachers and caregivers become more aware of the individual learning needs of all children.

TECHNOLOGY AND CHILDREN WITH SPECIAL NEEDS. *Assistive technology* is defined as any item, piece of equipment, or product system—whether acquired commercially off the shelf, modified, or customized—that is used to increase, maintain, or improve functional capabilities of individuals with disabilities (Individuals with Disabilities Act, 1997). Technology applications can be important in improving both the teaching and learning for children with special needs (Stremel, 2000). When developing an IFSP or IEP, the benefits of assistive technology must be considered for all children. A child who has challenges in communicating might use a program and a device that enable the child to use pictures to point to as a communication tool. Assistive technology is available to enhance learning in each developmental domain.

PROGRAM OPTIONS OR SETTINGS. Program options also provide a format to meet the diverse learning needs of children with special needs. Many options are available and can be combined or altered to meet individual needs. For example, a child could attend a second program concurrent with his early childhood program. The specialized program might provide therapy or specific resources at the same center or at another site (DEC, 2000). A young child who has developmentally delays in her speech or language would spend time with a speech/language therapist on a regular basis. The speech/language therapist would also collaborate with the preschool teacher to find ways that both might incorporate similar activities to help the child with her language development. Remember when Jodie's IFSP goals included expanding her sentence length beyond two-word responses? In this situation, the preschool teacher and assistants, parents, and speech/language therapist met to discuss this goal and how to help Jodie increase her vocabulary and sentence length in her natural environment (play, home, class). The collaboration of all who work with Jodie helped create a coherent approach to Jodie's language development.

When children are working with several specialists and professionals, regular communication between specialists and parents is essential to help everyone keep abreast of the child's progress. Lynn found these meetings very helpful: "I always felt involved in the decision making and was able to talk about what I saw Jodie doing at home." The nature of these collaborations or partnerships is often established by the early childhood specialist and her willingness to actively include all parties in the planning and assessing of a child's learning and development.

JOURNAL 12.3: What might be some benefits gained by people representing different programs and agencies if they work together to assess Jodie's needs and develop plans to guide her learning? ●

Special Education in the Public Schools

Once Jodie entered kindergarten, her education and services were provided by the local education agency. States differ on the age when local school districts begin providing special education services. Most start providing services through the school districts at age 3. The school district receives federal funding for special education, which is allocated according to the number of special education students enrolled in the district. This funding formula brings up the problem of labeling children and requiring children to fit into a specific category of need so that the district will receive funding. Often, a child may be functioning below grade level in some subject areas and need special services to support her learning. Unless her disability meets eligibility criteria and she needs special education in order to benefit from the education program, she may not be eligible for services.

REFERRING STUDENTS FOR SPECIAL EDUCATION SERVICES. You might be wondering how a child becomes eligible to receive special education services. Under Part B and Part C of IDEA, states are responsible for locating young children who have disabilities or possibly are at risk of developmental delays. This process is called *child-find,* with individuals and agencies throughout the community serving as initial contacts that refer a child suspected of having possible developmental delays for further screening. Screening measures are to be used for gathering information and must include family input. If the screening process identifies a child as having a possible problem, the child is then further evaluated, with the intent of establishing whether the child is eligible for services under IDEA.

The child must meet established federal and state criteria for eligibility. IDEA 97 requires that the evaluation be comprehensive and identify all of the child's special education and related service needs. The evaluation also must be sufficient to determine the current levels of performance of the child. With the information gained from the evaluative process, an IFSP or IEP is developed for the child. The IFSP or IEP will also include when and how the effectiveness of the program will be determined.

Special education programs at the school district level follow procedures and requirements monitored by the state department of education. If a district is not large enough to require full-time services of an occupational therapist, physical therapist, psychologist, speech therapist, or other specialist, it might contract with the county or several other districts to share a specialist. By law, school districts are required to provide the necessary services to each child identified with special needs as prescribed in the child's IEP. School districts must also provide necessary medical support to assist children with medical conditions to participate as fully as possible in their local school program.

The focus of education shifts gradually from the family unit to the child as the child moves through the school years, although many school districts continue parent education programs and parents often form support groups through formal associations, such as the ARC (previously called the Association of Retarded Citizens), or on an informal level. Children with more severe disabilities typically spend time in some type of career preparation or life skills program to prepare them for adulthood. The goal for these young adults is to learn skills needed to become as independent as possible when they leave school. Many of the skills learned in early childhood lay the foundation for adult skills. Learning to get along with others, follow directions, accept responsibility for one's own actions, share with others, and similar social skills are as important to a 30-year-old as to a 5-year-old. The social goals for Jodie as a 4-year-old would be modified to be developmentally and age appropriate, but would still focus on her learning to participate as a contributing and active member of society.

Role of Families in Early Childhood Special Education

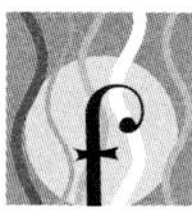

As discussed in several sections of this book, families are an integral part of early childhood education. This holds true in special education, as these families may need specific assistance in learning how best to help their child. Often, the role of the early childhood professional is to share day-to-day experiences of the child's interactions and activities at his setting, much like the communication you might have with all of your students' families. Many parents of children with special needs wish to hear good news about their child, and your feedback is important to them. A simple note or a quick chat at the door can help the family learn of their child's unique place in your program. Jerry appreciated notes home about Jodie's progress at preschool. He remembers, "After one particularly hard day at work, I arrived home to find a note from the preschool teacher describing Jodie's creative storytelling with her classmates. This was the first time Jodie had told stories at school and we were so glad to hear that her language was growing. That note made my day and my week!"

FAMILY-CENTERED APPROACH. A family-centered approach to early childhood education and to early special education have similar rationales. Finding out the priorities of the family is part of developing an individualized learning program for a child. For instance, if Jodie's family is interested in helping Jodie increase her vocabulary, the early intervention specialist, speech/language therapist, and early childhood professional would work with her family to identify specific goals for Jodie. These goals might include providing frequent and interesting opportunities for Jodie to communicate with other children and her family. When a family is more concerned with a child learning certain skills, it makes sense to focus learning activities in this direction and work together in providing activities that help the child accomplish these skills.

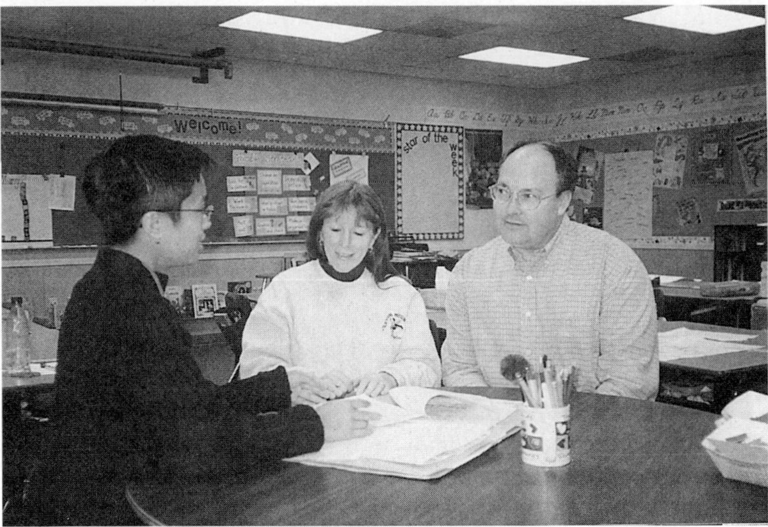

Families and teachers work together to communicate about a child's progress.

In order to know which areas are of interest to the family, an early childhood provider might spend time during a conference discussing areas that the family is concentrating on at home and successes and challenges they have faced. For a child with learning difficulties, it is critical for people to work together to make the child's learning more connected between home and her early childhood setting. This active partnership empowers the family as they work with their child and note their child's new accomplishments. The partnership you develop with this family may not differ much from those with other families. You will find that communicating the experiences, successes, and challenges that occur throughout a day helps you build on what the family is doing and enables the family to make connections with the activities in your setting.

Jodie's family is economically and educationally advantaged; Jerry and Lynn are college graduates, and they have the support of an extended family. Many families of children with disabilities are not as fortunate. Jerry and Lynn expressed many trials and tribulations they experienced when learning how to find the best services for Jodie in her early years. Remember their gratitude for the support from the families in their parent support group? This support was an essential resource in their understanding of Jodie's disability and their search to find services for Jodie.

JOURNAL 12.4: Imagine the many challenges that a single parent, perhaps a teen mother, would face as the mother of a child with Down syndrome. As a teacher, what community resources might you suggest to the family to help support them in their unique challenges? ●

Rationale for Early Intervention for Children with Special Needs

At some point in your career, you might be asked why there is a need for early intervention programs for children with special needs. It is important for you to be able to explain the rationale for such programs. Young children are typically in learning situations that allow them to grow and develop at their individual pace, which contributes to a nurturing setting for children with special needs. The early childhood profession views each child as an individual with appreciation for the diversity children bring to the setting. This approach to learning is congruent with the stance of special educators, who see individualized learning programs as the key to helping each child reach his potential.

EARLY INTERVENTION AND ITS INFLUENCE ON LATER LIFE. Early intervention for young children with special needs provides physical and emotional care that promotes self-efficacy and leads to positive outcomes (Werner, 2000). During the 1960s and the War on Poverty, one outcome was to provide early childhood programs for children living in poverty. The belief was that reaching children and their families while the children were young could make positive influences on their academic and social development. Results from a preschool project that followed children into early adulthood, the Perry Preschool Project, found that early intervention during preschool years had impacts in multiple areas, including higher academic performance, lower teenage pregnancy rate, higher enrollment at higher education levels, and higher high school graduation rate (Schweinhart & Weikart, 1985). Children in the Abecedarian Project were in high-quality child care settings from infancy through age 5. These children had higher mental test scores, enhanced language skills, and higher reading achievement scores than individuals without the early intervention (Campbell & Ramey, 1999). These researchers concluded that early intervention was a sound cost-effective program. Early intervention led to later cost savings that would not have occurred if these children had not participated in high-quality programs. For example, when the group was followed into adulthood, it was found that only 18 percent of the Perry Preschool group was on welfare, compared to 32 percent of the control group (made up of a similar population who had not attended the Perry Preschool.) This difference is reflected in savings with reduced costs of welfare for society. (The Perry Preschool Study and the Abecedarian Project are discussed further in Chapter 13, when we examine the economics of early childhood programs.)

For early childhood professionals and special educators, the findings that early intervention significantly affects later learning and success is evident in the results presented in these studies.

EARLY INTERVENTION AND PREVENTION. Early intervention and prevention are interwoven. Prevention and intervention work together around the same goal of helping each child reach his potential in his intellectual, physical, emotional, and social evelopment. The longitudinal studies support the long-term gains made by children who received early intervention services, both in personal growth and gains and in financial savings to society. In Part C of IDEA 1997, states are encouraged to provide services to infants and toddlers who are at risk of needing special education services in the future, thus providing preventive resources at critical stages of development. Clearly, early intervention and preventive services play an essential role in helping young children and their families.

JOURNAL 12.5: **What argument or rationale would you develop to the question, Why is it necessary to provide early intervention for children with special needs?** ●

PRINCIPLES AND INSIGHTS: A Summary and Review

You began this chapter with a quick visit to Jodie's home. Teachers and caregivers who have not worked with children with special needs often feel unqualified or uncertain about their expertise in special education. By meeting Jodie at her home, we hoped to dispel some of these feelings by sharing how Jodie is much like other children in her needs, interests, and support from her family.

The early intervention childhood specialist made regular home visits and involved Lynn and Jerry as she worked with Jodie. Struggles and challenges were discussed and plans were developed to help Jodie succeed. In a preschool program, you typically would notice when a child progresses in language development and begins talking in full sentences. With Jodie, progress was noted when she began moving from one-word responses to two-word phrases. Each small step was acknowledged, with future plans or learning goals built on her successful experiences and activities.

Take a few minutes to review your journal entries from this chapter and think about the impact of legislation on the programs and services that Jodie and her family experienced. You will likely recognize that through legislative decisions, support, resources, and an educational program were provided for Jodie and her family. Each of the programs she was involved in built on her strengths and prior accomplishments, and focused on specific goals.

Jodie's parents were partners in planning their child's programs and making decisions about her learning. Jodie often was involved with several different specialists, who collaborated to define individual learning activities and situations to help her meet learning goals established by her family and specialists.

Jodie also had input in her planning. She has certain likes and dislikes, as do all children, and her early childhood specialists designed experiences that allowed her to make choices and develop her own interests. Seeing each and every child as an individual, with unique dispositions and developmental patterns, enables you to reach the children you work with and create an optimal learning environment.

Working with children with special needs will be part of your future. Approximately 11 percent of the school-aged population of children are eligible for special education services. From reading this chapter, you now know that specialists are available to assist and support you, the child, and his family. You also know about the importance of including children with special needs and supporting their growth and development in early childhood programs, as both an intervention and a prevention practice. This knowledge, along with your introduction to Jodie and her experiences, provides an introduction to working with young children with special needs. Hopefully, you will have the opportunity to help children such as Jodie become active, eager learners in your early childhood program.

BECOMING AN EARLY CHILDHOOD PROFESSIONAL

Your Professional Portfolio

1. Describe two different settings in which Jodie received special education services during her early years. What was the role of the early childhood education specialist in each of these settings?
2. Interview a special education teacher or teacher assistant. Why did she choose this career? What education or training is required for his position? Ask her to describe a "typical" workday. What part of his job sounds the most rewarding to you? Summarize the interview findings and your thoughts about these findings in a short paper for your portfolio.

Your Professional Library

Chandler, P. (1994). *A place for me: Including children with special needs in early care and education settings.* Washington, DC: NAEYC.

Guralnick, G. (Ed.). (2001). *Early childhood inclusion: Focus on change.* Baltimore, MD: Paul H. Brookes.

Kostelnik, S., Onaga, E., Rohde, B., & Whiren, A. (2002). *Children with special needs: Lessons for early childhood professionals.* New York: Teachers College Press.

Lerner, J., Lowenthal, B., & Egan, R. (2003). *Preschool children with special needs: Children at risk and children with disabilities.* Boston: Pearson Education.

Odom, S. (2002). *Widening the circle: Including children with disabilities in preschool programs.* New York: Teachers College Press.

Sandall, S., McLean, M., & Smith, B. (2000). *DEC recommended practices in early intervention/early childhood special education.* Longmont, CO: Sporis West.

CHAPTER 13

The Changing World of Early Childhood

CHAPTER focus:

When you finish reading and reflecting on this chapter, you will be able to:

1. Summarize political influences on early childhood programs.
2. Describe several economic impacts on early childhood.
3. Discuss the social forces that influence early childhood.
4. Define, in your own words, *early childhood professional.*
5. Clarify and define your role as an advocate for early childhood.

"Nothing is more important to our shared future than the well-being of our children. . . . Just as it takes a village to raise a child, it takes children to raise up a village to become all it should be. The village we build with them in mind will be a better place for us all" (Clinton, 1996, p. 318). As you read this chapter and prepare to work with young children, you are learning and making decisions that will change your life as well as the lives of children. In the book *It Takes a Village and Other Lessons Children Teach Us,* Hillary Clinton (1996) reminds us that the way we raise our children influences their future as well as our own future and the quality of our lives.

As individuals and professionals, the economic, political, and social decisions you make individually and collectively about the care of and programs for young children demonstrate your commitment to young children. These decisions and actions are determined by members of a modern-day village, composed of people both near and far who share the raising of children. Years ago, villages were much simpler; one could easily recognize most of the members of one's village. Villages of today are much more complex; one probably will not know—or even see all the members who help raise one's children. Come meet Angela and some of the people helping to raise her.

Angela's Village

Angela Russo is 4 years old and lives in Brooklyn, New York. At first glance, it appears her village is quite small. Her mother, Marie, is a single parent working from 8:30 to 5:00 each day in a nearby law office. Living close by (each only several bus stops from Angela's apartment) are two sets of grandparents, Edward and Betty Deluiso, and Frank and Anna Russo. In the apartment upstairs live Mr. and Mrs. Ponzi, who occasionally watch Angela when her mother goes out for an evening. Emily Weiss, who cares for four young children in her home, one of whom is Angela, lives three blocks away. And finally, one of Angela's favorite stops, is the corner bakery, where Mrs. Gianolla lets Angela pick out a biscottini (an Italian cookie) when she and her mom stop in to buy bread.

Four blocks away is the public library, where Jerome Washington is the children's librarian. He knows that stories about cats are Angela's favorite books. She checks out at least one "cat" book each week. Jerome often puts aside a new book about cats, saving it for Angela.

Recently, Cindy Kim was at Angela's apartment building to inspect the building. Cindy is a county health inspector who has been trained in detecting levels of lead in buildings. Her report could have an impact on Angela's health.

Last week, Angela visited the local public health clinic for her latest immunization, administered by Jessica Pederson. Jessica reviewed Angela's medical record and discussed fluoride treatments with Angela and her mother.

Kent Larson is Marie Russo's employer. He has been reviewing employee benefit packages that provide child care benefits by deducting monthly amounts targeted for such benefits. The new plan would allow employees to chose from different options for child care.

All of these people make many decisions that have a direct impact on Angela. These are local people who are part of the village raising Angela. Angela's well-being is constantly influenced by decisions made at state, regional, and federal levels.

Politics, social forces, and economics influence the types of programs available for young children, the number of social services available for young children and their families, and the quality of these programs. The priority for the care of children is reflected in the support designated for early childhood programs and for families. Although politics, economics, and societal issues are often intertwined, each area will be examined separately, with a look at their impact on early childhood programs. You will also look at what these influences mean to the professional in early childhood education and the growing expectations and responsibilities of these professionals. Angela's life is influenced by political, economic, and social decisions, and yours is, too. Thus, it is advantageous for you to be knowledgeable of these powerful forces.

Politics and Early Childhood Programs

The influence of politics on the educational system in the United States has a long history. When discussing **political influence,** we are referring to the role of government (national, state, and local levels) as it affects early childhood programs and the support and funding that comes from the government. Private kindergarten programs in the United States began as early as 1860, later followed by nursery school programs for younger children. During the 1930s and the period of the Great Depression, the government sponsored nearly 3,000 child care programs to provide work for unemployed women as child care workers. When World War II began, the labor of women was essential to war-related employment, so child care was again supported by the government. Once the war ended in 1945, women generally returned to work at home and government support for child care was terminated.

Politics and Early Childhood Education in the 1960s

During the 1960s, the rapidly increasing number of children raised in poverty became unacceptable. Social consciousness was high and, as a nation, there was concern about the effects of poverty on young children. It was determined that early education programs were a major factor leading to later success in school and throughout life. Remember the Bereiter-Englemann program discussed in Chapter 5? This was a program of the 1960s, with a goal of preparing economically disadvantaged young children to succeed in school.

The concern and regard for equality in the nation led to the passage of the Economic Opportunity Act during the Lyndon B. Johnson administration. One of the major purposes of this act was to declare a "war on poverty" by disrupting the pattern of **inter-**

generational poverty. This meant it was necessary to find a way to assist families at or below the poverty level to prevent the children from becoming adults who repeat the same cycle with limited opportunities. Programs and support would be provided by the federal government for children and families at or below the poverty level.

Head Start and Early Head Start Programs

Through the Office of Economic Opportunity, Project Head Start was implemented in 1965 and continues today. Head Start and Early Head Start are comprehensive child development programs that serve children from birth to age 5 and their families. The overall goal of the programs is to increase school readiness of young children of low-income families (U.S. Department of Health and Human Services, 2003). Through government funding, services are provided in the areas of education and early childhood development; medical, dental, and mental health; nutrition; and parent involvement.

Over 20 million children from low-income families have received Head Start services in the past four decades (U.S. Department of Health and Human Services, 2003). Unfortunately, only 60 percent of children eligible to participate in Head Start do so, due to lack of funding (Children's Defense Fund, 2002). On a more positive note, funding for Head Start has increased significantly in the past few years. Early Head Start was implemented in 1994 to serve low-income families of infants and toddlers and pregnant women. Congress responded to evidence from research and practice that called for early intervention through high-quality programs. In 2002, the funding increased to serve approximately 62,000 infants and toddlers. The increase in funding for Head Start and Early Head Start signifies support from our political system for young children.

Several children who live in Angela's apartment building attend Head Start. If Marie Russo earned less money, it's possible that Angela could attend a Head Start program in her Brooklyn neighborhood, as well. By advocating for more funding to support Head Start programs and increasing accessibility to the program, legislators and Head Start advocates have become members of the village raising the children in Angela's neighborhood.

Other Government Programs

Other government-supported programs and/or legislation that affects young children include the Personal Responsibility and Work Opportunity Reconciliation Act of 1996 (welfare reform), Child and Adult Food Care Program, Child Care and Development Block Grant Act, Minority Education Programs, Elementary and Secondary Education Act (Title I programs), Goals 2000, and other legislation. Each of these government programs fund different types of activities related to young children and their developing needs. Let's take a brief look at these programs before moving to recent political agendas in education—No Child Left Behind and the Early Childhood Initiative.

WELFARE REFORM AND EARLY CHILDHOOD. In 1996, Congress enacted sweeping changes in the welfare system. The intent of the Personal Responsibility and Work Opportunity Reconciliation Act of 1996 is to move people from welfare to work (Gnezda, 1996). The passage of the Personal Responsibility and Work Opportunity Reconciliation Act (PRWORA) created a situation where most single mothers are required to work. As of 1999, in 16 states, mothers of children ages 3 to 6 months were required to participate in work-related activities (Committee for Economic Development, Research and Policy Committee, 2002). The work requirement increases the need for child care, which is already difficult to obtain for infants and toddlers, both in terms of quality and affordability. All children should have access to child care that meets the needs of the child and family. This child care should also foster child development and learning as well as meet professional standards (NAEYC, 1997b). The NAEYC developed a position statement on state implementation of welfare reform, urging early childhood advocates to become involved with legislators, organizations, and other officials in developing high standards for child care programs. At the same time, attention needs to be given to expanding the number of qualified providers and ensuring adequate assistance for families so they can afford quality child care (NAEYC, 1997b).

Legal immigrants were also cut from many social services under the welfare reform. Several changes were made to the welfare legislation in 1997 and 1998. The U.S. Immigration and Naturalization Service clarified that noncitizens can make use of noncash benefits, such as food stamps and Medicaid, without fear that they would be labeled a public charge (Children's Defense Fund, 2000). Hopefully, this policy will help alleviate some parents' anxiety of contacting public agencies.

There is much concern that more children will be forced into poverty with these reforms, and that problems associated with lack of food, medical care, housing, and other basic needs will become more prevalent. At the same time, this is an opportunity for early childhood advocates to work at their local and state levels to ensure that access to quality child care is available for all young children and families.

CHILD CARE AND DEVELOPMENT BLOCK GRANT. During the 1996 welfare reform, the Child Care and Development Block Grant (CCDBG) was created to provide subsidies for child care for low-income working families. In 2001, federal funding for CCDBG was $4.5 billion, which provides grants for states for subsidizing child care costs. The General Accounting Offices estimates that 1.3 million children under the age of 5 participated in CCDBG in 1999 (Committee for Economic Development, Research and Policy Committee, 2002). Each state sets subsidy levels and fee schedules.

TEMPORARY ASSISTANCE FOR NEEDY FAMILIES. Although many families that leave the welfare system have a parent working, often the job is at minimum wage, keeping the family near or below the poverty level. The Temporary Assistance for Needy Families program (TANF) is also a block grant provided to each state. The state is responsible for establishing criteria for granting aid to needy families.

CHILD AND ADULT CARE FOOD PROGRAM. Funding for food at child care centers is available through the Child and Adult Care Food Program (CACFP) sponsored by the U.S. Department of Agriculture (USDA). This program provides money and food to child care centers and homes. The intent of this program in regard to children is to improve the nutrition for children age 12 and under. In 1999, over 2,600,000 children participated in CACFP (Children's Defense Fund, 2000). Emily Weiss, Angela's caregiver, is eligible to receive supplemental funding for purchasing nutritious food for the children she cares for in her home.

As part of the welfare reform in 1996, major changes were made to restructure the CACFP. Food reimbursement rates are now established according to family income levels within the area where the child care provider resides or the family income levels of the providers. Child care providers who do not meet these requirements may apply for reduced funding, although there is concern that the amount of funding may be too low for these providers to continue with the program. CACFP also provides training and support networks.

AID FOR CHILDREN IN MIGRANT FAMILIES. The Migrant Education Program is authorized under Title I of the Elementary and Secondary Act and was created to support quality and comprehensive education programs for migrant children to help reduce the educational disruption and other problems that result from repeated moves (Migrant Education Program, 2003). To ensure participation of children, many of these programs for young children begin in the early morning hours, since the field workers may begin their day by 4:00 or 5:00 A.M. Migrant programs address learning at the early childhood, elementary, and secondary school levels. They have also developed systems to track students from location to location to facilitate the continuity of their schooling. The Office of Migrant Education has determined that developing a Records Transfer Initiative is of priority.

For example, the Rodriguez family moves each year from California in the late spring to Washington, where they prune fruit trees and work in the orchards until late October. They then move back to California to work in the fields from November until late spring. The Rodriguez family returns to work at the same farms and fields, so their children are able to attend the same schools each year. Each school tracks the children's progress and sends this information to other schools when the family moves. This communication helps teachers in planning for children's learning and in building continuity into their schooling.

TITLE I PROGRAMS. In 1965, legislation was passed to provide Title I funds to improve education for economically disadvantaged children. This was the Elementary and Secondary Education Act (ESEA). The ESEA provides funding for **compensatory education,** which is education that compensates or seeks to help children from low-income homes improve their school performance. Title I services are educational resources that target children functioning below their expected grade level and assist them in improving their basic skills, primarily in reading, language, and mathematics. Funding may also be used for counseling, parental involvement, and program improvement.

Title I programs vary among school districts, although many districts are attempting to move from a **pull-out model** (when a Title I teacher or assistant pulls a child from the classroom to work in another setting) to a model where the Title I teacher or assistant provides services within the child's classroom. A Title I teacher might be responsible for diagnosing and developing programs for individual children or for developing schoolwide programs that improve academic achievement. This federal program reaches approximately 11 million children annually, helping them succeed within their regular school program.

OTHER GOVERNMENT-SPONSORED SUPPORT. Additional government support sources include employer-supported (or sponsored) child care, which allows employers tax breaks for providing child care for their employees. Remember hearing earlier in this chapter about Kent Larson, Marie Russo's employer? He is selecting a new employee benefit plan that will provide support for child care benefits.

Another source of government involvement is found in the child care services provided by governmental agencies for the children of their employees. Also, earned income tax credits (EITC) are available for low-income families. The tax credit reduces the amount of tax that some of these families owe the government, whereas other families might receive a refund after deducting their earned income tax credit.

With this introduction to federal programs that affect early childhood education, let's now explore policies that focus directly on education.

GOALS 2000. A political agenda that directly influenced education from birth through adulthood is Goals 2000. During an Educational Summit in 1989, President George H. Bush met with governors and proposed six goals to improve the U.S. educational system by the year 2000. The goals were adopted in 1990 and titled *America 2000.* In 1994, two goals were added, which became law under the passage of Goals 2000: Educate America Act. A major function of Goals 2000 was to identify national standards for student learning and for evaluation of schools (Earley, 1994). The National Education Goals stated that by the year 2000:

1. All children in America will start school ready to learn.
2. The high school graduation rate will increase to at least 90 percent.
3. All students will leave Grades 4, 8, and 12 having demonstrated competency over challenging subject matter.
4. The Nation's teaching force will have access to programs for the continued improvement of their professional skills and the opportunity to acquire the knowledge and skills needed to instruct and prepare all American students for the next century.
5. United States students will be first in the world in mathematics and science achievement.
6. Every adult American will be literate and will possess the knowledge and skills necessary to compete in a global economy and exercise the rights and responsibilities of citizenship.

7. Every school in the United States will be free of drugs, violence, and the unauthorized presence of firearms and alcohol and will offer a disciplined environment conducive to learning.
8. Every school will promote partnerships that increase parental involvement and participation in promoting the social, emotional, and academic growth of children. (National Education Goals Panel, 1995)

Progress has been made in academic performance in mathematics and science, although insufficient gains have been realized in reading performance and in narrowing the gap in performance between White and minority students (National Education Goals Panel, 1999).

NO CHILD LEFT BEHIND ACT. In 2001, the No Child Left Behind Act was implemented across the United States. This was the reauthorization of the Elementary and Secondary Education Act and mandated that each state establish standards for what each child must know and be able to do in core academic areas. The standards are set at each grade level and students are tested on an annual basis. The current political climate is requiring schools to be accountable for what they teach and what their students learn.

The No Child Left Behind Act creates a challenge for early childhood educators committed to maintaining and promoting developmentally appropriate programs and curriculum for young children. Although the mandated act is for students in kindergarten through grade 12, there is concern that this and other legislation concerned about alignment with standards in the elementary schools will push the standards movement to the earlier years. Early childhood professionals who understand the importance of relevant learning experiences will need to work with parents and policymakers to ensure an infrastructure that supports developmentally appropriate programs (Raines & Johnston, 2003).

GOOD START, GROW SMART. The Bush Administration's early childhood initiative was established in 2002 to help states and local communities strengthen early learning for young children (Good Start, Grow Smart, 2002). The three major areas addressed include:

1. Strengthening Head Start with a new accountability system to ensure that each program assesses standards of learning in early literacy, numeracy, and language
2. Partnering with states to improve early childhood education through development of quality criteria in early literacy and alignment with K–12 standards
3. Providing information from research and current practices in early childhood education through a range of partnerships and research funding from the federal government

As you read through these goals for the early years (birth through age 5), notice a connection between these three major goals and the goals in the No Child Left Behind Act and the challenges raised in defining early childhood programs. Involvement of entire communities in supporting education from the prenatal period to adulthood is required to make significant progress in improving education for our nation's children.

As Americans become more concerned about the quality of the educational system, politicians have joined the debates about education and provided policies and guidelines for improving education. In order for these goals to be met, local and state agencies must be prepared to analyze their current educational programs and make changes necessary for alignment with national goals. In this example of the relationship between politics and education, take notice of the large influence legislation has on shaping the primary goals for the education of this country's children. When you vote for a certain legislator, you are also voting for her or his opinions about plans for early childhood programs. You can see why it is important to be an informed voter and make wise decisions, which come back to you in the form of political and economic support for programs.

JOURNAL 13.1: Find out who among your state representatives and legislators are working for improvements in education, child care, and other children's issues. Record your findings and share your thoughts on current proposed bills with your colleagues in class. ●

GOVERNMENT REGULATION AND EARLY CHILDHOOD PROGRAM STANDARDS. Specific program standards are developed and monitored by government agencies. There is an expectation that early childhood programs meet standards, whether these are child care centers, home care providers, preschool settings, or the early grades of elementary school. Standards might be in areas of health (e.g., requirement of a food handler's permit for cooking), safety (e.g., no open wiring), or program quality assurances (e.g., the number of children per adult). When thinking about working as a child care provider, you might assume that politics have little to do with your role as a professional in early childhood education. In reality, however, you might be surprised at the amount of involvement your local, state, and national government has in the area of early childhood programs. With the allocation of funding to the state level, states have increased responsibility in developing standards and criteria and in monitoring early childhood programs, with the intent of ensuring the safety and well-being of young children. For example, in most cases, state and local licenses are required to run a home care program, with approval granted after on-site visits document that criteria have been met or exceeded.

Angela's child care provider, Emily, has been visited by an early childhood specialist from the State Office for Services to Children and Families and has received approval for her setting. The early childhood specialist reviewed Emily's daily plans for the children's activities, examined the areas where the children played and rested during the day, and watched Emily interact with the children in her care. She discussed her observations with Emily, with a written report shared with Emily and filed at the state office. Emily also received approval for her nutrition program and exceeded the federal guidelines in providing healthy meals and snacks. You can see how a state agency monitors important guidelines for child care providers. This helps ensure that Angela receives quality child care while her mother is at work.

CHANGES IN GOVERNMENT POLICY. Many organizations contribute to the field of early childhood education at the national, state, and local levels. The *Early Learning Initiative* is an agenda of the Education Commission of the States (ECS), a nonprofit, nationwide organization that assists governors, legislators, state education officials, and others in identifying, developing, and implementing public policies to improve student learning at all levels (Education Commission of the States, 2000). This group is attempting to bring together knowledge and research from various agencies and organizations and synthesizing the information to help policymakers translate research and practice into good policy (Education Commission of the States, 2000). One example is highlighting the recent findings in brain development research and examining how these implications might affect early childhood programs and funding.

The locus of policy making, implementing, and funding of programs for young children is moving more toward state and local levels. An example of a local program that has yielded positive influences on young children and their families can be found in San Francisco. In 2000, Mayor Willie Brown assumed a lead role in implementing high-quality child care in this city. Accessibility to child care was increased through city-funded child care subsidies for working families. Incentives to reward child care workers for continuing their education and city-funded health benefits for family child care providers were made available. In addition, $4.1 million was directed to improve the wages of 1,000 community-based child care workers (Coleman Advocates for Children & Youth, 2000).

As decision-making processes move to the local level, families and child care providers will have a stronger voice in important decisions about their programs. Early childhood professionals will be working closer with other professionals in their "village." Although it takes more time and effort to work in collaboration with multiple agencies and professionals, the end result can be programs that better meet the needs of the local community and its children. Collaborations combine resources to strengthen the common or related programs and their effects on children and families.

Summary: Politics and Early Childhood Programs

Looking over the different governmental programs and agendas that support young children helps you recognize the role of federal funding and the government's influence on early childhood programs. Becoming an informed advocate for young children requires analyzing governmental policy and funding, and supporting legislators who promote funding in the best interests of young children.

As you think about the social and economic factors affecting early childhood programs, it's easy to see how political influences reflect the social and economic climate of a specific time. More mothers with young children are in the work force and in need of quality child care. The necessity for quality child care—prompted by political, social, and economic matters—creates an increase in the regulation and licensing involved in child care centers, whether at homes or other facilities. Welfare reform has created a high demand for more child care.

Angela is fortunate to be cared for by Emily while Marie is at work. Emily has met the requirements of the state agency for her child care program. This helps assure Marie that Emily is not only a warm, caring adult but that she also has specialized knowledge about young children and has created a safe learning environment for children. Angela's care and future education is influenced by today's political and economic climate. We'll now examine the larger picture of economics and its impact on early childhood education.

Economics and Early Childhood Education

Many of the programs for young children you read about earlier in this chapter were supported by the government and closely linked to economic factors of a specific time period. **Economics** can be thought of as the development and management affecting the overall financial climate in a country.

Economics and Availability of Early Childhood Programs

Remember reading about the need for child care while women worked in war-related employment during World War II? The economic needs of the United States became the reason for quick development of child care centers while mothers were working at shipyards and factories during the war.

Following World War II, preschool and kindergarten programs were primarily attended by middle-class children throughout the 1950s to 1970s. (The major exception was Project Head Start.) The predominant belief during this era was that young children should be home with their mothers during the day, and that those who could afford half-day nursery schools or kindergartens might choose to send their child to those programs. Thus, the economics of the day influenced what was available and who could access early childhood programs.

Economy, Early Childhood Programs, and Future Work Force

The economy of the United States is linked to the quality of child care in terms of the potential productivity of these future workers. The early experiences of a child have lasting impacts throughout life. Children growing up in poverty tend to be less productive and effective workers (Edelman, 2002). Availability of financially supported child care can make the difference between a family receiving welfare checks or being part of the work force. Marie wants to keep her job at the law office, and employee benefits for child care help Marie afford the child care she wants for Angela.

For the child living in poverty, participation in programs such as Head Start help with enrichment, social growth, and developmental learning before the child enrolls in school. It costs far less to invest in quality child care programs for young children than to pay for other programs for older youths and adults who were not successful in school or life. (See the Perry Preschool Project and the Abecedarian Project discussions later in this chapter.)

Early childhood experiences set the stage for later life, with quality early childhood programs providing the foundation for developing language skills, social competence, self-confidence, and ways of thinking about the world. This learning is necessary for success in school (Schoor, 1998), which later transfers into skills and knowledge required in successful employment. The nation's future economy is dependent on skilled, productive workers. Financial support of early childhood programs is a beginning in the development of the country's work force. When Marie picks up Angela at Emily's home, she is usually greeted by a content child ready to show Marie what she "learned" that day at Emily's house. Emily's knowledge of early childhood development and her ability to translate this into appropriate and fun activities for the children in her care is evident. Emily is certainly contributing to the healthy growth and development of Angela and other young children, and ultimately to the country's future economy.

Changes in the Work Force

The number of mothers of young children working outside the home has steadily increased. According to the U.S. Department of Labor (2001), in 2000, 73 percent of women with children were in the labor force. Marie is included in these statistics. Reasons for working vary from economic circumstances to a mother's desire to seek challenges outside of the home, or a combination of several reasons. Many households find that the income of the mother is required, either as the sole support in a single-parent home or to support the family. Whatever the reason, it is clear that the need for a variety of options of quality child care for young children is increasing. Child care programs such as the one Emily has developed must be available.

Employer- or company-based child care programs are increasing, as is the policy for paid leave for parents of newborn children. In the 1990s, the **Family Leave Act** was implemented to provide the option of unpaid leave from work to attend to family needs, which might include spending time with a newborn or with an aging parent, or taking care of a family emergency. This is a welcome support for families, especially considering the frequent conflict that occurs between balancing work and families. Studies are underway to investigate the benefits of allowing working parents to spend time with their newborns and to develop flexible work schedules that support more time with their families. A flexible work schedule or reduced work week would allow parents to spend time with their children and not be penalized in their workplace.

Not all costs can be determined by dollars alone. Supporting families and the time they spend with their children may become part of what attracts employees to a company and ensures their loyalty and long-term employment. More importantly, these options influence the long-term economic health of society. During Angela's first year, Marie worked at the law office four days each week, giving her more time with Angela. Marie also is able to bring work home during the week and leave the office early when either she or Angela have doctor appointments or other needs during the workday. The flexibility of her work schedule is important to Marie as she raises Angela.

Economics and Salaries of Early Child Care Providers

Equally important to consider when thinking about the economic impact on early childhood programs is the salary you, as an early childhood professional, will receive. Currently, the average annual salary of center-based child care teachers is approximately $14,500 (Center for the Child Care Workforce, 2003). This salary is close to the poverty level for a family of four, and less than half of the average salary of a beginning teacher. No wonder many early childhood professionals feel undervalued for their important contributions. Early childhood care providers have been subsidizing programs by contributing their time and expertise for salaries that are far below the value of their services.

The impact that low wages has on the morale and long-term commitment of those who care for young children must be considered. High turnover in teaching staff continues, with approximately one-third of the early childhood staff leaving their positions during a one-year period (Center for the Child Care Workforce, 2003). The high turnover rate of early childhood staff affects the continuity and quality of care the children receive, creating difficulties for young children and families as they adjust to a new child care provider and changes in their program.

Unfortunately, it is becoming harder to recruit talented people into the field of early childhood education just at the time when there is a rapid and steadily increasing demand for more early childhood professionals. Attention must be given to increasing the salaries and benefits for qualified staff, as well as giving more recognition to the important role they play in the healthy development of young children.

JOURNAL 13.2: **Why are you attracted to working in early childhood education? What kind of support and resources will sustain your interest in this profession?** ●

Economic Benefits of Early Childhood Education

Let's discuss informative studies that examined early childhood education in terms of economic value. The Perry Preschool Study (see Box 13.1) followed 123 children born between 1958 and 1962 into their early adulthood (Schweinhart et al., 1985).

HIGH SCOPE STUDY. A later study, the High Scope study, was conducted by many of the researchers involved in the earlier Perry Preschool Project. Their findings in 1993 supported the earlier findings of the Perry Preschool Project. Schweinhart and colleagues (1993) found that participation in a high-quality preschool created a framework for later success as an adult, "significantly alleviating the negative effects of childhood poverty on educational performance, social responsibility, adult economic status, and family formation" (p. 230). This same study also examined the cost of the preschool program and analyzed the actual costs with the benefits gained from preschool attendance. The researchers determined that taxpayers received a $7.16 return on each dollar invested in the preschool program.

ABECEDARIAN PROJECT. In 1999, initial findings from the Abecedarian Project, a longitudinal study that began when children were infants and followed them to age 21, examined the effects of early childhood intervention. The study found that low-income children who received quality early education and intervention scored higher on reading,

BOX 13.1 A Closer Look

Findings from the Perry Preschool Study

The Perry Preschool Study examined the economic effects of a quality preschool and looked at the **longitudinal** (long-term) effects. A primary author of this study, Lawrence Schweinhart, states, "More than other educational innovations, high-quality programs for young children living in poverty have demonstrated the promise of lasting benefits and return on investment" (1994, p. 1).

Children selected for this study lived in the attendance area of the Perry Elementary School in Ypsilanti, Michigan. The families in this neighborhood were primarily of low income and of African American descent. Researchers identified preschool-aged children in this attendance area and determined socioeconomic levels on the basis of the level of employment, parents' education level, and the ratio of rooms in the home to number of persons living in the home. Children were then given the Stanford-Binet Intelligence Test. Children with scores between 60 and 90 (100 represents an average intelligence score) became part of this study.

The researchers used a random method to assign children to the preschool group or to the group that would not attend preschool. This random assignment process helps make this study credible, as teachers, parents, or researchers did not influence which children would become preschool or nonpreschool participants. In fact, a toss of a coin was used to determine the assignment to the preschool or nonpreschool group, resulting in 58 children being assigned to the preschool group and 65 children assigned to the nonpreschool group. The backgrounds of the children in each group were significantly similar, leading to accurate comparisons between effects that can be attributed to participation in the preschool program.

The curriculum of the preschool program focused on intellectual and social development with preschool in session five days a week for 2½ hours each morning. In addition, teachers made home visits with the mother and child each week. Both groups of children were tested and interviewed at regular intervals, with researchers unaware of whether the child they were interviewing was part of the preschool or nonpreschool group.

The primary sources of data for the Perry Preschool Study were interviews when the child reached age 19, information from the elementary and secondary schools the child attended, police and court records, and social service records. The findings were reported in three major areas: schooling success, social responsibility, and socioeconomic success.

Within the category of *school success,* it was found that children who attended preschool continued in school longer, tested higher on functional competence, were less likely to be classified as mentally retarded, and were less likely to spend some of their school years in special education classes. When *social responsibility* was analyzed, it was found that the group of children who attended preschool were less likely to become pregnant as teenagers and less likely to be arrested than those who did not attend preschool. Finally, in *socioeconomic success,* almost twice as many from the group who attended preschool were employed. Nearly half as many of the preschool group received welfare benefits as compared to those who had not attended preschool. These findings support the long-term, critical impact that preschool or early childhood education can have on a person's life. Children in the Perry Preschool Study who attended preschool showed far more indicators of economic, social, and educational success than the group of children with similar backgrounds but without a preschool experience.

The other area the Perry Preschool Study examined was the economic costs of the program in relation to the long-term costs to society in supporting persons on welfare or in the criminal system. The cost analysis found that the money spent on preschool produced a return of 3½ times the initial investment (Schweinhart et al., 1985). This means that the initial investment (paying for the preschool program) led to a reduction of later costs to society—a strong justification for early childhood education as an economic benefit to society.

The authors of the Perry Preschool Project drew two major conclusions from their research. The first conclusion is specifically linked to the study results where the data proved that good preschool programs can help children move beyond the barriers created by poverty. The second conclusion comes from following these two groups of children for 20 years and noting the numerous long-term effects that preschool exerts on the overall quality of one's life. The economic benefits of prevention (through participation in preschool) versus intervention (paying for welfare benefits, criminal costs, or lower-skilled work force) show the long-term impact of quality early childhood education.

cognitive, and math tests in comparison to a group of children who did not receive intervention. Additionally, those who participated in high-quality child care as young children were more likely to attend college or hold skilled jobs in later life (Campbell & Ramey, 1999). The Abecedarian study provides evidence that early childhood education significantly improves the educational attainments of poor children through early adulthood (Campbell et al., 2001). You might be asked to explain to others the rationale for and benefits of good early childhood programs available for all children. Your response might include that benefits are found both in economic factors and in overall quality-of-life issues.

JOURNAL 13.3: You are talking with several acquaintances when one person mentions that preschool seems like a fun—but nonessential—experience. What might you say, drawing on your knowledge of the Perry Preschool Project and the Abecedarian Project? ●

Summary: Economics and Early Childhood Education

Economics greatly affects early childhood programs. With increasing numbers of mothers in the work force, the need for quality child care programs is essential not only to children but also to parents and society (Campbell & Ramey, 1999). A strong economy requires skilled and educated workers. The ability to learn and demonstrate the skills of a productive worker begin to be formed at an early age, hopefully with the guidance and support of a caring family and child care specialists.

We have looked at the support from Marie's employer for child care benefits and a flexible work schedule, the support from Emily in her planning activities that encourage creativity and exploration, and the support from programs that help young children become successful learners. These critical mainstays lead to a stronger economy for all of us.

Society and Early Childhood

Each society holds a different stance regarding the importance and value of supporting and educating its young children. In the United States, educational reform has become a priority. People are worried about the quality of education U.S. children are receiving. The concern with improving education in America reflects a current interest of society. The term **society** refers to a group of people who have common interests with shared institutions and a common culture that generalizes to the larger population.

Society and Educational Reform

In 1983, *A Nation at Risk,* a report about the state of U.S. schools, was published. This report immediately raised concerns about schooling and how schools were preparing the country's future leaders. Subsequent reports repeated the theme that children were not receiving the education they needed to be ready for the twenty-first century.

Thinking back to the political and economic issues discussed in the earlier sections of this chapter helps you see the close relationship between political, economic, and social factors that affect early childhood education. A major social unit that impacts and is impacted by political and economic factors is the family unit. Many of the programs you've been reading about in this chapter focus on both the young child and the family. Obviously, families exert a large influence on early childhood programs and practices.

Society and Families

Families make up a small, nuclear unit within society. The family of today varies greatly from the family of only one generation ago. Currently, children live in families that might look like one or more of the following:

- Blended families (parents remarrying and creating new family units)
- Single-parent households
- One parent working and one parent at home with the child or children
- Grandparents raising their grandchildren
- Teen parents
- Dual-career families (both parents working outside the home)
- Extended families (several families or generations living in a home)

Today, a minority of children live in a family structure with a father at work and a mother at home with the children. The changing family structure finds that only 40 percent of children born in recent years will live with both mother and father until they are age 18 (U.S. Bureau of the Census, 1998). Children come from families of diverse configurations. Changes in the family unit can create challenges for young children and their families.

Marie (Angela's mother) visited with a parent educator from the Family Services office in Brooklyn. After her divorce, she wanted some assistance in helping Angela adjust to their new family arrangement. Marie talked to the family services counselor several times and gain some insights into ways to help Angela as well as herself. Family Services provided another dimension to the composition of Angela's "village."

JOURNAL 13.4: You are reading a story to the 2- and 3-year-old children in your care. The story continually portrays a family with a mother and father living together in the same household. Several of your children live with one parent and two of the children live with their grandparents. What might you do to help them feel included in this story?

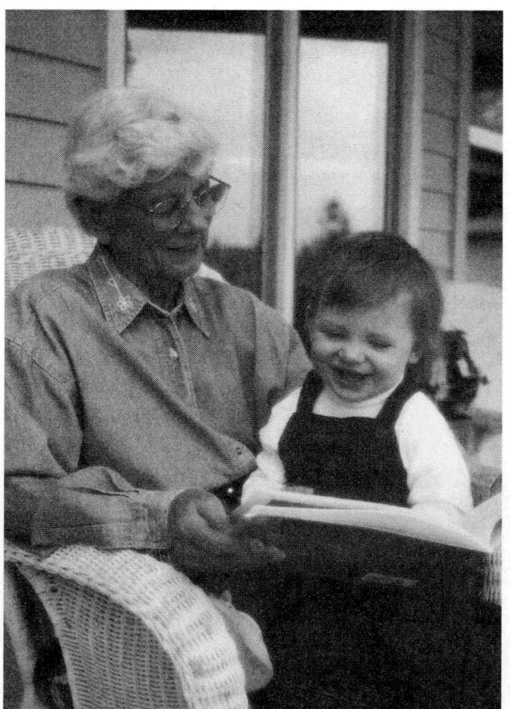

A young child enjoys reading with her grandmother.

As you look over the list of family structures, you will notice that in many of these situations the child will need child care services in order for the parent (or parents) to work. Again, do you see the close links between political, economic, and social impacts on child care? With the changing economic structure, many families face increased stress and pressures. When early childhood care programs become more family focused and view strengthening the family as an integral part of their curricula, staff work to support and educate families.

As the work force includes more working mothers, the need for more child care options increases. One solution that is popular with parents is employer-supported child care, as discussed in Chapter 7. Another option that helps parents of young children is a flexible work schedule that permits one or both parents to work at home part of the week. Other flexible schedules might allow for part-time work, working longer hours for three or four days instead of five days a week, working several days a week at home with a computer connection to the office, or working every other week. These trends of support for child care and for flexible work schedules by the workplace reflect society's valuing of children. Hopefully, the trends are indicative of future possibilities for supporting children and families.

Marie found support from her neighbors, Mr. and Mrs. Ponzi, who help when Marie has to work later than usual. Mr. Ponzi walks over to Emily's house and picks up Angela and brings her home for dinner. Marie's employer, Kent Larson, is aware of Marie's need to leave work on time to pick up Angela. He asks Marie to work late only on rare occasions when they must finish a project. Marie appreciates his sensitivity to her situation and to her commitment to Angela. Here, again, you can see the Ponzis and Kent Larson as "villagers" helping to raise Angela. Marie's situation is not uncommon—parents all over this country find themselves balancing the demands of work and family.

Society and Children in Need

In 2000, nearly 20 percent of children under age 6 lived in poverty (Children's Defense Fund, 2002). This situation creates a population of children who may have nutritional, learning, language, or emotional deficiencies. Imagine how difficult it would be for a 3-year-old child who is hungry and living in a stressful environment to learn to sing songs or to skip, hop, or jump. The family may be most concerned with having enough food for that day or securing employment, leaving little time and energy to create stimulating experiences for the 3-year-old. Unfortunately, there is a connection between poverty and school failure. Children who begin their school years behind other students have difficulty making up for lost time and often find school to be a discouraging and negative experience. This is how the cycle of poverty continues from generation to generation.

It is important for early childhood professionals to recognize the diversity of family structures and to find ways to support children and families in need. Divorce, long-term illness in the family, death, parent's loss of a job, remarriage, or a new baby can be stressful for children as well as adults. Children need support and comfort in their child care situation as they adjust to changes in home living situations. When the child care provider or teacher knows that a family is going through a difficult time, she can help parents seek support services and work with the child as he reacts to changes in his family situation. At this time, he needs a sensitive adult to help him during a stressful period.

A teacher or caregiver can provide much needed support and assistance during a time of need, such as helping the family understand that talking about the situation with the child (in terms the child comprehends) provides factual information for him. When a crisis occurs, children sense something is wrong, and when excluded from conversations, they may think the situation is worse than it is or feel left out of family concerns. Let's look at a scene from a preschool as an example.

Jermaine's grandmother is ill with cancer and was recently told by her doctor that she has approximately one to two months to live. Of course, his family is upset and talks frequently on the phone to other family members about grandmother's condition. Jermaine, who is 3 years old, hears some of these conversations and knows that his parents are visiting his grandmother often in the hospital. By sharing that his grandmother is very sick and will die soon, Jermaine has an opportunity to make some drawings for his grandmother, talk with her on the phone, make a special visit, and ask questions about dying. Jermaine's parents let him take the lead in asking questions as they talk with him at his level of understanding.

At the same time, Jermaine's parents have shared this information with his preschool teacher, Scott. Scott set up a hospital center in the classroom, with a stethoscope, surgical gowns and masks, a chair, and bed. He wants to provide an opportunity for Jermaine and other children to act out their feelings and to experience the hospital setting and procedures. He plans to stay close to this area when Jermaine begins playing, to assist in the play acting and to answer any questions that Jermaine might ask. This type of play setting is also helpful for children who might be entering the hospital or who have family members that are hospitalized.

Scott will also read some children's books about death and dying to the preschoolers. He knows that young children may assume guilt when a crisis occurs, whether it is death, divorce, family illness, or other crises. By reading books to the class, he can open up a discussion about how bad things happen sometimes, and that these bad things are not the child's fault.

In the classroom, Scott will expect Jermaine to follow his regular routine, but he knows there may need to be allowances so Jermaine can express his feelings in a safe and familiar environment. Scott has suggested to Jermaine's parents that they describe the hospital room and the grandmother's appearance before Jermaine's visit. This will help him when he enters the hospital for his special visit with his grandmother.

Most of these suggestions also apply to other situations, whether they are happy changes or unhappy events. Sharing about the upcoming birth of a sibling and preparing for the baby keeps the child part of an important family event. Coping with their parents' divorce is very difficult for young children. Strategies that Scott used in Jermaine's situation are transferable to a divorce situation also. Play opportunities, absolving the child from guilt about the divorce, talking about separation, and hearing stories about other families and divorce all assist the child in navigating through a crisis.

As a teacher or caregiver, there will be many times when one or more children in your setting face a major crisis or change. Most often, your role is one of support to the family as you provide opportunities for the child to face the difficult situation or change in a stable, caring environment.

Other children in need include those who need special education as part of their education program. It is estimated that over 11 percent of the children in the United States between the ages of 6 and 11 receive special education services (U.S. Department of Education, 2002). The first choice for services for these children is to be included in natural settings and receive additional assistance as needed. As you know from reading Chapter 12, federal funding is available for programs for children with special needs that support their growth and development.

For instance, Shantell, a 2-year-old child at a nearby child care center, has difficulty with large muscle motor development and requires the services of a physical therapist as part of her overall educational program. She recently learned to walk but is unstable and learning how to coordinate her steps. The physical therapist works with the staff at the center to develop a therapy program that fits the routine at Shantell's child care site. The therapist also assists the staff in developing activities to help Shantell practice her walking. This arrangement includes Shantell in activities at her site, with assurance that she will receive the special services appropriate to her needs.

As an early childhood professional, your attention will be drawn to children in need. The need might be related to a family's economic situation, other family situations, or a child's specific learning needs. Whether the need is temporary or ongoing, it must be addressed to help both the child and family. Let's now turn to other situations that will require your immediate attention and response.

Society and Child Abuse

A critical concern of early childhood professionals is also a major societal problem—the occurrence of child abuse. The following descriptions of child abuse and neglect were derived from the National Clearinghouse on Child Abuse and Neglect Information (U.S. Department of Health & Human Services, 2002). **Child abuse** is a form of mistreatment of a child, and it might occur in the form of physical, emotional, or sexual abuse. Any physical injury to a child, other than an accident, is considered **physical abuse.** Possible physical indicators include bruises and welts, burns, lacerations, or fractures. **Emotional abuse** is harm to a child's ability to think or have feelings. Emotional or mental abuse may take the form of extreme negative language or inhumane treatment of the child, such as ridicule, threats, confinement, or torture. **Sexual abuse** includes incidents of sexual contact. **Child neglect** is when a child's basic needs are not met through negligence or maltreatment of the child. A neglected child may lack food, appropriate clothing, hygiene, medical care, or supervision by a responsible adult.

Children who suffer child abuse may take years to recover from the abuse, often carrying the pain and emotional bruises through their entire lives. Unfortunately, the incidence of child abuse and neglect continues to increase, with 3 million children reported abused or neglected in the United States in 2001 (U.S. Department of Health and Human Services, 2003b). Of the 3 million reported cases of child abuse, nearly 1 million were substantiated. Among the children who were victims of *substantiated maltreatment* in 2001, 57 percent were neglected, 19 percent physically abused, 10 percent sexually abused, 7 percent emotionally abused, and 2 percent medically neglected.

One of these children who was reported as a victim was 6-year-old Taylor. He entered kindergarten reluctantly, seeming fearful of joining in any boisterous activity, such as playground games or group activities in the gym. His teacher thought perhaps he was quiet by nature and observed him, while also encouraging him to participate in activities where he seemed to be most comfortable. In October, Taylor was absent for several days. When he returned to school, his clothes were dirty and he was unwashed. He stayed near the door most of the morning. When his teacher talked with him about missing him while he was gone, Taylor told her he had been naughty and had to stay home. More conversations revealed that Taylor was punished frequently and made to sit in a chair for long periods of time. If he was "loud" at home, he was told that he was bad and left to sit in a chair for hours at a time.

Taylor's teacher began writing down the information and discussed these conversations with her school principal. Within a few weeks, she felt she had enough indicators of neglect to report her findings. Later, the teacher and principal learned that Taylor's mother was battling alcohol and drug problems and spent much of her afternoon sleeping. Taylor's teacher was knowledgeable about child abuse or neglect indicators, was alert to possible signs, involved the appropriate authorities, and collected information to document her observations. She was advocating for a child's right to a healthy environment and took the responsible steps to help both Taylor and his family.

What can you do about child abuse and neglect? Child care centers and early childhood programs that meet national accreditation standards with licensed or certified staff are seen as part of the solution to ensuring that children are cared for by professionals who provide safe environments. As a child care professional, you will often be the first person to see signs of abuse and neglect. In each state, if you suspect that a child is being abused or neglected, you are legally required to report this information to the appropriate authorities. Indicators of child abuse are listed in Figure 13.1.

As a caregiver or teacher of young children, you carry the responsibility to report signs or symptoms of child abuse and to help the child and family during this crisis. As an early childhood professional, you will be in a position to detect signs of child abuse or neglect and advocate for any child you suspect has been abused. The effects of child abuse and neglect affect a child's learning and development. For professional, ethical, and moral reasons, teachers and caregivers are in a position to commit to the well-being of children and families. Awareness of signs and indicators of child abuse is an important step in recognizing a child in need and in assisting the child and family in gaining help.

Support for the child is essential. The following steps outline suggestions to follow if you suspect child abuse:

1. Believe the child; children rarely lie about sexual abuse.
2. Commend the child for telling you what happened.
3. Convey your support for the child. Children's greatest fear is that they are at fault and responsible for the incident.
4. Temper your own reactions, recognizing that your perspective and acceptance are critical signals to the child.
5. Report the suspected abuse to the child's parent(s), the designated social service agency and/or the police.
6. Find specialized agencies that evaluate sexual abuse victims and a physician with the experience and training to detect and recognize sexual abuse. (U.S. Department of Health and Human Services, 1986)

Although these guidelines are developed for suspected sexual abuse, they are helpful to early childhood professionals when suspecting physical or emotional abuse of the young child. When in frequent contact with young children, you are often the first person outside the family to note abuse. You have a responsibility to help the child and family end the abuse and engage in the necessary social services to handle this problem.

FIGURE 13.1

Observational Chart of Child Behavior and Indicators of Abuse

Parent's Name ____________________

Child's Name ____________________

Date ________ Observer's Signature ____________________

Child:

____ receives a lot of spankings at home

____ complains that his/her parent is always angry

____ comes to school early and finds reasons to stay after school as long as possible

____ role-plays abusive parents in class or dramatizes abusive situations with puppets and toys or in artwork

____ abuses younger children

____ is frequently absent from school, many times with no explanations

____ wears clothing inappropriate to the weather (usually long sleeves and pants to hide bruises)

____ shows physical evidence of abuse (describe below)

____ shows aggressive behavior

____ is self-abusive or expresses suicidal ideas

Comments ____________________

____

____

____

____

____

____

____

____

Source: From *The Compassionate School* by Gertrude Morrow. Copyright © 1987. Reprinted with permission of Prentice Hall Direct an imprint of Pearson Education Co.

Society and Health Issues Affecting Young Children

The United States has one of the most advanced health care systems in the world; yet, many people are unable to afford health care or insurance. Twelve percent of the children in the United States were without health insurance in 2000 (Children's Defense Fund, 2002). Health care reforms have been proposed by Congress, with some states adopting health care plans that provide coverage to people with low incomes. Hopefully, the trend toward increasing accessibility to health care will enable more people to afford basic care.

In 1993 and 1994, the Childhood Immunization Initiative and the Vaccines for Children Program were launched. These programs have made great strides in increasing the number of children receiving vaccines by providing vaccines at numerous sites within communities. In 2000, nearly three out of four 2-year-olds were fully immunized (Children's Defense Fund, 2002). Angela received several of her immunizations through the Childhood Immunization Initiative at her local public health office. The success of these programs illustrates how public policy and cooperation among federal, state, and local agencies can result in enormous gains.

The State Child Health Insurance Program (CHIP) was enacted in 1997 to provide health insurance and medical care for low-income children. The CHIP statue provided $48 billion over a 10-year period to increase health coverage, expand Medicaid, establish a new state health program, or all of these. Each state has its own eligibility and program guidelines. By 2000, over 3.3 million children were enrolled in CHIP. Again, we see evidence of economic, political, and social forces joined together to implement policy that has a great impact on young children.

Society and Homeless Children

When you think of homelessness, you might picture an adult male living on the street, spending days on a park bench next to a shopping cart piled next to his possessions. Today, families with children are a growing group of homeless people. It is believed that over 100,000 children each night are homeless (Children's Defense Fund, 1997). This problem is made even more acute when many families are turned away from shelters because such shelters are not structured for families.

Children who are homeless tend to experience more severe health, developmental, and nutritional problems than other poor children. Without decent housing, it is difficult for poor families to access essential social services and obtain medical, educational, or nutritional support for the family.

If families continually move, school attendance or participation of children in child care centers is spotty or nonexistent. It is estimated that up to 50 percent of children who are homeless and of school age do not attend school. Reasons include lack of immunization records, the feeling that they will move again soon, reluctance of the child to adjust to another group of children and teachers, or lack of transportation to school. In some cities, schools for homeless children have become part of the shelter and social service network. These schools provide clothing, school supplies, and nutritious meals, but, most of all, they welcome children and develop school programs that fit individual learning needs.

In 2001, Congress reauthorized the Education for Homeless Children Program, which directed local school districts to allow homeless children to attend the school that their parent requests. Hopefully, the attention to the needs of homeless families will increase options to social, medical, and educational programs. Let's now turn our attention to another population that also needs societal support and resources.

Society and Teen Parents

Much progress has been made in the overall teen birth rate in the past decade. The reduction in teen birth rate has been attributed to federal, state, and community activities that support teen pregnancy prevention efforts. Bearing a child during adolescence is associated with long-term difficulties for the mother and child (Federal Interagency Forum on Child and Family Statistics, 2001). Adverse socioeconomic circumstances frequently accompany early childbearing and are linked to limited educational attainment of the mother, which, in turn, impacts the future employment and economic situation for the young family.

Becoming a parent with the support of a spouse is stressful for most young families. There are daily (hourly) challenges dealing with the demands and needs of an infant. Teenage parents often know less about child development and feel less positive about their role as a parents. Adolescent parents and their children can flourish when they are supported as they continue their education. In earlier chapters, you read about the impor-

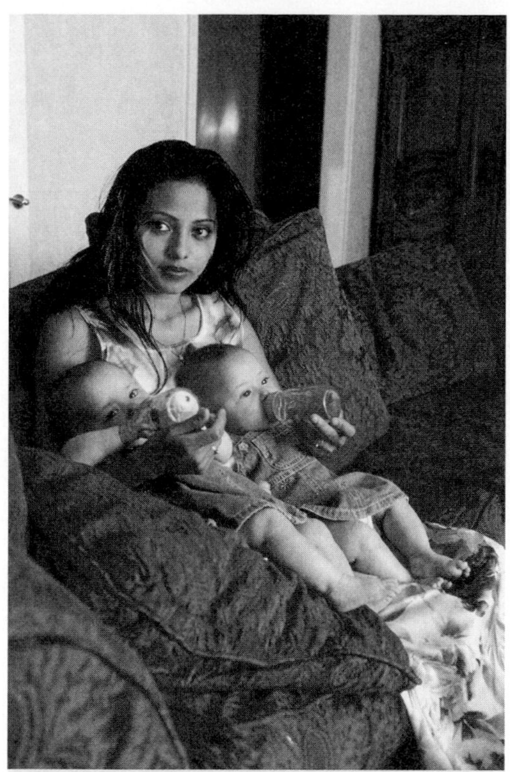
Young parents as well as infants need nurturing to support their growth.

tance of including the family in early childhood programs. With teen parents, this is critical. Teen parents need the opportunity to finish their education, with child care available (preferably on site, so they can visit the child during the day) and involvement in parent education classes and peer support groups facilitated by specialists. The financial and emotional support received by teen parents and their infants at this time may make the difference between the teens being able to finish school, experiencing success, and finding gainful employment to support themselves and their children.

In a situation with teen parents, the child care provider frequently finds herself nurturing both the infant and the teen parent. Teen families need support in their new role as a family. This support might include sharing information about child development, infant needs, and parenting skills. Teen families frequently need assistance in learning how to interact with their children. When a caregiver models comforting and nurturing behavior with teens' infants, she is providing one way for teen families to see how others interact with their children in a positive manner.

In many cities, programs combine all of these needs within a teen parent program—that is, continued education for the teen, parenting education for the teen mother and father, support for adolescent growth, and a quality infant program. In these programs for teen parents and their children, political, economic, and social factors work together to combine resources in one setting, helping teen families access supportive services.

Society and Community Involvementwith Young Children

The relationship between the child care setting or school and the community provides great potential with long-lasting impact for both the community and the children. Partnerships among senior citizens, businesses, local agencies, schools, child care centers, and community organizations create a collaboration built on providing the best possible programs for the young children in the community. For instance, the Lion's Club might hold fundraisers to assist children needing vision care, and a public school might share a visiting nurse with a preschool.

Sharing resources and opening up communication between agencies and organizations can lead to benefits for the entire community. Senior citizens might be interested in volunteering their time to read to young children or to help them make projects. When actively involved with young children, the senior citizen feels wanted and useful, while the children benefit from learning new skills and having an interested adult spend time with them.

Emily has invited the children's grandparents to visit during the late morning to read to the children or to simply watch them play. She wants grandparents to feel welcome and to be part of the growing-up period of their grandchildren. Angela's grandmother stops in each Thursday, often bringing a book to read to the children. Angela looks forward to her visit, as do the other children and Grandmom.

Businesses are often interested in promoting high-quality programs for young children, realizing that these young people are their future employees. Businesses recognize that the quality of the child care these children receive also affects their parents and the parents' ability to focus on their work. If employees are worried or concerned about adequate child care or about the quality of their children's programs, their attention at work is often distracted. Kent Larson understands these concerns and has offered Marie the opportunity to work at home when Angela is sick. This is an example where the employer, employee, and young child benefit from the work arrangement.

One way that businesses address the importance of early childhood programs is through volunteer work. Some businesses have initiated programs where employees may spend several hours a week volunteering in a school or early child care program. From the standpoint of the businesses, they know they are making a difference in the preparation of their future work force. Employees are able to share and improve their expertise with the children, and the children benefit from specialized knowledge and skills brought to them. For example, two bilingual employees of a company work with a class of 4- and 5-year-olds twice a week, teaching them Spanish words and phrases. The public school plans to implement a Spanish language program in the primary grades and is eager to receive students who have already started their language study.

In the larger picture, the essence of community (or village) permeates such collaborations. In this fast-paced world, where you might pass hundreds of people on the street and not recognize anyone, these community efforts help you learn about the place where you live and your common values and goals. Strong communities ensure there are safe places for children to play, recreational programs for all children, community centers for senior citizens, libraries with books for all interests, and family activities. Angela, Marie, the Ponzis, and Mrs. Deluiso have celebrated the last two Fourth of July holidays by watching an annual parade consisting of neighbors, representatives from local businesses, and, of course, police officers and the fire truck. This has become an important event for their village.

Some neighborhoods have given themselves a name (e.g., Rose City Neighbors) and hold special events each year. The families come together and celebrate new additions to families and share common activities and events. They have found a way to create a true community spirit that supports them and their families. The essence of community enlarges the single family unit to that of a strong, caring village, similar to the one that surrounds Angela.

The people in Angela's neighborhood represent many different cultures and ethnic groups. Recognizing and appreciating diversity will be part of your role as an early childhood professional.

Society and Diversity

The world is enlarging at the same time that it is shrinking. No longer is the place where someone lives defined merely as the name of a road or an apartment building. A place of residence might be connected to many other geographic areas via television, telephone, computers, and fax machines. There is continual access to news and information from around the world. A person could just as easily talk with someone in India via the Internet as walk across the street to visit with a friend. With the expansion of access to the world and global awareness, the importance of a shared world must be emphasized with young children.

It is the job of the caregiver or teacher of young children to bring a world perspective and to plan curriculum that responds to and appreciates cultural diversity (Trawick-Smith, 2003). Emily is aware of the different ethnic backgrounds of the children in her care. Each year, she talks to the families and asks each family to come to her home care and host one tradition connected to their cultural roots. Many of the books on her bookshelf depict children from different cultures and countries. She wants the children to be proud of their heritage and appreciate the diversity in their village.

DEMOGRAPHIC TRENDS. In the early 1990s, children attending school in California depicted a new demographic trend in the United States. A majority of public school children in six states are now from minority groups. Can *minority,* then, be an accurate term? The school-aged population in the largest cities in this country represent more children from cultures and races other than Caucasian. This means that children who are non-White can no longer be labeled as *minority children,* when, in fact, they compose the majority of the population in many cities, towns, and rural areas. In 1999, 40 percent of the total public elementary and secondary school population was made up of children of color (U.S. Department of Education, 2000).

What does this mean to early childhood programs? Children as young as 2 or 3 years of age notice racial and gender differences and are developing their thoughts about differences among their peers. Early childhood is a wonderful time to celebrate diversity, to share many cultures, and to learn about contributions of a many ethnic and racial groups. A **diversity perspective** means bringing a positive awareness and appreciation of differences among children into the curriculum of the young child (Trawick-Smith, 2003). Young children are open and receptive to learning about each other. These are the years when children can learn to appreciate diversity through the cultural activities and awareness that Emily promotes with the children in her care center.

CULTURAL PLURALISM. **Cultural pluralism** refers to studying, respecting, and celebrating the contributions made by people from many cultures. Numerous benefits can be gained from learning about each other's customs, beliefs, and traditions. Expectations for developmentally appropriate behavior and learning needs to be analyzed on an individual level to take into account the child's home experiences. Young children bring their cultures with them to their schools or centers. Children are learning through the lens of their culture. Acknowledging this culture and building on it affirms that this individual child is important, as is her family and her culture. Respect for diversity includes spending time learning about each child's background and family culture and using the children's interests and experiences to develop activities (Trawick-Smith, 2003).

At the same time, the teacher or caregiver must also examine his own cultural background and be prepared to share his traditions and beliefs with the children. When educating culturally diverse children, caregivers or "teachers must be sensitive to the similarities and differences between themselves and their students and their families" (Bowman, 1994, p. 224). Emily's roots are from Israel, and she shares stories, clothing, food, and customs from her country with the children. She actively encourages the children and families to share their cultures with the group of children.

It is helpful to look at your curriculum and materials as you determine whether you offer authentic situations to learn about cultures. Do you include many books and stories about children from different cultures? Are the children in these books portrayed accurately? What about your expectations for the children? Do you attempt to get to know each child on an individual level and base program decisions (including expectations for learning) on the child's interests, developmental level, and culture? All of these questions probe at the important issue of developing a curriculum around the knowledge and beliefs that the children in your care and their families bring with them. It is important to incorporate materials and activities that show respect and interest in each child's cultural background. It is also important to review your materials for possible bias.

Emily enjoys learning about the many countries and cultures of her children as the families bring their customs to her home and to the children in her care. She finds she is also a learner when she invites families to share their traditions and cultures with the children. Often, grandparents, relatives, and friends participate in events with the children, sharing their customs.

Sensitivity to a child's learning is critical to cultural pluralism. You will want the children in your care to feel positive about the diversity of cultures, find worth in all people, and believe that each person has something special to share with the group. Believing in the importance and worth of each child and her contribution to the larger group models the perspective that you hope to teach as you embrace cultural pluralism.

BILINGUAL EDUCATION. Providing second language instruction to children whose first language is not English is a controversial issue. As you recall from the discussion on bilingual education in Chapter 9, one perspective supports instruction in the native or home language, enabling the child to progress academically yet retain his primary language. A differing view suggests that the sooner the child learns English, the sooner she will become part of the classroom learning environment. Unfortunately, children who are taught in English only at an early age often forget their primary language and may experience difficulty with grasping concepts and understanding new ideas in an unfamiliar language.

Again, going back to the core belief that the learning of each child should be developmentally appropriate, accounting for her prior knowledge and her culture, you are better able to make sound decisions about bilingual instruction. Bilingual models that present concepts in the dominant language first and then in English have been shown to be successful (Garcia, 2002). These programs value the child's first language while helping the child become proficient in English.

Angela has always spoken English, but Grandma and Grandpa Russo have been teaching her Italian phrases, which she loves to hear. The grandparents speak Italian most of the time, having learned English as adults. They want Angela to learn Italian so she can communicate with them as well as learn the language of her heritage.

JOURNAL 13.5: You have a new child entering your group of 2-year-olds next week. The child is Vietnamese and has been in the United States since birth. How do you prepare for this child? What is some important information you want to gather before the child starts school? What are some resources for you in this area?

With regard to cultural diversity within a pluralistic society, you have an opportunity to influence how the young children in your care think about people from races or cultures different from their own. Modeling appreciation and awareness of diversity is essential to teaching young children to value diversity throughout their lives. The early childhood staff should also reflect the cultural composition of the children and families. Respect for cultures is shown in many forms, as modeled by Emily in her welcoming of families to share their traditions and her invitation to grandparents to become part of her program. In early childhood programs, frequent communication with families and hiring qualified staff that represent children of the community is essential to creating a village that values each member.

Summary of Political, Economic, and Social Influences on Early Childhood

Current trends in support for early childhood programs find political, economic, and social forces working together to promote and ensure continuity of services for young children. The federal government is allocating some of its power and funding responsibilities to state and local levels. At the local level, you will find that programs are likely to reflect community (or village) priorities of the local region.

Accountability for programs and for the learning of children is important for renewed funding of government-supported programs. Changes in society, economic status of the nation, and the political agenda bring changes in the care of young children. Early childhood professionals are becoming more involved and vocal in influencing policies that support the role of families and young children's development (Kagan, 1999). The role of advocacy by early childhood professionals is critical to improved programs for the care and education of all young children.

Advocacy: Why and How?

An **advocate** is one who understands issues and concerns in a specific field and takes an active stand, whether defending the current status or supporting changes to better the field. In this case, advocacy is taking a stance in support of quality early childhood programs that promote the healthy growth and development of children and their families. The intent of this chapter is to look at the influences of political, economic, and social forces on early childhood programs. You will want to bring this perspective with you while you explore what the early childhood professional can do to influence political, economic, and social agendas.

The Child Care and Development Block Grants, created in 1990, are an example of the influence made by a large, coordinated number of early childhood advocates. Their combined influence resulted in policy and economic decisions that affect a substantial number of children and programs. On the national and international levels, membership in professional affiliations and active participation through conferences, shared stories, and active communication have the potential to create changes in early childhood policies. The National Association for the Education of Young Children has developed and implemented guidelines and policies for ethical conduct, professional standards, and program accreditation. These policies are noted at the national, state, and local levels. Your involvement and voice in such an organization demonstrates your commitment to your profession and to quality programs for young children. This is part of being an advocate.

Modeling Advocacy

The act of advocacy models important behavior for young children; that is, it is a commitment to beliefs or causes and consequent actions that support an important cause. If you truly wish children to stand up for their rights and beliefs, you must model this behavior. When families see you taking a stance about early childhood issues, they recognize your commitment and dedication to improving or extending the quality of services and resources for children and families. Marie is aware of Emily's dedication to her work with young children and families. She knows that Emily is an advocate of her family and the other families associated with the child care program and that Emily will help them find resources or services when needed. Marie and Angela saw Emily assist a family when the parents needed help locating a nearby health clinic. Emily has developed a file and a directory of community resources to share with families.

Advocating for Children

When you share information with parents that helps them learn a new way to communicate with their children, you are demonstrating your advocacy to young children. Let's return to the story of Jodie and listen to a conversation between her preschool teacher, Karla, and her parents. As you listen, think about the role of an advocate and identify where you notice Karla assuming a child advocacy position.

Karla: Child Advocate

Lynn and Jerry are concerned about Jodie's language development. The 4-year-old has been using one-word responses most of the time at home and they are concerned about her progress. Lynn and Jerry wonder if it would be helpful to have the speech and language therapist come to the preschool and work with Jodie. Karla listens to their concerns. She tells them that she hears Jodie respond with two-word phrases occasionally, particularly when she is playing in the dramatic play area. Karla tells Lynn and Jerry that she will keep a checklist for a week and record some of Jodie's responses. She will then get in touch with them and help them decide if they would like to set up a meeting with the speech and language therapist.

Karla wants to follow up on Lynn and Jerry's observations and respond to their concerns. At the same time, she knows that Jodie becomes frustrated when she is pressured to increase her sentence length. Karla, wanting what is best for Jodie, will meet with the speech and language therapist to talk about options. She will then set up a meeting for Lynn, Jerry, the speech and language therapist, and herself to discuss ways to help Jodie.

The conversation ends with Lynn and Jerry making plans to call Karla next week and planning to write down any two- or three-word phrases that Jodie uses spontaneously. Karla suggests asking Jodie to share stories about her friends at school instead of asking her to say more words. The conversational context seems like a good idea to Jerry and Lynn, and they leave feeling relieved and heard.

Child advocacy assumes different shapes and roles. You can find many opportunities throughout a day to support the learning and development of young children, just as Karla did in her brief conversation with Jodie's parents. When you talk with your local librarian and keep her informed of current information for parents regarding finding quality child care (Robinson & Stark, 2002), you are advocating for families in your area. You will encounter opportunities in both your personal and professional life to advocate for children. At this point in your professional development, you may feel uncertain about how to fulfill that role. In the next section is a discussion of specific actions you might take to declare yourself a children's advocate.

Becoming a Children's Champion through Advocacy

Throughout this book, you have seen numerous references to the National Association for the Education of Young Children and the policies and actions pursued by the organization to improve early childhood experiences for each and every child. NAEYC (1995) outlines five steps that one can take to advocate for children and become a children's champion.

1. Speak out on behalf of children by communicating information about the necessity for quality experiences for young children. You can do this with friends, colleagues, legislators, letters to the local paper, or community leaders. Your opinion and voice can carry important information to people in a position to make decisions, whether as a voter or a politician.
2. Help one child beyond your family. Perhaps you live in a neighborhood where several school-aged children are home alone after school or in the early evening. This might be an opportunity for you to ask the family if you could plan an activity for their child one evening a week. Your time and energy with this child can make a difference to the child and to you as you participate in that child's development.
3. Be an informed voter in your community—research the decisions and stances that different public officials advocate for young children. Legislative decisions affect the funding and availability of early childhood programs and services (e.g., welfare reform). Your vote and voice are important to elected officials in making changes that support the growth and development of young children.
4. Explore the service opportunities within the organizations of which you are a member. Perhaps your church or club could raise funds for equipment for a child care center or volunteer to work two hours a month at a local school. Often, the suggestion of helping a neighborhood school, park, or child care center is enough to get others excited about the possibilities. These actions create potential for new partnerships to benefit young children.
5. Encourage others to join you in supporting young children and the availability of services and resources for young children. When you gather a group of friends together to prepare a garden plot for a nearby preschool program, you will likely enjoy the experience of working together. Beyond that, you are making a contribution. Watching the children planting and tending their vegetable plants promotes an even greater satisfaction in your advocacy role.

Committing yourself to implementing these five steps creates more children's champions—people willing to stand up for the rights and welfare of children. Acting together, we can improve public understanding, support, and funding of high-quality early childhood programs, making a difference for young children, their families, and the teaching profession (Robinson & Stark, 2002). By following these steps, you help build a better world for yourself as well as for children, creating a stronger village.

Advocacy is an essential element of professionalism. What is professionalism? How do you become a professional? These questions are addressed in the next section.

Professionalism in Early Childhood Education

You have read about the political, economic, and social forces influencing young children and the priority given to their care and development in today's world. You have also learned of some ways to advocate for improved conditions for children and for the profession of early childhood education. Now let's take some time to discuss professionalism and how one continues to grow in this profession.

Professionalism

A **professional** is someone who is educated, knowledgeable, dedicated to her profession, committed to completion of a specialized course of study, and in possession of a knowledge base essential to her specialty area. These terms might be used when describing a doctor, accountant, counselor, or teacher. Whatever the profession, there are certain standards of criteria to be met prior to becoming a professional.

Perhaps one of the more critical criteria of a professional is that of possessing specialized skills and knowledge. The erroneous belief that most anyone can work with young children must be eradicated. This belief should be replaced with the finding that there is a strong relationship between the quality of child care and the preparation and compensation of early childhood providers (National Institute of Health and National Institute of Child Health and Human Development, 2001). Emily wants to continue to learn about helping toddlers with language development. She contacted the local community college and is taking a course called Language Acquisition. She found many of the readings and course sessions relate directly to her interactions with her children, and has made changes in her communication patterns to promote their language development.

CONTINUED PROFESSIONAL DEVELOPMENT. As you begin your journey into early childhood education, you might be wondering about the meaning of professionalism and how this relates to different careers in early childhood. There are many different roles within the early childhood profession. Each of the roles requires different levels of preparation and professionalism. At the same time that NAEYC is considering requirements for increased preparation for all professionals, individual states are also examining licenses and standards for those working with young children. You are apt to see many changes in the requirements for licensure in the coming years.

CHILD DEVELOPMENT ASSOCIATE CREDENTIAL. The Child Development Associate (CDA) is a national-level credential that reflects an individual's ability to meet the needs of young children. This credential was developed by the Council for Early Childhood Professional Recognition as a national effort to assess and improve the skills and knowledge of caregivers and teachers in early childhood settings. An individual may meet the standards in one of two ways, either as part of a program in a postsecondary institution or through direct assessment. The direct assessment format is for candidates who have experiences in early childhood work and have demonstrated competence in the six CDA competency areas (see Table 13.1). These competencies reflect important skills and a knowledge base necessary for those who work with young children. Many programs, including Head Start, require their professionals to hold a CDA credential.

Becoming a Professional

So, you finish a course of study and are awarded a certificate or credential. Does this mean you are now a professional? And does this mean you have reached the end of your education?

TABLE 13.1 CDA Competency Goals and Functional Areas

CDA Competency Goals	Functional Areas
I. To establish and maintain a safe, learning environment.	**1.** *Safe:* Candidate provides a safe environment to prevent and reduce injuries. **2.** *Healthy:* Candidate promotes good health and nutrition and provides an environment that contributes to the prevention of illness. **3.** *Learning Environment:* Candidate uses space, relationships, materials, and routines as resources for constructing an interesting, secure, and enjoyable environment that encourages play, exploration, and learning.
II. To advance physical and intellectual competence.	**4.** *Physical:* Candidate provides a variety of equipment, activities, and opportunities to promote the physical development of children. **5.** *Cognitive:* Candidate provides activities and opportunities that encourage curiosity, exploration, and problem-solving appropriate to the developmental tasks and learning styles of children. **6.** *Communication:* Candidate actively communicates with children and provides opportunities and support for children to understand, acquire, and use verbal and nonverbal means of communicating thoughts and feelings. **7.** *Creative:* Candidate provides opportunities that stimulate children to play with sound, rhythm, language, materials, space and ideas in individual ways and to express their creative abilities.
III. To support social and emotional development and to provide positive guidance.	**8.** *Self:* Candidate provides physical and emotional security for each child and helps each child to know, accept and take pride in himself or herself and to develop a sense of independence. **9.** *Social:* Candidate helps each child feel accepted in the group, helps children learn how to communicate and get along with others, and encourages feelings of empathy and mutual respect among children and adults. **10.** *Guidance:* Candidate provides a supportive environment in which children can begin to learn and practice appropriate and acceptable behaviors as individuals and as a group.
IV. To establish positive and productive relationships with families.	**11.** *Families:* Candidate maintains an open, friendly, and cooperative relationship with each child's family, encourages their involvement in the program, and supports the child's relationship with his or her family.
V. To ensure a well-run purposeful program responsive to participant needs.	**12.** *Program Management:* Candidate is a manager who uses all available resources to ensure an effective operation. Candidate is a competent organizer, planner, record keeper, communicator, and cooperative co-worker.
VI. To maintain a commitment to professionalism.	**13.** *Professionalism:* Candidate makes decisions based on knowledge of early childhood theories and practices. Candidate promotes quality in child care services. Candidate takes advantage of opportunities to improve competence, both for personal and professional growth and for the benefit of children and families.

Source: Reprinted by permission of the Council for Early Childhood Professional Recognition. The Child Development Associate Assessment System and Competency Standards.

WHEN ARE YOU A PROFESSIONAL? Becoming a true professional takes dedication and commitment to the profession. This commitment begins during your course of study but becomes more apparent when you enter your first career job with young children. Your learning from courses and field experiences will guide you in your planning, decision making, and interactions with children, families, and colleagues. But you will also develop many new questions. Perhaps this is the key to defining a true professional—one who considers herself "unfinished" and acknowledges that she has much more to learn. Your continued thirst for knowledge and your commitment to reading and reflecting on your work is part of being a professional.

JOURNAL 13.6: As you think back to several of the early childhood professionals throughout this book, recall some of their professional activities and how their commitment to the profession translated into actions. Describe several ways that these professionals demonstrated their continued education or professional growth.

A LOOK AT ONE TEACHER'S COMMITMENT TO PROFESSIONALISM. Let's go back to Chapter 1, where you met Robin, the teacher of a multiage first/second-grade class, and take a look at professionalism through her work. Remember her dining room table covered with books, journals, and catalogs related to early childhood education? Recall her frequent conversations with other early childhood professionals about teaching, child development, and advocacy within the profession? Robin is committed to learning more and becoming the best teacher that she can be, even after 27 years of teaching. She is already considered an outstanding teacher and has received numerous awards and recognition for her teaching and dedication to her students.

Robin is not satisfied with the status quo; she wants to find more ways to reach her students and promote their successful learning. She enrolls in courses and workshops, and is a member of a study group that meets to share successful classroom practices as well as to help each other through struggles. Her students are fortunate. Not only do they have an exceptional teacher but they are also exposed to a model of lifelong learning. Robin brings innovative ideas to the classroom, shares her work with her students and their parents, and invites their input into her professional growth. You will want to remember some of her thoughts and priorities as you develop your own personal philosophy of early childhood education.

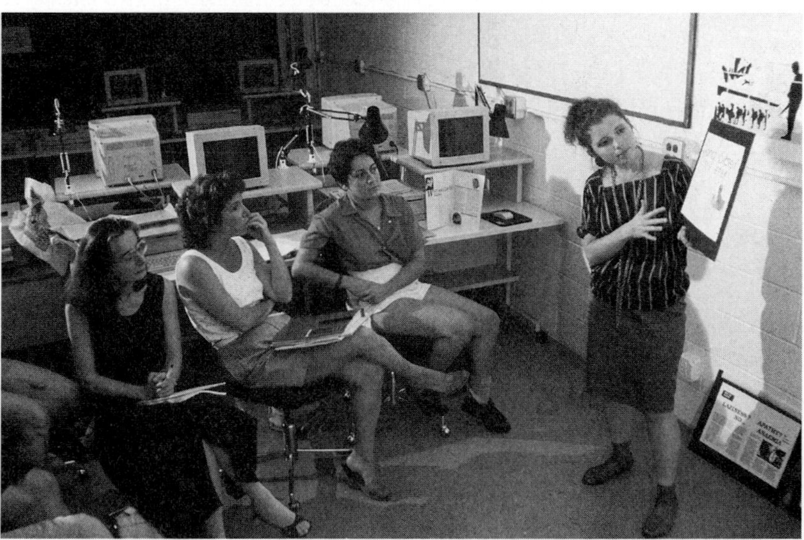

These teachers model a commitment to lifelong learning as they participate in a college course for educators.

Developing and Assessing Your Personal Philosophy of Education

What do you think is important in developing a good environment for optimal learning and development for children in your care? What do you want these children to leave with at the end of their time with you? What are important characteristics of an effective early childhood professional? The answers to these questions will grow from your personal philosophy of working with young children, and your personal philosophy will evolve with your experiences and your continuing education.

Each day you work with young children, you put your philosophy into practice. Taking time to think carefully through your philosophy helps you make decisions. Many professionals find it helpful to keep a journal to record thoughts about their personal philosophy and their interactions with children and families that emerge from their philosophy. Hopefully, your journal work here will begin a daily practice for you.

Articulating your thoughts or personal philosophy with someone you respect in your field is an excellent way to become more aware of your philosophy and to ensure that your actions really do reflect your beliefs. Working with young children is an important career—one that requires professionals who are willing to take the time and effort to examine their beliefs, biases, and goals for their work with children.

Taking time to reflect on your day also helps you make changes to improve your work and to congratulate yourself on good decisions that affect children in a positive way. You will also enjoy your work more when you add an intellectual dimension instead of merely reacting or going through an established routine. Making conscious choices and thoughtful decisions based on your personal philosophy of what is best for young children improves both your professional work and your programs for children. This is an essential element of both professional growth and professionalism. Another aspect of professionalism has been alluded to throughout these discussions. Continuing education provides new learning and extensions of your prior knowledge as you grow in your profession.

Continuing Education

The knowledge and experiences you bring to your first job in early childhood will form the foundation of your knowledge base. As you learn from your experiences, you will want to develop a continuing education plan for yourself. If you are employed at a large organization or a public school, topics of staff development might be selected by the school, with room for personal choices supported through tuition reimbursement programs. In smaller programs, such as Emily's child care program, you might need to actively seek further learning opportunities. These learning opportunities are available at national or local conferences, courses at a local community college, distance education programs through state agencies, or special programs offered on weekends.

Often, students of early childhood education have questions or interests in topics that were not included in their preparation. Perhaps you will find that you need more development in certain areas. Discussions about your personal development plans should occur with your supervisor or colleagues, helping you identify programs or courses that would assist you in gaining the knowledge you are seeking. Emily has a friend who is also involved in child care. She gets together with her friend about once a month to discuss their activities, plans, challenges, and changes they would like to make. Emily finds the interaction and support essential to her professional development. She appreciates having someone to share ideas with and to learn from in her career.

Remember Karla, Jodie's preschool teacher? Karla had limited experience working with children with special needs and wanted to learn more to help her be successful in teaching these children. She discussed her personal learning needs with her supervisor and found that the local community college offered two courses in special education of interest to her. The preschool agreed to pay 75 percent of the tuition for these courses, because they realize that Karla's knowledge would benefit the school. Karla also planned to visit other preschools known to have model inclusion programs. Having Jodie in her class prompted Karla to create her professional development plan.

One word of advice: No one is expected to know everything all at once. You will have many years to continue learning and trying out new ideas with the children in your care. However, it is helpful to develop a written professional development plan that assesses your areas of strengths and the areas that you wish to strengthen. Sharing and discussing your plans with your colleagues and your supervisor will enable you to identify areas of professional development and will provide a format for exchanging ideas and knowledge.

Your continuing education will most likely focus on your professional development goals and result in an expanding knowledge base. Right now, as you begin your studies in early childhood education, you might wonder about expectations for ethical behavior within your profession as well as guidelines or standards that guide moral and ethical decisions.

Professional Ethics

In 1998, the National Association for the Education of Young Children Association approved a revised Code of Ethical Conduct, which provides guidelines for those who work with young children. In 2003, an addendum to the Code of Ethical Conduct was adopted to address the ethical challenges facing early childhood teacher educators. The code provides guidelines that reflect a shared commitment of professional responsibility within the spirit of helping children and their families develop to their fullest potential.

One of the qualities or attributes expected of a professional is a commitment to ethical endeavors, as indicated in the Code of Ethical Conduct. The code establishes guidelines of professional responsibilities for early childhood professionals to follow in relationships with children, families, colleagues, and the larger community and society (Freeman, Feeney, & Moravcik, 2003).

Perhaps one of the more important guidelines for your work is to always consider the impact of your decisions on the child or children with whom you are working. Thinking in terms of what is best for the child helps you focus on each child's particular needs and shape your decisions to improve circumstances for that child. For example, let's say that during outside play, you notice that Raul is "clingy" and wants to stay near you. You know that his parents are considering a separation and that life at home is tense for the family. Typically, you might encourage Raul to become involved in an activity with other children, but you sense that his clinging to you is a security need, as you represent a comforting adult in his life. Your decision to spend extra time with him and also to let his parents know that their interactions with him are important is based on what you think is best for Raul at this time in his life.

As an early childhood education professional, you will face ethical decisions on a daily basis. Having guidelines and a framework to operate from in order to feel that you are doing your best to help children learn and develop will assist you greatly. The NAEYC Code of Ethical Conduct provides these important guidelines that should become part of your knowledge base as an early childhood professional. Another component of professionalism is becoming part of a professional organization, such as the NAEYC.

Professional Affiliations

Becoming an active member of a professional organization and having your voice heard is important in any profession. Early childhood education is in an evolving process of shaping programs and establishing certification and accreditation standards. Joining an organization that promotes thoughtful advancement of the state of young children demonstrates your commitment to children and to programs for children and their families. Most professional organizations sponsor conferences and publish journals with practical ideas for working with young children along with current research findings in the profession.

PROFESSIONAL ORGANIZATIONS. The National Association for the Education of Young Children is one of the largest organizations in early childhood education and is active in promoting high standards for program accreditation and for the quality of early childhood programs. The NAEYC also publishes two journals, *Young Children* and *Early Childhood Research Quarterly,* and sponsors an annual conference. Related regional conferences and workshops are offered across the country to promote professional development.

The World Organization for Early Education (also known as OMEP) works with the United Nations Educational, Scientific, and Cultural Organization (UNESCO) to support the improvement of young children's needs in the areas of education, development, health, and nutrition. This organization publishes *The International Journal of Early Childhood.*

The Association for Childhood International (ACEI) publishes two journals, *Childhood Education* and *Journal of Research in Childhood Education,* and sponsors an annual conference. This organization is concerned with improving education, programs, and practices for young children and supporting the professional development of teachers.

Each of these organizations provide numerous possibilities for learning more about early childhood, programs in early childhood, and professional growth opportunities. Joining one or more of these professional organizations is a way for you to stay informed in your profession and keep current with knowledge, issues, concerns, and research that affect early childhood. They are well worth your financial investment.

Emily is a member of NAEYC and receives their journal, *Young Children.* She often finds ideas to use in her program, which means that Angela benefits from the articles in the journal. The professional association of NAEYC has become part of Angela's village.

PROGRAM ACCREDITATION. Another area affected by professional organizations is accreditation of early childhood programs. Early childhood programs may seek accreditation from the NAEYC's National Academy of Early Childhood Programs. National accreditation is a voluntary process in which a center's administrators, staff, and parents join with representatives of the national Academy of Early Childhood Programs to determine whether the center's program meets the criteria for high-quality early childhood programs.

You might be thinking, Why would a center want to spend the time and money to go through the accreditation process? Suzane Gellens (2003), a director of an NAEYC-accredited child care center, presented several reasons for embarking on the accreditation process.

1. National accreditation provides recognition by the early childhood profession that the program meets high-quality standards.
2. The self-study presents a staff development process that empowers staff to analyze the program and their work, noting areas that are outstanding and areas needing improvement.
3. The accreditation criteria provide knowledge and procedures to regain program excellence.
4. Active involvement of families with the center provides support and resources for the accreditation commitment.

These statements strongly support the rationale for working toward and attaining national accreditation.

Summary of Professionalism

There are high expectations of professionals in early childhood education—and there should be. You will be entrusted with the care of young children, along with the expectation that you will create and sustain a rich, nurturing environment. This is a significant role, and one that touches many young lives as it builds the future.

Professional organizations provide support, research, dissemination of knowledge, and implementation of guidelines for the profession of early childhood educators. Working together with other professionals also helps you expand your knowledge base and learn from others in the profession. Joining a professional organization is another avenue in voicing your support for the future of young children and their families.

PRINCIPLES AND INSIGHTS: A Summary and Review

The African proverb woven throughout this chapter, "It takes a village to raise a child," serves as a reminder that we each play an essential role in raising young children in a healthy environment. This proverb advocates for a society that values children and recognizes the importance of providing for the emotional, physical, and intellectual development of each and every child.

Federal, state, and local policies clearly have an impact on the availability of programs and resources for young children and their families. Your vote and your interest in politics can significantly affect young children. As national policy and control is shifted to local efforts, your voice can make a difference to the young children in your village.

A nation's economy is only as strong as its people and their work skills. At a very young age, children begin learning some of the basic principles and values needed to be successful learners. As an early childhood professional, you will be creating environments where these skills can be practiced and valued. You will also have the opportunity to share with others the rationale for early childhood program on an economic level. Again, your active role with young children will contribute to strengthening and supporting your community or village.

Many of today's social issues have a direct impact on young children. Educational reform, need for universal health care, homelessness, and increasing diversity are some of the social issues we are currently experiencing. The early childhood professional who is knowledgeable about political, economic, and social issues and who advocates for resources and support for young children contributes to the well-being of his or her village.

When you enter the early childhood profession, you will be joining thousands of other professionals committed to improving their villages for the sake of young children. You've already begun the process of building that "best possible world" by choosing to study early childhood education. The more you learn about children and families, the better able you will be to contribute to the village goal: the well-being of children and of us all.

BECOMING AN EARLY CHILDHOOD PROFESSIONAL

Your Professional Portfolio

1. In Journal 13.1, you were asked to find the names of your state representatives and legislators. Write a letter to one of these politicians, advocating for a personal area of interest within the field of early childhood education. Include a copy of this letter in your portfolio.
2. Interview a teacher or caregiver who you admire and who works with young children. Perhaps you could visit, write to, or call a teacher from your childhood. Ask that person about attributes or qualities that she or he associates with a professional in early childhood. What suggestions does this person have regarding steps a beginner can take when starting the journey of professionalism? Record the ideas gained from this early childhood specialist, along with your thoughts about what makes this person exceptional.

Your Professional Library

Children's Defense Fund. (2002). *The state of children in America's union: A 2002 action guide to Leave No Child Behind.* Washington, DC: Author.

Kozol, J. (1992). *Savage inequalities: Children in America's schools.* New York: Crown.

Polakow, V. (Ed.). (2000). *The public assault on America's children: Poverty, violence and juvenile injustice.* New York: Teachers College.

Robinson, A., & Stark, D. (2002). *Advocates in action: Making a difference for young children.* Washington, DC: NAEYC.

Tertell, E., Klein, S., & Jewett, J. (Eds.). (1998). *When teachers reflect: Journeys toward effective, inclusive practice.* Washington, DC: NAEYC.

Tower, C. (2001). *Understanding child abuse and neglect* (5th ed.). Boston: Allyn & Bacon.

Washington, V., & Andrews, J. D. (Eds.). (1998). *Children of 2010.* Washington, DC: NAEYC.

Appendix A

Web Resources

Association for Childhood Education International (ACEI) This site, established by the oldest professional early childhood education organization, describes the association, its programs, and the services it offers to both teachers and families. **www.udel.edu/bateman/acei**

Child Welfare League of America (CWLA) The CWLA is the oldest and largest organization in the United States devoted entirely to the well-being of vulnerable children and their families. Its website provides links to information about issues related to morality and values in education. **www.cwla.org**

Children's Defense Fund (CDF) This organization seeks to ensure that every child is treated fairly. The site includes reports and resources regarding current issues facing today's youth, along with national statistics on various subjects. **www.childrensdefensefund.org**

Council for Exceptional Children (CEC) Information on identifying and teaching gifted children, attention deficit disorders, and other topics in disabilities and gifted education may be accessed at this site. **www.cec.sped.org/index.html**

Diversity Database This site offers access to multicultural and diversity resources. A further purpose of this site is to find ways to create a more responsive and respectful dialogue among family and schools. **http://www.inform.umd.edu/EdRes/Topic/Diversity**

Division for Early Childhood (DEC) The DEC advocates for the improvement of conditions for young children with special needs. Links to other sites are included. **http://www.dec-spec.org**

Early Childhood Art Activities This site features child-friendly art projects submitted by teachers. Activities include painting to music, pipe cleaner sculpture, dough recipes, and primary color mixing. **www.princetomol.com/groups/iad/lessons/early/early.html**

Early Childhood Education Online This site presents tips for observation and gives information on advocacy. **www.eme.maine.edu/ECEOL-L/**

Future of Children This research journal, published by the David and Lucile Packard Foundation, disseminates timely information on major issues related to the well-being of children. **www.futureofchildren.org**

I Am Your Child This resource is a national public awareness and engagement campaign to make early childhood development a top priority for our nation. **www.iamyourchild.org**

International Reading Association and National Council of Teachers of English Standards for the English language arts are outlined. **www.ncte.org**

International Society for Technology in Education The national educational technology standards are presented. **www.cnets.iste.org**

National Association for the Education of Young Children (NAEYC) This is the nation's largest organization of early childhood educators and others dedicated to improving the quality of programs for children from birth through third grade. NAEYC works to improve professional practice and working conditions in early childhood education and to build public support for high-quality early childhood programs. **www.naeyc.org**

National Association for the Education of Young Children Standards for early childhood professional preparation are presented. **www.naeyc.org/profdev/prep_review/preprev_standards_2001.asp**

National Association for the Education of Young Children and National Association of Early Childhood Specialists in State Department of Education A joint position statement on early learning standards is given: Creating the conditions for success. **www.naeyc.org/resources/positions_statements/earlylearn.pdf**

National Clearinghouse for Bilingual Education (NCBE) This website collects, analyzes, and disseminates information relating to the effective education of linguistically and culturally diverse learners in the United States. **http://www.ncbe.gwu.edu**

National Committee for Standards in the Arts Standards describe what every young American should know and be able to do in the arts. **www.artsedge.kennedy-center.org/professional_resources/standards**

National Council for the Social Studies Curriculum standards for social studies are presented. **www.socialstudies.org/standards/**

National Council of Teachers of Mathematics Standards and principles for school mathematics, along with other resources are provided. **www.nctm.org**

National Early Childhood Technical Assistance (NECTAS) NECTAS explores many areas related to children with special needs, including IDEA, inclusion, and a project database. **http://nectas.unc.edu**

National Head Start Association This is a national forum for the continued enhancement of Head Start services for children ages newborn through 5 years and for their families. **www.nhsa.org/index.htm**

National Research Council (NRC) This site lists the current national science education standards. **www.nap.edu/readingroom/books/nses.html**

National Resource Center for Health and Safety in Child Care Extensive links on information in health and safety in child care are provided. Health and safety tips are discussed, as are other child care information resources. **nrc.uchsc.edu**

PECentral This website on health and physical education provides information on developmentally appropriate physical education programs. **www.pecentral.org**

Southern Poverty Law Center This site includes lesson plans and resources designed to teach tolerance. **www.tolerance.org**

U.S. Department of Education Government Goals, projects, grants, and other educational programs are listed here as well as many links to teacher services and resources. **www.ed.gov/pubs/TeachersGuide**

Zero to Three This resource aims to strengthen and support families, practitioners, and communities to promote the healthy development of babies and toddlers. **www.zerotothree.org**

Appendix B

The National Association for the Education of Young Children's Code of Ethical Conduct

Preamble

NAEYC recognizes that many daily decisions required of those who work with young children are of a moral and ethical nature. The NAEYC Code of Ethical Conduct offers guidelines for responsible behavior and sets forth a common basis for resolving the principal ethical dilemmas encountered in early childhood education. The primary focus is on daily practice with children and their families in programs for children from birth to eight years of age: preschools, child care centers, family day care homes, kindergartens, and primary classrooms. Many of the provisions also apply to specialists who do not work directly with children, including program administrators, parent educators, college professors, and child care licensing specialists.

Standards of ethical behavior in early childhood education are based on commitment to core values that are deeply rooted in the history of our field. We have committed ourselves to:

- Appreciating childhood as a unique and valuable stage of the human life cycle
- Basing our work with children on knowledge of child development
- Appreciating and supporting the close ties between the child and family
- Recognizing that children are best understood in the context of family, culture, and society
- Respecting the dignity, worth, and uniqueness of each individual (child, family member, and colleague)
- Helping children and adults achieve their full potential in the context of relationships that are based on trust, respect, and positive regard.

The Code sets forth a conception of our professional responsibilities in four sections, each addressing an arena of professional relationships: (1) children, (2) families, (3) colleagues, and (4) community and society. Each section includes an introduction to the primary responsibilities of the early childhood practitioner in that arena, a set of ideals pointing in the direction of exemplary professional practice, and a set of principles defining practices that are required, prohibited, and permitted.

The ideals reflect the aspirations of practitioners. The principles are intended to guide conduct and assist practitioners in resolving ethical dilemmas encountered in the field. There is not necessarily a corresponding principle for each ideal. Both ideals and principles are intended to guide conduct and assist practitioners in resolving ethical dilemmas encountered in the field. They serve as guides to direct practitioners to those questions which, when responsibly answered, will provide the basis for conscientious decision making. While the Code provides specific direction for addressing some specific ethical dilemmas, many dilemmas will require the practitioner to combine the guidance of the Code with sound professional judgment.

The ideals and principles in this Code present a shared conception of professional responsibility that affirms our commitment to the core values of our field. The Code publicly acknowledges the responsibilities that we in the field have assumed and in so doing supports ethical behavior in our work. Practitioners who face ethical dilemmas are urged to seek guidance in the applicable parts of this Code and in the spirit that informs the whole.

Section I: Ethical Responsibilities to Children

Childhood is a unique and valuable stage in the life cycle. Our paramount responsibility is to provide safe, healthy, nurturing, and responsive settings for children. We are committed to supporting children's development by cherishing individual differences, by helping them learn to live and work cooperatively, and by promoting their self-esteem.

Ideals

I-1.1 To be familiar with the knowledge base of early childhood education and to keep current through continuing education and in-service training.

I-1.2 To base program practices upon current knowledge in the field of child development and related disciplines and upon particular knowledge of each child.

I-1.3 To recognize and respect the uniqueness and the potential of each child.

I-1.4 To appreciate the special vulnerability of children.

I-1.5 To create and maintain safe and healthy settings that foster children's social, emotional, intellectual, and physical development and that respect their dignity and their contributions.

I-1.6 To support the right of children with special needs to participate, consistent with their ability, in regular childhood programs.

Principles

P-1.1 Above all, we shall not harm children. We shall not participate in practices that are disrespectful, degrading, dangerous, exploitative, intimidating, psychologically damaging, or physically harmful to children. *This principle has precedence over all others in this Code.*

P-1.2 We shall not participate in practices that discriminate against children by denying benefits, giving special advantages, or excluding them from programs or activities on the basis of their race, religion, sex, national origin, or the status, behavior, or beliefs of their parents. (This principle does not apply to programs that have a lawful mandate to provide services to a particular population of children.)

P-1.3 We shall involve all of those with relevant knowledge (including staff and parents) in decisions concerning a child.

P-1.4 When, after appropriate efforts have been made with a child and the family, the child still does not appear to be benefiting from a program, we shall communicate our concern to the family in a positive way and offer them assistance in finding a more suitable setting.

P-1.5 We shall be familiar with the symptoms of child abuse and neglect and know and follow community procedures and state laws that protect children against abuse and neglect.

P-1.6 When we have evidence of child abuse or neglect, we shall report the evidence to the appropriate community agency and follow up to ensure that appropriate action has been taken. When possible, parents will be informed that the referral has been made.

P-1.7 When another person tells us of their suspicion that a child is being abused or neglected but we lack evidence, we shall assist that person in taking appropriate action to protect the child.

P-1.8 When a child protective agency fails to provide adequate protection for abused or neglected children, we acknowledge a collective ethical responsibility to work toward improvement of these services.

P-1.9 When we become aware of a practice or situation that endangers the health or safety of children, but has not been previously known to do so, we have an ethical responsibility to inform those who can remedy the situation and who can keep other children from being similarly endangered.

Section II: Ethical Responsibilities to Families

Families are of primary importance in children's development. (The term *family* may include others, besides parents, who are responsibly involved with the child.) Because the family and the early childhood educator have a common interest in the child's welfare, we acknowledge a primary responsibility to bring about collaboration between the home and school in ways that enhance the child's development.

Ideals

I-2.1 To develop relationships of mutual trust with the families we serve.

I-2.2 To acknowledge and build upon strengths and competencies as we support families in their task of nurturing children.

I-2.3 To respect the dignity of each family and its culture, customs, and beliefs.

I-2.4 To respect families' childrearing values and their right to make decisions for their children.

I-2.5 To interpret each child's progress to parents within the frame work of a developmental perspective and to help families understand and appreciate the value of developmentally appropriate early childhood programs.

I-2.6 To help family members improve their understanding of their children and to enhance their skills as parents.

I-2.7 To participate in building support networks for families by providing them with opportunities to interact with program staff and families.

Principles

P-2.1 We shall not deny family members access to their child's classroom or program setting.

P-2.2 We shall inform families of program philosophy, policies, and personnel qualifications, and explain why we teach as we do.

P-2.3 We shall inform families of and, when appropriate, involve them in policy decisions.

P-2.4 We shall inform families of and, when appropriate, involve them in significant decisions affecting their child.

P-2.5 We shall inform the family of accidents involving their child, of risks such as exposures to contagious disease that may result in infection, and of events that might result in psychological damage.

P-2.6 We shall not permit or participate in research that could in any way hinder the education or development of the children in our programs. Families shall be fully informed of any proposed research projects involving their children and shall have the opportunity to give or withhold consent.

P-2.7 We shall not engage in or support exploitation of families. We shall not use our relationship with a family for private advantage or personal gain, or enter into relationships with family members that might impair our effectiveness in working with children.

P-2.8 We shall develop written policies for the protection of confidentiality and the disclosure of children's records. The policy documents shall be made available to all program personnel and families. Disclosure of children's records beyond family members, program personnel, and consultants having an obligation of confidentiality shall require familial consent (except in cases of abuse or neglect).

P-2.9 We shall maintain confidentiality and shall respect the family's right to privacy, refraining from disclosure of confidential information and intrusion into family life. However, when we are concerned about a child's welfare, it is permissible to reveal confidential information to agencies and individuals who may be able to act in the child's interest.

P-2.10 In cases where family members are in conflict we shall work openly, sharing our observations of the child, to help all parties involved make informed decisions. We shall refrain from becoming an advocate for one party.

P-2.11 We shall be familiar with and appropriately use community resources and professional services that support families. After a referral has been made, we shall follow up to ensure that services have been adequately provided.

Section III: Ethical Responsibilities to Colleagues

In a caring, cooperative work place human dignity is respected, professional satisfaction is promoted, and positive relationships are modeled. Our primary responsibility in this arena is to establish and maintain settings and relationships that support productive work and meet professional needs.

A—Responsibilities to Co-Workers: Ideals

I-3A.1 To establish and maintain relationships of trust and cooperation with co-workers.

I-3A.2 To share resources and information with co-workers.

I-3A.3 To support co-workers in meeting their professional needs and in their professional development.

I-3A.4 To accord co-workers due recognition of professional achievement.

Principles

P-3A.1 When we have concern about the professional behavior of a co-worker, we shall first let that person know of our concern and attempt to resolve the matter collegially.

P-3A.2 We shall exercise care in expressing views regarding the personal attributes or professional conduct of co-workers. Statements should be based on firsthand knowledge and relevant to the interests of children and programs.

B—Responsibilities to Employers: Ideals

I-3B.1 To assist the program in providing the highest quality of service.

I-3B.2 To maintain loyalty to the program and uphold its reputation.

Principles

P-3B.1 When we do not agree with program policies, we shall first attempt to effect change through constructive action within the organization.

P-3B.2 We shall speak or act on behalf of an organization only when authorized. We shall take care to note when we are speaking for the organization and when we are expressing a personal judgment.

C—Responsibilities to Employees: Ideals

I-3C.1 To promote policies and working conditions that foster competence, well-being, and self-esteem in staff members.

I-3C.2 To create a climate of trust and candor that will enable staff to speak and act in the best interest of children, families, and the field of early childhood education.

I-3C.3 To strive to secure an adequate livelihood for those who work with or on behalf of young children.

Principles

P-3C.1 In decisions concerning children and programs, we shall appropriately utilize the training, experience, and expertise of staff members.

P-3C.2 We shall provide staff members with working conditions that permit them to carry out their responsibilities, timely and nonthreatening evaluation procedures, written grievance procedures, constructive feedback, and opportunities for continuing professional development and advancement.

P-3C.3 We shall develop and maintain comprehensive written personnel policies that define program standards and, when applicable, that specify the extent to which employees are accountable for their conduct outside the work place. These policies shall be given to new staff members and shall be available for review by all staff members.

P-3C.4 Employees who do not meet program standards shall be informed of areas of concern and, when possible, assisted in improving their performance.

P-3C.5 Employees who are dismissed shall be informed of the reasons for the termination. When a dismissal is for cause, justification must be based on evidence of inadequate or inappropriate behavior that is accurately documented, current, and available for the employee to review.

P-3C.6 In making evaluations and recommendations, judgments shall be based on fact and relevant to the interests of children and programs.

P-3C.7 Hiring and promotion shall be based solely on a person's record of accomplishment and ability to carry out the responsibilities of the position.

P-3C.8 In hiring, promotion, and provision of training, we shall not participate in any form of discrimination based on race, religion, sex, national origin, handicap, age, or sexual preference. We shall be familiar with laws and regulations that pertain to employment discrimination.

Section IV: Ethical Responsibilities to Community and Society

Early childhood programs operate within a context of an immediate community made up of families and other institutions concerned with children's welfare. Our responsibilities to the community are to provide programs that meet its needs and to cooperate with agencies and professions that share responsibility for children. Because the larger society has a measure of responsibility for the welfare and protection of children, and because of our specialized expertise in child development, we acknowledge an obligation to serve as a voice for children everywhere.

Ideals

I-4.1 To provide the community with high-quality, culturally sensitive programs and services.

1-4.2 To promote cooperation among agencies and professions concerned with the welfare of young children, their families, and their teachers.

I-4.3 To work, through education, research, and advocacy, toward an environmentally safe world in which all children are adequately fed, sheltered, and nurtured.

I-4.4 To work, through education, research, and advocacy, toward a society in which all young children have access to quality programs.

I-4.5 To promote knowledge and understanding of young children and their needs. To work toward greater social acknowledgment of children's rights and greater social acceptance of responsibility for their well-being.

I-4.6 To support policies and laws that promote the well-being of children and families. To oppose those that impair their well-being. To cooperate with other individuals and groups in these efforts.

I-4.7 To further the professional development of the field of early childhood education and to strengthen its commitment to realizing its core values as reflected in this Code.

Principles

P-4.1 We shall communicate openly and truthfully about the nature and extent of services that we provide.

P-4.2 We shall not accept or continue to work in positions for which we are personally unsuited or professionally unqualified. We shall not offer services that we do not have the competence, qualifications, or resources to provide.

P-4.3 We shall be objective and accurate in reporting the knowledge upon which we base our program practices.

P-4.4 We shall cooperate with other professionals who work with children and their families.

P-4.5 We shall not hire or recommend for employment any person who is unsuited for a position with respect to competence, qualifications, or character.

P-4.6 We shall report the unethical or incompetent behavior of a colleague to a supervisor when informal resolution is not effective.

P-4.7 We shall be familiar with laws and regulations that serve to protect the children in our programs.

P-4.8 We shall not participate in practices which are in violation of laws and regulations that protect the children in our programs.

P-4.9 When we have evidence that an early childhood program is violating laws or regulations protecting children, we shall report it to persons responsible for the program. If compliance is not accomplished within a reasonable time, we will report the violation to appropriate authorities who can be expected to remedy the situation.

P-4.10 When we have evidence that an agency or a professional charged with providing services to children, families, or teachers is failing to meet its obligations, we acknowledge a collective ethical responsibility to report the problem to appropriate authorities or to the public.

P-4.11 When a program violates or requires its employees to violate this Code, it is permissible, after fair assessment of the evidence, to disclose the identity of that program.

References

Ada, A. (1988). Creative reading: A relevant methodology for language minority children. In L. M. Malave (Ed.), *NABE '87. Theory, research and application: Selected papers.* Buffalo: State University of New York.

Advisory Committee on Head Start Quality and Expansion. (1994). Executive summary: The report of the advisory committee on Head Start quality and expansion. *Children Today, 22* (4), 5–8, 41.

Aeppli, W. (1986). *Rudolf Steiner: Education and the developing child.* Hudson, NY: Authroposophic Press.

Allen, K. E., & Marotz, L. R. (2003). *Developmental profiles* (4th ed.). Albany, NY: Delmar.

Allington, R. (1999). Start early, finish strong: Effective literacy instruction. *NYSAEYC Reporter, 36* (1), 4.

Althouse, R., Johnson, M. H., & Mitchell, S. T. (2003). *The colors of learning: Integrating the visual arts into early childhood curriculum.* New York: Teachers College Press.

American Association of University Women. (1992). *How schools shortchange girls.* Annapolis Junction, MD: Author.

American Federation of Teachers. (1999). *Teaching reading is rocket science.* Washington, DC: Author.

American Psychiatric Association. (1994). *Diagnostic and statistical manual of mental disorders, fourth edition (DSM-IV).* Washington, DC: Author.

Andrews, A., & Trafton, P. (2002). *Little kids—Powerful problem solvers: Math stories from a kindergarten classroom.* Portsmouth, NH: Heinemann.

Armstrong, T. (2000). *Multiple intelligences in the classroom* (2nd ed.). Alexandria, VA: ASCD.

Ashton-Warner, S. (1963). *Teacher.* New York: Simon & Schuster.

Association for the Gifted. (2001). *Diversity and developing gifts and talents: A national action plan.* Arlington, VA: Author.

Bassuk, E. L., & Rosenberg, L. (1990). Psychosocial characteristics of homeless children and children with homes. *Pediatrics, 85,* 257–286.

Beatty, J. (1995). *Converting conflicts in preschool.* Ft. Worth, TX: Harcourt Brace.

Beatty, J. (1996). *Skills for preschool teachers* (5th ed.). Englewood Cliffs, NJ: Merrill.

Begley, S. (1996, February 19). Your child's brain. *Newsweek,* pp. 55–61.

Benson, C. S., Buckley, S., & Elliorr, A. M. (1980). Families as educators: Time use contributions to school achievement. In J. Guthrie (Ed.), *School finance policy in the 1980's: A decade of conflict.* Cambridge, MA: Ballinger.

Bereiter, C., & Engelmann, S. (1966). *Teaching disadvantaged children in the preschool.* Englewood Cliffs, NJ: Prentice-Hall.

Bergen, D. (1988). *Play as a medium for learning and development.* Portsmouth, NH: Heinemann.

Bergen, D. (2003). Perspectives on inclusion in early childhood education. In J. P. Isenberg & M. R. Jalongo (Eds.), *Major trends and issues in early childhood education.* New York: Teachers College Press.

Berk, L. (2003). *Child development* (6th ed.). Boston: Allyn & Bacon.

Berk, L. E. (1984). Development of private speech among low-income Appalachian children. *Developmental Psychology, 20,* 271–286.

Berk, L. E. (1985). Why children talk to themselves. *Young Children, 40* (5), 46–52.

Berk, L. E. (1992). Children's private speech: An overview of theory and the status of research. In R. M. Diaz & L. E. Berk (Eds.), *Private speech: From social interaction to self-regulation.* Hillsdale, NJ: Erlbaum.

Berk, L. E. (1994). Vygotsky's theory: The importance of make-believe play. *Young Children, 50,* 30–39.

Berk, L. E. (2002). *Infants, children, and adolescents* (4th ed.). Boston: Allyn & Bacon.

Berliner, B. (2002). Educating homeless students. *National Association of Elementary School Principals, 20* (4), 3–6.

Bernhardt, J. (2000). A primary caregiving system for infants and toddlers: Best for everyone involved. *Young Children, 55* (2), 74–80.

Berns, R. (1997). *Children, families, communities: Socialization and support.* Forth Worth, TX: Harcourt Brace Jovanovich.

Berns, R. (2004). *Child, family, community* (4th ed.). New York: Holt, Rinehart and Winston.

Bernstine, N. (1997). Housing and homelessness. In Children's Defense Fund, *The state of America's children: Yearbook 1997.* Washington, DC: Children's Defense Fund.

Biber, B. (1988). The challenge of professionalism: Integrating theory and practice. In B. Spokek, O. N. Saracho, & D. L. Peters (Eds.), *Professionalism and the early childhood practitioner.* New York: Teachers College Press.

Biber, B., & Franklin, M. B. (1967). The relevance of developmental and psychodynamic concepts to the education of the preschool child. *Journal of the American Academy of Child Psychiatry, 6* (1–4), 5–24.

Birch, L. L., Johnson, S., & Fisher, J. A. (1995). Children's eating: The development of food-acceptance patterns. *Young Children, 50* (2), 71–78.

Black, J., & Puckett, M. (2000). *The young child: Development from prebirth through age eight.* Englewood Cliffs, NJ: Merrill.

Bloom, P. (1993). But I'm worth more than that: Addressing employee concerns about compensation. *Young Children, 48* (3), 65–68.

Bodrova, E., & Leong, D. (1996). *Tools of the mind: The Vygotskian approach to early childhood education.* Englewood Cliffs, NJ: Prentice-Hall.

Bodrova, E., & Leong, D. J. (2003). Do play and foundational skills need to compete for the teacher's attention in an early childhood classroom? *Young Children, 58* (3), 10–17.

Bolenbaugh, S. (2000, July). Activity-based developmental learning in a collaborative first grade classroom. *Young Children,* pp. 30–32.

Bomba, A. K., Oakley, C. B., & Knight, K. B. (1996). Planning the menu in the child care center. *Young Children, 51* (6), 62–67.

Bowlby, J. (1962/1982). *Attachment and loss, Vol. 2. Attachment.* New York: Basic Books.

Bowman, B. T. (1993). *Head Start: Then and now.* Unpublished paper.

Bowman, B. T. (1994). The challenge of diversity. *Phi Delta Kappan, 76* (3), 218–224.

Bredekamp, S. (Ed.). (1987). *Developmentally appropriate practice in early childhood programs serving children from birth through age 8.* Washington, DC: National Association for the Education of Young Children.

Bredekamp, S. (1995). What do early childhood professionals need to know and be able to do? *Young Children, 50* (2), 67–69.

Bredekamp, S., & Copple, C. (1997). *Developmentally appropriate practice in early childhood programs* (2nd ed.). Washington, DC: National Association for the Education of Young Children.

Bredekamp, S., & Rosegrant, T. (1994). Learning and teaching with technology. In J. L. Wright & D. D. Shade (Eds.), *Young children: Active learners in a technological age* (pp. 53–62). Washington, DC: National Association for the Education of Young Children.

Bredekamp, S., & Willer, B. (1993). Professionalizing the field of early childhood education: Pros and cons. *Young Children, 48* (3), 82–84.

Brewer, J. A., & Kieff, J. (1996/1997). Fostering mutual respect for play at home and school. *Childhood Education, 73* (2), 92–96.

Bromer, J. (1999). Cultural variations in child care: Values and actions. *Young Children, 54* (6), 72–78.

Bronfenbrenner, U., & Crouter, A. (1982). Work and family through time and space. In S. B. Kammerman & C. D. Hayes (Eds.), *Families that work: Children in a changing world.* Washington, DC: National Academy Press.

Bronson, M. B. (1995). *The right stuff: Selecting play materials to support development.* Washington, DC: National Association for the Education of Young Children.

Bronson, M. B. (2000). Recognizing and supporting the development of self-regulation in young children. *Young Children, 55* (2), 32–37.

Brown, L., Branston-McLean, M. B., Baumgart, D., Vincent, L., Falvey, M., & Schroeder, J. (1979). Using the characteristics of current and subsequent least restrictive environments as factors in the development of curriculum content for severely handicapped students. *AAESPH Review, 4,* 407–424.

Bruner, J. S. (1951). Personality dynamics and the process of perceiving. In R. Blake & G. Ramsey (Eds.), *Perception: An approach to personality.* New York: Ronald Press.

Bruner, J. S. (1966). *Toward a theory of instruction.* New York: Vintage Books.

Bruner, J. S. (1971). *The relevance of education.* New York: Norton.

Bruner, J. S. (1985a). On teaching thinking: An afterthought. In S. F. Chipman, J. W. Segan, & R. Glasser (Eds.), *Thinking and Learning Skills* (vol. 2). Hillsdale, NJ: Erlbaum.

Bruner, J. S. (1985b). Vygotsky: A historical and conceptual perspective. In J. Wertsch (Ed.), *Culture, communication, and cognition* (pp. 22–34). New York: Cambridge University Press.

Bruner, J. S. (1990). *Acts of meaning.* Cambridge, MA: Harvard University Press.

Bruner, J. S., Goodnow, J. J., & Austin, G. A. (1956). *A study of thinking.* New York: Wiley.

Bullough, R. V., Jr. (1994). Personal history and teaching metaphors. *Teacher Education Quarterly, 21* (1), 107–120.

Bullough, R. V., Jr., & Gitlin, A. (1995). *Becoming a student of teaching.* New York: Garland.

Buskin, M. (1975). *Parent power: A candid handbook for dealing with your child's school.* New York: Walker & Co.

California Child Care Health Program. (2000). *Serving children in biracial/bi-ethnic families: A supplementary diversity curriculum for the training of child care providers.* Oakland, CA: Author.

California Tomorrow. (1999). Helping children develop a sense of identity. *Scholastic Early Childhood Today,* pp. 14–16.

Campbell, F., Pungello, E., Miller-Johnson, S., Burchinal, M., & Ramey, C. (2001). The development of cognitive and academic abilities: Growth curves from an early childhood educational experiment. *Developmental Psychology, 37* (2), 231–242.

Campbell, F., & Ramey, C. (1999). *Early learning, later success. The Abecedarian Study.* Chapel Hill, NC: The Franklin Porter Graham Child Development Center.

Cantor, N. (1990). From thought to behavior: "Having" and "doing" in the study of personality and cognition. *American Psychologist, 45* (6), 735–750.

Capezzuto, S., & Da Ros-Voseles. (2001). Using experts to enhance class projects. *Young Children, 56* (2), 84–85.

Cartwright, S. (1999). What makes good early childhood teachers? *Young Children, 54* (4), 4–7.

Cassidy, D., Mims, S., Rucker, L., & Boone, S. (2003). Emergent curriculum and kindergarten readiness. *Childhood Education, 79* (4), 194–199.

Center for Children in Poverty. (2001). *Child poverty fact sheet.* New York: Columbia University.

Center for the Child Care Workforce. (2003). *Overview of the staffing crisis.* Washington, DC: Author.

Chaille, C. & Britain, L. (1997). *The young child as scientist: A constructivist approach to early childhood science education.* New York: HarperCollins.

Chaille, C., & Silvern, S. (1996). Understanding through play. *Childhood Education, 72* (5), 274–277.

Chatterji, P., & Markowitz, S. (2000). *The impact of maternal alcohol and illicit drug use on children's behavioral problems: Evidence from the children of the national longitudinal survey of youth.* Cambridge, MA: National Bureau of Economic Research.

Checkley, K. (1997). The first seven . . . and the eighth: A conversation with Howard Gardner. *Educational Leadership,* 55 (1), 8–13.

Children's Defense Fund. (1991). *The state of America's children: Yearbook 1991.* Washington, DC: Author.

Children's Defense Fund. (1994a). *The state of America's children: Yearbook 1994.* Washington, DC: Author.

Children's Defense Fund. (1994b). *Wasting America's future.* Washington, DC: Author.

Children's Defense Fund. (1995). *The state of America's children: Yearbook 1995.* Washington, DC: Author.

Children's Defense Fund. (1996). *The state of America's children: Yearbook 1996.* Washington, DC: Author.

Children's Defense Fund. (1997). *The state of America's children: Yearbook 1997.* Washington, DC: Author.

Children's Defense Fund. (2000). *Yearbook 2000: The state of America's children.* Washington DC: Author.

Children's Defense Fund. (2002). *The state of children in America's union: An action guide to leave no child behind.* Washington, DC: Author.

Children's Defense Fund. (2003). *Child care basics.* Washington, DC: Author.

Children's Services Division and the State Office for Services to Children and Families. (1995). *Recognizing and reporting child abuse and neglect: An explanation of Oregon's mandatory reporting law.* Salem, OR: Author.

Chilman, C. (1966). *Your child from 6–12.* Washington, DC: U.S. Department of Health, Education, and Welfare.

Church, E. B. (2003). Group time: Have a question session. *Scholastic Early Childhood Today, 17* (6), 44–45.

Church, E. B. (2003). Introduction to outdoor games. *Early Childhood Today, 17* (8), 57–59.

Clark, P., & Kirk, E. (2000). All-day kindergarten. *Childhood Education, 76* (4), 228–231.

Clements, D., & Samura, J. (2002). The role of technology in early childhood learning. *Teaching Children Mathematics, 8* (6), 340–343.

Clifford, R. (1997). Welfare reform and you. *Young Children, 52* (2), 2–3.

Cline, D. B., & Ingerson, D. (1996). The mystery of Humpty's fall: Primary school children as playmakers. *Young Children, 51* (6), 4–10.

Clinton, H. R. (1996). *It takes a village and other lessons children teach us.* New York: Simon & Schuster.

Coleman Advocates for Children & Youth. (2000, August 7). Child care history in the making. *The New York Times* (advertisement), p. A-21.

Coleman, J. S., & Hoffer, T. (1987). *Public and private high schools: The impact of communities.* New York: Basic Books.

Committee for Economic Development. (1991). *The unfinished agenda: A new vision for child development and education.* New York: Author.

Committee for Economic Development, Research and Policy Committee. (2002). *Preschool for all: Investing in a productive and just society.* Washington, DC: Author.

Coontz, S. (1997). *The way we really are: Coming to terms with America's changing families.* New York: Basic Books.

Copple, C. (Ed.). (2003). *A world of difference: Readings on teaching young children in a diverse society.* Washington, DC: NAEYC.

Corson, P. (2000). Laying the foundation for literacy: An anti-bias approach. *Childhood Education, 76* (6), 385–389.

Cost, Quality, and Child Outcomes Study Team. (1995). *Cost, quality, and child outcomes in child care centers: Executive summary.* Denver: Economics Department, University of Colorado at Denver.

Crain, W. (1980). *Theories of development: Concepts and applications.* Englewood Cliffs, NJ: Prentice-Hall.

Crockett, R. O. (1997, January 16). Mentor Graphics shores up top ranks. *The Oregonian,* p. C1.

Cunningham, A., & Shagoury, R. (2004). *Kindergarten comprehension.* Portland, ME: Stenhouse.

Curran, D. (1985). *Traits of a healthy family.* Minneapolis, MN: Winston Press.

DeJong, L. (2003). Using Erikson to work more effectively with teenage parents. *Young Children, 58* (2), 87–94.

Derman-Sparks, L. (1989). *Anti-bias curriculum: Tools for empowering young children.* Washington, DC: National Association for the Education of Young Children.

Derman-Sparks, L. (1992). "It isn't fair!" Antibias curriculum for young children. In B. Neugebauer (Ed.), *Alike and different: Exploring our humanity with young children.* Washington, DC: National Association for the Education of Young Children.

Derman-Sparks, L. (1998). Activism and preschool children. In E. Lee, D. Menkart, & M. Okazawa-Rey (Eds.), *Beyond heroes and holidays: A practical guide to K–12 anti-racist, multicultural education, and staff development.* Washington, DC: Network of Educators on America.

Derman-Sparks, L. (2003). Markers of multicultural/antibias education. In C. Copple (Ed.), *A world of difference: Readings on teaching young children in a diverse society.* Washington, DC: NAEYC.

DeVries, R., & Zan, B. (1994). *Moral classrooms, moral children: Creating a constructivist atmosphere in early education.* New York: Teachers College Press.

Diffily, D., & Morrison, K. (1996). *Family-friendly communication for early childhood programs.* Washington, DC: National Association for the Education of Young Children.

DiNatale, L. (2002). Developing high-quality family involvement programs in early childhood settings. *Young Children, 57* (5), 90–95.

Division for Early Childhood. (1993). *DEC position on inclusion.* Reston, VA: Council for Exceptional Children, Division for Early Childhood.

Division for Early Childhood of the Council for Exceptional Children (DEC). (2000). *Division for Early Childhood position on inclusion.* Denver, CO: Author.

Dixon-Krauss, L. (1995). Partner reading and writing: Peer social dialogue and the zone of proximal development. *Journal of Reading Behavior, 27* (1), 45–63.

Dombro, A. L. (1995). Sharing the care: What every provider and parent needs to know. *Children Today, 23* (4), 22–25.

Donovan, C. A., Milewicz, E. J., & Smolkin, L. B. (2003). Beyond the single text: Nurturing young children's interest in reading and writing for multiple purposes. *Young Children, 58* (2), 30–36.

Douglass, A. (1996). Rethinking the effects of homelessness on children: Resiliency and competency. *Child Welfare, 75* (6), 741–751.

Driscoll, A. (1995). *Cases in early childhood education: Stories of programs and practices.* Boston: Allyn & Bacon.

Duke, N. K. (2003). Information books in early childhood. *Young Children, 58* (2), 14–20.

Durkin, D. (1966). *Children who read early.* New York: Teachers College Press.

Earley, P. (1994). Goals 2000: *Educate America Act—Implications for teacher educators.* Washington, DC: AACTE Publications.

Early Childhood Assessments Resource Group. (1998). *Principles and recommendations for early childhood assessments.* Washington, DC: National Education Goals Panel.

Early, D., Pianta, R., & Cox, M. (1999). Kindergarten teachers and classrooms: A transition context. *Early Education and Development, 10* (1), 25–46.

Edelman, M. (2002). In *The state of America's union: A 2002 action guide to Leave No Child Behind.* Washington, DC: Children's Defense Fund.

Education Commission of the States. (2000). *Early learning: Improving results for young children.* Denver, CO: Author.

Education Week. (2002, January 10). In early-childhood education and care: Quality counts, pp. 8–9.

Edwards, C., Gandini, L., & Forman, G. (1995). *The hundred languages of children: The Reggio Emilia approach to early childhood education.* Norwood, NJ: Ablex.

Ehrle, J., Adams, G., & Tout, T. (2001). *Who's caring for our youngest children: Child care patterns of infants and toddlers.* Washington, DC: The Urban Institute.

Eisenberg, N. (1992). *The caring child.* Cambridge, MA: Harvard University Press.

Elkind, D. (1981). *The hurried child.* Reading, MA: Addison-Wesley.

Elkind, D. (1994). *A sympathetic understanding of the child, birth to 16* (3rd ed.). Boston: Allyn & Bacon.

Elkind, D. (2003). The lasting value of true play. *Young Children, 58* (3), 46–51.

Epstein, J. L. (1992). *School and family partnerships.* Baltimore: Center on Families, Communities, Schools, and Children's Learning, Johns Hopkins University.

Epstein, J., Jansorn, N. R., Salinas, K. C., Sanders, M. G., Simon, B. S., & VanVoorhis, F. L. (2002). *School, family and community partnerships: Your handbook for action* (2nd ed.). Thousand Oaks, CA: Corwin. ED 467082.

Erikson, E. H. (1968). *Identity: Youth and crisis.* New York: Norton.

Erikson, E. H. (1974). Once more the inner space: Letter to a former student. In J. Strouse (Ed.), *Woman and analysis* (pp. 320–340). New York: Grossman.

Espinosa, L. (2002). *High-quality preschool: Why we need it and what it looks like.* New Brunswick, NY: National Institute for Early Education Research.

Espiritu, E., Meier, D. R., Villazana-Price, N., & Wong, M. K. (2002). A collaborative project on language and literacy learning. *Young Children, 57* (5), 71–78.

Federal Interagency Forum on Child and Family Statistics. (2001). *America's Children: Key national indicators of well-being, 2001.* Washington, DC: Author.

Feeney, S., Christensen, D., & Moravcik, E. (2000). *Who am I in the lives of children*? Englewood Cliffs, NJ: Merrill.

Fischer, M., & Gillespie, C. (2003). Computers and young children's development. *Young Children, 58* (4), 85–91.

Flavell, J., Miller, P., & Miller, S. (1993). *Cognitive development* (3rd ed.). Englewood Cliffs, NJ: Prentice-Hall.

Foster, S. W. (1984). An introduction to Waldorf education. *Clearinghouse, 57* (5), 228–230.

Franklin, M. B., & Biber, B. (1977). Psychological perspectives and early childhood education: Some relations between theory and practice. In L. G. Katz, M. Z. Glockner, S. T. Goodman, & M. J. Spencer (Eds.), *Current issues in early childhood education* (Vol. 1). Norwood, NJ: Ablex.

Freeman, N., Feeney, S., & Moravcik, E. (2003). Ethics and the early childhood educator: A proposed addendum to the NAEYC Code of Ethical Conduct. *Young Children, 58* (3), 82–86.

Freiberg, H., & Driscoll, A. (2000). *Universal teaching strategies* (3rd ed.). Boston: Allyn & Bacon.

Frieberg, H., & Driscoll, A. (1996). *Universal teaching strategies* (2nd ed.). Boston: Allyn & Bacon.

Friedman, D. (2001). Employer supports for parents with young children. In R. Behrman (Ed.), Caring for infants and toddlers. *Future of Children, 11* (1). Los Altos, CA: David and Lucile Packard Foundation.

Frost, J. (1991). *Play and playscapes.* Albany, NY: Delmar.

Gable, S. (2002). Teacher-child relationships throughout the day. *Young Children, 57* (4), 42–47.

Gadsden, V., & Ray, A. (2002). Engaging fathers: Issues and considerations for early childhood educators. *Young Children, 57* (6), 32–42.

Galinsky, E. (1999). *Ask the children: What America's children really think about working parents.* New York: Families & Work Institute.

Galinsky, E. (2000). Findings from *Ask the Children* with implications for early childhood professionals. *Young Children, 55* (3), 64–68.

Gallahue, D. (1982). *Developmental movement experiences for children.* New York: Wiley.

Gandini, L. (1993). Fundamentals of the Reggio Emilia approach to early childhood education. *Young Children, 49* (1), 4–8.

Garcia, E. (1991). *The education of linguistically and culturally diverse students: Effective instructional practices.* Santa Cruz, CA: National Center for Research on Cultural Diversity and Second Language Learning.

Garcia, E. (1997). The education of Hispanics in early childhood: Of roots and wings. *Young Children, 52* (3), 5–14.

Garcia, E. (2002). *Student cultural diversity: Understanding and meeting the challenge.* Boston: Houghton Mifflin.

Gardner, H. (1993a). *Education the unschooled mind: A science and public policy seminar.* Washington, DC: American Educational Research Association.

Gardner, H. (1993b). *Multiple intelligences: The theory in practice.* New York: BasicBooks.

Gardner, H. (1999). *Intelligence reframed: Multiple intelligences for the 21st century.* New York: Basic Books.

Garwood, S., Phillips, D., Harman, A., & Zigler, E. (1989). As the pendulum swings: Federal agency programs for children. *American Psychologist, 44* (2), 434–438.

Gellens, S. (2003). Seeking NAEYC Accreditation restored our program's quality. *Young Children, 58* (3), 96–102.

Gerber, M. (Ed.). (1979). *A manual for parents and professionals: Resources for infant educators.* Los Angeles: Resources for Infant Educators.

Gerber, M. (1981). What is appropriate curriculum for infants and toddlers? In B. Weissbourd & J. S. Musick (Eds.), *Infants: Their social environments* (pp. 77–85). Washington, DC: National Association for the Education of Young Children.

Gestwicki, C. (2000). *Home, school and community relations* (4th ed.). Albany, NY: Delmar.

Gibbs, J. (1989). Biracial adolescents. In J. Gibbs & L. Huang (Eds.), *Children of color.* San Francisco: Jossey-Bass.

Gillespie, C. W. (2000). Six Head Start classrooms begin to explore the Reggio Emilia Approach. *Young Children, 55* (4), 21–27.

Ginsburg, H., & Opper, S. (1969). *Piaget's theory of intellectual development: An introduction.* Englewood Cliffs, NJ: Prentice-Hall.

Ginsburg, H., & Opper, S. (1988). *Piaget's theory of intellectual development* (3rd ed.). Englewood Cliffs, NJ: Prentice-Hall.

Gnezda, M. (1996). Welfare reform: Personal responsibilities and opportunities for early childhood advocates. *Young Children, 52* (1), 55–58.

Goffin, S. (1992). Federal legislation of importance to early childhood education: A chronology. In L. Williams & D. Fromberg (Eds.), *Encyclopedia of early childhood education* (pp. 58–64). New York: Garland.

Goffin, S. (1994). *Curriculum models and early childhood education.* New York: Macmillan.

Golinkoff, R., & Hirsh-Pasek, K. (1999). *How babies talk.* East Rutherford, NJ: Penguin Putnam.

Gonzalez-Mena, J., & Bhavnagri, N. (2000). Diversity and infant/toddler caregiving. *Young Children, 55* (5), 31–35.

Gonzalez-Mena, J., & Bhavnagri, N. P. (2003). Diversity and infant/toddler caregiving. In C. Copple (Ed.), *A world of difference: Readings on teaching young children In a diverse society.* Washington, DC: NAEYC.

Gonzalez-Mena, J., & Eyer, D. M. (2003). *Infants, toddlers, and caregivers* (6th ed.). New York: McGraw-Hill.

Gonzalez-Mena, J., & Peshotan Bhavnagri, N. (2002). Diversity and infant/toddler caregiving. *Young Children, 55* (5), 31–35.

Good Start, Grow Smart. (2002). *Good start, grow smart: The Bush administration's early childhood initiative.* Washington, DC: Government Printing Office.

Gordon, A., & Browne, K. (1993). *Beginnings and beyond: Foundations in early childhood education* (3rd ed.). Albany, NY: Delmar.

Gordon, L. (1988). Job descriptions for infant care programs: Directors, teachers, and assistants. In P. Greenberg (Ed.), *Setting up for infant care: Guidelines for centers and family day care homes* (pp. 45–49). Washington, DC: National Association for the Education of Young Children.

Gowen, J. W. (1995). The early development of symbolic play. *Young Children, 50* (3), 75–84.

Grant, R. (1990). The special needs of homeless children: Early intervention at a welfare hotel. *Topics in Early Childhood Special Education,* 10 (4), 76–91.

Greenberg, P. (1990). Before the beginning: A participant's view. *Young Children, 45* (6), 41–52.

Greenberg, P. (1993). *Character development: Encouraging self-esteem & self- discipline in infants, toddlers, and two-year-olds.* Washington, DC: National Association for the Education of Young Children.

Greenspan, S. I. (1995). *First feelings: Milestones in the emotional development of your baby and child.* New York: Viking.

Greenspan, S., & Meisels, S. (1996). Toward a new vision for the developmental assessment of infants and young children. In S. Meisels & E. Fenichel (Eds.), *New visions for the developmental assessment of infants and young children.* Washington, DC: Zero to Three.

Guddemi, M. P. (2002). The important role of quality assessments for children ages 3–8 years. In J. Wall & G. R. Walz (Eds.), *Measuring up: Assessment issues for teachers, counselors, and administrators.* Greensboro, NC: ERIC Counseling and Student Services Clearinghouse.

Gullo, D. F., & Clements, D. H. (1984). The effects of kindergarten schedule on achievement, classroom behavior, and attendance. *Journal of Educational Research, 78* (1), 51–56.

Guralnick, M. (2001). *Early childhood inclusion: Focus on change.* Baltimore, MD: Brookes.

Haight, W. L., & Miller, P. J. (1993). *Pretending at home: Early development in a sociocultural context.* Albany: State University of New York Press.

Harris, T., & Fuqua, J. D. (2000). What goes around comes around: Building a community of learners through circle times. *Young Children, 55* (1), 44–47.

Hartley, R. (1971). Play: The essential ingredient. *Childhood Education, 48* (2), 80–84.

Haugland, S. (2000). Early childhood classrooms in the 21st century: Using computers to maximize learning. *Young Children, 55* (1), 12–18.

Haugland, S., & Gerzog, G. (1998). *The developmental software scale for web sites.* Cape Girardeau, MO: K. I. D. S. & Computers.

Haugland, S., & Wright, J. (1997). *Young children and technology: A world of discovery.* Boston: Allyn & Bacon.

Hawkins, D. (1973). How to plan for spontaneity. In C. Silberman (Ed.), *The open classroom reader.* New York: Random House.

Head Start Bureau, Department of Health and Human Services. (1995). *Program information report.* Washington, DC: Author.

Heleen, O. (1992). *Is your school family-friendly?* Alexandria, VA: Association of Elementary School Principals.

Helen Gordon Child Development Center. (1996–97). *Parent handbook: Helen Gordon Child Development Center.* Portland, OR: Author.

Helm, J. H., & Beneke, S. (2003). *The power of projects: Meeting contemporary challenges in early childhood classrooms—Strategies and solutions.* Washington, DC: NAEYC.

Helm, J. H. & Katz, L. (2001). *Young investigators: The project approach in the early years.* Washington, DC: NAEYC.

Helm, J. H., & Lang, J. (2003). Overcoming the ill effects of poverty. In J. H. Helm & S. Beneke (Eds.), *The power of projects.* New York: Teachers College Press.

Henderson, A. T. (1981). *The evidence grows.* Boston: National Committee for Citizens in Education.

Henderson, A. T. (1987). *The evidence continues to grow.* Boston: National Committee for Citizens in Education.

Henderson, A. T., & Berla, N. (1996). *The family is critical to student achievement: A new generation of evidence.* Washington, DC: Center for Law and Education.

Hendrick, J. (1990). *Total learning: Curriculum for the young child.* Columbus, OH: Merrill/Macmillan.

Hendrick, J. (1996). *The whole child: Developmental education for the early years.* Englewood Cliffs, NJ: Prentice-Hall.

Hess, R. D. (1970). Social class and ethnic influences upon socialization. In P. H. Mussen (Ed.), *Carmichael's manual of child psychology* (3rd ed., Vol. 2). New York: Wiley.

Hestenes, L., & Carroll, D. (2000). The play interactions of young children with and without disabilities: Individual and environmental influences. *Early Childhood Research Quarterly, 15* (2), 229–246.

Hetherington, E. M. (1972). The effects of father absence on personality development in adolescent daughters. *Developmental Psychology, 7,* 313–326.

Hetherington, E. M., Cox, M., & Cox, R. (1976). Divorced fathers. *The Family Coordinator, 25* (4), 417–428.

Hetherington, E. M., Cox, M., & Cox, R. (1985). Long-term effects of divorce and remarriage on the adjustments of children. *Journal of American Academy of Psychiatry, 24* (5), 518–830.

Heward, W. L. (1996). *Exceptional children: An introduction to special education* (5th ed.). Englewood Cliffs, NJ: Prentice-Hall.

Hewes, D. W. (1996). *NAEYC's first half century: 1926–1976.* Washington, DC: National Association for the Education of Young Children.

Hilgard, E., & Bower, G. (1975). *Theories of learning* (4th ed.). Englewood Cliffs, NJ: Prentice-Hall.

Hill, L., Strommel, A., & Wu, V. (2002). Teaching kindness and compassion in a diverse world. *Early Childhood Today, 17* (3), 39–44.

Hitz, R., & Driscoll, A. (1988). Praise or encouragement? New insights into praise: Implications for early childhood teachers. *Young Children, 43* (5), 6–13.

Hochschild, A. (1997, April 20). There's no place like work. *The New York Times Magazine.*

Hoffman, L. W. (1989). The effects of maternal employment in the two-parent family. *American Psychologist, 44* (2), 283–292.

Hollich, G., Hirsh-Pasek, K., & Golinkoff, R. (2000). Breaking the language barrier: An emergent coalition model for the origins of word learning. *Monographs for the Society for Research in Child Development, 65* (3), 1–138.

Honig, A. (2002). Encourage cooperation and communication. *Scholastic Early Childhood Today, 17* (3), 26–27.

Honig, A. (2002). Signals that say "I want (or need) it." *Early Childhood Today, 17* (2), 26–27.

Honig, A. (2003). Activities that promote curiosity and choice making. *Scholastic Early Childhood Today, 17* (4), 30–31.

Honig, A. (2003a). Helping babies become independent. *Scholastic Early Childhood Today, 17* (6), 25–27.

Honig, A. (2003b). Beauty for babies. *Scholastic Early Childhood Today, 17* (7), 22–25.

Honig, A. S. (1985). High quality infant/toddler care: Issues and dilemmas. *Young Children, 41* (1), 40–46.

Honig, A. S. (1995). Singing with infants and toddlers. *Young Children, 50* (5), 72–78.

Howes, C. (1988). Peer interaction of young children. *Monographs of the Society for Research in Child Development, 53* (1), Serial No. 217.

Hughes, F. P. (1991). *Children, play, and development.* Boston: Allyn & Bacon.

Humpal, M. E., & Wolf, J. (2003). Music in the inclusive environment. *Young Children, 58* (2), 103–107.

Hurwitz, S. (2003). To be successful—Let them play. *Childhood Education, 79* (2), 101–102.

Hurwitz, S. C. (1998). War nurseries—Lessons in quality. *Young Children, 53* (5), 37–39.

Huttenlocher, J., Haight, W., Bryk, A., Seltzer, M., & Lyons, T. (1991). Early vocabulary growth: Relation of language input and gender. *Developmental Psychology, 27* (2), 236–248.

Individuals with Disabilities Education Act Amendments of 1997. (1997). P. L. 105–117, 105th Congress, 1st session.

Individuals with Disabilities Education Act, 20 U.S. C. § 1412(5)(B); 34 C. F. R. 300.551. (1990).

International Reading Association and the National Association for the Education of Young Children. (1998). *Overview of learning to read and write: Developmentally appropriate practices for young children.* Washington, DC: NAEYC.

International Reading Association and the National Association for the Eduation of Young Children. (2000). Learning to read and write: Developmentally appropriate practices for young children. In S. Neuman, C. Copple, & S. Bredekamp (Eds.), *Learning to read and write.* Washington, DC: Author.

Isenberg, J., & Jalongo, M. (1993). *Creative expression and play in the early childhood curriculum.* New York: Macmillan.

Jabs, C. (1996, November). Your baby's brain power. *Working Mother,* pp. 24–28.

Jacobson, L. (2002). ESEA includes new requirements on educating homeless students. *Education Week, 21* (43), 1.

Jewett, J., & Peterson, K. (2003). Stress and young children. *ERIC/EECE Newsletter, 15* (1), 1–2.

Johnson, J., & McCracken, J. (Eds.). (1994). *The early childhood career lattice: Perspectives on professional development.* Washington, DC: National Association for the Education of Young Children.

Johnson, J. E., Christie, J. F., & Yawkey, T. D. (1987). *Play and early childhood development.* Glenview, IL: Scott Foresman.

Jones, E. (1984). Training individuals: In the classroom and out. In J. Greenman & R. Fuqua (Eds.), *Making day care better: Training, evaluation, and the process of change.* New York: Teachers College Press.

Jones, E. (1986). *Teaching adults: An active learning approach.* Washington, DC: National Association for the Education of Young Children.

Jones, E. (1993). *Growing teachers: Partnerships in staff development.* Washington, DC: National Association for the Education of Young Children.

Jones, E. (2003). Playing to get SMART. *Young Children, 58* (3), 32–35.

Jones, E., & Nimmo, J. (1994). *Emergent curriculum.* Washington, DC: National Association for the Education of Young Children.

Jones, J., & Courtney, R. (2002). Documenting early science learning. *Young Children, 57* (5), 34–40.

Jones, V., & Jones, L. (2004). *Comprehensive classroom management: Creating communities of support and solving problems* (7th ed.). Boston: Allyn & Bacon.

Jusczyk, P. W. (1997). *The discovery of spoken language.* Cambridge, MA: MIT Press.

Kagan, S. (1999). A5: Redefining 21st century early care and education. *Young Children, 54* (6), 2–3.

Kagan, S. L. (1994). Readying schools for young children: Polemics and priorities. *Phi Delta Kappan, 76* (3), 226–233.

Kamii, C. (1989). *Young children continue to reinvent arithmetic—2nd grade: Implications of Piaget's theory.* New York: Teachers College Press.

Kamii, C., & DeVries, R. (1978). *Physical knowledge in preschool education: Implications of Piaget's theory.* Washington, DC: National Association for the Education of Young Children.

Katz, L. (1992). *What should young children be learning?* Urbana, IL: ERIC Clearinghouse on Elementary and Early Childhood Education, University of Illinois, ED 290 554.

Katz, L. (1993a). Dispositions: Definitions and implications for early childhood practices. In *Perspectives from ERIC: EECE.* Monograph series No. 4. Urbana, IL: ERIC Clearinghouse on Elementary and Early Childhood Education.

Katz, L. (1993b). *Dispositions as educational goals.* Urbana, IL: ERIC Clearinghouse on Elementary and Early Childhood Education, University of Illinois, ED 363 454.

Katz, L. (1994). Perspectives on the quality of early childhood programs. *Phi Delta Kappan, 76* (3), 200–205.

Katz, L., & Chard, S. (2000). *Engaging children's minds: The project approach.* Norwood, NJ: Ablex.

Katz, L., & Raths, J. D. (1985). Dispositions as goals for teacher education. *Teaching and Teacher Education,* 1 (4), 301–307.

Katz, P. (1982b). A review of recent research in children's attitude acquisition. In. L. Katz (Ed.), *Current topics in early childhood education* (vol. 4). Norwood, NJ: Ablex.

Kavale, K., & Forness, S. (2000). Policy decisions in special education. In R. Gersten, E. Schiler, & S. Vaughn (Eds.), *Contemporary special education research* (pp. 281–326). Mahwah, NJ: Erlbaum.

Kelman, A. (1990). Choices for children. *Young Children, 45* (3), 42–45.

Kim, Y. A. (2003). Necessary social skills related to peer acceptance. *Childhood Education, 79* (4), 234–238.

King, E., Chipman, M., & Cruz-Janzen, M. (1994). *Educating young children in a diverse society.* Boston: Allyn & Bacon.

Kirk, S., Gallagher, J., & Anastasiow, N. (2003). *Educating exceptional children* (10th ed.). Boston: Houghton Mifflin.

Kisker, E., Hofferth, S., Phillips, D., & Farquhar, E. (1991). *A profile of child care settings: Early education and care in 1990.* Washington, DC: U.S. Department of Education, Office of the Under Secretary.

Klein, T. P., Wirth, D., & Linas, K. (2003). Play: Children's context for development. *Young Children, 58* (3), 38–45.

Klein, T., Bittle, C., & Molnar, J. (1993). No place to call home: Supporting the needs of homeless children in the early childhood classroom. *Young Children, 48* (6), 22–31.

Kohlberg, L. (1976). The development of children's orientations toward a moral order. Sequence in the development of moral thought. In P. B. Neubauer (Ed.), *The process of child development* (pp. 143–163). New York: Jason Aronson.

Kohn, A. (1999). Rewards versus learning: A response to Paul Chance. *Phi Delta Kappan, 74* (10), 783–787.

Kohn, M. L. (1977). *Class and conformity: A study in values.* Chicago: Chicago University Press.

Kontos, S., & Wilcox-Herzog, A. (2001). How do education and experience affect teachers of young children? *Young Children, 56* (4), 85–91.

Kopp, C. B. (1982). Antecedent of self-regulation: A developmental perspective. *Developmental Psychology, 18,* 199–214.

Kostelnik, M. J., Soderman, A. K., & Whiren, A. P. (1993). *Developmentally appropriate programs in early childhood education.* New York: Merrill.

Kramer, J. (1994). In D. E. Day & S. G. Goffin (Eds.), *New perspectives in early childhood teacher education* (pp. 31–33). New York: Teachers College Press.

Krashen, S. (1996). *Under attack: The case against bilingual education.* Culver City, CA: Language Education Associates.

Krashen, S. (1999). *Condemned without a trial: Bogus arguments against bilingual education.* Portsmouth, NH: Heinemann.

Kuhl, P. K. (1992, October). *Infants' perception and representation of speech: Development of a new theory.* Paper presented at the International Conference on Spoken Language Processing, Banff, Alberta, Canada.

Lally, J. R. (1995). The impact of child care policies and practices on infant/toddler identity formation. *Young Children, 51* (1), 58–67.

Lally, J. R., Griffin, A., Fenichel, E., Segal, M., Szanton, E., & Weissbourd. B. (1995). *Caring for infants and toddlers in groups: Developmentally appropriate practice.* Washington, DC: Zero to Three.

Lamb, M. (1981). The development of father-infant relationships. In M. Lamb (Ed.), *The role of father in child development* (2nd ed.). New York: Wiley.

Leachman, G., & Victor, D. (2003). Student-led class meetings. *Educational Leadership, 60* (6), 64–68.

Lerner, J., Lowenthal, B., & Egan, R. (2003). *Preschool children with special needs: Children at risk and children with disabilities.* Boston: Allyn & Bacon.

Lombardi, J. (1990). Head Start: The nation's pride, a nation's challenge. *Young Children, 45* (6), 22–29.

Lundgren, D., & Morrison, J. (2003). Involving Spanish-speaking families in early education programs. *Young Children, 58* (3), 88–95.

Maier, H. (1978). *Three theories of child development* (3rd ed.). New York: Harper & Row.

Mamchur, C. (1983). Heartbeat. *Educational Leadership, 40* (4), 14–20.

Manfredi-Pettit, L. (1993). Child care: It's more than the sum of its tasks. *Young Children, 79* (1), 40–42.

Marcon, R. A. (2003). Growing children: The physical side of development. *Young Children, 58* (1), 80–87.

Marshall, H. (1995). Beyond "I like the way. . . ." *Young Children, 50* (2), 26–28.

Maslow, A. (1987). *Motivation and personality* (3rd ed.). New York: Harper & Row.

Maxim, G. W. (1989). *The very young child.* (3rd ed.). Englewood Cliffs, NJ: Merrill/Prentice-Hall.

McAfee, O., & Leong, D. (1997). *Assessing and guiding young children's development and learning.* Boston: Allyn & Bacon.

McBride, B. A., & Lee, M. (1995). *Child care on the community college campus: The relationship between teaching and service.* Presented at the National Organization of Child Development Laboratory Schools preconference, NAEYC annual conference, Dallas, TX.

McBride, S. L. (1999). Family-centered practices. *Young Children, 54* (3), 62–68.

McCall, K. P. (1990). *Educating homeless children and youth: A sample of programs, policies, and procedures.* Cambridge, MA: Center for Law and Education.

McCollum, J. A., & Maude, S. P. (1993). Portrait of a changing field: Policy and practice in early childhood special education. In B. Spodek (Ed.), *Handbook of research on the education of young children* (pp. 352–371). New York: Macmillan.

McCune, L. (1986). Symbolic development in normal and atypical infants. In G. Fein & M. Rivkin (Eds.), *The young child at play.* Washington, DC: National Association for the Education of Young Children.

McDermott, K. (1999). Helping primary school children work things out during recess. *Young Children, 54* (4), 82–84.

McLean, M., Bailey, D. B., & Wolery, M. (1996). *Assessing infants and preschoolers with special needs.* Englewood Cliffs, NJ: Prentice-Hall.

McLean, S. V., Haas, N., & Butler, B. (1994). Kindergarten curriculum: Enrichment and improvishment. *Early Childhood Development and Care, 101,* 1–12.

McLoyd, V. C. (1990). The impact of economic hardship on black families and children: Psychological distress, parenting and socioemotional development. *Child Development, 61,* 190–198.

McMullen, M. B. (1999). Achieving best practices in infant and toddler care and Education. *Young Children, 54* (4), 69–76.

Meisels, S. (1996). Charting the continuum of assessment and intervention. In S. J. Meisels & E. Fenichel (Eds.), *New visions for the developmental assessment of infants and young children* (pp. 27–52). Washington, DC: Zero to Three: National Center for Infants, Toddlers, and Families.

Meisler, S. (1992, May 4). Gap between rich, poor now widest on record. *Washington Post,* p. A1.

Mello, R. (2001). Building bridges: *How storytelling influences teacher/student relationships.* Paper presented at the Storytelling in America Conference, Ontario.

Mello, R. (2004). Telling tales: The journey of a storyteller. In R. Berger & R. Quinney, (Eds.), *Once upon a time: Storytelling and social inquiry.* Boulder, CO: Lynne Rienner Publishers.

Mentor Graphics Child Development Center. (1996). *Mentor Graphics parent handbook.* Wilsonville, OR: Author.

Michnik Golinkoff, R., & Hirsch-Pasek, K. (1999). Small talk. *Working Mother,* pp. 47–49.

Migrant Education Program. (2003). *General program information.* Washington, DC: U.S. Department of Education.

Miller, D. (2002). *Reading with meaning.* Portland, ME: Stenhouse.

Miller, K. (1995). Caring for the little ones. *Child Care Information Exchange, 105,* 23–24.

Miller, K., & Gelman, R. (1983). The child's representation of number: A multidimensional scaling analysis. *Child Development, 54,* 1470–1479.

Miller, R. (1996). *The developmentally appropriate inclusive classroom in early eduation.* Albany, NY: Delmar.

Miller, S. (2003). How children build skills through art. *Scholastic Early Childhood Today, 17* (7), 26–28.

Moles, O. (1992). *Schools and families together: Helping children learn more at home.* Washington, DC: U.S. Department of Educational Research and Improvement.

Molnar, J., Rath, W., & Klein, T. (1990). Constantly compromised: The impact of homelessness on children. *Journal of Social Issues, 46* (4), 109–124.

Montessori, M. (1964). *The Montessori method.* (A. E. George, Trans.). New York: Schocker.

Morrison, G. (2003). *Early childhood education today.* Englewood Cliffs, NJ: Prentice-Hall.

Morrison, J. W., & Rogers, L. S. (1996). Being responsive to the needs of children from dual heritage backgrounds. *Young Children, 52* (1), 29–33.

Morrison, N. (1995). Successful single-parent families. *Journal of Divorce and Remarriage, 22,* 286–287.

Morrow, G. (1987). *The compassionate school: A practical guide to educating abused and traumatized children.* Englewood Cliffs, NJ: Prentice-Hall.

Moyer, J. (2001). The child-centered kindergarten: A position paper. *Childhood Education, 77* (3), 161–166.

Nagel, N. G. (1996). *Learning through real-world problem solving: The power of integrative teaching.* Thousand Oaks, CA: Corwin.

Nagel, N., & Swingen, C. (1998). Students' explanations of place value in addition and subtraction. *Teaching Children Mathematics, 5* (3), 164–170.

National Association of Early Childhood Specialists in State Departments of Education. (2000). *Unacceptable trends in kindergarten entry and placement.* Endorsed by NAEYC in 2001. Washington DC: NAEYC.

National Association for the Education of Young Children. (1990a). *The demand and supply of child care in 1990: Joint findings from the National Child Care Survey 1990 and a profile of child settings.* Washington, DC: U.S. Department of Health & Human Services, Office of Policy and Planning, U.S. Department of Education.

National Association for the Education of Young Children. (1990b). NAEYC position statement on school readiness. *Young Children, 46* (1), 21–23.

National Association for the Education of Young Children. (1990c). *What are the benefits of high quality early childhood programs?* Washington, DC: Author.

National Association for the Education of Young Children. (1995). NAEYC—A community of learners. *Young Children, 51* (1), Annual Report.

National Association for the Education of Young Children. (1996a). NAEYC position statement: Technology and young children—Ages three through eight. *Young Children, 51* (6), 11–16.

National Association for the Education of Young Children. (1996b). *Responding to linguistic and cultural diversity: Recommendations for effective early childhood education.* Washington, DC: Author.

National Association for the Education of Young Children. (1997a). *Guidelines for appropriate curriculum content and assessment in programs serving children 3 through 8 years of age.* Washington, DC: Author.

National Association for the Education of Young Children. (1997b). NAEYC position statement on state implementation of welfare reform. *Young Children, 52* (2), 42–45.

National Association for the Education of Young Children. (2001). Five essential lessons learned from NAEYC's first 75 years. *Young Children, 56* (1), 51–52.

National Association for the Education of Young Children. (2001). *NAEYC Standards for early childhood professional preparation.* Washington, DC: Author.

National Association for the Education of Young Children & National Association of Early Childhood Specialists in State Departments of Education. (1990). *Guidelines for appropriate curriculum content and assessment in programs serving children ages 3 through 8.* Washington, DC: NAEYC.

National Association for the Education of Young Children & National Association of Early Childhood Specialists in State Departments of Education (2002). *Early learning standards: Creating the conditions for success.* Washington, DC: NAEYC.

National Association for the Education of Young Children & National Council of Teachers of Mathematics. (2002). *Early childhood mathematics: Promoting good beginnings.* Washington, DC: NAEYC.

National Center for Children in Poverty. (1995, April). *Number of poor children under six increased from 5 to 6 million, 1987–1992.* Washington, DC: Author.

National Center for Children in Poverty. (2001). *Child poverty fact sheet.* New York: Author.

National Center for Early Development and Learning. (2002). *Child care licensing: NCEDL Spotlights.* Chapel Hill, NC: Author.

National Center for Education Statistics. (2003). *Public school student, staff and graduate counts by state, school year 2001–02.* Table 5: Percentage of public school membership by race/ethnicity and state. Washington, DC: Author.

National Council for the Social Studies. (1994). *Expectations of excellence: Curriculum standards for social studies.* Washington, DC: Author.

National Council for the Social Studies. (1998). *Ten thematic strands in social studies.* Washington, DC: Author.

National Council of Teachers of Mathematics. (2000). *Principles and standards for school mathematics.* Reston, VA: Author.

National Education Association. (1998). *Promoting quality in early care and education: Issues for schools.* Washington, DC: Author.

National Education Goals Panel. (1995). *1995 National education goals report.* Washington, DC: Author.

National Education Goals Panel. (1999). *The National Education Goals report: Building a nation of learners, 1999.* Washington, DC: U.S. Government Printing Office.

National Institute of Child Health and Human Development. (1997). *Mother-child interaction and cognitive outcomes associated with early child care: Results of the NICHD study.* Bethesda, MD: Author.

National Institute of Child Health and Human Development. (1999). *NICHHD study of early child care.* Washington, DC: Author.

National Institute of Child Health and Human Development. (2002). Early child care and children's development prior to school entry: Results from the NICHD study of early child care. *American Educational Research Journal, 39* (1), 133–164.

National Institute of Health and National Institute of Child Health and Human Development. (2001). *NIH Backgrounder: Preschoolers who experience higher quality care have better intellectual and language skills.* (Press release, April). Washington DC: Author.

National Research Council. (1996). *National standards for science education.* Washington, DC: National Academy Press.

National Research Council and Institute of Medicine. (2000). *From neurons to neighborhoods: The science of early childhood development.* Committee on Integrating the Science of Early Childhood Development. Jack P. Shonkoff and Deborah A. Phillips, Eds. Board on Children, Youth, and Families, Commission on Behavioral and Social Sciences and Education. Washington, DC: National Academy Press.

Nazario, C. R. (1999). *Intergenerational child care.* Vienna, VA: National Child Care Information Center.

Nelson, C. (1997). The new nuclear family: Grandparenting in the nineties. *Black Child, 2* (5), 9–11.

Neugebauer, B. (1992). What are we really saying to children? Criteria for the selection of books and materials. In B. Neugebauer (Ed.), *Alike and different: Exploring our humanity with young children.* Washington, DC: National Association for the Education of Young Children.

Neugebauer, R. (1991a, October/November). Churches that care: Status report #2 on church-housed child care. *Child Care Information Exchange,* pp. 41–45.

Neugebauer, R. (1991b). Status report #2 on employer child care. *Child Care Information Exchange,* 80, 5–9.

Neugebauer, R. (2002). Employer child care growth slows with the economy. Status report #12 on employer child care. *Child Care Information Exchange, 147,* 58–61.

Neuman, S. B., Copple, C., & Bredekamp, S. (2000). *Learning to read and write.* Washington, DC: National Association for the Education of Young Children.

New, R. (1994). Culture, child development, and developmentally appropriate practices. In B. L. Mallory & R. S. New (Eds.), *Diversity and developmentally appropriate practices: Challenge for early childhood education.* New York: Teachers College Press.

Newberger, J. (1997). New brain development research—A wonderful window of opportunity to build public support for early childhood education! *Young Children, 52* (4), 4–9.

O'Brien, L. M. (2003). The rewards and restrictions of recess. *Childhood Education, 79* (3), 161–166.

Okagaki, L., & Diamond, K. (2000). Responding to cultural and linguistic differences in the beliefs and practices of families with young children. *Young Children, 55* (3), 74–80.

Olson, L. (1991, March 6). Social woes pose threat to reform, C. E. D. maintains. *Education Week,* pp. 1, 18.

Oppenheimer, T. (1999). Schooling the imagination. *The Atlantic Monthly, 284* (3), 71–83.

Oregon Department of Education. (1995). *Oregon prekindergarten program requirements.* Salem, OR: Author.

Osborn, D. (1991). *Early childhood education in historical perspective* (3rd ed.). Athens, GA: Education Associates.

Owens, C. (1999). Conversational science 101A: Talking it up! *Young Children, 54* (5), 4–9.

Parker, J. G., & Gottman, J. M. (1989). Social and emotional development in a relational context: Friendship interaction from early childhood to adolescence. In T. J. Berndt & G. W. Ladd (Eds.), *Peer relations in child development.* New York: Wiley.

Patton, C. (1993). What can we do to increase public knowledge about child development and quality child care? *Young Children, 49* (1), 30–31.

Pellegrini, A. D. (1988). Elementary school children's rough and tumble play. *Developmental Psychology, 24,* 802–806.

Pellegrini, A. D. (1989). So what about recess, really? *Play and Culture, 2,* 354–356.

Pellegrini, A. D., & Boyd, B. (1993). The role of play in early childhood development and education: Issues in definition and function. In B. Spodek (Ed.), *Handbook of research on the education of young children.* New York: Macmillan.

Pellegrini, A. D., & Perlmutter, J. C. (1988). Rough-and-tumble play on the elementary school playground. *Young Children, 44* (2), 14–17.

Perkins, D., Jay, E., & Tishman, S. (1993). New conceptions of thinking: From ontology to education. *Educational Psychologist,* 28 (1), 67–85.

Perry, B. D. (2003). Why young children are curious? *Early Childhood Today, 17* (4), 26–27.

Perry, J. (2003). Making sense of outdoor play. *Young Children, 58* (3), 26–30.

Phillips, C. B. (1994). The challenge of training and credentialing early childhood educators. *Phi Delta Kappan, 76* (3), 214–217.

Piaget, J. (1952). *The origins of intelligence in children.* New York: International Universities Press.

Piaget, J. (1962). *Play, dreams, and imitation in childhood.* New York: Norton.

Piaget, J. (1963). *The origins of intelligence in children.* New York: Norton.

Piaget, J. (1969). *Science of education and the psychology of the child.* New York: Viking.

Piaget, J., & Inhelder, B. (1969). *The psychology of the child.* New York: Basic Books.

Pinker, S. (1994). *The language instinct.* New York: Morrow.

Poulton, S., & Sexton, D. (1995/1996). Feeding young children: Developmentally appropriate considerations for supplementing family care. *Childhood Education, 72* (2), 66–71.

Powell, D. R. (1989). *Families and early childhood programs.* Washington, DC: National Association for the Education of Young Children.

Pratt, C. (1948). *I learn from children.* New York: Harper & Row.

Rafferty, Y., & Shinn, M. (1991). The impact of homelessness on children. *American Psychologist, 46* (11), 1170–1179.

Raines, S., & Johnston, J. (2003). Developmental appropriateness: New contexts and challenges. In J. Isenberg & M. Jalongo (Eds.), *Major trends and issues in early childhood education* (2nd ed., pp. 85–96). New York: Teachers College Press.

Ramsey, P. G. (1991). *Making friends in school: Promoting peer relationships in early childhood.* New York: Teachers College Press.

Reer, L. (2004, September). Personal communication.

Richards, L. N., & Schmiege, C. J. (1993). Problems and strengths of single-parent families: Implications for practice and policy. *Family Relations, 42,* 278.

Roberts, L. C., & Hill, H. T. (2003). Using children's literature to debunk gender stereotypes. *Young Children, 58* (2), 39–42.

Robinson, A., & Stark, D. (2002). *Advocates in action: Making a difference for young children.* Washington, DC: NAEYC.

Rogers, C., & Sawyer, J. (1988). *Play in the lives of children.* Washington, DC: National Association for the Education of Young Children.

Rogoff, B., Mistry, J., Göncü, A., & Mosier, C. (1993). Guided participation in cultural activity by toddlers and caregivers. *Monographs of the Society for Research in Child Development, 55* (8, Serial No. 236).

Root, M. P. P. (1996). *The multiracial experience: Racial borders as the new frontier.* Thousand Oaks, CA: Sage.

Ross, H. S., & Lollis, S. P. (1987). Communication within infant social games. *Developmental Psychology, 23,* 241–248.

Rubin, K. H. (1980). Fantasy play: Its role in the development of social skills and social cognition. In K. H. Rubin (Ed.), *Children's play.* San Francisco: Jossey-Bass.

Rubin, K. H., Fein, G. G., & Vandenberg, B. (1983). Play. In E. M. Hetherington (Ed.), *Handbook of child psychology* (vol. 4). New York: Wiley.

Rubin, K. H., & Howe, N. (1986). Social play and perspective taking. In G. Fein & M. Rivkin (Eds.), *The young child at play.* Washington, DC: NAEYC.

Rushton, S., & Larkin, L. (2001). Shaping the learning environment: Connecting brain research to developmentally appropriate practices. *Early Childhood Education Journal, 29* (1), 25–33.

Russell, A. (1994). Our babies, our future. *Carnegie Quarterly, 39* (2), 1–11.

Russell, C. (1999). Only 10% of day care is rated excellent. *The Washington Post,* pp. 1–4.

Rust, F. O. (1994). From a child's point of view. *Journal of Early Childhood Teacher Education, 15* (3), 3–6.

Rutledge, K. (1995a). National accreditation: What is it? *Oregon Association for Young Children Bulletin, 31* (1), 1, 8.

Rutledge, K. (1995b). Why should MY center become accredited? *Oregon Association for Young Children Bulletin, 31* (1), 8–9.

Sandall, S. (2003). Play modifications for children with disabilities. *Young Children, 58* (3), 54–55.

Sandall, S., McLean, M., & Smith, B. (2000). *DEC recommended practices in early intervention/Early childhood special education.* Longmont, CO: Sopris West.

Sanders, S. (2002). *Active for life: Developmentally appropriate movement programs for young children.* Washington, DC: NAEYC.

Santrock, J. W. (1990). *Children.* Dubuque, IA: Brown.

Scales, B., Almy, M., Nicolopoulou, A., & Ervin-Tripp, S. (1991). *Play and the social context of development in early care and education.* New York: Teachers College Press.

Schneider, J., & Houston, P. (1993). *Exploding the myths: Another round in the education debate.* Washington, DC: American Association of Educational Service Agencies.

Schoor, L., with Schoor, D. (1998). *Within our reach: Breaking the cycle of the disadvantaged.* New York: Anchor.

Schram, S. (1991). Welfare spending and poverty: Cutting back produces more poverty, not less. *The American Journal of Economics and Sociology, 59* (20), 129–140.

Schreiber, M. E. (1999). Time-outs for toddlers: Is our goal punishment or education? *Young Children, 54* (4), 22–25.

Schulman, M., & Mekler, E. (1985). *Bringing up a moral child.* Reading, MA: Addison-Wesley.

Schwartz, W. (2003). The identity development of multiracial youth. *Connections, 31* (3), 10–13.

Schweinhart, L. (2001). Recent evidence on preschool programs. *ERIC Clearing House on Elementary and Early Childhood Education.* Washington, DC: Office of Educational Research and Improvement.

Schweinhart, L. J. (1994). Lasting benefits of preschool programs. *ERIC Digest,* EDO-PS-94-2.

Schweinhart, L. J., Barnes, H. V., & Weikart, D. P. (with Barnett, W. S., & Epstein, A. S.). (1993). *Significant benefits: The High/Scope Perry Preschool Study through age 27.* Ypsilanti, MI: High/Scope Press. Monographs of the High/Scope Educational Research Foundation, no. 10.

Schweinhart, L. J., Berrueta-Clement, J. R., Barnett, W. S., Epstein, A. S., & Weikart, D. P. (1985). The promise of early childhood education. *Phi Delta Kappan, 66* (8), 548–553.

Schweinhart, L. J., & Weikart, D. P. (1985). Evidence that good early childhood programs work. *Phi Delta Kappan, 66* (8), 545–551.

Seefeldt, C. (1987). *The early childhood curriculum: A review of current research.* New York: Teachers College Press.

Seefeldt, C., & Galper, A. (2000). *Active experiences for active children: Social studies.* Columbus, OH: Merrill.

Seligson, M. (2001). School-age child care today. *Young Children, 56* (1), 90–94.

Siegel, B. (2002). In R. Neugebauer (Ed.), Employer child care growth slows with the economy. Status Report #12 on Employer Child Care. *Child Care Information Exchange, 147,* 58–61.

Simons, R. L., & Associates. (1996). *Understanding differences between divorced and intact families.* Thousand Oaks, CA: Sage Publications.

Sloane, M. (1999). All kinds of projects for your classroom. *Young Children, 54* (4), 17–20.

Smilansky, S. (1968). *The effects of sociodramatic play on disadvantaged preschool children.* New York: Wiley.

Smith, B., & Rapport, M. J. (1999). *IDEA and early childhood inclusion.* Denver, CO: The Collaborative Planning Project.

Smith, P. K. (1989, April). *Rough and tumble play and its relationship to serious fighting.* Paper presented at the biennial meeting of the Society for Research in Child development, Kansas City, MO.

Snider, M., & Fu, V. (1990). The effects of specialized education and job experience on early childhood teachers' knowledge of developmentally appropriate practice. *Early Childhood Research Quarterly, 5,* 69–78.

Sobel, D. (1994). Authentic curriculum. *Holistic Education Review, 7,* 33–43.

Spodek, B. (1986). *Today's kindergarten: Exploring the knowledge base, expanding the curriculum.* New York: Teachers College Press.

Spodek, B. (1988). Conceptualizing today's kindergarten curriculum. *The Elementary School Journal, 89* (2), 203–211.

Spodek, B. (1993). *Handbook of research on the education of young children.* New York: Macmillan.

Spodek, B., & Saracho, O. N. (1994). *Right from the start: Teaching children three to eight.* Boston: Allyn & Bacon.

Staley, L., & Portman, P. (2000). Red Rover, Red Rover: It's time to move over. *Young Children, 55* (1), 67–72.

Stone, J. (1993). Caregiver and teacher language—Responsive or restrictive? *Young Children, 48* (4), 12–18.

Stone, J. (2001). *Building classroom community: The early childhood teacher's role.* Washington, DC: NAEYC.

Stone, S. J. (1995/1996). Integrating play into the curriculum. *Childhood Education, 72* (2), 104–107.

Stott, F., & Bowman, B. (1996). Child development knowledge: A slippery base for practice. *Early Childhood Research Quarterly, 11* (3), 169–184.

Stremel, K. (2000). DEC recommended practices in technology applications. In S. Sandall, M. McLean, & B. Smith (Eds.), *DEC recommended practices in early intervention/Early childhood special education.* Longmont, CO: Sopris West.

Strickland, D. (1994). Educating African-American learners at risk: Finding a better way. *Language Arts, 71,* 328–336.

Stroufe, L. A., Cooper, R., & DeHart, G. (1992). *Child development: Its nature and course.* New York: McGraw-Hill.

Swaminathan, S., & Wright, J. (2003). In J. Isenberg & M Jalongo (Eds.), *Major trends and issues in early childhood education: Challenges, controversies, and insights* (2nd ed., pp. 136–149). New York: Teachers College Press.

Swap, S. (1987). *Enhancing parent involvement in schools.* New York: Teachers College Press.

Szanton, E. (2001). For America's infants and toddlers, are important values threatened by our zeal to "teach"? *Young Children, 56* (1), 15–21.

Thouvenelle, S., & Bewick, C. (2003). *Completing the computer puzzle: A guide for early childhood educators.* Boston: Allyn & Bacon.

Trawick-Smith, J. (2003). *Early childhood development: A Multicultural perspective* (3rd ed.). Upper Saddle River, NJ: Merrill Prentice Hall.

U.S. Bureau of the Census. (1997). *Statistical Abstract of the United States: 1997* (117th ed.). Washington, DC: Author.

U.S. Bureau of the Census. (1998). *Statistical abstract of the United States: 1998* (118th ed.). Washington, DC: Author.

U.S. Census Bureau. (2000). *Census 2000 supplementary survey.* Washington, DC: Author.

U.S. Department of Education. (1991). *A profile of child care settings: Early education and care in 1990.* Washington, DC: Author.

U.S. Deparment of Education. (1993). *National excellence: A case for developing America's talent.* Washington, DC: Author.

U.S. Department of Education. (1996a). *Eighteenth annual report to Congress on the implementation of the Individuals with Disabilities Education Act.* Washington, DC: Author.

U.S. Department of Education. (1996b, November). Teachers volunteer to train colleagues in using technology. *Community Update, 41,* 1.

U.S. Department of Education. (1997). *Digest of education statistics, 1997,* NCES 98–015, by Thomas D. Snyder. Production Manager: Charlene M. Hoffman. Program Analyst: Claire M. Geddes. National Center for Education Statistics. Washington, DC: Author.

U.S. Department of Education, National Center for Education Statistics. (2000). *America's kindergartners: Findings from the early childhood longitudinal study, kindergarten class of 1998–99.* Washington, DC: Author.

U.S. Department of Education, Office of Special Education Programs. (2002). *The twenty-third annual report to Congress on the implementation of the Individuals with Disabilities Education Act.* Washington, DC: Author.

U.S. Department of Education. (2001). *The twenty-third annual report to Congress on the implementation of the Individuals with Disabilities Education Act.* Washington, DC: Author.

U.S. Department of Health and Human Services. (1986). *Child sexual abuse prevention—Tips to parents.* Washington, DC: Author.

U.S. General Accounting Office. (1995). *Infants and toddlers: Dramatic numbers living in poverty.* Washington, DC: Author.

U.S. Department of Health and Human Services. (1999, October 1). *About Head Start—Early Head Start.* Washington, DC: Author.

U.S. Department of Health and Human Services. (2000, June 16). *HHS fact sheet.* Washington, DC: Author.

U.S. Department of Health and Human Services. (2002). *National Clearinghouse on Child Abuse and Neglect Information.* Washington, DC: Author.

U.S. Department of Health and Human Services. (2003a). *Head Start Fact Sheet.* Washington, DC: Author.

U.S. Department of Health and Human Services. (2003b). National Clearinghouse on Child Abuse and Neglect Information and National Adoption Information Clearinghouse. *Child Maltreatment 2001: Summary of key findings.* Washington, DC: Author.

U.S. Department of Labor. (1999). *Marital and family characteristics of the labor force from the March 1999 Current Population Survey.* Washington, DC: Bureau of Labor Statistics.

U.S. Department of Labor. (2001). *Bureau of Labor Statistics, 2001.* Washington, DC: Author.

Uhrmacher, P. B. (1993). Coming to know the world through Waldorf education. *Journal of Curriculum and Supervision, 9* (1), 87–104.

Vance, E., & Jimenez Weaver, P. (2002). *Class meetings: Young children solving problems together.* Washington, DC: National Association for the Education of Young Children.

Vandell, D., & Su, H. (1999). Child care and school-age children. *Young Children, 54* (6), 62–71.

VanHoorn, J., Nourot, P., Scales, B., & Alward, K. (1999). *Play at the center of the curriculum.* Columbus, OH: Merrill.

Veatch, J. (1991). *Whole language and its predecessors: Commentary.* Paper presented at the annual meeting of the College Reading Association, Crystal City, VA.

Vecchiotti, S. (2001). *Kindergarten: The overlooked school year.* New York: Foundation for Child Development.

Viadero, D. (1990, November 28). Battle over multicultural education rises in intensity. *Education Week,* pp. 1, 11, 13.

Villegas, A. M. (1991). *Culturally responsive pedagogy for the 1990s and beyond.* Trends and Issues Paper No. 6. Washington, DC: ERIC Clearinghouse on Teacher Education.

Vinovskis, M. A. (1993). Early childhood education then and now. *Daedalus, 122* (1), 1–18.

Vold, E. B. (2003). Young children's affirmation of differences: Curriculum that is multicultural and developmentally appropriate. In J. P. Isenberg & M. R. Jalongo (Eds.), *Major trends and issues in early childhood education.* New York: Teachers College Press.

Vygotsky, L. S. (1962). *Thought and language.* Eugenia Hanfmann & Gertrude Vakar (Trans. & Eds.). Cambridge, MA: MIT Press. New York: Wiley (joint publishers).

Vygotsky, L. S. (1978). *Mind in society: The development of higher psychological processes.* Cambridge, MA: Harvard University Press.

Vygotsky, L. S. (1986). *Thought and language.* Cambridge, MA: MIT Press.

Walker, C., Kragler, S., Martin, L., & Arnett, A. (2003). Facilitating the use of informational texts in a 1st grade classroom. *Childhood Education, 79* (3), 152–159.

Ward, C. (1996). Adult intervention: Appropriate strategies for enriching the quality of children's play. *Young Children, 51* (3), 20–24.

Washington County Community Action Organization. (1996). *Washington County Head Start parent handbook.* Hillsboro, OR: Author.

Wasserman, S. (1990). *Serious players in the primary classroom.* New York: Teachers College Press.

Weitzman, L. (1985). *The divorce revolution.* New York: Free Press.

Werner, E. (2000). Individual differences needs: A thirty-year study of resilient high-risk infants. *Zero to Three, 8,* 1–5.

West, J., Denton, K., & Germino-Housken, E. (2000). *America's kindergartners.* Washington, DC: National Center for Education Statistics.

Wetsit, D. (2002). Head Start: Teaching those who teach our most precious. *Tribal College Journal of American Indian Higher Education, 14* (2), 52–53.

Wheatley, K. F. (2003). Promoting the use of content standards: Recommendations for teacher educators. *Young Children, 58* (2), 96–103.

Wheeler, T., & Martin, H. (2000). Personal communication. Monterey Bay, CA.

White, V. F., Buchanan, T. K., Hinson, J. M., & Burts, D.C. (2001). Primary teachers: Five portraits. *Young Children, 56* (1), 22–32.

Whitebok, M., & Bellm, D. (1999). *Taking on turnover: An action guide for child care center teachers and directors.* Washington, DC: Center for the Childcare Workforce.

Whitebrook, M., Phillips, D., & Howes, C. (1993). *National Child Care Staffing Study revisited: Four years in the life of center-based child care.* Oakland, CA: Child Care Employee Project.

Whitehead, C. A. (1994). Seeking common ground: The family child care perspective. In J. Johnson & J. McCracken (Eds.), *The early childhood career lattice: Perspectives on professional development.* Washington, DC: National Association for the Education of Young Children.

Williams, J., & Best, D. (1990). *Measuring sex stereotypes: A multination study* (rev. ed.). Newbury Park, CA: Sage.

Wing, L. A. (1995). Play is not the work of the child: Young children's perceptions of work and play. *Early Childhood Research Quarterly, 10* (2), 223–247.

Winter, S. (1997). "SMART" planning for inclusion. *Childhood Education, 74* (4), 212–218.

Winter, S. (1999). *The early childhood inclusion model: A program for all children.* Olney, MD: Assocation for Childhood Education International.

Witherell, C. S. (1991). Narrative and the moral realm: Tales of caring and justice. *The Journal of Moral Education, 20* (3), 237–241.

Witt, S. D. (2000). The influence of television on children's gender role socialization. *Childhood Education, 76* (5), 322–324.

Wittmer, D. S. (1996). Starting to share. *Scholastic Early Childhood Today, 11* (3), 28–29.

Wolery, M., & Wilbers, J. (1994). Introduction to the inclusion of young children with special needs in early childhood programs. In M. Wolery & J. Wilbers (Eds.), *Including children with special needs in early childhood programs* (pp. 1–22). Washington, DC: NAEYC.

Wolfe, B. L. (1994). Effective practices in staff development: Head Start experiences. In J. Johnson & J. McCracken (Eds.), *The early childhood career lattice:*

Perspectives on professional development. Washington, DC: NAEYC.

Wong Fillmore, L., & Snow, C. (2002). What teachers need to know about language. In C. Adgar, C. Snow, & D. Christian (Eds.), *What teachers need to know about language.* Washington, DC: Office of Educational Research and Improvement.

Wood, D. J., Bruner, J. S., & Ross, G. (1976). The role of tutoring in problem solving. *Journal of Child Psychology and Psychiatry and Allied Disciplines, 17,* 89–100.

Woolfolk, A. E. (1995). *Educational psychology* (6th ed.) Boston: Allyn & Bacon.

Woolfolk, A. E. (2004). *Educational psychology* (9th ed.). Boston: Allyn & Bacon.

Wortham, S. (2003). Assessing and reporting young children's progress. In J. P. Isenberg & M. Renck Jalongo (Eds.), *Major trends and issues in early childhood education.* New York: Teachers College Press.

Zahn-Waxler, C., & Radke-Yarrow, C. (1984). Roots, motives, and patterns in children's prosocial behavior. In E. Stabb. D. Bar-Tal, J. Karylowski, & J. Reykowski (Eds.), *Development and maintainence of prosocial behavior: International perspecitves on positive behavior.* New York: Plenum.

Zeavin, C. (1997). Toddlers at play: Environments at work. *Young Children, 52* (3), 72–77.

Zigler, E., & Muenchow, S. (1992). *Head Start: The inside story of America's most successful educational experiment.* New York: BasicBooks.

Zigler, E., Styfco, S., & Gilman, E. (1993). In E. Zigler & S. Styfco (Eds.), *Head Start and beyond* (pp. 1–41). New Haven, CT: Yale University Press.

Name Index

Subject Index